COMPLETE GUIDE TO RS232 AND PARALLEL CONNECTIONS

A Step-by-Step Approach To Connecting Computers, Printers, Terminals, and Modems

Martin D. Seyer

PRENTICE HALL, Englewood Cliffs, New Jersey 07632

Library of Congress Cataloging-in-Publication Data

Seyer, Martin D.
    Complete guide to RS232 and parallel connections : a step-by-step
  approach to connecting computers, printers, terminals, and modems /
  Martin D. Seyer.
        p.   cm.
    Includes index.
    ISBN 0-13-160201-2.   ISBN 0-13-783515-9 (pbk.)
    1. Computer input-output equipment--Handbooks, manuals, etc.
  2. Computer interfaces--Handbooks, manuals, etc.   I. Title.
  II. Title: Complete guide to RS 232 and parallel connections.
  TK7887.5.S46 1988
  621.398'5--dc19   88-10095
                                                               CIP

Cover design: Photo Plus Art
Manufacturing buyer: Mary Ann Gloriande

 © 1988 by Prentice-Hall, Inc.
A Division of Simon & Schuster
Englewood Cliffs, New Jersey 07632

The publisher offers discounts on this book when ordered
in bulk quantities. For more information, write:
    Special Sales/College Marketing
    Prentice Hall
    College Technical and Reference Division
    Englewood Cliffs, NJ 07632

Printed in the United States of America

10 9 8 7 6 5 4 3 2 1

ISBN 0-13-783515-9   {PBK}
ISBN 0-13-160201-2

Prentice-Hall International (UK) Limited, *London*
Prentice-Hall of Australia Pty. Limited, *Sydney*
Prentice-Hall Canada Inc., *Toronto*
Prentice-Hall Hispanoamericana, S.A., *Mexico*
Prentice-Hall of India Private Limited, *New Delhi*
Prentice-Hall of Japan, Inc., *Tokyo*
Simon & Schuster Asia Pte. Ltd., *Singapore*
Editora Prentice-Hall do Brasil, Ltda., *Rio de Janeiro*

CONTENTS

1. CONNECTING PRINTERS WITH RS232 INTERFACES, 1

General printer information: interfaces, speed, flow control, parity and character length, printer emulation, line-ending sequences, ABC switches, 1–3

Tutorial Module

2. CONNECTING PRINTERS WITH PARALLEL INTERFACES, 63

General parallel printer information: parallel interface, data and ground leads, control leads, busy signal, online/select mode, paper-out condition, printer reset, timing leads, printer emulation, buffers, ABC switches, IBM parallel connector, options, interfaces, flow control, speed, parity and character length, 63–70

3. CONNECTING MODEMS, 81

General modem information: speed, 103 compatibility, 212 compatibility, auto detection, auto answer, command results, local echo, status of leads, Hayes compatibility, port profile, modem tests, local self-test, analog loopback test, end-to-end self-test, digital loopback test, 81–87

4. CONNECTING TERMINALS, 158

General terminal information: proprietary versus nonproprietary terminals, VT100 compatibility, X3.64, Termcap/Terminfo, speed, flow control, duplex, DTE/DCE emulation, parity, echoplex, line-ending sequence, 158–65

5. CONNECTING COMPUTERS, 211

General computer information: compatibility, options, flow control, XMODEM, connector sizes, DTE/DCE port emulation, communication software, emulation, 211–14

6. SPECIAL TOOLS FOR CONNECTIONS: SOFTWARE, HARDWARE, AND CABLE DESIGNS, 271

LIST OF TUTORIAL MODULE CONNECTORS

Tutorial module connectors	Connections	Features
1–1 DB25-DB25	PC/XT and HP LaserJet	Hardware flow control Using a voltage-ohm meter Cable continuity check Printer symptoms and cures
1–2 DB9-DB25	PC/AT and HP LaserJet	Hardware flow control 9-pin connections
1–3 DB9-DB25	UNIX system and printer	Software flow control
1–4 DB9-DB25	Terminal and printer	Print Online Hardware flow control Using break-out box
1–5 DB25-DB25	Terminal and printer	Print Online Software flow control
1–6 DB25-DB25	UNIX system and printer	Software flow control
1–7 DB25-DB25	Printer and modem	Software flow control Keyboard dialing Line ending sequences
1–8 DB9-DB25	Printer and multiuser	Software flow control
1–9 DB25-DB25	Printer and two computers	ABC switch Flow control
2–1 DB25-36pin	PC and parallel printer	IBM parallel interfaces
2–2 DB25-36pin	PC and two printers	ABC switch
2–3 36pin-36pin	MUM and parallel printer	Parallel interface Hardware flow control
3–1 DB25-DB25	PC and modem	Hayes options Using break-out box DCE/DTE emulation Sex changer Using flat ribbon cables Communication software Modem symptoms and cures

LIST OF FIGURES

LIST OF TABLES

PREFACE

My first book, *RS232 Made Easy,* was written to provide the reader with a solid understanding of the leads in the RS232-C interface, focusing on the interaction of leads between data terminal equipment (DTE) and data communication equipment (DCE). Its key features included the appendices, which allowed a quick assessment of the pinouts of over 200 devices and allowed the reader to easily design the cable to connect these together.

This text, *Complete Guide to RS232 and Parallel Connections: A Step-by-Step Approach to Connecting Computers, Printers, Terminals, and Modems,* is a continuation of the first book, but uses tutorial modules designed to cover just about every possible connection being done today with serial and parallel interfaces, to enable the user to connect a multitude of devices together. Covered are computers, modems, terminals, and printers.

In the step-by-step, methodical approach to connecting any two devices established here, the user is offered a "profile" that can be used to analyze a port on a device. By completing the "port profiles" and adhering to the straightforward steps and tools provided, the user can quickly and easily connect any different number of devices together. It is the hope of the author that vendors will eventually standardize their documentation to conform to the "port profile" format, allowing the end users to complete their connections more easily. You, the end user and systems implementers deserve this!

A review of more than 300 devices has been included in the appendices of this text to continue the momentum established in the first book. The material was provided by various vendors, whose contributions are greatly appreciated. The user should consult this handbook's information, keep it updated, and use it frequently.

Users and vendors are encouraged to send any supporting information, device port profiles, or other comments to Prentice Hall for incorporation in future revisions. The author and publisher want to continue to provide you with the best tools available for easier connections.

Martin D. Seyer

ACKNOWLEDGMENTS

The author and publisher would like to extend a special thanks to the support organizations of the following companies for providing the most frequently asked questions they receive from their customers regarding the connections of computers, modems, printers, and terminals.

AMP Inc.
Black Box Corporation
ECZEL Corporation
Heathkit
inmac
Jensen Tools
Lyben Computer Systems
MiSCO
NCR Direct Marketing Division
Pryor Catalog Sales Corporation
R+R Direct
Specialized Products Company
The Drawing Board-Computer Supplies Division
Thomas Computer Corporation
TRW
Valiant UNIVERSALmicro
Visible Computer Supply Corporation

1

CONNECTING PRINTERS
WITH RS232 INTERFACES

When printers are to be connected to various devices, such as terminals or computers, the user should have a good feel for what is necessary for a successful connection. Printers, or other hardcopy devices such as plotters, should be easily connected to computers. However, in reality this can be one of the most difficult connections that exists.

The complexity derives from the fact that there are so many variations to the interfaces that are present on printers with serial ports. In addition, the options of the printers must be set up for proper functioning with the attached device. This chapter highlights step-by-step approaches to connecting printers with RS232 interfaces to a multitude of devices. Chapter 2 focuses on the same connections, but it features printers with parallel interfaces. Many of the concepts will be the same, but the user should be familiar with a number of printer and interface features prior to attempting printer connections. The following discussions highlight the concepts and options that are important when connecting printers with RS232 interfaces.

INTERFACES

Many printers offer a serial or a parallel port, or both. This option generally exists because some printers offer one or more ports as a standard feature. Or perhaps an option is available to get a different interface. Set this option to match whatever port you are planning on using in the printer. If the printer is to be connected with a serial port, then set the switches so they enable the serial port and disable the parallel port.

SPEED

The printer will probably offer an interface speed ranging from 110 to 9600 bits per second (bps). With serial ports, the two device port speeds must match. This speed will be different from the actual print speed. However, the interface supports high speeds to match those of the device to be connected. The computer or terminal that is to be connected to the printer probably can output data at speeds up to 9600 bps, or even 19,200 bps. The printer port must match this speed of the attached device.

FLOW CONTROL

How then can a printer's port operate at 9600 bps when the actual print speed is 180 characters per second (cps)? Good question! With 10 bits per character (including parity, data, and start and stop bits), 9600 bps equates to 960 cps. If the printer can only print at 180 cps, what happens to the other 780 characters? Another good question! Without a feature known as flow control, part of the data sent to the printer would be lost.

Printers are slower devices than computers or terminals. Due to the printing technology available today and the inherent mechanical processes involved in printing, printers will probably never be as fast as computers. Yet printers need to be able to receive and print all the data that an attached device outputs. When a slower device is receiving data from a faster device, it must have the ability to regulate the flow of data, or it will never be able to print all the data that are being sent its way. The printer uses ''flow control'' as a method of temporarily halting the output of data to it. The printer controls when to resume the outputting of data. By regulating the flow of data, the slower-speed printer can successfully print information being sent to it through a high-speed interface.

There are two different flow control techniques used by printers. One is hardware flow control. With this technique, a lead in the RS232 interface on the printer is used to signal to the attached device when it is ''all right'' to send data. The other method is software flow control. With software flow control, a character is sent by the printer that implies that data output should be temporarily halted. When the printer is ready to receive more data, it sends a different character to signal that more data may be output by the attached device. These characters must be received and interpreted by the attached device. Let's look at a typical scenario involving flow control.

Several printer conditions rely on the use of flow control. They are the relatively slow nature of the printer, buffer control, paper out, offline mode, and paper jam. If the printer cannot receive any more data, it must indicate this to the attached device. When one of these conditions occurs, the printer uses the flow control technique, either hardware or software, to stop and resume the data flow.

When hardware flow control is used, a lead in the RS232 interface is held ''on'' by the printer, as long as none of the foregoing conditions applies. Typical leads used by the printer for this are 20, 11, 19, or 4. Once an error condition occurs, the printer lowers this lead. By connecting this lead to certain lead(s) in the attached-devices port, the printer can control the output of data. The tutorial modules in this chapter feature these types of connections. Once the error condition clears, the printer turns this lead back on as an indication that it is ready to receive more data from the attached computer or terminal.

When software flow control is used, the printer transmits a character to regulate the data flow. When one of the aforementioned conditions occurs and the printer needs to halt the data flow, it will transmit a character to the attached device. Normally, the software flow control characters are XON/XOFF, ETX/ACK, and ENQ/ACK. Assuming that XON/XOFF is being used, the printer will send an XOFF character to halt the data flow. The attached computer or terminal will receive this character and interpret it to mean that the printer cannot receive any more data for now. Once the error condition clears on the printer, it sends an XON character to the computer or terminal. The device receives this and interprets the character as a sign to resume data flow. This continues throughout the printing cycle, to ensure that no data are lost. Through this, or the hardware flow control technique, slower-speed printing can occur, regardless of the port speed.

PARITY AND CHARACTER LENGTH

Eight-bit characters are typically used, without the need for parity. However, 7-bit characters with even or odd parity can be used. The important point is that the character settings should match those of the attached computer or terminal. If the computer is set up for 8-bit data characters with parity, set the printer the same way. Otherwise, the data may be garbled due to incompatible formats. Be consistent at both ends.

PRINTER EMULATION

Because of the widespread use of some printers, such as the Texas Instruments 800 series, HP LaserJet Plus, Qume Sprint series, and Epson printers, support for their control codes and print formatting are included with several different printers. This implies that an Okidata printer can print the output from applications that are outputting data formatted for an Epson printer. Features such as compressed print, bold print, and superscript are supported on the Okidata just as the Epson handles them. This feature eliminates the need for changes in the application to support the printer.

This is an application compatibility issue, not a hardware interface compatibility issue. If a printer emulates a different printer, this does not imply that the serial interface is exactly the same. For example, a printer emulating an Epson printer may require a different cable than an Epson printer would. Printer emulation does not always imply hardware port emulation. This is cited only because there could be a difference in the cable required.

LINE-ENDING SEQUENCES

A computer or terminal will end a line with one of two characters, line feed or carriage return, or a combination of both. The printer may receive either of these and misinterpret them based on its option setting.

Printers sometimes offer the option of interpreting the receipt of a line feed as a carriage return and a line feed. Hence the attached device outputs a sentence with a line feed at the end. When the printer receives this, it advances the paper one line feed and returns the print head to the left side of the paper (carriage return).

The printer could also be set up to add a line feed any time it receives a carriage return. As long as the attached unit is outputting only a carriage return at the end of a line, single spacing will function as desired. However, if the attached device is sending both a carriage return and a line feed, the printer will add a line feed, causing double spacing to occur. Or if the printer is awaiting a line feed and only receives a carriage return, overwriting could occur. The line-ending sequences can cause unnecessary grief in a connection. Check this option carefully.

ABC SWITCHES

An ABC switch is a device that connects multiple devices together by the mere flick of a switch. A single computer connected to a switch can access one of two different printers as needed. Conversely, a single printer can be shared by more than one computer. The devices are connected to the switch, so that the common unit is connected to port C. The other two devices are connected to ports A and B. When the switch is in position "A," devices connected to ports A and C are connected. In position "B," devices on ports B and C can communicate. The switches took their name from the foregoing relation. ABCDE switches provide more than two devices to be shared by a single device. These switches can be used to optimize an installation and reduce overall expenses.

The foregoing features were listed to provide you with a general understanding of some issues surrounding the connection of printers with serial ports. The next section features many different connections involving printers, terminals, and computers. Different elements of serial interfacing will be highlighted in each tutorial module, such as different-size connectors and hardware versus software flow control. You are encouraged to review each of these for a complete understanding of different serial connections with printers.

Tutorial Module 1-1: Connecting an HP LaserJet to an IBM PC/XT

This discussion will focus on connecting an IBM PC/XT with a serial port to an HP LaserJet printer. Any compatible, such as a Compaq Portable or the AT&T PC 6300, may be substituted in this exercise. We will refer to the computer generically as a PC. The serial port for an IBM PC/XT may be obtained from a number of sources: dedicated asynchronous communication adapters (ACA), graphics boards, multifunction boards, and so on. Depending on the IBM PC or compatible, the serial port may be included with the basic system. For purposes of this case study, assume that the RS232 port has been installed on the PC, whether it is built on or has been purchased separately.

The HP LaserJet is shipped standard with an RS232-compatible serial port. Any of the LaserJet family of printers can be substituted here. We will denote the printer as merely the HP. Figure 1–1 depicts the connection that we will be attempting.

The steps we will follow are common to all our tutorial modules:

STEPS FOR CONNECTION

1. Determine compatibility (should it work?).
2. Determine signs of success.
3. Determine the type of connector used.

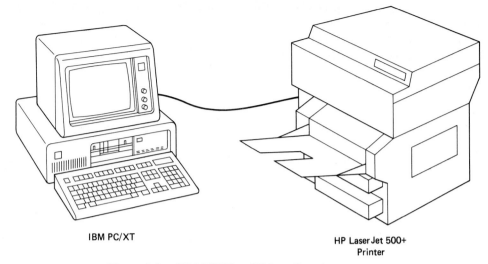

IBM PC/XT

HP LaserJet 500+
Printer

Figure 1–1. IBM PC/XT-to-HP LaserJet printer.

4. Determine gender of the ports.
5. Determine which leads (pins) are provided by each device.
6. Determine which leads are required to be on by each device.
7. Design the cable.
8. Build the cable.
9. Test the cable for continuity.
10. Cable the two systems together with the cable.
11. From step 2, measure success.

1. Determine compatibility

Prior to attempting this feat, the user should determine whether the connection is possible. The options and interfaces dictate whether the two devices are compatible. The best manner of determining compatibility is to check the documentation for both devices. When this information is not available, use the procedure described here to determine if the two can communicate. If all else fails, ask around to see if anyone has made the same or a similar connection. Connecting the PC and the HP printers is a common occurrence. For completeness, however, we will follow the steps just listed for determining compatibility.

When connecting a printer to a PC, the two ports must allow for the same type of parameters. The two devices must support a common communication mode, speed, character format, and protocol. Using the printer and computer SCS^{TM} (Software cabling system) port profile forms, we can lay out the specifics of each port as shown in Table 1–1.

From the information just given, which was taken directly from users' manuals, the two systems appear to be compatible. The common options between the two appear to be asynchronous transmission, 9600 bps, 8 data bits, 1 stop bit, no parity, full duplex operation, and hardware flow control.

The PC supports software flow control only when the application that is using the port supports it. Refer to Tutorial Module 4-2 on connecting a PC emulating a VT100 terminal for more information about when the PC could use software flow control.

The user should select the highest port speed common to both devices, except where there is no flow control. If no flow control, be aware that the user could lose some data if one of the devices cannot keep up. At 9600 bps and no flow control used while printing is occurring, the printer would never be able to halt data transfer long enough to empty its buffer, handle paper-out conditions, and so on. Consult the discussion on flow control for further explanations and examples of the usefulness of flow control.

2. Determine signs of success

Now that the determination has been made that the HP appears to be compatible with the PC, the user needs to know, in advance, the signs of a successful connection. Merely physically connecting the two devices together is a milestone, but this usually does not complete the setup. Prior to beginning any connection, ensure that the user knows when he or she has completely and successfully connected the PC/XT to the HP LaserJet.

TABLE 1–1. HP LASERJET PORT PROFILE

Printer SCS port profile

Underline if supported; circle if selected.

Model: LaserJet _____   Vendor: Hewlett-Packard   Port: RS232
Interface type: <u>serial</u> parallel
Port type: <u>DB25</u> 9-pin 5-pin 8-pin/modular 20mA Centronics

Gender: male <u>female</u>

Pin #	Function	Direction	Pin #	Function	Direction
1	Chassis Ground	to from <u>n/a</u>	14		to from n/a
2	Transmit Data	to <u>from</u> n/a	15		to from n/a
3	Receive Data	<u>to</u> from n/a	16		to from n/a
4		to from n/a	17		to from n/a
5		to from n/a	18		to from n/a
6		to from n/a	19		to from n/a
7	Signal Ground	to from <u>n/a</u>	20	Data Terminal Ready	to <u>from</u> n/a
8		to from n/a	21		to from n/a
9		to from n/a	22		to from n/a
10		to from n/a	23		to from n/a
11		to from n/a	24		to from n/a
12		to from n/a	25		to from n/a
13		to from n/a			

Complete the next section only with 36-pin cinch connector.

26		to from n/a	27		to from n/a
28		to from n/a	29		to from n/a
30		to from n/a	31		to from n/a
32		to from n/a	33		to from n/a
34		to from n/a	35		to from n/a
36		to from n/a			

Flow control technique: <u>XON/XOFF</u> ENQ/ACK STX/ETX (Hardware) _____
Flow control lead(s): 4 11 19 <u>20</u> __ __ __

Leads that must be on: 5 6 8 __ __ __
   Speeds: 110 <u>300 1200</u> 1800 <u>2400 4800</u> (9600) 19.2k 56k _____
   Parity: even odd space mark (none)
   Char-length: 7 (8) __
   # stop bits: (1) 1.5 2
   Line-ending sequence: <u>cr</u> lf cr/lf cr/lf/lf

Mode: <u>async</u> sync   sync timing leads:

#	Function	Direction
15		to from
17		to from
24		to from

Printer compatibility modes: Epson MX Diablo 630 <u>HP LaserJet</u> HP ThinkJet NEC 3500 IBM Graphics IBM Color Printronix TI-810

Notes: _____
_____
_____

TABLE 1–1. (*Continued*)

Computer SCS port profile

Underline if supported; circle if selected.

Model: PC/XT _____ Vendor: IBM _____ Port: ACA _____
Port type: <u>serial</u> parallel
Port: <u>DB25</u> 9-pin 5-pin 8-pin/modular 20mA Centronics

Gender: <u>male</u> female

Pin #	Function	Direction	Pin #	Function	Direction
1		to <u>from</u> n/a	14		to from n/a
2	<u>Transmit Data</u>	to <u>from</u> n/a	15		to from n/a
3	<u>Receive Data</u>	to <u>from</u> n/a	16		to from n/a
4	<u>Request to Send</u>	to <u>from</u> n/a	17		to from n/a
5	<u>Clear to Send</u>	to <u>from</u> n/a	18		to from n/a
6	<u>Data Set Ready</u>	to <u>from</u> n/a	19		to from n/a
7	<u>Signal Ground</u>	to from <u>n/a</u>	20	<u>Data Terminal Ready</u>	to <u>from</u> n/a
8	<u>Data Carrier Detect</u>	to <u>from</u> n/a	21		to from n/a
9		to from n/a	22	<u>Ring Indicator</u>	to from n/a
10		to from n/a	23		to from n/a
11		to from n/a	24		to from n/a
12		to from n/a	25		to from n/a
13		to from n/a			

Complete the next section only with 36-pin cinch connector.

26	_____	to from n/a	27	_____	to from n/a
28	_____	to from n/a	29	_____	to from n/a
30	_____	to from n/a	31	_____	to from n/a
32	_____	to from n/a	33	_____	to from n/a
34	_____	to from n/a	35	_____	to from n/a
36	_____	to from n/a			

Flow control technique: XON/XOFF ENQ/ACK STX/ETX (Hardware) _____
Leads that must be on: <u>5</u> <u>6</u> 8 __ __ __ __

Options:
   Speeds: <u>110 300 600 1200</u> 1800 2400 4800 (9600) 19.2 56k _____
   Parity: <u>even odd</u> space mark (none)
   Char-length: 7 (8) __
   # stop bits: (1) 1.5 2
   Line-ending sequence: cr lf <u>cr/lf</u> cr/lf/lf
   Disconnect sequence: EOT DEL ~. _____

Mode: <u>async</u> sync isoch   sync timing leads:

#	Function	Direction
15	_____	to from
17	_____	to from
24	_____	to from

Notes: _____
_____
_____

Our goal is to connect the printer to the PC so that we may obtain hardcopy of documents, spreadsheets, desktop publishing output, and so on. Success will be determined by our ability to print information on the printer.

When connecting printers, getting the connection made for output is 95 percent of the task. But we must also ensure that the printer will not lose data when long documents are being printed. Specifically, flow control must function properly to prevent loss of data due to buffer overrun, paper-out conditions, offline condition, or other printer error conditions. Our success will be measured by being able to print a copy of the PC screen contents. But also our ability to print long documents, handle error conditions, or halt printing when the printer is offline must be allowed. We will test each of these conditions to ensure success.

3. Determine type of connector

By consulting the documentation of both devices, we can quickly determine the type of connector provided by each device.

On the IBM PC, multiple connectors (ports) may be located on the back of the PC. They may be many different sizes. Locate the RS232 serial port. It is usually labeled COM1, COM2, RS232, or serial. If the port is not labeled, consult the documentation to determine which port is the RS232. It is important that the correct port is used for this connection.

The standard serial port on most IBM PCs and compatibles is a DB25-size connector. A DB25 connector is shaped like a ''D'' and has up to 25 pins or sockets for pins. Usually, all 25 pins are present, but this should not always be assumed. Some vendors may leave some pins out because they are never used.

The DB25-size connector is the most common port on the PC. However, with the introduction of the PC/AT computer, a 9-pin serial interface entered the picture. Refer to the tutorial modules involving the PC/AT for interfacing using this size connector (Tutorial Modules 1-2, 3-2, 4-3, 5-3, 5-5).

The HP LaserJet provides a standard DB25 connector. It is a 25-pin type connector.

4. Determine gender of ports

The IBM PC may have multiple ports, serial and parallel. IBM implemented its parallel port using a DB25 connector. This could be confusing, but the difference is evident by looking at the ports. If a parallel and serial port are present, there is an easy way to distinguish between the two. The IBM parallel port on a PC is usually a DB25 connector. This is a female port, with 25 sockets for pin insertion. The RS232 port is a DB25P, or male, connector. The PC end of the cable we will design will be of female gender. We will connect the completed cable to the male DB25 port.

The HP only has one DB25-size connector. This port is female, implying that this end of our cable will be male. There will be no confusion as to which cable end goes where, as they will only fit one way.

5. Determine leads provided by each device

The user should find out the leads and their directions for the PC port, as well as the HP port. The goal is to determine which leads are provided by the PC port and which should be used in the cable construction.

A port has four categories of leads: ground, data, control, and timing. Ignore the timing category of leads, as we are building a cable to function in an asynchronous environment. The ground leads, usually pins 1 and 7 in a DB25-size connector, have no direction, so they too can be ignored for now. However, these leads must be included in the cable.

Specifically, we are interested in determining which data and control leads are provided by the computer and printer. ''Provided by the computer or printer'' implies that the device is the source of the lead. The direction of the lead is ''from'' the device. There are multiple methods of determining which leads are provided by a computer.

To determine the direction of the RS232 leads that are used, consult the documentation. Usually the users' manuals or application programmers' guides give the RS232 port pinout descriptions. Eventually, it is hoped, all vendors will provide SCS port profiles or similar information in a nice, concise fashion for the user. If the user does not have the documentation, a break-out box (BOB) is one of the best means of identifying the leads that are provided by the computers. Consult Chapter 5, Tutorial Module 5-1, ''Connecting a PC to a UNIX System,'' for step-by-step approach using a break-out box. Another technique involves the use of a volt-ohm meter (VOM). We will use a VOM to determine the leads that are ''provided'' by each device in this example.

If a break-out box is not available to provide port analysis, a VOM can be used to determine which leads (pins) are provided by each computer. Although this tool does not allow for detection of any input leads required by a port, it is still a great tool for port analysis. In this discussion, a Tandy Corporation ArcherKit VOM will be used.

The first step is to enable the port. This is accomplished by using the Mode command as in the following:

MODE LPT1:=COM1

This standard MS-DOS command sets up the serial port, usually denoted as COM1, to be the printer port. Any output destined for a printer will now be routed to the serial port. The user normally holds the Shift key and the Prt Sc key simultaneously to dump a picture of the screen to the printer. Do this now to enable the serial (COM1) port.

Note: Substitute COM2 for COM1 as appropriate. This will usually be the case when a board-level modem or even a mouse is already set up to use COM1. The COM is merely a mnemonic address that identifies the device.

This should cause an attempt to dump a copy of the PC's screen out the serial port, as if a printer were attached. The data will not actually flow because the port requirements have still not been satisfied, but will allow us to analyze further the PC's port.

Turn on the VOM and connect the probes to it. Ensure that the batteries are good, or that the power is on, by doing a resistance test and ensuring scale movement. Once you're confident that the VOM is operational, you can proceed. If multiple scales of measurement are provided on the VOM, set it to the 15 DC volts level (Figure 1–2). The RS232 standard allows signals to be from −15 to +15 volts. Select the scale that can measure at least up to +15 DC V.

The VOM may now be used to determine which signals are provided by the PC port. There are 25 possible pins or sockets in a DB25-size connector. Some or all of the 25 may be present. The user can test each one of them and check for a positive voltage to determine if they are signals "from" the PC port. The pins are numbered from 1 through 25. If the interface conforms to the RS232 standard, which the PC's port does, pin 1 can be on either the right- or left-hand side of the port, depending on your relative viewing position.

There are easy means of locating pin 1 on a port. Sometimes, the port actually has the pins numbered. If not, don't fret, because if you know the difference between a male and female port, the numbering is easy. The male port has pins, the female port has sockets. There are two rows of pins/sockets, one with 13, the other with 12, totaling 25. Prior to locating pin 1, ensure that you are viewing the port just as the text is referencing it. The text assumes that you are looking at the port with the pins/sockets facing you and the 13 pins/sockets on top. Look at Figure 1–3 for a reference.

If the port is female, and viewing it as just described, socket 1 will be in the upper right-hand corner. The socket numbers progress from right to left, with 13 being the last pin on the top row. Socket 14 begins on the right side of the connector on the bottom row of sockets. Numbering progresses from right to left, with socket 25 on the left end of the bottom row.

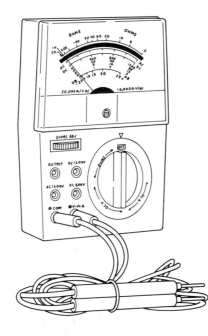

Figure 1–2. Voltage-Ohm Meter with scales.

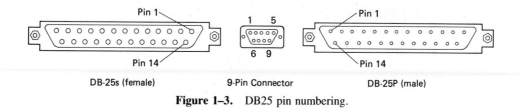

Figure 1–3. DB25 pin numbering.

If the port is male, the number is just the opposite. Pin 1 is the upper left side of the top row of pins. Pin 14 is on the left side of the bottom row of pins. Numbering progresses from left to right. From this you can deduce that when a male connector is plugged into a female connector, the pins will match up. Pin 1 will be connected to socket 1, pin 2 to socket 2, and so on.

The purpose for understanding this bearing is to provide the user a means of locating the ground signals of the port. Leads 1 and 7 are Protective Ground and Signal Ground, respectively. When using the VOM to detect which leads are present, a ground is required. One of these leads, or another ground, should be used for ground purposes. The term "pin" will be used synonymously with socket or leads, as the industry refers to this in this manner.

With the ground probe touching one of these pins, or a ground, take the + volt probe and scan it across every pin or socket to see if any of the pins or sockets yields some sort of reading. This is a "sanity check" to ensure that the port is enabled and that the VOM is grounded and working. Switch the ground to pin 1/7 or an external ground if the port is enabled and your scanning still yields no measurement. Proceed once a reading is detected. If none is noted, recheck the ground, port-enabling shift Prt SC and Mode command, and VOM. If nothing shows up, either the port has no output signals or the VOM cannot be used.

Touch each lead, 2 through 6 and 8 through 25, one at a time. Note the meter on the VOM as you touch each lead. When pin 2 is touched, the needle or scale should indicate a negative reading. This lets us know that the PC is providing a negative DC voltage level on this lead. Hence the direction of pin 2 is "from" the PC. Even though there is no positive reading, the lead is still present. The RS232 standard uses negative DC voltage levels for signals.

Proceeding to pin 3 with the + volt probe, we get no reading or needle movement. This indicates one of two things: either the lead is not used by the port, or this lead is an input lead to the PC. Consulting the documentation, the user can determine that indeed pin 3, Receive Data, is used but is an input signal "to" the port. Hence the HP being connected to the PC provides this signal.

By touching pin 4 with the probe, the VOM should register a positive voltage measurement, usually in the +10–13 volt range. This imples that this signal is "from" the PC port and is "on." Proceed with signals 5 and 6. They are the same status as pin 3. Skipping to pins 8 through 19, the same is noted—no measurement. Pin 20, however, is of similar status as pin 4. Pin 20 is an output signal "from" the PC and is "on." Pins 21 through 25 should yield no measurement, indicating that they are input signals, or not used at all. In review, we now know that pins 2, 4, and 20 are output signals from the PC. This is the same conclusion we arrived at using a break-out box in Chapter 5.

HP leads provided. The same approach should be taken to analyze the HP printer port as we did with the IBM PC or compatible. This section will not repeat all the same activities as with the PC port, but will note the differences. A VOM will be used in the text, although the documentation and a BOB may be used just as easily.

Locate the serial port on the HP printer. Ensure that the LaserJet printer is turned on. This will be evident by numbers being displayed on the status display on the front operator control panel. This two-digit display, located on the left side of the panel, gives printer status and printer error information. If the printer is turned on and the wrong cable, or no cable, is connected to the port, the number should be flashing. This indicates that an error condition has occurred. The digit "40" should be displayed, indicating that a line error has occurred. This is our signal that the cable is incorrect.

Don't be alarmed if the printer shows a different error code. Multiple error conditions could be occurring simultaneously. Our goal, however, is to prevent this error condition from occurring.

To determine which leads are provided by the HP port, use the VOM as we did in the PC exercise. Because the port is female, viewing it as described, pin 1 will be in the upper right-hand corner. The pin numbers progress from right to left, with 13 being the last pin on the top row. Pin/socket 14 begins on the right side of the connector on the bottom row of pins/sockets. Numbering progresses from right to left, with pin/socket 25 on the left end of the bottom row.

Once you have your bearings, locate the ground leads. Pins 1 and 7 are Protective Ground (PG) and Signal Ground (SG), respectively. When using the VOM to detect which leads are present, a ground is required. One of these pins or another ground should be used for ground purposes.

With the ground probe touching one of these pins, or a ground, take the + volt probe and scan it across every pin or socket to see if any of the pins or sockets yield some sort of reading. This is a sanity check to ensure that the port is enabled and that the VOM is grounded and working. In the case of our female port, ensure that the probe actually touches the metal inside the socket. The user may need to use a paper clip or another object to extend the probe. You can usually unfold a paper clip and wrap it around the probe, leaving one end extended out as a smaller probe than that provided by the VOM. Switch the ground to pin 1/7 or an external ground if the port is enabled and your scanning still yields no measurement. Proceed once a reading is detected. If none is noted, recheck the ground, power on the HP, and VOM. If nothing shows up, either the port has no output signals or the VOM cannot be used.

Touch each lead, 2 through 6 and 8 through 25, one at a time. Note the meter on the VOM as you touch each lead. This is the same procedure as used with the PC port analysis.

When pin 2 is touched, the needle or scale should indicate a negative reading. This lets us know that the HP is providing a negative DC voltage level on this lead. Hence the direction of pin 2 is "from" the HP.

Proceeding to pin 3 with the + volt probe, we get no reading or needle movement. This indicates one of two things: either the lead is not used by the port, or this lead is an input lead to the PC. Consulting the documentation, the user can determine that indeed pin 3, Receive Data, is used but is an input signal "to" the HP port. Hence the device being connected to the PC provides this signal.

By touching pin 4 with the probe, the VOM does not register a positive voltage measurement. This implies that pin 4 is not provided as an output signal, that it is not present, or that it is an input signal. Judging from our "data leads," pin 2 was an output signal. This implies a data terminal equipment (DTE) port. We should review our handy port analysis tables to determine the normal signals provided be DTE-type ports. Table 1–2 outlines the various assumptions that hold true 90 percent of the time.

As a DTE class of port, the foregoing generality holds true. The HP port does not quite adhere to these guidelines, but it is close. Upon detecting that pin 2 is an output signal, we could assume that the port was DTE. However, this would imply that pin 4 was also an output signal, according to our table. Our findings do not indicate this, so we should not assume that the port is a DTE port. However, we should check pin 20 for its status before judgment is passed.

Jumping ahead of our structured approach, repeat the step used to assess pin 4. This time, however, check pin 20 for its presence and direction. The VOM should register a reading indicating that pin 20 is present and is indeed an output signal. Hence, with the exception of pin 4, the port looks as if it is a DTE port. If documentation is available, our assessment is correct, even if pin 4 is not provided by the printer.

Continuing with the port assessment, proceed with signals 5 and 6. They are the same status as pin 3. Skipping to pin 8 through 19, the same is noted—no measurement. Pin 20 was already tested and confirmed as an output signal. Pins 21 through 25 should yield no measurement, indicating that they are input signals or are not used at all. In review, we now know that pins 2 and 20 are output signals from the HP and can assume that pins 1 and 7 are ground leads.

Which signal within in the HP port is used for hardware flow control? We only have one to choose from, pin 20. We will treat this lead as if it is to be used for this function. It will control the input signals required by

TABLE 1–2. SUMMARY OF DTE/DCE SIGNAL RELATIONS

Output leads	Port type	Input leads required
2, 4, 20	Data terminal equipment	3, 5, 6, 8
3, 5, 6, 8	Data communications equipment	2, 4, 20

Notes: The table assumes conformity to Electronics Industry Association (EIA) RS232 standard. Pins 2 and 3 are assumed to be data leads, while 4, 5, 6, 8, and 20 are control leads. Pins 1 and 7 are assumed to be ground leads.

the PC to regulate the output of data to be printed. Consulting the documentation for the HP, both hardware and software flow control are supported. Pin 20 is indeed used for hardware flow control.

We now know which leads (pins) are provided by each device. Table 1–3 outlines the leads provided. A cross-over cable is required to connect the HP (DTE) to the PC (DTE). A straight-through cable, 1–1, 2–2, 3–3, 4–4, will not work, as the direction of the leads will clash. To complete the cabling requirements, review the next section, which describes how to ascertain which leads are required by each of the ports to function. Once this is known, we can design and construct the cable.

6. Determine leads required to be on

We now have determined which leads are provided by each. This was done by either consulting the documentation or a VOM. The next step is to determine which leads are input signals to the PC and printer ports, in other words, which leads should be on for data transmission and reception.

First, let's look at the PC's port. Recall that we attempted to perform a screen print from the PC keyboard. The port became enabled, yet the output did not actually occur. We are able to detect this, noting that the cursor on the screen did not progress line by line until the screen had been output through the serial port. Furthermore, by monitoring pin 2 with the VOM or BOB, we would see no fluctuation on pin 2, Transmit Data, which is the lead used by the PC to send the bits of the character to an attached device. We need to determine the appropriate input signals that must be on for the computer to output data.

The easiest way is to consult the documentation once again. This is the quickest way to note all the input signals for a port. However, this can be misleading, as not all the signals may be required prior to data transmission. This is a great source to identify the signals "to" the PC port. From this we find that pin 3 (Receive Data), pin 5 (Clear to Send), pin 6 (Data Set Ready) pin 8 (Data Carrier Detect), and pin 22 (Ring Indicator) are input signals to the PC port. As mentioned, not all these leads must be on for output to occur. From previous experience, only pins 5 and 6 are required for a printer connection. When using communication software such as Crosstalk XVI, pin 8 must also be on. Pin 22 is used as an indication that an incoming call is being received. This allows the port to get the modem to answer a call. Pin 22 is not required to be on for data transmission, especially in our printer connection. From these input leads, pins 5, 6, and 8 should be on for our connection. Ignore pin 3 for now as it is a data lead. This matches the guidelines set forth in Table 1–2.

A VOM can assist in finding input leads without the documentation. Unfortunately, the only way to accomplish this is through trial and error. Since we already know the output signals of the PC's port, pins 2, 4, and 20, we can attempt to determine which of the leads must be on. Ignore pin 3 for now, as it is a data lead.

The user should somehow connect pin 4 and/or 20 to pins 5, 6, and 8. Shielded wire can be used for this. Jumper the ends of four separate wires together, and connect them to pins 20, 5, 6, and 8. The tricky part is getting the wires to stay connected to the pins in the PC port. Because we are testing the port only, electrical tape can be used to build a receptacle around the end of the wire. This strawlike piece can then be slid onto one of the pins. Repeat this for the other three pins.

Once the connections are made, set up the VOM to monitor pin 2 of the interface. Use the probes to connect to pin 7 and pin 2. Ensure that the proper scale and settings are being used on the VOM to measure up to 15 volts DC.

Earlier, the Mode command was covered as a means of enabling the RS232 port. Type "MODE LPT1:=COM1" followed by a return, and then hold down the Shift key simultaneously with the Prt Sc key. This enables the serial port as the printer port and dumps a copy of the screen contents through that port. The cursor should scan the screen while it dumps the screen information out the port. Pin 2 was an output signal from the PC for all the data bits, so the VOM's needle/indicator should be registering a reading. If the needle of the VOM is held on and movement is almost nonexistent, there is no cause for concern. The reason for little or no noticeable fluctuation, corresponding to the on/off condition for the ones and zero bits, is the speed of the

TABLE 1–3. LEADS PROVIDED BY PC AND HP LASERJET

Device	Lead #	Function	Direction
PC	2	Transmit Data	from
	4	Request to Send	from
	20	Data Terminal Ready	from
HP	2	Transmit Data	from
	20	Data Terminal Ready	from

port. The data are being output at a high rate of speed, probably 9600 bps. To slow down the output, the user can change the speed of the port with the mode command. Type the following to reduce the speed of the port to 300 bps:

```
MODE COM1:300      followed by a return
MODE LPT1:=COM1    followed by a return
```

This should allow you to see the on/off representation of the ones and zero bits of the characters. You still won't be able to recognize specific characters. At 300 bps, an average of 30 characters is being output each second. This was calculated by dividing the bit rate, 300 bps, by the number of bits per character, including start and stop bits, 10, to yield 30 cps. However, the data transmission should be apparent.

The purpose of this exercise has been to satisfy the input signals necessary for the PC to output data. From this, the user can assess that pins 5, 6, and 8 are required prior to data transmission. To confirm this, do the screen dump routine as before. Monitor the output on the screen or VOM. Watch what happens if you disconnect pin 5 or pin 6. The screen dump should halt. Reconnect it! The screen dump should continue. If you halt it too long, the PC will abort the output. But for our purposes, try this to conclude that pins 5 and 6 must be on for the PC to output data through the RS232 port. Pin 8 does not impact output when connecting printers, but does in communicating environments. We will treat it just like pins 5 and 6 for completeness.

This is an example of hardware flow control in action. Flow control using the pins of the RS232 interface was discussed earlier in this chapter. Refer to it for clarification. However, the user now knows how to determine which leads are input and which must be on for data transmission to occur.

HP LaserJet. Determine leads required to be on. This step of port analysis involving a printer is not quite as easy as is analysis of the PC port, the reason being that the printer cannot dump information out of the port. Hence, we cannot use trial and error to determine which leads must be on.

The best method is to consult the documentation, or our charts that outline generalities of ports. We had determined that pin 20 was the only output control signal in the HP port and that it was a DTE interface. We would be led to believe that pins 5, 6, and 8 should be on prior to being able to receive data from an attached computer. This would be a good bet. However, the HP does not require any input control signals to be present for it to receive data. This is often the case with printers, as they don't transmit data unless software flow control is used.

If the documentation were not available, the assumption that 5, 6, and 8 were input signals to the HP should not cause any problems. The resulting cable design to include these would simply not serve any purpose.

7. Design the cable

We know what the RS232 hardware requirements are at both ports of the PC and the HP devices. A quick review of our SCS port profile summarizes our findings:

Computer SCS port profile

Underline if supported; circle if selected.

Model: PC/XT _____   Vendor: IBM _____   Port: ACA _____
Port type: <u>serial</u> parallel
Port: <u>DB25</u> 9-pin 5-pin 8-pin/modular 20mA Centronics

Gender: <u>male</u> female

Pin #	Function	Direction	Pin #	Function	Direction
1	_____	to from n/a	9	_____	to from n/a
2	Transmit Data	to from n/a	10	_____	to from n/a
3	Receive Data	to from n/a	11	_____	to from n/a
4	Request to Send	to from n/a	12	_____	to from n/a
5	Clear to Send	to from n/a	13	_____	to from n/a
6	Data Set Ready	to from n/a	14	_____	to from n/a
7	Signal Ground	to from n/a	15	_____	to from n/a
8	Data Carrier Detect	to from n/a	16	_____	to from n/a

Gender: <u>male</u> female

Pin #	Function	Direction	Pin #	Function	Direction
17	_____	to from n/a	22	Ring Indicator	to from n/a
18	_____	to from n/a	23	_____	to from n/a
19	_____	to from n/a	24	_____	to from n/a
20	Data Terminal Ready	to <u>from</u> n/a	25	_____	to from n/a
21	_____	to from n/a			

Complete the next section only with 36-pin cinch connector.

Pin #	Function	Direction	Pin #	Function	Direction
26	_____	to from n/a	27	_____	to from n/a
28	_____	to from n/a	29	_____	to from n/a
30	_____	to from n/a	31	_____	to from n/a
32	_____	to from n/a	33	_____	to from n/a
34	_____	to from n/a	35	_____	to from n/a
36	_____	to from n/a			

Flow control technique: XON/XOFF ENQ/ACK STX/ETX (Hardware) _____
Leads that must be on: <u>5 6 8</u> __ __ __ __

Options:
    Speeds: <u>110 300 600 1200</u> 1800 <u>2400 4800</u> (9600) 19.2 56k _____
    Parity: <u>even odd</u> space mark (none)
    Char-length: 7(8) __
    # stop bits: (1) 1.5 2
    Line-ending sequence: cr lf <u>cr/lf</u> cr/lf/lf
    Disconnect sequence: EOT DEL ~. _____
    Mode: <u>async</u> sync isoch   sync timing leads:

#	Function	Direction
15	_____	to from
17	_____	to from
24	_____	to from

Notes: _____
_____
_____

Printer SCS port profile

Underline if supported; circle if selected.

Model: LaserJet _____   Vendor: Hewlett-Packard   Port: RS232
Interface type: <u>serial</u> parallel
Port type: <u>DB25</u> 9-pin 5-pin 8-pin/modular 20mA Centronics

Gender: male <u>female</u>

Pin #	Function	Direction	Pin #	Function	Direction
1	Chassis Ground	to from <u>n/a</u>	10	_____	to from n/a
2	Transmit Data	to <u>from</u> n/a	11	_____	to from n/a
3	Receive Data	<u>to</u> from n/a	12	_____	to from n/a
4	_____	to from n/a	13	_____	to from n/a
5	_____	to from n/a	14	_____	to from n/a
6	_____	to from n/a	15	_____	to from n/a
7	Signal Ground	to from n/a	16	_____	to from n/a
8	_____	to from n/a	17	_____	to from n/a
9	_____	to from n/a	18	_____	to from n/a

Gender: male <u>female</u>

Pin #	Function	Direction	Pin #	Function	Direction
19	_____	to from n/a	23	_____	to from n/a
20	Data Terminal Ready	to from n/a	24	_____	to from n/a
21	_____	to from n/a	25	_____	to from n/a
22	_____	to from n/a			

Complete the next section only with 36-pin cinch connector.

Pin #	Function	Direction	Pin #	Function	Direction
26	_____	to from n/a	27	_____	to from n/a
28	_____	to from n/a	29	_____	to from n/a
30	_____	to from n/a	31	_____	to from n/a
32	_____	to from n/a	33	_____	to from n/a
34	_____	to from n/a	35	_____	to from n/a
36	_____	to from n/a			

Flow control technique: <u>XON/XOFF</u> ENQ/ACK STX/ETX (Hardware) _____
Flow control lead(s): 4 11 19 <u>20</u> __ __ __

Leads that must be on: 5 6 8 __ __ __ __
Options:

    Speeds: 110 <u>300 1200</u> 1800 <u>2400 4800</u> (9600) 19.2k 56k _____
    Parity: even odd space mark (none)
    Char-length: 7 (8) __
    # stop bits: (1) 1.5 2
    Line-ending sequence: <u>cr</u> lf cr/lf cr/lf/lf

    Mode: <u>async</u> sync

#	Function	Direction
15	_____	to from
17	_____	to from
24	_____	to from

sync timing leads:

Printer compatibility modes: Epson MX Diablo630 <u>HP LaserJet</u> HP ThinkJet NEC 3500 IBM Graphics IBM Color Printronix TI-810

Notes: _____
_____
_____

It can be easier to analyze the cable pinouts if grouped by function. The function of leads is outlined in the EIA RS-232-C standard document. Once we group the foregoing pinouts into the four categories of ground, data, control, and timing, the cable design will be much easier. The foregoing chart could be rearranged as shown in Table 1–4.

We are now ready to design the cable by looking at each category of leads of both ports. A few general rules should be established prior to any cable design.

CABLE DESIGN: GENERAL RULES

1. Connect like categories of leads together.
2. Always connect an "out" to an "in" and an "in" to an "out."
3. A lead that is input should only be connected to another lead that is an input, if both of these are connected to an output lead.
4. In synchronous connections, use only one source of timing, or minimize the number used.

Keeping these general rules in mind, let's design the cable.

Ground leads. First, deal with the ground leads—they are probably the easiest leads to handle. Protective Ground is provided to protect the user from sustaining a shock in the case of an electrical short. Pin 1 is generally the protective ground lead of most RS232 interfaces. It is also frequently referred to as Chassis Ground or Frame

TABLE 1–4. PC AND HP LASERJET LEADS GROUPED BY CATEGORY

IBM PC/XT		HP LaserJet
Ground Leads		
		1 Protective Ground
Signal Ground	7	7 Signal Ground
Data Leads		
Transmit Data (out)	2	2 Transmit Data (out)
Receive Data (in)	3	3 Receive Data (in)
Control Leads		
Request to Send (out)	4	
Clear to Send (in)	5	
Data Set Ready (in)	6	
Data Carrier Detect (in)	8	
Data Terminal Ready (out)	20	20 Data Terminal Ready (out)
Timing Leads		
n/a		

Ground. In this tutorial module, the PC port documentation does not indicate the presence of a Protective Ground. This is not a show stopper because a Protective Ground is provided within the PC itself. It may be isolated from the interface. Nonetheless, we will allow for it in our interface. The HP provides for it. We will merely connect the two Protective Ground leads, pins 1 and 1, together.

Signal Ground signals are the key ground leads in the interface. These leads are used as a reference point for all the other signals in the interface. When the voltage level, as outlined in the RS232-C standard, is to be ±5 volts, this is relative to Signal Ground. Both the interfaces provide a Signal Ground lead, found on pin 7 of the ports. These two leads should be connected to provide a common Signal Ground for the two interfaces. Table 1–5 summarizes these two connections, completing the design for the ground category of leads.

Data leads. The next category of leads to tackle is the data leads. There are only two possible connections for these, so we can quickly lay out the cabling of the data category. The Transmit Data lead, with a direction of out/from, is the lead on which data will be sent out of a computer. The PC will send all its data on the Transmit Data lead. Likewise, the HP will send its characters on this lead. The only characters that the HP will be transmitting are the flow control characters, XON/XOFF. This will only be done if software flow control will be used. Pin 2 is the Transmit Data lead for both computers. General rule 2 indicated to connect an output lead to an input lead. Both number 2 pins are output signals. Hence, we should not connect them "straight through."

The Receive Data lead, pin 3 on both parts, is the lead that is used by the devices to receive data. Any data that the PC is to receive are expected to arrive on pin 3. Since the HP is sending its data out on pin 2, destined for the PC, this lead should be connected to the Receive Data lead of the PC. By connecting the HP's pin 2 to the PC's pin 3, the PC will receive whatever information the HP sends it, specifically the software flow control characters. The converse is true! Connect the Transmit Data lead of the PC, pin 2, to the Receive Data

TABLE 1–5. GROUND LEAD CONNECTIONS

PC		HP	
Function	Pin #	Pin #	Function
Protective Ground	1 ------- 1		Protective Ground
Signal Ground	7 ------- 7		Signal Ground

LEGEND: The "-------" refers to connecting the two leads together. Pin 1 in the PC end of the cable will be connected to pin 1 at the HP end of the cable by means of a conductor between the two pins. This is commonly referred to as a "straight-through" connection. Pins 1 and 7 will be "straight through" from end to end.

TABLE 1–6. DATA LEAD CONNECTIONS

PC			HP
Function	Pin #	Pin #	Function
Transmit Data	2 ------⟩	3	Receive Data
Receive Data	3 ⟨-----	2	Transmit Data

LEGEND: The "------⟩" refers to connecting the two leads together. It differs from the "straight-through" connection in that there is a "cross-over" connection. Pin 2 at the PC end of the cable is connected to pin 3 at the HP end of the cable, with a piece of wire or conductor between them. The "------⟩" also indicates that a direction of a lead is involved. This is included for clarity only, as there are no special wire connections involved. The same type of connections are made as "straight-through" ones. The only difference is that different pins are connected at each end of the cable.

lead of the HP, to allow the HP to get data from the PC. We now have allowed for data to be output by one device and received (input) by the other. Table 1–6 depicts the data category portion of the cable design.

Earlier, we indicated that there were only two possible connections with the data leads. The two possibilities were (1) "straight through" yielding pin 2 connected to pin 2 and pin 3 to pin 3, and (2) "crossed over," yielding pin 2 at one end of the cable connected to pin 3 at the other end, and vice versa. The only other possibility for data lead design appears when there is only a Receive Data lead on a printer's port. This is possible when printers are involved and no software flow control is supported. In this case there will be no characters transmitted and, hence, no need for a Transmit Data lead from a printer. Our HP does support this and does include this pin number.

Control leads. This is generally the toughest category of leads to understand. However, by keeping the general rules for cable design in mind, even the control leads can be easily tackled. The control leads that we have to work with are given in Table 1–7.

Within the control lead category, the direction of the leads is extremely important. Note the directions of the leads, specifically that pins 5, 6, and 8 in the PC port are input leads. Clear to Send (CTS), Data Set Ready (DSR), and Data Carrier Detect (DCD) are input signals expected by the PC to indicate the status of the connection to the HP. In the software that controls the PC's RS232 serial port, a special code is included to monitor the status of these three leads. If they are on, the PC will interpret this as meaning that the connection to the other device is OK. If they are off (low), the PC will assume that the attached device is turned off, an error condition has occurred, or nothing is connected. Because of this monitoring, the cable we design can use this as an advantage. The cable will be designed so that whenever the HP is turned on and its port is enabled, the PC will detect this by watching pins 5, 6, and 8. The completed cable will allow all this to take place without any involvement required by the users of the systems.

Recall that whenever the HP's port was enabled, pin 20 was on. This lead was Data Terminal Ready (DTR). If the printer were turned off or taken offline, an error condition had occurred, or the ports were not active, this lead would be off. Note the direction of this lead as output.

Apply our general rule 2, and connect an output to an input lead. If we connect pin 20 at the HP end of the cable, "crossed over" to pins 5, 6, and 8 at the PC end of the cable, what are the results? As long as the

TABLE 1–7. PC AND HP LASERJET CONTROL LEADS

PC		HP	
Request to Send (out)	4		
Clear to Send (in)	5		
Data Set Ready (in)	6		
Data Carrier Detect (in)	8		
Data Terminal Ready (out)	20	20	Data Terminal Ready (out)

TABLE 1–8. PC/XT-TO-HP CONTROL LEADS

PC	Pin #	Pin #	HP
Clear to Send (in)	5 ⟨--|------- 20		Data Terminal Ready (out)
Data Set Ready (in)	6 ⟨--|		
Data Carrier Detect (in)	8 ⟨--|		

Legend: The "⟨--" indicates a "cross-over" connection. This implies a connection from pin 20 at the HP end of the cable across to pins 5, 6, and 8 at the PC end of the cable. Pins 5, 6, and 8 are said to be "jumpered" together. Pin 20 should be connected to one of the leads, for example, pin 5. Pins 6 and 8 are then connected together and then to pin 5 to allow pin 20 at one end and pins 5, 6, and 8 to be all "jumpered" together. This daisy chaining allows pin 20 to control the status, on/off condition, of the PCs pins. DO NOT connect pins 5, 6, and 8 "straight through" to the other end of the cable. Make the connections only as depicted. Improper connection could cause the status of these leads to be improperly controlled.

HP port is active, pin 20 will be on. If it is on, and connected to pins 5, 6, and 8 at the PC end, these leads should also be turned on. This is merely a voltage level applied at one end of a wire and conducted across the wire to the other end. Now the PC will be able to know the status of the HP by monitoring pins 5, 6, and 8. When the HP port is enabled, pins 5, 6, and 8 will be on. When the HP port is inactive, pins 5, 6, and 8 will be off. Table 1–8 depicts the "cross-over" connection.

The HP had no input leads that were to be on for data transmission. Our earlier port analysis determined this to be the case. However, chances are that your printer, other than an HP, had the same input lead requirements as the PC. If this is the case, repeat the "cross-over" connection as in Table 1–8, but in the reverse direction. Table 1–9 shows how the completed control lead category would be in such a case.

Referring to Table 1–9, note that pin 4 at the PC port was not used at all. The signal direction for this lead is out/from. We have taken care of all input signal requirements, so this pin serves no purpose in our cable design. Implicit with pin 20's function name (Data Terminal Ready) is reference to the readiness of the DTE. There will be cases when pin 4 will be used to control the status of input signals. But for now we will ignore this pin.

Timing leads. We will exclude the timing category of leads. Because both ports are asynchronous, we do not have to contend with any timing leads in the RS232 interface. Refer to Chapter 3 on connecting modems for further clarity on the timing leads.

THE CABLE HAS BEEN COMPLETELY DESIGNED

Table 1–10 depicts the final cable design with special notes about the design.

TABLE 1–9. PC/XT-TO-HP CONTROL LEAD DESIGN

PC	Pin #	Pin #	HP
Clear to Send (in)	5 ⟨--|------- 20		Data Terminal Ready (out)
Data Set Ready (in)	6 ⟨--|		
Data Carrier Detect (in)	8 ⟨--|		
Data Terminal Ready (out)	20 ---	|--⟩ 5	Clear to Send (in)
		|--⟩ 6	Data Set Ready (in)
		|--⟩ 8	Data Carrier Detect (in)

Legend: Connect pin 20 from the HP end across to pins 5, 6, and 8 as previously described. "Cross-over" pin 20 from the PC end of the cable to pins 5, 6, and 8 at the HP end of the cable, with single wire between them in the cable. Then "jumper" 5, 6, and 8 together at the HP end of the cable. Whenever the PC port is enabled, pins 5, 6, and 8 will be on at the HP end of the cable. It is worth reiterating that the latter "cross-over" is only required if your printer, instead of the HP, has leads that must be on for data transmission.

TABLE 1–10. COMPLETED PC-TO-HP CABLE DESIGN

PC				HP	
Function	Pin #		Pin #	Function	
Protective Ground	1	-------	1	Protective Ground	
Signal Ground	7	-------	7	Signal Ground	
Transmit Data (out)	2	------〉	3	Receive Data (in)	
Receive Data (in)	3	〈------	2	Transmit Data (out)	
Clear to Send (in)	5	〈--|---	20	Data Terminal Ready (out)	
Data Set Ready (in)	6	〈--|			
Data Carrier Detect (in)	8	〈--|			
{Data Terminal Ready (out)	20	-------|--〉	5	Clear to Send (in)	
		|--〉	6	Data Set Ready (in)	
		|--〉	8	Data Carrier Detect (in)	}

Notes:

1. Pin 1 in the PC end of the cable will be connected to pin 1 at the HP end of the cable by means of a wire between the two pins. Pin 7 will also be "straight through" from end to end.

2. Pin 2 at the PC end of the cable is connected to pin 3 at the HP end of the cable, with a piece of wire between them. The converse is true with the HP's pin 2 "crossed over" to the PC's pin 3.

3. "Cross-over" pin 20 from the HP end of the cable to pin 5 at the PC end of the cable with single wire between them in the cable. Then "jumper" 5, 6, and 8 together at the PC end of the cable. Repeat this in the reverse within the { } braces if your printer has input lead requirements as discussed in the text. In our tutorial module, the absence or presence of the reverse "cross-over" should not impact our connection.

8. Building the cable

Now that we have a cable design, we are ready to build the cable. Tutorial Module 5–1 includes a step-by-step approach to building this cable. The genders involved are the same, female at the PC end of the cable and male at the HP end of the cable. Follow this procedure exactly, substituting the HP end for the 3B1 computer for the actual cable construction. Pin 22 should be excluded, as Ring Indicator is not applicable to a computer-printer connection. The cable constructed should be as that outlined in Table 1–11.

TABLE 1–11. PC/XT-TO-HP CABLE DESIGN

HP A end		PC B end
1	-------	1
7	-------	7
2	〈--| X	2
	|--〉	3
	|--〉	2
3	〈--| X	3
	X |--〉	5
	X |--〉	6
	X |--〉	8
20	----| X	20
4	----| X	4
22	----| X	22

Legend: Pin 20 is used to control the status of 5, 6, and 8 at the opposite connector. Pins 5, 6, and 8 are *not* "straight through." Pin 4 should not be "straight through." Pin 22 may be "straight through" and not cause any harm, yet may be removed like pin 4. "X" indicates no connection.

9. Test for continuity

Once the cable has been constructed, it is worthwhile to perform a continuity check. A continuity check will determine the lead makeup of the cable, specifically the leads that are ''straight through,'' ''jumpered,'' or ''crossed over.'' Specific test equipment is available for this cable test, but a BOB or a VOM can be used.

First, let's use a VOM to check our continuity in the cable. This will be a pin-by-pin test. Make notes as you progress to ensure completeness. Practice logging them using a chart such as the following. Lines will be drawn to identify which conductors are connected, once we identify the connections (Table 1–12):

TABLE 1–12. BLANK FORM FOR CONTINUITY CHECK

Connector end A (Male)	Connector end B (Female)
1	1
2	2
3	3
.	.
.	.
.	.
25	25

Because one of the cable ends is female, getting to each of the sockets may be difficult. It would probably be better if you opened the hoods, commonly referred to as covers, surrounding the connectors at both ends of the cable. This would permit easy access to the leads. This is done by unscrewing the cover screws that hold the connector together. Refer to Figure 1–4. Some connectors may merely pop apart, not involving screws. The connector is put together with two halves. By removing the screws, the hood can be taken apart, thus exposing the leads on the back side of the DB25 connector. Another technique would be to wrap a paper clip around the end of the probe. The end of the opened paper clip can easily fit into the slots of the female connectors. Either way, we need to make contact with the metal slots and pins.

With the hood removed, we can begin our test. Using a VOM, set the meter to the 1-ohm scale. Once set up, touch the two probes together and note the meter reading. We are looking for a similar reading during the continuity check. We will refer to the different probes as red and black, the cable ends as connector A and connector B, and the pins/wires by number. Connector A will be the HP end; connector B will be the PC end of the cable. The wires in the cable may be different colors. There is inconsistency among the color coding of leads, so we will not reference the colors.

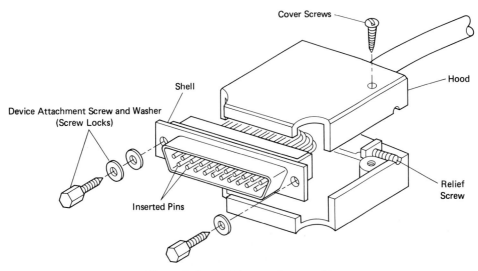

Figure 1–4. DB25 connector assembly.

Recall the reference number associated with the pin number of the connector. The goal is to determine which conductors in the cables are connected. Place the black probe into pin 1 of the cable end. Holding this in place, touch every lead 2, 3, 4, . . . , 25 individually within the same connector. Record any local jumperings. For example, in our PC-HP cable, leads 5, 6, 8 were connected together in the PC end connector.

With the black probe still in socket 1, test leads 1, 2, 3, 4, . . . , 25 of the other connector at the other end of the cable. Log your findings.

Once this step is complete, move the black probe to lead 2, testing leads 1, 3, 4, 5, . . . , 25 on the local connector and leads 1, 2, 3, 4, . . . , 25 in the other connector. Log and repeat this for all 25 leads. Once you have tested leads 1–25 at one end, and their connections to the other side of the cable, you need only test the other connector for local jumperings. Some cables may have lead 4 looped back to 5, 6, and 8 in the same connector. Ours won't, but you should always check the second connector. Log your findings.

Your logging should match that as depicted in Table 1–11. If it does not, correct the problem, and recheck it. Once the cable is built to your satisfaction, replace the hood/covers around each connector. Label each end of the cable with notations such as "IBM PC end" and "HP end." Keep a summary of the "cross-overs" that can be attached to the cable with tape. Permanent tagging and logging will save you much time in the future when dealing with the systems or reusing the cable. Turn to the discussion of "SCS RS232 Cable Designer" in Chapter 6 for other information on cable logging.

10. Cable the two systems

With the cable you have just constructed, plug the connectors into the computers. Be sure that connector A is plugged into the HP and that connector B is plugged into the PC serial port. Our cable will only allow it to be connected in one manner due the differences in gender. However, depending on the systems you are connecting, the gender of both ends of the cable could be the same. If they are labeled, the choice will be easy.

Screw the connectors onto the ports they are plugged into. As computers are moved slightly, this will prevent the cable from being disconnected. This could be devastating if you are in the middle of a large file transfer and the two systems become unplugged. You are now prepared to attempt to dump information from the PC to the HP LaserJet.

11. Measure success

With the cable constructed, and the two systems cabled together, the user can begin to use the printer. The printer, if in the Online mode, is ready for the PC to dump data to it for printing. The PC can only do this if the serial port has been properly set up for use as a printer port.

At the PC, setting up the serial port as the default printer port is fairly easy. Merely power up the computer as you normally would, if it is not already on. Once you are at the DOS prompt, usually the "A⟩" or "C⟩" prompt, begin to set up the serial port. Consult the Computer Port Profile sheet for the PC port options to be used that are common with the HP. The common options between the two are asynchronous transmission, 9600 bps, 8 data bits, 1 stop bit, no parity, full duplex operation, and hardware flow control. If the serial port being used on the PC is COM1, typing the following will set up the port.

```
MODE COM1:96,N,8,1,P     followed by a return
MODE LPT1:=COM1          followed by a return
```

You've seen this before. The first command line options the port, COM1. Substitute COM2 as appropriate. The "96" establishes the speed, the "N" indicates no parity, the "8" is 8 bits per character, and the "1" is 1 stop bit. The newly introduced item is the "P." When setting up or administering a PC port for connection to a printer, this is an important parameter. Including the "P" indicates that a printer is attached. This allows the port to send appropriate line-ending sequences. But, also, it allows for the hardware flow control to be recognized properly. Include this in your command line to ensure completeness. If you do not include this, errors could occur when flow control begins to be used. Transfer these two command lines to your autoexec.bat file to be executed each time you boot your computer.

The default settings of the HP printer should do just fine, as they match the common options. Be sure that the HP is turned on and is online.

Test out the connection by printing a copy of the screen contents of the PC. This is done by holding the Shift key simultaneously with the Prt Sc key. The contents of the screen should be output to the HP LaserJet printer. After approximately 5 to 10 seconds, the printing should be complete. This was the sign of success that you noted earlier. CONGRATULATIONS! You have successfully completed the connection of the PC/XT to an HP LaserJet printer. There is only one other item that you must check to ensure 100 percent success—flow control.

Recall that our true sign of success when connecting a printer to a computer was the ability to print data. Not only do we want to be able to print data, but we must be able to print lots of it without losing any. Printers have various error conditions that can occur when receiving and printing data sent from a computer. Refer to the section in this chapter about printer flow control for a discussion of the error conditions: paper-out, buffer overrun, printer offline, printer error.

We must check to see if the flow control incorporated into the cable actually functions. The best way to accomplish this is to create an error condition while the printer is receiving data from the PC. We will take the HP offline to create such an error condition. Our "sign of success" will be a clean hardcopy of what we are printing, despite the error condition.

To send a listing of the directory that you are in on the PC out to the printer, use the "print online" capability of the PC. Holding down the Ctrl key simultaneously with the Prt Sc key will set up a Print Online (POL) condition. In this mode, everything that is displayed on the PC's screen will be also dumped to the printer. Test this mode by issuing a directory listing command as in the following:

CD /   followed by a return
DIR   followed by a return

This will move you to the root directory and list all the files in that directory using the long directory format. As this is displayed on the screen, you should also get a hardcopy sent to the HP. You will not notice that a hardcopy is being printed on the LaserJet, as if you were connecting a dot-matrix printer. The dot-matrix printer prints either a character or line at a time, allowing you to see/hear it as it is printing. The HP LaserJet is a page printer. Hence, a page of information is queued prior to its actually being printed. You can, however, look at the HP's panel on the front of the printer. Here are excerpts from the HP LaserJet's documentation that describe how to detect what is occurring.

> . . . flashing ready indicator . . . means that the printer is receiving data . . . if the memory contains less than a page of data, pressing the form feed key will print . . .

In summary, our directory listing may only fill a partial page of memory. If this is the case, pressing the Form feed key on the panel will give you a hardcopy of the incomplete page. Do this to ensure that our command sequence is working.

If the information displayed on the screen, but not on the printer, ensure that the Mode command was issued correctly and that the cable is properly connected. Be sure that there are no other error conditions indicated on the HP's panel, such as "out of paper."

We are now ready to test the flow control. Hit the Online key on the printer panel to ensure readiness to receive data. This should turn on the ready light. Issue the same DIR command to send the information out to the printer. Quickly touch the Online key on the printer panel. This should take the printer offline, a signal to the PC that it should stop sending data. If our flow control is functioning, the directory listing on the PC's screen should be halted. If it has, and you know that you are not at the end of the directory listing, press the Online key on the printer panel again. This should put the printer in the Online mode again, allowing the PC to continue dumping the directory listing to the printer. Hit the Online key a couple of more times to ensure that the flow control is working. Once the directory listing is finished, pressing the Ctrl key and the Prt Sc key again will turn the Print Online capability off at the PC.

Take the HP "offline" and hit the Form feed key on the panel. This should allow the printing of the incomplete page. Press the Online key to put the LaserJet back in the Ready condition. Compare the hardcopy of the directory listing with that on the screen of the PC. If it is the same, CONGRATULATIONS! You have built the proper cable, taking into account such complicated factors as flow control and all port options.

If you are unable to get a hardcopy of your desired output, a couple of possibilities exist. Table 1–13 lays out the steps to be taken if the "signs of success" are not evident. Try each of these separately to isolate the problem. One or more of them may be causing the problem.

If you follow the steps in Table 1–13 and still don't achieve "success," consult the vendors. You may have a computer hardware or software problem that is beyond the scope of the interfacing discussion in this book.

TABLE 1–13. CHECKLIST FOR PRINTER CONNECTION FAILURES

1. The cable is not securely connected, is connected to the wrong port, or has the wrong ends connected to the wrong port.
2. The computer or printer is not on. Be sure that the HP and the PC are up and running.
3. Your serial port on the PC is not optioned properly. Reissue the Mode command using the proper options.
4. Your serial port is not set up as the default printer port. Set up the COM1 (or COM2) port to be the default, using the MODE LPT1=COM1 sequence.
5. Options are set incorrectly at the HP. The factory setting should have worked. Perhaps they have been altered or were not set correctly to begin with. Make sure that the options match at both ports, specifically the speed, character length, parity, and duplex.
6. Check to see that there are no printer error conditions. The HP will not print if the printer is out of paper, offline, paper jam, in test mode, and so on. Reset the printer to clear any of these conditions. For a more complete listing, consult the documentation.
7. Be sure that the PC was in the POL condition when the test was attempted. If a screen dump was being tried, this should not have mattered.
8. Recheck the cable design and continuity.

Tutorial Module 1-2: Connecting an HP LaserJet to an IBM PC/AT

This tutorial module is a mirror image of Tutorial Module 1–1 except that the port to which we will be connecting the LaserJet printer will be a 9-pin RS232 port. This will impact our cable design and cable construction, but the other steps will be exactly the same. We will not repeat the steps other than the cable design portion.

Steps 1–6

Refer to Tutorial Module 1–1. The only difference is that the port analysis would have yielded the port profile shown in Table 1–14 for the PC/AT, due to the 9-pin male serial port. (Refer to Tutorial Module 4–3 for a step-by-step analysis of the AT port.)

7. Design the cable

Upon review of the foregoing, you will note that the same leads are supported in the interface as the PC/XT in Tutorial Module 1-1. The only difference is the pin numbers. Look at the functions of each of the leads laid out in Table 1–15, and note the cross-reference of the leads. Armed with this information, you can substitute the AT pin numbers in the cable that was designed for the XT-to-LaserJet connection. Review Table 1–11 for the XT-to-LaserJet cable design. The substitution of pin numbers would be as that outlined in Table 1–16.

8–11.

Repeat the procedures outlined in Tutorial Module 1–1 to complete the cable construction, connection, and testing. At the PC/AT cable end, use a 9-pin female connector; the HP end should be a male DB25 connector. CONGRATULATIONS!

Tutorial Module 1-3: Connecting a QMS Laser Printer to a Plexus Computer

In this tutorial module, a QMS printer will be connected to a multiuser computer system. The keys in this exercise are the multiple ports available on the computer. The QMS printer could easily be another printer in this example. However, the Plexus P15 and P20 computers offer a variety of serial ports. These ports vary by the number of pins, size connector, and pin functions. This case study will show you how to connect the QMS printer to all these ports, even though they may not be labeled for printer connection.

The Plexus documentation indicates that the ports in Table 1–17 are available for connection to TTY-type devices. These are the ports provided by the motherboard itself of a P/15 or P/20 computer system. Other ports are provided by ports boards, referred to as intelligent communication processors (ICPs) and communication processors (ACPS). The following ports (Table 1–18) are provided by each of these boards that can be used on multiple Plexus computers. Be sure that you know which port type you are working with in this tutorial module.

TABLE 1–14. SCS PORT PROFILE FOR PC/AT

Computer Port Profile

Underline if supported; circle if selected.

Model: PC/AT _____   Vendor: IBM _____   Port: COMM _____

Port type: <u>serial</u> parallel

Port: DB25 <u>9-pin</u> 5-pin 8-pin/modular 20mA Centronics

Gender: <u>male</u> female

Pin #	Function	Direction	Pin #	Function	Direction
1	Carrier Detect	to from n/a	14	_____	to from n/a
2	Receive Data	to from n/a	15	_____	to from n/a
3	Transmit Data	to from n/a	16	_____	to from n/a
4	Data Terminal Ready	to from n/a	17	_____	to from n/a
5	Signal Ground	to from n/a	18	_____	to from n/a
6	Data Set Ready	to from n/a	19	_____	to from n/a
7	Request to Send	to from n/a	20	_____	to from n/a
8	Clear to Send	to from n/a	21	_____	to from n/a
9	Ring Indicator	to from n/a	22	_____	to from n/a
10	_____	to from n/a	23	_____	to from n/a
11	_____	to from n/a	24	_____	to from n/a
12	_____	to from n/a	25	_____	to from n/a
13	_____	to from n/a			

Complete the next section only with 36-pin cinch connector.

26	_____	to from n/a	27	_____	to from n/a
28	_____	to from n/a	29	_____	to from n/a
30	_____	to from n/a	31	_____	to from n/a
32	_____	to from n/a	33	_____	to from n/a
34	_____	to from n/a	35	_____	to from n/a
36	_____	to from n/a			

Flow control technique: XON/XOFF ENQ/ACK STX/ETX Hardware _____

Leads that must be on: 8 6 1 __ __ __

Options:

    Speeds: 110 300 600 1200 1800 2400 4800 9600 19.2 56k _____

    Parity: even odd space mark none

    Char-length: 7 8 ____

    # stop bits: 1 1.5 2

    Line-ending sequence: cr lf cr/lf cr/lf/lf

    Disconnect sequence: EOT   DEL   ~. _____

    Mode: async sync isoch

	sync timing leads:	
#	Function	Direction
15	_____	to from
17	_____	to from
24	_____	to from

Notes: The options of this port are set up using the MS-DOS Mode command. Your application may do this automatically or through a menu-driven interface.

To which port should the QMS printer be connected? You decide, as this tutorial module will provide for connection to the five different types. The key part to this tutorial module will be the cable design step, as five different cables will be designed. The steps used for connection are no different from those in any other tutorial module and are as follows:

The Cable Has Been Completely Designed

TABLE 1–15. CROSS-REFERENCE OF AT AND PC/XT PINOUTS

Lead function	AT lead #	PC/XT lead #
Transmit Data	3	2
Receive Data	2	3
Request to Send	7	4
Clear to Send	8	5
Data Set Ready	6	6
Signal Ground	5	7
Data Carrier Detect	1	8
Data Terminal Ready	4	20
Ring Indicator	9	22

TABLE 1–16. IBM PC/AT-TO-HP LASERJET CABLE DESIGN

PC		AT		HP	
Function	Pin #	pin #		Pin #	Function
Signal Ground	7	5	-------	7	Signal Ground
Transmit Data (out)	2	3	------)	3	Receive Data (in)
Receive Data (in)	3	2	⟨------	2	Transmit Data (out)
Clear to Send (in)	5	8	⟨--|---	20	Data Terminal Ready (out)
Data Set Ready (in)	6	6	⟨--|		
Data Carrier Detect (in)	8	1	⟨--|		

NOTES: The HP had no input lead requirements; hence a 4-conductor cable can be used. The ''--'' indicates a ''straight-through'' connection, while the ''--)'' implies a ''cross-over.'' The ''⟨--\|--'' implies ''jumpering.''

TABLE 1–17. PLEXUS PORTS PROVIDED BY MOTHERBOARD

Port #	Type connector	# of signals	Comments
Port 0	9-pin	3	Reserved for console
Port 1	9-pin	3	No hardware handshake
Port 2	9-pin	3	No hardware handshake
Port 3	9-pin	3	No hardware handshake
Port 4	9-pin	7	Signals provided for modems
Port 5	9-pin	7	Signals provided for modems
Port 6	25-pin	12	Include timing lead support
Port 7	25-pin	12	Include timing lead support

TABLE 1–18. ICP AND ACP PORTS

Port #	Type connector	# of signals	Comments
ICP	25-pin	11	Include timing lead support
ACP	9-pin	9	Timing leads (3 and 5) are supported only on ports 0–7 on the ACP

1. Determine compatibility (should it work?).
2. Determine signs of success.
3. Determine the type of connector used.
4. Determine gender of the ports.
5. Determine which leads (pins) are provided by each device.
6. Determine which leads are required to be on by each device.
7. Design the cable.
8. Build the cable.
9. Test the cable for continuity.
10. Cable the two systems together with the cable.
11. From step 2, measure success.

1. Determine compatibility

The QMS printer provides an asynchronous port supports speeds up to 9600 bps, 8 bits per character, XON/XOFF, no parity, full duplex, and 1 stop bit. This matches that of any of the ports on the Plexus computers; hence, the two systems are compatible. A separate SCS port profile for each port will not be provided in this tutorial module; however, a summary of the leads will be included in the ensuing steps.

2. Determine signs of success

As the UNIX system is the operating system governing the Plexus computers, use the other tutorial modules' signs of success for this step and step 11. Refer to Tutorial Module 1–6 for complete details.

3. Determine type of connector

4. Determine gender of ports

Table 1–19 lists the different genders and types of connectors used on the various Plexus ports, as well as the QMS KISS printer.

TABLE 1–19. SUMMARY OF PLEXUS AND QMS KISS CONNECTORS

Device	Port #	Type connector	Gender
P/15/20	0–5	DB9	Female
P/15/20	6–7	DB25	Female
ICP	0–7 (8–15)	DB25	Female
ACP	0–15	DB9	Female
QMS-KISS	RS232	DB25	Female

5. Determine leads (pins) provided by each device

6. Determine leads required to be on

Consult the documentation to determine the leads provided by each of the Plexus computer ports, as well as the QMS printer. The ports on the Plexus computers, regardless of connector, emulate DTE. This means they provided data terminal equipment signals. They are summarized in Table 1–20:

TABLE 1–20. PORT PINOUTS FOR PLEXUS COMPUTER PORTS AND QMS KISS PRINTER

P/15/20: Ports 0–3 on Motherboard (DB9F)	
Function	Lead #
Transmit Data (out)	1
Receive Data (in)	6
Signal Ground	8

* * *

The Cable Has Been Completely Designed

25

TABLE 1–20. *(Continued)*

P/15/20: Ports 4–5 on Motherboard (DB9F)

Function	Lead #
Transmit Data (out)	1
Request to Send (out)	2
Data Terminal Ready (out)	4
Receive Data (in)	6
Clear to Send (in)	7
Signal Ground	8
Data Carrier Detect (in)	9

* * *

P/15/20: Ports 6–7 on Motherboard (DB25F)

Function	Lead #
Frame Ground	1
Transmit Data (out)	2
Receive Data (in)	3
Request to Send (out)	4
Clear to Send (in)	5
Signal Ground	7
Data Carrier Detect (in)	8
Transmit Clock (in)	15
Receive Clock (in)	17
Data Terminal Ready (out)	20
Ring Indicator (in)	22

* * *

ICP: Ports 0–7 (or 8–15 on P/15/20) (DB25F)

Function	Lead #
Transmit Data (out)	2
Receive Data (in)	3
Request to Send (out)	4
Clear to Send (in)	5
Data Set Ready (in)	6
Signal Ground	7
Data Carrier Detect (in)	8
Speed Select (out)	11
Transmit Clock (in)	15
Receive Clock (in)	17
Data Terminal Ready (out)	20

* * *

ACP: Ports 0–15 (DB9F)

Function	Lead #
Transmit Data (out)	1
Request to Send (out)	2
Receive Clock (in)	3
Data Set Ready (out)	4
Transmit Clock (in)	5
Receive Data (in)	6
Clear to Send (in)	7
Signal Ground	8
Data Carrier Detect (in)	9

* * *

TABLE 1–20. *(Continued)*

QMS KISS printer (DB25F) Function	Lead #
Chassis Ground	1
Transmit Data (out)	2
Receive Data (in)	3
Request to Send (out)	4
Data Set Ready (in)	6
Logic Ground	7
Data Terminal Ready (out)	20

As you can see, the pinouts vary between the various Plexus computer ports. A number of them provide for timing leads which will be ignored, as well as the Ring Indicator leads, as no synchronous devices or modems are involved.

7. Design the cable

The cables necessary to connect the different computer ports to the QMS printer port will now be designed. Standard logic prevails for connecting the devices as outlined in the rules for cable design (see Table 1–21).

8. Build the cable

9. Test for continuity

10. Cable the two systems together

11. Measure success

Follow steps 8–11 according to the same procedures in Tutorial Module 1–1 and 1–6. The gender of the connectors at the end of each cable will be male, regardless of 9-pin or 25-pin connector. Once the cable is constructed, have the Plexus systems administrator set up the port so a printer is supported, with the common options of 9600 bps, XON/XOFF, 8 data bits, 1 stop bit, full duplex, and no parity. The QMS KISS printer should match these, paying particular attention to the flow control option. Disable the DTR data throttle option, disable the RTS data throttle, and enable the XON/XOFF options. CONGRATULATIONS!

Tutorial Module 1–4: Connecting an AT&T 5310 Teleprinter to an Auxiliary Port of a Wyse W-85 Terminal

Occasionally it is necessary to use a terminal that has a printer attached to it, as when a terminal is to access a computer and print a copy of the information sent to the terminal from the computer. This is often referred to as a POL function. In this scenario, a printer is attached to an auxiliary port of the terminal, not the main/communication port.

Tutorial Module 1–4 will center on this requirement and use a Wyse WY-85 as the terminal, with an AT&T 5310 printer attached to it. The terminal or printer may vary in your scenario, but the concepts of what to look for and check will be the same. An Epson, Mannesmann Tally, Star Micronics, NEC, or Toshiba printer, to name just a few, could be used, as long as an RS232 interface is provided on these. The cable and options may be different, but the concept is the same. Figure 1–5 depicts the connection covered in this module. This tutorial module is equally applicable to those installations where a terminal and printer are remotely connected to a computer using modems.

We will follow the steps common to all our tutorial modules:

STEPS FOR CONNECTION

1. Determine compatibility (should it work?).
2. Determine signs of success.
3. Determine the type of connector used.
4. Determine gender of the ports.
5. Determine which leads (pins) are provided by each device.
6. Determine which leads are required to be on by each device.

The Cable Has Been Completely Designed

TABLE 1–21. CABLE DESIGNS BETWEEN PLEXUS COMPUTER PORTS AND QMS KISS PRINTER

P/15/20: Ports 0–3 on Motherboard

Function	Lead #		Lead #	Function
Signal Ground	8	-------	7	Logic Ground
Transmit Data (out)	1	------⟩	3	Receive Data (in)
Receive Data (in)	6	⟨------	2	Transmit Data (out)
		|--	20	Data Terminal Ready (out)
		|-⟩	6	Data Set Ready (in)

* * *

P/15/20: Ports 4–5 on Motherboard

Function	Lead #		Lead #	Function
Signal Ground	8	-------	7	Logic Ground
Transmit Data (out)	1	------⟩	3	Receive Data (in)
Receive Data (in)	6	⟨------	2	Transmit Data (out)
Data Terminal Ready (out)	4	------⟩	6	Data Set Ready (in)
Data Carrier Detect (in)	9	⟨------	20	Data Terminal Ready (out)
Clear to Send (in)	7	⟨------	4	Request to Send (out)

* * *

P/15/20: Ports 6–7 on Motherboard

Function	Lead #		Lead #	Function
Signal Ground	7	-------	7	Logic Ground
Frame Ground	1	-------	1	Chassis Ground
Transmit Data (out)	2	------⟩	3	Receive Data (in)
Receive Data (in)	3	⟨------	2	Transmit Data (out)
Clear to Send (in)	5	⟨------	4	Request to Send (out)
Data Carrier Detect (in)	8	⟨------	20	Data Terminal Ready (out)
Data Terminal Ready (out)	20	------⟩	6	Data Set Ready (in)

* * *

ICP: Ports 0–7 (or 8–15 on P/15/20)

Function	Lead #		Lead #	Function
Signal Ground	7	-------	7	Logic Ground
Transmit Data (out)	2	------⟩	3	Receive Data (in)
Receive Data (in)	3	⟨------	2	Transmit Data (out)
Clear to Send (in)	5	⟨------	4	Request to Send (out)
Data Set Ready (in)	6	⟨-|----	20	Data Terminal Ready (out)
Data Carrier Detect (in)	8	⟨-|		
Data Terminal Ready (out)	20	------⟩	6	Data Set Ready (in)

* * *

ACP: Ports 0–15 (DB9F)

Function	Lead #		Lead #	Function
Transmit Data (out)	1	------⟩	3	Receive Data (in)
Data Set Ready (out)	4	------⟩	6	Data Set Ready (in)
Receive Data (in)	6	⟨------	2	Transmit Data (out)
Clear to Send (in)	7	⟨------	4	Request to Send (out)
Signal Ground	8	-------	7	Logic Ground
Data Carrier Detect (in)	9	⟨------	20	Data Terminal Ready (out)

* * *

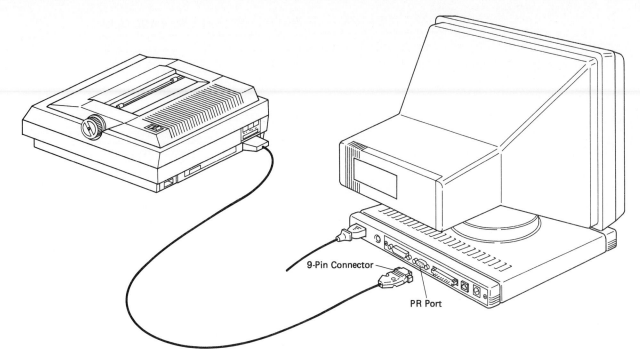

Figure 1–5. Wyse terminal with locally attached serial printer.

7. Design the cable.
8. Build the cable.
9. Test the cable for continuity.
10. Cable the two systems together with the cable.
11. From step 2, measure success.

1. Determine compatibility

The two devices will work together, providing that they have the same interfaces, speeds, character lengths, parity, transmission mode, and flow control. The user should perform port profile analysis on each prior to answering this question. Table 1–22 highlights the port analysis results, obtained from the standard user documentation. The common options between the two of them appear to be asynchronous, 7 data bits, even parity, 1 stop bit, hardware flow control, and 9600 bps. Either hardware or software flow control may be used here. We will design the cable to support both, but we will use hardware flow control in our tutorial module. The speed of 9600 bps was chosen to match the speed of the terminal-to-computer speed. Refer to Figure 1–5. We are assuming a local connection of the terminal to a computer, with the attached printer. If your terminal is connected to a modem, set up the printer to match the speed of the line, normally 1200 bps in the case of a 212a modem attached to the terminal. This is an important point having to do with flow control. We will discuss this point later in the tutorial module. For now, match the speed of the printer-terminal connection to that of the terminal-computer (or modem) connection.

2. Determine signs of success

Our printer-terminal connection will be successful if we can perform a Print online function without loss of data. The attached computer would be sending information to the terminal, with the printer producing a hardcopy of the same information. We must be assured that the printer does not lose any of the information. In other words, flow control must function between the printer and terminal as well as between the terminal and computer. Our success will be complete if we can print a long document from the computer, through the terminal, to the printer.

3. Determine type of connector

First, we will analyze the Wyse terminal. The WY-85 terminal has multiple connectors on the back of the base of the unit. View it or consult the documentation for a description of each. Viewing the back of the base unit, from left to right, it provides COMM, PR, 20mA, TEST, and KYBD ports. The one of interest to us is the

TABLE 1–22. TERMINAL PORT PROFILE FOR WYSE WY-85 TERMINAL

Underline if supported; circle if selected.

Model: Wy-85 _____ Vendor: Wyse _____ Port: PR _____

Port type: DB25 <u>9-pin</u> 5-pin 8-pin/modular 20mA Centronics

Gender: <u>male</u> female

Pin #	Function	Direction	Pin #	Function	Direction
1	<u>Shield Group</u>	to from <u>n/a</u>	14	_____	to from n/a
2	<u>Transmit Data</u>	to <u>from</u> n/a	15	_____	to from n/a
3	<u>Receive Data</u>	<u>to</u> from n/a	16	_____	to from n/a
4	<u>Request to Send</u>	to <u>from</u> n/a	17	_____	to from n/a
5	<u>Determined Ready</u>	to <u>from</u> n/a	18	_____	to from n/a
6	<u>Data Set Ready</u>	to <u>from</u> n/a	19	_____	to from n/a
7	<u>Signal Ground</u>	to from <u>n/a</u>	20	_____	to from n/a
8	_____	to from n/a	21	_____	to from n/a
9	_____	to from n/a	22	_____	to from n/a
10	_____	to from n/a	23	_____	to from n/a
11	_____	to from n/a	24	_____	to from n/a
12	_____	to from n/a	25	_____	to from n/a
13	_____	to from n/a			

Complete the next section only with 36-pin cinch connector.

26	_____	to from n/a	27	_____	to from n/a
28	_____	to from n/a	29	_____	to from n/a
30	_____	to from n/a	31	_____	to from n/a
32	_____	to from n/a	33	_____	to from n/a
34	_____	to from n/a	35	_____	to from n/a
36	_____	to from n/a			

Flow control technique: <u>XON/XOFF</u> (Hardware) _____

Flow control lead(s): 4 11 19 20 __ __ __

Leads that must be on: 5 <u>6</u> 8 __ __ __ __

Printer port: serial   parallel

   Flow control: XON/XOFF Hardware _____

   FC lead(s): 4 11 19 20 __ __ __   Connector DB25 Centronics

Options:

   Speeds: 110 300 600 1200 1800 2400 4800 (9600) 19.2 56k _____

   Parity: (even) odd space mark none

   Char-length: (7) 8 ____

   # stop bits: (1) 1.5 2

   Line ending sequence: cr lf cr/lf cr/lf/lf

   Mode: async sync isoch   sync timing leads:

#	Function	Direction
15	_____	to from
17	_____	to from
24	_____	to from

Terminal compatibility: ANSI X3.64 VT100 VT220 VT52 _____

TABLE 1–22. (*Continued*)

Printer Port Profile for 5310 Printer

Underline if supported; circle if selected.

Model: 5310 printer _____ Vendor: AT&T _____ Port: RS-232-C _____

Interface type: <u>serial</u> parallel

Port type: <u>DB25</u>   9-pin   5-pin   8-pin/modular 20mA Centronics

Gender: <u>male</u> female

Pin #	Function	Direction	Pin #	Function	Direction
1	Frame Ground	to from <u>n/a</u>	14	_____	to from n/a
2	Send Data	to <u>from</u> n/a	15	_____	to from n/a
3	Receive Data	<u>to</u> from n/a	16	_____	to from n/a
4	Request to Send	to <u>from</u> n/a	17	_____	to from n/a
5	_____	to from n/a	18	_____	to from n/a
6	Data Set Ready	<u>to</u> from n/a	19	SRTS	to <u>from</u> n/a
7	Signal Ground	to from <u>n/a</u>	20	Data Terminal Ready	to <u>from</u> n/a
8	Data Carrier Detect	<u>to</u> from n/a	21	_____	to from n/a
9	_____	to from n/a	22	Ring Indicator	<u>to</u> from n/a
10	_____	to from n/a	23	_____	to from n/a
11	SRTS	to <u>from</u> n/a	24	_____	to from n/a
12	Speed Mode	<u>to</u> from n/a	25	_____	to from n/a
13	_____	to from n/a			

Complete the next section only with 36-pin cinch connector.

26	_____	to from n/a	27	_____	to from n/a
28	_____	to from n/a	29	_____	to from n/a
30	_____	to from n/a	31	_____	to from n/a
32	_____	to from n/a	33	_____	to from n/a
34	_____	to from n/a	35	_____	to from n/a
36	_____	to from n/a			

Flow control technique: <u>XON/XOFF</u> ENQ/ACK STX/ETX (Hardware) _____

Flow control lead(s): 4 <u>11</u> (19) 20 __ __ __

Leads that must be on: 5   <u>6</u>   <u>8</u> __ __ __ __

Options:

    Speeds: <u>110</u> 300 600 1200 1800 2400 4800 (9600) 19.2 56k _____

    Parity: (even) odd space mark none

    Char-length: (7) 8 __

    # stop bits: (1) 1.5 2

    Line-ending sequence: cr lf cr/lf cr/lf/lf

    Mode: async sync   sync timing leads:

#	Function	Direction
15	_____	to from
17	_____	to from
24	_____	to from

    Printer compatibility modes: Epson MX Diablo 630 HP LaserJet HP ThinkJet NEC 3500 IBM Graphics IBM Color Printronix TI-810

Note: Pins 11 and 19 are active only if flow control option value is E.A.

The Cable Has Been Completely Designed

9-pin port labeled "PR." Do not use the COMM port, as this is for connection to our computer, or to a modem. The PR port is for attachment of a local printer to the terminal. Notice, if you have ATs in your office, that this port resembles the 9-pin AT port. This resemblance is in size, shape, and gender only. The pinouts are different, as we will review. The Wyse WY-85 terminal does provide a 9-pin port for a printer.

The 5310 provides a 25-pin DB25 connector, labeled EIA (RS232). It is different from the Wyse PR connector. Hence, we will need to construct a DB25 to 9-pin cable to connect the two devices together.

4. Determine gender of ports

The Wyse terminal provides a 9-pin "male" port. The terminal end of the cable will be a female 9-pin connector. The 5310 provides a DB25P port. This is a male port, implying that the printer end of the cable needs to be a female gender connector. We now know the gender of both ports. Update the port profile sheets with this information.

5. Determine leads provided by each device

6. Determine leads required to be on

With the Wyse terminal, a break-out box cannot be used, unless the BOB provides a 9-pin tester. If this is available, use it. Otherwise, a VOM could be used in the same manner as in other case studies. The simplest approach is to review the documentation to arrive at which signals are provided (output) and required (input) by the terminal. Table 1–23 outlines those leads as listed in the user's manual. A standard BOB or VOM may be used to analyze the 5310 printer port. However, consulting the documentation, the user can arrive at the pinouts summarized in Table 1–24.

7. Design the cable

At this point, we are ready to design the cable necessary to connect the AT&T 5310 printer, or printer of your choice, to the Wyse terminal. Prior to cable design, it is worthwhile to review the rules for cable design as in the following.

CABLE DESIGN: GENERAL RULES

1. Connect like categories of leads together.
2. Always connect an "out" to an "in" and an "in" to an "out."
3. A lead that is input should only be connected to another lead that is an input, if both of these are connected to an output lead.
4. In synchronous connections, only use one source of timing. (Because the 5310 to Wyse connection is asynchronous, this point is not applicable.)

TABLE 1–23. WYSE TERMINAL PR PORT LEADS

Function	Lead #	
Shield Ground (PG)	1	
Transmit Data (out)	2	
Receive Data (in)	3	
Request to Send (out)	4	
Data Terminal Ready (out)	5	
Data Set Ready (in)	6	(flow control)
Signal Ground	7	

NOTES: Lead 6 must be on before data will be output by the terminal to the printer on pin 2. This lead is our flow control lead for hardware flow control. The lead numbering for this port is from left to right, top to bottom. If you are facing the pins of the port, lead 1 is in the top row, leftmost position. Lead 5 is in the top row, rightmost position, lead 6 is the leftmost position of the bottom row of leads, while lead 9 is the rightmost in the same row.

TABLE 1–24. 5310 PRINTER EIA (RS232) PORT LEADS

Function	Lead #
Frame Ground	1
Send Data (out)	2
Receive Data (in)	3
Request to Send (out)	4
Data Set Ready (in)	6
Signal Ground	7
Data Carrier Detect (in)	8
Secondary Request to Send (out)	11
Speed Mode Indication (in)	12
Secondary Request to Send (out)	19
Data Terminal Ready (out)	20
Ring Indicator (in)	22

NOTES: Pins 11 and 19 are active only if flow control option value is EIA. If Secondary Request to Send option value is EIA (hardware flow control), then these pins will be on when the printer can receive data into the buffer and when there is paper in the printer. Choose one of them for hardwood flow control lead (out). Pin 20 also provides the online/offline status for the printer. Leads 6 and 8 should be on for the printer to receive data.

The easiest way to tackle the leads is to separate them by category of ground, data, control, and timing. Timing leads are not appropriate, as this is an asynchronous connection. Table 1–25 outlines the various leads separated by category.

The ground leads are the easiest to tackle. Connect the two Protective Grounds together "straight through." Do the same for the Signal Ground leads as depicted in Table 1–26. The data category of leads should be tackled next, as you can apply our cable design rules, 1 and 2. Connect like categories of leads together; connect "ins" to "outs," and vice versa (Table 1–27).

The most difficult lead category is the control category. However, if you tackle the inbound leads, one at a time, it is not so bad. Determine which leads are involved in hardware flow control, both inbound and outbound, to ensure the proper cable design. Reviewing Table 1–23, note that the Wyse PR port has one input control lead.

TABLE 1–25. WYSE WY-85 TERMINAL AND AT&T 5310 PRINTER LEADS SEPARATED BY CATEGORY

Function	Wyse lead #	5310 lead #	Function
Shield Ground (PG)	1	1	Frame Ground
Signal Ground	7	7	Signal Ground
Transmit Data (out)	2	2	Send Data (out)
Receive Data (in)	3	3	Receive Data (in)
Request to Send (out)	4	4	Request to Send (out)
Data Terminal Ready (out)	5	6	Data Set Ready (in)
Data Set Ready (in)	6	8	Data Carrier Detect (in)
		11	Secondary Request to Send (out)
		12	Speed Mode Indication (in)
		19	Secondary Request to Send (out)
		20	Data Terminal Ready (out)
		22	Ring Indicator (in)

The Cable Has Been Completely Designed

TABLE 1–26. WYSE PR-TO-AT&T 5310 GROUND LEADS

Function	Wyse lead #	5310 lead #	Function
Shield Ground (PG)	1 -------	1	Frame Ground
Signal Ground	7 -------	7	Signal Ground

TABLE 1–27. WYSE PR-TO-AT&T 5310 DATA LEADS

Function	Wyse lead #	5310 lead #	Function
Transmit Data (out)	2 ------⟩	3	Receive Data (in)
Receive Data (in)	3 ⟨------	2	Send Data (out)

LEGEND: Connect the outbound data lead from the Wyse printer port "crossed over" to the inbound data lead in the 5310 printer port. Repeat this for the outbound 5310 data lead.

Lead 6 is the input control lead that the terminal monitors to determine the status of the attached device. This lead will be connected to the outbound control lead that gives the status of the attached printer. On the 5310, both leads 11 and 19 are on whenever the printer has space in its buffer to receive data as well as has paper in the printer. The Secondary Request to Send option must be set to "EIA" for this to be the case. Also, be aware that the 5310 can "INVert" this signal level. This would yield a negative voltage on leads 11 and 19 when the printer was ready to receive. Do not set the printer up to invert the signal. You want a "positive" voltage on these leads if the printer can receive data, as the Wyse terminal looks for a "high" signal. Our cable design should allow lead 6 at the Wyse end to be connected to the 5310 outbound flow control leads, either 11 or 19. Our cable design will use pin 19. Table 1–28 outlines the flow control lead design of the Wyse PR to AT&T 5310 cable.

Now that flow control has been achieved, you should look at the remaining input leads, as these are the ones that need to be on before the terminal and printer can communicate. The outbound control leads are on, but don't need to be dealt with, as long as the input control lead requirements have been met. All the Wyse input control leads (the only one) have been satisfied with our flow control design. Look at the input control leads of the 5310 to complete our cable design.

The AT&T 5310 printer has several input control leads, as listed in Table 1–24. Let's put aside the ones that are not applicable. Pin 22, Ring Indicator, and pin 12, Speed Mode Indicator, are input control leads used whenever a modem is to be connected to the printer. Ignore these as this is not appropriate in this tutorial module. With these two leads aside, only leads 6 and 8 remain. Data Set Ready and Data Carrier Detect are input control leads that need to be on for the printer to be in "line" mode or online. If we want these leads to indicate that status of the attached Wyse terminal, then one of the output control leads from the terminal should be connected to these two leads.

The Wyse WY-85 PR port has two leads, 4 and 5, that can be used to control the status of the input control leads of the printer. In this tutorial module, lead 5, Data Terminal Ready, will be used. Our design should connect this lead, "crossed over" to the printer end of the cable and "jumpered" to both leads 6 and 8. Now, as long as the terminal port is enabled, pin 5 will be on. When pin 5 is on, by virtue of its connection, leads 6 and 8 will be on at the printer interface. This was our goal, shown in Table 1–29.

TABLE 1–28. WYSE PRINTER PORT-TO-AT&T 5310 FLOW CONTROL LEAD DESIGN

Function	Wyse lead #	5310 lead #	Function
Data Set Ready (in)	6 ⟨------	19	Secondary Request To Send

LEGEND: Lead 19 at the printer end of the cable should be "crossed over" to lead 6 at the Wyse end of the cable. This will allow pin 19 to determine the status of the lead 6 at the terminal's printer port, allowing hardware flow control.

TABLE 1–29. FLOW CONTROL DESIGN FOR 5310 TELEPRINTER TO WY-85 TERMINAL

Function	Wyse lead #	5310 lead #	Function
Data Terminal Ready (out)	5 -----:--⟩	6	Data Set Ready (in)
	:--⟩	8	Data Carrier Detect (in)

LEGEND: The output control lead, 5, from the terminal port should be "crossed over" to the input control leads of the printer. Leads 6 and 8 should be "jumpered" together at the printer end of the cable and have a conductor in the cable connecting them to pin 5 at the Wyse end of the cable.

This satisfies all our input control leads and completes our cable design. The completed cable design for connecting an AT&T 5310 to a printer port on Wyse Wy-85 terminal is summarized in Table 1–30.

8. Build the cable

9. Test for continuity

Using the various techniques described in earlier case studies, construct the cable. Recall that a female 9-pin connector is needed at the terminal end. The 5310 printer end of the cable required a female DB25 connector. The Wyse terminal connector supports 9 pins, but only uses 7; hence, a cable with seven conductors maximum may be used. Once the cable is constructed, be sure that the "straight-throughs," "jumperings," and "cross-overs" are as you desired the cable to be. Refer to other sections on the best way to check for continuity.

10. Cable the two systems together

Once you're satisfied that the cable is constructed according to your design, cable the 5310 printer to the Wyse terminal. The cable will only go one way, since there are two different-size connectors involved. Screw the connectors to the ports securely and proceed to the testing of your success.

11. Measure success

From step 2, we will rejoice when we are able to print a hardcopy of all the data that are sent from the attached computer to the terminal. The feature that allows this to happen is termed Print online. POL has the terminal pass everything received through the printer port. The Wyse WY-85 terminal provided us this printer port labeled PR. We are ready to test this POL function.

The terminal-to-printer connection options should match those of the terminal-to-computer options. Specifically, the speeds, parity, character length, and stop bit options should be the same. If your terminal is locally attached to a computer, then more than likely the speed will be 9600 bps. If your terminal is connected to a remote computer via modems, then more than likely the line speed will be 1200 bps. The attached printer, and terminal "PR" ports, should be optioned to match this speed. The other agreed-to options are 7 data bits, even parity, 1 stop bit, and hardware flow control. We have already designed and constructed the cable to support hardware or

TABLE 1–30. WYSE WY-85 PRINTER PORT-TO-AT&T 5310 PRINTER CABLE DESIGN

Function	Wyse lead #	5310 lead #	Function
Shield Ground (PG)	1 -------	1	Frame Ground
Signal Ground	7 -------	7	Signal Ground
Transmit Data (out)	2 ------⟩	3	Receive Data (in)
Receive Data (in)	3 ⟨------	2	Send Data (out)
Data Set Ready (in)	6 ⟨------	19	Secondary Request to Send
Data Terminal Ready (out)	5 ---:--⟩	6	Data Set Ready (in)
	:--⟩	8	Data Carrier Detect (in)

LEGEND: The "------⟩" implies a "cross-over" between leads. The "5 ---:--⟩ 6" implies a "jumpering" between leads 6 and 8 at one "   :--⟩ 8" end of the cable, with a conductor between these two leads and lead 5 at the other end of the cable.

The Cable Has Been Completely Designed

software flow control. We will test the hardware flow control capability, but the software flow control is just as applicable.

There are two means of testing out our Print online feature. One is with a printer attached to the "PR" port. The other utilizes a break-out box. First, we will ensure that hardware flow control functions in a POL condition.

To test the terminal-printer connection with a break-out box, the terminal needs to be set up prior to this experiment. The options that should be set are duplex and flow control. Flow control, previously mentioned, should be set to be hardware flow control. This implies that, ultimately, the attached printer will raise and lower a lead that the terminal should interpret for flow of data. You should set your terminal to be "half duplex" to allow the terminal to display locally any information that you type on the keyboard. On the Wyse WY-85, this is done by hitting Function key 3. Go into the "Comm" options and set the "Echo:" option to "on." This echoes all input on the screen.

Enter the "Printer-1" options and set the "Handshake:" option to be DTR. This sets up the printer port to support hardware flow control. Review Table 1–29 and note that lead 6 is the input control lead for hardware flow control. This lead will be monitored by the terminal to determine when to stop and resume data flow to the attached printer. You could set this option to both hardware and software flow control if you desire. Some terminals do not support "both" as an option for flow control, so we will select hardware.

Enough about options. With a break-out box, we can fake out the PR port to think that a printer is attached. We will use a Black Box tristate BOB, but others will do. Attach the cable to the terminal that was constructed in the earlier steps of this tutorial module. Review Table 1–23 and note which leads are input control leads, output control leads, and the output data lead of the printer port. Note that lead 6 of the Wyse printer port is the input control lead.

With hardware flow control enabled on the terminal, as long as this lead is on, the printer will be assumed to be online, all right, and ready to receive data. If this lead is off, then data flow will halt and resume only after the lead is on again. Our cable from Table 1–30 connected the 5310 printer output flow control lead, 19, through the cable to lead 6. Also the output data lead from the Wyse printer port, lead 2, was "crossed over" to lead 3 at the printer end of the cable.

Connect the break-out box to the DB25 end of the cable. We need to apply a positive voltage to pin 19 at the printer end of the cable. Use one of the leads at the printer end of the cable that is held on by the Wyse printer port and "jumper" it on the BOB to lead 19. You should be able to use lead 5, 6, or 8, as these were "jumpered" locally and "crossed over" to lead 5 of the terminal end of the cable. Otherwise, you can use a positive source on the BOB itself to keep lead 19 high, and subsequently lead 6 at the terminal end. As long as lead 19 is on, and hence lead 6, the terminal will think a printer is attached, alive, and well. Pin 3 on the BOB is the data lead that we want to monitor, as this is the data lead to the printer.

With the terminal optioned as outlined, type some data on the keyboard. Enter enough to fill several lines on the screen. We will now check the flow control by performing a "Print local" function. Most terminals support this as a standard feature. The Wyse offers Function key 2 to print a copy of the screen contents. With some information on the screen of the terminal, hit the Print local key. This should dump the screen contents out the terminal's printer port. Watch the break-out box, specifically the data lead lamp, for monitoring the pin 3. It should be fluctuating, indicating that the screen contents are being dumped to an imaginary printer. Had a printer been attached, it would have printed the contents of the screen.

As the data are being output, disconnect lead 19 so it goes "off." This mimics the hardware flow control function by turning off lead 6 in the Wyse's printer port. Note the data lead on the break-out box. It should cease to fluctuate, indicating that data flow has stopped. To resume the data flow, reconnect pin 19 to the voltage source. The break-out box lamp for the data lead should once again be fluctuating, representing data flow. This test did not actually test the POL function, but affirms that hardware flow control within the terminal and our cable is functioning.

To test the flow control function with a printer, connect the printer to the terminal with the cable. With the printer online and full of paper, and the lid closed, repeat the test. This time, as the data are being printed, take the printer offline somehow, either by raising the lid or using the Online button of the printer. The flow of data should cease. Put the printer back online for a continuation of the data flow. Be sure that you have not lost any data. You have now tested the flow control from the printer, up to and including the terminal.

You now should test the POL function using the attached computer. As stated, this tutorial module assumes that the terminal and printer are locally attached to a computer. Hardware flow control is being used, although software flow control could just as easily been used. If your terminal and printer are remote from the computer, separated by modems and telephone lines, you should use software flow control. This includes the terminal, printer, and remote computer. Select whatever flow control is appropriate for your installation.

Enter a command on the terminal keyboard that will cause the computer to send you a file for displaying on the screen. If you are attached to a UNIX system, you can "cat" a file. The goal is to display a standard ASCII file that you can print on the printer and check out the flow control. The longer the file, the better. While you are receiving the information on the terminal, put the terminal in POL mode. Most terminals offer this as a key sequence. The Wyse WY-85 is put in Copy Print mode, or Print online mode, by holding down the Ctrl key and hitting Function key 2 simultaneously. In this mode, any data received from the attached computer, or entered on the keyboard, will be dumped to the printer. If you have not yet begun to display a file, enter the commands to do this. As the data are being received by the terminal, they should now also be printed on the printer. Check flow control by taking the printer offline. This should halt the flow of data from the computer. The only exception to this might be if the printer you are using has a large buffer that allows it to receive data continually. However, eventually the buffer should fill up, and the printer will exercise flow control with the data flow suspended. By putting the printer back online, the data flow should resume. This is flow control in action. CONGRATULATIONS!

Hitting the Ctrl and Function key 2 sequence again takes the terminal out of the POL mode. If the flow control does not appear to work in any of these tests, check the options and cabling; then repeat the tests. Double check to ensure that the options are set consistently among the computer, terminal, and printer. Particularly, the flow control method should be consistent.

Tutorial Module 1-5: Connecting an AT&T 5310 Teleprinter to the Auxiliary Port of an AT&T 610 Terminal

This module is exactly like Tutorial Module 1-4, except for the type of connector found on the back of the 610 terminal, used for printer connection. In Tutorial Module 1-4, a Wyse WY-85 terminal was used. This terminal provided a 9-pin connector, similar in size to that found on an IBM PC/AT. In this tutorial module the 610 is used, because it provides a standard DB25S-size port for local printer connection. Steps 1–6 and 8–11 will be ignored as they are a duplication of Tutorial Module 1-4. However, we will review the port profiles, design the appropriate cable, and summarize the options required on the 610 to support the 5310 printer. Figure 1–6 outlines the connection that is covered in this tutorial module.

The 610 port profile is shown in Table 1–31. Refer to Table 1–24 for a review of the 5310 port. With the

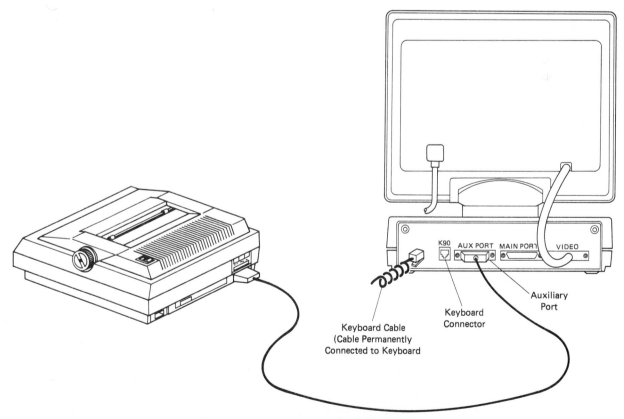

Figure 1–6. AT&T 610 with auxiliary printer.

TABLE 1–31. AT&T 610 PORT PROFILE

Terminal Port Profile

Underline if supported; circle if selected.

Model: 610 family _____ Vendor: AT&T _____ Port: AUX _____
Port type: DB25 9-pin 5-pin 8-pin/modular 20mA Centronics

Gender: male <u>female</u>

Pin #	Function	Direction	Pin #	Function	Direction
1	<u>Frame Ground</u>	to from n/a	14	_____	to from n/a
2	<u>Send Data</u>	<u>to</u> from n/a	15	_____	to from n/a
3	<u>Receive Data</u>	to <u>from</u> n/a	16	_____	to from n/a
4	<u>Request to Send</u>	<u>to</u> from n/a	17	_____	to from n/a
5	<u>Clear to Send</u>	to <u>from</u> n/a	18	_____	to from n/a
6	<u>Data Set Ready</u>	to <u>from</u> n/a	19	_____	to from n/a
7	<u>Signal Ground</u>	to from n/a	20	Data Terminal Ready	<u>to</u> from n/a
8	<u>Carrier Detect</u>	to <u>from</u> n/a	21	_____	to from n/a
9	_____	to from n/a	22	_____	to from n/a
10	_____	to from n/a	23	_____	to from n/a
11	_____	to from n/a	24	_____	to from n/a
12	_____	to from n/a	25	_____	to from n/a
13	_____	to from n/a			

Complete the next section only with 36-pin cinch connector.

26	_____	to from n/a	27	_____	to from n/a
28	_____	to from n/a	29	_____	to from n/a
30	_____	to from n/a	31	_____	to from n/a
32	_____	to from n/a	33	_____	to from n/a
34	_____	to from n/a	35	_____	to from n/a
36	_____	to from n/a			

Flow control technique: <u>XON/XOFF</u> Hardware _____
Flow control lead(s): 4 11 19 20 __ __ __
Leads that must be on: 5 6 8 __ __ __ __
Printer port: serial   parallel
   Flow control: XON/XOFF Hardware _____
   FC lead(s):   4 11 19 20 __ __ __   Connector DB25 Centronics

Options:
   Speeds: 110 300 600 1200 1800 2400 4800 9600 19.2 56k _____
   Parity: even odd space mark none
   Char-length: 7 8 __
   # stop bits: 1 1.5 2
   Line-ending sequence: cr lf cr/lf cr/lf/lf

Mode: async sync isoch   sync timing leads:

#	Function	Direction
15	_____	to from
17	_____	to from
24	_____	to from

   Terminal compatibility: ANSI X3.64 VT100 VT220 VT52 _____

NOTES: Pins 4 and 5 are tied together at the terminal so that when the attached device turns on lead 4, it receives the same signal on pin 5. Leads 6 and 8 are always on when the terminal has power. The AUX port only supports software flow control. This port emulates a DCE interface and is expecting to be connected to DTE.

Connecting Printers with RS232 Interfaces   Chap. 1

610 providing a female port and the 5310 printer equipped with a male port, our cable will have one of each gender. Note that the 610 printer port is emulating a DCE port. The port is set for connection to a piece of data terminal equipment such as our 5310 printer. Refer to the earlier discussion in this chapter of DTE/DCE port emulation.

The cable design should be laid out to support software flow control, as hardware flow control is not supported by the 610 terminal. There are many different possibilities with this in mind. Table 1–32 outlines the easiest for the 610 AUX port–to–5310 port cable design. Remember that the 610 end of the cable will need a male connector, while the 5310 requires a female connector.

Tutorial Module 1-6: Connecting a Toshiba P351 to a Pyramid Technology 90mx or 98x Computer Set

This module will feature the connection of a printer with a DB25-type connector to a multiuser micro with a DB25 connector. The printer to be used will be the Toshiba P1351 series. Toshiba provides the same type of interface in models P1340, P1350, P351, P341, and P321 and the PageLaser12, so substitute if necessary.

The computer featured is a UNIX-based multiuser micro offered by Pyramid Technology, the 90 series. The models 90mx, 90x, and 98x all get their serial interfaces using Pyramid's intelligent terminal processor (ITP). As this is a UNIX system, the ports require some setup to be performed by the systems administrator. This tutorial module will not delve into the UNIX administration function, but merely hint at where this should be done. Furthermore, the ports in a UNIX system are generally referenced as "ttyxxx," where "xxx" is some number. This module will feature the port ttyi05 as the one to which the printer will be connected, so adjust your nomenclature accordingly.

The steps we will follow for this tutorial module are common to all our reviews:

STEPS FOR CONNECTION

1. Determine compatibility (should it work?).
2. Determine signs of success.
3. Determine the type of connector used.
4. Determine gender of the ports.

TABLE 1–32. AT&T 610 AUX PORT-TO-AT&T 5310 PRINTER CABLE DESIGNS

Function	610 lead #		5310 lead #	Function
Frame Ground (PG)	1	-------	1	Frame Ground
Signal Ground	7	-------	7	Signal Ground
Transmit Data (in)	2	⟨------	2	Send Data (out)
Receive Data (out)	3	------⟩	3	Receive Data (in)
Request to Send (in)	4	:⟨-----	4	Request to Send (out)
Clear to Send (out)	5	:-----⟩	5	Clear to Send (ignored)
Data Set Ready (out)	6	------⟩	6	Data Set Ready (in)
Signal Ground	7	-------	7	Signal Ground
Data Carrier Detect (out)	8	------⟩	8	Data Carrier Detect
Data Terminal Ready (in)	20	⟨------	20	Data Terminal Ready (out)

LEGEND: Leads 4 and 5 can be excluded from the cable, as they serve no purpose. The 5310 ignores the input lead 5, which is internally tied within the terminal to lead 4. This is a "straight-through" cable; hence a ribbon cable may be used with a male connector at one end and a female connector at the other end.

OPTION NOTES:

1. Software flow control should be used in the printer, terminal, and computer.
2. The printer speed and 610 port speed should match that of the MAIN port.
3. The options of the COMM port should be used in the printer.
4. The Print Online function is enabled on the 610 by depressing the Ctrl key and Function key 4 simultaneously. Then press the key labeled Print Online. An asterisk in the screen label key indicates that the POL mode is enabled. Pressing the Function key again toggles this mode.

5. Determine which leads (pins) are provided by each device.
6. Determine which leads are required to be on by each device.
7. Design the cable.
8. Build the cable.
9. Test the cable for continuity.
10. Cable the two systems together with the cable.
11. From step 2, measure success.

1. Determine compatibility

Should the Toshiba 1351 work with the Pyramid 90x? UNIX is known for its support of asynchronous devices. As both these device ports are asynchronous, more than likely they are compatible. SCS port profiles should be completed for both these devices to determine absolute compatibility. Consult the documentation to fill in the profiles and assess whether they will function together or not. Table 1–33 outlines the port profiles for each of the devices. The common options between the ports are 9600 bps, 7 data bits, even parity, 1 stop bits, XON/XOFF flow control, full duplex.

2. Determine signs of success

Once the Toshiba printer is connected to the Pyramid computer, we will know we are successful if we can redirect some output directly to the printer. The output should be in correct form, meaning that there should be no undesired double spacing, no overwriting, no errors, and no loss of data (flow control). We will test the system by redirecting some output to the printer.

3. Determine type of connector

4. Determine gender of ports

By physically viewing the ports or consulting the documentation, the user should determine the type of connector used on both systems, as well as the gender. In our tutorial module, the Pyramid computers, using the ITP (Intelligent Terminal Processor), provide a DB25P connector, implying a 25-pin male connector. The Toshiba P351, on the other hand, provides a female 25-pin connector DB25S. Hence, our cable will have a female connector at one end, with a male connector at the other allowing for easy distinction for the connection.

5. Determine leads (pins) provided by each device

6. Determine leads required to be on

These next two steps have to do with the pinouts of the ports. The leads that are provided by each device can be determined by consulting the documentation, using a VOM, or by using a break-out box. Once these output leads are determined, the user can usually surmise what the input leads are. This is done by categorizing the port as emulating either DTE or DCE. If DTE, then the input leads are normally those provided by a piece of DCE, and vice versa. However, the documentation should be consulted to confirm this, as there are many variances from the standard interface. Consult Table 1–33 for a summary of the input and output leads of both device ports.

7. Design the cable

Once the ports have been totally analyzed, a cable may be designed. Separate the leads from Table 1–33 into the categories ground, data, and control for ease of cable design. Ignore the timing category, as this is an asynchronous connection. Table 1–34 lays out the separated categories of leads for both devices.

CABLE DESIGN: GENERAL RULES

1. Connect like categories of leads together.
2. Always connect an ''out'' to an ''in'' and an ''in'' to an ''out.''
3. A lead that is input may be connected to another lead that is an input, only if both these are connected to an output lead.
4. In synchronous connections, only use one source of timing. (Because the 90x-to-P351 connection is asynchronous, this point is not applicable.)

TABLE 1–33. PYRAMID 90X AND TOSHIBA P351 PORT PROFILES

Computer Port Profiles for

Underline if supported; circle if selected.

Model: 90mx, 90x, 98x Vendor: Pyramid Tech. Port: ITP RS232 __
Port type: <u>serial</u> parallel
Port: <u>DB25</u> 9-pin 5-pin 8-pin/modular 20mA Centronics

Gender: <u>male</u> female

Pin #	Function	Direction	Pin #	Function	Direction
1	Frame Ground	to from <u>n/a</u>	14	_____	to from n/a
2	Transmit Data	to <u>from</u> n/a	15	_____	to from n/a
3	Receive Data	<u>to</u> from n/a	16	_____	to from n/a
4	Request to Send	to <u>from</u> n/a	17	_____	to from n/a
5	Clear to Send	<u>to</u> from n/a	18	_____	to from n/a
6	Data Set Ready	<u>to</u> from n/a	19	_____	to from n/a
7	Signal Ground	to from <u>n/a</u>	20	Data Terminal Ready	to <u>from</u> n/a
8	Carrier Detect	<u>to</u> from n/a	21	_____	to from n/a
9	_____	to from n/a	22	Ring Indicator	<u>to</u> from n/a
10	_____	to from n/a	23	_____	to from n/a
11	_____	to from n/a	24	_____	to from n/a
12	_____	to from n/a	25	_____	to from n/a
13	_____	to from n/a			

Complete the next section only with 36-pin cinch connector.

26	_____	to from n/a	27	_____	to from n/a
28	_____	to from n/a	29	_____	to from n/a
30	_____	to from n/a	31	_____	to from n/a
32	_____	to from n/a	33	_____	to from n/a
34	_____	to from n/a	35	_____	to from n/a
36	_____	to from n/a			

Flow control technique (XON/XOFF) ENQ/ACK STX/ETX Hardware ____
Leads that must be on: 5 6 <u>8</u> __ __ __ __

Options:
Speeds: 110 300 600 1200 1800 2400 4800 (9600) 19.2 56k _____
Parity (even) odd space mark none
Char-length: (7) 8 __
stop bits: (1) 1.5 2
Line-ending sequence: cr lf cr/lf cr/lf/lf
Disconnect sequence: EOT DEL ~. _____

Mode: async sync isoch   sync timing leads:

#	Function	Direction
15	_____	to from
17	_____	to from
24	_____	to from

Notes: _____
_____
_____

The Cable Has Been Completely Designed

TABLE 1–33. *(Continued)*

Printer Port Profile

Underline if supported; circle if selected.

Model: P351 _____ Vendor: Toshiba _____ Port: RS232C _____
Interface type: <u>serial</u> parallel
Port type: <u>DB25</u> 9-pin 5-pin 8-pin/modular 20mA Centronics

Gender: male <u>female</u>

Pin #	Function	Direction	Pin #	Function	Direction
1	<u>Frame Ground</u>	to <u>from</u> n/a	14	<u>Fault</u>	to <u>from</u> n/a
2	<u>Send Data</u>	to <u>from</u> n/a	15	_____	to from n/a
3	<u>Receive Data</u>	<u>to</u> from n/a	16	_____	to from n/a
4	<u>Request to Send</u>	to <u>from</u> n/a	17	_____	to from n/a
5	<u>Clear to Send</u>	to <u>from</u> n/a	18	_____	to from n/a
6	<u>Data Set Ready</u>	to <u>from</u> n/a	19	<u>Data Terminal Ready</u>	to <u>from</u> n/a
7	<u>Signal Ground</u>	to from <u>n/a</u>	20	<u>Data Terminal Ready</u>	to <u>from</u> n/a
8	_____	to from n/a	21	_____	to from n/a
9	_____	to from n/a	22	_____	to from n/a
10	_____	to from n/a	23	_____	to from n/a
11	_____	to from n/a	24	_____	to from n/a
12	_____	to from n/a	25	_____	to from n/a
13	_____	to from n/a			

Complete the next section only with 36-pin cinch connector.

26	_____	to from n/a	27	_____	to from n/a
28	_____	to from n/a	29	_____	to from n/a
30	_____	to from n/a	31	_____	to from n/a
32	_____	to from n/a	33	_____	to from n/a
34	_____	to from n/a	35	_____	to from n/a
36	_____	to from n/a			

Flow control technique (XON/XOFF) ENQ/ACK STX/ETX <u>Hardware</u> _____
Flow control lead(s): 4 11 <u>19</u> <u>20</u> <u>14</u> __ __
Leads that must be on: 5 6 8 __ __ __ __

Options:
    Speeds: 110 300 600 1200 1800 2400 4800 (9600) 19.2 56k _____
    Parity (even) odd space mark none
    Char-length: (7) 8 ____
    # stop bits: (1) 1.5 2
    Line-ending sequence: cr lf cr/lf cr/lf/lf

Mode: async sync   sync timing leads:

#	Function	Direction
15	_____	to from
17	_____	to from
24	_____	to from

Printer compatibility modes: Epson MX Diablo630 HP LaserJet HP ThinkJet NEC 3500 IBM
    Graphics IBM Color Printronix TI-810

Note: The flow control option is switch selectable.

TABLE 1–34. PYRAMID TECHNOLOGY 90X AND TOSHIBA P351 LEADS BY CATEGORY

Function	90x lead #	P351 lead #	Function
Ground			
Frame Ground	1	1	Frame Ground
Signal Ground	7	7	Signal Ground
Data			
Transmit Data (out)	2	2	Send Data (out)
Received Data (in)	3	3	Received Data (in)
Control			
Request to Send (out)	4	4	Request to Send (out)
Clear to Send (in)	5	5	Clear to Send (in)
Data Set Ready (in)	6	6	Data Set Ready (in)
Data Carrier Detect (in)	8	8	Carrier Detect (in)
	n/a	14	Fault (out)
	n/a	19	Data Terminal Ready Alternate (out)
Data Terminal Ready (out)	20	20	Data Terminal Ready (out)
Ring Indicator (in)	22	n/a	

First, connect the ground and data leads. The same ground leads should be connected "straight through." Hence, the cable should have pin 1 at one connector, connected across the cable to pin 1 at the other cable. Pin 7 should be designed in the same manner.

As rules 1 and 2 state, the data output lead from one device should be connected to the data input lead at the other device. The cable design should allow for the Pyramid's pin 2 to be crossed over to pin 3 of the Toshiba printer. The same is true from the Toshiba's perspective. Table 1–35 outlines these category designs.

The timing category of leads is not applicable in this cable design, so proceed to the control category. It was determined earlier (in step 1) that XON/XOFF flow control would be used. Because of this, there is no need to deal with the output hardware flow control leads of the printer. It is better when software flow control is to be used not to use the hardware flow controls if avoidable. The reason for this is that the computer, in some UNIX systems, may misinterpret the received signal given. An example is in order.

Most UNIX systems will accept software flow control on their serial ports, but not all of them support hardware flow control. A serial computer port set up for XON/XOFF expects the input control leads to be on whenever the opposite device, in this case, a printer is connected. If the printer suddenly appears not to be connected, most UNIX systems will abort the print job. This could be catastrophic in some cases. The intent of flow control is to regulate the flow, not cut it off. If the printer supports both hardware and software flow control, and exercises both simultaneously, this could confuse the computer it is attached to. Read on for an example of what can happen.

If a printer needs to suspend temporarily the flow of data it is receiving from the computer due to a buffer overflow condition, it will send and XOFF character to the computer. Consult the special section in this text regarding flow control for further details of this interaction. If, however, the printer is also exercising hardware flow control at the same time, it would lower the output hardware flow control lead. With the Toshiba, this is lead 14, 19, or 20. Assume that pin 14 is being used to keep the input control leads on at the computer through "cross-overs." When the buffer overrun occurs, not only does the printer send an XOFF character, it also lowers pin 14, causing the input control leads of the computer to be lowered. The UNIX system you are using may well

TABLE 1–35. PYRAMID 90X AND TOSHIBA P351 GROUND AND DATA LEAD DESIGN

Function	90x lead #	P351 lead #	Function
Frame Ground	1 -------	1	Frame Ground
Signal Ground	7 -------	7	Signal Ground
Transmit Data (out)	2 ------⟩	3	Received Data (in)
Received Data (in)	3 ⟨------	2	Send Data (out)

The Cable Has Been Completely Designed

interpret this as a disconnect from the printer and kill the print job. This destroys the intent of flow control. Fortunately, some printers allow you to option which method of flow control will be exercised in the printer, but *not all do*! To be safe, it is better, if possible, not to use output hardware flow control leads of a printer in the cable design, UNLESS you are sure that the two flow control methods operate in a "one or the other" fashion, NOT BOTH! You can test this, if you have a break-out box, by causing a paper-out condition at the printer and monitoring the hardware flow control lead. Otherwise, consult the documentation.

Now back to our cable design. With the foregoing example, you should not count on using the leads 14, 19, or 20 in the cable design unless you simply must. This leaves pin 4 as the only available output control lead from the printer. Review the input control lead requirements at the Pyramid's port. You may ignore Ring Indicator, as this pertains only to a modem connection. Note that this leaves Clear to Send, Data Set Ready, and Data Carrier Detect, with Data Carrier Detect being a *must*. Since pin 4 is available from the printer, and software flow control is to be used, connect it "crossed-over" to these input leads as in Table 1–36. If, however, your computer system will not abort a print job upon 5, 6, and 8 going low, then you can connect pin 14, 19, or 20 across to them for hardware flow control. Our module will not!

The Toshiba's input control leads are the same and should be connected to an output control lead from the Pyramid port. You can use either pin 4 or 20 from the Pyramid to keep these leads on. Our design will use pin 20 as in Table 1–36. This completes the cable design between the Pyramid ITP and the Toshiba P351 series printers.

8. Build the cable

9. Test for continuity

10. Cable the two systems together

Build the cable using a female DB25 connector at the Pyramid cable end and a male connector for the Toshiba port. Label the cable. Once built, test the cable for continuity and use it to connect the two devices.

11. Measure success

Our success is the ability to print information from the Pyramid system. Testing this can be twofold. If the systems administrator has set up the Toshiba to be the system printer that a print spooler uses, then issue the command sequence normally associated with dumping a file to the printer. The syntax for this command is something like "lp filename" followed by a return. This can be done from one of the terminals on the system. CONGRATULATIONS!

If this is not functioning, then the user can write directly to the device port. From step 1, note that we assumed that the port "ttyi05" was to be used. Once the printer is connected to this port, the user can issue a command under UNIX that redirects output to that port. You can enter the command sequence "ls ⟩ /dev/tty105" to list a directory and, instead of displaying it on the terminal, send it the printer. The printer should print this directory listing almost immediately. If nothing happens, check the "tty" address, the cable, the physical connection, the printer condition, printer options, and power. The systems administrator should be consulted to ensure that the Pyramid port was properly set up to match the printer options.

TABLE 1–36. PYRAMID 90X-TO-TOSHIBA P351 CABLE DESIGN

Function	90x lead #	P351 lead #	Function
Frame Ground	1 -------	1	Frame Ground
Signal Ground	7 -------	7	Signal Ground
Transmit Data (out)	2 ------⟩	3	Received Data (in)
Received Data (in)	3 ⟨------	2	Send Data (out)
Clear to Send (in)	5 ⟨--|---	4	Request to Send (out)
Data Set Ready (in)	6 ⟨--|		
Data Carrier Detect (in)	8 ⟨--|		
Data Terminal Ready (out)	20 ---|--⟩	5	Clear to Send (in)
	|--⟩	6	Data Set Ready (in)
	|--⟩	8	Carrier Detect (in)

LEGEND: The "-------" indicates a "straight-through" connection. The "arrowhead" is provided to illustrate direction of a lead only and a "cross-over." The "\|--⟩" indicates local "jumpering" in a connector.

If printing occurs, but there are error conditions, correct them through the various options outlined in the printer symptom/solution section. CONGRATULATIONS!

Tutorial Module 1-7: Connecting an AT&T 5310 Teleprinter to a Hayes Smartmodem 1200

In this tutorial module a teleprinter will be connected to a modem. The goal is to demonstrate that a printer/keyboard combination, referred to as a teleprinter, can communicate to a remote computer system. The teleprinter can interact with an intelligent modem, such as the Hayes Smartmodem, and use the keyboard dialing features to establish a connection as depicted in Figure 1–7.

We will use an AT&T 5310 teleprinter and connect it to a Hayes Smartmodem 1200. Substitute the teleprinter of your choice in this exercise, as most of them behave the same and provide probably the exact interface as the AT&T 5310. The 5310 is a descendant of the original teletype terminals; hence, most other vendors follow suit on this type of teleprinter design. Our goal will be to connect these two pieces of equipment together and then communicate with another computer system, such as a UNIX system, mainframe, time-sharing system, or some other teleprinter. We will follow our standard approach to connecting two devices together:

STEPS FOR CONNECTION

1. Determine compatibility (should it work?).
2. Determine signs of success.
3. Determine the type of connector used.
4. Determine gender of the ports.
5. Determine which leads (pins) are provided by each device.
6. Determine which leads are required to be on by each device.
7. Design the cable.
8. Build the cable.
9. Test the cable for continuity.
10. Cable the two systems together with the cable.
11. From step 2, measure success.

1. Determine compatibility

Complete an SCS port profile analysis for each of the devices. This will aid in determining the compatibility between the teleprinter and the modem. Previous tutorial modules provided us this information, as outlined in Table 1–37. However, you should consult the device documentation to complete your own port profiles, if you are interfacing different devices.

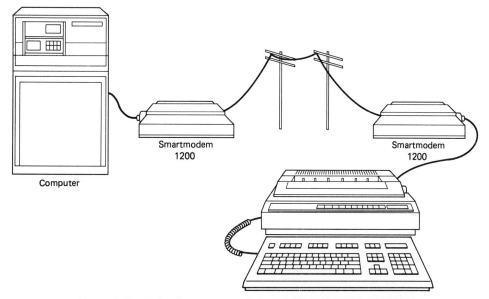

Figure 1–7. Teleprinter-to-computer connection using dial-up network.

The Cable Has Been Completely Designed

TABLE 1–37. AT&T 5310 TELEPRINTER AND HAYES SMARTMODEM 1200 PORT PROFILES

Printer Port Profile

Underline if supported; circle if selected.

Model: 5310 printer _____ Vendor: AT&T _____ Port: RS232-C _____
Interface type: serial parallel
Port type: DB25 9-pin 5-pin 8-pin/modular 20mA Centronics

Gender: male female

Pin #	Function	Direction	Pin #	Function	Direction
1	_____	to from n/a	14	_____	to from n/a
2	_____	to from n/a	15	_____	to from n/a
3	_____	to from n/a	16	_____	to from n/a
4	_____	to from n/a	17	_____	to from n/a
5	_____	to from n/a	18	_____	to from n/a
6	_____	to from n/a	19	_____	to from n/a
7	_____	to from n/a	20	_____	to from n/a
8	_____	to from n/a	21	_____	to from n/a
9	_____	to from n/a	22	_____	to from n/a
10	_____	to from n/a	23	_____	to from n/a
11	_____	to from n/a	24	_____	to from n/a
12	_____	to from n/a	25	_____	to from n/a
13	_____	to from n/a			

Complete the next section only with 36-pin cinch connector.

Pin #	Function	Direction	Pin #	Function	Direction
26	_____	to from n/a	27	_____	to from n/a
28	_____	to from n/a	29	_____	to from n/a
30	_____	to from n/a	31	_____	to from n/a
32	_____	to from n/a	33	_____	to from n/a
34	_____	to from n/a	35	_____	to from n/a
36	_____	to from n/a			

Flow control technique: XON/XOFF ENQ/ACK STX/ETX Hardware _____
Flow control lead(s): 4 11 19 20 __ __ __
Leads that must be on: 5 6 8 __ __ __ __

Options:
    Speeds: 110 300 600 1200 1800 2400 4800 9600 19.2 56k _____
    Parity: even odd space mark none
    Char-length: 7 8 __
    # stop bits: 1 1.5 2
    Line-ending sequence: cr lf cr/lf cr/lf/lf

Mode: async sync   sync timing leads:

#	Function	Direction
15	_____	to from
17	_____	to from
24	_____	to from

Printer compatibility modes: Epson MX Diablo 630 HP LaserJet HP ThinkJet NEC 3500 IBM Graphics IBM Color Printronix TI-810

Notes: _____
_____
_____

TABLE 1–37. *(Continued)*

Modem Port Profile

Underline if supported, circle if selected.

Model: Smartmodem 1200 ___ Vendor: Hayes ____ Port: RS 232C ____
Port type: serial
Port: DB25 9-pin 8-pin/modular 20mA _____

Gender: male female

Pin #	Function	Direction	Pin #	Function	Direction
1	_____	to from n/a	14	_____	to from n/a
2	_____	to from n/a	15	_____	to from n/a
3	_____	to from n/a	16	_____	to from n/a
4	_____	to from n/a	17	_____	to from n/a
5	_____	to from n/a	18	_____	to from n/a
6	_____	to from n/a	19	_____	to from n/a
7	_____	to from n/a	20	_____	to from n/a
8	_____	to from n/a	21	_____	to from n/a
9	_____	to from n/a	22	_____	to from n/a
10	_____	to from n/a	23	_____	to from n/a
11	_____	to from n/a	24	_____	to from n/a
12	_____	to from n/a	25	_____	to from n/a
13	_____	to from n/a			

Leads that must be on: 4 20 __ __ __ __

Options:
Speeds: 110 300 600 1200 1800 2400 4800 9600 19.2 56k _____
Compatibility: 103 212 V.22bis _____
Parity: even odd space mark none
Char-length: 7 8 __
stop bits: 1 1.5 2
Line-ending sequence: cr lf cr/lf cr/lf/lf
Auto answer: yes no RTS/CTS delay: ____
Disconnect sequence: EOT DEL ATZ _____
Intelligent modems . . . dialing technique: Touch-tone Pulse
  Compatibility: Hayes _____
  Command line prefix: AT _____ Dial command: D _____
  Touch-tone dial: T ____ Pulse dial: P ____ Pause: , ____
  Wait for dial tone: W ____ Wait for quiet answer: @ ____
  Flash: ! ____ Dial stored number: S ____
  Return to command state after dialing: ; ____
  Escape sequence: + + + ____ Switch-hook control: H ____
  Store phone#: &Z ____
  Mode: async sync isoch

sync timing leads:

#	Function	Direction
15	_____	to from
17	_____	to from
24	_____	to from

Notes: Parity modes are 7 bit, 1–2 stop bits, with odd, even, or fixed parity, *or* 8 bit, 1–2 stop bits, and no parity at 1200 bps. At 300 bps, 7–8 bit, 1–2 stop bits, with odd, even, or no parity.

The Cable Has Been Completely Designed

From the preceding, it appears that the two devices will work together. For the record, just about any 212-compatible modem will work with these teleprinters. Several teleprinters on the market are limited to 300 bps operation, depending on vintage. The 5310 will operate at the 1200 bps speed. The other common options appear to be 1200 bps, 8 data bits, even parity, full duplex, and 1 stop bit. We will use these later when we test the connection.

2. Determine signs of success

The teleprinter-to-modem connection will be complete if we can initiate a call from the keyboard of the teleprinter, using the intelligent modem. Furthermore, the connection should be established to a remote computer with the data exchange being error free. For sanity reasons, we will also ensure that flow control functions to prevent loss of data. Assume that the data are being printed too fast for us, and we want to suspend the data flow to review a section that has just been printed. Upon satisfactory halting of data flow, we will resume the reception of data. This will assure us that flow control is functioning properly.

3. Determine type of connector

4. Determine gender of ports

The AT&T 5310 teleprinter provides a DB25P connector, implying a male connector. Our cable at this end will need a female 25-pin connector on it. The Hayes Smartmodem 1200 provides a DB25S connector, indicating a female gender. This end of our cable will need a male 25-pin connector.

5. Determine leads (pins) provided by each device

6. Determine leads required to be on

These port analyses have been completed in other modules, so we will not repeat the details of this step. Table 1–38 summarizes the leads provided by each of the ports laid out in the completed port profiles.

7. Design the cable

From the port profiles, you should separate the leads in both ports by category. This will allow you to come up with the best design for the cable required to connect the teleprinter to the modem. Table 1–39 provides this separation of categories.

Apply the following rules when designing the cable.

CABLE DESIGN: GENERAL RULES

1. Connect like categories of leads together.
2. Always connect an "out" to an "in" and an "in" to an "out."
3. A lead that is input may be connected to another lead that is an input, only if both these are connected to an output lead.
4. In synchronous connections, only use one source of timing. (Because the teleprinter to Hayes Smartmodem 1200 connection is asynchronous, this point is not applicable.)

First, tackle the ground leads. Merely connect the same ground leads together. In our case, pin 1 at one of the cable should be connected to lead 1 at the other end of the cable. The same is true for pin 7, as outlined in Table 1–40.

The next category to tackle is the data leads. Look at the Transmit Data leads of both ports. Note that one is input on pin 2, while the other is output on pin 2. Applying rules 1 and 2 for cable design, you should connect lead 2 at one end of the cable "straight through" to the other end of the cable. Also review the Receive Data leads, noting their directions at each port. Repeat a "straight-through" connection for pin 3 as in Table 1–41. Thus far, the cable has been a "straight-through" cable, hinting that a ribbon cable may be used.

No timing leads are present, as this is an asynchronous connection, so we will next tackle the control leads and complete this cable design. First, look at the input control leads of the Hayes modem in Table 1–39. Lead # 20, Data Terminal Ready, is the only input control lead required by the modem. The 5310 provides Data Terminal Ready as an output control signal. Rules 1 and 2 apply, allowing pin 20 to pass straight through the cable, from end to end.

Now that the input control leads from the modem have been taken care over, bounce over to the teleprinter port, summarized in Table 1–39. Leads 6, 8, 12, and 22 are the input control leads. Their corresponding functions

TABLE 1–38. AT&T 5310 AND HAYES SMARTMODEM 1200 LEADS

Printer Port Profile

Underline if supported, circle if selected.

Model: 5310 printer _____ Vendor: AT&T _____ Port: RS232-C _____
Interface type: serial parallel
Port type: DB25 9-pin 5-pin 8-pin/modular 20mA Centronics

Gender: male female

Pin #	Function	Direction	Pin #	Function	Direction
1	Frame Ground	to from n/a	14		to from n/a
2	Send Data	to from n/a	15		to from n/a
3	Receive Data	to from n/a	16		to from n/a
4	Request to Send	to from n/a	17		to from n/a
5		to from n/a	18		to from n/a
6	Data Set Ready	to from n/a	19	Secondary Request to Send	to from n/a
7	Signal Ground	to from n/a	20	Data Terminal Ready	to from n/a
8	Carrier Detect	to from n/a	21		to from n/a
9		to from n/a	22	Ring Indicator	to from n/a
10		to from n/a	23		to from n/a
11	Secondary Request to Send	to from n/a	24		to from n/a
12	Speed Mode	to from n/a	25		to from n/a
13		to from n/a			

Complete the next section only with 36-pin cinch connector.

Pin #	Function	Direction	Pin #	Function	Direction
26		to from n/a	27		to from n/a
28		to from n/a	29		to from n/a
30		to from n/a	31		to from n/a
32		to from n/a	33		to from n/a
34		to from n/a	35		to from n/a
36		to from n/a			

Flow control technique: XON/XOFF ENQ/ACK STX/ETX Hardware _____
Flow control lead(s): 4 11 19 20 __ __ __

Leads that must be on: 5 6 8 __ __ __ __
Options:
  Speeds: 110 300 600 (1200) 1800 2400 4800 9600 19.2 56k _____
  Parity (even) odd space mark none
  Char-length: 7 (8) __
  # stop bits: (1) 1.5 2
  Line-ending sequence: cr lf cr/lf cr/lf/lf
  Mode: async sync   sync timing leads:

#	Function	Direction
15		to from
17		to from
24		to from

  Printer compatibility modes: Epson MX Diabloc 630 HP LaserJet HP ThinkJet NEC 3500 IBM Graphics IBM
    Color Printronix TI-810

NOTES: Pins 11 and 19 are active only if flow control option value is EIA. If secondary request to send option value is EIA (hardware flow control), then these pins will be on when the printer can receive data into the buffer, and when there is paper in the printer. Choose one of them for hardware flow control lead (out). Pin 20 also provides the online/offline status for the 5310 printer. Leads 6 and 8 should be on for the printer to receive data.

The Cable Has Been Completely Designed

TABLE 1–38. (*Continued*)

Modem Port Profile

Underline if supported; circle if selected.

Model: Smartmodem 1200 _____ Vendor: Hayes _____ Port: RS 232C _____
Port type: <u>serial</u>
Port: <u>DB25</u> 9-pin 8-pin/modular 20mA _____

Gender: male <u>female</u>

Pin #	Function	Direction	Pin #	Function	Direction
1	<u>Protective Ground</u>	to from <u>n/a</u>	14	_____	to from n/a
2	<u>Transmit Data</u>	<u>to</u> from n/a	15	_____	to from n/a
3	<u>Receive Data</u>	to <u>from</u> n/a	16	_____	to from n/a
4	_____	to from n/a	17	_____	to from n/a
5	<u>Clear to Send</u>	to <u>from</u> n/a	18	_____	to from n/a
6	<u>Data Set Ready</u>	to <u>from</u> n/a	19	_____	to from n/a
7	<u>Signal Ground</u>	to from <u>n/a</u>	20	Data Terminal Ready	<u>to</u> from n/a
8	<u>Carrier Detect</u>	to <u>from</u> n/a	21	_____	to from n/a
9	_____	to from n/a	22	Ring Indicator	to <u>from</u> n/a
10	_____	to from n/a	23	_____	to from n/a
11	_____	to from n/a	24	_____	to from n/a
12	<u>High Speed Indicator</u>	to <u>from</u> n/a	25	_____	to from n/a
13	_____	to from n/a			

Leads that must be on: 4 20 __ __ __ __

Options:
  Speeds: 110 300 600 (1200) 1800 2400 4800 9600 19.2 56k _____
  Compatibility: 103 212 V.22bis _____
  Parity: (even) odd space mark none
  Char-length: 7 (8) _____
  # stop bits: (1) 1.5 2
  Line-ending sequence: cr lf cr/lf cr/lf/lf
  Auto answer: yes no RTS/CTS delay: _____
  Disconnect sequence: EOT DEL ATZ _____
  Intelligent modems . . . Dialing technique: Touch-tone Pulse
    Compatibility: Hayes _____
    Command line prefix: AT _____ Dial command: D _____
    Touch-tone dial: T _____ Pulse dial: P _____ Pause: , _____
    Wait for dial tone: W _____ Wait for quiet answer: @ _____
    Flash: ! _____ Dial stored number: S _____
    Return to command state after dialing: ; _____
    Escape sequence: +++ _____ Switch-hook control: H _____
    Store phone #: &Z _____
  Mode: async sync isoch   sync timing leads:

#	Function	Direction
15	n/a_____	to from
17	n/a_____	to from
24	n/a_____	to from

Notes: Parity modes are 7 bit, 1–2 stop bits, with odd, even, or fixed parity, or 8 bit, 1–2 stop bits and no parity at 1200 bps. At 300 bps, 7–8 bit, 1–2 stop bits, odd, even, no parity.

TABLE 1–39. AT&T 5310 AND HAYES SMARTMODEM 1200 LEADS SEPARATED BY CATEGORY

Function	5310 lead #	Hayes lead #	Function
Ground			
Frame Ground	1	1	Protective Ground
Signal Ground	7	7	Signal Ground (common return)
Data			
Send Data (out)	2	2	Transmit Data (in/to)
Receive Data (in)	3	3	Receive Data (out/from)
Control			
Request to Send (out)	4	5	Clear to Send (out/from)
Data Set Ready (in)	6	6	Data Set Ready (out/from)
Data Carrier Detect (in)	8	8	Carrier Detect (out/from)
Secondary Request to Send (out)	11		
Speed Mode Indication (in)	12	12	High Speed Indicator (out/from)
Secondary Request to Send (out)	19		
Data Terminal Ready (out)	20	20	Data Terminal Ready (in/to)
Ring Indicator (in)	22	22	Ring Indicator (out/from)

TABLE 1–40. GROUND LEADS FOR TELEPRINTER-TO-MODEM CABLE DESIGN

Function	5310 lead #	Hayes lead #	Function
Protective Ground	1 -------	1	Protective Ground
Signal Ground	7 -------	7	Signal Ground

LEGEND: The "--------" indicates a "straight-through" connection, from one end of the cable to the other.

TABLE 1–41. DATA LEAD DESIGN FOR TELEPRINTER-TO-MODEM CONNECTION

Function	5310 lead #	Hayes lead #	Function
Transmit Data (out)	2 ------)	2	Transmit Data (in)
Receive Data (in)	3 (------	3	Receive Data (out)

LEGEND: The "------)" indicates a "straight-through" connection from one end of the cable to the other.

are Data Set Ready, Carrier Detect, Speed Mode Indication, and Ring Indicator. As before, look for the corresponding leads from the modem, noting their direction. Exactly the same lead numbers are provided by (from/out) the Hayes modem. Applying rules 1 and 2 as before, connect each of these leads independently from end to end in the cable. Specifically, connect lead 6 at one end of the cable to lead 6 at the other cable end. Repeat this for leads 8, 12, and 22. Table 1–42 outlines the completed control lead design.

Pins 4, 11, and 19 are provided by 5310, but are not supported by the Hayes modem. As they are output control leads, we need not concern ourselves with them.

Reviewing all the subset designs, a "straight-through" cable can be used here. Even though leads 4, 11, and 19 will be included in the "straight-through" cable, they will not cause any problems. Hence, our design is for a "straight-through" cable. Either a flat ribbon cable or a cable with leads 1, 2, 3, 6, 7, 8, 12, 20, and 22 can be used, as summarized in Table 1–43.

The Cable Has Been Completely Designed

TABLE 1–42. CONTROL LEAD DESIGN FOR TELEPRINTER-TO-MODEM CONNECTION

Function	5310 lead #		Hayes lead #	Function
Request to Send (out)	4			n/a
Data Set Ready (in)	6	⟨------	6	Data Set Ready (out)
Data Carrier Detect (in)	8	⟨------	8	Data Carrier Detect (out)
Secondary Request to Send (out)	11			n/a
Speed Mode Indication (in)	12	⟨------	12	High Speed Indicator
Secondary Request to Send (out)	19			n/a
Data Terminal Ready (out)	20	------⟩	20	Data Terminal Ready (in)
Ring Indicator (in)	22	⟨------	22	Ring Indicator

LEGEND: The ''⟨------'' indicates a ''straight-through'' connection between the leads from one end of the cable to the other.

TABLE 1–43. AT&T 5310-TO-HAYES SMARTMODEM CABLE DESIGN

Function	5310 lead #		Hayes lead #	Function
Protective Ground	1	-------	1	Protective Ground
Transmit Data (out)	2	------⟩	2	Transmit Data (in)
Receive Data (in)	3	⟨------	3	Receive Data (out)
Data Set Ready (in)	6	⟨------	6	Data Set Ready (out)
Signal Ground	7	-------	7	Signal Ground
Data Carrier Detect (in)	8	⟨------	8	Data Carrier Detect (out)
Speed Mode Indication (in)	12	⟨------	12	High Speed Indicator
Data Terminal Ready (out)	20	------⟩	20	Data Terminal Ready (in)
Ring Indicator (in)	22	⟨------	22	Ring Indicator

LEGEND: This is a ''straight-through'' cable. The arrows are given for illustrating direction only. Even if there are more leads in the cable that are also ''straight through,'' then they probably will not cause any concern when the cable is built.

8. Build the cable

The steps in this cable construction are covered in Tutorial Module 1-1. The 5310 end of the cable should have a female 25-pin connector, while the Hayes Smartmodem 1200 end should be a male 25-pin connector. A flat ribbon cable may be used here, and is probably the easiest to construct, as you merely crimp the connector onto the cable at each end, aligning up pin 1 at one end to pin 1 at the other end, and so on. Double check to ensure that the pins line up, one for one, throughout the cable.

9. Test for continuity

10. Cable the two systems together

Check out the continuity of this cable using one of the techniques described in Tutorial Module 5-1. Once you are convinced that it is complete, connect the teleprinter to the modem with it. There should be no confusion for the connection, as the genders will guide you to the appropriate port.

11. Measure success

Our goal was to connect the teleprinter to the modem, allowing you to communicate with another computer system or teleprinter. Because the modem is intelligent, we need to test out our ability to ''keyboard dial.'' This is the ability to wake up the modem by entering a keyboard sequence and then enter the phone number on the keyboard, causing the modem to dial the desired number. Once the far end answers, we should concern ourselves with the ability to regulate the data flow using flow control. Set up the two devices to have the common options of 1200 bps, 7 data bits, 1 stop bit, full duplex, and even parity.

The first step will be to check our ability to communicate locally with the modem. A standard telephone could be attached to the modem for manual dialing of other desired number, but this is nineteenth-century stuff. The twentieth-century technique is to "keyboard dial." With the teleprinter powered on, and in the Online mode, be sure that the modem is powered up. When both devices have power, we are ready to communicate with the modem.

Wake up the modem by entering the appropriate "attention" sequence. Review our Hayes port profile, or the user's documentation, and note that the "AT" sequence is used to wake up the modem. At the keyboard of the 5310, enter a return "AT" and another return/enter key. If all is well, you should receive an "OK" message on your teleprinter's paper. If you do not receive this "OK" message, check your cabling for completeness, as well as the power to each device. Be sure that the 5310's EIA port is being used. Insert a break-out box to monitor the RS232 lead activity if you have one.

If you receive garbled characters, then recheck your options in the 5310. If you are receiving double characters for all those you enter, then the duplex option is probably set wrong in your teleprinter. Set this option to full duplex. If you do not see any characters you type, check the Hayes option switches located behind the front faceplate of the modem. Ensure that switch 4 is in the "up" position to echo characters back to you while in the command state. The command state allows you to perform keyboard dialing and other modem features. Be sure that your teleprinter has paper in it and that it is in the Online state. If you still get no response to your "wake-up" sequence, then check the rest of the modem switches. The default settings should be "OK" for this connection. However, the author recommends changing switch 1. They are outlined in Table 1–44.

At this point, we will assume that you have received the "OK" message indicating that the Hayes Smartmodem is ready for your next command. All commands should be preceded with the "AT" sequence. We now want to dial the number of the remote entity, be it a computer or another teleprinter. To do this, enter "ATDT8511234" followed by a Return key. This should cause the modem to dial the number "8511234."

Substitute the number to be dialed, ensuring that you dial the appropriate access code if you are behind a PBX. Separate the access code from the main number with a comma if an access code is used. The comma allows for a brief pause between dialings to allow for a second dial tone if behind a PBX. The "D" indicates that the number to follow should be dialed. The "T" preceding the number indicates that touch-tone dialing is used. Substitute a "P" if pulse or rotary dialing is used with your phone number. If your volume control of the modem's speaker is turned up, you should hear the actual dialing of the remote system as well as the ringing of the telephone network. If you did not hear dial tone prior to the dialing of the number, then be sure that the phone line is connected to the "line" jack on the back of the Hayes Smartmodem. If the phone line connected is to the wrong jack on the back of the modem, your modem will not function correctly.

After a brief moment, you should hear a strange "high-frequency" noise indicating that the far-end system has automatically answered your call. If you do not get this, then the other device is not set up for auto answer of calls, or it is not ready to receive a call. If the remote computer or device is not powered up, then the call will not be answered. The port must be enabled and configured properly to accept incoming calls. The same holds true for the modem. Without power, the call will not be answered.

The "high-frequency" noise is answer tone, or carrier. This is the signal used to carry your data between the two systems. After about a second, the tone should disappear, indicating that your modem has synchronized with the remote system. You should now be connected to the remote system. The Hayes Smartmodem 1200 will let you know if this happens through messages that your teleprinter should display/print. A "Connect" message will be displayed if the telephone connection is set up between your teleprinter and the remote device. If something

TABLE 1–44. HAYES SMARTMODEM 1200 OPTION SETTINGS

Switch	Setting	Function
1	up	Allows DTE to control status of lead 20.
2	up	Responds with English word result codes.
3	down	Outputs result codes to the teleprinter.
4	up	Echoes characters while in Command state.
5	down	Yields no auto answer (set this per your desires).
6	down	Forces pin 8 (DCD) to be true, so teleprinter functions.
7	up	Allows for use of RJ11 jack.
8	down	Enables modem command recognition (keyboard dialing).

else occurred resulting in a failure, the modem will send you an appropriate error message, such as Error or No Carrier. Retry if this occurs.

If you still cannot get a connection, try to call another known device or system to ensure that it is the remote's problem, and not a local one. If the same holds true regardless of which remote system you call, then recheck all your local options and cabling.

At this juncture, we will assume that you have successfully dialed another computer system. Hit the Return key several times to allow the remote system to select the appropriate speed. If the remote system is a UNIX computer, a "login:" prompt should appear. Login as appropriate, entering your ID, and if needed, a password (heaven forbid if the UNIX system is not password protected).

If you get garbled characters, then the parity, character lengths, stop bits, or speed options are mismatched. Check them and correct them in the 5310 teleprinter so they are the same. If, after they are set up properly, you still get garbled characters, then you may have a poor-quality telephone line. Disconnect and retry. Normal disconnection from a UNIX system is accomplished by entering a Control-d sequence. A hard disconnect can be accomplished by powering off the Hayes modem for a couple of seconds.

Double characters indicate that your duplex is wrong. The far-end device is echoing each character that you send it. Also, your teleprinter is locally echoing the same characters; hence, the duplication. Change the 5310 option to support "Echo off" or full duplex. This will not allow the 5310 locally to echo each entered character but rather rely on the far end system to send the characters back to you.

If you are receiving multiple lines of data from the far-end system, and your teleprinter is overwriting on the same line, then the line-ending settings are wrong. Furthermore, if double spacing is occurring, the same option is wrong. For overwriting, you need to enable an "LF" upon reception of a carriage return from the remote end. For double spacing, the far end is sending you both a carriage return and a line feed, so you need to disable interpreting the carriage return as a CR/LF.

The 5310 offers a couple of options that impact these conditions. There are two options: AUTO LF ON CR(LFON) and AUTO CR ON LF(CRON). If the LFON option is set to "Yes," the teleprinter will perform both a CR and an LF when a CR is received. Setting it to "No" performs only a CR, which is the default setting. So if overwriting occurs, change the LFON option to "Yes."

The CRON option, if set to "Yes," causes the teleprinter to perform a CR and LF when a LF is received. If "No," then an LF is interpreted as only an LF. The default is "No." Most UNIX systems output only an LF at the end of each line, so you probably receive something along the lines, as in Table 1–45.

Play with both these options to get the received text to appear as it should, single spaced without overwriting. At this point you should be sending and receiving short messages back and forth. Recall that this was two-thirds of our success, with only the ability to control the data flow left to test. The 5310 supports software flow control, XON/XOFF, as should your remote system. To test this aspect, you should enter a request for the remote system to send you a large text file. If a UNIX system is called, then the "Cat" command can be used followed by a filename. Enter the appropriate command sequence to get a large file sent your way. As it is being received, enter the flow control sequence to halt the transmission of data. The XOFF character serves this purpose and is entered by holding down the Ctrl key and "s" key simultaneously on the 5310's keyboard. This sends the XOFF character to the remote system. If software flow control is functioning properly, the far-end system should temporarily halt the output of data to you. To resume the transmission, enter a Ctrl-q, or XON, to resume the transmission. CONGRATULATIONS! Update your profiles with any other notations that you uncovered.

If flow control is functioning, you should be able to enter alternating Control-s's and Control-q's to regulate the flow of data. If this is not occurring, then the far-end system is not set up to support XON/XOFF. Check to be sure that it will support software flow control using XON/XOFF and that it is optioned accordingly.

TABLE 1–45. IMPROPER LINE-ENDING SEQUENCE SETTINGS

this is a
    test message
        to illustrate the CRON option set to "NO."
Change this option to "yes" to get the received messages to appear as follows:
this is a
test message
to illustrate the CRON option set to "YES."

This connection will illustrate the connection of a 9-pin connector found on any of the Prime computers, models 2350, 2450, 2655, 9655, 9755, or 9955. This 9-pin interface supports asynchronous operation. This tutorial module will focus on connecting a C.ITOH 8510 printer, although other printers such as the 1550 series have the same interface. The steps used in this module will be the same as those used in all the other modules.

STEPS FOR CONNECTION

1. Determine compatibility (should it work?).
2. Determine signs of success.
3. Determine the type of connector used.
4. Determine gender of the ports.
5. Determine which leads (pins) are provided by each device.
6. Determine which leads are required to be on by each device.
7. Design the cable.
8. Build the cable.
9. Test the cable for continuity.
10. Cable the two systems together with the cable.
11. From step 2, measure success.

1. Determine compatibility

The best means of determining compatibility is to prepare an SCS port profile for each of the two devices. Consult the documentation for each to complete the profiles as much as possible. As this tutorial module proceeds, you can update the profiles. Tables 1–46 and 1–47 outline the port profile information pulled directly from the user's documentation.

Reviewing the two profiles, the two devices will work together as they both support asynchronous operation at 9600 bps, 8 data bits, no parity, 1 stop bit, XON/XOFF flow control, and full duplex operation.

2. Determine signs of success

How will you know if you are successful? Issue a standard Prime computer Print command to test out the ability to send information to the printer. The flow control should also be tested by printing a very long document. If both these can be satisfied, then success has been obtained.

3. Determine type of connector

4. Determine gender of ports

The Prime computers provide a 9-pin female connector, while the C.ITOH 8510 printer provides a male 25-pin port. Hence, our cable will require a 9-pin male connector at one end, with a DB25S at the other end.

5. Determine leads (pins) provided by each device

6. Determine leads required to be on

Next the user should analyze the pinouts of both ports. A break-out box, a VOM, or the documentation should be used to determine the output and input leads of the both ports. They are summarized in Tables 1–48 and 1–49. The reader should update the port profiles with this information.

7. Design the cable

Armed with the foregoing information, the reader can proceed to design the cable, keeping in mind the standard rules of cable design.

CABLE DESIGN: GENERAL RULES

1. Connect like categories of leads together.
2. Always connect an "out" to an "in" and an "in" to an "out."
3. A lead that is input may be connected to another lead that is an input only if both these are connected to an output lead.

The Cable Has Been Completely Designed

TABLE 1–46. PORT PROFILES FOR PRIME COMPUTER'S 9-PIN ASYNCHRONOUS PORT

Computer Port Profile

Underline if supported; circle if selected.

Model: 2350 _____ Vendor: Prime _____ Port: async _____

Port type: <u>serial</u> parallel

Port: DB25 <u>9-pin</u> 5-pin 8-pin/modular 20mA Centronics

Gender: male <u>female</u>

Pin #	Function	Direction	Pin #	Function	Direct
1	_____	to from n/a	14	_____	to from n/a
2	Transmit Data	to <u>from</u> n/a	15	_____	to from n/a
3	Receive Data	<u>to</u> from n/a	16	_____	to from n/a
4	Request to Send	to <u>from</u> n/a	17	_____	to from n/a
5	Clear to Send	<u>to</u> from n/a	18	_____	to from n/a
6	_____	to from n/a	19	_____	to from n/a
7	Signal Ground	to from <u>n/a</u>	20	_____	to from n/a
8	Data Carrier Detect	<u>to</u> from n/a	21	_____	to from n/a
9	Data Terminal Ready	to <u>from</u> n/a	22	_____	to from n/a
10	_____	to from n/a	23	_____	to from n/a
11	_____	to from n/a	24	_____	to from n/a
12	_____	to from n/a	25	_____	to from n/a
13	_____	to from n/a			

Complete the next section only with 36-pin cinch connector.

26	_____	to from n/a	27	_____	to from n/a
28	_____	to from n/a	29	_____	to from n/a
30	_____	to from n/a	31	_____	to from n/a
32	_____	to from n/a	33	_____	to from n/a
34	_____	to from n/a	35	_____	to from n/a
36	_____	to from n/a			

Flow control technique: (XON/XOFF) ENQ/ACK STX/ETX Hardware _____

Leads that must be on: 5 6 8 __ __ __ __

Options:

  Speeds: 110 300 600 1200 1800 2400 4800 (9600) 19.2 56k _____

  Parity: even odd space mark (none)

  Char-length: 7 (8) __

  # stop bits: (1) 1.5 2

  Line-ending sequence: cr lf cr/lf cr/lf/lf

  Disconnect sequence: EOT DEL ~. _____

Mode: async sync isoch   sync timing leads:

#	Function	Direction
15	_____	to from
17	_____	to from
24	_____	to from

Notes: _____
_____
_____

TABLE 1–47. C.ITOH ELECTRONICS 8510 PRINTER PORT PROFILE

Printer Port Profile

Underline if supported; circle if selected.

Model: 8510 printer _____ Vendor: C.ITOH _____ Port: RS232 _____
Interface type: <u>serial</u> parallel
Port type: <u>DB25</u> 9-pin 5-pin 8-pin/modular 20mA Centronics

Gender: <u>male</u> female

Pin #	Function	Direction	Pin #	Function	Direction
1	Frame Ground	to from n/a	14	Fault	to <u>from</u> n/a
2	Transmit Data	to <u>from</u> n/a	15		to from n/a
3	Receive Data	<u>to</u> from n/a	16		to from n/a
4	Request to Send	to <u>from</u> n/a	17		to from n/a
5	Clear to Send	<u>to</u> from n/a	18		to from n/a
6	Data Set Ready	<u>to</u> from n/a	19		to from n/a
7	Signal Ground	to from n/a	20	Data Terminal Ready	to <u>from</u> n/a
8	Data Carrier Detect	<u>to</u> from n/a	21		to from n/a
9		to from n/a	22		to from n/a
10		to from n/a	23		to from n/a
11		to from n/a	24		to from n/a
12		to from n/a	25		to from n/a
13		to from n/a			

Complete the next section only with 36-pin cinch connector.

26		to from n/a	27		to from n/a
28		to from n/a	29		to from n/a
30		to from n/a	31		to from n/a
32		to from n/a	33		to from n/a
34		to from n/a	35		to from n/a
36		to from n/a			

Flow control technique (XON/XOFF) ENQ/ACK STX/ETX <u>Hardware</u> _____
Flow control lead(s): <u>4</u> 11 <u>19</u> <u>20</u> __ __ __
Leads that must be on: 5 <u>6</u> 8 __ __ __ __
Options:
   Speeds: <u>110 300 600 1200 1800 2400 4800 (9600)</u> 19.2 56k _____
   Parity: even odd space mark (none)
   Char-length: 7 (8) __
   # stop bits: (1) 1.5 2
   Line-ending sequence: cr lf cr/lf cr/lf/lf

Mode: async sync   sync timing leads:

#	Function	Direction
15		to from
17		to from
24		to from

Printer compatibility modes: Epson MX Diablo 630 HP LaserJet HP ThinkJet NEC 3500 IBM Graphics IBM Color Printronix TI-810

Notes: _____
_____
_____

The Cable Has Been Completely Designed

TABLE 1–48. PINOUTS OF PRIME COMPUTER'S 9-PIN ASYNC PORT

Function	Lead #
Transmit Data (out)	2
Receive Data (in)	3
Request to Send (out)	4
Clear to Send (in)	5
Signal Ground	7
Data Carrier Detect (in)	8
Data Terminal Ready (out)	9

TABLE 1–49. PINOUTS FOR C.ITOH 8510 PRINTER

Function	Lead #
Frame Ground	1
Transmit Data (out)	2
Receive Data (in)	3
Request to Send (out)	4
Clear to Send (in)	5
Data Set Ready (in)	6
Signal Ground	7
Data Carrier Detect (in)	8
Fault (out)	14
Data Terminal Ready (out)	20

4. In synchronous connections, only use one source of timing. (Because the Prime-to-C.ITOH printer connection is asynchronous, this point is not applicable.)

Table 1–50 summarizes the leads of both ports, separated by category. Work through each category of leads, ground, data, and control to complete the cable design. Reviewing the ports, the read should note that both ports provide the standard signals associated with DTE products, implying that the ports are expecting a DCE port to be connected. Hence a null modem cable will be required to connect the two devices together.

TABLE 1–50. PINOUTS OF PRIME COMPUTER AND C.ITOH 8510 PRINTER

Function	Lead #	Lead #	Function
Ground			
	n/a	1	Frame Ground
Signal Ground	7	7	Signal Ground
Data			
Transmit Data (out)	2	2	Transmit Data (out)
Receive Data (in)	3	3	Receive Data (in)
Control			
Request to Send (out)	4	4	Request to Send (out)
Clear to Send (in)	5	5	Clear to Send (in)
	n/a	6	Data Set Ready (in)
Data Carrier Detect (in)	8	8	Data Carrier Detect (in)
Data Terminal Ready (out)	9	14	Fault
		20	Data Terminal Ready (out)

In a null modem cable, to connect two pieces of DTE together, the ground leads should be connected "straight through" from end to end in the cable. Furthermore, the outbound data lead from one device should be "crossed over" to the inbound data lead of the other device. Repeat the data cross-over in the other direction. Consult Table 1–51 for a depiction of these connections.

This leaves only the control leads to deal with. Recall that XON/XOFF flow control, or software flow control, is going to be used between the two systems. However, the printer does support hardware flow control with leads 4, 14, or 20, depending on the printer. Since hardware flow control is not going to be used, our cable will include only lead 20. Feel free to use one of the other outbound control leads in your cable. Knowing that lead 20 will be used to connect to the input control leads of the Prime computer port, review the input leads required. Note that leads 5 and 8 are input leads for the Prime port. Connect lead 20 at the printer end of the cable across to both leads 5 and 8 at the Prime end. This fulfills the input control leads for the Prime computer.

Because XON/XOFF is used with the C.ITOH printer, the documentation indicates that lead 6 must be on to receive data. Hence, an output lead from the Prime computer port will be connected across to this lead. For completeness, we will also connect pin 8 to this. Pin 9, Data Terminal Ready, of the Prime port will be used. The only remaining input lead in the printer port is lead 5, Clear to Send. This lead could also be tied to 6 and 8. However, we will use a different output control lead in the Prime port, pin 4. This will allow all three input leads of the printer port to be on whenever the Prime port is active. Table 1–51 summarizes the completed cable necessary to connect the two systems.

8. Build the cable

9. Test for continuity

10. Cable the two systems together

11. Measure success

Build the cable in the normal manner; then test it for continuity. Once you have the cable constructed and are comfortable that the leads are laid out and connected per our design, cable the two systems together. There is no chance for error as the cable ends have different connector types for easy match-up with the proper port.

Once connected, attempt to perform a print operation in the Prime computer system. If the desired output does not appear on the printer, consult the section on common printer problem symptoms and solutions for items to check. Be sure that you test the printer by printing a long enough document to ensure that software flow control is functioning. CONGRATULATIONS!

Tutorial Module 1-9: Connecting a Single Printer to Multiple Computers Using an ABC Switch

Have you ever needed to share a printer with more than one computer? With a local area network, this becomes quite easy. However, if the two computer systems are too diverse, are not physically connected, or lack supporting software, this can be difficult to accomplish. The user will have to unplug the printer from one computer

TABLE 1–51. CABLE DESIGN FOR PRIME COMPUTER TO C.ITOH PRINTER

Function	Prime Lead #		C.Itoh Lead #	Function
Signal Ground	7	-------	7	Signal Ground
Transmit Data (out)	2	------)	3	Receive Data (in)
Receive Data (in)	3	(------	2	Transmit Data (out)
Request to Send (out)	4	------)	5	Clear to Send (in)
Data Terminal Ready (out)	9	----|--)	6	Data Set Ready (in)
		|--)	8	Data Carrier Detect (in)
Clear to Send (in)	5	(--|---	20	Data Terminal Ready (out)
Data Carrier Detect (in)	8	(--|		

LEGEND: The "-------" indicates a "straight-through" connection, while the "------)" indicates a "cross-over" between lead #s. The "---\|--)" is a notation implying that certain leads in the same connector "\|--)" should be connected together.

and reconnect it to the other one whenever printing is to be done. There is often a strong need to share a device, such as a printer, easily between two computers.

Switches, units that connect multiple devices together by the mere flick of a finger, will solve this problem. A single computer connected to a switch can access both a dot-matrix and letter-quality printer with a single DOS device address. A similar switch could allow a computer to share both a modem and printer in the same fashion. Two computers can share the same printer or multiple printers even when different operating systems are used on each computer. Many possibilities exist. Both serial and parallel versions are available, with the serial version being featured in this case study. Some are activated manually; others accept control characters for software control. The manually operated switches are the most common and easiest to use and hence will be featured.

The generic name "ABC switch" is used to classify these switches. The reason for this is that the devices (ports) are labeled A, B, C, and so on. The goal of the switches is to connect the devices connected to ports A and B to the device connected to port C. The ports can increase in number, with usually the nomenclature progressing along with the alphabet. These switches used to be called EIA switches, because of the widespread use of the EIA RS232 interface, and in some cases, they still are. However, because Centronics parallel ports have become more prevalent, this tag became inappropriate. Hence, ABC switches denote either serial or parallel versions. The user should note which version is required. Consult Chapter 2 for using serial ABC switches when an IBM PC parallel port is involved.

The simplest of the serial switches is an ABC switch, supporting three devices. With an ABC switch, there are two possible settings. With the switch in the "A" position, the devices connected to ports A and C are connected together. With the switch in the "B" position, devices on ports B and C are connected.

One factor to consider is the number of leads that are supported through the switch. Some serial switches may switch all 25 leads of the RS232 standard. Others may not pass all leads, supporting only the leads used in most asynchronous environments. In this case hardware flow control must be considered, as pins 11 and 19 may not necessarily be supported, as they are not used in all environments. Even though they are prevalent printer hardware flow control leads, modems don't use them. Hence, consider the number of leads supported when using an ABC switch. Later in this section you will learn how to overcome this by strategic placement of the custom-built cable versus a standard ribbon cable. If the unit is to be used in a synchronous configuration, even more leads could be required to support the timing leads. Because leads 15, 17, and 24 are used in synchronous environments, the unit should support 25 leads to be the most flexible.

The only factor with which a user should be concerned is the gender of the connectors on the boxes. Check out the genders of the device ports and your inventory of cables. If reviewed properly prior to the ABC switch purchase, you could minimize the number of cables that may have to be purchased. If your device ports are all female, and your cables have male connectors at both ends, select an ABC switch with DB25S (female) ports. With proper selection, you will not need to purchase an entire new set of cables or purchase gender changers. If you can plan for this, some money might be saved that would otherwise be spent on cable purchases.

Assume that the user has an IBM PC/XT and an IBM PC/AT that are to share a single QMS laser printer. The user could unplug the laser printer from each of the computers and connect it to the one that was to be used. However, this could be cumbersome after awhile. As an alternative a serial ABC switch could be used to allow printer sharing between the two personal computers with the flip of a switch.

A quick review of the SCS port profiles for each device provides the user with some useful information. The information is summarized in Table 1–52. Select a serial ABC switch to match the genders of the cables that you have or plan to use.

An assumption will be made that hardware flow control is used. Because each of the ports is emulating DTE, a null modem cable(s) will be required to connect the devices together. The actual cable design has been covered in previous tutorial modules. Refer to those respective modules for detailed analysis on the port profiles and the ultimate cable designs. This poses a question: Where should the null modem cable be? Figure 1–8 diagrams possible locations of the NMC.

Two null modem cables could be required if the NMC is not properly located. If the NMC is not connected to the printer and port C on the ABC switch, then two NMCs would be required. In this case, a straight-through cable would be used to connect the printer to port C. Duplicate NMCs could add unnecessary expense to the configuration.

To optimize the connection and cabling, construct the null modem cable necessary to connect an XT to the QMS printer. Place this cable between the QMS printer and port C of the ABC switch. With this in place, "straight-through" cables can be used to connect the PC/XT to port A of the ABC switch. Because the AT has a 9-pin port, and the ABC switch has a 25-pin port, construct/acquire a DB9-to-DB25 adapter cable. This adapter

TABLE 1–52. PORT INFORMATION FOR XT, AT, AND QMS KISS PRINTERS

Device	PC/XT	PC/AT	QMS	
	DB25P male	DB9P male	DB25S female	Function
Port Gender Pinouts	n/a	n/a	1	Chassis Ground
	2	3	2	Transmit Data (out)
	3	2	3	Receive Data (in)
	4	7	4	Request to Send (out)
	5	8	n/a	Clear to Send (in)
	6	6	6	Data Set Ready (in)
	7	5	7	Logic Ground
	8	1	n/a	Data Carrier Detect (in)
	20	4	20	Data Terminal Ready (out)

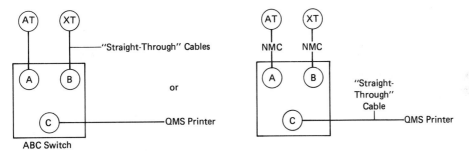

Figure 1–8. Null modem cable with ABC switch.

cable should bring out the pinouts to match that of the PC/XT port at the DB25 end. This cable could be equivalent to one necessary to connect an AT to a stand-alone modem, except for possible gender differences. Connect the AT to port B of the ABC switch with this cable. You now have a single NMC in the configuration, with two straight-through cables.

When the switch is in the "A" position, the PC/XT could use the QMS laser printer. In the "B" position, the PC/AT could access the printer. This allows a single device to be shared by multiple computers. This same scenario could be used to connect a modem to multiple computers. The two computers need not be both MS-DOS computers. A mixture of operating systems, such as MS-DOS and UNIX, could be present in your configuration. The key to success is to have a common speed, character length, parity, flow control, and duplex among the three devices to be connected. If any of these options is different, the resulting configuration may not function correctly without the constant changing of setup options. CONGRATULATIONS!

SERIAL PRINTER INTERFACING: MOST FREQUENTLY ASKED QUESTIONS

Question 1. When a printer/plotter supports DTR flow control, what does this mean?

Answer 1. The connotation is that hardware flow control is supported. RS-232 nomenclature for the lead that is used to provide hardware flow control in this case is Data Terminal Ready (DTR). Other references include SRTS for Secondary Request to Send, and Busy for any number of different leads.

Question 2. How can a user tell if the end of the cable is male or female?

Answer 2. Without exploiting the details of the birds and the bees, a male connector has pins protruding from it, while a female connector has holes (sockets/receptacles) for the pins (up to 25) to fit into.

Question 3. What is a break-out box?

Answer 3. A break-out box (BOB) is a useful tool for interfacing devices. It breaks out leads, or allows the user to monitor, open, close, or cross-over the leads of an interface. The most popular BOB is for RS232-C interfaces. However, parallel versions are also available. The user can determine whether a port emulates DTE or DCE using a break-out box with lamps that indicate on/off conditions of the leads of a ports.

Question 4. What is the difference between hardware and software flow control?

Answer 4: Software flow control involves the transmission and reception of an ASCII character to regulate the flow of data. Hence this technique uses the transmit data lead in an RS232-C interface. Hardware flow control uses the on/off condition of a port lead to accomplish the same data flow control. A lead in the port will be kept on as long as data can be received, but dropped/lowered when no more may be received. Both accomplish the same goal.

Question 5. Which is better—serial or parallel interfaces for printers?

Answer 5. If the distance between a printer and attached device exceeds 6–10 feet, perhaps a serially interfaced printer may be more appropriate. Because the RS232-C standard allows distances of up to 50 feet, this may be a better selection.

Speeds can be a factor if long documents will be printed and a buffer is involved. Because 9600 or 19200 bps are the top speeds found in a printer's serial port, a document of 2000 characters would take about 2–3 seconds (2000 char times 10 bits/char divided by 9600 bps). With a parallel interface, which is typically operating in the 1000s-of-characters-per-second range, the same document takes only 1 second. This is not that big a deal unless you are printing lengthy documents or a large number of documents. The times stated here reflect the time required for a computer to send the document to the printer—not the time of the actual printing. Print speed dictates actual throughput rates.

As more print servers are being used with local area networks, the number of users placing demands on a printer increases. Here the speed of the interface could be an issue, but the buffer size and management of the buffer really play a larger role. Once the printer's buffer is filled, the server cannot send any more data until buffer memory is released. The interface speeds are not that big of a factor, but the location of the printer is extremely important. A print server is set up to allow multiple users to share a single printer. The printer is attached to a computer on a network. The computer that is attached to the printer may not be centrally located. With a parallel-interfaced printer, the distance of 6–10 feet may not allow easy access to the printer by all users. However, with an RS232 interface, the distance of 50 feet (or more) could offer users more flexibility.

Question 6. What is "polarity"?

Answer 6. When hardware flow control is used, one of the port's leads of a printer will reflect the readiness of the printer to receive data. Polarity is often an option allowing the user to establish whether an "on or off" condition indicates the printer's readiness. If the attached computer needs leads on to operate, the polarity of the printer should be set to "HI." This implies that it will have a positive voltage on the hardware flow control lead as long as the printer is ready. When it is not ready, a negative or "off" condition will occur. Because this output control lead is connected to the computer's input leads, the computer will be able to interpret the off condition as a signal to stop sending data. If the computer needs to see a lead come on, or go "HI" to indicate an error condition, then polarity should be set to "low."

Question 7. When connecting a printer to a computer, it is usually necessary to use eight wires in the cable. But to connect a terminal, only three wires are required. Why the difference?

Answer 7. A couple of factors determine the number of pins required in a cable. It is possible to use only three pins to connect a printer to a computer. Factors such as flow control, error condition indications, interface indicators, protective grounding requirements, and port requirements dictate the number of required conductors.

Review the known minimal number of leads that are required for printer connection. These are receive data (usually lead 3) and signal ground (almost always lead 7). Protective ground (pin 1) is not usually needed. Hence only two leads are required thus far.

The use of flow control requires one additional lead. When hardware flow control is used, normally one of the leads 4, 11, 19, or 20 is used. Software flow control uses pin 2 as transmit data to send the XON/XOFF sequences. Hence flow control requires one more lead, bringing the total thus far to three.

Occasionally a printer uses more than one lead to indicate printer conditions when hardware flow control is used. Pin 20 may be used to indicate if the printer lid is open, while pin 19 in the same printer will indicate buffer status and paper out conditions. If multiple printer conditions are indicated on more than one hardware lead, this adds to the pin requirements. However, this is not normally the case because the flow control lead handles this.

A printer may have input leads that must be on for the printer to receive data, or as an indication that there is an attached computer. If the printer provides an output lead, such as 4 or 20, one of these can be locally looped back to the input leads. As long as 4 or 20 is on, the input leads will be on. Hence no other leads are required. If the printer does not provide any output control leads, then a lead from the computer will have to be used for this purpose, thus requiring another conductor in the cable.

If the printer uses the flow control technique, software, or a single hardware lead to indicate all error conditions, and any printer input control leads can be satisfied by a printer output control lead, a cable with only three conductors may be used. Local jumpering requires pins/sockets in the connector, not conductors/wires in the cable.

On the other hand, a terminal normally uses software flow control, and hence requires no extra leads. The XON/XOFF technique uses the same lead (usually pin 2) as the keyboard operate does for sending data. Hence, pins 2, 3, and 7 are required. Most terminals and computers don't require any input control signals, or they are locally jumpered in the connector.

2

CONNECTING PRINTERS
WITH PARALLEL INTERFACES

To this point the tutorials, how tos, and optimizations have been oriented toward environments where an RS232 port was used. With the increasing population of PCs in office environments, their requirements for serial interfacing will grow rapidly. Paralleling this growth, pardon the pun, is the need for hardcopy devices associated with each PC, terminal, supermicro, minicomputer, or network. The early hardcopy devices, mainly printers and plotters, used either a proprietary interface or the RS232 serial interface. More and more of the printers available today are being used with a parallel interface instead of either of the other interface types.

The parallel interface has been evolving over many years, but has really settled down since the advent of the PCs. Many different vendors offered their own versions of parallel interfaces. If a computer vendor offered a computer with a proprietary parallel interface, and its printer was the only device that supported this interface, guess whose printer was purchased? This condition of proprietary interfaces was also true of the serially interfaced terminals prior to the RS232 standard. This was great for the computer vendor, but not very appealing for the end user. The purchaser of the system was limited to the selection of printers that the computer vendor offered. Nonetheless, many printers were sold with computer systems.

The end users began to speak out against this, a cry that was heard by various printer and computer companies. One noted printer company, Centronics, had been fine tuning its printers to be flexible enough for about all types of parallel interfacing. In particular, the four categories of leads, the same ones in the RS232 standard, were included in the Centronics interface. Computer and peripheral companies began to offer ports that resembled this otherwise proprietary interface. The term "Centronics parallel interface" was born. Today, the reference to a parallel interface usually implies Centronics compatibility.

This chapter will review the elements of the Centronics-compatible parallel interface that is offered on the vast majority of computer and hardcopy devices. In the past any terminal that supported an attached printer connected to that printer through an RS232 interface. Times are changing due to the popularity of interfacing printers using the parallel interface. Now several terminal vendors selling asynchronous terminals will offer a parallel port for printer connection. The IBM PC entry this decade spawned a slight variation of the Centronics-compatible parallel interface, the IBM parallel interface. The IBM parallel interface will be featured here as well.

Prior to the presentation of tutorial modules that highlight parallel interfacing, we should review the elements of the parallel interface. If you already have a good understanding of the Centronics interface, proceed directly to the tutorial modules.

PARALLEL INTERFACE

The Centronics parallel interface is a 36-pin interface that uses an Amphenol 57 series connector. Cable lengths of 6 and 9 feet are common cable lengths. This footage is not the limit of the interface, as this author has successfully run a 15-foot parallel cable between the PC and printer. Ask the peripheral vendor about the distance allowed when you are preparing to make a purchase.

The Centronics interface offers the same category of leads as does the RS232 serial interface: ground, data, control, and timing. A key difference is that the parallel interface only allows data to be transferred in one direction, from the computer to the peripheral. This is different from the serial interfaces that allow two-way data exchange. There are a lot of similarities in concept between the serial and parallel interfaces. The next section discusses the different lead categories of the parallel interface and compares them to the serial interface. The data and ground categories will be covered together to ease the explanations. If the reader is interested in seeing the actual lead interaction of the Centronics parallel interface, a parallel interface break-out box (BOB) should be used. There are several models available on the market, such as the Black Box Catalog SAM Centronics 20. These types of BOBs allow the user to monitor lead interaction and perform lead jumperings similar to those in an RS232 interface.

DATA AND GROUND LEADS

In serial transmission, the bits of a character were transmitted one at a time. The receiving machine had to know character length, start/stop bits, speed, and parity to decipher the characters for proper handling. The parallel interface contrasts with the serial by allowing the computer to transmit all a character's bits simultaneously instead of one at a time to the printer. Picture the runners in a 100-yard dash. They all start at the same time, and if all goes well, all arrive at nearly the same time. The data bits are transmitted in a similar fashion. RS232 offered a single lead, Transmit Data, for the passing of the data bits serially. To transmit all the bits at once requires eight separated data leads. The Centronics standard sets aside pins 2 to 9 for data transmission. Each of the data leads has a corresponding ground lead for signal-level reference. Whereas RS232 sets aside only one lead (pin 7) for this, the Centronics interfaces use pins 20–27 as a ground reference for each data lead. These ground leads are often termed "returns" and are paired with each data lead. Refer to Table 2–1 for the list of the data leads with these return leads. As with the RS232 interface, the ground leads have no direction. These paired ground leads have a ± 0 V level.

By having eight data leads, all the data bits of a character are transmitted from the computer to the printer at the same time. This allows for very fast transmission of the data. Thus, the speed of the interface is not expressed in bits per second. Rather, characters per second (cps) are used, with a typical speed of 5000 cps. This is the speed of the interface. This does not automatically imply that a parallel interface on a printer is faster than a serial port. The speed of the printing dictates how much actual throughput can be expected, even though the interface can pump a lot of data.

The other ground leads are found on leads 14 and/or 16, as well as lead 17. Leads 14/16 are the signal reference for the control leads. The frame or chassis ground lead is lead 17.

TABLE 2–1. DATA AND ASSOCIATED LEADS OF PARALLEL INTERFACE

Function	Data, ground lead pair
Data bit 1	2, 20
Data bit 2	3, 21
Data bit 3	4, 22
Data bit 4	5, 23
Data bit 5	6, 24
Data bit 6	7, 25
Data bit 7	8, 26
Data bit 8	9, 27

CONTROL LEADS

The interface has set aside a control lead for the printer to indicate to the attached computer that a character has been received. This is lead 10, and is termed the "acknowledgment" lead. Lead 10 is an output signal from the printer to the attached computer. Once a code is sent to the printer, the computer should receive this signal pulse before a new code or character is sent. There is an associated "return" lead for the "acknlg" lead found on lead 28.

Other control functions must allow for conditions of paper-out, printer in offline mode, and other printer error or fault conditions. Because of the high-speed capability of the parallel interface, control leads are imperative to control the transmission of data between the two devices. Flow control must be maintained so that the computer knows when data may be transmitted.

BUSY SIGNAL

If the printer cannot receive any more data, it must indicate this to the attached computer. Sound familiar? It should. This is the flow control portion of the interface, similar in concept to the serial counterpart. RS232 supported either hardware or software flow control. Full duplex was required for software flow control, using XON/XOFF or ETX/ACK, because actual characters were transmitted by the printer back to the computer. Because the parallel interface is unidirectional, or simplex, only hardware flow control is possible. Pin 11 is used for this function. As long as pin 11, known as the Busy signal, is off/low, data may be transmitted by the computer if the ACK lead allows it. A Busy condition causes the printer to turn on pin 11 as an indication for the computer to cease transmission. The printer turns this lead on if the printer is offline, in an error condition, or if the printer buffer is full and the printer needs to catch up. Once the printer is placed in Online mode or the error condition clears, this lead goes off/low once again. This is a signal to the computer to resume transmission. Pin 29 is the ground return for the Busy signal.

The Busy lead functions exactly as the hardware flow control in RS232. The difference is in the state of the lead and the corresponding condition. Pins 11, 19, or 20 in RS232 were generally on as an indication to the computer that data could be transmitted. The Centronics parallel Busy lead is off, as an indication to continue transmission.

Lead 32 is the Fault signal. When this lead is on, then no error conditions exist at the printer. This lead goes off when the printer is out of paper, the printer is "offline" or deselected, or any other "not ready" conditions exist. The Fault and Busy leads sound very similar. However, they differ in the following manner. The Busy lead only comes on to stop the flow of data from the attached computer. Many conditions can cause the need for this lead to come on, including buffer control, paper out, offline condition, and so on. The Fault lead is always off unless any of the preceding conditions is present, except for buffer control. Buffer control is not considered an error condition. When the buffer is full, the Busy lead will come on to regulate the flow of data from the computer. During this time, the fault light stays lit as it does when there are no "error" conditions in the printer. Hence, when the Busy lead is on and the Fault lead is on, there is no major problem at the printer. However, if the Busy light is on and the Fault light is off, then there is a printer problem, not just a buffer control situation. To summarize, the Busy lead regulates the flow, while the Fault lead indicates an error condition.

ONLINE/SELECT MODE

The parallel port on a printer normally has a special lead that it uses to tell the computer that it is online and ready. If pin 13 is on, the computer should interpret this to mean that the printer is in the Online mode. This lead is also referred to as the Select lead, meaning that a "select" code has been received by the printer. If the printer is online, this lead remains on. Should the user take the printer offline, then this lead will go off, and the Busy lead will come on. The computer recognizes the flow control action and halts data transmission.

PAPER-OUT CONDITION

Should the printer run out of paper, an indication is passed to the attached computer. Found on pin 12, the PE (paper empty) signal is a paper-out signal "from" the printer. If this lead goes on, the computer should halt transmission to prevent loss of data. The printer will bring this lead on, as well as the Busy lead, without lowering its Select lead. Hence, when a paper-out condition occurs, the following leads will be on in the interface: ACK, Busy, PE, SEL, and Fault. Once the paper-out condition clears and the printer is back online, only the ACK and SEL leads will be on. The ACK will actually go on and off with each received piece of data. The use of this lead in conjunction with the Fault lead allows the attached computer to identify what the problem is with the printer.

PRINTER RESET

If the computer desires to reset the printer and clear its buffer, a lead is provided in the interface for this function. Lead 31 is on unless a reset is desired. Lowering of this lead is equivalent to powering the printer off and back on again. This lead is "to" the printer, "from" the attached computer. The Ground/Return lead for this signal is found on lead 30.

TIMING LEADS

All that remains is the timing category for the data transmission. RS232 had separate Transmit and Receive Timing leads for synchronous connections. The Centronics standard offers on a Transmit lead, as the interface is simplex. Pin 1 or the Data Strobe lead provides for the synchronization necessary to receive data. This is an input clock for the printer and allows for reading of the parallel data bits. The strobe is of short duration, about 1 microsecond or so. Once a character is read in, the strobe goes off for a short duration and then goes low again to receive the next characters. Refer to Figure 2–1 for the timing diagram of the parallel interface. Note the interaction of the ACK and Busy leads as discussed before.

PRINTER EMULATION

A printing characteristic worth mentioning is "printer emulation." Because of the widespread use of some printers, such as Texas Instruments 800 series, HP LaserJet Plus, Qume Sprint series, Epson printers, and so on support for their control codes and print formatting is included with several different printers. This implies that an Okidata printer can print from applications that are outputting data that has been formatted for an Epson printer. Features such as compressed print, bold print, and superscript are supported on the Okidata just as the Epson would handle them.

This is an application compatibility issue, not a hardware interface compatibility issue. If a printer emulates a different printer, this does not imply that the parallel (or serial) interface is exactly the same. Chances are that if both devices conform to the Centronics parallel standard, then the two interfaces will be exactly the same. However, there are no guarantees. This is cited only because there could be a difference in the cable required.

The interface study is now complete. A summary of the Centronics parallel interface appears in Table 2–2. Review this and the previous sections to ensure a complete understanding of the interface.

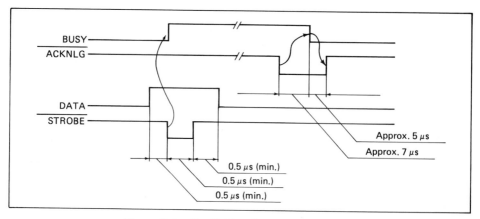

Figure 2–1. Parallel interface timing diagram.

TABLE 2–2. CENTRONICS PARALLEL INTERFACE SUMMARY

Pin	Signal	Pin	Signal
1	DATA STROBE	19	Twisted Pair Ground
2	Data Bit 1	20	Twisted Pair Ground
3	Data Bit 2	21	Twisted Pair Ground
4	Data Bit 3	22	Twisted Pair Ground
5	Data Bit 4	23	Twisted Pair Ground
6	Data Bit 5	24	Twisted Pair Ground
7	Data Bit 6	25	Twisted Pair Ground
8	Data Bit 7	26	Twisted Pair Ground
9	Data Bit 8	27	Twisted Pair Ground
10	ACKNOWLEDGE	28	Twisted Pair Ground
11	BUSY	29	Twisted Pair Ground
12	PAPER OUT	30	INPUT PRIME RETURN
13	SELECT	31	INPUT PRIME
14	GROUND	32	FAULT
15	Not Used	33	GROUND
16	GROUND	34	Not Used
17	CHASSIS GROUND	35	Not Used
18	+5V	36	Not Used

BUFFERS

As the user knows, or will soon find out, the printer is not quite as fast as the computer to which it is attached. When long print jobs are planned, the user often has a need to dump the data quickly and proceed on to more application work, leaving the printer to complete the print job at its own pace. A stand-alone buffer box can be acquired to provide this functionality.

These buffers come in a variety of memory sizes and features. They are being featured here to highlight the interfaces. Buffer boxes can be acquired with serial or parallel interfaces, or both. This allows the user much flexibility. An example is the computer that only has a serial interface but the user has obtained a printer with a parallel port. A buffer could be purchased, not only to provide a spooling function to offload the computer but to also solve the interface incompatibility.

The computer could communicate serially to its port on the buffer, with all the normal flow control features supported. The buffer box would then output these data to the printer through a parallel port. The printer would communicate with the buffer box just as if a computer were connected. All flow control and error conditions are dealt with by the buffer box. The converse arrangement is also possible, with a parallel interface on the computer and a serial port for the printer. The user would interface the devices to the buffer box, just as they would connect the computer and printer. The tutorial modules should be reviewed for the appropriate interfacing. The only caution is that, assuming a parallel port is available on both the computer and printer, get the two devices working without the buffer, prior to attempting to install the buffer box between them.

ABC SWITCHES

An ABC switch is a device that connects multiple devices together by the mere flick of a switch. A single computer connected to a switch can access one of two different printers, as needed. A single printer can be shared by more than one computer. The devices are connected to the switch, so that the common unit is connected to port C. The other two devices are connected to ports A and B. When the switch is in position "A," devices connected to ports A and C are connected. In position "B," devices on ports B and C can communicate. (The switches took their name from the foregoing relation.) ABCDE switches provide more than two devices to be shared by a single device.

The point for the user is that the switches are a "pass-through" device. The switches add no cross-over leads. The connections A-C and B-C are "straight through." If the ABC switch is for parallel connections, then all 36 pins will typically be provided. Build or select your cables to make the separate connections accordingly.

IBM PARALLEL CONNECTOR

Now that we have laid out the Centronics parallel standard, a variation of this will be discussed. IBM gets all the credit for this, as its PCs, and all compatibles, offer a Centronics-type port that uses a different connector, that of an RS232 interface. Yes, a DB25 connector with 25 pins is used for a parallel port. This means that some of the 36 pins are not used or they are shifted around. More important, though, is the cord plug compatibility issue. Most printers with parallel interfaces use an Amphenol-type connector as previously mentioned. This is also termed a champ connector. Even with a shoehorn, you cannot plug a DB25 connector into a champ receptacle. Because of this physical incompatibility, a conversion cable must be purchased.

At one end of the conversion cable is a DB25 connector. At the other is the Amphenol connector most printers are used to being cabled with (see Figure 2–2). The gender of the DB25 connector on the conversion cord is male. This is because the port on the PC is female. A quick way to determine which port on the back of a PC is the parallel port is by looking at the gender. All female ports should be parallel, while the male ports are serial. This conversion cable allows a standard printer to be connected to an IBM PC, or compatible, parallel port. The pin assignments at the PC's DB25 port are shown in Table 2–3. Table 2–4 then shows what an adapter cable could look like with a DB25 and Amphenol connector at each end.

OPTIONS

When connecting a printer to another device, the options must be set up properly. Because more and more printers offer both serial and parallel ports, the options required will vary. The next section summarizes some of the options with which the reader should be familiar when connecting a printer with a parallel port.

INTERFACES

This option generally exists because some printers offer one or more ports as a standard feature. Or perhaps an option is available to get a different interface. Set this option to match whatever port you are planning on using in the printer.

FLOW CONTROL

This option becomes irrelevant when a parallel interface is being used, as the flow can only be hardware flow control. This is inherent in the standard, as opposed to a serial, port. The setting of this option should not matter.

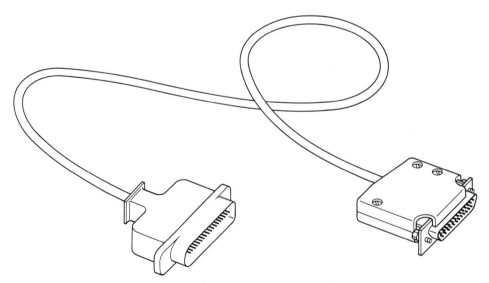

Figure 2–2. PC-to-printer converter cable.

TABLE 2–3. IBM PARALLEL PORT
PINOUT

DB25 Pin #	Function
1	Strobe
2	Data bit 0
3	Data bit 1
4	Data bit 2
5	Data bit 3
6	Data bit 4
7	Data bit 5
8	Data bit 6
9	Data bit 7
10	Acknowledge
11	Busy
12	Paper end (out of paper)
13	Select
14	Auto feed
15	Error
16	Initialize printer (reset)
17	Select input
18–25	Ground

TABLE 2–4. PC PARALLEL-
TO-CENTRONICS
AMPHENOL CABLE LEAD
LAYOUT

DB25	Amphenol
1	1
2	2
3	3
4	4
5	5
6	6
7	7
8	8
9	9
10	10
11	11
12	12
13	13
14	14
15	32
16	31
17	36
18	33
19	19
20	21
22	25
23	27
24	29
25	30

Flow Control

SPEED

This is another option that becomes irrelevant when a parallel port is used. With serial ports, the two device port speeds must match. A strobe lead in a parallel interface provides the data rate. Ignore this option when parallel ports are being used.

PARITY AND CHARACTER LENGTH

Because the bits of a character are being sent at the same time, 7-bit characters are typically used, without the need for parity.

The other printer options should be the same regardless of the port that is being used. Check each of them to ensure that they are set to meet your needs, and match those of the attached device.

Tutorial Module 2-1: Connecting a PC to a Printer with a Parallel Interface

In this module, a step-by-step approach will be taken to connecting a PC or compatible to a printer with a Centronics parallel interface. Here we will highlight the use of a PC due to the parallel port being implemented with a DB25-type connector. The general text in this chapter covered this parallel implementation, and this tutorial module will feature the conversion cable necessary to connect the two devices together.

The discussion will feature an IBM PC/XT throughout. It is important to note that any of the compatibles, such as the AT&T PC 6300 series, Compaq Deskpro series, and PC Limited series, can be substituted throughout. Furthermore, any of the laptop computers that offer a parallel port using a DB25 connector can be used here also. This would include the NEC MultiSpeed, Toshiba 1100 series, Toshiba 3100, and others. Substitute your computer here as appropriate, as the word "PC" will reference all the foregoing as well as many unlisted computers.

The printer that will be featured here is the Epson FX-80 as it offers a standard Centronics parallel interface. Many other printers offer this same interface, such as the Epson MX series, the C.ITOH series, the Toshiba series, the Genicom 3000 series, the Citizen printers, and many more. As long as your printer conforms to the Centronics parallel standard, as outlined earlier in this chapter's text, it may be substituted here.

The steps we will follow for these modules are common to all our reviews:

STEPS FOR CONNECTION

1. Determine compatibility (should it work?).
2. Determine signs of success.
3. Determine the type of connector used.
4. Determine gender of the ports.
5. Determine which leads (pins) are provided by each device.
6. Determine which leads are required to be on by each device.
7. Design the cable.
8. Build the cable.
9. Test the cable for continuity.
10. Cable the two systems together with the cable.
11. From step 2, measure success.

1. Determine compatibility

2. Determine signs of success

Should the PC and Epson work? Both these devices offer Centronics-compatible parallel interfaces. They merely use different-size connectors. However, the signal levels are the same. As long as the proper conversion cable is used, the two should work together. Our success will be the ability to print a file or print a copy of the screen contents on the attached printer.

3. Determine type of connector

4. Determine gender of ports

Review the documentation to determine the connectors and gender of the ports for each of the devices. The PC offers a DB25s connector. This is a female connector. Depending on your PC, this port could come standard with your computer or be obtained with an add-on board. Nonetheless, the gender of this port, female, is a good way to differentiate it from the RS232 ports on a PC. RS232 ports are male; parallel ports are female.

The Epson offers a female Amphenol/Cinch connector with 36 pins. This is easily differentiated from a serial port. Depending on the model printer that you are using, both a parallel and serial port may be offered. The 36-pin port is the one we are going to use, as this is the parallel port. Fill in an SCS (Software Cabling System) port profile with the information gathered thus far.

5. Determine leads (pins) provided by each device

6. Determine leads required to be on

Review the documentation for each port to determine which leads are provided by each device, as well as which ones must be on. The easiest way to review the leads is to look at their functions and corresponding directions. Table 2–5 lists the leads of both devices. Parallel interfaces are simplex, that is, transferring data in only one direction, from the computer to the printer. This differs from RS232 serial interfaces, which can be bidirectional. Because of this, the lead functions and directions are fairly standard. The receiving devices, in this case a printer, will have certain leads that it provides, as well as expects to see. The computer, because it is outputting the information, will have the reverse direction of each lead. The key variance in parallel interfacing is either the lead numbers or the lack of a lead. Fortunately, 100 percent conformance to the Centronics parallel interface is more common than 100 percent conformance to the serial standards.

7. Design the cable

From the foregoing you can see that the port on a 25-pin parallel port offers a subset of functions compared to the Centronics 36-pin interface. Nonetheless, the two systems are compatible with the proper cable. The cable can be designed by locating the common functions provided in both ports and connecting these together. The rules of cable design, in particular connecting an output to an input, are appropriate here. Once the common functional leads are connected, the remaining leads will be dealt with or ignored. Should the user desire, the leads can be separated by category of leads.

The first category of leads is ground (Table 2–6). The parallel interface offers a common Return or Signal Ground for each data lead, as well as the Strobe, Acknowledge, Busy, and Reset leads. Most cable designs for this type connection will merely connect the ground leads together. The printer has leads 19–30 set aside for signal grounding, while the PC parallel port has leads 18–25 for this purpose. Connect these leads together as outlined in Table 2–7. The 36-pin interface provides a lead, 16, for Signal Ground. Many times vendors connect all the Signal Ground leads to lead 16 so signal grounds are all based from the same level. This would allow for a single lead in the interface to be connected across to all the returns. Most devices internally jumper all these leads together anyway. This case study will not feature this, although you may need to add it in your connection. This takes care of the ground category of leads.

The next category is data. Because the bits of a character are transmitted at the same time in parallel, eight leads are set aside for this purpose. The PC and printer both have these Data leads, the only difference being the direction of the leads. The Data leads are output from the PC and input to the printer due the simplex (one-way) nature of the parallel interface. Merely connect the Data leads together in the interface, paying attention to the data bit numbers. It is important to connect bit 1 from the PC's port to bit 1 of the printer's port, and so on, for proper reception of the data characters.

The control category of leads are the next area to tackle. Review the control-type leads in the interface. The best way is to look at the PC's interface first as there are fewer leads. Match up the common functions, noting their directions relative to the PC and the printer. The leads for the Acknowledge, Busy, Paper end/out, Select, and Auto feed functions all have matching leads in both interfaces, with exactly the same lead numbers. Connect these together as shown in Table 2–8. Another important lead is the Fault lead found on leads 15 and 32 of the PC and printer ports, respectively. These two leads should also be connected.

Most printers, including the Epson, support a Reset function in the interface. Lead 31 of the Centronics standard provides for this and is found on lead 16 of the PC's DB25 port. Connect these two together. The Reset/Init/Prime function is not supported on all printers. There are other leads in the interface, but are typically not included in PC-to-printer cables. Hence, add the control leads, found in Table 2–9, to your cable design.

The only remaining category of leads is timing. In a parallel interface, the timing lead is a strobe that times the output of the parallel data bits. This is found on lead 1 of both interfaces; hence, these two should be connected. Note in Table 2–10, the completed cable design, that the directions do not conflict for the timing leads, as well as the other categories.

TABLE 2–5. PC AND EPSON PARALLEL PORT PINOUTS

Function	PC lead #	Epson lead #	
Timing Lead			
Data strobe (from)	1	1	Data strobe (to)
Data Leads			
Data bit 0 (from)	2	2	Data bit 0 (to)
Data bit 1 (from)	3	3	Data bit 1 (to)
Data bit 2 (from)	4	4	Data bit 2 (to)
Data bit 3 (from)	5	5	Data bit 3 (to)
Data bit 4 (from)	6	6	Data bit 4 (to)
Data bit 5 (from)	7	7	Data bit 5 (to)
Data bit 6 (from)	8	8	Data bit 6 (to)
Data bit 7 (from)	9	9	Data bit 7 (to)
Control Leads			
Acknowledge (to)	10	10	Acknowledge (from)
Busy (to)	11	11	Busy (from)
Paper end (to)	12	12	Paper end (from)
Select (to)	13	13	Select (from)
Auto feed (from)	14	14	Auto feed (to)
Error (to)	15	—	
Init (from)	16	—	
Select in (from)	17	—	
	—	31	Prime/init/reset (to)
	—	32	Fault (from)
	—	35	+5 V (from)
	—	36	Select in (to)
Ground Leads			
	—	16	Signal ground
	—	17	Chassis ground
Ground	18	—	
Ground	19	19	Ground
Ground	20	20	Ground
Ground	21	21	Ground
Ground	22	22	Ground
Ground	23	23	Ground
Ground	24	24	Ground
Ground	25	25	Ground
	—	26	Ground
	—	27	Ground
	—	28	Ground
	—	29	Ground
	—	30	Ground
	—	33	Ground

NOTES: Leads 14, 15, 18, and 33 may vary depending on the printer you are using. They are typically used as ground leads. Lead 35 on a 36-pin connector may sometimes have no connection. Note that only 25 leads are supported on the PC port due to the DB25 connector being used.

TABLE 2–6. GROUND LEAD CROSS-OVERS

Function	PC lead #		Epson lead #	Function
Ground	18	-|--|-	19	Ground
Ground	19	-| |-	20	Ground
Ground	20	-| |-	22	Ground
Ground	21	-| |-	22	Ground
Ground	22	-| |-	23	Ground
Ground	23	-| |-	24	Ground
Ground	24	-| |-	25	Ground
Ground	25	-| |-	26	Ground
Ground		|-	27	Ground
Ground		|-	28	Ground
Ground		|-	29	Ground
Ground		|-	30	Ground

TABLE 2–7. DATA LEADS OF DB25-TO-CENTRONICS CABLE

Function	PC lead #		Epson lead #	Function
Data bit 0 (from)	2	-----)	2	Data bit 0 (to)
Data bit 1 (from)	3	-----)	3	Data bit 1 (to)
Data bit 2 (from)	4	-----)	4	Data bit 2 (to)
Data bit 3 (from)	5	-----)	5	Data bit 3 (to)
Data bit 4 (from)	6	-----)	6	Data bit 4 (to)
Data bit 5 (from)	7	-----)	7	Data bit 5 (to)
Data bit 6 (from)	8	-----)	8	Data bit 6 (to)
Data bit 7 (from)	9	-----)	9	Data bit 7 (to)

NOTE: The connections are "straight through." The arrows are used for illustrative purposes only.

TABLE 2–8. CONTROL LEADS OF PC-TO-CENTRONICS CABLE DESIGN

Function	PC lead #		Epson lead #	Function
Acknowledge (to)	10	-------	10	Acknowledge (from)
Busy (to)	11	-------	11	Busy (from)
Paper end (to)	12	-------	12	Paper end (from)
Select (to)	13	-------	13	Select (from)
Auto feed (from)	14	-------	14	Auto feed (to)

NOTE: These leads are "straight through."

TABLE 2–9. MORE CONTROL LEADS OF PC-TO-CENTRONICS CABLE DESIGN

Function	PC lead #		Epson lead #	Function
Error (to)	15	-------	32	Fault (from)
Init (from)	16	-------	31	Prime/Init/Reset (to)

TABLE 2–10. COMPLETE PC-TO-CENTRONICS PARALLEL CABLE DESIGN

FUNCTION	PC lead #		Epson lead #	FUNCTION
Data strobe (from)	1	-------	1	Data strobe (to)
Data bit 0 (from)	2	------)	2	Data bit 0 (to)
Data bit 1 (from)	3	------)	3	Data bit 1 (to)
Data bit 2 (from)	4	------)	4	Data bit 2 (to)
Data bit 3 (from)	5	------)	5	Data bit 3 (to)
Data bit 4 (from)	6	------)	6	Data bit 4 (to)
Data bit 5 (from)	7	------)	7	Data bit 5 (to)
Data bit 6 (from)	8	------)	8	Data bit 6 (to)
Data bit 7 (from)	9	------)	9	Data bit 7 (to)
Acknowledge (to)	10	-------	10	Acknowledge (from)
Busy (to)	11	-------	11	Busy (from)
Paper end (to)	12	-------	12	Paper end (from)
Select (to)	13	-------	13	Select (from)
Auto feed (from)	14	-------	14	Auto feed (to)
Error (to)	15	-------	32	Fault (from)
Init (from)	16	-------	31	Prime/Init/Reset (to)
Ground	18	-|---|-	19	Ground
Ground	19	-| |-	20	Ground
Ground	20	-| |-	22	Ground
Ground	21	-| |-	22	Ground
Ground	22	-| |-	23	Ground
Ground	23	-| |-	24	Ground
Ground	24	-| |-	25	Ground
Ground	25	-| |-	26	Ground
		|-	27	Ground
		|-	28	Ground
		|-	29	Ground
		|-	30	Ground

NOTE: Your cable may not need to include the leads for the Reset function, as not all printers support it. Furthermore, the ground leads may need to be connected to lead 16 of the 36-pin port.

8. Build the cable

9. Test for continuity

10. Cable the two systems together

Parallel cables are more difficult actually to build than are serial cables. There are several reasons for this. The printer connectors are not as readily available as the serial connections. Furthermore, over 20 solder connections must be made on each side of the cable. Finally, improperly constructed cables can generate significant levels of RFI (radio frequency interference). For example, to reduce RFI, the cable must be assembled with the wires wrapped in twisted pairs. Because of this, parallel cables are not quite as easy to construct as serial ones. Standard cables are available for this PC-to-printer connection that was just described. The user is encouraged to purchase one of these prefabricated cables or to have an experienced technician actually build the cable.

Once the cable is acquired or built, be sure that the leads are crossed over and straight through as designed. Cable the two systems together with this cable. If the PC-to-printer cable is not long enough to reach between the two devices, or the user wants them farther apart, an easy solution exists. Because the PC end of the cable is a DB25 connector (male), an RS232 ribbon cable can be used as an extension cable. Be sure that the cable is a ribbon cable or contains all 25 leads. This extension cable will require a male gender at one end, with a female at the other.

A total distance between the PC and printer greater than 15 feet is not recommended, though that distance has been extended to as much as 20 to 25 feet. If you are using ribbon cable with snap-on DB25 connectors, you can move them to the proper-length cable as appropriate. Be sure that the PC-to-printer cable works prior to inserting this type of extension cable in between the PC and printer. Once you are assured of this, play with the extension cable length until the printer works, shortening it and snapping on the DB25 connector at various points.

11. Measure success

With the PC and printer connected with the cable, you are ready to test the system. Your success will be your ability to print information on the printer. To test this, you can print a file in a couple of ways. The file should be of significant length to ensure that flow control functions properly. To test this, you can issue a Print command. Another way is to enable the Print Online function by holding the Ctrl key down while hitting the Prt Sc key and then releasing them both. With the latter, anything that is displayed on the screen will also be sent to the printer. By displaying a file using the "type" command, the user will be able to ensure that the printer works.

A couple of areas are worth checking before you actually attempt to test the printer. The printer options should be checked first. If your printer offers both parallel and serial ports, typically an option has to be set to enable the port you are going to use. Check to make sure that the options are set to use the parallel port.

Another option that should be checked is the Print mode option. A number of printers offer the ability to emulate an IBM Graphics printer. If your printer offers this option, it is sometimes desirable to enable this emulation so the screen and other graphics can be printed. If not, your printer may misinterpret the graphic control sequences and misprint the information, or not print it at all.

Often there is an option for the printer to read either 8 or 7 bits from the data leads. This option is normally set for 8 bits.

Power up the PC as you normally would. Be sure that printer is cabled properly to the PC. Check to see that paper is in the printer, that power is applied to the printer, and that the printer is in the Online mode. You are ready to test the printer. The IBM PC offers the ability to print a duplicate of the information that appears on your screen. To enable this POL function, hit the Prt Sc key while holding down the Cntl key. Upon releasing these, the PC will enter the Print Online mode. Pressing this combination again disables the POL function. While in POL mode, display the directory on your disk by entering the command "dir." This should display the contents of your disk drive that you are currently on. In addition to this being displayed on the screen, your printer should be producing a hardcopy of the directory as it is displayed. If you get a hardcopy that mirrors the directory displayed on your screen, CONGRATULATIONS!

If for some reason you do not, then make sure that you were in the POL mode. Repeat the key combination, Cntl and Prt Sc, to enable POL. Repeat the test. If this still does not work, try to "print" a file by entering the command Print filename, substituting an ASCII file on your system. This should send the file out to your printer.

If you still do not get a hardcopy on the printer, be sure that the printing is not being redirected to a serial port. The Mode command allows this. To ensure that the printing is not being redirected, enter Mode lpt1: followed by the Enter key to disable any redirection that might have been set up. Also, check to see that the printer has paper, and is in the Online mode. Double check the optioning on the printer. Last, check to see that the two devices are properly cabled together.

If you get a hardcopy of the information, but the formatting appears to be wrong, refer to the Chapter 1 discussion on correcting printer problems. In particular, problems of double spacing and overwriting can be cured through correct optioning.

Tutorial Module 2-2: Connecting Multiple Devices with Parallel Ports to a Single PC

If more than one device with a Centronics parallel interface is to be used with a PC, the availability of RS232-type devices can be capitalized on. A good example of this would be ABC switches designed for use with RS232 devices. The idea of the extension cord, highlighted in Tutorial Module 2-1, could be applied if both a plotter and printer are to share a single parallel port on the PC. The ABC switch must provide all 25 leads to function here. Because the PC has a DB25 port, a ribbon cable or one with all 25 leads could connect the PC's parallel port to port C of the ABC switch. Then two DB25-to-Centronics cables, designed in Tutorial Module 2-1, could be connected to ports A and B of the switch, with the other end connected to the printer and plotter. Refer to Figure 2–3. Now the PC's single parallel port can be shared by both devices. Of course, parallel ABC switches are available to perform the same function. This is provided to aid the user in optimizing connection where possible.

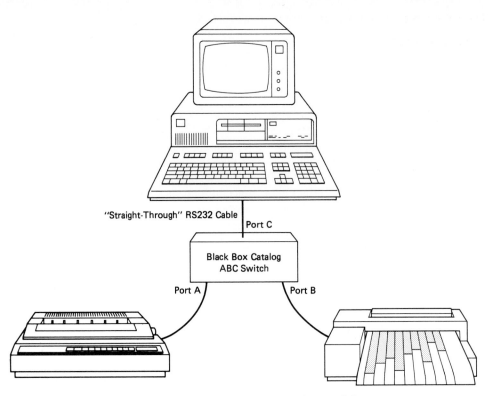

Figure 2–3. RS232 ABC switch connecting parallel ports.

Tutorial Module 2-3: Connecting a Parallel Printer to a Multiuser Micro

This module will highlight the connection of a printer with a parallel port to a multiuser micro (MUM). This is a common connection involving printers with Centronics-compatible interfaces. Most microcomputers now offer the same Centronics-compatible interface for these connections. The Centronics interface is closely conformed to with only minor variances in the pinouts between the different devices. This tutorial module will feature an AT&T 3B2/400 UNIX computer being connected to a Toshiba P351 printer. The interfaces on these devices are very similar, with only slight variances. Many other devices can be substituted in this module, as long as they offer 36-pin Centronics-compatible ports.
The steps we follow for this module are common to all our reviews:

1. Determine compatibility

2. Determine signs of success

The 3B2 computer system supports a Centronics parallel port on the I/O ports board. Devices that conform to this standard should physically work with the system. The Toshiba P351 does indeed conform to the standard; hence, it should work. UNIX does enter into the picture and complicate the compatibility issue. The UNIX spool facility, "lp," should support this printer for a proper working environment. The system administrator or computer vendor should be consulted prior to the connecting the printer to the system to ensure that the two are indeed compatible. The Toshiba will work with the 3B2 and other UNIX systems.
The user's goal is to print information directly onto the attached printer or have their application do this. Success will be measured by this ability. Beyond the physical connection of a printer, certain parameters must be set up prior to the printer functioning properly. UNIX must know about the printer, what port it is connected to, the "interface" profile to use, if it is the default printer for "lp," and so on. The systems administration can set this up for the user once the printer has been physically connected to the system. This tutorial module will not attempt to cover the systems administration of adding a printer, but rather will focus on the physical interfacing. However, upon proper setup, the user should be able to issue an "lp" command and print a file.

3. Determine type of connector used

4. Determine gender of ports

Both the 3B2 and the Toshiba P351 printers have the same female connectors. Hence, our cable will consist of 36-pin male connectors at both ends.

5. Determine leads (pins) provided by each device

6. Determine leads required to be on

The documentation should be consulted to determine the pinouts of both ports. The user will find that the two ports are very, very similar with only slight differences, allowing for easy cable design. The key difference will be in the direction of the leads. Table 2–11 summarizes the pinouts, separated by function.

TABLE 2–11. PC AND EPSON PARALLEL PORT PINOUTS

Function	3B2 lead #	Toshiba lead #	
Timing Lead			
Data strobe (from)	1	1	Data strobe (to)
Data Leads			
Data bit 0 (from)	2	2	Data bit 0 (to)
Data bit 1 (from)	3	3	Data bit 1 (to)
Data bit 2 (from)	4	4	Data bit 2 (to)
Data bit 3 (from)	5	5	Data bit 3 (to)
Data bit 4 (from)	6	6	Data bit 4 (to)
Data bit 5 (from)	7	7	Data bit 5 (to)
Data bit 6 (from)	8	8	Data bit 6 (to)
Data bit 7 (from)	9	9	Data bit 7 (to)
Control Leads			
No connection	10	10	Acknowledge (from)
Busy (to)	11	11	Busy (from)
Paper end (to)	12	12	Paper end (from)
Select (to)	13	13	Select (from)
No connection	18	18	+5 volts
Input prime (from)	31	31	Prime/init/reset (to)
Fault (to)	32	32	Fault (from)
Ground Leads			
±0 volts signal ground	14	14	±0 volts signal ground
Ground	16	16	±0 volts
Frame ground	17	17	Chassis ground
Ground	19	19	Ground
Ground	20	20	Ground
Ground	21	21	Ground
Ground	22	22	Ground
Ground	23	23	Ground
Ground	24	24	Ground
Ground	25	25	Ground
Ground	26	26	Ground
Ground	27	27	Ground
Ground	28	28	Ground
Ground	29	29	Ground
Ground	30	30	Ground
Ground	33	33	Ground

7. Design the cable

Review the lead functions in the pinouts of both ports. The directions are about the only thing that differ. Note that they are all the same, except for leads 10 and 18, which are not supported by the 3B2. The similarity is due to the nature of the parallel interface and, moreover, the Centronics parallel interface.

Parallel interfaces support simplex transmission; that is, data flow in only one direction. This differs from the bidirectional data transmission of the RS232 interface. This factor, coupled with the standard Centronics leads and their functions, allows for simple cable design. The user merely connects the common functions together, ensuring that there are no conflicting direction of leads. Refer to other tutorial modules for all the rules of cable design. But the most important rule is "connect an output to an input," and vice versa. All the signals, except for 10 and 18, functionally match, with opposite signal directions. Hence, the cable design would be as that outlined in Table 2–12.

The only leads not featured in the cable are leads 10 and 18. Lead 10 is an Acknowledge lead from the printer. The 3B2 does not support this lead. Having the lead in the cable will not cause a problem, as the 3B2 does ignore it. The Toshiba provides +5 V on lead 18. The 3B2 once again does not need this voltage level. It

TABLE 2–12. PARALLEL CABLE DESIGN FOR AT&T 3B2-TO-TOSHIBA P351 PRINTER

Function	3B2 lead #	Toshiba lead #	
Data strobe (from)	1	------- 1	Data strobe (to)
Data bit 0 (from)	2	------- 2	Data bit 0 (to)
Data bit 1 (from)	3	------- 3	Data bit 1 (to)
Data bit 2 (from)	4	------- 4	Data bit 2 (to)
Data bit 3 (from)	5	------- 5	Data bit 3 (to)
Data bit 4 (from)	6	------- 6	Data bit 4 (to)
Data bit 5 (from)	7	------- 7	Data bit 5 (to)
Data bit 6 (from)	8	------- 8	Data bit 6 (to)
Data bit 7 (from)	9	------- 9	Data bit 7 (to)
No connection	10	------- 10	Acknowledge (from)
Busy (to)	11	------- 11	Busy (from)
Paper end (to)	12	------- 12	Paper end (from)
Select (to)	13	------- 13	Select (from)
±0 volts signal ground	14	------- 14	±0 volts signal ground
Ground	16	------- 16	±0 volts
Frame ground	17	------- 17	Chassis ground
No connection	18	------- 18	+5 volts
Ground	19	------- 19	Ground
Ground	20	------- 20	Ground
Ground	21	------- 21	Ground
Ground	22	------- 22	Ground
Ground	23	------- 23	Ground
Ground	24	------- 24	Ground
Ground	25	------- 25	Ground
Ground	26	------- 26	Ground
Ground	27	------- 27	Ground
Ground	28	------- 28	Ground
Ground	29	------- 29	Ground
Ground	30	------- 30	Ground
Input prime (from)	31	------- 31	Prime/Init/Reset (to)
Fault (to)	32	------- 32	Fault (from)
Ground	33	------- 33	Ground

NOTE: All the leads are "straight-through" connections from one end of the cable to the other.

is better to leave this lead out of the cable if possible, as there is no need to exert unnecessary voltage levels in an interface, although the two devices will function with it present.

8. Build the cable

9. Test for continuity

10. Cable the two systems together

Because there are no special cross-overs involved in this cable, the user is encouraged to buy a prebuilt cable. This will minimize the potential problem of cable and lead continuity that arises when a custom cable is built with the soldering of leads and connectors. Acquire a cable, if possible, that has a connector that is at a 90-degree angle with the actual cable. This will allow easy installation into the 3B2. This is not a requirement, but merely a nicety.

11. Measure success

Your success will depend on your ability to send a file to the printer. As indicated, there is more than mere physical connection of a printer to a UNIX system. Have the systems administrator of the UNIX system add the printer. This is normally done through a menu-driven administration program. The printer will be added to the system, with the appropriate entries made to indicate the port where the printer was attached. Furthermore, a "model" profile would be associated with the printer. The administrator can specify the number of copies to be printed by the printer, whether a header and trailer sheet are provided with each print request, and other sundry items. Refer to one of the books available on systems administration of UNIX systems for further information. It is beyond the scope of this text to cover these complex areas.

The options of the printer should be checked. In particular, the option that specifies the type of port used in a printer should be set to parallel. Printers today may offer both serial and parallel interfaces. If this option is set to serial, and you are interfacing through the parallel port, the printer will not function. Double check to make sure of a proper option setting.

Once the systems administrator has defined the printer to the system and has enabled the printer, the user should attempt to send a file to the printer. The normal sequence necessary to accomplish this from a terminal on a UNIX system is, "lp filename." This command sequence, followed by the Enter key, causes UNIX to print a copy of the file specified in filename. Be aware that the "lp" command invokes a spool function. Thus, your print request is queued and printed when possible. Your output may not appear on the printer immediately, but should be printed shortly. UNIX provides a command that allows the user to check the status of the printer and its queue. The "lpstat -t" command sequence will list the printers, their status, and the print requests that are queued for printing. Upon issuance of this command, determine if your print has been scheduled for printing. If it has been, the printer should print the file soon. Correct any formatting problems, such as overwriting and double spacing through the line feed option. CONGRATULATIONS!

If you encounter problems, check that you entered the proper command sequence. Reenter it to be sure. If you still don't have success printing the file, make sure that the printer has paper, is powered on, is cabled properly, and is in the Online mode. Then involve the systems administrator to ensure proper software setup. Also ensure that the printer is enabled.

PARALLEL INTERFACING: MOST FREQUENTLY ASKED QUESTIONS

Question 1. Why does the distance for running parallel Centronics cable vary for different equipment?

Answer 1. The distance between devices has to do with signal levels outputted or expected by two attached devices. Because the parallel standards have a signal range for each signal, and signals fade as distances increase, the distance between two devices will vary. If a vendor's port outputs signals that are near the lower level allowed by the standard, then the distance allowed could be reduced.

Another factor is the type of equipment that is cabled, or where the cabling is "ran." Heavy machinery such as air conditioners, compressors, etc., cause interference that can cause signal power loss. Pay attention to where cabling is ran.

Question 2. How can a printer with a Centronics-compatible 36-pin port be connected to a 25-pin port of an IBM PC/XT/AT? The number of pins don't match.

Answer 2. The Centronics standard allows for 36 pins, some of which are not used. Also each signal lead has a separate ground lead associated with it. By sharing a common signal ground lead, the number of leads required are reduced. Also several of the leads in the 36-pin interface are not required for the PC connection. By crossing over leads within the cable, in particular the signal ground leads, the number of conductors can be reduced to twenty-five. The reason the printer end has the 36-pin connector is because not all computers will have the 25-pin connector like a PC. Hence a cross-over cable allows most printers with 36-pin connectors to be connected to PCs. These same printers can also be connected to other computers that have 36-pin ports by using a straight-through cable with 36-pin connectors at each end.

Question 3. What does it mean to be "HP compatible" or "Epson compatible"?

Answer 3. Printer compatibility can mean many things. When referring to interfacing, Centronics compatible implies that a printer conforms to the interface standard that the Centronics printer company established. A printer that is HP or Epson compatible typically supports the same escape sequences as the printer they emulate. If a printer offers Epson compatibility, the same escape sequence used to shrink the print can be used on the non-Epson printer. This is important from an application software standpoint. A variety of printers can be selected for use with a system as long as the application can easily support them. Printer compatibility allows for this. Some printers may offer multiple compatibility modes, i.e., both HP and Epson. The reason for this is that not all application programs may support the HP printer, but they almost all support an Epson printer. Hence the printer with more compatibility modes offers much flexibility.

Question 4. What is the difference between an ABC switch and an EIA switch?

Answer 4. The use of a box to connect a single device to more than one device first involved interfaces that were RS232 compatible. The Electronics Industry Association, EIA, defined the RS232 standard, hence the term EIA switch. Vendors of such EIA switches labeled the device ports A, B, and C, with C being connected to the common device. They became known as both ABC switches and EIA switches in the industry.

With the advent of a standard parallel interface, the Centronics parallel standard, it was inappropriate to refer to switches for parallel interfaces as EIA switches, and the tag, ABC switches, became the standard. Although there are those in the industry who still denote all switches as EIA switches, EIA switches should be limited to those that switch RS232 devices.

Question 5. Why is software flow control not used in parallel connections?

Answer 5. Parallel connections are simple, implying only a single direction of data transmission. XON/XOFF involves the transmission of a character to the device that is sending data, simultaneous with the reception of data (full-duplex). Therefore a hardware lead is raised and lowered for flow control. Software flow control will not work in a parallel connection.

3

CONNECTING MODEMS

A stand-alone piece of computer or terminal equipment is becoming a thing of the past. As the need to access, exchange, upload, or download information increases, more and more systems have the need to communicate. This basic need for communication with other computer systems dictates the need for connecting a modem to your computer system. The modem allows a digital piece of equipment to access another digital piece of computer equipment, using standard telephone lines. The telephone lines in use today are predominantly analog. The modem is used to convert a signal transmitted from an attached computer, terminal, or printer (DTE) to analog and modulate this signal on the network, to be received at the other end of the network by another modem. This remote modem receives the analog signal, demodulates the signal, and presents the information to the attached digital equipment. The term modem (short for MOdulator-DEModulator) describes the piece of equipment that sends and receives information on an analog network. This chapter is dedicated to easing the connection of modems to all different types of computers, terminals, printers, and other modems.

The marketplace is driving the features of modems and their capabilities. During the early days of communication, speeds of 75 baud and 110 baud were prevalent, with 300 baud being considered high speed. Today, this is slow. The most common speed used for dial-up communication is 1200 bits per second (bps), with 2400 and 9600 bps being the speeds that many of the modems vendors are targeting over the next five years. The users are demanding higher speeds because of the heavy data exchange capabilities. Electronic mail alone is causing users to review the current speeds of their systems. When the user adds uploading and downloading of data files and programs, the speed and throughput of a modem can be critical. Modem vendors are responding with higher-speed modems.

Furthermore, as workstations become more intelligent, the demand for more intelligent modems increases. The user expects the modem to buffer the data to be sent, monitor the quality of the line, provide selection of the optimal transmission speed for a line, provide error-free transmission with automatic error detection and correction, buffer the data, and provide inherent protocols. This list of demands continues to grow.

Regardless of the demands expected from the modems, all of them will provide the same basic functionality of converting digital signals to analog and back to digital when used in pairs. The variations will be features above this basic functionality to meet specific user requirements. There are a significant number of options and features that any modem user should understand. The next section highlights these. The tutorial modules that follow cover the connection of modems to computers, to printers, to terminals, and to other modems.

SPEED

This feature tends to be one of the main points that separates the different modems. When a user is destined to use, acquire, connect, or call a modem, this is one of the most important pieces of information to be known. The user's modem must be able to communicate with the remote system at a common speed. Without this, the two systems cannot communicate. A modem may offer several speeds, such as 110 to 300 and 1200 bps. Once the remote system's modem speed is known, the user must communicate with it at the same speed.

103 COMPATIBILITY

A standard in the industry has been set by AT&T over the years for low-speed communication. The modem that has been sold to address the 0–300 bps transmission rate is the AT&T 103J modem. There have been many variations of this modem, but it is the standard for low-speed communications. Hence other modem vendors have made modems that emulate this modem. The term ''103 compatible'' has emerged to imply that a modem is compatible with the AT&T 103 modem series. These modems communicate at speeds of from 0 to 300 bps. They use a modulation technique known as frequency shift keying, FSK. This technique uses different well-defined frequencies to represent the ones and zeros of the data bits, in both directions. Compatible means that the modem can communicate with any other modem that conforms to the standard.

212 COMPATIBILITY

As with 103J compatibility, AT&T has set the standard for the 1200 bps, full duplex, dial-up modem. The 212 modem is an industry standard for the medium-speed modem marketplace. The 212 uses a different modulation technique, known as phase shift keying, PSK. The bits of the data are modulated using different phases of a signal. Hence, modems that are 212 compatible also use the PSK modulation technique at 1200 bps. The reason for citing ''at 1200 bps'' is that the 212 also supports the same lower-speed environment provided by the 103 modem. Hence a true 212-compatible modem supports speeds of 0–300 and 1200 bps operation. Some modems offer 212 compatibility at the higher speed, yet may not offer 103J compatibility. Check for this if the lower-speed operation is important to you. Because of this dual speed capability, most of the bulletin boards, news networks, and electronic mail services use 212-compatible modems. This allows access by users with 103-type modems as well as 212 modems.

AUTO DETECTION

Depending on the modem used, the speed may be set automatically based on the modulation technique used, or the user can set the speed manually. The called modem will monitor the line to determine the type of modulation technique used and adjust the speed accordingly. Certain leads in the RS232 interface are used as either ''speed select'' or ''speed indicator'' functions. When these leads are supported by both the DTE and DCE, a lead will be on to indicate whether the higher speed is to be used or if the modem is actually using the higher speed.

AUTO ANSWER

This feature is used by all bulletin boards, time-sharing systems, UNIX-based systems, and electronic mail systems, to name just a few. Auto answer is the ability of a modem and attached device to answer an incoming call, unattended. Unattended implies that a person need not be there to answer the telephone attached to a modem and put the modem in ''data'' modem. This is a common feature of most dial-up modems.

This modem feature typically relies on the attached device to enable this capability, but not always. If a modem offers this option, the RS232 interface normally plays an integral part in this. Pin 20, Data Terminal Ready, controls whether or not the modem automatically answers an incoming call. If the modem is set up for auto answer, it will receive the incoming call just as you would hear a phone ring. The modem logic then checks to see if DTR is turned on. If so, the modem will answer the incoming call automatically. If DTR is not on, the modem will not answer the call, with the calling party getting a continuous ring.

If the DTR is on and the modem has power applied to it, the call will be answered. The attached device, be it a computer, printer, or terminal, can control how long the connection is established with the DTR lead. If the device lowers DTR, then the modem will disconnect from the line. Placing the device offline will typically cause DTR to be lowered, hence dropping the connection. Powering off either the device or modem will drop the connection.

There are modems that offer an option to ignore the status of the DTR lead. With this option enabled and the modem set up for auto answer, the incoming call will be answered regardless of the status of the DTR lead. If you want the attached device to control the auto answer, be sure that the DTR option is set properly. If your device is powered off, then the incoming call will not be answered.

COMMAND RESULTS

Intelligent modems offer commands allowing the attached device to cause actions or enable features. Different types of dialing, stored numbers, auto answer, disconnect, and so on are supported through the issuance of these commands to the modem. Depending on the command used, result codes are given by the modem. Typically, once the command has been completed, the modem will send a result code. These intelligent modems generally offer an option for the results to be displayed in either plain English words or digits. If a keyboard operator, on a terminal, computer, or other device, is issuing the commands, the English words are more desirable. If, however, a program such as a communication software program on a PC is communicating with the modem, then the digits may be more appropriate. Often this communication software will support either method, transparently, to the user.

LOCAL ECHO

Intelligent modems offer the ability locally to echo the characters of a command back to the attached device. Recall that the term echoplex has been used to describe a full duplex environment. With echoplex, a sending device relies on the remote system to echo back the characters. The sending device does not display them until they receive them from the far end. If a device, attached to a modem, is issuing modem commands with the echoplex (full duplex) option enabled, the user will not be able to see what he or she is typing. The "local echo" option within a modem provides for this echoplexing feature. However, this is only active during the modem command interaction. Once a connection is established to a remote system, the local modem disables the echoplexing feature, allowing the remote system to assume this responsibility.

STATUS OF LEADS

Indicator lights are found on the front of many modems, whether they are intelligent or not. These lights permit a visual check of the modem's status, the attached device status, and the line condition. Typically, lamps are present for modem ready, terminal ready, send and receive data, offhook condition, carrier detect, and high-speed indication. Table 3–1 highlights the indicators and their meanings.

HAYES COMPATIBILITY

The industry often speaks of "Hayes compatible" when referencing modems or "support for Hayes modem." What exactly is this? A standard existed in the industry for the 300 bps modem as well as the 1200 bps. AT&T set the standard for the 103J (300 bps) and the 212A (300/1200 bps) modems. The industry was full of 103- and 212-compatible modems.

Hayes Microcomputer Products added luster to this compatibility by offering "intelligence" to these compatible modems, namely, microprocessors that supported commands, offered auto dialing, stored numbers, and so on. At the same time, Hayes introduced a set of commands that allowed the attached device to communicate with the modem. These commands provided the aforementioned features as well as others.

One of the most notable was the dialing sequence. The Hayes Smartmodem series of modems supported an attention code, AT, that preceded all commands. This was the first step of what has grown to be known as

TABLE 3–1. BREAKOUT BOX INDICATORS

Lamp	Meaning
Modem ready	Typically lights when power is applied.
Terminal ready	Typically lights when the attached device is on supplying DTR. If modem is optioned to ignore DTR, this lamp is on when power is applied to the modem, just as the modem ready indicator.
Send data	Lights whenever data are sent from the attached device to/through the modem.
Receive data	Lights whenever data are received off the line by the modem.
Offhook	When the telephone line is being used, this is lit.
Carrier detect	Lights when the modem has detected a carrier signal from a distance modem.
High speed	If a modem supports multiple speeds, this lamp is lit when the higher speed is being used.

"Hayes compatible." This sequence, AT, is followed by any number of difference commands to enact the features of the modem. The Hayes documentation indicates that the "A" allows the modem to determine the speed at which the attached device is communicating. The "T" indicates the word length and parity.

In addition to the AT attention command, one of the most prominently used commands is the dialing command. Depending on the type of dialing—pulse or touch-tone—the command to dial a number is "DP" or "DT," preceded by the "AT" sequence. After the DT or DP sequence, the actual telephone number follows. The "," is used to cause a pause, allowing the modem to wait for a second dial tone. To disconnect the call, a "ATZ" sequence is used. These sequences comprise some of the basic Hayes Smartmodem commands.

Many vendors offer "Hayes compatibility" in their modems. What is this? This implies those modems support at least the foregoing commands plus a few more. By the strictest definition, modems that boast Hayes compatibility should support the entire set of Hayes Smartmodem commands. Consult Appendix I for a complete listing of these commands. However, modem vendors will claim Hayes compatibility and support a subset of all the commands.

The key to how big an issue this is can be the software that drives the devices attached to the Hayes or compatible modem. Some communication software requires strict conformance to the standard; others need a minimal command set. Prior to buying a compatible, be sure that the communication software that you are planning to use does indeed function with the modem. In the case of a terminal or printer, generally this is not an issue as there is no communication software. However, with a PC, mini, or mainframe, this could be an issue.

It is important to note that modems that boast Hayes compatibility don't necessarily mimic the modem 100 percent. This is not even related to the commands supported. Rather, this refers to the RS232 interface on the modem. The Hayes Smartmodem 1200 has a different interface than the Hayes Smartmodem 2400. An AT&T modem, a Ventil, NEC, Bizcomp, and others may support the Hayes command set, but offer a slight variation on the RS232 interface. This is cited only because when interfacing to equipment, the cable required could be slightly different from one normally used for a Hayes Smartmodem. Consult the appendices for further information about the compatible modems and their interfacing to the different equipment.

PORT PROFILE

The bulk of the modems offered today provide a female port for connection. This port is normally a DB25-type connector ready for connection to a piece of data terminal equipment. Modem ports, due to the modem's being a DCE device, provide signals according to the RS232 standard. In other words, they provide signals such as Clear to send, Data set ready, Data Carrier detect, and Ring Indicator. Hence, the industry claims that these ports emulate DCE. The port is ready for connection to a piece of DTE, normally with a straight-through cable. The tutorial modules will elaborate on this issue and its impact on connections.

MODEM TESTS

Modems typically have built-in diagnostics for testing the modem functionality. These diagnostics, typically referred to as tests, allow the user to isolate problems. There are generally four different tests that are possible on a modem. Although these may vary, they are typically the local self-test, the analog loopback test, the end-to-end self-test, and the digital loopback test. These tests will be explained in the next sections. A key point in understanding these is to locate just what in a modem connection the test is actually checking out. Normally, indicator lights are provided to show the results of the test. Refer to your modem's documentation for the specific results you should expect.

In cases of suspected trouble, first perform the local self-test. If the modem passes the test, then perform the analog loopback test. If the test fails, the trouble is in the DTE or connections from the DTE to the modem. If both tests pass, perform either the end-to-end test or the digital loopback test. Figure 3–1 provides a flow chart useful in using these tests to diagnose a modem connection.

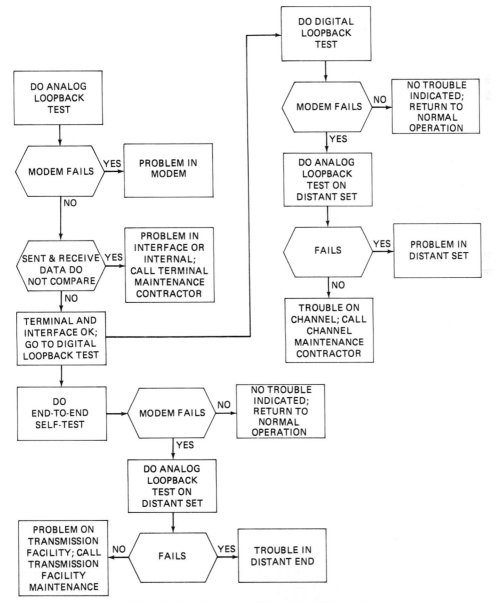

Figure 3–1. Modem trouble isolation flowchart.

LOCAL SELF-TEST

This test checks out the operation of the modem. Functionally, what is occurring is that onboard diagnostics are being performed throughout the circuitry on the modem chips. This is accomplished through a pattern generated within the modem that is measurable. The modem typically provides a word/pattern generator and word comparator for this testing. The word comparator compares what is received to a known pattern that the generator sent, to determine the health of the modem. If the two are the same, the test passes. This self-test generator is used with some of the other tests to send, receive, and compare test patterns.

ANALOG LOOPBACK TEST

This is used to check the operation of the modem with the attached DTE. Refer to Figure 3–2 for a pictorial representation of what is occurring in an analog loopback test. When the modem is in this mode, the modem is utilizing the transmitter normally used to output the data to the line. This test loops back this transmitter to the modem's receiver. At the keyboard of the attached device, the user can enter information and have the modem locally echo it back to them. This test checks out the transmitter and receiver of the modem. It is termed "analog," because it occurs on the line side (analog) of the modem. The telephone line supports analog signals, while the RS232 interface supports digital signals. If the user receives the characters that they type, the transmitter and receiver of the modem pass the test. This, in conjunction with the local self-test, can diagnose the health of your local modem.

END-TO-END SELF-TEST

To perform this test, the distant-end modem, as opposed to your locally attached modem, needs to be able to support the self-test feature. This test checks the local and remote modems as well as the telephone line connecting them. The only piece that it does not check is the RS232 (digital) interface side of the distant modem. The DL test does this.

Figure 3–3 outlines the connections and what is occurring in the end-to-end self-test. With this test, different from the previous ones, a connection has to be made between the two modems. Once a connection is made, both modems are placed in self-test modem. Both modems, through the word generators and word comparators, transmit test messages to each other and compare them. This test generally requires an attendant at each end. A lamp is provided to indicate the results of this test.

DIGITAL LOOPBACK TEST

The distant-end modem must be equipped with a self-test feature for this test also. A connection should be established between the two modems for this test as with the end-to-end test. The local modem, through the self-test function, transmits test messages to the distant end where it is then looped back. The local modem then

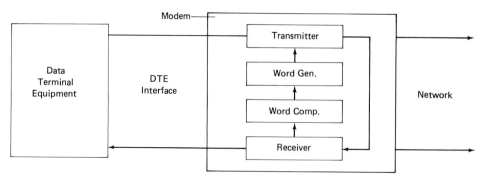

Figure 3–2. Analog loopback test.

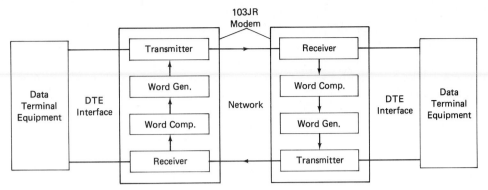

Figure 3–3. End-to-end self-test.

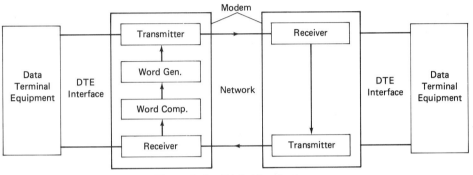

Figure 3–4. Digital loopback test.

compares the received message with the transmitted modem to see if the modem, circuit, and DTE connections pass the test. Figure 3–4 shows what is occurring within the modems for this test to occur.

These explanations were provided to establish a basis on which a deeper understanding of "modem connections" can be built. The tutorial modules for this chapter feature a variety of installations involving modems with terminals, printers, computers, and even other modems. Each tutorial module is designed to show a different issue surrounding the connection of modems to other devices.

Tutorial Module 3-1: Connecting an IBM PC/XT to a Hayes Smartmodem 1200

In this tutorial module, the discussion will focus on connecting an IBM PC/XT with a serial port to a Hayes Smartmodem 1200. This is the stand-alone modem that utilizes an RS232 interface on the PC. For connection of such a modem to a 9-pin connector such as that found on the IBM PC/AT or Toshiba 1100/3100, refer to Tutorial Module 3-2; other than the physical connections, the process will be the same. Any compatible, such as a Compaq Portable or the AT&T PC 6300, may be substituted in this exercise. We will generically refer to the computer as a PC.

The serial port for an IBM PC/XT may be obtained from a number of sources: dedicated asynchronous communication adapters (ACAs), graphics boards, multifunction boards, and so on. Depending on the IBM PC or compatible, the serial port may be included with the basic system. For purposes of this tutorial module, assume that the RS232 port has been installed on the PC, whether it is built on or has been purchased separately.

Furthermore, elsewhere within this book sections describe how to analyze the port on an IBM PC/XT; the proceedings of this tutorial module will not duplicate this text. Rather, a summary will be provided for the port along with the references of where the reader may go for the detailed analysis.

This tutorial module will feature a Hayes Smartmodem 1200, referred to as merely the "modem." The user may have a different modem to be connected. Substitution of other vendors' products, such as AT&T, Ventel, Penril, Bizcomp, and so on, are fine. The only point is that the exercise will assume that the modem to be connected is an intelligent one. By "intelligent," the modem will be required to support autocall and keyboard dialing. Non intelligent modems may be used, but the discussion surrounding the step "Determine signs of success" will not be applicable. Figure 3–5 depicts the connection.

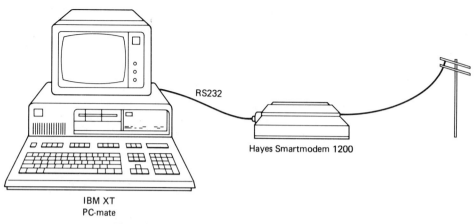

RS232

Hayes Smartmodem 1200

IBM XT
PC-mate

Figure 3–5. IBM PC/XT to Hayes Smartmodem.

The steps we will follow, common to all our tutorial modules, are as follows:

STEPS FOR CONNECTION

1. Determine compatibility (should it work?).
2. Determine signs of success.
3. Determine the type of connector used.
4. Determine gender of the ports.
5. Determine which leads (pins) are provided by each device.
6. Determine which leads are required to be on by each device.
7. Design the cable.
8. Build the cable.
9. Test the cable for continuity.
10. Cable the two systems together with the cable.
11. From step 2, measure success.

1. Determine compatibility

Prior to attempting the connection, the user should make a determination as to whether the connection is possible. The best way to determine compatibility is to check the documentation for both devices. When this cannot be done, use the procedure that follows to determine if the two can communicate. If all else fails, ask around to determine if anyone has done the same or a similar connection. Connecting these two devices is a common occurrence. For completeness, however, we will follow the steps for determining compatibility.

When connecting a modem to a PC, the two ports must allow for the same type of parameters. The two devices must support a common communication mode, speed, and character format. Using the modem and computer profile forms, we can lay out the specifics of each port as in Table 3–2. Fill in as much as is known at this time; fill in any blanks as you proceed. From the information in the tables, which was taken directly from the users' manuals, the PC and the modem appear to be compatible. The common options between the two appear to be asynchronous transmission, 1200 bits per second, 8 data bits, 1 stop bit, no parity, and full duplex operation.

The PC only supports software flow control when the application that is using the port supports it. Refer to the module on connecting a PC emulating a VT100 terminal for more information about when the PC could use software flow control. In the case of the Hayes Smartmodem 1200, flow control is not an issue. The modem is merely a conduit for the information flow from the PC to the other system. Flow control is an issue between the PC and the other computer that it connects to using communication. Refer to the earlier text in this chapter for a complete discussion of flow control when two communicating computers are involved.

2. Determine signs of success

Now that the compatibility determination has been made, the user needs to know, in advance, the signs of a successful connection. Merely physically connecting the modem to the PC is a milestone, but this usually does not complete the setup. The user needs to be assured that communication is possible, using the modem, between the PC and another PC. This communication could be to another PC, a bulletin board, an electronic mail service,

TABLE 3–2. SCS PORT PROFILES FOR IBM PC AND HAYES SMARTMODEM

Personal Computer Port Profile

Underline if supported; circle if selected.

Model: PC/XT _____ Vendor: IBM _____ Port: ACA _____

Port type: <u>serial</u> parallel
Port: DB25 9-pin 5-pin 8-pin/modular 20mA Centronics

Gender: male female

Pin #	Function	Direction	Pin #	Function	Direction
1	_____	to from n/a	14	_____	to from n/a
2	Transmit Data	to <u>from</u> n/a	15	_____	to from n/a
3	Receive Data	<u>to</u> from n/a	16	_____	to from n/a
4	Request to Send	to <u>from</u> n/a	17	_____	to from n/a
5	Clear to Send	<u>to</u> from n/a	18	_____	to from n/a
6	Data Set Ready	<u>to</u> from n/a	19	_____	to from n/a
7	Signal Ground	to <u>from</u> n/a	20	Data Terminal Ready	to <u>from</u> n/a
8	Data Carrier Detect	<u>to</u> from n/a	21	_____	to from n/a
9	_____	to from n/a	22	Ring Indicator	<u>to</u> from n/a
10	_____	to from n/a	23	_____	to from n/a
11	_____	to from n/a	24	_____	to from n/a
12	_____	to from n/a	25	_____	to from n/a
13	_____	to from n/a			

Complete the next section only with 36-pin cinch connector.

26	_____	to from n/a	27	_____	to from n/a
28	_____	to from n/a	29	_____	to from n/a
30	_____	to from n/a	31	_____	to from n/a
32	_____	to from n/a	33	_____	to from n/a
34	_____	to from n/a	35	_____	to from n/a
36	_____	to from n/a			

Flow control technique: XON/XOFF ENQ/ACK STX/ETX Hardware _____
Leads that must be on: 5 6 8 __ __ __ __

Options:
   Speeds: <u>110 300 600 1200 1800 2400 4800 9600</u> 19.2 56k ____
   Parity: <u>even</u> <u>odd</u> space mark none
   Char-length: <u>7</u> <u>8</u> __
   # stop bits: <u>1</u> <u>1.5</u> 2
   Line-ending sequence: cr lf cr/lf cr/lf/lf
   Disconnect sequence: EOT DEL ~. _____
   Mode: async sync isoch   sync timing leads:

#	Function	Direction
15	_____	to from
17	_____	to from
24	_____	to from

Notes: _____
_____
_____

TABLE 3–2. (*Continued*)

Modem Port Profile

Underline if supported; circle if selected.

Model: Smartmodem 1200 _____ Vendor: Hayes _____ Port: RS 232C _____

Port type: serial
Port: DB25 9-pin 8-pin/modular 20mA _____

Gender: male female

Pin #	Function	Direction	Pin #	Function	Direction
1	Protective Ground	to from n/a	14	_____	to from n/a
2	Transmit Data	to from n/a	15	_____	to from n/a
3	Receive Data	to from n/a	16	_____	to from n/a
4	_____	to from n/a	17	_____	to from n/a
5	Clear to Send	to from n/a	18	_____	to from n/a
6	Data Set Ready	to from n/a	19	_____	to from n/a
7	Signal Ground	to from n/a	20	Data Terminal Ready	to from n/a
8	Data Carrier Detect	to from n/a	21	_____	to from n/a
9	_____	to from n/a	22	Ring Indicator	to from n/a
10	_____	to from n/a	23	_____	to from n/a
11	_____	to from n/a	24	_____	to from n/a
12	High Speed	to from n/a	25	_____	to from n/a
13	_____	to from n/a			

Leads that must be on: 4 20 __ __ __ __

Options:
    Speeds: 110 300 600 1200 1800 2400 4800 9600 19.2 56k _____
    Compatibility: 103 212 V.22bis _____
    Parity: even odd space mark none
    Char-length: 7 8 __
    # stop bits: 1 1.5 2
    Line-ending sequence: cr lf cr/lf cr/lf/lf
    Auto answer: yes no RTS/CTS delay: _____
    Disconnect sequence: EOT DEL ATZ _____
    Intelligent modems . . . Dialing technique: Touch-tone Pulse
        Compatibility: Hayes _____
        Command line prefix: AT _____ Dial command: D _____
        Touch-tone dial: T _____ Pulse dial: P _____ Pause: , _____
        Wait for dial tone: W _____ Wait for quiet answer: @ _____
        Flash: ! _____ Dial stored number: S _____
        Return to command state after dialing: ; _____
        Escape sequence: +++ _____ Switch-hook control: H _____
        Store phone #: &Z _____
    Mode: async sync isoch   sync timing leads:

#	Function	Direction
15	_____	to from
17	_____	to from
24	_____	to from

Notes: Parity modes are 7 bit, 1–2 stop bits with odd, even, or fixed parity, *or* 8 bit, 1–2 stop bits, and no parity at 1200 bps. At 300 bps, 7–8 bit, 1–2 stop bits, odd, even, no parity.

an electronic news service, or to a UNIX system. Prior to beginning any connection, be sure that the user knows when he or she has completely and successfully connected the PC/XT to the modem.

Success will be determined by the ability to dial another computer system with the Hayes modem. Not only must we be able to dial a number from the PC using the modem, but we must also be able to login to other systems. We will access two services with the PC to test both dialing and communicating capabilities. The first will be a UNIX multiuser computer. If properly connected to this computer, we will be successful if we receive a "login:" prompt. The second service will be AT&T Mail, which provides a similar "login:" prompt. Hence in this connection, we will know when we are successful when the login prompt occurs, and we can type in our ID with the UNIX system receiving it.

As a special note, the PC and Hayes may be physically connected properly yet the user may not be able to login successfully. This tutorial module focuses on how to connect the PC to the Hayes physically, not on how to perform systems administration to set up UNIX ports or AT&T Mail. Consult the support organizations for each of these to ensure that you have the telephone access numbers, speeds, and login IDs prior to attempting to measure our success. In our discussion, the MS-DOS port on the IBM PC will be set up using the terminal emulation package, Crosstalk XVI; hence, it will be included in the discussion. Look for the "login:" prompt to determine when we have been successful.

3. Determine type of connector

By consulting the documentation of both devices, we can quickly determine the type of connector provided by each device. However, we can determine this by examining the ports on both the PC and the Hayes.

On the IBM PC, there may be multiple connectors (ports) on the back of the PC. Previous tutorial modules highlighted the easiest means of determining the type of connector provided. Consult Tutorial Module 5-1 in Chapter 5. From this, the analysis indicated that the port was a DB25P port. Refer to Tutorial Module 3-2 for analysis of an AT-size 9-pin port.

The Hayes modem connector is found on the back of the modem. This connector is in the center of the modem and is labeled "RS 232C." It is a 25-socket DB25S connector. More than likely, not all 25 sockets are used, as we will see. But it is a DB25-size connector.

4. Determine gender of ports

At the IBM PC there may be multiple ports, serial and parallel. Refer to Tutorial Module 5-2 in Chapter 5 to locate the serial connector. From this we have concluded that the DB25 connector is of male gender. You will see references to a DB25P and DB25S connector. The P denotes pins, or a male port; the S denotes sockets, or female. The PC end of the cable we will design will be of female gender. We will connect the completed cable to the male DB25, or DB25P port.

The Hayes modem only has one DB25-size connector. This port is female, implying that this end of our cable will be male. There will be no confusion as to which cable end goes where, as our cable will only fit one way.

5. Determine leads (pins) provided by each device

6. Determine leads required to be on

The user should find out the leads and their directions for the PC port as well as the modem port. The goal is to determine which leads are provided by the ports and which should be used in the cable construction.

A port has four categories of leads: ground, data, control, and timing. Ignore the timing category of leads, as we are building a cable to function in an asynchronous environment. The ground leads, usually pins 1 and 7 in a DB25-size connector, have no direction, so they too can be ignored for now. However, these leads must be included in the cable.

Specifically we are interested in determining which data and control leads are provided by the computer and modem. "Provided by the computer or modem" implies that the device is the source of the lead. The direction of the lead is "from" the device. There are multiple methods of determining which leads are provided by a computer.

The best possible method to determine the direction of the RS232 leads that are used is to consult the documentation. Usually, the users' manuals or application programmers' guides give the RS232 port pinout descriptions. If you do not have the documentation, you can use a break-out box (BOB) to identify the leads that are provided by the computers.

Which leads are provided by the PC? Consult Chapter 5, Tutorial Module 5-1, "Connecting a PX/XT to a

TABLE 3–3. PC-PROVIDED LEADS

Device	Lead #	Function	Direction
PC	2	Transmit Data	from
	4	Request to Send	from
	20	Data Terminal Ready	from

UNIX computer,'' for a step-by-step approach using a break-out box or Chapter 1, Tutorial Module 1-1, for a step-by-step port analysis using a volt-ohm meter (VOM). In either of these port analyses, we conclude that the leads in Table 3–3 are provided by the PC port. Which leads are provided by the Hayes modem? As with any port, the user can use one of three approaches to determining which leads are provided by a device: (1) consulting the documentation, (2) using a break-out box, or (3) using a VOM. A break-out box will be used to determine the control and data leads with directions, provided in the Hayes modem port.

We will use a tristate break-out box. Refer to Chapter 5, Tutorial Module 5-2, for the difference in break-out boxes and their use. In summary, a tristate break-out box offers indicators for three different levels of a lead: on, off, or not present. Be sure that the break-out box you are using is turned on and operational before testing the modem.

Connect the male connector of the BOB to the female connector on the back of the modem. Power up the Hayes modem. Upon ensuring that the modem power cord is connected to an outlet as well as to the modem itself, turn the on/off switch on the back of the modem to the on position. Looking at the front panel of the modem, several lights should be on, indicating that power is applied. If no lights are present, check the power cord and the outlet to be sure that all is well.

When the power is on and the BOB is connected, look at the indicators of the BOB. Depending on the options set in the Hayes modem, several lights are on. The tristate BOB indicates that Clear to Send, Data Set Ready, and Data Carrier Detect are on (red lamps). These are leads 5, 6, and 8, respectively.

If these three lamps are not on, more than likely the modem is optioned differently than the factory settings. Our tutorial module will warrant the changing of a couple of the switches. It is worthwhile to check to see how the modem is actually optioned. Using a small screwdriver, pry the front faceplate off the modem from either side. You should see a row of eight switches on the left of the modem. The factory settings are depicted in Table 3–4. If your BOB shows the three leads on—Clear to Send, Data Set Ready, and Data Carrier Detect— change switch 6. With switch 6 ''up,'' this enables the ''to be'' connected PC to determine if a carrier signal is coming from a distant modem. This status will occur on pin 8, Data Carrier Detect. We want pin 8 to fluctuate, depending on whether a connection is established to another computer. Our PC communication software will automatically check pin 8 for the status of the circuit. If we misoption switch 6, the communication software will never know if a connection has been established or disconnected. Be sure that switch 6 is ''up.'' Watch the BOB, specifically Data Set Ready and Data Carrier Detect, when you flip switch 6 ''up.'' These two lamps should go off, or turn green, if a tristate BOB is used. We will assume that switch 6 is in the ''up'' position and

TABLE 3–4. FACTORY SETTING OF HAYES SMARTMODEM OPTIONS

Switch	Position	Description
1	Down	Forces pin 20 on always.
2	Up	Causes modem to respond with English words.
3	Down	Sends result codes to the PC.
4	Up	Causes modem to echo characters in Command mode.
5	Down	Prevents auto answering of calls.
6	Down	Forces pin 8 on always.
7	Up	Allows RJ11 modular jack connection.
8	Down	Enables Modem command recognition.

TABLE 3–5. HAYES SMARTMODEM-PROVIDED LEADS

Lead #	Function	Direction
3	Receive Data	from Hayes
5	Clear to Send	from Hayes
6	Data Set Ready	from Hayes
8	Data Carrier Detect	from Hayes

that Data Set Ready and Data Carrier Detect lamps are in the "low" state. Check this to ensure that the PC actually works without pin 6 high, due to switch 6.

If you have the faceplate off, note the row of lights across the front of the modem (eight of them). The second to last lamp from the right, if you are facing the front of the modem, will probably be on. Flip switch 1 to the "up" position and watch this lamp. The light on the front of the modem should turn off as you flip the switch. This observation will be explained as we proceed. However, we want switch 1 to be in the "up" position.

From this, we can see that pins 5, 6, and 8 are signals provided by the Hayes modem. These signals are output from modem and input to the PC. If these leads are output signals, then usually the Receive Data lead, pin 3, is also output. If you are using a tristate BOB or a VOM, you can confirm this, even though lead 3 will not be on. With a tristate BOB, note the lamp for monitoring pin 3. It will be a different color from the lamp for pin 5, probably green. This indicates that this lead is present, but in the off state for voltages (i.e., negative DC voltage). Thus far, we have the leads shown in Table 3–5 as output signals from the Hayes modem.

With a regular BOB, there is no easy way to assert that pin 3 is also an output signal from the modem, as it is only turned on when data are being received. It fluctuates to the bits of the characters received by the modem from the line. However, if we review our general interface guidelines in Table 3–6, we can make certain assumptions. We have noted that pins 5, 6, and 8 are output leads from the Hayes modem. This appears to indicate that the modem port is a DCE interface. Certainly it makes sense that a modem would be DCE. Reviewing Table 3–5, with 5, 6, and 8 as output leads, you could surmise that pin 3, Receive Data, is also an output lead. In fact this is the case, as data received from the phone line are presented to the PC on this lead, making it an output lead from the modem.

Normally when dealing with DCE, such as a modem, a couple of other control leads could be involved. How does a modem let an attached PC or other device know that someone is calling? If someone is going to access your PC from another location, do you want the modem to answer the call automatically? The PC to which we are attaching the modem must be able to know when a call is coming in. A special control lead is available in the RS232 standard allowing for such an indication and is pin 22 as defined by the standard. This lead, known as Ring Indicator, is a signal provided by DCE that indicates when someone, or something such as a computer, is calling the phone number to which your modem is attached. Refer to the discussion earlier in this chapter for the interaction of Ring Indicator and data terminal.

When interfacing with a modem, or other DCE, this lead should be checked. It more than likely will be required in the cable we ultimately use to connect the modem to DTE. With our tristate BOB, pin 22 should register a reading. This lead, like our Receive Data lead, is present but in the off condition. The lamp for this lead should be green. Hence, it is a signal provided by the Hayes modem. A dual-state BOB would not indicate presence on this lead because it only registers leads that are "on."

Review the Hayes Modem Port Profile and note the speeds that the modem supports. The Hayes modem supports multiple speeds from 0–300 and 1200 bps. An attached computer needs to know at which speed the modem is operating. The Hayes modem, and all other AT&T 212-compatible modems, can figure out which speed to operate at when another computer calls them. However, the PC must be notified of the speed to use.

TABLE 3–6. GENERAL GUIDELINES OF PIN DIRECTIONS

Output leads	Port type	Input leads required
2, 4, 20	Data Terminal Equipment	3, 5, 6, 8
3, 5, 6, 8	Data Communication Equipment	2, 4, 20

TABLE 3–7. OUTPUT LEADS FROM HAYES SMARTMODEM 1200

Lead #	Function	Direction
3	Receive Data	from Hayes
5	Clear to Send	from Hayes
6	Data Set Ready	from Hayes
8	Data Carrier Detect	from Hayes
12	High Speed Indicator	from Hayes
22	Ring Indicator	from Hayes

The RS232 standard allows for multispeed indications. The standard allows for pin 12 to be used to denote the higher speed of a piece of DCE. Because the Hayes modem can operate at either 0–300 or 1200, it notifies the PC, using pin 12, which speed it is operating at. We can confirm this using a tristate BOB, dual-state BOB, or a VOM. More than likely with a BOB, there is no dedicated lamp for monitoring the status of pin 12, as it is normally used only with DCE. However, most BOBs provide a separate lamp for testing any of the leads in the interface. Using a jumpering wire, or unfolded paperclip, touch the lamp probe to pin 12. Upon touching the two together, the lamp should light. If this lamp is lit (normally red), then the Hayes modem is set up for the higher speed of 1200 bps. If lower speed is being used, then pin 12 will be off, or low. This confirms that this signal is an output signal from the Hayes. The Hayes modem, as with most 212-type modems, provides a lamp on the front of the modem to indicate whether the high speed is being used. Looking at the front of the Hayes modem, the leftmost lamp should be illuminated, indicating that the high speed, 1200 bps, is being used. Table 3–7 outlines all the signals provided by (from) the Hayes modem.

Determine which leads are required to be on. We now have determined which leads are provided by each. The next step is to determine which leads are input signals to the PC and printer ports; in other words, which leads should be on for data transmission and reception.

First, let's look at the PC's port. Consult Chapter 5, Tutorial Module 5-2, for a complete walk-through of how this is determined on the PC. Table 3–8 summarizes the findings of the leads that are input to the PC's port. Of these leads, pins 5, 6, and 8 must be on for data transmission to occur. Which leads are required to be on with the Hayes modem port? This step of port analysis involving a modem is not as easy as the PC port, the reason being that the modem cannot dump information out of the port. Hence, we cannot use trial and error to determine which leads must be on.

The best method is to consult the documentation, or our charts that outline generalities of ports. We had determined that pins 5, 6, and 8 were output control signals of the modem port. Consulting Table 3–5, you can see that our generalities surrounding a DCE port hold true. Pins 2, 4, and 20 are input signals to the modem. The truth is that pin 4 is absent from the interface. This variation from the norm will not cause us any problems when we do the interfacing, even though our PC had this signal as an output. Table 3–9 depicts our analysis of the input signals to the modem.

It is appropriate at this point to ensure that the computer and modem port profiles are updated to include our findings (see Table 3–10). Note the pinouts in the profile, as they are complete allowing us to proceed and design the cable necessary to connect the PC to the Hayes modem.

7. Design the cable

We know what the RS232 hardware requirements are at both ports, the PC and the modem devices. It can be easier to analyze the cable pinouts if grouped by function. This function is that as outlined in the EIA RS232-

TABLE 3–8. IBM PC/XT INPUT SIGNALS

Pin #	Description	Direction
3	Receive Data (in)	to PC
5	Clear to Send (in)	to PC
6	Data Set Ready (in)	to PC
8	Data Carrier Detect (in)	to PC
22	Ring Indicator	to PC

TABLE 3–9. INPUT SIGNAL REQUIRED
BY THE HAYES MODEM

Pin #	Function	Direction
2	Transmit Data	to Hayes
20	Data Terminal Ready	to Hayes

C standard document. Once we group the pinouts into the four categories—ground, data, control, and timing—the cable design will be much easier. These profiles could be rearranged as shown in Table 3–11. We are now ready to design the cable by looking at each category of leads of both ports. General rules have been established to aid our cable design. Refer to Appendix L for the elaboration on each of the following general rules:

CABLE DESIGN: GENERAL RULES

1. Connect like categories of leads together.
2. Always connect an "out" to an "in" and an "in" to an "out."
3. A lead that is input may be connected to another lead that is an input, only if both these are connected to an output lead.
4. In synchronous connections, use only one source of timing. (Because the PC-to-Hayes connection is asynchronous, this point is not applicable.)

Ground leads. First, the ground leads should be considered. They are probably the easiest leads to handle. Protective Ground is provided to protect the user from being shocked, in the case of an electrical short of some sort. Pin 1 is generally the Protective Ground lead of most RS232 interfaces. It is also frequently referred to as Chassis Ground, or Frame Ground. In our case study, the PC port documentation does not indicate that a Protective Ground is present. This is not a show stopper because a Protective Ground is provided within the PC itself. It may be isolated from the interface. Nonetheless, we will allow for it in our cable because the modem provides for it. Our cable will have a conductor in the wire to connect the two Protective Ground leads, pins 1 and 1 at both ends, together.

Signal Ground signals are the key ground leads in the interface. These leads are used as a reference point for all the other signals in the interface. When the voltage level, as outlined in the RS232-C standard, is to be +5 volts, this is relative to Signal Ground. Both the interfaces provide a Signal Ground lead, found on pin 7 of the PC and modem ports. These two leads should be connected together to provide a common reference signal for the two devices. Table 3–12 summarizes these two connections, completing the design for the ground category of leads.

Data leads. The next category of leads to tackle is the data leads. There are only two possible connections for these, so we can quickly lay out the cabling of the data category. Either pin 2 is connected at one end of the cable to pin 2 at the other end of the cable, or pin 2 at one end is connected to pin 3 at the other end.

The PC will send all its data on the Transmit Data lead, pin 2. The modem will receive these characters on pin 2 and transmit them across the telephone line to the other computer. We know this from the Hayes port profile indicating that the transmit data lead is an "input" lead. General rule 2 indicated to connect an output lead to an input lead. Hence, we should connect pin 2 at the PC end of the cable "straight through" to pin 2 at the other end (modem end) of the cable.

The Receive Data lead, pin 3 on both devices, is the lead that is used by the computers to receive data. Any data that the PC wants to receive is expected to arrive on pin 3. What does the modem do with the data it receives off the telephone line? It presents this received data to the PC, or any other attached device, using pin 3. Our modem port analysis indicated that pin 3 was an "output" lead. Since the modem is sending its data out on pin 3, destined for the PC, this lead should be connected to the Receive Data lead of the PC. By connecting the modem's pin 3 to the PC's pin 3, the PC will receive whatever information the modem presents to it. Lead 3 in the cable should also be "straight through" from end to end, the same as pin 2.

We now have allowed for data to be output by one device and received (input) by the other. Table 3–13 depicts the data category portion of the cable design.

Earlier, we indicated that there were only two possible connections with the data leads. The two possibilities were "straight through," yielding pin 2 connected to pin 2 and pin 3 to pin 3, or "crossed over," yielding pin

Digital Loopback Test

TABLE 3–10. SCS PORT PROFILES FOR IBM PC-TO-HAYES SMARTMODEM CONNECTION

Computer Port Profile

Underline if supported; circle if selected.

Model: PC/XT _____ Vendor: IBM _____ Port: ACA _____

Port type: <u>serial</u> parallel
Port: <u>DB25</u> 9-pin 5-pin 8-pin/modular 20mA Centronics

Gender: <u>male</u> female

Pin #	Function	Direction	Pin #	Function	Direction
1	_____	to from n/a	14	_____	to from n/a
2	Transmit Data	to <u>from</u> n/a	15	_____	to from n/a
3	Receive Data	<u>to</u> from n/a	16	_____	to from n/a
4	Request to Send	to <u>from</u> n/a	17	_____	to from n/a
5	Clear to Send	<u>to</u> from n/a	18	_____	to from n/a
6	Data Set Ready	<u>to</u> from n/a	19	_____	to from n/a
7	Signal Ground	to from <u>n/a</u>	20	Data Terminal Ready	to <u>from</u> n/a
8	Data Carrier Detect	<u>to</u> from n/a	21	_____	to from n/a
9	_____	to from n/a	22	Ring Indicator	<u>to</u> from n/a
10	_____	to from n/a	23	_____	to from n/a
11	_____	to from n/a	24	_____	to from n/a
12	_____	to from n/a	25	_____	to from n/a
13	_____	to from n/a			

Complete the next section only with 36-pin cinch connector.

#	Function	Direction	#	Function	Direction
26	_____	to from n/a	27	_____	to from n/a
28	_____	to from n/a	29	_____	to from n/a
30	_____	to from n/a	31	_____	to from n/a
32	_____	to from n/a	33	_____	to from n/a
34	_____	to from n/a	35	_____	to from n/a
36	_____	to from n/a			

Flow control technique: XON/XOFF ENQ/ACK STX/ETX Hardware _____
Leads that must be on: <u>5</u> <u>6</u> <u>8</u> __ __ __ __

Options:
   Speeds: 110 300 600 (1200) 1800 2400 4800 9600 19.2 56k _____
   Parity: even odd space mark (none)
   Char-length: 7 (8) __
   # stop bits: (1) 1.5 2
   Line-ending sequence: cr lf cr/lf cr/lf/lf
   Disconnect sequence: EOT DEL ~. _____
   Mode: async sync isoch   sync timing leads:

#	Function	Direction
15	_____	to from
17	_____	to from
24	_____	to from

Notes: _____
_____
_____

TABLE 3–10. *(Continued)*

Modem Port Profile

Underline if supported; circle if selected.

Model: Smartmodem 1200 _____ Vendor: Hayes _____ Port: RS232C _____

Port type: <u>serial</u>
Port: <u>DB25</u> 9-pin 8-pin/modular 20mA _____

Gender: male <u>female</u>

Pin #	Function	Direction	Pin #	Function	Direction
1	Protective Ground	to from <u>n/a</u>	14	_____	to from n/a
2	Transmit Data	<u>to</u> from n/a	15	_____	to from n/a
3	Receive Data	to <u>from</u> n/a	16	_____	to from n/a
4	_____	to <u>from</u> n/a	17	_____	to from n/a
5	Clear to Send	to <u>from</u> n/a	18	_____	to from n/a
6	Data Set Ready	to <u>from</u> n/a	19	_____	to from n/a
7	Signal Ground	to from <u>n/a</u>	20	Data Terminal Ready	<u>to</u> from n/a
8	Data Carrier Detect	to <u>from</u> n/a	21	_____	to from n/a
9	_____	to from n/a	22	Ring Indicator	to <u>from</u> n/a
10	_____	to from n/a	23	_____	to from n/a
11	_____	to from n/a	24	_____	to from n/a
12	High-Speed Indicator	to <u>from</u> n/a	25	_____	to from n/a
13	_____	to from n/a			

Leads that must be on: 4 20 __ __ __ __

Options:
   Speeds: 110 300 600 (1200) 1800 2400 4800 9600 19.2 56k _____
   Compatibility: 103 (212) V.22bis _____
   Parity: even odd space mark (none)
   Char-length: 7 (8) __
   # stop bits: (1) 1.5 2
   Line-ending sequence: cr lf cr/lf cr/lf/lf
   Auto answer: yes no RTS/CTS delay: _____
   Disconnect sequence: EOT DEL ATZ _____
   Intelligent modems . . . Dialing technique: Touch-tone Pulse
     Compatibility: Hayes _____
     Command line prefix: AT _____ Dial command: D _____
     Touch-tone dial: T _____ Pulse dial: P _____ Pause: , _____
     Wait for dial tone: W _____ Wait for quiet answer: @ _____
     Flash: ! _____ Dial stored number: S _____
     Return to command state after dialing: ; _____
     Escape sequence: +++ _____ Switch-hook control: H _____
     Store phone #: &Z _____
   Mode: async sync isoch   sync timing leads:

#	Function	Direction
15	_____	to from
17	_____	to from
24	_____	to from

Notes: Parity modes are 7 bit, 1–2 stop bits with odd, even, or fixed parity, *or* 8 bit, 1–2 stop bits, and no parity at 1200 bps. At 300 bps, 7–8 bit, 1–2 stop bits, odd, even, no parity.

TABLE 3-11. IBM PC/XT AND HAYES SMARTMODEM LEADS GROUP BY CATEGORY

IBM PC/XT			Hayes modem
Ground Leads			
		1	Protective Ground
Signal Ground	7	7	Signal Ground
Data Leads			
Transmit Data (out)	2	2	Transmit Data (in)
Receive Data (in)	3	3	Receive Data (out)
Control Leads			
Request to Send (out)	4		
Clear to Send (in)	5	5	Clear to Send (out)
Data Set Ready (in)	6	6	Data Set Ready (out)
Data Carrier Detect (in)	8	8	Data Carrier Detect (out)
		12	High Speed Indicator (out)
Data Terminal Ready (out)	20	20	Data Terminal Ready (in)
Ring Indicator (in)	22	22	Ring Indicator
Timing Leads			
n/a			

TABLE 3-12. GROUND LEADS OF PC-HAYES CABLE

PC Function	Pin #	Pin #	Hayes modem Function
Protective Ground	1 -------	1	Protective Ground
Signal Ground	7 -------	7	Signal Ground

LEGEND: The "-------" refers to connecting the two leads together. Pin 1 in the PC end of the cable will be connected to pin 1 at the modem end of the cable by means of a wire between the two pins. This wire is termed a "conductor." This is commonly referred to as "straight through." Pin 7 will be "straight through" from end to end.

TABLE 3-13. PC-HAYES MODEM DATA LEAD CONNECTIONS

PC Function	Pin #	Pin #	Hayes modem Function
Transmit Data	2 ------⟩	2	Transmit Data
Receive Data	3 ⟨------	3	Receive Data

LEGEND: The "------⟩" refers to connecting the two leads together. The "------⟩" also indicates that a direction of a lead is involved. This arrow is included for clarity only, as there are no special wire connections involved. The source of pin 2 is the PC, with the source of pin 3 being the Hayes modem. Pin 2 at the PC end of the cable is connected to pin 2 at the modem end of the cable, with a piece of wire between them.

2 at one end of the cable connected to pin 3 at the other end, and vice versa. The only other possibility for data lead design appears when there is only a Receive Data lead on a device's port. This is possible when printers are involved. Consult the printer chapter (Chapter 1) for further details about this.

Control leads. This is generally the toughest category of leads to understand. However, by keeping the general rules for cable design in mind, even the control leads can be easily tackled. The control leads that we have to work with are shown in Table 3-14.

TABLE 3–14. PC-HAYES MODEM CONTROL LEADS

IBM PC/XT	Control leads		Hayes modem
Request to Send (out)	4		
Clear to Send (in)	5	5	Clear to Send (out)
Data Set Ready (in)	6	6	Data Set Ready (out)
Data Carrier Detect (in)	8	8	Data Carrier Detect (out)
		12	High Speed Indicator (out)
Data Terminal Ready (out)	20	20	Data Terminal Ready (in)
Ring Indicator (in)	22	22	Ring Indicator (out)

Which of these control leads must be on for each device to function? Consulting our port profiles, we note that the PC/XT requires that pins 5, 6, and 8 be on to allow data transmission. We will deal with these leads first.

Once we know that these control leads are required, we should review the same leads in the modem interface to determine if we can use them as input to the PC/XT leads. Consulting our modem port profile, review pins 5, 6, and 8. These leads are "out" from the modem's perspective. These leads' functions match those of the PC/XT, exactly. Clear to Send, Data Set Ready, and Data Carrier Detect are the same leads in both interfaces. The only difference is the direction of the leads. They are all input in the PC port and output in the modem port. Applying our rule 2, always connect an "out" to an "in," these leads can be connected "straight through." Table 3–15 depicts this portion of the cable involving these control leads.

The only other input lead in the PC/XT port that needs to be on is pin 22, Ring Indicator. Ring Indicator is the lead that denotes, to the PC, the existence of an incoming call. This input signal should be connected to the lead from the modem that is used to indicate this. Pin 22 in the modem port is an output lead used for this purpose. "Connecting an output to an input lead," conductor 22 in our cable, should be "straight through" from end to end. Consult Table 3–16 for this control lead design.

This completes all the input control signals in the PC's port. Looking at the Hayes modem port, there is only one input lead, pin 20. Data Terminal Ready is an input lead to the modem, indicating the readiness of the "to be" attached device. The PC offers this lead as an output signal. Our port analysis proved that this lead would be on once the PC port was enabled. We should connect this lead "straight through" as we did the other control leads to allow DTR to function between the PC and the modem. Table 3–17 shows this connection. By taking a look at the input leads first in our cable design, we can be confident that the cable will satisfy the required leads of both ports. These leads were satisfied by using the corresponding output leads. Not all cables will be this simple, but we are nearing the completion of our cable design. The cable appears to be what is termed a "straight-through" cable.

TABLE 3–15. INPUT CONTROL LEADS OF PC-TO-HAYES CABLE

IBM PC		Hayes	
Function	lead #	lead #	Function
Clear to Send (in)	5 ⟨------ 6		Clear to Send (out)
Data Set Ready (in)	6 ⟨------ 6		Data Set Ready (out)
Carrier Detect (in)	8 ⟨------ 8		Carrier Detect (out)

TABLE 3–16. RING INDICATOR CONDUCTORS

IBM PC		Hayes modem
Ring Indicator (in)	22 ⟨------ 22	Ring Indicator (out)

LEGEND: The "⟨------" indicates a "straight-through" connection. The head on the arrow is used to indicate direction. There is nothing special about the conductor in the cable. The arrow is used for illustrative purposes only.

TABLE 3–17. DATA TERMINAL READY CONNECTOR

IBM PC			Hayes modem
Data Terminal Ready (out)	20 ------⟩	20	Data Terminal Ready (in)

LEGEND: This conductor is "straight through," from end to end in the cable. Our modem is optioned to use pin 20. If the modem is optioned differently, this lead is not really required. Consult the earlier section in this chapter for clarification on the function of pin 20.

Let's look at the remaining signals, leads 4 and 12. Pin 4 is an output signal provided by the PC port. It is on whenever the port is enabled. The modem does not utilize pin 4. Some modems do use this signal. You can include it in the output cable for completeness. Simply include conductor 4, from end to end in the cable.

This leaves pin 12, the High-Speed Indicator provided by the Hayes. Recall that this signal was used to indicate that the higher of the two speeds, 300 and 1200, was being used in a connection. The PC port does not support this signal, as it expects the communication software or user to be smart enough to figure the speed. Hence, this lead serves no function in our cable, but we can include it for completeness. The reason for including this and pin 4 will become obvious when we actually construct our cable, as this will allow us to use a flat ribbon cable. Table 3–18 depicts these two leads.

This completes our cable design. We have accounted for the ground, data, and control leads in the cable. Because this is an asynchronous connection, the timing leads are not required. Hence, our design did not include them. If we were to use a flat ribbon cable to construct the cable, these leads would be included. This should cause no problem in our connection of the two devices. Table 3–19 depicts the completed cable design. The next step is to construct the cable.

TABLE 3–18. REQUEST TO SEND AND HS INDICATOR LEADS

IBM PC			Hayes modem
	n/a ⟨------	12	High-Speed Indicator (out)
Request to Send (out)	4 ------⟩	n/a	

LEGEND: Both these leads are "straight through." Your cable design does not have to include them, but ours will for completeness. This will permit a flat ribbon cable to be used in our cable design.

TABLE 3–19. IBM PC/XT-TO-HAYES SMARTMODEM 1200 CABLE DESIGN

PC Function	Pin #	Pin #	Hayes modem Function
Protective Ground	1 -------	1	Protective Ground
Signal Ground	7 -------	7	Signal Ground
Transmit Data	2 ------⟩	2	Transmit Data
Receive Data	3 ⟨------	3	Receive Data
Request to Send	4 ------⟩	4	n/a (optional)
Clear to Send	5 ⟨------	5	Clear to Send
Data Set Ready	6 ⟨------	6	Data Set Ready
Data Carrier Detect	8 ⟨------	8	Data Carrier Detect
n/a	12 ⟨------	12	High-Speed Indicator (optional)
Data Terminal Ready	20 ------⟩	20	Data Terminal Ready
Ring Indicator	22 ⟨------	22	Ring Indicator

LEGEND: All these conductors are "straight through" (i.e., pin 1 at one end of the cable is connected through to pin 1 at the other end of the cable). Conductors 4 and 12 are optional as they are not used when connecting a PC to a Hayes Smartmodem 1200.

8. Build the cable

Now that we have a cable designed for connecting the PC to the modem, we should physically construct the cable. The design section referred to a "straight-through" cable. This is a cable in which all the conductors (wires) are "straight through" from end to end. There are many ways to construct a "straight-through" cable. One of the easiest is to use flat ribbon cable.

Flat ribbon cable is normally cable that is flat and is offered with different numbers of connectors. Usually these are noted as DBxx connectors, such as DB9, DB15, and DB25. We are interested in the DB25 cable that is about $1\frac{1}{2}$ inches wide. All 25 conductors are present in the cable from end to end. This cable can be purchased at varying lengths, but the RS232-C recommends this length not exceed 50 feet. Purchase the flat ribbon cable to satisfy the distance between the PC and the modem. Because "straight-through" cables are so usable and interchangeable, it is advisable to make the cable at least 5 feet in length. This is an overkill because your modem will probably sit on top of the PC, yet could aid use if later used in another connection.

The ribbon cable normally has a fixed price, which may include the actual connectors, and a cost per foot of cable price. When you purchase the cable, be sure to determine if the fixed price includes the connectors. If you plan on building more than one cable, you should consider purchasing bulk ribbon cable, as this could reduce the cost of the cable.

In this cable construction section, we assume that the connectors are not included in with the purchased ribbon cable. The user needs to connect one to each end of the cable. Prior to getting these connectors, the user should review the port profiles to determine the gender required at each end of the cable. The gender will be the opposite of that in the actual device port. The IBM PC had a male port, indicating that connector at this end of the cable should be female. The Hayes Smartmodem 1200 has a female port, demanding a male connector at the modem end of the cable. Once constructed, there will be only one way that the cable can be plugged in, as the genders will match.

Obtain both a female and male connector to use on the ribbon cable. These can be obtained one by one, or by the box. You should keep a mixture of male and female DB25 connectors on hand if you are building multiple cables.

When constructing a cable with ribbon cable, the connectors are snapped onto the flat cable. The user must ensure that pin 1 in one connector is connected to the same conductor as pin 1 in the other connector. This is the trickiest part. It might be worthwhile to mark one edge of the ribbon cable at each end as a reference. Mark the same conductor at both ends.

The connector is actually two pieces, one plastic piece that has the metal pins/sockets and one plastic piece that tightly fastens the connector to the ribbon cable. The connector comes apart as shown in Figure 3–6.

The PC end connector will be a female connector. Remove the back piece on the connector, the one without the metal pins in it. Locate pin 1 in this connector. Review Figure 3–3 to determine which pin is 1 in a female versus male connector. Take the ribbon cable and place the marked edge of the cable so this conductor

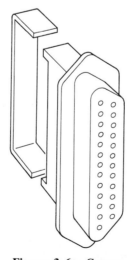

Figure 3–6. Connector, unassembled, for ribbon cables.

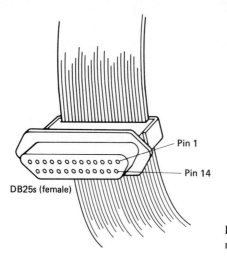

Pin 1

Pin 14

DB25s (female)

Figure 3–7. Ribbon cable being attached to female connector.

lays on the back of the female connector as shown in Figure 3–7. We made this mark on the edge of the cable earlier.

Be sure that the cable is lying flat on the back of the connector. Using your thumb, or a solid object such as a screwdriver head, mash the cable against the metal pieces in the back of the connector. The object is to make contact between the individual wires in the cable and the associated pins in the connector. Be sure that the cable is pressed firmly onto the back of the connector. Once this is complete, replace the second piece of plastic associated with the connector. Press the piece firmly into place. This piece usually has snaps on each side that will hold it into place firmly once it is properly seated. Work with it until the connector is in place.

The modem connector will be a male DB25 connector. This will be connected to the other end of the ribbon cable. Locate pin 1 in this connector, and align it on the same conductor to which pin 1 of the other end is connected. As before, consult Figure 1–3 to get the proper orientation as to which pin is pin 1 in the connector. DOUBLE CHECK. Once pin 1 of the male connector is aligned with the same conductor as pin 1 of the female connector, repeat the foregoing steps of attaching the connector to the cable.

9. Test for continuity

You have now completed the construction of the cable. It is a good habit to check the cable to ensure that the conductors are "straight-through" from end to end. This is important, because you had to mash the connector physically onto the cable, hoping to make contact between the metal contacts and the wires of the ribbon cable. Consult Tutorial Module 1–1 on how to use a VOM to test this or Tutorial Module 1–4 when using a BOB to check continuity.

Once this is completed, you have a "straight-through" cable. All conductors, leads 1–25, are present. Even though the PC and Hayes modem don't support all the leads, the cable provides them. This will not cause any problems and will allow us flexibility to use the cable elsewhere if needed.

Gender flexibility. A simple addition to this cable will allow it to be used in all environments requiring a "straight-through" cable, regardless of the gender requirements. If another male and female connector are available, a very flexible cable can be constructed. Near the end of the cable with the male connector, we can snap on a female connector. At the opposite end of the cable, we can add a male connector. These connectors should be snapped on approximately 3–4 inches from the cable ends, respectively. As before, align the pins up before assembly, and check for continuity after completed.

With these two additional connectors added to our cable, this cable can be used in any "straight-through" connection. If the connection of two devices involves a cable with male connectors at each end, the cable will work. If female-female cable is needed, this cable will also work. This type cable, shown in Figure 3–8, is very flexible.

10. Cable the two systems together

Now that we have constructed our cable, it is time to cable the PC to the Hayes modem. Because our cable will only work one way, the female end at the PC and the male end at the modem port, plug it in. Fasten the cable to each port with the small bolts provided. It is a good habit to use these bolts, even though the ribbon cable and connectors will probably fit snugly onto the ports.

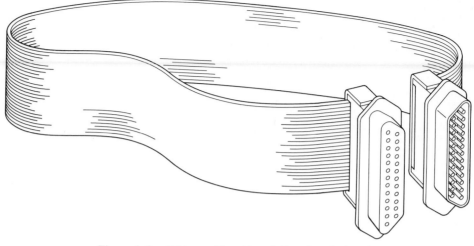

Figure 3–8. Ribbon cable with male/female at both ends.

11. Measure success

We have physically connected the PC to the Hayes modem at the juncture. The critical test is our ability to use the modem to dial another computer system or service and login. We will first dial in and login to a UNIX system.

To use the Hayes Smartmodem 1200, we will use a communication software program. We have used Crosstalk XVI in some of the other examples. To test this connection, we will use a "freeware" program called Procomm version 2.3. You can substitute a favorite communication software package here, as the concepts will be the same.

After the connection of the PC/XT and the modem with the ribbon cable, check the modular cord for the phone line. On the back of the Hayes Smartmodem, there is a four-pin modular receptacle, labeled "telco." If you are looking at the back of the modem, it is on the right-hand side. Plug the modular cord that comes with the modem into this receptacle. Plug the other end of the RJ-11C cord into the wall outlet for the phone line. Be sure that these cords fit snugly into the receptacles.

The next step is to connect the power cord to the modem. This cord will only fit into the back of the modem one way. Hence, plug the power cord into the modem and also to an electrical outlet. Once this is complete, the switch on the back of the modem needs to be flipped to the "on" position. The modem is on when this switch is in the "up" position. Do this now. Check the front panel of the modem for red lights. You will know you are successful if one or more of these lights are lit. If not, check the connections and option switches as outlined earlier in this chapter.

Now that we have power, we are ready to begin the "successful" communication to a remote system. This connection will be to an AT&T 3B2/300 Supermicro. We will know success by being able to both dial a number and establish a connection, as well as receiving the "login:" prompt. If we get to this point, and are able to type the login ID, then we will assume success.

If you are fortunate enough to have a computer port profile for the 3B2, consult it. Compare the Hayes and IBM PC profiles to obtain the common options. We will assume that the line settings are to be 1200 bps, no parity, 8 data bits, and 1 stop bit, as the 3B2 port profile may not be available.

Load the Procomm communication software by typing "Procomm." Prior to this make sure that you are in the proper directory or disk drive that contains "Procomm." Once loaded, the screen should display the following message:

    ALT-F10 HELP   S ANSI-BBS S HDX S 9600 N81 S LOG CLOSED S PRT OFF S CRLF S CR

This status line tells us a number of things, beginning in position 3. We are operating with the PC set to half duplex, 9600 bits per second, no parity check, 8 bits per character, and 1 stop bit. The "CR" indicates that a Carriage return (Enter key) will be interpreted as a carriage return. These differ from our desired line settings, so we should change them.

You can set these up within Procomm by hitting the Alt key and Function key 10 simultaneously. This will bring up the help screen as depicted in Figure 3–9.

```
┌─────────────────────────────────────────────────────────────────────────┐
│                            ProComm  Help                                  │
│                                                                           │
│   MAJOR FUNCTIONS          UTILITY FUNCTIONS          FILE FUNCTIONS       │
│                                                                           │
│  Dialing Directory  ...... Alt-D   Program Info ............. Alt-I   Send Files ......... PgUp │
│  Automatic Redial ...... Alt-R    Setup Screen ............. Alt-S   Receive Files ...... PgDn │
│  Keyboard Macros ...... Alt-M     Kermit Server Cmd ......... Alt-K  Directory ......... Alt-F │
│  Line Settings  ........ Alt-P    Change Directory ........... Alt-B  View a File ........ Alt-V │
│  Translate Table ....... Alt-W    Clear Screen ............. Alt-C   Screen Dump ...... Alt-G │
│  Editor .............. Alt-A      Toggle Duplex ............. Alt-E  Log Toggle ....... Alt-F1 │
│  Exit ............... Alt-X       Hang Up Phone ............ Alt-H   Log Hold ........ Alt-F2 │
│  Host Mode .......... Alt-Q       Elapsed Time ............. Alt-T                          │
│  Chat Mode .......... Alt-O       Print On/Off .............. Alt-L                          │
│  DOS Gateway ........ Alt-F4      Set Colors ............. Alt-Z                             │
│  Command Files ...... Alt-F5      Auto Answer .............. Alt-Y                           │
│  Redisplay .......... Alt-F6      Toggle CR-CR/LF ......... Alt-F3                           │
│                                   Break Key .............. Alt-F7                            │
└─────────────────────────────────────────────────────────────────────────┘
```

Figure 3–9.   HELP screen of ProComm communication software.

By hitting the Alt key and the ''p'' key simultaneously, the line settings will be displayed. We need to change the setup to be 1200 bps instead of 9600 and keep the other settings. By selecting number 8 and hitting the Enter key, this should select the desired line settings. Hit the Esc key once this has been done. We are now ready to dial the phone number of the remote computer system.

To dial the number, hold the Alt key and ''d'' key down momentarily. This displays the dialing directory. Typing an ''m'' selects the manual dial mode. A prompt occurs for the number to dial. Input the number to be dialed, followed by the enter key. If the modem is properly cabled and set up, the sequence, ''ATDT5551212'' should appear, with the ''5551212'' being your desired phone number. You should hear dial tone, followed by the dialing of the number. This dialing will be a sequence of different frequencies, one per digit to be dialed. If you get to the point of hearing the dialing occur, then you are 50 percent successful. The only remaining test is to ensure that you can actually communicate with the far-end computer system.

If you do not complete the dialing, several items are worth checking.

1. Check that the phone line works. Usually you can connect any telephone to the phone plug outlet and check to see if you can call a local number.
2. Check that a modular cord is connecting the modem to the outlet in checkpoint 1.
3. Check that your cable is securely connected to the PC and the modem.
4. Check that the modem is optioned as discussed in this case study.
5. Check that Procomm, or your communication software, is set to the proper speed, parity, character length, and COM1/2 (port) settings. This is done via software commands.
6. Be sure that the power cable is plugged into the modem and the modem is turned on. Light indicators on the front should be present.

If these items check out, you could have a bad modem, computer port, or communication software. Have each of these checked. If the dialing occurs correctly, and ringing is noted, then you should be successfully calling the desired computer. After several rings, the far-end computer should answer the call. If the far end computer, 3B2, does not answer the call, check the following:

1. Check that you are dialing the correct number. If you are calling from behind a PBX, you may need to include a dial access code. This is usually a ''9'' or an ''8,'' but check to make sure.
2. Check that the 3B2 computer is up and running, with this port enabled.
3. Check with the 3B2 systems analyst or systems administrator to ensure that the modem you are calling is set up to receive calls and automatically answer.

Momentarily you should hear an ear-piercing tone if the 3B2 modem answers the call. Once this tone is heard, the local Hayes modem goes into Online mode. The UNIX system will attempt to figure out the speed with which the two modems will operate. You may need to hit a couple of Enter keys for this to occur. You should receive characters on your screen indicating a successful connection. Normally, the UNIX system prompts you with a ''login'' message. You should type in your login. If you don't have a login, obtain one for the 3B2 administrators. In any event, log into the system by typing in your ID followed by a return.

If you see double characters for each character you enter, then the duplex is set up wrong. In half duplex, your local computer will display on the screen everything that you enter on the keyboard. If the far-end computer is operating in full duplex, commonly referred to as echoplex, then it will echo back to you everything that you enter on the keyboard. Double characters indicate that you should set your options to be full duplex, to match the far-end system. In this setting, your computer will not display each character as you enter them, but rather let the far end computer echo them back to your screen. Change the duplex setting to full duplex to rid you of the double characters. Alt and "e" will change the duplex within Procomm.

After you enter the login ID, you should receive a prompt for a password. A slight problem exists, as the word "password" is not legible. Several problems could exist. Usually if you are getting something, yet it is garbled, then the line settings are wrong. We can check them and try something different until it works. Most UNIX systems use even parity, 7 character bits, and 1 stop bit. Change the settings to match this. Using Procomm, this is done by hitting the Alt-p key combination. Select item 2 to set up the communication software as 1200 bps, 7 bits, even parity, with 1 stop bit. Hit the Esc key to return to the Online mode. You should permanently save these settings if you will be calling this system frequently.

Now attempt to enter your password. At this point this case study will assume that you have successfully logged onto the UNIX system. We will now explore possible problems with the data that you are receiving from the far-end 3B2 computer system.

Depending on the system you are connected to, you may see double spacing between the lines of data, split sentences, or overwriting of what you receive. Table 3–20 depicts the possible conditions that could occur and the possible resolutions of each situation. All this information should be noted in the port profiles for future reference. At this point things should be "humming" and you can be confident of a successful connection. You have successfully connected an IBM PC/XT to a Hayes Smartmodem. CONGRATULATIONS!

Tutorial Module 3-2: Connecting a Hayes Smartmodem 2400 to an IBM PC/AT

In this tutorial module we will connect a Hayes Smartmodem 2400 to an IBM PC/AT to illustrate the cabling requirements between a DB25 port on a modem and a 9-pin connector on an AT or compatible. If you are using a board in the AT that provides a DB25 (25-pin) port instead of the 9-pin port, refer to Tutorial Module 3–1. The semantics involved in port setup will be the same as in Tutorial Module 3–1, so we will not repeat all the steps. However, we will walk through the cable design section to highlight the differences between a PC/XT and PC/AT port. Furthermore, we will discuss the setup procedures for the Hayes Smartmodem 2400 modem, as they are different from those of the Smartmodem 1200. First, review the steps for connection used in all approaches. We will note which are not going to be repeated.

TABLE 3–20. POSSIBLE CHARACTER DISPLAY PROBLEMS AND RESOLUTIONS

If the data you receive look like:	Problem	Resolution
1. line 1 (your output will vary) line 2 (your output will vary) line 3	Too many line feeds.	(only) Ensure that CR/LF is not being performed.

2. line 1
    line 2
        line 3
	No carriage return is being performed.	Change option so receipt of line feed is interpreted as CR/LF, or have sending device output CR/LF instead of only LF.

3. lines 1, 2, 3 overwriting each other causing illegible lines	No line feed is being performed.	Change option so that receipt of line ending sequence is interpreted as CR/LF, instead of just a CR. Sending device could also be optioned to output a LF with each CR. Insure that receiving device is not stripping out the CR or LF character.

STEPS FOR CONNECTION

1. Determine compatibility (should it work?); see Tutorial Module 3–1.
2. Determine signs of success; see Tutorial Module 3–1.
3. Determine the type of connector used.
4. Determine gender of the ports.
5. Determine which leads (pins) are provided by each device.
6. Determine which leads are required to be on by each device.
7. Design the cable.
8. Build the cable; see Tutorial Module 4–3.
9. Test the cable for continuity; see Tutorial Module 1–1.
10. Cable the two systems together with the cable; see Tutorial Module 3–1.
11. From step 2, measure success; see Tutorial Module 3–1.

At this point the author assumes that you are convinced that the two devices are compatible and that the signs of success will be our ability to issue commands to the modem. We will rejoice when we reach the point where we can call a remote system, login, and communicate with it. We will now proceed to step 3 and determine the types of connectors used.

3. Determine type of connector used

The Hayes Smartmodem 2400 has the same type of connector as the Smartmodem 1200. Consult the documentation, or eyeball the back side of the modem to confirm that it is a DB25-size port. The PC/AT has a 9-pin connector as the default RS232 port. If you are using a board in the AT that provides a DB25 (25-pin) connector, refer to Tutorial Module 3–1 for this modem connection. This case study is focusing on the 9-pin connector that is found on most ATs and laptops such as the Toshiba 3100.

4. Determine gender of ports

The Hayes Smartmodem incorporates a female connector, DB25s. The 9-pin connector on the AT provides us a male interface. Our cable will require a male DB25 connector and a female 9-pin D subminiature connector.

5. Determine leads (pins) provided by each device

We need to find out which leads are provided by the Hayes Smartmodem 2400. One might assume that this modem provides the same leads as the Smartmodem 1200. This is not 100 percent true. The modems are very close except for a couple of differences. The foremost is that this modem supports both asynchronous and synchronous communication. When connecting a standard AT serial port to the modem for uploading and downloading of files, asynchronous transmission will be used. This is the present case.

However, if a port in the AT is to be used for communication in an IBM synchronous network, such as 3270, 2780/3780, or SNA (Systems Nework Architecture), then this modem could be used. However, the standard AT serial does not provide for synchronous capabilities. A special board needs to be purchased to provide a synchronous serial interface. Refer to Tutorial Module 3–5 for further discussion of synchronous environments. There we will highlight the differences between the Hayes Smartmodem 2400 in a synchronous versus asynchronous environment. Here we will merely point out the leads provided by the modem.

Which leads are provided by the 2400? The best means of determining this is to consult the documentation. However, we will use a tristate break-out box to assess which leads are "from" the modem. Connect the BOB to the RS232C port on the back of the modem. Turn the modem on! Also be sure that your break-out box has power. Our tristate is battery powered, so we will turn it on. The BOB lights up like a Christmas tree. Table 3–21 outlines the lights that are present on our BOB. Also provided is a cross-reference for normal break-out boxes that are not tristate. Recall that tristate BOBs show three states of a lead: high, low, and not present.

Receive Data is the lead that the Hayes presents the data it receives from the telephone line, so this is a normal output line from a modem. The Clear to Send, Data Set Ready, and Data Carrier Detect leads are also status leads from the modem. These three leads can be optioned to be on all the time, regardless of the condition of the telephone line. Ring Indicator turns on if there are incoming calls, so the attached device can detect this.

The transmit and receive timing leads will be ignored in our exercise and deferred until Tutorial Module 3–5 for a synchronous connection. Excluding these leads, the port is the same as the Hayes Smartmodem 1200. One lead that the 1200 provided was lead 12, High-Speed Indicator. If you can monitor this lead on your break-out box, you will also see that this lead is provided by the Smartmodem 2400. Consulting the documentation, it

TABLE 3–21. SMARTMODEM 2400-PROVIDED LEADS INDICATED BY A BREAKOUT BOX

Function	Lamp status	Lamp status
Receive Data	Low (green)	Off
Clear to Send	High (red)	On
Data Set Ready	High (red)	On
Data Carrier Detect	High (red)	On
Transmit Clock (DCE)	High/low (*)	Off/on fluctuation
Receive Clock (DCE)	High/low (*)	Off/on fluctuation
Ring Indicator	Low (green)	Off

NOTES: (*) This lead is fluctuating from high to low, or from red to green, at a very rapid rate. On a regular break-out box, the clock leads may not have a lamp for monitoring. However, if you can connect one of these leads to a lead that has a lamp on your BOB, then you should see this on/off fluctuation, or at least a pale red, indicating that the lead is fluctuating. The reason for the rapid rate of fluctuation is that these leads are the timing leads. The clock pulses that are used in a synchronous environment are on these leads. We can ignore them in our AT-to-Hayes connection.

can be noted that also pin 23, Select Alternate Rate, is used for the same function. For Bell operation, 1200 bps would be the speed if either of these leads was on. For CCITT operation, these signal 2400 bps operation. Table 3–22 outlines the Hayes-provided leads.

PC/AT lead analysis has been done in another section. Refer to Tutorial Module 4–3 to see how we arrive at the results summarized in Table 3–23.

6. Determine leads required to be on

Consulting the documentation is the best source of information for the input leads to both the modem and the AT. However, in the case of a modem, if our output control leads are any indication of compatibility to the RS232 standard, we may be able to make accurate assumptions. The modem is classified as DCE, data communication

TABLE 3–22. HAYES-PROVIDED SIGNALS

Function	Lead #
Receive Data	3
Clear to Send	5
Data Set Ready	6
Data Carrier Detect	8
Select Alternate Rate	12
Transmit Clock (DCE)	15 (n/a in this case study)
Receive Clock (DCE)	17 (n/a in this case study)
Ring Indicator	22
Select Alternate Rate	23 (same as lead 12)

TABLE 3–23. PORT ANALYSIS FINDINGS FOR AT

IBM PC/AT	
3	Transmit Data (from)
4	?? control lead (from)
7	?? control lead (from)

equipment. This implies that a piece of DTE, such as the AT, is to be connected to the port. DTE normally has output control leads of Request to Send and Data Terminal Ready, as well as the Transmit Data lead. The RS232 standard has this functions on leads 4, 20, and 2, respectively. The Hayes modem conforms to the standard, so we can surmise that it will require the same leads, 4, 20, and 2, as input leads. Confirm this with the documentation. If you are using a different modem, one of the leads, 4 or 20, may not be required, but otherwise the port conforms to the standard. The Hayes Smartmodem 1200 does not require pin 4, yet conforms to the RS232 standard, whereas the 2400 does use this lead. Check this lead in particular if you are using a different modem.

Another lead is supported as an input lead on the Smartmodem 2400. This is lead number 24, Transmit Clock (DTE source). If the modem is NOT going to provide timing in a "synchronous" connection, then the attached device gives the modem the timing signal on this lead. However, in our tutorial module, timing leads are not of value, so we will ignore this lead. Table 3–24 outlines the input leads "to" the modem. The PC/AT input leads have previously been analyzed in Tutorial Module 1–2. Consult this to discover the results summarized in Table 3–25.

7. Design the cable

We may now begin to design the cable necessary to connect the modem to the AT. Prior to designing this cable, the user should review the SCS port profile analysis forms. These are presented in Tables 3–26 and 3–27. We should separate the categories of leads by functions of ground, data, and control to ease our design. Table 3–28 has the leads of both ports separated by category. With leads separated by function, the user can get a good look at what needs to be incorporated into the cable design. Prior to this design, we should review our cable design rules.

CABLE DESIGN: GENERAL RULES

1. Connect like categories of leads together.
2. Always connect an "out" to an "in" and an "in" to an "out."
3. A lead that is input may be connected to another lead that is an input only if both are connected to an output lead.
4. In synchronous connections, only use one source of timing. (Because the AT-to-Hayes Smartmodem 2400 connection is asynchronous, this point is not applicable.)

TABLE 3–24. INPUT LEADS "TO" THE HAYES SMARTMODEM 2400

Function	Lead #
Transmit Data	2
Request to Send	4
Data Terminal Ready	20
Transmit Clock (DTE)	24

NOTES: Ignore lead 24 as we are interested in only those leads used in an asynchronous connection such as our AT to Hayes modem.

TABLE 3–25. INPUT CONTROL LEADS OF AT PORT

1	Carrier Detect
2	Receive Data
6	Data Set Ready
8	Clear to Send
9	Ring Indicator

TABLE 3–26. HAYES SMARTMODEM 2400 MODEM PORT PROFILE

Underline if supported; circle if selected.

Model: Smartmodem 2400   Vendor: Hayes_____   Port: RS232C_____

Port type: serial
Port: DB25   9-pin 8-pin/modular 20mA _____

Gender: male female

Pin #	Function	Direction	Pin #	Function	Direction
1	Protective Ground	to from n/a	14		to from n/a
2	Transmit data	to from n/a	15	Transmit Timing	to from n/a
3	Receive Data	to from n/a	16		to from n/a
4	Request to Send	to from n/a	17	Receive Timing	to from n/a
5	Clear to Send	to from n/a	18		to from n/a
6	Data Set Ready	to from n/a	19		to from n/a
7	Signal Ground	to from n/a	20	Data Terminal Ready	to from n/a
8	Data Carrier Detect	to from n/a	21		to from n/a
9		to from n/a	22	Ring Indicator	to from n/a
10		to from n/a	23	Same as 12	to from n/a
11		to from n/a	24	Receive Timing (DTE)	to from n/a
12	Select Alt-Rate	to from n/a	25		to from n/a
13		to from n/a			

Leads that must be on: 4 20 __ __ __ __

Options:
   Speeds: 110 300 600 1200 1800 (2400) 4800 9600 19.2 56k _____
   Compatibility: 103 212 V.22bis _____
   Parity: even odd space mark (none)
   Char-length: 7 (8) __
   # stop bits: (1) 1.5 2
   Line-ending sequence: cr 1f cr/1f cr/1f/1f
   Auto answer: yes no RTS/CTS delay: __
   Disconnect sequence: EOT DEL ATZ_____
   Intelligent modems. . . . Dialing Technique: Touch-tone Pulse
     Compatibility: Hayes _____
     Command line prefix: AT _____ Dial command: D _____
     Touch-tone dial: T __ Pulse dial: P __ Pause: , __
     Wait for dial tone: W __ Wait for quiet answer: @ __
     Flash: ! __ Dial stored number: S __
     Return to command state after dialing: ; __
     Escape sequence: + + + __ Switch-hook control: H __
     Store phone #: &Z __

   Mode: async sync isoch   sync timing leads:

#	function	direction
15	Transmit timing	to from
17	Receive Timing	to from
24	Receive Timing (DTE)	to from

Notes: Parity modes are 7 bit, 1–2 stop bits with odd, even, or fixed parity, *or* 8 bit, 1–2 stop bits, and no parity at 1200 bps. At 300 bps, 7–8 bit, 1–2 stop bits, odd, even, no parity.

TABLE 3–27. PC/AT COMPUTER PORT PROFILE

Underline if supported; circle if selected.

Model: PC/AT _____ Vendor: IBM _____ Port: COMM _____

Port type: <u>serial</u> parallel

Port: DB25 <u>9-pin</u> 5-pin 8-pin/modular 20mA Centronics

Gender: <u>male</u> female

Pin #	Function	Direction	Pin #	Function	Direction
1	<u>Carrier Detect</u>	<u>to</u> from n/a	14	_____	to from n/a
2	<u>Receive Data</u>	to from n/a	15	_____	to from n/a
3	<u>Transmit Data</u>	to <u>from</u> n/a	16	_____	to from n/a
4	<u>Data Terminal Ready</u>	to <u>from</u> n/a	17	_____	to from n/a
5	<u>Signal Ground</u>	to from <u>n/a</u>	18	_____	to from n/a
6	<u>Data Set Ready</u>	<u>to</u> from n/a	19	_____	to from n/a
7	<u>Request to Send</u>	to <u>from</u> n/a	20	_____	to from n/a
8	<u>Clear to Send</u>	<u>to</u> from n/a	21	_____	to from n/a
9	<u>Ring Indicator</u>	<u>to</u> from n/a	22	_____	to from n/a
10	_____	to from n/a	23	_____	to from n/a
11	_____	to from n/a	24	_____	to from n/a
12	_____	to from n/a	25	_____	to from n/a
13	_____	to from n/a			

Complete the next section only with 36-pin cinch connector.

#	Function	Direction	#	Function	Direction
26	_____	to from n/a	27	_____	to from n/a
28	_____	to from n/a	29	_____	to from n/a
30	_____	to from n/a	31	_____	to from n/a
32	_____	to from n/a	33	_____	to from n/a
34	_____	to from n/a	35	_____	to from n/a
36	_____	to from n/a			

Flow control technique: XON/XOFF ENQ/ACK STX/ETX Hardware _____

Leads that must be on: 8, 6, 1 _____ __

Options:

    Speeds: <u>110 300 600 1200 1800</u> (2400) 4800 9600 19.2 56k _____

    Parity: <u>even</u> odd space mark (none)

    Char-length: 7 (8) __

    # stop bits: (1) 1.5 2

    Line-ending sequence: cr lf cr/lf cr/lf/lf

    Disconnect sequence: EOT DEL ~. _____

Mode: async sync isoch		sync timing leads:	
	#	function	direction
	15	_____	to from
	17	_____	to from
	24	_____	to from

Notes: The options of this port are set up using the MS-DOS Mode command. Your application may do this automatically or through a menu-driven interface.

The ground leads are the easiest in that the Signal Ground leads in both ports are merely connected to one another. The Protective Ground leads are not really required in the cable, as the AT does not offer it in the 9-pin port. It has an isolated ground; hence, protective ground can be ignored in our design, resulting in the design outlined in Table 3–29.

The next category of leads to tackle are the data leads. Applying cable design rules 1 and 2, the data leads present no problems. Note the function of Transmit Data. In the Hayes port, this is lead 2 and an input signal.

TABLE 3–28. HAYES SMARTMODEM 2400 AND
IBM PC/AT LEADS SEPARATED BY CATEGORY

| Smartmodem 2400 | IBM PC/AT | |
| | Hayes | PC/AT |
Function	Lead	Lead
Ground		
Protective Ground	1	n/a
Signal Ground	7	5
Data		
Transmit Data	2	3
Receive Data	3	2
Control		
Request to Send	4	7
Clear to Send	5	8
Data Set Ready	6	6
Data Carrier Detect	8	1
Data Terminal Ready	20	4
Data Rate Selector	12	n/a
Data Rate Selector	23	n/a
Timing (not used in asynchronous connections)		
Transmit Timing (DCE)	15	n/a
Receive Timing (DCE)	17	n/a
Transmit Timing (DTE)	24	n/a

TABLE 3–29. GROUND LEADS
IN HAYES-AT CABLE

Function	Hayes Lead	PC/AT Lead
Signal Ground	7 -------	5

LEGEND: Lead 7 of the Hayes port should
be "straight through" to lead 5 in the AT
port. Ground leads have no direction.

Transmit Data is an output lead found on pin 3 of the AT port. Rule 1 indicates to connect an "out" to an "in." Because these are not only the same category of leads but also the same functions, merely connect them together. The same holds true for the Receive Data leads, as summarized in Table 3–30.

Control lead design. Now that the ground and data leads have been taken care of, and the timing leads ignored, the only category of leads left is the control leads. As with the data leads, apply rules 1 and 2 for an easy connection of the control leads Request to Send, Clear to Send, Data Set Ready, Data Carrier Detect, Data

TABLE 3–30. DATA LEAD DESIGN FOR HAYES-TO-AT

Function	Hayes Lead	PC/AT Lead	
Transmit Data (in)	2	⟨------ 3	Transmit Data (out)
Receive Data (out)	3	------⟩ 2	Receive Data (in)

LEGEND: The "⟨------" indicates that a "straight-through" connection is
involved. Connect pin 3 at the 9-pin (AT end) connector through the cable
to pin 2 at the Hayes (DB25) end of the cable.

TABLE 3–31. CONTROL LEAD CABLE DESIGN FOR AT-HAYES
SMARTMODEM 2400

Function	Hayes	AT	
Request to Send (in)	4 ⟨------ 7		Request to Send (out)
Clear to Send (out)	5 ------⟩ 8		Clear to Send (in)
Data Set Ready (out)	6 ------⟩ 6		Data Set Ready (in)
Data Carrier Detect (out)	8 -----⟩ 1		Data Carrier Detect (in)
Data Terminal Ready (in)	20 ⟨------ 4		Data Terminal Ready (out)
Ring Indicator (out)	22 ------⟩ 9		Ring Indicator (in)

LEGEND: The "⟨------" indicates a "cross-over" connection between the pins at the opposite ends of the cable.

Terminal Ready, and Ring Indicator. Because these are not only the same category of leads but also the same functions, merely connect them together. The Request to Send leads should be connected "straight through" from one connector across the cable to the other connector. The same is true for the other control leads. Table 3–31 outlines the corresponding lead numbers for these control leads for both the modem and AT end of the cable.

Consulting Table 3–27 the user sees that the IBM PC/AT port does not support the other control signals, Select Alternate Rate. If it were an input signal, we would have to somehow satisfy it. As this is an output signal from the Hayes modem, we need not worry about it. Table 3–32 outlines the completed design for the IBM PC/AT to Hayes Smartmodem 2400 cable.

Steps 8–11 are no different in this connection from any others. Hence, refer to any of the other tutorial modules for a step-by-step procedure to build the cable, check for continuity, and physically cable the systems together. To measure your success, apply the same techniques used in Tutorial Module 3–1, as the AT-modem connection will behave in the same fashion as the XT-modem connection. The only difference is how the modems are optioned. The Smartmodem 1200 has dip switches and a command language, whereas the Smartmodem 2400 uses only a command language.

The next section will highlight how the Smartmodem 2400 is optioned, because it is different from the Smartmodem 1200. Once the modem is optioned properly, follow the steps for measuring success found in Tutorial Module 3–1 to test out your PC/AT to Smartmodem 2400 connection. The steps are exactly the same as an IBM PC/XT-to-modem connection. Hence, follow these steps precisely.

Optioning the Hayes Smartmodem 2400. The Hayes modem is shipped from the factory with options set to allow operation in most PC-to-modem environments. Some of the factory-set options are as follows:

TABLE 3–32. PC/AT-TO-HAYES SMARTMODEM 2400 CABLE
DESIGN

Function	Hayes Lead	PC/AT Lead	
Signal Ground	7 ------- 5		
Transmit Data (in)	2 ⟨------ 3		Transmit Data (out)
Receive Data (out)	3 ------⟩ 2		Receive Data (in)
Request to Send (in)	4 ⟨------ 7		Request to Send (out)
Clear to Send (out)	5 -----⟩ 8		Clear to Send (in)
Data Set Ready (out)	6 ------⟩ 6		Data Set Ready (in)
Data Carrier Detect (out)	8 ------⟩ 1		Data Carrier Detect (in)
Data Terminal Ready (in)	20 ⟨------ 4		Data Terminal Ready (out)
Ring Indicator (out)	22 ------⟩ 9		Ring Indicator (in)

LEGEND: The "⟨------" indicate "cross-overs" between the two opposite ends of the cable. Merely connect the lead numbers as indicated. The resulting cable breaks out the 9-pin AT-type connector to be a standard IBM PC/XT serial port.

1. 2400 bps
2. Bell 212A operation at 1200 bps
3. Even parity
4. Auto answer disabled
5. Command echo on
6. All result codes enabled
7. Modem ignores DTR
8. Data Carrier Detect always on
9. Data Set Ready always on

The last three options are the ones that we will change for our AT connection. It is not imperative that these be changed, but the author prefers it this way.

The modem has a built-in command language that is supported. The Hayes 1200 bps modems also have a command language, but they have physical switches in addition. The 2400 does not have switches. The user accesses the commands from the attached devices keyboard. In our case, the PC/AT is used: the user runs communication software, and the software emulates the user typing the commands at a keyboard to set up and control the modem. This all happens transparent to the user. However, if a user has a terminal, such as a AT&T 610 or DEC VT100, connected to the modem, he or she will enter these commands from a keyboard. We will walk you through the sequences you can enter from the PC/AT once communication software is loaded. We will use ProComm, but you can use your favorite software package.

Command lines must begin with the letters "AT." This is often referred to as the "ATtention" code. Once the modem receives these two characters, it knows that one or more commands follow. Because the modem only accepts these two entries for the attention code, it compares what you type in to determine quickly the line settings at which you are operating. There are a limited number of combinations of number of data bits, parity, number of stop bits, and speeds. So the modem merely checks your input against all these possibilities to assess how your PC port is optioned. The modem then updates its memory to store these settings. This is why you can easily communicate with the command language of the Hayes modem. The modem keeps these settings even when power is turned off.

Armed with this knowledge, let's proceed to set up the modem the way we want. The command line structure, or syntax, is "AT" followed by option command settings. If you desire to see the modem command line interaction, type in an "AT" followed by a carriage return. The modem should respond with an "OK" message. If your sequence looks similar to this, "aatt," then your duplex setting should be changed to full. If the "OK" message appears two lines after your "AT" input, then you should change the command software to not add a line feed upon receipt of a carriage return. This may need to be changed back depending on the system you ultimately connect to. However, for clarity, be sure that you are getting single spacing.

To see what the settings are, you may enter the sequence "AT&V." This will display the current settings. It may appear to be garbage now, but this list will mean more to you once you know what to look for. In particular, look in the top line for the sequences "&D0," "&S0," and "&C0." These are the options that we will be changing in the next section. They should appear on the first line of display, once you enter the "AT&V" command.

We are interested in setting up the modem to let the telephone line dictate the status of Data Carrier Detect. The option command for this is "&Cx," where x is either a 0 or a 1. Issuing the command "AT&C1" followed by carriage return yields the desired result of having DCD track the state of carrier sent from the remote station.

Data Set Ready was also to be dictated by the actual state of the modem instead of always being on. To set up the modem for this, issue the command "AT&S1" followed by a carriage return. This option causes DSR to operate as it is supposed to, according to the EIA RS232-C standard.

The last option to be set up was Data Terminal Ready, DTR. We want the modem to monitor this lead rather than ignore it. This will let the modem know when the port on the PC/AT is active. There are four possible settings on this option. The command "AT&D2" is the setting. This causes the modem to go onhook (hang up) and disable "auto answer" if it detects an "on-to-off" transition of this lead. If our PC/AT loses power, the user exits the communication software, or the AT is merely not running; then DTR will be off. The modem will know not to answer an incoming call if either of these conditions is present.

We should enable auto answer. This will allow other devices to call into the PC/AT. Ignore this if you do not plan on allowing remote access to your system. The command "AT SO=1" should be entered to have the modem automatically answer an incoming call. The reason for a factory setting of "no auto answer" is because a phone may be connected to share the same line as the modem. If an incoming call is detected, the modem would answer the call before you had a chance to pick up the attached phone. Set this option to suit your environment. Furthermore, the number of rings prior to answer can be adjusted when there is an attached phone.

Tutorial Module 3–3: Connecting a Modem to an Apple IIe/IIc

This module covers the connection of a Hayes Smartmodem 1200 to an Apple II Plus. A serial port will be provided through the use of a SeriALL card from Practical Peripherals, Inc. Different Apple models offer similar serial ports as that covered in this tutorial module. The modem will be connected to the computer using the RS232 port on this card. The goal is to allow the Apple user to be able to communicate with a remote system, such as the Dow Jones News/Retrieval System, CompuServe, ATTMail, or another computer system. This tutorial module will test out the Apple/modem connection by dialing into a UNIX system. References to the Apple will imply the RS232 port on the SeriALL board, as they will be treated as one device.

The steps we will follow for this tutorial module are common to all our reviews:

STEPS FOR CONNECTION

1. Determine compatibility (should it work?).
2. Determine signs of success.
3. Determine the type of connector used.
4. Determine gender of the ports.
5. Determine which leads (pins) are provided by each device.
6. Determine which leads are required to be on by each device.
7. Design the cable.
8. Build the cable.
9. Test the cable for continuity.
10. Cable the two systems together with the cable.
11. From step 2, measure success.

1. Determine compatibility

The SeriALL card provides an RS232-compatible port that can be used to connect a printer, modem, or another computer. The Hayes Smartmodem 1200 is an industry standard modem supporting asynchronous operation

TABLE 3–33. SERIALL BOARD OPTION SETUP FOR HAYES SMARTMODEM

Switch		
SW1–1	On	XON/XOFF enabled
–2	On	Communications modem
–3	Off	No printer type
–4	Off	No printer type
–5	Off	No printer type
–6	Off	No auto 300/1200 baud
–7	Off	Send line feed after carriage return
–8	Off	No Apple IRQ interrupt
SW2–1	Off	1200 baud
–2	On	1200 baud
–3	On	1200 baud
–4	On	1200 baud
–5	On	1 stop bit
–6	On	8 data bits
–7	On	no parity
–8	On	no parity

NOTE: Also the jumper should be in the HHS-5 position, with the SeriALL cable plugged into the Modem position on the board.

at speeds up to 1200 bps. The common parameters between the devices are 1200 bps, asynchronous operation, 8 bits, no parity, stop bit. The SeriALL has two sets of option switches: SW1 and SW2. Table 3–33 outlines the settings of these switches for ultimate connection of a Hayes or compatible modem to the serial port. The Hayes Smartmodem should have the switched set to the factory settings (see Table 3–34).

2. Determine signs of success

The goal of this connection is to bring communications to the Apple computer. You will know that you have been successful if you can dial into a remote computer system, a UNIX system in this tutorial module, to send and receive data. Your success will be the ability to dial a number, connect to a system, login, and send and receive information. The ability to regulate the flow between the two systems is also important. Hence, the flow control mechanisms must also be tested to ensure that the Apple operator can stop the data flow when desired.

3. Determine type of connector used

4. Determine gender of ports

The Apple II serial port is a DB25 connector provided by the SeriALL board. A cable is provided for connection onto the board that yields a DB25S or female connector. The Hayes Smartmodem 1200 also provides a DB25S female port. Hence the cable necessary to connect the two devices will have a male connector at each end.

5. Determine leads (pins) provided by each device

6. Determine leads required to be on

Consult the documentation to determine which leads are present and which signals are provided by each port as well as which ones must be on. Refer to the tutorial modules that include the Hayes Smartmodem 1200 for the details of performing port analysis on the modem port. The Apple port pinouts are found in Table 3–35.

TABLE 3–34. HAYES SMARTMODEM 1200 SWITCH SETTINGS FOR APPLE CONNECTION

Switch	Setting	Function
1	Up	Does not force DTR lead on.
2	Up	Causes Smartmodem 1200 to respond to commands with word result codes.
3	Down	Sends result codes from modem.
4	Up	Causes Smartmodem 1200 to echo characters during Command mode.
5	Down	Prevents auto answering of incoming calls (change if desired).
6	Up	Forces DCD(8) on.
7	Up	Uses RJ11 modular telephone jack.
8	Down	Enables Smartmodem 1200 commands recognition.

TABLE 3–35. PINOUTS FOR PRACTICAL PERIPHERALS SERIALL CARD FOR APPLE II

Pin	Function
1	Protective Ground
2	Transmit Data (out)
4	Request to Send (out)
5	Clear to Send (in)
6	Data Set Ready (in)
7	Signal Ground
8	Data Carrier Detect (in)
20	Data Terminal Ready (out)

Digital Loopback Test

TABLE 3–36. PINOUTS OF
HAYES SMARTMODEM 1200

Pin	Function
1	Protective Ground
2	Transmit Data (in)
3	Receive Data (out)
5	Clear to Send (out)
6	Data Set Ready (out)
7	Signal Ground
8	Carrier Detect (out)
12	High Speed Indicator (out)
20	Data Terminal Ready (in)
22	Ring Indicator (out)

The Apple port on this board emulates DTE. However, the input signals 5, 6, and 8 do not have to be on for the computer to output data. This can be tested by enabling the slot that the SeriALL card is in. The user can type ''PR#4'' followed by an Enter key to send the data out the port. If a break-out box is connected, pin 2, Transmit Data, will flicker according to the data bits being output. The pinouts of the Hayes Smartmodem 1200 are summarized in Table 3–36, taken from other tutorial modules.

The modem can be optioned to not require any leads to be on. However, this tutorial module has set the modem options so that DTR, pin 20, must be on for the modem to execute commands. With the modem set this way, lead 20 must be on. Other than that, no leads are required by the modem. Note the direction of the leads. In particular, look at leads 3, 5, 6, and 8. These signals are all output from the modem. The other leads, 2 and 20, are input signals. The port on the modem emulates DCE. This is normal, as modems are data communication equipment.

7. Design the cable

Now that the pinouts are known for both the Apple and Hayes devices, the user can design the cable. The Apple board, when the ''modem'' setup is followed, is emulating data terminal equipment. The modem, as just cited, is DCE. From this relationship, a ''straight-through'' cable should meet our needs. Review the leads, category by category, noting their directions. Consult Table 3–37 for the actual cable designs. Note that not all leads are connected, as both devices do not require all the same leads. However, the essential leads have been accounted for with associate directions.

8. Build the cable

9. Test for continuity

TABLE 3–37. APPLE-TO-HAYES SMARTMODEM 1200 CABLE DESIGN

Function	Apple lead #	Hayes lead #	Function
Protective Ground	1 -------	1	Protective Ground
Transmit Data (out)	2 -------	2	Transmit Data (in)
Receive Data (in)	3 -------	3	Receive Data (out)
Clear to Send (in)	5 -------	5	Clear to Send (out)
Data Set Ready (in)	6 -------	6	Data Set Ready (out)
Signal Ground	7 -------	7	Signal Ground
Carrier Detect (in)	8 -------	8	Carrier Detect (out)
Data Terminal Ready (out)	20 -------	20	Data Terminal Ready (in)

NOTE: A ''straight-through'' cable is possible here. Even though some of the leads are not required, such as lead 4, a ribbon cable or other ''straight-through'' cable can be used here. The important point is the genders, with a male connector being required at both ends.

10. Cable the two systems together

Once you are comfortable with the cable design, construct it or acquire the "straight-through" cable. The other sections outline how physically to build the cable. Once it is built, check it out for good continuity and then connect the modem to the computer with the newly acquired/built cable. You are now ready to test out the connection.

11. Measure success

Your success will be your ability to dial another computer system or service, establish the connection, and exchange data successfully. The first step is to ensure that the modem and SeriALL board are optioned correctly. With the power off, check the options as outlined in step 1 of this tutorial module. Install the SeriAll board in one of the available slots in the Apple computer. The assumption made here is that it is in slot 4, but this is not a requirement. With the modem cabled to the board, be sure that the modem is turned on and has power applied to it. The modem should be connected to the telephone line using a modular cord. With a DOS disk in the drive, turn on the Apple computer, and you are ready to check out the connection.

When the Apple computer has been powered up, with the user having the "right-bracket" prompt on the screen, type in "PR#4" and "IN#4" followed by the Enter key. This should allow all typed data to go out to the device attached to the board in slot 4. Now if you enter data followed by the return, the modem should try to interpret the characters. However, the Apple interprets input instead. For example, if you enter the dialing sequence necessary to dial using a Hayes modem, ATDT5551212, you will get an error message from the Apple. You need to disable the Apple's local interpretation of the command, so the modem can interpret your entries. The Apple offers a Terminal mode function to get around this. To go to Terminal mode, enter a "Control-a" followed by a "t." This places the Apple in Terminal mode, a condition that will cause the Apple to merely pass through the keyboard input. Now enter the dialing sequence ATDT5551212, substituting your desired number. You should hear the modem go offhook and the digits being dialed.

The far-end system should answer the call if it is set up for auto answer of incoming calls. Since we are dialing a UNIX system, the remote system answers the call, waiting for the user to enter a couple of return keys. This allows the UNIX system to determine the speed of the port. Once the UNIX system adjusts to the correct speed, the user should see the "login:" prompt. Complete the login and password sequence. If you do not get to this point, refer to the sections on diagnosing modem problems to correct garbled characters, overwriting, double spacing, and so on.

Once you are logged in, you should check out the flow control mechanisms. The SeriALL board supports XON/XOFF, just as the remote UNIX system does. To determine if this works, list a file by issuing the "cat filename" sequence. If you don't know what files are available, the "ls" command will give you a directory listing. "Cat"ing the file will cause the UNIX system to output the file contents to your Apple computer. To regulate the flow, enter a Control-s sequence from the Apple keyboard. This is done by holding down the Ctrl key while hitting the "s" key on the Apple's keyboard. This should halt the output of the file to your display. If this does not stop the flow, with the file contents being output completely to your Apple display, retry it. If the same thing occurs the second time, one or both of the computers are not set up properly. Review the options set forth earlier in this tutorial module and correct the situation.

To resume the outputting of the file, enter a Control-q sequence. CONGRATULATIONS!

Tutorial Module 3–4: Connecting a Hayes Smartmodem 2400 to a WYSE WY-85 Terminal

Often it becomes necessary to have a terminal with a modem at a site that can dial into a remote computer system. Today many PCs with terminal emulators are being used instead of a stand-alone terminal. However, the arrangement depicted in Figure 3–10 is still popular today. We will connect a Wyse WY-85 terminal to a Hayes Smartmodem 2400 and attempt to access a remote computer system. This arrangement is very similar to Tutorial Module 1–7, where a teleprinter used an intelligent modem, except that the speed of operation will be twice as fast and the optioning will be different. We will not repeat step-by-step procedures, but summarize where appropriate. We will follow the normal steps to get the connection in place between the terminal and modem.

STEPS FOR CONNECTION

1. Determine compatibility (should it work?).
2. Determine signs of success.
3. Determine the type of connector used.

Digital Loopback Test

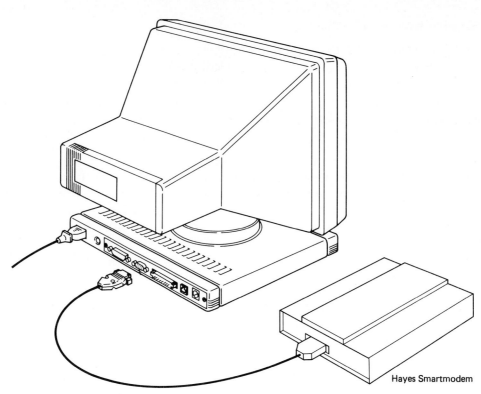

Figure 3–10. Wyse WY-85 terminal with Hayes Smartmodem 2400.

4. Determine gender of the ports.
5. Determine which leads (pins) are provided by each device.
6. Determine which leads are required to be on by each device.
7. Design the cable.
8. Build the cable.
9. Test the cable for continuity.
10. Cable the two systems together with the cable.
11. From step 2, measure success.

1. Determine compatibility

Review each of the SCS port profiles to determine if the two devices are compatible. A quick review of each indicates that the two are compatible with the common features and options of asynchronous, 2400 bps, 7 data bits, even parity, 1 stop bit, and full duplex operation. The information for these profiles was obtained from the device documentation. Be aware that although 2400 bps is supported, the remote system or "called" system will need to support 2400 bps operation, or the speed will be lowered to the common speed. The common speed will probably be 1200 bps. During our test for success, step 11, we will see if this is done automatically or needs to be reset manually, and how.

2. Determine signs of success

The reason for an installation depicted in Figure 3–10 is for remote access to a computer or message system. The installation may not need the power of local processing, which rules out the need for a PC and associated software. Furthermore, maybe the terminal limits the need for the sophistication required of a local computer. Whatever the reason, the goal is to provide a setup that allows a user to access a remote system using a dial-up telephone line. Our success will be measured by our ability to call a remote system, exchange data, and control the flow of the data.

Furthermore, the intelligent features of the Hayes modem should be capitalized on to ease the connection from start to finish. The Wyse terminal supports the defining of certain function keys to allow quick input. We will use these to aid in the communication with the remote system, as well as the local communication with the modem.

3. Determine type of connector

4. Determine gender of ports

The port on the Wyse terminal and Hayes Smartmodem have already been analyzed in the text. The Wyse WY-85 terminal provides a male DB25 connector. The Hayes Smartmodem 2400 provides a female 25-pin connector. This indicates that our cable will need a female DB25S connector for the Wyse end of the cable, with a DB25P connector at the modem end. The modem port emulates data communication equipment, DCE. What should the Wyse terminal emulate? DTE! Without advancing to the next step, you may guesstimate that a "straight-through" cable might work here. Proceed for comfirmation of this.

5. Determine leads (pins) provided by each device

6. Determine leads required to be on

Refer to Tutorial Module 4–3 for a step-by-step approach to analyzing the Wyse WY-85 terminal port, labeled "COMM." Tutorial Module 3–2 discusses how to assess leads in the Hayes Smartmodem 2400 port, tagged "RS232C." Table 3.38 summarizes the leads of both ports, separated by category.

7. Design the cable

Tackle ground leads first. The Protective Grounds should be connected "straight through" to one another. The Signal Grounds should also be connected with a conductor from one end of the cable to the other as depicted in Table 3–39.

Data leads: Next we tackle the data leads. There are only two possible connections for these, so we can quickly lay out the cabling of the data category. Either pin 2 is connected at one end of the cable to pin 2 at the

TABLE 3–38. WYSE WY-85 TERMINAL AND HAYES SMARTMODEM 2400 LEADS

Function	Wyse lead	Hayes lead	Function
Ground			Ground
Shield Ground	1	1	Protective Ground
Signal Ground	7	7	Signal Ground
Data			Data
Transmit Data (out)	2	2	Transmit Data (in)
Receive Data (in)	3	3	Receive Data (out)
Control			Control
Request to Send (out)	4	4	Request to Send (in)
Clear to Send (in)	5	5	Clear to Send (out)
Data Set Ready (in)	6	6	Data Set Ready (out)
Data Carrier Detect (in)	8	8	Data Carrier Detect (out)
Data Terminal Ready (out)	20	20	Data Terminal Ready (in)
Speed Indicator (in)	12	12	Select Alternate Rate (out)
Speed Selector (out)	23	23	Select Alternate Rate (out)
Timing (not used in asynchronous connections)			
	n/a	15	Transmit Clock (out)
	n/a	17	Receive Clock (out)
	n/a	24	Transmit Clock (in)

NOTES: The Wyse terminal should be optioned for EIA modem so that the leads Clear to Send, Data Set Ready, and Data Carrier Detect will be monitored. In this mode, the terminal will only send data if these leads are on. The Hayes always has Clear to Send held high (on). However, the modem can be optioned to maintain Data Set Ready and Data Carrier Detect on at all times or to let the condition of the line dictate the status of these leads. The author recommends that you option the modem to let the line determine the state of these leads. Also if lead 12 to the Wyse terminal is on, the terminal will transmit and receive data at 1200 bps, regardless of the speed selected in the setup.

Digital Loopback Test

TABLE 3–39. GROUND LEAD DESIGN FOR WYSE
WY-85-TO-HAYES SMARTMODEM 2400

Function	Wyse lead #	Hayes lead #	Function
Protective Ground	1 ------- 1		Protective Ground
Signal Ground	7 ------- 7		Signal Ground

LEGEND: The "-------" indicates a "straight-through" connection, from one end of the cable to the other.

other end, or it is "crossed over" to pin 3. The terminal will send all its data on the Transmit Data lead, pin 2. The modem will receive these characters on pin 2 and transmit them across the telephone line to the other computer. We know this from the Hayes port profile indicating that the Transmit Data is an input lead. The Receive Data lead, pin 3 on both devices, is the lead that is used by the terminal to receive data. Any data that the terminal wants to receive are expected to arrive on pin 3. What does the modem do with the data it receives from the telephone line? It outputs it to the terminal on lead 3. Hence we should connect lead 2 at both ends of the cable "straight through." The same holds for lead 3. We now have allowed for data to be output by one device and received (input) by the other. Table 3–40 depicts the data category portion of the cable design.

No timing leads are present, as this is an asynchronous connection, so we will next tackle the control leads and complete this cable design. First, look at the input control leads of the Hayes modem in Table 3–28. Leads 20, Data Terminal Ready, and 4, Request to Send, are the only input control leads required by the modem. The Wyse terminal provides Data Terminal Ready as an output control signal as well as Request to Send. Rules 1 and 2 apply, allowing pin 20 to pass straight through the cable, from end to end. Repeat the same for pin 4.

Now that the input control leads of the modem have been taken care of, bounce over to the terminal port, summarized in Table 3–28. Leads 5, 6, 8, and 12 are the input control leads. Their corresponding functions are Clear to Send, Data Set Ready, Carrier Detect, and Speed Indicator. As before, look for the corresponding leads from the modem, noting their direction. Exactly the same lead numbers are provided by (from/out) the Hayes modem. Applying rules 1 and 2 as before, connect each of these leads independently from end to end in the cable. Specifically, connect lead 5 at one end of the cable to lead 5 at the other cable end. Repeat this for leads 6, 8, and 12. Table 3–41 outlines the completed control lead design, with the exception of leads 22 and 23.

Note that pin 22 is not supported by the Wyse terminal. For this reason, the cable design could include this lead for completeness, especially if a flat ribbon cable is to be used. The Hayes supports this lead and outputs a signal on lead 22 if an incoming call is detected. However, the Wyse terminal will ignore this signal.

The only remaining control lead is found on lead 23. This lead in both devices is the speed selection lead. The only conflict is that both devices output a signal on this lead. If we connect lead 23 from end to end in the cable, this would violate rule 2 of cable design. We SHOULD NOT connect two output leads together. Although the two devices may work together, damage could be caused by this, perhaps shorts or grounding out. It is highly recommended that these two leads not be connected. If a ribbon cable is being used, then cut lead 23 somewhere in the cable so that it does not pass from end to end in the cable.

8. Build the cable

9. Test for continuity

TABLE 3–40. DATA LEAD DESIGN FOR THE WYSE
WY-85-TO-HAYES SMARTMODEM 2400 CABLE

Function	Wyse lead #	Hayes lead #	Function
Transmit Data (out)	2 ------) 2		Transmit Data (in)
Receive Data (in)	3 (------ 3		Receive Data (out)

LEGEND: The "------)" indicates a "straight-through" connection from one end of the cable to the other. There are no "cross-overs." The arrow heads are used to indicate direction only.

TABLE 3–41. CONTROL LEAD DESIGN FOR TERMINAL-TO-MODEM CONNECTION

Function	Wyse lead #	Hayes lead #	Function
Request to Send (out)	4 ------)	4	Request to Send (in)
Clear to Send (in)	5 <------	5	Clear to Send (out)
Data Set Ready (in)	6 <------	6	Data Set Ready (out)
Data Carrier Detect (in)	8 <------	8	Data Carrier Detect (out)
Speed Mode Indication (in)	12 <------	12	High Speed Indicator
Data Terminal Ready (out)	20 ------)	20	Data Terminal Ready (in)

LEGEND: The "<------" and "------)" indicates a "straight-through" connection between the leads from one end of the cable to the other.

10. Cable the two systems together

Steps 8–10 should be completed in normal fashion. Consult the other chapters for tips on how to build the cable, noting that a flat ribbon cable may be used if pin 23 is snipped at some point. At one end of the cable should be a male connector, with a female connector at the other end. Check the cable for continuity in the normal manner, but double check to ensure that lead 23 does not pass from end to end in the cable. Once satisfied, cable the two systems together with the cable. The cable will only fit one way, as each device has the opposite gender of port. Securely fasten the cable to each port and proceed to measure your success in the next step.

11. Measure success

How will we know if we are successful in this terminal-to-modem connection? There are three milestones to reach. The first is to communicate locally between the terminal and the intelligent modem, the second is to communicate with a remote system, and the third is to regulate the flow of data between the two communicating systems. This third milestone will be the testing of software flow control, XON/XOFF.

Once the two systems are cabled together, power each of them up. First, let's look at the common options from step 1 of asynchronous operation, 2400 bps, 7 data bits, even parity, 1 stop bit, and full duplex operation. Set up these options following the standard procedures outlined in the user's manual. Specifically, we are interested in the "Comm" option setup, reached by hitting Function key 3 and Arrow keys.

Set up the terminal to these options by hitting the Function key 3, using the Right Arrow key to highlight the "Comm" screen label and the space bar to get into the communication subset of options. Set up the options as outlined in the compatibility step of this tutorial module. Use the Arrow keys to highlight the option and the space bar to step through the options to set them to

Transmit: 2400 bps

Receive: 2400 bps

Data Bits: 7

Parity: Even

Parity Check: Off

Echo: Off

Down Arrow key: Moves to next Comm subset

Handshake: XOFF

Stop Bits: 1

Port: EIA data (This is important until the modem is set up properly.)

Disconnect: 2 sec

Xmt Limit: none

Once set up, hit Function key 3, and position the highlight on the "Save" screen label using the Right Arrow and hit the space bar. This saves the options and returns you to the Online state of the terminal. If you have a break-out box, insert it between the terminal and modem at this time. You can monitor the RS232 activity

Digital Loopback Test

occurring between the two devices. If not, don't fret, as the conditions will be detailed in this text. Monitor the status of leads 15 and 17, as you will see the *timing* element spoken of in the RS232 interface as these leads will be fluctuating constantly. This represents the timing signals used in a synchronous environment. They are not used in our connection, as we are dealing with an asynchronous terminal.

When you have the terminal optioned and the Hayes Smartmodem 2400 has the factory setting of the options, be sure that the power is applied to both devices, and they are cabled. At the upper left position of the Wyse terminal, the word "LINE" should appear indicating that the terminal is in the Online mode. Hit the Return key a couple of times to see if any activity occurs. Probably nothing happens, except that you hear beeps when keys are depressed. This is due to the setting of the terminal options Port: EIA data and Echo: Off. The terminal ignores the status of the leads 5, 6, and 8 and relies on the "to be connected" system to echo back the characters as they are typed. The modem was set up to have leads 6 and 8 on whenever the modem is powered up, not to behave according to the RS232 standard, and thus not to indicate the true status of the line condition. Since there is no connection to a remote system, these two leads would normally be turned off. However, because the terminal is ignoring the leads, local communication with the modem is possible, regardless of the status of these leads. See the following "Caution."

Caution: If the option of the terminal is set up to be Port: EIA modem and the Hayes modem is set up to represent the actual state of the leads 5, 6, and 8, then you will not be able to communicate locally with the intelligent modem. At the same time, you will not be able to change the terminal option easily to be Port: EIA data. In the computer industry, this is known as a "deadly embrace," whereby two entities are each waiting for the other to take an action before they will/can do anything. In this case, the terminal needs these leads up, whereas the modem will bring them up only if a connection to a remote system is established. Once in this standoff situation, you cannot enter the terminal Option setup mode, or at least the author could not figure out how to do this. The only way around this was to fiddle around with the RS232 leads in the terminal's port. TURN THE TERMINAL OFF.

If you don't have a BOB, the idea is to "jumper" lead 4 or 20 back to leads 5, 6, and 8. Then turn the terminal back on. This should keep leads 5, 6, and 8 on, faking the terminal into believing that a connection is established. At this point, hit Function key 3 and reset the Port option to be "Port: EIA" data. Save these options so you don't get into this lockup position.

With the options on the terminal set correctly, hit the Return key a couple of times on the terminal keyboard. The cursor should advance down the screen a couple of lines. The modem is echoing these characters as it awaits command input. On the terminal keyboard, enter the characters "AT" followed by a Return. You should get an "OK" message. If not, it could be that your terminal is set up incorrectly or the modem is not set up according to the factory options. The factory options allow the modem to echo your commands and results. We will assume that this is occurring. If you are getting double characters, reset the terminal "Echo" option to "off."

Take a moment to go back into the terminal options. Check the speed of the terminal. If set per the previous instructions, the transmit and receive speeds are set to 2400 bps. If you have a BOB in the interface and monitor lead 12, it would be on, indicating that speeds of greater than 300 bps are being used. Change the transmit and receive speeds to be 300 bps. Then exit the option Setup mode. Now enter the same "AT" sequence from the terminal's keyboard followed by a Return key. The modem echoes the characters and gives you the same "OK" result message. This is part of the modem's built-in intelligence—to detect the correct speed to operate at. If a BOB was used, now pin 12 will be in the "off" state, indicating the 300 bps mode. This is the function of the speed indicator lead of the RS232 interface. To satisfy your curiosity, try the same test at 1200 bps and then return the speed options to 2400 bps, both transmit and receive speeds.

Entering the "AT" command wakes up the modem or gets it attention. Tutorial Module 1–7 goes into great detail about how to enter Hayes commands to operate the modem. However, we would like to show you how to change the Hayes modem so that leads 6 and 8 represent the actual status of the line. The Smartmodem 2400 modem is set up through commands entered at the attached device, not switches like the Smartmodem 1200.

All commands are preceded by the "AT" sequence. To fetch the factory configuration profile, enter "AT&F" followed by a Return key. This will restore to active memory the factory option settings. The sequence to change the modem so that leads 6 and 8 is done by setting one of the switches/registers in the modem. Enter the command "AT&C1&S1&W" followed by a Return key. This command sets the options so that the leads Carrier Detect and Data Set Ready indicate the actual status of the lines. If you have a break-out box between the two devices, the Data Set Ready and Carrier Detect lamps should go off once this command is successfully entered. Now these two leads will represent the actual state of the line condition. This may be desirable in your configuration.

To return this option to its previous state, enter the command sequence "AT&C&S&W" followed by a Return key. These two leads will now come back on in the interface.

With the factory settings in the modem, and the terminal set up as previously indicated, we have completed one-third of our measure for success: local communication with the intelligent modem. We should now test the ability to dial out and establish a connection to a remote system. We will access a remote UNIX system that has a 2400 bps modem. After this is complete, we will dial the same system's 1200 bps modem. Now for the actual dialing.

Plug the telephone line from the wall outline into the back of the Smartmodem 2400 modem port, labeled "to line." Make sure that you are not plugging the phone line into the "to phone" port as you will get a "NO DIALTONE:" message. At the terminal keyboard, enter the sequence "ATDT######" followed by a Return, substituting the phone number for the pound signs. The "D" instructs the modem to dial, with the "T" indicating touch-tone dialing. Substitute "P" if rotary dialing is normally used. Allow for access behind a PBX if appropriate, normally entering a "9" to get an outside line.

Upon entering the dialing command, you should hear the dialing. If the far-end computer system is set up to auto answer your call, and is powered up, then you should hear it answer the phone. Upon answer, you will hear a high-pitched-frequency answer tone or carrier. Momentarily, it will go away, indicating that you are online. The local modem will give you a message "CONNECT 2400," indicating that you are setup with the remote system at 2400 bps. If you are dialing a UNIX system, then it needs to figure out the speed that you are communicating at because its modem is more than likely multispeed. Hit the Return key once to allow the UNIX system to figure out the speed. In some cases the Break key may be needed instead of the Return key. Once you receive the login prompt, login as appropriate and proceed to the next section where we test for flow control. If you are getting garbled characters, check the character length and parity options to be sure that they match what the far end is expecting. The UNIX system that this author dialed into sent double prompts. Changing the option "Newline" to "off" cured this problem.

Let's try the same dialing sequence, but this time dialing to a 1200 bps modem on the UNIX system. For curiosity's sake, leave the terminal speed set to 2400. Once you are connected to the far end, the local modem will give you a message "CONNECT 1200," indicating that you have reached a 1200 bps modem. However, when you hit the Return key a couple of times to let the far end know your speed, you get garbage characters. This is because the terminal is outputting data at 2400 bps, yet the far end and modems are transmitting data at 1200 bps. With the connection still in place, bounce into the Option mode and change the Transmit and Receive Speed options to 1200 bps. Exit the Setup mode and then hit a couple of Return keys. Now you should get the "login:" message from the UNIX system. This assumes that your parity and characters match. You are now connected to the remote system and can proceed upon a successful login to test out the data flow control.

Whether you have dialed into a 2400 or 1200 bps modem, and have logged into the system, you need to feel comfortable that flow control is functioning. This is the third and final step of our testing to measure for a successful connection of the terminal and modem. Once you are into the remote system, you will be using software flow control to regulate the data flow. This is the XON/XOFF protocol, as it is often referred to. The easiest way to check this out is to have a long listing generated from the remote system. There are several ways to test this. One such way is to "cat" or display a file. Another way is to list the files in a lengthy directory, such as the "root" directory. Either way, generate a long listing. At some point during the reception of the data, halt the transmission of the data by entering an XOFF character. This is done by hitting a Control-s sequence on the terminal keyboard. If flow control is functioning, the outputting of data (and your reception of it) should halt. To resume enter a Control-q key sequence. This generates the XON character that, when received by the far-end computer, should be interpreted as the signal to resume outputting of the information. Repeat this to see the interactions. CONGRATULATIONS!

If for some reason your XOFF sequence does not halt the transmission of data, check your terminal option. Be sure that the Handshake option is set up to be XON/XOFF. If this end is set correctly, check with the remote system's administrator to ensure that software flow control is set up for the port you are dialing into, as well as for your particular ID. This can be extremely important if a printer is attached to the back of the terminal you are using. The printer will definitely at times need to halt the flow of data. The printer may run out of paper, be taken offline, or have some other error condition. The flow control option should work between a terminal and remote computer system before you give up on this tutorial module.

Tutorial Module 3-5: Connecting a Modem to a UNIX System

This tutorial module concerns the connection of a modem to a UNIX system. There are many possible modems that could be substituted in this tutorial module, as well as many different UNIX-based computers that could have been featured here. The idea will be to connect the system physically, but also to give the user a feel for the UNIX system setup necessary to add an intelligent modem. This will become increasingly more important as 80386 computers with UNIX enter the market. This tutorial module will give you a feeling for what is involved in connecting a Hayes or Hayes-compatible modem to a Pyramid Technology Corporation computer. Any UNIX system with an RS232 port can be substituted in this case study, providing that the appropriate cable can be designed.

This module will walk through the steps necessary to cable the modem to the computer successfully. The same steps (1–11) from previous tutorial modules will be followed here.

1. Determine compatibility

The UNIX operating system is known for its open architecture allowing many different types of devices to be interfaced and function well. The Pyramid Technology computers, featuring UNIX, support this principle of open architecture. The modem, for example, a QUBIE' 1200E, Penril DataComm Cadet 1200, Hayes 1200, or Hayes Smartmodem 2400, can be connected. The list of modems that will function with this type of computer system is almost endless. The key here is whether the modem is to be used for incoming calls only, outgoing calls only, or both. This dictates what setup must occur in the UNIX system as well as whether the "intelligence" in the modems is important. We are featuring a Hayes-compatible modem and will assume that the port is for incoming and outgoing calls. With UNIX's open architecture, and the "smarts" of the modem, outgoing and incoming calls are possible, making the two systems compatible.

To analyze the two systems, complete (SCS) (Software Cabling System) port profiles for each to determine common options. The Pyramid supports different speeds using an RS232 interface in its intelligent terminal processor (ITP) up to 19,200 bps; half or full duplex; 5, 6, 7, or 8 bits per character; odd, even, or no parity; with 1 to 2 stop bits in an asynchronous environment. There are multiple ports on the ITP offering these same options. Depending on the modem, the same options, other than speeds, are supported. In the case of the Penril, QUBIE', and Hayes Smartmodem 1200, the maximum speed supported is 1200 bps. Should a Hayes Smartmodem 2400 be used, then speeds up to 2400 bps are possible. The point here is that the two devices are compatible.

2. Determine signs of success

Once connected, how will the user know if they are successful? UNIX offers flexible communication capabilities. If you have properly designed, built, and connected the cable between the modem and UNIX system, along with correct optioning and UNIX system setup, the user should be able to place outgoing data calls using the intelligence of the modems. Specifically, UNIX offers the "cu" command, allowing the user to place a call from one of the terminals on the computer. This tutorial module will walk the user through setup and ultimately a call being placed from this system to another computer. If you are able to dial, establish a connection, and transmit and receive data, you will have achieved success.

3. Determine type of connector

The port analysis should continue for each device with the determination of the type of connector used on each system. The Pyramid ITP uses a 25-pin connector that provides RS232C-compatible signals. The modem also supports the same type and size of connector. Hence our cable for connecting the two systems will have DB25-type connectors at each end.

4. Determine gender of ports

The next step is to assess the gender of each port. Just about all (never say all) modems provide a female port, DB25S. The modems mentioned in this tutorial module conform to this conjecture. The Pyramid ITP's ports are male connectors. Hence our ultimate cable will have a male connector at one end with a female at the other end.

5. Determine leads (pins) provided by each device

6. Determine leads required to be on

The Pyramid ITP's port pinouts are listed in the user's manual listing the hardware specifications. On any ITP port connector, Transmit Data and Data Terminal Ready signals are provided. These signals are output from the ITP. They are found on leads 2 and 20, respectively. The usual ground leads are also provided on pins 1 and 7.

As for the leads that are required by the UNIX port, leads 3 and 8 are input signals to the ITP. The port looks for Receive Data and Data Carrier Detect signals to be transmitted from the modem to the port. This is

TABLE 3–42. PINOUTS FOR
PYRAMID TECHNOLOGY
CORPORATION'S ITP PORTS

Function	ITP lead #
Protective Ground	1
Signal Ground	7
Transmit Data (out)	2
Receive Data (in)	3
Request to Send (out)	4
Data Carrier Detect (in)	8
Data Terminal Ready (out)	20

NOTE: The documentation indicates that optionally eight leads instead of only the foregoing six can be used. This would include leads 5 and 6, Clear to Send and Data Set Ready. These signals are not required in our cable, but could be included for completeness.

true for most UNIX systems. The data lead is required for sure. However, the important point here is that Data Carrier Detect is almost always required to be on for the UNIX system to function. This stems from the conformity of the early UNIX systems to the RS232 standard. Lead 8 is Data Carrier Detect, and was present when a remote terminal had dialed into the computer, assuming full duplex. If the connection was broken, or the remote terminal disconnected purposely, then this lead turned off. UNIX capitalized on this to "kill" the process for that port. Once this lead turned on again, through another connection, UNIX began the appropriate process for activating the port. The same is true for a locally connected terminal. As long as the terminal is powered on, if the proper cable is used, this lead should be on. Refer to Tutorial Module 4–1 for specifics on a locally attached terminal to a UNIX system. This practice is not limited to UNIX systems; rather, it is used by many different computer systems. Table 3–42 summarizes the pinouts for the ITP port.

Now the reader should analyze the modem's port. Consult the modem's documentation to obtain the pinouts for the port (Tables 3–43, 3–44, 3–45, and 3–46). This tutorial module has alluded to the fact that a Hayes-compatible modem is being featured in this tutorial module. An important point here is that Hayes compatibility does not ensure that exactly the same port pinouts are present. Rather, Hayes compatibility implies that the modem at one end of a circuit can communicate with a Hayes at the other end. Furthermore, the Hayes offers a command set that has become a standard in the industry. Hayes compatibility implies that the commands used for dialing and disconnecting other systems will be the same as those in the Hayes Smartmodem 1200 command set. To repeat, this does not imply that the ports are exactly the same. The user can, however, be assured that they will be very similar. This tutorial module will list several intelligent modems that offer Hayes compatibility to point out that there a minor differences in the port pinouts.

TABLE 3–43. HAYES
SMARTMODEM 1200 PINOUTS

Function	Hayes lead #
Protective Ground	1
Transmit Data (in)	2
Receive Data (out)	3
Clear to Send (out)	5
Data Set Ready (out)	6
Signal Ground	7
Data Carrier Detect (out)	8
High Speed Indicator (out)	12
Data Terminal Ready (in)	20
Ring Indicator (out)	22

TABLE 3–44. HAYES
SMARTMODEM 2400 PINOUTS

Function	Hayes lead #
Protective Ground	1
Transmit Data (in)	2
Receive Data (out)	3
Request to Send (in)	4
Clear to Send (out)	5
Data Set Ready (out)	6
Signal Ground	7
Data Carrier Detect (out)	8
Select Alternate Rate (out)	12
Transmit Clock (out)	15
Receive Clock (out)	17
Data Terminal Ready (in)	20
Ring Indicator (out)	22
Select Alternate Rate (out)	23
Transmit Clock (DTE) (in)	24

NOTE: Pins 15, 17, and 24, are appropriate
only when the modem is being used in a synchronous environment, not in this tutorial module.

TABLE 3–45. QUBIE' 1200E MODEM
PINOUTS

Function	QUBIE' lead #
Protective Ground	1
Transmit Data (in)	2
Receive Data (out)	3
Request to Send (in)	4
Clear to Send (out)	5
Data Set Ready (out)	6
Signal Ground	7
Data Carrier Detect (out)	8
Data Terminal Ready (in)	20
Ring Indicator (out)	22

Your modem's pinouts may actually be a little different from those in Tables 3–43 through 3–46. The actual pinouts could affect the cable that you use. More than likely, a ''straight-through'' cable will be used to connect the modem to your computer, as most computer ports emulate DTE. This means that they provide the signals and directions in a port that is ready to be connected to a piece of DCE, such as an intelligent modem. Check to be sure!

7. Design the cable

You are now ready to design the cable necessary to connect the modem physically to your UNIX system. This cable will vary depending on the modem you are using and its required input signals as well as the options that are set. Before actually laying out the designs, it is important to point out a couple of possible modem options that impact the cable design.

Some modems, such as the Hayes Smartmodem 1200, offer an option that forces the DTR (pin 20) lead to be on, allowing execution of the modem's commands. If this option is on, then the DTR lead from the UNIX system may not need to be provided in the cable. However, if the option is not set to force this lead on automatically,

TABLE 3–46. PENRIL CADET 1200 MODEM PINOUTS

Function	Penril lead #
Protective Ground	1
Transmit Data (in)	2
Receive Data (out)	3
Clear to Send (out)	5
Data Set Ready (out)	6
Signal Ground	7
Data Carrier Detect (out)	8
Positive Test Voltage (out)	9
Negative Test Voltage (out)	10
Speed Indicate (out)	12
Data Terminal Ready (in)	20
Ring Indicator (out)	22

the lead from the attached computer must be provided for. This author recommends that the cable design provide for this lead regardless of the setting of this option. The reason for citing this distinction is for those cables that may have minimal leads available. This option could reduce the number of leads required.

All the modems featured here provide a DCE-type interface for direct connection to a piece of DTE or port-emulating DTE. Our UNIX system does indeed emulate DTE, implying that the signals from the RS232 standard normally provided and required are present in the Pyramid system. Because this tutorial module features four different modems with slightly different port pinouts, the cable designs will be shown separately. Notes will be provided explaining the minor differences in cable design. Refer to Tables 3–47 through 3–50 for actual cable designs necessary to connect the modems to the Pyramid Technology Corporation UNIX system. These conform to our cable design "rules" discussed at length in the other tutorial modules.

If you are using a different UNIX-based computer whose port does not provide pin 4, Request to Send, and a modem that does require pin 4 to be on, then the cable cannot be a "straight-through" one. However, minor alterations will make this cable work. Assume that your UNIX computer does not provide pin 4, but does provide lead 20 (output) and your modem requires it to be on. By jumpering the leads in Table 3–51 the two systems should work.

What if your UNIX-based computer port requires leads 5 and 6 to be on, but your modem only provides lead 8, Carrier Detect, as an output control signal? Fret not! The jumperings in Table 3–52 could be made to allow the modem to function with your system.

8. Build the cable

9. Test for continuity

TABLE 3–47. PYRAMID'S ITP UNIX PORT-TO-QUBIE' MODEM CABLE DESIGN

Function	ITP lead #	QUBIE' lead #	Function
Protective Ground	1 -------	1	Protective Ground
Transmit Data (out)	2 -------	2	Transmit Data (in)
Receive Data (in)	3 -------	3	Receive Data (out)
Request to Send (out)	4 -------	4	Request to Send (in)
Signal Ground	7 -------	7	Signal Ground
Data Carrier Detect (in)	8 -------	8	Data Carrier Detect (out)
Data Terminal Ready (out)	20 -------	20	Data Terminal Ready (in)

NOTES: A "straight-through" ribbon cable with all 25 leads will work here. Leads 5 and 6 are optional, as the Pyramid system does not require them.

TABLE 3–48. PYRAMID'S ITP UNIX PORT-TO-PENRIL DATACOMM
CADET MODEM CABLE DESIGN

Function	ITP lead #	CADET lead #	Function
Protective Ground	1 ------- 1		Protective Ground
Transmit Data (out)	2 ------- 2		Transmit Data (in)
Receive Data (in)	3 ------- 3		Receive Data (out)
Signal Ground	7 ------- 7		Signal Ground
Data Carrier Detect (in)	8 ------- 8		Data Carrier Detect (out)
Data Terminal Ready (out)	20 ------- 20		Data Terminal Ready (in)

NOTES: A ''straight-through'' ribbon cable with all 25 leads will work here. Leads 5 and 6 are optional, as the Pyramid system does not require them. Note that lead 4 is absent, as the Penril modem does not support it. A cable with lead 4 present will still work properly. Also, the Penril pinouts have more than the foregoing leads present. Because the Pyramid does not require them, or use them, they are ignored.

TABLE 3–49. PYRAMID'S ITP UNIX PORT-TO-HAYES SMARTMODEM
1200 MODEM CABLE DESIGN

Function	ITP lead #	HAYES lead #	Function
Protective Ground	1 ------- 1		Protective Ground
Transmit Data (out)	2 ------- 2		Transmit Data (in)
Receive Data (in)	3 ------- 3		Receive Data (out)
Signal Ground	7 ------- 7		Signal Ground
Data Carrier Detect (in)	8 ------- 8		Data Carrier Detect (out)
Data Terminal Ready (out)	20 ------- 20		Data Terminal Ready (in)

NOTES: A ''straight-through'' ribbon cable with all 25 leads will work here. Leads 5 and 6 are optional, as the Pyramid system does not require them. Note that lead 4 is absent, as the Hayes modem does not support it. A cable with lead 4 present will still work properly. Also, the Hayes pinouts have more than the foregoing leads present. Because the Pyramid does not require them, or use them, they are ignored.

TABLE 3–50. PYRAMID'S ITP UNIX PORT-TO-HAYES SMARTMODEM
2400 MODEM CABLE DESIGN

Function	ITP lead #	HAYES lead #	Function
Protective Ground	1 ------- 1		Protective Ground
Transmit Data (out)	2 ------- 2		Transmit Data (in)
Receive Data (in)	3 ------- 3		Receive Data (out)
Request to Send (out)	4 ------- 4		Request to Send (in)
Signal Ground	7 ------- 7		Signal Ground
Data Carrier Detect (in)	8 ------- 8		Data Carrier Detect (out)
Data Terminal Ready (out)	20 ------- 20		Data Terminal Ready (in)

NOTES: A ''straight-through'' ribbon cable with all 25 leads will work here. Leads 5 and 6 are optional, as the Pyramid system does not require them. Also, the Hayes pinouts have more than the foregoing leads present. Because the Pyramid does not require them, or use them, they are ignored.

10. Cable the two systems together

The next three steps should be completed in the normal fashion. Note the gender requirements of the cable. Your computer port may vary, but more than likely it will be male, with the modem port being female. Hence, build the cable accordingly, with a female connector for the computer end and a male plug at the modem

TABLE 3–51. INPUT CONTROL LEAD CONNECTIONS FOR MODEM

Function	Computer lead #		Modem lead #	Function
Data Terminal Ready (out)	20	---|--)	4	Request to Send (in)
		|--)	20	Data Terminal Ready (in)

TABLE 3–52. INPUT CONTROL LEAD CONNECTIONS FOR COMPUTER

Function	Computer lead #		Modem lead #	Function
Clear to Send (in)	5	⟨--|---	8	Data Carrier Detect (out)
Data Set Ready (in)	6	⟨--|		
Data Carrier Detect (in)	8	⟨--|		

end. Be sure that continuity for the individual conductors exists according to your design. Connect the two systems together once you are satisfied that the proper cable has been built and tested.

11. Measure success

As indicated earlier, the actual success of our connection will be the ability to use the modem to place a call to a remote system for transmitting and receiving information. However, beyond physically connecting the modem to the computer, other items must be tended to. Specifically, the UNIX operating system has some requirements for defining the port, as well as the modem. The systems administrator should be involved to ensure proper setup. Several files are involved including gettydefs, Devices, and /dev entries. The user should ensure that the "basic networking utilities" are installed. The next section describes some typical entries for UNIX system. Your actual entries may vary slightly, but the same type of information should be used. An explanation of the normal location of the appropriate systems files, and their syntax, will be provided.

First, check the port to which the modem is being connected. The appropriate drivers must be installed, as well as defined. UNIX provides the "tty" drivers, or they may be supplied as you purchase the ports board. However they are obtained, the port must be defined properly for connection of a modem.

Consult with the systems administrator to ensure that this is done. To summarize what is required to add a modem to a System V UNIX system, entries must be made in several system files. An entry is required in the /etc/inittab, /usr/lib/uucp/Devices, and /usr/lib/uucp/Dialers files to turn on the port.

The format of the entry in the inittab file is: "id:rstate:action:process". The explosion of the parameters of such an entry are as follows:

> id = usually last two digits of the tty number
> rstate = runstate

> where
> > 2—multiuser by convention
> > 3—net state starting w/ SVR3
> > s—single user state
> > 0—powerdown
> > 5—firmware state

> action = what to do in this state
> respawn—if the process stops, generate a new one

process = the program to run; usually /etc/getty. With SVR2 at AT&T, /usr/lib/uucp/uugetty has been used to allow a modem be used for both outgoing and incoming communications.

An example entry for a Hayes Smartmodem 1200 used in an AT&T 3B2 UNIX System environment is as follows:

> "14:2:respawn:/etc/getty tty14 1200".

Digital Loopback Test

If the modem is going to be used for communications with other systems either with uucp, or even with cu, an entry in the /usr/lib/uccp/Devices file is needed. The format is: "Type Line Line2 Class Dialer-Token Pairs" where:

Type = Direct—provides a way to communicate directly with the modem. This is convenient for manually setting soft options

= ACU—indicates that the modem is the autodial type. There are other entries possible for data pbx's or for hard wired connections to other systems.

Line = the tty port to which the modem is connected.

Line2 = indicates the port to which an external dialing device would be attached. Place a hyphen here as a null entry

Class = indicates the speed, although in some installations it is a way to differentiate modems of the same speed which are attached to different networks.

Dialer = Token pairs—usually indicates which entry in the Dialers file contains the template for calling another system.

A sample entry for a Hayes Smartmodem 1200 could be:

"ACU tty14—1200 hayes"

The /usr/lib/uucp/Dialers file contains entries that provide a template for calling another system. It is of the form: "dialer substitutions expect-send pairs" format, where:

dialer—matches the entry in the Dialer-Tokens pairs entry
in the Devices file.
substitutions—mappings from the 801 automatic calling unit
characters where = means "wait for dialtone" and—
means
"pause for"
expect-send pairs—the template to the dial function in the
form of
expected responses and sent characters. Escapes exist
to indicate
pause ($\frac{1}{4}$ to $\frac{1}{2}$ sec), delay($\sim$2 sec), telephone number,
etc

An entry for Hayes could be:

"hayes   =,−,   """ \dAT\r\c\ OK\r \EATDT\T\r\c\ CONNECT"

The files, Devices and Dialers, are used in a version of uucp, referred to as HoneyDanBer, which is the current version. In the older versions of uucp, the Devices file was L.dev, and the autodialer information was not supported directly. Hence it was usually embedded in the L.sys file. To clarify which version you have, as well as to better understand the entries and interactions of the files, please contact the systems administrator. The appropriate UNIX System V manuals contain this information in greater detail.

Once these entries have been made, attempt to test the system and modem capabilities. From a terminal on the system, login as you normally would. This tutorial module assumes that you have permission to access the modem for outgoing calls. If this is not the case, "beat up" on the systems administrator. Well, maybe you should just consult with him or her to obtain access to a modem that supports outgoing traffic. Our tutorial module will use the "cu" command, short for Call UNIX, to test the outgoing capability of the system.

The "cu" command allows a user to establish a connection between two systems. The remote system you are attempting to call does not have to be another UNIX system. The key is that the remote system have a compatible modem and that you have permission to login to the system. The reference to a compatible modem here is not one of "Hayes" compatibility. The issue is the speed and modulation technique used. AT&T established the standard for low-speed modems (i.e., 1200 bps). Its modem, model 212A, is the standard for full duplex, 1200 bps, asynchronous, dial-up modems. This same model can communicate with 103J modems and compatibles. If your local modem is a 212A-compatible modem, then the remote systems should offer 212A- or 103J-compatible communications. If you are using a 2400 bps modem, such as the Hayes Smartmodem 2400, it is compatible with the 212As, at the lower speed of 1200. The point here is that the remote modem should be compatible with yours.

The cu command necessary to dial out of your UNIX system and connect to a remote system is as follows:

cu [-s speed] [-l line] [-h] [-t] [-ol-e] telno | systemname [1]

To dial another computer within our scenario, the command line would be as simple, as follows:

cu -s 1200 5551212   (followed by the enter key)

Some UNIX systems require that a ''-l line'' be given. Do so if your system needs it. Furthermore, if the administrator has ''named'' another computer (i.e., made an entry in the /usr/lib/uucp/Systems files), you can substitute the system name instead of the phone number. This author has an entry for the AT&T electronic mail service, called ATTMAIL, so the command would be ''cu -s 1200 attmail.'' If there is a problem locally, you will get an error message that identifies the source of the problem. Furthermore, all the modems could be in use. In this case, the UNIX system would give you a message similar to ''Connect failed: DEVICE LOCKED'' or ''Connect failed: DEVICE UNAVAILABLE.'' Try again in a few moments.

If you are successful in dialing and connecting to a remote computer, the local UNIX system will give you a message, ''Connected,'' or something similar. At this point, hit the Enter key several times so the proper speed can be set up between the two machines. You should receive a ''login:'' prompt of some kind, depending on which remote system you dialed. If you reach the point where you get this prompt, you have reached ''third base''; you are almost home. Enter your login ID as you normally would.

The only thing left to check is whether the parity, character length, duplex, and line-ending sequences are correct. If the characters are garbled, check the speed, parity, and character-length options. If you don't see what you type, other than a password entry, then the duplex needs to be changed to half duplex. Check the cu command for this option, ''-h.'' If you overwrite each line, then the line-ending sequence should be changed to line feed, as UNIX expects this. If you are double spacing when single spacing is desired, the far end may be sending multiple line feeds. Change these options as appropriate. If necessary, disconnect and retry the ''cu'' command with the new options. Disconnecting may be accomplished by entering a ''~.'' (''tilde period'') and the Enter key. CONGRATULATIONS! The outdialing capability of the system has been tested.

What about the incoming capabilities? What if a remote user is wanting access to your UNIX system through the newly connected modem? That user will dial your number and expect a UNIX ''login:'' prompt upon establishing a connection. Will the modem on the UNIX system automatically answer the incoming call? That depends on the settings within the modem. Be sure that the modem has been optioned to answer incoming calls automatically. If the UNIX port is on, and the modem has this option set correctly, the incoming call will be answered by the modem. This is 50 percent of the test, the ability to establish a connection from a remote device calling into a UNIX system. The systems administrator must also set up appropriate entries in the file so that once the UNIX system answers the call, a ''login'' prompt will be started. A sample entry for this was highlighted earlier in this section.

If both of these are tended, and the phone line is connected properly to the modem, attempt to dial into the UNIX system. Once the UNIX system modem receives ringing, it should answer the call and return carrier back to you. From the user's PC or terminal, hit the Return/Enter key several times. This allows the UNIX system to determine the speed with which to operate. Once it figures the speed, the user should see the ''login:'' prompt. Enter your login ID followed by a Return key. Then key in the password if prompted. Your login ID should have been echoed back to you from the UNIX system, with the password not echoed.

If the far-end UNIX system does not answer the call, check that you are dialing the correct number. Redial if appropriate. If the modem does not answer your call, the modem is misoptioned, powered off, improperly

---

[1] -s option is for setting the desired speed (1200).
-l option is for selecting the device (default is usually fine).
-h option is for ''half duplex'' or local echo (fdx is assumed).
-t option is used when dialing an ASCII terminal (ignore here).
-ol-e is used to set the parity to (o)dd or (e)ven.
telno | systemname is used to enter a telephone number or system name:
   (= is used for secondary dial tone, i.e., 9=13145551212.
   − is used for delays).

connected to the phone line, not connected to the UNIX system, not cabled properly to the UNIX system, or defective. Check each of these to ensure that all pieces are properly connected and functioning.

If you do get the far-end modem to answer your call, but you are not receiving the "login" prompt, then either the UNIX system entries are incorrect or your line settings are way off. Be sure that your local PC or terminal is properly connected to its modem, with the options set per outlined in the terminal or PC-to-modem tutorial modules. The options of speed, character length, parity, and stop bits should be double checked. If they are correct, then the systems administrator for the UNIX system should be consulted to ensure that the modem's port will initiate a login prompt upon auto answer of your incoming call.

If you do get the "login" prompt, but are not successful logging in, reenter the login sequences when prompted. If you are still not successful, check to see that your login ID is correct. Also be sure that the password is entered correctly. Often, the parity, speed, and character lengths cause problems. Make sure that your settings match those expected by the UNIX system. Consult the section on line settings to cure the problems of double characters, double spacing, overwriting, and so on. Correct them to enable you to receive and send characters correctly. CONGRATULATIONS!

Tutorial Module 3-6: Connecting Modems or Digital Service Units (DSUs) in a 3270 Point-to-Point Environment

As PCs have become increasingly prevalent, a significant number of modems have been required to connect these personal computers to other computer systems. The bulk of these have been asynchronous modems, as discussed in the other tutorial modules. However there is another world of connectivity that deals with synchronous modems. This world is made up of products such as 3270s, 2780/3780s, mainframes, packet devices, or emulators running on different computers.

In the synchronous world, product families are typically connected to larger computers for online-type applications, batch file transfers, or host-to-host communications. IBM has been a major proponent of synchronous communications for support of its online mainframe applications. This section will not delve into the specifics of an SNA architecture, or any other synchronous architectures. However, the user should recognize these terms. Vendors of a specific network architecture offer introductory materials that explain the goal, design, and plans for their network offerings. The reader is encouraged to consult this documentation for future references.

What is this tutorial module going to cover? One of the more difficult components of a synchronous network is timing. Synchronous modems have various options that can be set for an optimal network. Furthermore, often the setting of those options determines the cables required to connect the modems to the computers, printers, nodes, or other modems. This module will highlight these two areas of timing options and the resulting cables in a point-to-point circuit. Modems will be featured here, although digital service units (DSUs) for digital networks can be substituted through this and the next tutorial module. If you are dealing in a multipoint circuit, refer to Tutorial Module 3–7. The standard steps for connection will be followed, but first it is worthwhile to cover some basic definitions involved in synchronous connections.

Point-to-Point

A point-to-point circuit is a network whereby two devices are connected with a circuit. This circuit can be provided by telephone wires, twisted pair, microwave, or satellite connections. The media used will not impact our cabling and connections. The important point is that the connection is viewed as depicted in Figure 3–11. This is shown to distinguish it from the multipoint networks that will be covered in the next tutorial module. The connection between the two endpoints can be either a permanent/private line or a dial-up connection. Slight variances occur in the required RS232 cables and optioning. This module will assume a private line and will point out some of the differences in a dial-up environment.

Figure 3–11. Point-to-point connections.

Timing

In all the other tutorial modules, timing was not a factor in the connections. This was due to the nature of the asynchronous mode of operation. Each character, framed by a start and stop bit, provides the timing function. This is in sharp contrast with the synchronous networks that require one or more timing sources to function.

The devices that are attached to the network rely on a timing source to dictate the rate at which they transmit and receive data. One of the devices—the computer, modem, node, or mainframe—should provide the timing. The RS232 interface allows for the use of such timing leads. The EIA standard offers three leads to accommodate this requirement. Refer to "RS232 Made Easy" for further description of the leads, though this discussion provides a synopsis of the functions of the leads.

The RS232 standard sets aside three leads to be used for timing. The three leads are Transmit Timing, Receive Timing, and another Transmit Timing. These leads are found on pins 15, 17, and 24, respectively. The Transmit Timing is a signal that indicates the rate at which devices should send their data. Think of this as a clock pulse, a very quick one. Typical speeds in synchronous environment range from 1200 to 1.5 mbps, with 9600 being a very common speed. Devices connected together latch onto this timing source and use it to regulate the flow of data bits.

The reason for two Transmit Timing leads is that, relative to a device, the transmit timing can be internal or external. For example, if a mainframe is connected to a synchronous modem as depicted in Figure 3–12, there are a couple of possible sources of timing. In most cases, the modem (network) should provide the timing. If the modem in our diagram provides the transmit timing, this is an output signal found on lead 15 of the RS232 interface. The attached mainframe can then use this rate, an input signal, to transmit its data.

However, there are those instances where it is desirable for the mainframe to provide the timing. If this is the case, then pin 15 is not used. Rather, the second transmit timing lead, pin 24, is used for the timing signal. The RS232 standard refers to this as the Transmit Timing–DTE source. This distinguishes it from the DCE-provided timing found on lead 15, sources from the modem, or other communication device. If the DTE is to provide the timing, then the modem will look for a timing source on lead 24 to transmit the data actually over the network. It is important to note the direction of the lead. If lead 24 is used, or DTE-provided Transmit Timing, lead 24 is input to the modem and output from the DTE (mainframe). In the other case of DCE-provided Transmit Timing, the timing source on lead 15 is from the modem and to the DTE.

Receive timing. The Receive Timing is the opposite of the Transmit Timing in that this rate is the speed at which a device will receive data. The RS232 standard dedicates lead 17 for this function. The source of the Receive Timing in Figure 3–12 is the modem, which is typical. As such, the Receive Timing signal is an output signal from the DCE (modem) to the DTE (mainframe).

Timing options. Now that a general understanding surrounding timing leads and their function has been established, certain options need to be covered. Specifically, devices will commonly offer the options of internal versus external timing, as well as slave timing. Each of these deserves special attention, as they will impact the cables that will be required when connecting synchronous devices together.

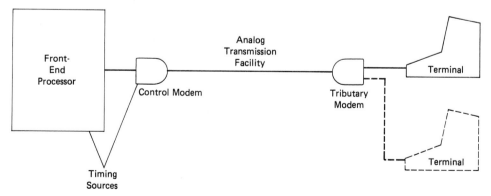

Figure 3–12. Two timing sources.

1. INTERNAL VERSUS EXTERNAL TIMING. Probably the most significant keyword involved in understanding timing options is "relative." If a device is optioned for internal timing, then the timing is internal relative to that device. In our example from Figure 3–12, the modem was to provide the timing. To have this occur, the modem should be optioned for "internal timing." This implies that the modem is to provide timing, and this timing source will occur on lead 15 of the RS232 interface.

However, in this same setup, when optioning the mainframe or communication processor, the timing option would be set to external. Relative to the computer, the timing is to be provided by an external source, the modem.

Sounds simple enough! The purpose for this belaboring is the RS232 interface. If a modem is optioned for internal timing, the timing lead is an output signal from the modem on lead 15. If, however, the modem is optioned for external timing, the timing is an input signal found on lead 24.

This is just the opposite at the attached device (mainframe). If the mainframe is optioned for external timing, then it looks to lead 15 for the timing signal. If it is optioned for internal timing, then it provides an output signal on lead 24. This will be true of the relationship between any piece of DTE and DCE. Remember "relative"!

2. SLAVE TIMING. One other timing option is that of slave timing. Slave timing refers to an ability of a piece of equipment, usually a modem (DCE), to derive timing from the signal that it receives from the circuit. The modem then uses this derived timing signal as its transmit timing. An example is in order!

Refer to Figure 3–13, which represents the other end of our point-to-point circuit. If the modem in the figure is optioned for slave timing, then it will monitor the signals that it receives from the network (or other modem) and derive a clock signal. This timing signal is looped up to the Transmit Timing component of the modem. Through the RS232 interface, this derived Transmit Timing signal is then provided on lead 15 of the interface to the attached DTE. In our example, the 3270 controller has no idea of this option, as it is getting its timing signal on lead 15 of the interface, just as it is used to getting.

The key here is that in this circuit there is a single source of timing. The Transmit Timing signal, provided by the modem in Figure 3–11, is that single source. This signal, originated by the clock in this modem, is received at the far-end modem in Figure 3–13. This received signal is presented to the attached 3270 controller on lead 17, but also looped up to become that modem's Transmit Timing signal. This signal is then received back at the original end of the circuit (the mainframe's modem). From this signal, the Receive Timing signal is derived and passed to the mainframe on lead 17. The goal in designing any synchronous network is to minimize the number of timing sources. Limiting it to one is usually the most desirable to maintain "synchronization" throughout the network.

Having covered some key definitions, this tutorial module will proceed to the step-by-step procedure of connecting a mainframe and a 3270 controller together with synchronous modems in a point-to-point network. Figure 3–14 lays out the desired connection. We will now follow the standard guidelines for connecting devices. These connections will involve the use of three or four port profiles, as multiple modems and other devices are involved.

1. Determine compatibility

2. Determine signs of success

Should this connection work? Greater powers than you and I say that it will, including the mammoths, AT&T and IBM. I will take their word for it. Actually, the SCS port profiles should be completed in the normal fashion. Consult the documentation to fill in the blanks. If you have the luxury of owning a break-out box, connect it to one of the modems. Monitor lead 15 of one of the modems. Be sure that the modem is optioned

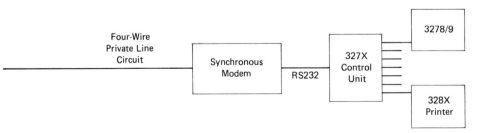

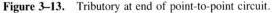

Figure 3–13. Tributary at end of point-to-point circuit.

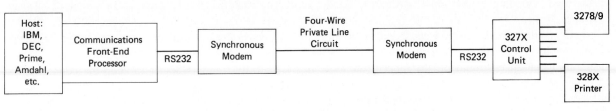

Figure 3–14. Mainframe-to-3270 point-to-point circuit.

for internal timing. Lead 15 should be on. Actually, it should be fluctuating at such a rapid rate that it appears to be on at all times. This rapid fluctuation, often not noticeable because of the speed, is the timing signal. Refer to steps 5 and 6 for the completed Port Profiles.

The signs of success are not that easily pinned down in these connections. Mere successful connection and optioning of the devices does not guarantee success. Many other elements enter the picture. Some include the circuit itself, the mainframe and communication processor software, the 3270 cluster options, the attached 3270 device options, and so on. This list goes on, but you should be confident that the cabling between the modems and their associated devices is correct. Furthermore, you should be sure that the timing options are tended to. The ultimate signs of success are your abilities to send and receive data over the network. It is not possible for this tutorial module to delve into all the different scenarios to walk the reader through all the testing. Work closely with the systems analysts and vendors to strive for the ability to communicate between the devices.

3. Determine type of connector

4. Determine gender of ports

Most pieces of DTE in the mainframe environment have DB25P (male) ports, while the DCE (modems) typically have female connectors. Not all 25 pins are required, but the connector is a 25 pin/socket connector.

5. Determine leads (pins) provided by each device

6. Determine leads required to be on

There are four ports involved in this connection. The first port to be analyzed is the communication processor. Most mainframes provide channels, which are used to connect to secondary devices. These devices are typically disk drive systems, tape systems, or communication systems. In our tutorial module, a communication processor will be assumed, although your connection may vary from this. The communication processor's role is to allow multiple slower-speed ports to work through only a single channel on the mainframe.

The communication processor, often referred to as a front-end processor (FEP), is a channel-attached device. This means that it is connected to the mainframe through one of the channels. On the network side of the FEP, RS232 ports are provided. This is where our modem will be connected. In IBM vernacular, a model 3074, 3705, or 3725 is common. If other mainframes are used, the term ''communication adapter'' is common. Whatever is present in your configuration, perform port analysis on the RS232 port that is to be connected to the modem. For ease of reference, we will refer to the modem connected to the FEP or communication adapter as ''control.'' The far-end modem will be the ''tributary'' modem.

Protective Ground and Signal Ground for the FEP conform to the RS232 standard. Protective Ground is found on lead 1, while Signal Ground is on lead 7. Depending on the attached modem, Protective Ground may or may not be used. Our scenario will use it for complete electrical short protection.

The data leads of a FEP port are also fairly straightforward. Transmit data are found on lead 2 of the port. It is an output signal and is used by the FEP to send data to the far end, through the modems. The FEP looks on lead 3 for its Received Data.

With most FEPs, the port can be set up to be full duplex or half duplex. In a point-to-point connection, full duplex should be used. The reason for this is that milliseconds of delays occur in a half duplex environment. Furthermore, there is no advantage of half duplex in a point-to-point environment, when a private line connection exists between the two endpoints. When the FEP is optioned for FDX, Request to Send (pin 4) will be on whenever the port is active. Regardless of the condition of lead 5, Clear to Send, or whether data are being sent or not, Request to Send will be on. This differs from half duplex. If optioned for HDX, the FEP will only raise Request to Send, if it is ready to send some data. The attached modem will only raise Clear to Send in response to this if the circuit is not being used by the other end device. Recall that HDX implies that two-way, non-simultaneous transmission is possible, allowing only one end to transmit data at a time. Assume that FDX is being used. This implies that pin 4, Request to Send, will be on when the port is active as an output signal from the FEP.

Depending on the FEP, Data Terminal Ready, pin 20, may also be provided when the port is active. Synchronous private line modems usually ignore this lead, whereas synchronous dial-up modems depend on this lead. In a dial-up environment, the modem monitors this lead to determine whether to keep the connection or disconnect. When Data Terminal Ready is on, the modem will keep the connection. If Data Terminal Ready is lowered (turned off) by the FEP, the modem will drop the line, causing a disconnect. Our point-to-point private line modem will ignore this lead as the circuit is present at all times. For completeness, indicate in the SCS Port Profiles that this lead is present.

With leads 4 and 20 being the two output control signals of the port, what control leads are required by the FEP? The common signals specified by the RS232 standard are Clear to Send, Data Set Ready, and Receive Line Signal Detector. These are found on leads 5, 6, and 8. Clear to Send is the signal that the FEP looks at to determine if the channel is available to send data on. This is only appropriate in a half duplex environment. Our scenario is full duplex, so the circuit is always free for the mainframe to send data. Hence, the FEP typically ignores this signal.

Data Set Ready, lead 6, is the signal that the FEP looks at to determine if the modem is on. In a private line modem, Data Set Ready will be on if the modem has power applied to it. This is in contrast with a dial-up synchronous modem. Most dial-up synchronous modems turn this lead on only once the connection is established. This tutorial module will assume that the FEP expects this lead to be on, even though the modem should provide this if it has power to it.

Received Line Signal Detect, lead 8, is monitored by the FEP. If this lead is on, then the far-end (tributary) 3270 controller has its Request to Send lead on. This is the case if the 3270's modem is optioned for Switched Carrier, Switched Request to Send. Carrier is transmitted whenever the 3270 controller turns on Request to Send. This will send a signal to the FEP end found on lead 8. This lead is commonly referred to as Carrier Detect because the far end, through its Request to Send lead, is causing its modem to transmit carrier to the mainframe. This carrier is detected by the FEP modem, and the signal on lead 8 provides the status. If the lead is on, then carrier is detected from the far end. If no carrier is detected, lead 8 will be off. If this lead is off, the far end does not have its Request to Send lead on, one of the modems is powered off or faulty, or there is a problem in the private line. Nonetheless, this is a very important lead for the FEP. It is even more important in the tutorial module for multipoint private lines.

We have covered the ground, data, and control leads of a synchronous port on a mainframe communication processor. What about the timing leads of a synchronous port? After all, these leads are what distinguished a synchronous environment from an asynchronous one. Refer back to the first part of this tutorial module for definitions of the various timing options. Most FEPs offer the capability to provide the timing for a network. This author recommends that you let the network (modems or DSUs) provide the timing. If you do, the FEP will be optioned for external timing, which means that the attached communication device will provide the timing.

According to the RS232 standard, DCE-provided timing is found on lead 15, Transmit Timing. The FEP looks on lead 15 for the clock pulse with which it should output data. Hence, lead 15 is an input signal. The Receive Timing lead is found on pin 17. The FEP will receive its data at the rate found on this lead, implying that this too is an input signal. This completes the lead analysis for the FEP port. As a reminder, your port may differ slightly in the control category and protective ground leads; however, the data and timing leads will probably match 100 percent. Table 3–53 outlines the completed port profile for the FEP. Adjust yours accordingly.

The next port to be analyzed will be that of the modem or digital service unit. Because each modem at both ends of the circuit will be the same, this tutorial module will analyze only one of them. Duplicate the port profiles for the far-end modem or DSU. The only difference between the two could be the option settings relating to timing. As this tutorial module proceeds, this potential difference will be exploited.

First the ground leads. Protective Ground is found on lead 1, just as the standard states. Signal Ground is on pin 7 of the interface.

As for the data leads, they are no different from most modems. Transmit Data is an input lead found on pin 2. It will receive data on this lead from the attached piece of DTE and send it out over the circuit. The actual Receive Data lead, pin 3, is used by the modem to present the data it receives from the circuit to the attached device. Hence, pin 3 is an output signal from the modem or DSU to the attached device.

What about the control leads for the modem or DSU? The standard allows for leads 4, 5, 6, 8, and 20 to be used for control leads. Ring Indicator and the secondary leads are not important in this point-to-point private line environment, so they are ignored. Of these five leads, which are input and which are output, or which are provided versus required by the modem?

TABLE 3–53. IBM 3705 FRONT-END PROCESSOR PORT PROFILE

Computer Port Profile

Underline if supported; circle if selected.

Model: 3705 front-end proc. __ Vendor: IBM _____ Port: synchronous

Port type: <u>serial</u> parallel
Port: <u>DB25</u> 9-pin 5-pin 8-pin/modular 20mA Centronics

Gender: <u>male</u> female

Pin #	Function	Direction	Pin #	Function	Direction
1	Frame Ground	to from <u>n/a</u>	14	_____	to from n/a
2	Transmit Data	to <u>from</u> n/a	15	Transmit Timing	<u>to</u> from n/a
3	Receive Data	<u>to</u> from n/a	16	_____	to from n/a
4	Request to Send	to <u>from</u> n/a	17	Receive Timing	<u>to</u> from n/a
5	Clear to Send	<u>to</u> from n/a	18	_____	to from n/a
6	Data Set Ready	<u>to</u> from n/a	19	_____	to from n/a
7	Signal Ground	to from <u>n/a</u>	20	Data Terminal Ready	to <u>from</u> n/a
8	Receive Line Signal Detector	<u>to</u> from n/a	21	_____	to from n/a
9	_____	to from n/a	22	_____	to from n/a
10	_____	to from n/a	23	_____	to from n/a
11	_____	to from n/a	24	_____	to from n/a
12	_____	to from n/a	25	_____	to from n/a
13	_____	to from n/a			

Complete the next section only with 36-pin cinch connector.

Pin #	Function	Direction	Pin #	Function	Direction
26	_____	to from n/a	27	_____	to from n/a
28	_____	to from n/a	29	_____	to from n/a
30	_____	to from n/a	31	_____	to from n/a
32	_____	to from n/a	33	_____	to from n/a
34	_____	to from n/a	35	_____	to from n/a
36	_____	to from n/a			

Flow control technique: XON/XOFF ENQ/ACK STX/ETX Hardware protocol
Leads that must be on: 5 6 8 __ __ __ __

Options:
Speeds: <u>110 300 600 1200 1800 2400 4800</u> (9600) 19.2 56k _____
Parity: <u>even odd space mark none</u>
Char-length: <u>7 8</u> __
stop bits: <u>1 1.5 2</u>
Line-ending sequence: cr 1f cr/1f cr/1f/1f
Disconnect sequence: EOT DEL ~. _____
Mode: async sync isoch   sync timing leads:

#	Function	Direction
15	Transmit	(to) from
17	Receive	(to) from
24	Transmit	to <u>from</u>

Notes: The flow control is left up to the protocol that is defined for the port. Normally, the attached modem should provide the timing.

The output signals from the modem are Clear to Send, Data Set Ready, and Received Line Signal Detector. These signals are used to provide status information to the attached device. Clear to Send, lead 5, is turned on by the modem upon receipt of a Request to Send signal. Hence, pins 4 and 5 work closely together. In a full duplex environment, the DTE will keep Request to Send on at all times; hence, the modem will turn on Clear to

Send. Clear to Send is used by the modem to provide a status of the "readiness" of the modem and circuit for data transmission.

Not all modems have the options Continuous Carrier, Switched Request to Send or Continuous Request to Send. However, if yours provides it, the modem should be optioned for Continuous Carrier, Continuous Request to Send so the modem will continuously transmit carrier to the far end and provide Clear to Send on whenever Request to Send is on. Refer to the section on multipoint private lines for further information about this option and its relevance. For this exercise, set the option for continuous versus switched carrier. Refer to Tutorial Module 3–7 on multipoint circuits for the use of the Switched Carrier, Switched Request to Send discussion. Hence, pin 4 is an input signal, whereas pin 5 is an output signal from the modem.

In a private line environment, the synchronous modem will turn on Data Set Ready, pin 6, whenever the modem has power. The exception to this is when the modem is in an error condition or is malfunctioning. Data Set Ready is, however, an output lead from the modem. If a dial-up synchronous modem were being used, this lead would be active once a connection were established. However, in our private line modem, this lead is on at all times, barring any error conditions. This lead is used to provide the "status" of the modem or data set.

Lead 8 is an important one for our environment. The modem uses this lead to provide the status of the actual line. Received Line Signal Detector, or Carrier Detect, will be on depending on the far-end's condition. The state of this lead is determined by the condition of the far-end's Request to Send lead. Lead 8 of the modem and our control end (mainframe) interface will be on if the tributary (3270 controller) has its Request to Send on. Recall that our environment was full duplex, which implied that both DTEs keep Request to Send up at all times. Hence lead 8, Carrier Detect, should also be on at all times. The modem uses this lead to indicate if it is receiving carrier from the other end. This is a good way to see if the actual circuit is present. The absence of Data Carrier Detect in a full duplex, Continuous Carrier, Continuous Request to Send environment is a good sign that there is something wrong on the circuit. The far-end controller is powered off, the modems are not functioning, or the circuit is down. This is a very important status lead. Most FEPs will use this lead for status information. Hence, lead 8 is an output lead from the modem to the locally attached device.

Although our mainframe-to-3270 controller connection is full-duplex, it is worthwhile to cover the impact of these leads in a half duplex environment. This is relevant as most dial-up synchronous environments, such as those using an AT&T 201C or compatible modem, will be HDX. In a half duplex environment, either the control or tributary end will have "control" of the circuit at any given moment, but not both. By the HDX definition, it is either the FEP or the 3270 controller. The way that one of the ends gets control is by raising its Request to Send lead (pin 4).

For example, assume that the mainframe end desires to transmit information. The FEP would turn on pin 4. The modem, upon detection of this lead, will check to see if it is receiving carrier. Remember that if the far end has its Request to Send lead on, then carrier is being transmitted. If the modem senses carrier, it will not turn on the Clear to Send lead as a signal to the FEP that the other end has control of the circuit (HDX). However, if carrier detect is not on, the modem will turn on its Clear to Send lead (pin 5) as a signal to the FEP that it now has control of the circuit. This interaction occurs locally at both ends to control the use of the two-way, nonsimultaneous circuit. The leads Request to Send, Clear to Send, and Data Carrier Detect play a key role in the control of the communication channel.

It is worth noting at this point that most null modem cables for asynchronous environments honor this interaction in their designs. Although a number of possibilities exist for building various null modem cables, the original ones took into account this interaction. Normally, see Table 3–54; pin 4 was looped back to pin 5 and across to the other device's pin 8. Looking in the other direction, the same connections were made.

Now back to our private line modem port analysis—the only control lead left is lead 20. Data Terminal Ready is an input signal to the modem. The modem typically ignores this signal, although it could check this

TABLE 3–54. CONTROL LEADS OF A STANDARD NULL MODEM CABLE

	Computer leads		Peripheral leads	
Request to Send	4	--|---⟩	8	Carrier Detect
Clear to Send	5	⟨-|		
Carrier Detect	8	⟨---|--	4	Request to Send
		|-⟩	5	Clear to Send

lead to determine if the attached device were powered up with the port enabled. Most modems assume that the attached device, in a private line environment, will be on and will act on receipt of the other control leads.

If, however, this were a point-to-point dial-up synchronous environment, lead 20 plays a major role. The modem will establish and keep a connection with another device, if this lead is on. Hence, this input signal to the modem is the DTE's means of controlling whether to establish, maintain, or disconnect a connection to a remote device. As long as Data Terminal Ready is on, the modem will keep connections established. However, if the FEP were to lower DTR, the modem would interpret this as a sign to disconnect the circuit. Our scenario includes private line connections only; hence this signal plays a minor role. However, for completeness, our ultimate cable design should allow for this lead.

The only category of leads left to discuss is the timing category. We will review the Transmit and Receive Timing leads relative to the modem, along with the appropriate options, for our point-to-point private line. [The RS232 standard [allows to] leads, 15 and 17 for timing leads provided by DCE, or modems/DSUs.] If a modem is to provide the transmit timing, it should do so on lead 15. The modem should be optioned for internal timing to allow this signal to occur on lead 15. As an output signal from the modem, the attached DTE will use this clock rate to send information. The modem attached to the FEP should be optioned for internal timing. This, paired with the FEP optioned for external timing, will allow a single source of timing at this end of the circuit. The receive timing is provided by the modem. The modem then passes this clock rate to the DTE as a signal on lead 17. Hence, both 15 and 17 are output signals from the modem and input to the DTE. This takes care of the options and timing leads at the "control" modem of our circuit.

What about the far end of the circuit, the one where the 3270 controller is attached to its modem? The same two signals will be present, leads 15 and 17, both as output leads from the modem. The modem will provide to the controller the transmit timing rate on lead 15. The controller will send its data at this rate. The controller will also know the rate at which to receive data by looking at the clock signal on lead 17 provided by the modem. Our cable must provide for these two leads at this end, just as the control-end cable does. As a matter of fact, the two cables will be exactly alike.

The key at this end of the circuit is what timing signal the modem provides to the 3270 controller. Recall from the earlier discussion of timing options that a slave option was available in addition to an internal timing option. Slave timing allowed a modem to derive a timing signal from the received signal and use this same signal as the Transmit Timing signal that it provided to attached device. This allowed for a single source of timing in a network, which is desirable in complex, extended circuits. Now the modem still provided the necessary Transmit Timing signal to the attached 3270 controller, but it was the same timing signal as that used at the far-end modem for data transmission.

Should a modem offer a slave timing option at the tributary site, it is not necessary to enable this option in a point-to-point network. This will not impact the cable design. If the tributary modem does not offer a slave timing option, and the user wants a single source of timing, the cable between the modem and the 3270 controller can be altered to allow for the same functionality. The next section will cover this cable building, as our case study assumes that internal timing will be used at both ends of the point-to-point circuit and builds the cable accordingly.

The goal of the salve timing option is to use the derived Receive Timing signal as the Transmit Timing signal. To build a cable that accomplishes this in the absence of a slave timing option, the user should option the modem for external timing. Then cut the Transmit Timing lead between the modem and 3270 controller. Pin 15 should not go "straight through." Then merely connect the modem's lead 17 to the 3270 controller's Transmit and Receiving Timing leads, 15 and 17, as well as to the modem's lead 24. Table 3–55 depicts this design.

TABLE 3–55.   TIMING LEAD DESIGN WITH NO SLAVE TIMING OPTION IN A MODEM

	Modem leads	3270 leads	
Transmit Timing (out)	15 X |--)	15	Transmit Timing (in)
Receive Timing (out)	17 ---|--)	17	Receive Timing (in)
Transmit Timing (in)	24 (--| X		

NOTE: The "X" implies that there is no "straight-through" connection on lead 15. Leads 17 and 24 on the modem side should be connected to leads 15 and 17 in the 3270 controller port. The modem should be optioned for external timing.

TABLE 3–56. SYNCHRONOUS MODEM PORT PROFILE

Underline if supported; circle if selected.

Model: Dataphone I-9600 Vendor: AT&T _____ Port: RS232 ____

Port type: <u>serial</u>
Port: <u>DB25</u> 9-pin 8-pin/modular 20mA _____

Gender: male <u>female</u>

Pin #	Function	Direction	Pin #	Function	Direction
1	_____	to from n/a	14	_____	to from n/a
2	<u>Transmit Data</u>	<u>to</u> from n/a	15	Transmit Timing (DCE)	to <u>from</u> n/a
3	<u>Receive Data</u>	to <u>from</u> n/a	16	_____	to from n/a
4	<u>Request to Send</u>	<u>to</u> from n/a	17	Receive Timing (DCE)	to <u>from</u> n/a
5	<u>Clear to Send</u>	to <u>from</u> n/a	18	_____	to from n/a
6	<u>Data Set Ready</u>	to <u>from</u> n/a	19	_____	to from n/a
7	<u>Signal Ground</u>	to from <u>n/a</u>	20	Data Terminal Ready	<u>to</u> from n/a
8	<u>Received Line Signal Detect</u>	to <u>from</u> n/a	21	_____	to from n/a
9	_____	to from n/a	22	_____	to from n/a
10	_____	to from n/a	23	_____	to from n/a
11	_____	to from n/a	24	Transmit Timing (DTE)	<u>to</u> from n/a
12	_____	to from n/a	25	_____	to from n/a
13	_____	to from n/a			

Leads that must be on: 4 20 __ __ __ __

Options:
    Speeds: 110 300 600 1200 1800 <u>2400</u> <u>4800</u> ⓐ9600 19.2 56k _____
    Compatibility: 103 212 V.22bis _____
    Parity: even odd space mark none
    Char-length: 7 8 ____
    # stop bits: 1 1.5 2
    Line-ending sequence: cr 1f cr/1f cr/1f/1f
    Auto answer: yes no   RTS/CTS delay: ____
    Disconnect sequence: EOT   DEL _____
    Intelligent modems. . . .Dialing Technique: Touch-tone Pulse
        Compatibility: Hayes _____
        Command line prefix: AT _____ Dial command: D _____
        Touch-tone dial: T ____ Pulse dial: P ____ Pause: , ____
        Wait for dial tone: W ____ Wait for quiet answer: @ ____
        Flash: ! ____ Dial stored number: S ____
        Return to command state after dialing: ; ____
        Escape sequence: +++ ____ Switch-hook control: H ____
        Store phone #: &Z ____
    Mode: async sync isoch

Sync timing leads:

#	Function	Direction
15	Transmit	to ⓐfrom
17	<u>Receive</u>	to ⓐfrom
24	<u>Transmit</u>	<u>to</u> from

Notes: _____
_____
_____

Now the modem is set to receive its timing on lead 24 because of the external timing option. Your cable has looped the Receive Timing lead, which came from the far-end modem, back into lead 24. From this signal, the modem will phase lock its clock rate to the clock rate on 24. Furthermore, the 3270 will have the same clock rate for its transmit and receive timing. WHA! LA! You now have a single source of timing.

By building the timing leads of the cable, this performs the same function as if the modem were optioned for slave timing and the cable had the leads 15 and 17, connected "straight through." Our tutorial module cable design will have these leads "straight through," with the modem optioned for internal timing. Review the modem port profile with the updated findings as found in Table 3–56. Yours may vary depending on whether you are using a different speed modem, different vendor's modem, or a DSU. Furthermore, some modems, such as AT&T's older modems, provided 5 volts on leads 9 and 10 for testing purposes. We will ignore these leads.

The only port left to perform analysis on is the 3270 controller port. This port will be the same as the FEP port. One possible exception exists. Depending on the modem of 3270 or compatible controller, lead 24 may not be supported. The controller may not be capable of supplying a timing source. Ignore lead 24 for our purposes, as it is not used anyway, and duplicate the FEP port profile for the 3270 controller.

7. Design the cable

You now have all the leads that are provided and required for each device in the point-to-point network. Review each of the ports. The rules to cable design are the same as before.

CABLE DESIGN: GENERAL RULES

1. Connect like categories of leads together.
2. Always connect an "out" to an "in" and an "in" to an "out."
3. A lead that is input may be connected to another lead that is an input only if both these are connected to an output lead.
4. In synchronous connections, only use one source of timing. (Select either the FEP or the modem, but not both, as the source of timing.)

The FEP and 3270 controller are emulating a DTE interface and are expecting to be connected to DCE equipment. The modems provide DCE interfaces and are expecting to be connected to DTE. Because all four pieces of equipment conform to the RS232 interface, the cabling is a piece of cake. "Straight-through" cables can be used to connect the FEP to the local modem and to connect the 3270 controller to its modem. Table 3–57 lays out the cables required for our connection. If you are using a Dataphone II modem with an RS449 port, the adapter cable will be required instead of a "straight-through" cable. For other type modems and DSUs, however, there are no "cross-overs" that are required in your "straight-through" cable.

8. Build the cable

9. Test for continuity

TABLE 3–57. CABLE DESIGN FOR FEP AND 3270 CONTROLLER-TO-MODEM CONNECTION

	FEP/3270 leads		Modem leads	
Transmit Data (out)	2	-------	2	Transmit Data (in)
Receive Data (in)	3	-------	3	Receive Data (out)
Request to Send (out)	4	-------	4	Request to Send (in)
Clear to Send (in)	5	-------	5	Clear to Send (out)
Data Set Ready (in)	6	-------	6	Data Set Ready (out)
Signal Ground	7	-------	7	Signal Ground
Carrier Detect (in)	8	-------	8	Carrier Detect (out)
Transmit Timing (in)	15	-------	15	Transmit Timing (out)
Receive Timing (in)	17	-------	17	Receive Timing (out)
Data Terminal Ready (out)	20	-------	20	Data Terminal Ready (in)

NOTE: The "-------" indicates a "straight-through" connection of the leads.

10. Cable the two systems together

Either acquire a ribbon cable or other type and ensure that the required leads are present. Check the cable for continuity to ensure that the leads are "straight through" and not "crossed over." Be sure that the genders are correct on the cable. The FEP and 3270 controllers, depending on your models, will provide a male port, requiring a female cable end. The modems generally have a female port, requiring a male connector. Cable the FEP to the modem and the 3270 controller to its modem.

11. Measure success

As indicated earlier in step 2, mere cabling, optioning, and connection are minor aspects necessary for a successful connection of these synchronous devices. Architectures and protocols dictate the need for other complex setups. Work closely with systems analysts and vendors to ensure total success in connecting the synchronous modems and associated devices. CONGRATULATIONS!

Tutorial Module 3-7: Connecting Modems in a 3270 Multipoint Environment

In the synchronous world, product families are typically connected to larger computers for online-type applications, batch file transfers, or host-to-host communications. IBM has been a major proponent of synchronous communications for support of its online mainframe applications. These online applications supported many users simultaneously. For example, a mainframe that had a database management system could support many users banging away doing data entry, inquiry, and report generation. It was not practical to connect a single terminal into the mainframe on a dedicated port. Furthermore, most users were not located in the same floor, building, or even the same city as the mainframe computer. Hence, the need for permanent connections, with port sharing, was born.

The history of this evolution is interesting but not important to our tutorial module. The result is a network of devices and computers, commonly referred to as multipoint private lines. Figure 3–15 depicts graphically a typical multipoint network with multiple controllers and terminals connected to a port on a mainframe's front-end processor.

In the past, the 3270 devices were the dominant devices used in multipoint private lines. However, IBM's relatively recent introduction of application program-to-program communication (APPC) will expand the use of synchronous environments to PCs and UNIX systems in a big way. APPC is one piece involved in an overall architecture referred to as SNA. Data exchanges among PCs, minicomputers, supermicros, terminals, and mainframes will take on a new dimension. APPC allows "peers" to communicate with one another, without relying totally on mainframe capabilities.

Whether the synchronous networks involve 3270 terminals, personal computers, mainframes, minis, supermicros, or other nodes, the user is faced with a task of maintaining continuity throughout the network. Specifically, in multipoint networks, the timing element takes on greater importance. It is desirable to minimize the number of different timing elements in a single network. Our point-to-point discussion in Tutorial Module 3–6 featured

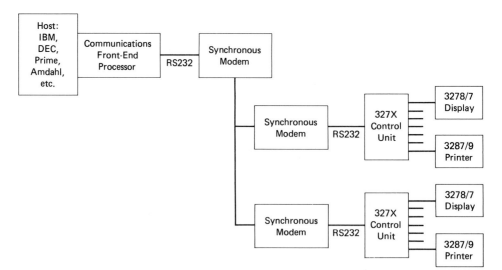

Figure 3–15. Typical multipoint network diagram.

two sources of timing, as only two endpoints were involved. However, when more than two endpoints are in a network, as the case with multipoint networks, the user should plan the network with minimal timing sources. This tutorial module will highlight the design of a multipoint network, featuring the necessary cables, but with heavy emphasis placed on the timing element of the interfaces.

Prior to pursuing the tutorial module, several definitions must be covered. If the different elements and options involved in timing are new to you, consult Tutorial Module 3–6, where these are covered in detail. In a multipoint environment, the list of terms that need to be understood grows.

Multipoint

This term applies to a network scheme whereby at one end of a circuit there is a single device, such as a FEP, and multiple endpoints to the circuit at the other end. Refer to Figure 3–15 for a depiction of this scenario. The concept evolved out of the situations whereby the line capacity (speed) is many times greater than the amount required for any single terminal. Hence line sharing was born. Multiple endpoints share a line used to communicate with a host system. The nature of the application dictates how many endpoints are practical on the same line.

Control

In a multipoint network where multiple terminals are accessing a central computer, one of the circuits is designated as the "control" end. This is typically the mainframe end. One of the reasons for this tag is that the mainframe (FEP) controls the line. The modem associated with the host is referred to as the "control modem."

In a 3270 environment, the host has the responsibility to maintain control of the network. Terms such as polling and selection are involved in the communication protocol of a multipoint private line environment with 3270s. These are "invitations to send" and "invitations to receive," respectively. The reader should refer to *Communications Architecture for Distributed Systems*, by R. J. Cypser (Addison-Wesley Publishing Company, 1978), for further information about protocols and networking.

Tributary

Conversely, the tributary refers to the multipoint end of the circuit. From Figure 3–15, the tributaries are the multiple 3270 controllers. The modems are referred to as "tributary modems." This nomenclature becomes important when it comes to optioning the modems. Depending on whether a modem is a control modem or tributary modem, the options will vary, specifically as it pertains to the timing options.

Switched Carrier, Switched Request to Send

This is normally an option within a modem that determines the condition of the carrier from an endpoint. This controls the carrier control method. It is necessary in multipoint applications for the tributaries to transmit carrier only when they are ready to transmit. If all the endpoints transmitted carrier simultaneously, a "conflicting carrier" condition would occur, not allowing for proper signal modulation. Only one endpoint should be transmitting at any given moment. The host is controlling which endpoint sends and receives through its polling and selection. Once an endpoint is "invited to send," it raises its Request to Send. The local modem gives a Clear to Send after a certain number of milliseconds. The controller then can transmit. Once it is finished transmitting its data, it lowers its Request to Send lead. This is known as Switched Carrier, Switched Request to Send. Carrier is transmitted from the tributary modem to the control modem, only while Request to Send is on. Lead 8, Carrier Detect at the control modem/host interface, will be on/off to match the condition of the tributary's Request to Send lead. In a multipoint circuit, the tributary modems should all be optioned for Switched Carrier, Switched Request to Send.

Continuous Carrier, Continuous Request to Send

In our scenario, the control location (host) should be set to this option. The reason is that the control location can transmit carrier at all times without conflict. This has to do with the circuit layout in the network. The outgoing signals are bridged to be received by all the multiple tributary locations. Any inbound signal to the host will be received by only the host, not the other tributary locations. The protocol binary synchronous communications (BSC) or synchronous data link control (SDLC) will take care of which tributary responds upon receipt of information from the network. However, it is important to note that all tributaries will receive carrier at all times when this option is set to CC, CRTS, and is desirable. Hence the host/FEP will be optioned to for full duplex or Continuous Request to Send, so that carrier is transmitted at all times. This is the opposite of the tributary locations. When set to this option, the user could monitor the RS232 interface at any one of the tributary locations and see that lead 8, Carrier Detect, would be on at all times. It does not fluctuate as the same lead at the host end, as cited previously. Because the host modem (control) is continually transmitting carrier, the Carrier Detect lead at the tributary modem should always be on. If this lead is not on at the tributary, then there is a problem with the circuit or the tributary modem. In a point-to-point circuit, both ends should be set up with this option.

Continuous Carrier, Switched Request to Send

This third option allows for carrier to be continuously transmitted, without the Request to Send lead held on. Once Request to Send is raised, Clear to Send is provided after millisecond(s) of delay.

Protocols and Architectures

Protocols are laws of communications; architectures are the states that issue the laws. This is a very-high-level view of complex data communication components. There are various architectures in use in DC environments, with SNA being one of the most prominent. Within SNA, different protocols may be used, with SDLC being the most prevalent. This tutorial module will not expound on these, but merely suggest that the reader understand that the devices involved in a network, DTE, must understand the laws and states to function. The modems in a network are typically transparent to the protocols and architectures, as they are merely vehicles to allow two endpoints to communicate. The data terminal equipment, host/controllers, actually must conform to the architecture and protocols. The modems need to support the communication modes. In our tutorial module, the mode is synchronous. With a decent understanding of some terminology used in a multipoint environment, the user is ready to proceed to actual connection involving DTE and DCE in a multipoint environment. As previously cited, this tutorial module will feature a simple multipoint environment, but will point to the issues involved in more complex extended circuits. The steps involved will mirror those of the other case studies. Because several of the modems and controllers were covered in Tutorial Module 3–6, they will not be repeated here other than in summary form.

1. Determine compatibility

2. Determine signs of success

Should this connection work? Greater powers than you and I, including AT&T and IBM, say that it will. As with Tutorial Module 3–6, I will take their word for it. The SCS port profiles should be completed in the normal fashion. Consult the documentation to fill in the blanks. The ultimate signs of success are your abilities to send and receive data over the network. It is not possible for this module to delve into all the different scenarios to walk the reader through all the testing. Work closely with the systems analysts and vendors to strive for the ability to communicate between the devices.

3. Determine type of connector used

4. Determine gender of the ports

Most pieces of DTE in the mainframe environment have DB25P (male) ports, while the DCE (modems) typically have female connectors. Not all 25 pins are required, but the connector is a 25-pin/socket connector.

5. Determine leads (pins) provided by each device

6. Determine leads required to be on

Each of these ports was analyzed in Tutorial Module 3–6. Refer to that module for a detailed look at each of these ports. Table 3–58 summarizes the port profiles.

The only port analysis left to perform is on the 3270 controller port. This port will be the same as the FEP port. One possible exception exists. Depending on the modem of 3270 or compatible controller, lead 24 may not be supported. The controller may not be capable of supplying a timing source. Ignore lead 24 for our purposes, as it is not used anyway, and duplicate the FEP port profile for the 3270 controller.

TABLE 3–58. IBM 3705 FRONT-END PROCESSOR PORT PROFILE

Computer Port Profile

Underline if supported; circle if selected.

Model: 3705 front-end proc.__ Vendor: IBM _____ Port: synchronous

Port type: <u>serial</u> parallel
Port: <u>DB25</u> 9-pin 5-pin 8-pin/modular 20mA Centronics

Gender: <u>male</u> female

Pin #	Function	Direction	Pin #	Function	Direction
1	Frame Ground	to from <u>n/a</u>	14		to from n/a
2	Transmit Data	to <u>from</u> n/a	15	Transmit Timing	<u>to</u> from n/a
3	Receive Data	<u>to</u> from n/a	16		to from n/a
4	Request to Send	to <u>from</u> n/a	17	Receive Timing	<u>to</u> from n/a
5	Clear to Send	<u>to</u> from n/a	18		to from n/a
6	Data Set Ready	<u>to</u> from <u>n/a</u>	19		to from n/a
7	Signal Ground	to from <u>n/a</u>	20	Data Terminal Ready	to <u>from</u> n/a
8	Received Line Signal Detect	<u>to</u> from n/a	21		to from n/a
9		to from n/a	22		to from n/a
10		to from n/a	23		to from n/a
11		to from n/a	24	Transmit Timing	to <u>from</u> n/a
12		to from n/a	25		to from n/a
13		to from n/a			

Complete the next section only with 36-pin cinch connector.

Pin #	Function	Direction	Pin #	Function	Direction
26		to from n/a	27		to from n/a
28		to from n/a	29		to from n/a
30		to from n/a	31		to from n/a
32		to from n/a	33		to from n/a
34		to from n/a	35		to from n/a
36		to from n/a			

Flow control technique: XON/XOFF ENQ/ACK STX/ETX Hardware protocol
Leads that must be on: 5 6 8 __ __ __ __

Options:
    Speeds: <u>110 300 600 1200 1800 2400 4800 (9600) 19.2 56k</u> _____
    Parity: even odd space mark none
    Char-length: 7 8 ____
    # stop bits: 1 1.5 2
    Line-ending sequence: cr 1f cr/1f cr/1f/1f
    Disconnect sequence: EOT DEL ~. _____

Mode: async sync isoch	#	Sync timing leads: Function	Direction
	15	Transmit	(to) from
	17	Receive	(to) from
	24	Transmit	to <u>from</u>

Notes: The flow control is left up to the protocol that is defined for the port. Normally the attached modem should provide the timing.

TABLE 3–58. (*Continued*)

Modem Port Profile

Underline if supported; circle if selected.

Model: Dataphone I-9600 Vendor: AT&T _____ Port: RS232 ____
Port Type: <u>serial</u>
Port: <u>DB25</u> 9-pin 8-pin/modular 20mA _____

Gender: male <u>female</u>

Pin #	Function	Direction	Pin #	Function	Direction
1	_____	to from n/a	14	_____	to from n/a
2	Transmit Data	<u>to</u> from n/a	15	Transmit Timing (DCE)	to <u>from</u> n/a
3	Receive Data	to <u>from</u> n/a	16	_____	to from n/a
4	Request to Send	<u>to</u> from n/a	17	Receive Timing (DCE)	to <u>from</u> n/a
5	Clear to Send	to <u>from</u> n/a	18	_____	to from n/a
6	Data Set Ready	to <u>from</u> n/a	19	_____	to from n/a
7	Signal Ground	to from <u>n/a</u>	20	Data Terminal Ready	<u>to</u> from n/a
8	Received Line Signal Detect	to <u>from</u> n/a	21	_____	to from n/a
9	_____	to from n/a	22	_____	to from n/a
10	_____	to from n/a	23	_____	to from n/a
11	_____	to from n/a	24	Transmit Timing (DTE)	<u>to</u> from n/a
12	_____	to from n/a	25	_____	to from n/a
13	_____	to from n/a			

Leads that must be on: 4 20 __ __ __ __

Options:
Speeds: 110 300 600 1200 1800 <u>2400</u> <u>4800</u> (9600) 19.2 56k _____
  Compatibility: 103 212 V.22bis _____
  Parity: even odd space mark none
  Char-length: 7 8 __
  # stop bits: 1 1.5 2
  Line ending sequence: cr 1f cr/1f cr/1f/1f
  Auto answer: yes no RTS/CTS delay: ____
  Disconnect sequence: EOT DEL _____
  Intelligent modems . . . Dialing technique: Touch-tone Pulse
    Compatibility: Hayes _____
    Command line prefix: At _____ Dial command: D _____
    Touch-tone dial: T ____ Pulse dial: P ____ Pause: , ____
    Wait for dial tone: W ____ Wait for quiet answer: @ ____
    Flash: ! ____ Dial stored number: S ____
    Return to command state after dialing: ; ____
    Escape sequence: +++ ____ Switch-hook control: H ____
    Store phone #: &Z ____
  Mode: async sync isoch

Sync timing leads:

#	Function	Direction
15	Transmit	to (from)
17	Receive	to (from)
24	Transmit	<u>to</u> from

Notes: _____
_____
_____

7. Design the cable

You now have all the leads that are provided and required for each device in the multipoint network. Review each of the ports. The rules to cable design are the same as before.

CABLE DESIGN: GENERAL RULES

1. Connect like categories of leads together.
2. Always connect an "out" to an "in" and an "in" to an "out."
3. A lead that is input may be connected to another lead that is an input only if both these are connected to an output lead.
4. In synchronous connections, only use one source of timing. (Select either the FEP or the modem, but not both, as the source of timing.)

The FEP and 3270 controllers are emulating a DTE interface and are expecting to be connected to DCE equipment. The modems provide DCE interfaces and are expecting to be connected to DTE. Because all four pieces of equipment conform to the RS232 interface, the cabling is a piece of cake. "Straight-through" cables can be used to connect the FEP to the local modem and to connect the 3270 controllers to their local modems.

Table 3–59 lays out the cables required for our connection. If you are using a Dataphone II modem with an RS449 port, the adapter cable will be required instead of a straight-through cable. For other-type modems and DSUs, no "cross-overs" are required in your straight-through cable. Each 3270 controller would require this same cable for connection to the local modem.

Each modem in the multipoint network should be optioned for internal timing. It is recommended that each of them also be set up as "master" as opposed to "slave" timing if such an option exists. The slave option will be covered in the extended circuit section. Point 4 of the cable design rules applies to extended circuits. Furthermore, the control modem should be optioned for Continuous Carrier, Continuous Request to Send, while the tributary modems should be optioned for Switched Carrier, Switched Request to Send.

8. Build the cable

9. Test for continuity

10. Cable the two systems together

Either acquire a ribbon cable or other type and ensure that the foregoing leads are present. Check the cable for continuity to ensure that the leads are "straight through" and not "crossed over." Be sure that the genders are correct on the cable. The FEP and 3270 controllers, depending on your models, will provide a male port, requiring a female cable end. The modems generally have a female port, requiring a male connector. Cable the FEP to the modem and the 3270 controller to its modem.

TABLE 3–59. CABLE DESIGN FOR FEP AND 3270 CONTROLLER-TO-MODEM CONNECTION

	FEP/3270 leads	Modem leads	
Transmit Data (out)	2 -------	2	Transmit Data (in)
Receive Data (in)	3 -------	3	Receive Data (out)
Request to Send (out)	4 -------	4	Request to Send (in)
Clear to Send (in)	5 -------	5	Clear to Send (out)
Data Set Ready (in)	6 -------	6	Data Set Ready (out)
Signal Ground	7 -------	7	Signal Ground
Carrier Detect (in)	8 -------	8	Carrier Detect (out)
Transmit Timing (in)	15 -------	15	Transmit Timing (out)
Receive Timing (in)	17 -------	17	Receive Timing (out)
Data Terminal Ready (out)	20 -------	20	Data Terminal Ready (in)

NOTE: The "-------" indicates a "straight-through" connection of the leads.

11. Measure success

As indicated earlier, mere cabling, optioning, and connection are minor aspects necessary for a successful connection of these synchronous devices in a multipoint network. Architectures and protocols dictate the need for other complex setups. Work closely with systems analysts and vendors to ensure total success in connecting the synchronous modems and associated devices. CONGRATULATIONS!

Tutorial Module 3-8: Connecting Devices in an Extended Circuit

The previous tutorial modules involving synchronous modems dealt with the connection of point-to-point and multipoint networks. The larger the network, with the greater geography that they span, the more likely a different circuit may be used. Circuits can become quite complex as they span the continental United States. Portions of the circuits can be extended beyond a given endpoint to offer service to a different location. These are called extended circuits and are depicted in Figure 3–16.

The best way to visualize an extended circuit is by looking at a point-to-point circuit. At one of the endpoints, a piece of DTE such as a controller could be connected. In addition to, or in lieu of, the DTE, another modem could be connected that is connected to another circuit. This circuit can be point to point or multipoint and is considered the extended circuit. The point-to-point circuit that this extended piece is connected to is termed the "backbone" circuit. As a matter of fact, the backbone portion of the network does not need to be point to point, but can be multipoint as well. These networks can get to be fairly complex, as "doubly extended circuits" are possible with circuits on both sides of the backbone circuit.

The coupling of terms describes the various locations on these circuits. The multipoint control and multipoint tributaries refer to the two ends of a multipoint circuit. Extended control and extended tributary refer to the ends of an extended circuit. What is your guess as to what the backbone control and backbone tributary terms refer? Many other combinations of these terms refer to specific locations on the complete circuit. This tutorial module will feature a simple point-to-point circuit with a single point-to-point extension as shown in Figure 3–16. Furthermore, the backbone tributary modem will have a local 3270 controller connected to it in addition to the extended circuit. Tutorial Modules 3–6 and 3–7 covered the port analysis of the DTE and modems involved in our scenario. They will not be reanalyzed here, but merely summarized as we proceed through the steps for connection.

The backbone portion of this network will be operated at 9600 bps and will be a point-to-point circuit. The 9600 bps modem offers multiple ports, as different-speed devices/modems can be attached to the backbone tributary modem. If AT&T 209- or 2096-compatible modems are used in a point-to-point configuration, the attached device can operate at 9600 bps. These types of modems can also support the attachment of multiple lower-speed devices. In our example, the 3270 that is locally attached to the backbone tributary modem will be operating at 4800 bps. The extended circuit and modems will operate at 2400 bps. Higher speeds are possible, with the backbone modem capabilities dictating the actual throughput that is possible. The extended modems will be of the AT&T 201C- or 2024-compatible type. The optioning and timing issues should be the same across all vendors' modems. The only difference might be with the slave timing option, which will be highlighted later in this tutorial module.

1. Determine compatibility

2. Determine signs of success

These extended circuits are commonly included in national network designs. The 3270 controller functions here just as it would in a straight point-to-point or multipoint environment. The modems and DTE are compatible with the same complex signs of success as the other types of circuits.

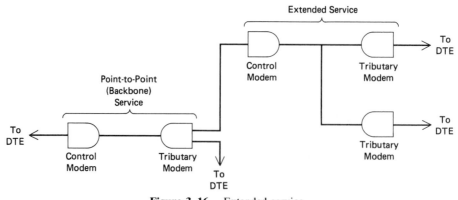

Figure 3–16. Extended service.

3. Determine type of connector used

4. Determine gender of ports

Review the port profiles from the previous tutorial modules. The additional pieces of DCE in our configuration are the extended control and extended tributary modems. Depending on the type of modems used, the interface may or may not be the same as our others. This tutorial module features 201C-type modems operating at 2400 bps. These modems feature DB25S connectors.

5. Determine leads (pins) provided by each device

6. Determine leads required to be on

What about the EIA interface signals of the modems? Review the port profiles from previous case studies for the 9600 bps modems, the FEP, and the 3270 controller. The additional modems comprising our extended piece of this circuit offer an EIA RS232-compatible interface. The signals are common to most of the synchronous modems. Hence, the signals that are important to our exercise are outlined in the Table 3–60.

7. Design the cable

Now that we know what we are dealing with regarding port profiles, the cables necessary to connect the devices together will be covered. Review Figure 3–16 for an understanding of how many different cables will be required. There are five EIA cables required in this tutorial module: FEP to backbone control, FEP to backbone control, backbone tributary to 3270 controller, backbone tributary to extended control modem, and extended tributary modem to 3270 controller. There will be two ports in the FEP for each of the separate connections to the 3270 controllers, one for the point-to-point simple circuit and one for the point-to-point extended circuit. This a minor, but often overlooked, requirement. The 9600 bps bandwidth of the circuit is being split into a 4800 bps connection and the extended 2400 bps circuit. The 9600 bps modems are often referred to as multiplexors because of this.

The cable requirements for connecting the two FEP ports to the two separate ports on the backbone control modem are the same. The cable is a "straight-through" cable, with leads 15 and 17 present to handle the timing leads. The reason for this type of cable, versus a "cross-over" cable, is that the FEP emulates DTE while the modem emulates DCE. Both devices conform to the EIA RS232 standard for the signals 1–8, 15, 17, and 20; hence, a "straight-through" cable will work. Depending on the vendor's modem you are using, other leads may be present but not used. Examples include +5 volts, −5 voltage level, and dibit clock receiver. Our cable(s), necessary to connect the FEP ports to the backbone control modem ports, are outlined in Table 3–61. The optioning of these two ports, as it relates to the two most important factors of timing and carrier control, will be covered later in this chapter.

The next cable required is that of connecting the 3270 controller to the backbone tributary modem. We are assuming that the speed of this port will be 4800 bps; hence the controller should be optioned for this speed. The cable required for this connection will be the same as that just designed for the FEP connections. A "straight-through" cable will be used to connect the controller to the modem port.

TABLE 3–60. SIGNALS COMMON TO SYNCHRONOUS PRIVATE LINE MODEMS

Lead #	Function	Direction
1	Protective Ground	n/a
2	Transmit Data	In (to)
3	Receive Data	Out (from)
4	Request to Send	In
5	Clear to Send	Out
6	Data Set Ready	Out
7	Signal Ground	n/a
8	Receive Line Signal Detector	Out
15	Transmit Timing (DCE)	Out
17	Receive Timing (DCE)	Out
20	Data Terminal Ready	To
24	Transmit Timing (DTE)	To

TABLE 3–61. FEP-TO-BACKBONE CONTROL MODEM

Function	FEP lead #		Modem lead #	Function
Protective Ground	1	-------	1	Protective Ground
Transmit Data (out)	2	-------	2	Transmit Data (in)
Receive Data (in)	3	-------	3	Receive Data (out)
Request to Send (out)	4	-------	4	Request to Send (in)
Clear to Send (in)	5	-------	5	Clear to Send (out)
Data Set Ready (in)	6	-------	6	Data Set Ready (out)
Signal Ground	7	-------	7	Signal Ground
Carrier Detect (in)	8	-------	8	Carrier Detect (in)
Transmit Timing (in)	15	-------	15	Transmit Timing (out)
Receive Timing (in)	17	-------	17	Receive Timing (out)
Data Terminal Ready (out)	20	-------	20	Data Terminal Ready (in)

NOTE: Two of these cables are required. The FEP typically has a male port, while the modem has a female port, so plan on a cable accordingly.

This leaves two cables to design: the cable to connect to two collocated modems together back to back and the pigtail end of the circuit. The "pigtail" is commonly used to refer to the portion of the circuit where the other 3270 controller will connect to the lower-speed modem. These two cables are the most difficult ones to design in our network. Their design cannot fully be understood, until the concepts of synchronized timing and carrier control are covered.

Synchronized timing. In synchronous networks, the fewer the timing sources, the better. In an extended circuit, it is imperative that the timing be consistent throughout the circuit, from backbone to pigtail. This is to prevent conflicting clocks, or timing signals that are slightly out of phase, from interfering with normal data transmission. The best means of controlling this is to have a single source of timing. In a point-to-point circuit, such as those cited in Tutorial Module 3–6, this was not as important. However, in this tutorial module it is of paramount significance. This tutorial module will highlight how to design the cables and option the equipment to maintain synchronization throughout the network with minimal timing sources.

To minimize the sources of timing, the backbone control modem should be optioned for internal timing. The FEP attached to it will be optioned to let the network (DCE) provide the timing. The cable previously designed will allow the modem to present both transmit and receive timing using leads 15 and 17, respectively.

The backbone tributary modem could be set up to provide a timing source. There is typically the choice of internal versus external timing and then slave timing. The modem will use internal timing, so that it does not look to lead 24 for the timing source. However, unless the slave timing option is selected, our network will already have two sources of timing. We have not even addressed the extended piece of the circuit. Slave timing allows the modem to derive its timing from the received signal from the backbone control modem. This signal is then used to provide the Transmit Timing signal for data from the backbone tributary to the backbone control modem and FEP. Furthermore, the Receive Timing is the same signal as the derived signal, still with only one source of timing. Hence, we have four RS232 leads, 15 and 17 at the control modem and 15 and 17 at the tributary modem, driven by the same timing source in the control modem. So far so good—a single source of timing!

For the 3270 controller attached to this backbone tributary modem, these timing leads will be provided on leads 15 and 17. Hence, this portion of the network will work from the single source of timing.

With the extended piece of the network, the modem options and a "cross-over" cable are required. To reach our goal of a single source of timing to drive the network, we must continue to follow the flow of the timing signal into the extended control modem. Review the options, internal versus external timing. If internal timing is selected, the extended control modem would provide its own clock. This would be a second source of timing, a point we are trying to avoid. This leaves us with external timing. When external timing is selected, the modem expects the timing signal to appear on lead 24. This is an input signal to the modem. The modem then synchronizes its pulse rate to this clock signal for transmission of data.

We now have a dilemma in that the modem is looking for a timing signal on lead 24. If an FEP or other

DTE were being connected to the modem, then this signal would normally be output on lead 24 from the DTE. However, we are connecting modems back to back. How are we going to get the "single" timing lead to provide an input signal to the extended control modem? A "cross-over" cable! Review the backbone tributary signals and note that the Receive Timing signal is an output signal that normally provides the received timing signal to the attached device. This, from our slave option, was synchronized with our single timing source at the backbone control modem. We should design a cable that connects lead 17 (Receive Timing) from the backbone tributary modem to lead 24 (Transmit Timing, DTE) of the extended control modem. Because of the "external timing" option, the extended control modem will use the timing source from our single source at the backbone control modem.

Continue following this to the "pigtail" end of the extended circuit. As with our other modems, the extended tributary modem will provide a Receive Timing signal from its received signal. This should represent the same signal as the "single-source" timing. The attached 3270 controller will receive its data at this rate. What about the timing for data destined from the 3270 controller all the way back to the FEP? Once again the options and cable design play a key role. Review the timing options for the pigtail modem. The choice is either internal or external. If you select internal, then the modem will provide another timing signal from its internal clock crystal. This goes against the grain! If you select external, the signal found on lead 24 will be used as the Transmit Timing signal. We want our single source to provide this so the cable between the extended tributary modem and 3270 controller should loop back leads 17 to 24 as in Table 3–62.

By including this in our cable design, the 3270 controller will have a Transmit Timing signal that stems from our "single source." Follow this signal back to the extended control modem. It will appear on the Receive Timing lead at modem. The collocated backbone tributary modem needs a Transmit Timing signal from the "single source." Logic says to duplicate the earlier 17-to-24 "cross-over" and option the backbone tributary modem for external timing. However, earlier we optioned it for slave timing, which did derive the Transmit Timing for this modem from its own Receive Timing lead. This Transmit Timing signal was then received at the other end (backbone control modem) on the Receive Timing lead, lead 17, and presented to the FEP as the Receive Timing signal. CONGRATULATIONS! You have a single source of timing through the complex extended circuit to allow for synchronization.

For completeness, and ease of connecting the collocated modems—backbone tributary to extended control— the "cross-over" of lead 17 to 24 is included in both directions. This is shown in Table 3–62. By including this, the ultimate cable may be plugged into both modems without regard for the proper cable-end matchup. Because both modems will have female ports, the cable ends will both be male.

8. Build the cable

9. Test cable for continuity

10. Cable the two systems together

11. Measure success

The last four steps should be completed in the normal fashion. Refer to earlier discussion for reference points on measuring success. CONGRATULATIONS!

For ease of reference, Figure 3–17 provides a summary of modem options required for complex synchronous private line networks. These are only the options relating to carrier and timing control.

TABLE 3–62. TIMING LEAD IN EXTENDED TRIBUTARY MODEM-TO-DTE CABLE

Function	Modem lead #	3270 lead #	Function
Transmit Timing (out)	15 -------	15	Transmit Timing (in)
Receive Timing (out)	17 ---|---	17	Receive Timing (in)
Transmit Timing (in)	24 ⟨-|		

NOTE: The extended tributary modem will be optioned for external timing, which forces the modem to look for its Transmit Timing signal on lead 24. This cable tricks the modem by using its own Receive Timing signal to provide the Transmit Timing signal.

Carrier Control. In the tutorial module for multipoint circuits, 3–7, it was noted that conflicting carriers cause problems. In particular, if more than one endpoint of the multipoint end of the circuit transmitted carrier simultaneously, the data would be garbled. This could occur because the signals would be modulated on two different carrier frequencies. For this reason, the multipoint tributary modems were optioned for Switched Carrier, Switched Request to Send. Hence, the carrier that was sent from the tributaries back to the FEP was only sent by the 3270 controller that had control of the channel. Once completed, the 3270 dropped carrier by dropping request to send. The next 3270 would send carrier when prepared to transmit information.

In a point-to-point circuit, normally carrier control is not as critical. Because only two endpoints are involved, there should be no possibility of conflicting carrier. Nonetheless, if two circuits are involved as in an extended circuit, the ultimate endpoints need to know if carrier is being transmitted from end to end in the circuit. The carrier control options of the modems, along with good cable design, will allow for this. If the extended portion of the circuit is a multipoint circuit, then the carrier control is the same as in a simple circuit.

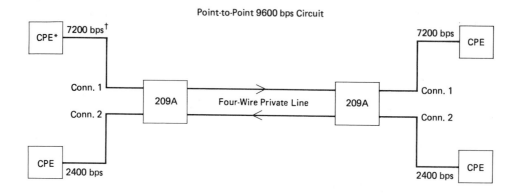

Point-to-Point 9600 bps Circuit

Select	Data Set 209A Options	Select
Internal	Transmitter Timing	Internal
Continuous	Carrier Control	Continuous
Per CPEs	Request-to-Send Control	Per CPEs

*Customer-provided equipment.

†Speeds can vary as long as consistent at both ends.

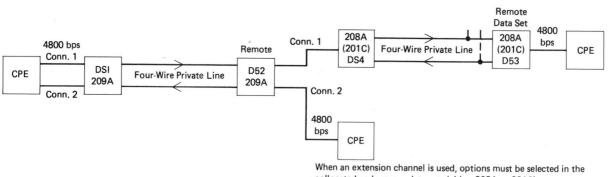

When an extension channel is used, options must be selected in the collocated and remove data sets (either 208A or 201C).

Central Select	Data Set 209A Options	Remote Select
Internal*	Transmitter Timing	Internal*
Continuous	Carrier Control	Continuous*
Per CPE	Request-to-Send Control	Continuous with Exten Channel (cont. or switched w/o exten channel)
Out	Slaved Timing	In (with extension channel) Out (without extension channel)

*Required

Collocated Select	Data Set 208A Options on Point-to-Point Extension Channel	Remote Select
External*	Transmitter Timing	External*
Switched*	Carrier Control	Continuous
Switched*	Request-to-Send Operation	0 or 8 MS per CPE
Collocated Select	Data Set 201C Options on Point-to-Point Extension Channel	Remote Select
External*	Transmitter Timing	External*
Switched*	Carrier Control	Continuous

Figure 3–17. Carrier and timing options in complex synchronous networks. 209S, 208S, and 201S are 9600, 4800, and 2400 b_{ps} modems, respectively.

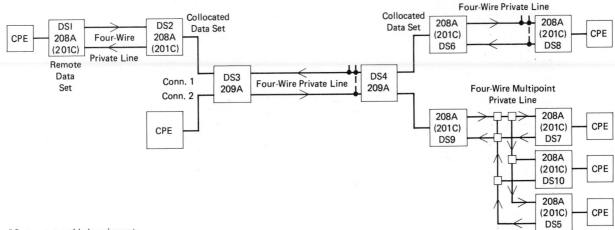

Doubly Extended Multipoint Circuit

*Customer-provided equipment.

Remote Select	Data Set 208A Options on Point-to-Point Extension Channel	Collocated Select
External*	Transmitter Timing	External*
Continuous	Carrier Control	Switched*
0 or 8 ms per CPE	Request-to-Send Operation	Switched*
Remote Select	Data Set 201C Options on Point-to-Point Extension Channel	Collocated Select
External*	Transmitter Timing	External*
Continuous	Carrier Control	Switched*

Select	Data Set 209A Options	Select
Internal*	Transmitter Timing	Internal*
Continuous*	Carrier Control	Continuous*
Continuous†	Request-to-Send Control	Continuous†
Out In	Slaved Timing	In Out

*Implies that the option is required.
†Not required except for multipoint.

Collocated Select	Data Set 208A Options on Multipoint Extension Channel	Remote Select
External*	Transmitter Timing	External*
Switched*	Carrier Control	Switched*
Switched*	Request-to-Send Operation	Switched*
Collocated Select	Data Set 201C Options on Multipoint Extension Channel	Remote Select
External*	Transmitter Timing	External*
Switched*	Carrier Control	Switched*

Figure 3–17. (*Continued*)

To maintain carrier control throughout the network and its extension, this tutorial module will now follow the "carrier" through the network as in the timing module. The options and cable design will once again play a key role in proper network setup. The impact when a multipoint extended circuit is involved will be highlighted as we progress through out study of a point-to-point extension.

Our goal is to avoid conflicting carrier problems that arise when more than one endpoint is transmitting carrier. This could potentially occur at a multipoint circuit. A general rule is that the multipoint endpoint modems of a circuit should always be optioned for Switched Carrier, Switched Request to Send. A point-to-point private line should be set up for Continuous Carrier. The only exception to this is a point-to-point dial-up line that may only support half duplex operation. In this case, Switched Carrier will be used.

Option the backbone control modem for Continuous Carrier. In a point-to-point circuit, this will allow carrier to be transmitted to the other end of the circuit. The FEP will be optioned for full duplex or Continuous Request to Send. From earlier discussions, as well as sections in *RS232 Made Easy*, when Request to Send is on at one end of the circuit, the other end will sense carrier and indicate this on lead 8, Carrier Detect. Hence, the backbone tributary modem will receive carrier and keep lead 8 on.

The attached device, normally DTE, would accept this signal as an input signal, indicating that carrier was being received from the far end. However, we are attaching another modem back to back, the extended control modem. Because both modems have DCE interfaces, lead 8 is an output signal for both of them. One golden rule for cable design: "Never connect an output to an output." Hence "cross-overs" are needed.

TABLE 3–63. CARRIER CONTROL LEADS IN AN EXTENDED CIRCUIT

Backbone tributary modem				Extended control modem	
Function	Lead #		Lead #		Function
Carrier Detect (out)	8	------⟩	4		Request to Send (in)
Request to Send (in)	4	⟨------	8		Carrier Detect (out)

If a modem is expecting Request to Send, lead 4, to be on for it to transmit carrier, then the device attached to the extended control modem should provide a signal on lead 4. Our attached device is another modem, with lead 4 being its input signal for Request to Send. Any ideas on which leads to cross? Lead 8 should be crossed over to lead 4. Repeat this in the other direction. Table 3–63 depicts this design. As long as carrier is being received by the backbone tributary modem on 8, then the extended control modem will have a signal on lead 4.

Option on the extended control modem for Switched Carrier, Switched Request to Send. This will allow the received carrier of one modem to control the sending carrier of the extended control modem. Follow the carrier signal through the extended circuit. Since lead 8 is crossed over to lead 4, carrier will be transmitted by the extended control modem. This carrier will in turn be received at the pigtail end of the circuit at the extended tributary modem. This modem will give an indication that it is receiving carrier by turning on lead 8, Carrier Detect, as an output signal. The attached device, 3270 controller, will then be able to monitor this lead.

In a multipoint circuit, the bridging in the network will allow this carrier to be received by all endpoints. The user should not have to do anything to allow this other than specify "multipoint" when the circuit is ordered. The network provided will ensure that the bridging occurs.

What about carrier control in the other direction? This is where the point-to-point versus multipoint distinction occurs. In a point-to-point environment, the extended modem should be optioned for Continuous Carrier. This will transmit carrier to the extended control modem, which provides an indication on lead 8. Through our "cross-over" cable, the collocated backbone tributary modem will have Request to Send on. This is immaterial, as the backbone tributary should be optioned for Continuous Carrier, Continuous Request to Send as there will be only one carrier signal possible in the backbone point-to-point circuit. This carrier signal will be received by the backbone control modem with a signal on lead 8 to the FEP for carrier detect. CONGRATULATIONS! Carrier control has been obtained.

In a multipoint environment, the attached 3270 controllers bring up their Request to Send leads when invited to send information on the network. The protocols ensure that only one 3270 responds at a time. However, the optioning of the modems are important to ensure that carrier is transmitted only when it should be. With a multipoint line, only one of the endpoints should be transmitting carrier at any given time. The modems should be optioned for Switched Carrier, Switched Request to Send to support this. With this setup, whenever a 3270 controller raises Request to Send, carrier will be transmitted. Following this to the other end, our "cross-over" cable will allow the extended control modem to indicate a received carrier on lead 8 and onto lead 4 of the backbone tributary modem.

The key here is that only the multipoint endpoint that is transmitting is actually sending carrier due to the Switched Carrier option. If all the multipoint modems were optioned for Continuous Carrier, then the extended control modem would be receiving multiple carriers, resulting in conflicting carrier signals that could mess up data modulation.

The cable designs have been elaborate thus far for the extended piece, but the only remaining control category leads are Data Terminal Ready and Data Set Ready. Data Terminal Ready is an input signal to the modem indicating the readiness of the attached DTE, while Data Set Ready indicates the status of the modem to the attached DTE. Our attached DTE is nonexistent, but rather is an attached modem. These two signals need to be "crossed-over" as in Table 3–64. Now as long as power is applied to the modems, and they are functioning properly, Data Set Ready will be on. This in turn keeps Data Terminal Ready high on the collocated modem.

What about the data leads? They need to be crossed over between the collocated modems. Lead 2 from one modem should be connected to lead 3 in the other modem's port, and vice versa. The easiest method of understanding this is to follow the data through as it passes from end to end in the circuit. The backbone control modem receives its data from the FEP on lead 2. These data are transmitted to the backbone tributary (BT) modem, thanks to our timing setup. These received data are output on the BT's lead 3. Normally, this is an

TABLE 3–64. EQUIPMENT CONTROL LEADS IN EXTENDED CIRCUIT

Backbone tributary modem			Extended control modem	
Function	Lead #	Lead #		Function
Data Set Ready (out)	6 -----⟩	20		Data Terminal Ready (in)
Data Terminal Ready (in)	20 ⟨-----	6		Data Set Ready (out)

input data lead to a piece of DTE. However, our extended control modem's lead 3 is an output just as the BT's. Crossing this lead over to the extended control modem's Transmit Data signal, lead 2, the data will be sent to the pigtail end of the circuit. It is presented to the attached 3270 controller as received data on lead 3. Repeat this in the other direction to assure yourself that you need to cross the two data leads between the collocated modems.

The only category of leads left between the collocated modems is ground. The ground leads, Protective Ground and Signal Ground, should be connected "straight through" on leads 1 and 7, respectively. Table 3–65 summarizes the completed back-to-back modem design for modems in an extended circuit.

This completes the cable design for the collocated modems. But what about the pigtail-end cable for connecting the extended tributary modem to the 3270 controller? The timing information was covered in the earlier section on timing. Specifically, lead 17 was looped back to lead 24 for the modem. This coupled with the external timing option allows synchronization. However, how does the 3270 obtain the timing signals for transmitting and receiving data? The external option causes the modem to phase lock its timing crystal to the signal found on lead 24. This same signal is then output on lead 15 as transmit timing to the attached 3270. This occurs in most modems with this option. However, some of them may not actually output this signal on lead 15. To be safe, you can connect lead 17 to 15 as well as lead 24. Now all three leads contain the same timing signal. Ensure that leads 15 and 17 go through the cable to the 3270 controller. If you are sure that the modem, when optioned for external timing, provides this same timing signal out on lead 15, then connect lead 15 "straight through" without connecting it to lead 17.

What about the other category of leads—ground, data, and control? The rest of the cable is a "straight through" cable. Table 3–66 outlines the cable design.

This concludes the option changes that we sought. If you want to permanently save these changes, then enter "AT&W" followed by a Carriage Return. This saves these options even when the modem is turned off. The factory settings for the modem would have worked, yet the author prefers to see the RS232 interface function according to the standard.

When a modem claims that it offers Hayes compatibility, the foregoing commands, along with many more, cause the modem to behave just like the Hayes Smartmodem would. Furthermore, the modem gives the same results and result codes as the Hayes modems do.

TABLE 3–65. COMPLETE CABLE DESIGN FOR COLLOCATED MODEMS IN EXTENDED CIRCUIT

Function	Modem lead #	Modem lead #	Function
Protective Ground	1 -------	1	Protective Ground
Signal Ground	7 -------	7	Signal Ground
Transmit Data (in)	2 ⟨------	3	Receive Data (out)
Receive Data (out)	3 ------⟩	2	Transmit Data (in)
Carrier Detect (out)	8 ------⟩	4	Request to Send (in)
Request to Send (in)	4 ⟨------	8	Carrier Detect (out)
Data Set Ready (out)	6 ------⟩	20	Data Terminal Ready (in)
Data Terminal Ready (in)	20 ⟨------	6	Data Set Ready (out)
Receive Timing (out)	17 ------⟩	24	Transmit Timing (in)
Transmit Timing (in)	24 ⟨------	17	Receive Timing (out)

TABLE 3–66. PIGTAIL CABLE DESIGN FOR EXTENDED TRIBUTARY MODEM-TO-3270 CONNECTION

Function	Modem lead #	3270 lead #	Function
Protective Ground	1 -------	1	Protective Ground
Signal Ground	7 -------	7	Signal Ground
Transmit Data (in)	2 -------	2	Transmit Data (out)
Receive Data (out)	3 -------	3	Receive Data (in)
Request to Send (in)	4 -------	4	Request to Send (out)
Clear to Send (out)	5 -------	5	Clear to Send (in)
Data Set Ready (out)	6 -------	6	Data Set Ready (in)
Carrier Detect (out)	8 -------	8	Carrier Detect (in)
Data Terminal Ready (in)	20 -------	20	Data Terminal Ready (out)
Transmit Timing (out)	15 ---|---	15	Transmit Timing (in)
Receive Timing (out)	17 ---|---	17	Receiving Timing (in)
Transmit Timing (in)	24 ⟨-|		

NOTE: The reason for connecting all the timing leads together is that certain modems may not output transmit timing on lead 15, even though they are optioned for external timing.

MODEM INTERFACING: MOST FREQUENTLY ASKED QUESTIONS

Question 1. Why can't a null-modem cable be used to connect two synchronous DTE devices together (back to back)?

Answer 1. The requirement for timing in a synchronous connection restricts the use of a standard null-modem cable. Normally two synchronous DTE devices, such as a mainframe and a 3270 controller, are connected with synchronous modems between them. The modems provide the necessary timing. When connecting them back to back, the timing source(s) is lost. If one of the DTE devices can provide the timing, then a null-modem cable, with added leads for the timing, may be used. Otherwise, a synchronous modem eliminator is required to provide the timing as well as the null-modem cable function.

Question 2. Why can't an asynchronous modem support synchronous devices?

Answer 2. One of the principles of asynchronous transmission is the framing of each character with a start and stop bit. These enclosing bits provide the timing. With synchronous communications, a timing source is used by the attached device for outputting the data. Without a clock pulse, the DTE would never send out data. An asynchronous modem does not provide the timing lead, nor allow for such transmission. Thus asynchronous modems cannot support synchronous transmission. However, some low-speed dial-up modems now offer both asynchronous and synchronous transmission capabilities. The attached device's transmission technique should match that of the modem.

Question 3. What is "AT" compatibility when referring to intelligent modems?

Answer 3. "AT" compatibility describes a modem's ability to support a standard command set. This standard was established by Hayes Microcomputer Products with its Smartmodem series of modems. The sequence, "AT," short for Attention, preceded the bulk of the commands that the modem accepted. As software programmers and users made use of this command set in the Hayes modems, other modem vendors offered the same support. Modems with "AT" compatibility support the same, a super-set, or subset of the Hayes Smartmodem series commands.

Question 4. Why are all 1200 baud modems not compatible?

Answer 4. 1200 bps indicates the speed of the modem. Other factors such as modulation techniques determine if two modems can communicate. AT&T offered the 212A modem that used one modulation technique at 300 bps and a different technique at 1200 bps. Furthermore, the 212A was a full-duplex modem. Some 1200 bps modems are half-duplex only, making them incompatible with a 212A modem.

Question 5. What is the normal gender of a modem?

Answer 5. Almost all modems are provided with a female connector. This is the recommendation as outlined in the RS232-C standard. The standard indicates that a female connector should be associated with, but not necessarily physically attached to, the DCE equipment. This implies that a cable could extend from the modem device with a female connector at the end of the cable. However, most modems have the female connector mounted directly on the back of the modem. The standard suggests that DTE devices provide male connectors.

Question 6. What is security dial back, and how does it work?

Answer 6. This is a feature of a computer, or possibly a modem, that protects a computer system from illegal access by unauthorized users. The concept stems from the fact that most users access a computer system from stable points, normally their office and/or home. The terminals, or PC, used to access remote computer systems have modems and associated phone numbers. The dial-back feature allows the remote computer system to store information about users, such as their phone numbers associated with their modems. Once a user dials in, the computer system can then accept a login, or immediately prompt the user for the phone number from where he or she is calling. A disconnect occurs with the computer checking its database and calling the input number. If the number matches a database entry, then the computer knows who the user should be. Once the computer's outbound call is answered by the computer/terminal of the originator of the session, the login prompt is issued. Comparisons are made to determine that logins, passwords, and phones numbers are valid. Otherwise, a disconnect occurs to close out the session.

4

CONNECTING TERMINALS

If you have just purchased a computer system, the power is waiting to be unleashed by you. Now the time has come to connect a terminal to the multiuser system. The computer vendor indicated that, depending on the terminal purchased, the system can do marvelous things. The terminal vendor, if different from the computer vendor, swears that even a child can connect the terminal to the computer. Of course, the caveat is that the correct cabling is used.

Probably the best example of this is the addition of a terminal to an IBM PC/AT, or 80386 machine. The computer can support more than one user at the same time. To date there has not really been a need for two users to share the system. As users become more reliant upon the information in the computer, it may make sense to share the same information. What was a simple installation may now be considered to be a bit more sophisticated.

The other popular area requiring a terminal-to-computer connection is the multi user micro (MUM). Computers such as the AT&T 3Bs, NCR Tower, and Altos systems are classic examples of supermicros. Each of these requires a terminal to be added to the system for user interaction with the programs. This is in contrast to a PC, which has the cathode ray tube and keyboard as part of the system. The popularity of UNIX is pushing use of these types of systems into more and more companies as they appear to economical. The cost of adding another user is minimal, as only another terminal is needed. With UNIX, just about any asynchronous ASCII terminal may be used.

If an additional terminal is going to be added to the computer system that has already been running, the potential headache has probably already been alleviated. The question is: Has a similar device been added in the past? Or is this a different product? If a similar device has been added, it is hoped that the installation procedures have been documented, allowing for a mere repeating of the cabling and system setup. If a different terminal is to be connected, the first step should be to determine whether or not the terminal will work with the computer.

How does the user know if a particular terminal will work with the computer? Several factors are involved that must be analyzed to ensure whether the connection is feasible. The user must determine if the terminal and computer are compatible.

PROPRIETARY VERSUS NONPROPRIETARY TERMINALS

Proprietary Terminal Required

The first determination is that of the nature of the port on the computer. Does a port support a variety of terminals, or are only specific devices supported? Some computer systems were designed for general and specific applications that use unique terminals. These ports are generally designed by the computer vendor to support only a limited type of terminal. That is, the vendor has intentions of selling its own proprietary terminals and, thus, programs the port to only work with their terminals, or 100 percent compatibles. Often the applications dictate this, but generally this is dictated by the vendor who is building to an overall proprietary architecture.

Probably the best example of this is the IBM System 34/36/38 computer family. These devices do not work with just any terminal; for example, a Digital Equipment Corporation (DEC) VT100 terminal is not supported by the system. IBM offers the 5250 series of terminals. These terminals, or 5250 compatibles, are required for connection to the computer. Hence if you are trying to connect an asynchronous ASCII-type terminal to the computer, it cannot be done.

Other minicomputer manufacturers include NEC, Tandem, Centurion, Burroughs, and Wang. In many of these cases, the applications justified the use of a special type of terminal. Wang offers many word processing features on its computers that require dedicated terminals.

These examples are only a few of many that require attention. The key point is that there are no guarantees that any terminal will work with any computer. Thus, the first step is to determine if a unique terminal is required to work with the computer system. If the system only accepts a proprietary or specific terminal, be sure that the terminal you are connecting is the specific terminal required.

The other option is to acquire a 100 percent-compatible terminal. Using the IBM System 36, for example, a 5250 series terminal is required. The user needs either an IBM 5251 terminal or compatible to work. Other vendors, such as Control Concepts, offer terminals that look like and behave like the 5251. Matching keyboards, CRTs, and ports are included in these terminals. These terminals may be connected successfully to the computer system. Determine early on whether proprietary or specific terminals are required.

Nonproprietary Requirements

Once it is determined that more than just the vendor's terminals will work with the computer, the user has a wider variety of terminals from which to choose. Operating systems are evolving to support this concept. The UNIX system is a good example. It will support a number of different terminals. This is made possible not so much due to connectivity, but mainly due to the software definition of how the terminal is set up. Refer to the discussion later in this chapter for more information on interfacing to UNIX systems.

How will you know for sure if the terminal will work? Research the characteristics of the terminal. Typically, the model number and name brand of the terminal are often sufficient to determine if it is compatible with the computer system. Other factors that tend to be important are the transmission mode, asynchronous or synchronous, speeds, emulation, duplex, and so on. Armed with this information, you will be ready to determine the compatibility with the computer system.

Asynchronous Versus Synchronous

There are two general modes in which ports on a computer and terminal operate, asynchronous and synchronous. There is a third mode termed *isochronous*. However, the number of ports supporting this mode is not as great as for the other two modes.

Most multiuser microsystems offer RS232-compatible interfaces. The computers are designed to communicate with an attached terminal at speed of up to 19,200 bps. Speeds of this magnitude are possible because of the limited distance between the terminal and the computer. This distance accommodates the asynchronous mode of transmission rather nicely. Asynchronous transmission allows character transmission at sporadic intervals due to its own inherent timing feature.

The concept of enclosing a character with a start and stop bit is known as asynchronous transmission. The start bit indicates to the receiving entity the time to start looking for the bits of the character; the stop bit lets the entity know when the entire character has arrived. The "timing" for the beginning and end of the character is provided by the start and stop bits. Because of this, it is said that, in asynchronous transmission, the start and stop bits provide the timing. Each character is individually synchronized (timed).

TABLE 4–1. POPULAR ASYNCHRONOUS
TERMINALS

Vendor	Model
Applied Digital Data System (ADDS)	Regent
AT&T Information Systems	4410
AT&T Information Systems	5410
AT&T Information Systems	610
Digital Equipment Corp. (DEC)	VT52
Digital Equipment Corp. (DEC)	VT100
Digital Equipment Corp. (DEC)	VT220
Hazeltime	1420
Hewlett-Packard (HP)	2621
Hewlett-Packard (HP)	2624
IBM Corporation	3101
Lear-Siegler	ADM3A
Televideo	910
Televideo	925

The synchronous mode of transmission allows high speeds of data transmission. It accomplishes this through its timing function. For ports that are to be used in a synchronous environment, the discussion will be deferred until later in this chapter. The key determination is whether the port is an asynchronous port or synchronous. Whichever, the terminal must match.

The connection of terminals to MUMs is typically done using an asynchronous interface. This is primarily due to the cost, price/performance, and limited complexity of the hardware involved. More than likely, if a multiuser system and UNIX operating system are being used, then you can almost be sure that the asynchronous mode will more than likely be used. Even when UNIX is not used, most minicomputers and supermicros do support asynchronous ASCII terminals.

If the port supports asynchronous terminals, how can you tell if a terminal is compatible? The easiest means is to check the terminal's user's guide documentation. If this is not available, ask someone. Should neither of these be available, call the vendor. Some of the popular asynchronous ASCII terminals are listed in Table 4–1.

VT100 COMPATIBILITY

The terminals, because of their popularity, are imitated by many plug-compatible manufacturers. Terminal manufacturers produce terminals that offer emulation. For example, AT&T offers the 610 terminal, which is DEC VT100 compatible. This implies that the terminal behaves the same as the DEC VT100 terminal. Most computers and applications that support the DEC VT100 also will support the AT&T 610.

The DEC VT100 terminal is only one of the terminals that is flattered by plug-compatible manufacturers. The Tektronix graphics terminals, HP 2600s, ADDS Regent, and others have their share of lookalikes. In addition, many software packages are available to run on the IBM PC and Apple computers to make them emulate these popular terminals. With these software packages, the personal computers can appear as a terminal to the computer to which they are connected. This allows them to work with the applications on that computer. A word of caution, however. Being a compatible terminal or PC software emulation package offering terminal capabilities does not necessarily imply that the hardware interface (i.e., RS232) has exactly the same pinouts. However, the terminal should be functionally equivalent to the terminal being emulated.

X3.64

One of the reasons for the popularity of the DEC VT100 is that it conforms to an American National Standards Institute (ANSI) standard for data terminal equipment (DTE). The ANSI X3.64 standard lays out the commands that a terminal should accept and interpret to ensure proper functionality across a wide range of computer systems. The intent is that as long as this standard is conformed to, applications written for it will support those terminals.

The standard lists a series of escape sequences along with their corresponding actions. A terminal that conforms to the standard will receive these sequences from the computer with which it is connected. Upon receipt, the terminal should interpret these escape sequences as dictated in the standard. An example is in order.

Assume that a supermicro is running a program that accepts data from a user at a DEC VT100 terminal. Probably once the user has logged onto the terminal, the data entry application software will want to paint a form on the terminal for operator input. Prior to doing this, the terminal screen probably needs to be erased, as it likely has characters left on it from the login sequence. How does the software in the computer erase the screen of the terminal? If the program is written with the X3.64 escape sequences in mind, and the terminal is a DEC VT100 or compatible, the solution is quite simple. The standard indicates that the terminal will interpret the receipt of the escape sequence "Escape [2J" to mean clear the screen. Upon receipt, the terminal should erase the screen. Other functions include positioning the cursor anywhere on the screen, setting up protected fields, setting up field attributes (blink, reverse video, underscore, etc.), reading the screen, and resetting the terminal, to name just a few. Each one of these actions has a control code sequence that dictates what action should occur at the terminal. Consult Appendix H for a listing of popular terminals and their escape sequence, including those of the DEC VT100 (X3.64) class terminal.

Getting back to our example, once the screen is cleared, the application would set up the blank form on the screen. What if the application is to be used by a number of different users on a variety of terminals? If a mixture of DEC VT100s, HP 2621s, and IBM 3101s is to be used to access the data entry application, how will this be handled. The HP 2621 and IBM 3101 do not conform to the X3.64 standard as the VT100 does. The application will have to have the ability to send separate escape sequences depending on which terminal is used. The exception to this is if the computer is using the UNIX operating system. UNIX computers have a utility known as either "Termcap" or "Terminfo" that does for the application what the X3.64 did for the terminals.

TERMCAP/TERMINFO

These utilities offer an application program the opportunity to not worry about the terminal that ultimately will be using it. Termcap (all discussions are equally applicable to Terminfo) have mnemonics which equate to the functions discussed earlier, such as clear screen and home the cursor. The list of these functions is rather extensive.

The concept is to create an entry in the Termcap database for any terminal that might be used on the computer system, regardless of application. For every terminal that is entered into Termcap, the escape sequences that it interprets for the functions (clear screen, home cursor, blink, etc.) are included. Once these mnemonics are equated to specific escape sequences, the terminal is considered to be supported by Termcap.

The system merely needs to know which terminal is being used. This is usually set up at login time. Within UNIX System V, the user's ".profile" (read "dot profile") can include this definition. The command sequence is as simple as "TERM=vt100." Once this information is exported with "export TERM," the application is home free. It merely uses the mnemonics to communicate with the terminal, with Termcap translating the mnemonics into the appropriate escape sequences.

The intent here is not to be on a UNIX soapbox but, rather, to give the readers a means of determining if their terminals may be used with a computer system. If the terminal is listed in Termcap/Terminfo, chances are good that the terminal will work with the computer system.

SPEED

Be sure that the speeds offered by the computer are similar to those of the terminal. It is not important that the terminal support all the speeds of the computer, and vice versa. But there needs to be a common one. For example, a terminal may support speeds of 110, 300, 600, 1200, 1800, 2400, 4800, 9600, and 19,200 bps (bits per second). The computer may only support speeds of 300, 1200, 2400, 4800, and 9600. As long as there is one common speed, the two are compatible.

What are typical speeds? Typically, computer ports that are expecting connection of a terminal directly to a port (see the next section for discussion of local versus remote) operate at speeds up to 19,200 bps. However, 9600 bps is a very common speed. This allows for relatively high-speed interaction between the user and the computer application.

Speeds of 19,200 bps are feasible if the ports of both the computer and terminal are indeed capable of these speeds. Often, the computer port can physically clock the data out at 19,200 bps but may have trouble accepting characters at that high rate.

This is usually the case when the port on the computer does not have what is referred to as intelligent I/O (input/output). Intelligent I/O generally implies that a microprocessor is present to drive the port(s). This computer chip is dedicated to managing the input and output operation of the port. The chip usually has its own memory that it can utilize, allowing for fast speeds.

This is in contrast to computer systems that use the main computer chip to drive I/O in addition to all the other computer operations. When I/O operations must be handled along with the standard demands of the application and system software, the throughput speed of the port is somewhat limited.

An example is in order. Assume that the computer system is performing a spreadsheet recalculation. Along with this, assume that the operating system, such as UNIX, offers a feature known as file hardening. File hardening is a nifty feature that aids in the reliability of data. Operating systems with this feature write copies of memory to disk on a predetermined schedule. In case of a power outage, only the data altered in memory since the last automatic memory save (file hardening) is lost. In addition to this, the user at a terminal is entering data onto the screen. Also, electronic mail has been initialized automatically by the system, per the system administrator's beckoning. To summarize, we have at least four potential operations occurring on the system.

What if all these occurred at once? The central computer is a very, very fast processor, yet it can get bogged down. In a multitasking system, as just described, the computer allocates its processing time to each task based on some algorithm that it took the labs years to develop. If, for some reason, the user types at approximately 80 characters per minute (not a chance with this author!), and the other three operations are in motion, we can now understand why the speed may be limited. If the computer is in the middle of a recalculation on the spreadsheet, and is set to process the electronic mail request next, it may not get to the process of accepting the input from the keyboard that is smokin' from the burst of input. Regardless of how fast the computer is, the system can only service each process one at a time. Depending on the speed of the computer, it may be able to keep up with a 9600 bps port, but not a 19,200 bps port. Unless previously tested, it is usually safe to operate most computer ports at 9600 bps. Most terminals can operate at 19,200 bps, but because of the foregoing, the computer port may limit the operation to 9600 bps.

FLOW CONTROL

Once the speed of the terminal, or PC emulating a terminal, is decided upon, another issue crops up. At speeds of 9600 bps, the data output from the computer to the terminal zips across the interface at a rapid pace. Even at 1200 bps, the actual character output is approximately 120 characters per second (cps). Regardless of speeds, there are occasions when either end—the computer or terminal—may want temporarily to halt the reception of data. The receiving device needs to have a means of indicating to the transmitting device to halt transmission of information. This means is a technique termed flow control. Flow control is a common practice when a printer, or lower-speed device, can't keep up with the outputting device.

However, it is just as important when connecting a terminal device to a computer port. Flow control becomes an issue when a printer is connected to the back of the terminal instead of the computer the terminal is attached to. Certain terminals offer a printer, or auxiliary port for local attachment of a printer. These terminals offer a Print Online (or POL) feature, enabling anything that is sent to the terminal to be printed on the printer. While the terminal may be able to keep up with the high-speed transfer of data, an attached printer may not. Normal printer conditions of buffer overrun, out-of-power condition, or paper jam demand the use of flow control.

One of the best examples of the need for flow control is the case when a PC is being used as a terminal, connected directly to a multiuser computer. For this explanation, assume that an IBM PC with Procomm communication software is emulating a VT100 terminal. If this terminal (PC with emulator software) is receiving a large file from the computer to which it is attached, chances are good that the user wants to save this information onto his disk drive.

Typical emulation software collects a certain amount of data from the source computer and keeps it in main memory (RAM). The source computer is the system that is dumping the information. The information is said to be downloaded from the source computer. Once the emulation software has received a preset amount of data from the source, it is necessary to write this information on the disk drive. Keep in mind that the PC is no different from the most powerful computer in that it can only do one operation at a time. If it merely begins to write the collected information to the disk drive, the source computer will continue downloading data. Without the source pausing until the PC can complete its disk I/O operation, the newly received data will be lost.

Fret not! Flow control is the means with which a PC can notify the source computer to halt downloading temporarily until the PC is ready to receive more information. There are several methods of flow control, but the principle is the same. The receiving computer transmits a character to the source computer which is interpreted by the source computer to halt transmission. When the receiving computer is ready to once again receive more information, it transmits another character to the source computer. The source interprets this character as a sign that it may resume downloading. The PC, which is controlling the on/off of transmission, can halt transmission for as long as is required to write the data onto disk.

The most popular method of flow control used in asynchronous transmission, and hence in a direct terminal-to-computer connection, is XON/XOFF. In our previous example, the PC would send an XOFF character to the source computer to halt transmission. Upon completion of the disk drive write, an XON would be sent from the PC to the source. The source would receive the XON character and resume transmission.

Why the lengthy discussion on flow control? As more and more PCs are being used as terminals on multiuser systems, the uploading and downloading of files increases. In these cases, it is important that both ends—the PC and the source computer—use the same flow control technique.

The previous discussions centered on the use of a terminal directly connected to the port on a computer. This is commonly referred to as a locally attached device. These factors are as equally important to those terminals that access computers from remote locations. As more and more PCs are purchased for use in the home, the accessing of the office computer remotely is becoming more commonplace. When this occurs, the elements of flow control, speed, and so on are just as important to guarantee a successful connection.

DUPLEX

The feature of flow control is made possible by the capability of data transmission in both directions simultaneously. That is, even while the source computer was downloading information to the PC, the PC could send the XOFF character to the source computer. This is known as full duplex transmission. Just about all computer ports work in a full duplex mode, with this being their typical mode. The same is true for terminals, PCs emulating terminals, and printers. This used to be a lot bigger issue than it is today. However, be aware that both the terminal and computer should be set up to operate in the same mode.

Half duplex is another mode of transmission that allows transmission of data in both directions, with one exception. It only allows this transmission in one direction at a time. In our previous example of the computer and the PC, XON/XOFF flow control would not have worked. With the computer downloading the information to the PC, the XOFF could not have been sent simultaneously to halt transmission. This mode is rarely used when connecting a terminal to a computer, but the user should be aware that it is generally offered as an option on both the computer port and the terminal.

However, it has taken on a new role in most devices today. Local echo of whatever is typed on the keyboard is provided by the half duplex option. Typically, when a terminal is connected to a computer, full duplex is used. This allows the computer to echo any character that is typed on the keyboard back to the screen. Echoplex is the term that describes this function.

However, in some cases, it may be desirable for the terminal to not rely on the computer for this. In those cases, the half duplex option functions as a local echoer of all typed characters. If the computer you are connecting does not have the capability of echoing your input, select the half duplex option on the terminal.

DTE/DCE EMULATION

The RS232 port on terminals can be one of two types. The serial ports can emulate data terminal equipment (DTE) or data communication equipment (DCE). The RS232 standard supports the interconnection of both DTE and DCE devices for serial communications. As such, the device's ports can take on the characteristics of either DTE or DCE. This means that a port that looks like DTE provides the leads and expects the leads, as laid out in the RS232 standard for DTE equipment. The same is true for DCE ports. DTE ports provide the signals Transmit Data (2), Request to Send (4), and Data Terminal Equipment (20), while DCE ports provide Receive Data (3), Clear to Send (5), Data Set Ready (6), and Data Carrier Detect (8). Consult Appendix A for a complete listing of the leads and their direction.

An explanation is in order. Typically, a computer, terminal, or printer is referred to as DTE. These type devices offered RS232 ports that were equipped for direct connection to a modem. The modem was termed DCE as it was the data communication equipment that allowed remote systems to exchange data over the communications network. If a device, such as a computer, was to be connected to a modem, a straight-through cable could be used. This straight-through cable had pin 1 at one end of the cable connected to pin 1 at the other end of the cable. Leads 2–25 would also be connected in a similar fashion. This was possible because of the strict conformance to the RS232 standard. Hence, the computer port was emulating DTE, while the modem port was emulating DCE.

Terminals would also have ports that emulated DTE. This would allow them to also be connected to modems for dial-up access to remote computer systems. As minicomputers and micros began to appear within companies, the issue of what a port looked like became increasingly important. If a minicomputer, such as a Digital Equipment Corporation PDP series computer, offered an asynchronous serial port, it was typically configured to emulate DTE. That is, a modem could be directly connected to the computer with a straight-through cable.

If, however, a terminal, such as the DEC VT100, was to be locally connected to the computer, a null modem cable (NMC) was required. These NMCs are covered thoroughly in this text. An NMC was required because two devices, both with DTE ports, were to be connected back to back. They were connected in such a fashion that they were fooled into behaving as if they were each connected to a modem. In reality, the leads were crossed to fake them out. As the bulk of users of these types of computers were all located in the same department of a business, or in the same building, modems were not required. The exception could be one modem on the system for remote access. Since this was the rule rather than the exception, computer vendors and terminal vendors began to provide solutions for connections that would not require expensive null modem cables. That is, they would change what the port on the device would emulate, so that a device with the opposite-type port could be directly connected with a straight-through cable.

If a computer port is configured to emulate DCE, or provide the RS232 signals normally provided by a modem, then a terminal (DTE) could be directly connected to the port with a straight-through cable. The terminal would have a port said to be emulating DTE. With the computer port emulating DCE, this type connection would be no different from a terminal-to-modem connection. This direct connection was less expensive than was using a null modem cable. Hence, a reference is made to what the computer port is emulating or looking like. In this case the computer port is emulating DCE. Printers, terminals, and other computers can be connected with a straight-through cable to this computer port.

Because some computers will have modems connected to them, it is not always desirable for the computer port to emulate DCE. This would require null modem cables to connect the modems to the computer ports, as this is a DCE-to-DCE connection. Anytime the same type of emulated ports are being connected, an NMC is required. Hence, most of the computer manufacturers left their ports emulating DTE. However, the several terminal vendors responded by having their ports emulate DCE. This is the reverse of what has just been described. When connecting a DTE computer port to a DCE terminal port, a straight-through cable can be used. The same is true for printers being connected to computers.

From this one can see the importance of understanding the type of port that a device is emulating. One cannot assume that, because a computer, terminal, or printer is normally classified as a piece of terminal equipment, it has a DTE-type port. Conversely, don't make the assumption that a piece of DCE, such as a protocol converter, offers a DCE-type port. It is more common, as a matter of practice, for a computer, terminal, or printer, to offer a different interface from DTE. However, it is imperative that the user understand that there could be a difference that would impact the cable required to connect two devices together.

Gender of Ports

Typically, DTE provide male connectors on their ports. Modems and other DCE provide female ports. This is a guideline and not a hard-and-fast rule. When the concept DTE/DCE emulation comes into play, the gender guidelines become nonexistent. Be aware that you cannot judge the type of port—DTE or DCE—by the gender of the port. However, either male or female ports will impact the type of cable ultimately required to connect two devices together.

PARITY

The computer system to which the terminal is being connected should dictate the parity setting in a terminal, whether it is remote or locally attached. Parity is a technique that allows for the detection of an error in a transmitted character. If you are expecting the letter "A" and you get something else, chances are that the parity is set improperly in your device or you had a parity error. A parity error is an alteration of the bits of a character so that an even or odd number of bits is not received as desired. On a terminal, you will be able to see if any parity errors have occurred because the character that you are expecting will be different. There are five typical settings for the type of parity that a device can have: even/odd/space/mark/none. Be consistent at both ends.

ECHOPLEX

A technique that works hand in hand with the parity setting is echoplex. Echoplex is the technique of allowing the remote device to which you are connected to send back every character as you type in on the keyboard. If you type "hello" on the keyboard without the echoplex option, your terminal will display the characters as they are typed. However, by the time the far end receives the characters, there could have been noise or a hit on the line, inducing errors. Your data would have been received by the computer in error.

However, if you let the far end echo your characters back to you, rather than the terminal displaying them locally, you would see any errors that occur. You could backspace and correct any errors. The echoplex option is often confused with full duplex versus half duplex. Conceptually, they are similar. Echoplexing requires a full duplex circuit, whereas no echoplexing does not. Typically, terminals and other devices offer one or both of these options. This author recommends echoplex where possible.

LINE-ENDING SEQUENCE

This is a fairly straightforward concept that can cause a lot of heartburn. It is very important that both devices—the terminal and connected computer—set these options with coordination. This is extremely important, as devices can interpret the characters they receive in a number of different manners, as well as transmit different sequences.

A terminal can typically be set up to send a carriage return, line feed, or both whenever the return key is typed. This should be set up to meet the requirements of the attached computer, either local or remote. If the attached computer system needs a line feed as the end of line sequence, option your terminal to output only a line feed. If the remote system will interpret either a line feed or a carriage return as a line feed, this option becomes less critical. Your terminal can also be optioned to interpret the receipt of one of these characters. Typical setups include the interpretation of a received line feed as a carriage return line feed, or just a line feed. Double spacing could occur, as well as overwriting on your screen of each line. Coordinate these options between the two devices. Often trial and error is an easy way to find the correct settings.

The options and concepts presented in this chapter should give the reader a better understanding of some of the generic issues involved when connecting terminals to different devices. The tutorial modules that follow will review the specifics of terminal interfacing through the step-by-step approach.

Tutorial Module 4-1: Connecting a DEC VT100 to UNIX Systems

A VT100-compatible will work here. The only caveat is that the RS232 interfaces may not be exactly the same. Earlier in the text, we noted that VT100 compatibility does not imply that the terminal has the same RS232 interface as the VT100. Rather, it is functionally equivalent, implying that the terminal will obey and respond to the same screen commands. However, this tutorial module will be easily adapted to the terminal of your choice.

To add some discipline to our approach, we will adhere to our different steps for connection. We will vary slightly from this as we are featuring two different computer systems. The intent here is to show two separate ports—one that emulates DTE as well as a DCE port—and the impact this has on the cable. An assumption will be made that UNIX Systems V is running on both these systems for clarity.

STEPS FOR CONNECTION

1. Determine compatibility (should it work?).
2. Determine signs of success.
3. Determine the type of connector used.
4. Determine gender of the ports.
5. Determine which leads (pins) are provided by each device.
6. Determine which leads are required to be on by each device.
7. Design the cable.

8. Build the cable.
9. Test the cable for continuity.
10. Cable the two systems together with the cable.
11. From step 2, measure success.

1. Determine compatibility

Prior to attempting this feat, the user should make a determination as to whether the connection is possible. Determine compatibility by checking the documentation for both devices. When this is not possible, the following procedure is a good method of determining if the two can communicate. If all else fails, ask around to determine if anyone has done the same or a similar connection.

One of the first items to check is compatibility between the ports. Consult the documentation to determine the possibilities of the terminal and computer ports. DEC VT100 compatibility with UNIX systems is pretty common. Hence, from a software standpoint, they should work together. What about the physical compatibility? The DEC VT100 terminal offers operation at speeds up to 19,200 bps, asynchronous mode, 7 or 8 bits per character, even-odd-no parity options, as well as XON/XOFF support. The UNIX systems support this same set of options. The common options between the ports could be 9600 bps, 7 data bits, and even parity, with XON/XOFF for flow control.

2. Determine signs of success

How will the user know if the connection is totally successful. The goal is to connect a terminal locally to the computer system for input, inquiry, or retrieval of information. The user will know when the VT100 has been successfully interfaced to the computer system when he or she can ''login:'' to the system. Furthermore, the user should have the ability to regulate the flow of data being output by the computer system. The XON/XOFF facility must function properly to constitute total success.

3. Determine type of connector used

4. Determine gender of ports

All systems involved—the DEC VT100, as well as the Altos 586/8600 and the Convergent Technology MegaFrame—offer DB25-type interfaces. They all offer ports that conform to the RS232 interface signal levels. The key difference is the gender of the ports. The DEC VT100 terminal is equipped with a male DB25P connector, as is the Altos 586. The Convergent Technology MegaFrame has a female connector for the serial port. This will impact the ultimate cable for connection.

5. Determine leads (pins) provided by each device

6. Determine leads required to be on

A break-out box can be used to determine the leads that are provided on each port. Refer to the other case studies for the techniques used for this type of port analysis. In this case study, the information will be pulled

TABLE 4–2. DEC VT100 RS232 PORT PINOUTS

Function	VT100 lead #
Protective Ground	1
Transmit Data (out)	2
Receive Data (to)	3
Request to Send (out)	4
Signal Ground	7
Secondary Ready to Send (out)	11
Data Terminal Ready (out)	20

NOTE: Your model of the VT100 line, or compatible, may support more leads. The leads in the table are those found in the basic VT100 terminal. In particular, you may have support for leads 5, 6, and/or 8 in addition to those shown here. This tutorial module will ignore them.

TABLE 4-3. CONVERGENT
TECHNOLOGY MEGAFRAME PORT
PINOUTS

Function	MegaFrame lead #
Protective Ground	1
Transmit Data (out)	2
Receive Data (to)	3
Request to Send (out)	4
Clear to Send (in)	5
Data Set Ready (in)	6
Signal Ground	7
Carrier Detect (in)	8
Data Terminal Ready (out)	20

from the device documentation as displayed in Tables 4–2, 4–3, 4–4. Once the pinouts are known, an assessment of the type device that the ports are emulating will be made. Once the information is known, fill in a Software Cabling System (SCS) port profile for each device for future reference.

Reviewing the pinouts for the DEC VT100, note the leads 2, 4, and 20. These leads are output relative to the DEC VT100 terminal. These are signals outlined in the RS232 standard provided by DTE. The input signal, Receive Data, is "to" the VT100. From this you can assess that the port on the terminal is emulating data terminal equipment, DTE. If your terminal differs from this by providing leads 5, 6, and/or 8, it too emulates DTE. This is an important point to note in your SCS port profile for later cable selection when connecting the terminal to the computer.

As with the VT100 terminal, this computer port has output signals of 2, 4, and 20, hinting that this is a DTE-type interface. Review the input signals Clear to Send, Data Set Ready, Carrier Detect, and Receive Data on leads 5, 6, 8, and 3, respectively. These leads conform to the RS232 standard confirming that this port is emulating a DTE interface.

Compare these pinouts with those of the Convergent Technology MegaFrame. In particular, note the direction of the leads. Although the functions and pin assignments are equivalent, the directions are just the opposite. If you were to review the RS232 standard in Appendix A, Receive Data (3), Clear to Send (5), Data Set Ready (6), and Data Carrier Detect (8) are leads "from" data communications equipment, DCE. The leads in this port have the same "from" direction. Also the other leads, Transmit Data, Request to Send, and Data Terminal Ready, have the opposite direction from what you would expect from a computer port. This port is emulating a DCE-type port. Refer to the discussion earlier in this chapter for further details on this and the impacts. If a piece of data transmission equipment is being connected to this type port, then more than likely a straight-through cable can be used. During the next section of cable design, you will see the difference between a DTE-to-DTE and a DTE-to-DCE connection.

TABLE 4-4. ALTOS 586/8600
PORT PINOUTS

Function	Altos lead #
Protective Ground	1
Transmit Data (to)	2
Receive Data (from)	3
Request to Send (to)	4
Clear to Send (from)	5
Data Set Ready (from)	6
Signal Ground	7
Carrier Detect (from)	8
Data Terminal Ready (to)	20

Line-Ending Sequence

TABLE 4–5. GROUND LEADS OF THE DEC VT100 AND ALTOS 586/8600 PORTS

Function	VT100 lead #	Altos lead #	Function
Protective Ground	1 ------- 1		Protective Ground
Signal Ground	7 ------- 7		Protective Ground

7. Design the cable

Now that the pinouts are known, you should update a port profile form for future references. Once these pins are known, the cable can be designed. Even though all three pieces of equipment are classified as data terminal equipment, our pinouts proved that the port on the Altos actually emulated DCE. This will impact our cable design. When connecting a DTE port to another DTE port, provided that they conform to the RS232 standard, then a standard null modem cable will work. When connecting a DTE-type port to a DCE port, then a straight-through cable can be used. Once again, the ports must otherwise conform to the RS232 standard. Let's explore each of these connections by designing cables for each.

The first to be covered will be the DEC VT100-to-Altos 586/8600 cable. This is a DTE-to-DCE connection. From the earlier premise, a straight-through cable should work here. The best way to determine this is to separate the leads into the categories of ground, data, control, and timing. As these are all asynchronous ports, ignore the timing category of leads.

Table 4–5 outlines the ground leads of both the DEC and Altos ports. The grounds are simple, as the user should merely connect "like" ground leads together. Hence, our cable design should connect pin 1 at one end of the cable to pin 1 at the other end of the cable. Connect the two Signal Ground leads together, and then repeat this for the Protective Ground leads.

The next category of leads is the data leads. Included in this are Transmit Data and Receive Data. In one device, Transmit Data is an output lead, while in the other, it is an input lead. The same holds true for the Receive Data lead. Consult the general cable design rules for assistance in the design of this and other category of leads.

CABLE DESIGN: GENERAL RULES

1. Connect like categories of leads together.
2. Always connect an "out" to an "in" and an "in" to an "out."
3. A lead that is input may be connected to another lead that is an input, only if both these are connected to an output lead.

Adhering to rules 1 and 2, the data leads are straightforward. Connect the Transmit Data (out) lead of the VT100 terminal straight through to the Transmit Data (in) lead of the Altos port. This connects pin 2 at both ends of the cable together. Repeat the operation for the Receive Data leads, connecting leads 3 together at both cable ends as outlined in Table 4–6.

If this is done, then any data output from the terminal on lead 2 will be received by the Altos computer on its input data lead, 2. Also the terminal will receive any data output by the Altos computer system. Thus far the cable design has been "straight through," as suggested in a DTE-to-DCE connection.

Because the timing leads are not appropriate here, the only category of leads remaining is the control leads. Review the control leads of both devices noting the directions of the leads. The Altos port offers support for more leads than does the VT100 terminal. In particular, Clear to Send, Data Set Ready, and Data Carrier

TABLE 4–6. DATA LEADS OF DEC VT100 AND ALTOS 586/8600

Function	VT100 lead #	Altos lead #	Function
Transmit Data (out)	2 ------- 2		Transmit Data (in)
Receive Data (in)	3 ------- 3		Receive Data (out)

TABLE 4–7. DEC VT100-to-ALTOS 586/8600 CABLE DESIGN

Function	VT100 lead #	Altos lead #	Function
Protective Ground	1 ------- 1		Protective Ground
Transmit Data (out)	2 ------- 2		Transmit Data (in)
Receive Data (in)	3 ------- 3		Receive Data (out)
Request to Send (out)	4 ------- 4		Request to Send (in)
Clear to Send (in)	5 ------- 5		Clear to Send (out)
Data Set Ready (in)	6 ------- 6		Data Set Ready (out)
Signal Ground	7 ------- 7		Protective Ground
Data Carrier Detect (in)	8 ------- 8		Data Carrier Detect (out)
Data Terminal Ready (out)	20 ------- 20		Data Terminal Ready (in)

NOTE: Leads 5, 6 and 8 are included for completeness as your terminal may require these leads to be on when connecting it to the Altos. The basic DEC VT100 does not support them, so they are not required.

Detect are absent from the VT100 port pinouts. Your terminal may actually have these leads. Be sure to include them as we proceed.

The control leads of the VT100 are Request to Send and Data Terminal Ready. These are output control leads ''from'' the terminal. The Altos computer port has these functions, on the same leads, but as input signals. As with the data leads, these can be connected straight through. Pin 4 at one end of the cable should have a conductor between it and pin 4 of the other end of the cable. The same holds true for pin 20. Whenever Request to Send is on at the terminal, the Altos will have its Return to Send lead on. When the VT100 has lead 20 on, which will be true when the terminal has power and is not in ''local'' mode, the Altos will know that the terminal is connected because its lead 20 is also on. Refer to Table 4–7 for these control leads as well as the completed cable design for DTE-to-DCE connections.

This completes the cable design for a DTE-to-DCE connection. What about connecting the DEC VT100 to the Convergent Technology MegaFrame computer? This is DTE-to-DTE connection that normally requires a null modem cable. The easiest way to design this cable, and determine if the premise of an NMC holds true, is to again design the cable by separate lead category. The same rules for cable design will be used throughout.

The ground leads will be connected, just as in the straight-through cable, as depicted in Table 4–5. This brings you to the data category of leads. Review Tables 4–2, 4–3, and 4–4 for the data lead pinouts. The Transmit Data leads appear on the same lead, pin 2. They do, however, have the same direction, ''out.'' The cable design rules don't allow an ''out'' to be connected to another ''out'' lead. An ''out'' should only be connected to an ''in.'' The same is true for the receive leads, in that they have the same directions, ''in.'' The goal is to have the output data lead from one device be connected to the input data lead at the other device. This will allow data being output by the VT100 to be received by the attached MegaFrame computer. To accomplish this, connect lead 2, the output data lead, of the VT100 across to lead 3, the input data lead, of the MegaFrame. Table 4–8 outlines this connection from one end of the cable to the other. The same connection holds true from the MegaFrame's transmit data lead perspective. It should be connected to the input lead on the VT100 port.

The only remaining category of leads is control. This is the most difficult category in our cable design. It is imperative that you keep the cable design rules in mind in this section. The goal is to ensure that any control leads that a device expects to be on are on at the appropriate time. Hence, the important leads are the input control leads. These leads need to be on for the interface to function. The output control leads will be used to keep these leads on as they have a positive voltage level when they are on.

Back-to-back pieces of DTE are being connected here. Hence, the cable should be designed to let each

TABLE 4–8. DATA LEAD DESIGN FOR VT100-TO-CONVERGENT TECHNOLOGY MEGAFRAME

Function	VT100 lead #	MegaFrame lead #	Function
Transmit Data (out)	2 ------) 3		Receive Data (in)
Receive Data (in)	3 (------ 2		Transmit Data (out)

TABLE 4-9. REQUEST-TO-SEND/CLEAR-TO-SEND CONNECTION IN NULL MODEM CABLE

Function	MegaFrame lead #
Request to Send (out)	4 --|
Clear to Send (in)	5 ⟨-|

NOTE: Do this at both ends of the cable for completeness, even though the basic DEC VT100 does not require Clear to Send to be on.

DTE behave as if an attached DCE were connected. The understanding of the Clear to Send, Data Set Ready, and Data Carrier Detect functions are necessary to design the cable. The reader is encouraged to read *RS232 Made Easy* for a complete description of each of these leads.

Clear to Send is a signal that is expected by most DTE, excluding the DEC VT100, to allow for a settling of the line when a modem is connected. Typically, the DTE raises Request to Send and, after a certain number of milliseconds, receives the Clear to Send. Hence, our cable design should allow for Clear to Send to come on when the DTE raises Request to Send. The best way for Clear to Send to come on when Request to Send is turned on by the DTE is to connect the two leads together at the cable end. By connecting these two leads together at the end of the cable that is to be plugged into the MegaFrame port, the result is achieved. Hence, whenever the MegaFrame port has Request to Send on, it will have Clear to Send on. Table 4-9 shows this connection. If your terminal also supports Clear to Send, then repeat this for the terminal cable end.

The pertinent lead is Data Carrier Detect. This lead is normally on whenever carrier is being received across a telephone line when modems are involved. Because no modems are involved in a back-to-back DTE connection, the line is not present. Yet the MegaFrame expects to receive an indication of when carrier is present. Request to Send controls carrier. When the DTE at one end of a circuit raises Request to Send, then Data Carrier Detect will be on at the other end, and the DTE will detect it. This null modem cable needs to mimic this indicator. Once again, the easiest way for data carrier at one end to be controlled by Request to Send at the other end is to connect the two leads together. Connect pin 4 at one end of the cable across to pin 8 at the other end, as shown in Table 4-10. The cable now has two leads, Clear to Send locally and Data Carrier Detect remotely, being controlled by the request to send.

The only input control lead left is Data Set Ready. In a dial-up environment, this lead is turned on by the modem once a connection is established with a remote system. Hence, the MegaFrame expects to see this lead on. The DEC VT100 does not require this lead to be on, yet your terminal may. If the Data Set Ready lead is to be on so the DTE knows when a connection is made, then without modems, this also needs to be mimicked. Review the function of the Data Terminal Ready lead in the VT100. As long as the terminal has power and is in the Online mode, this lead will be on. By connecting the DTR lead at one end of the cable across to lead 6, Data Set Ready, at the other end of the cable, the DTE will know when the other DTE is online. This online condition equates to a connection when modems are involved. Table 4-11 outlines this cross-over connection that has DTR from one DTE control Data Set Ready in the other DTE.

This takes care of all the input control leads of both interfaces. The complete cable design is outlined in Table 4-12. This is a standard null modem cable that is used to connect two pieces of DTE back to back.

TABLE 4-10. REQUEST-TO-SEND/DATA-CARRIER-DETECT CONNECTION IN NULL MODEM CABLE

Function	MegaFrame lead #	VT100 lead #	
Request to Send (out)	4 --|---⟩	8	Data Carrier Detect (in)
Clear to Send (in)	5 ⟨-|		

NOTE: Do this at both ends of the cable for completeness, even though the basic DEC VT100 does not require DCD to be on.

TABLE 4–11. DTR/DSR CONNECTION IN NULL MODEM CABLE

Function	VT100 lead #		MegaFrame lead #	
Data Terminal Ready (out)	20	------⟩	6	Data Set Ready (in)

NOTE: Do this at both ends of the cable for completeness, even though the basic DEC VT100 does not require DSR to be on.

TABLE 4–12. NULL MODEM CABLE FOR DEC VT100-TO-MEGAFRAME

Function	VT100 lead #		MegaFrame lead #	
Protective Ground	1	-------	1	Protective Ground
Signal Ground	7	-------	7	Protective Ground
Transmit Data (out)	2	------⟩	3	Receive Data (in)
Receive Data (in)	3	⟨------	2	Transmit Data (out)
Request to Send (out)	4	--|---⟩	8	Data Carrier Detect (in)
Clear to Send (in)	5	⟨-|		
Data Carrier Detect (in)	8	⟨---|--	4	Request to Send (out)
		|⟩	5	Clear to Send (in)
Data Terminal Ready (out)	20	------⟩	6	Data Set Ready (in)
Data Set Ready (in)	6	⟨------	20	Data Terminal Ready (out)

NOTE: The basic DEC VT100 does not need leads 5, 6, and 8 to be on, yet they are included for completeness. The above is a standard null modem cable.

8. Build the cable

9. Test for continuity

10. Cable the two systems together

Acquire or build a null modem cable for the DEC VT100-to-Convergent Technology connection, or the straight-through cable for the DEC VT100-to-Altos connection. These cables are fairly common. The key here is the genders. Refer to other tutorial modules for general cable building guidelines. If you construct your own cable, be sure and check for continuity. Once the cable is complete, connect the two systems together.

11. Measure success

The user will determine success by the ability to "login" on the UNIX system as well as to regulate the flow of information from the attached computer. With multiuser systems, there is much more to interfacing than just physically connecting the two systems together. Correct entries must be made in the UNIX systems files for the terminals to function. Refer to the "inittab" discussion in Tutorial Module 3–5. It is not the intention of this text to make you systems administrators of UNIX. Consult with the systems administrator to ensure that the port you are connected to is set up properly. The documentation for UNIX outlines the entries necessary for direct connection of terminals to the system. Furthermore, typically menu-driven interfaces provide automatic generation of the necessary entries. Depending on which version of UNIX you are running, the filenames containing the entries will vary. This is the first step to ensuring success.

Next check the options on the terminal to be sure that they match those of the UNIX system port. The common options outlined earlier were 9600 bps, 7 data bits, and even parity. Double check these to be sure that they are set properly in the VT100. With the terminal plugged into the systems, you can begin testing by powering up the terminal. If the UNIX entries are correct, you should get the "login:" prompt. Attempt to log in to the system with your ID and password. If you get logged in, attempt to list the contents of a file by using the "cat" command. This will allow you to test the flow control capability. The format for this command is "cat filename" followed by a Return key. As the file is being displayed on the screen, temporarily halt the output by hitting the "s" key while holding down the Control key. This sends an XOFF character. The display should be suspended.

To continue, enter a Control-q sequence to send an XON character. The displaying of the file should continue at this point. CONGRATULATIONS!

Should you not get the "login:" prompt, check the terminal options again. If they check out, be sure the terminal is connected to the correct port with the right cable and that the terminal has power. If you still do not get a prompt, consult the systems administrator.

If you get the information on the screen, but it is garbled, check the speed, character length, and parity options. Set them correctly, or through trial and error, determine the correct settings. If you get double spacing, or overwriting of data, the line-ending sequence option is set incorrectly. Double spacing typically means that your terminal is interpreting the receipt of a carriage return as a carriage return/line feed. If the attached system is sending out both a carriage return and a line feed, your system is adding an extra line feed. If you are overwriting all the data, then your terminal is expecting a line feed but is not receiving one. The far-end system is probably not sending one. Set the option so that receipt of a carriage return is interpreted as a carriage return and line feed. If you get a stair-step effect, your terminal is not receiving a carriage return as the attached computer is only sending out a line feed. You need to change the options so that receipt of a line feed is interpreted as a carriage return and line feed. Set these to match the requirements so that you get single spacing of the information. CONGRATULATIONS!

Tutorial Module 4-2: Connecting a PC Emulating a Terminal to a Computer

This module is exactly the same as in Tutorial Module 5–1. Refer to that Module for the details of what is involved in connecting the PC to a computer.

Tutorial Module 4-3: Connecting a Wyse Terminal to an IBM PC/AT

In this exercise we will be connecting a Wyse terminal, model WY-85, to an IBM PC/AT. Here we will refer to the terminal as a Wyse and the computer as an AT. Many other terminals may be connected to the AT, but we will use the WY-85. It offers VT52, VT100, and VT220 terminal compatibility. The AT can be a host of different compatibles, the key point being that we will be interfacing the terminal to a 9-pin RS232 port. Furthermore, a UNIX operating system will be running on the AT to support the use of a locally attached terminal. There are many cards that offer ports for connecting terminals to ATs as well as many different operating systems. Conceptually, this type connection will be the same regardless. This exercise will focus on how to construct a cable to connect the 9-pin AT port to a standard DB25-size connector. Figure 4–1 depicts the connections that we will be attempting. The steps we will follow are common to all our tutorial modules:

STEPS FOR CONNECTION

1. Determine compatibility (should it work?).
2. Determine signs of success.
3. Determine the type of connector used.

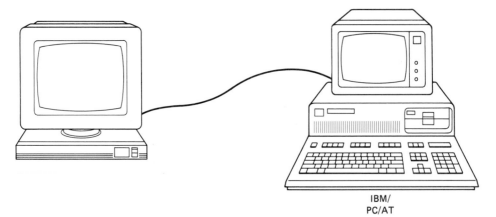

IBM/
PC/AT

Figure 4–1. IBM PC/AT-to-Wyse WY-85 terminal.

4. Determine gender of the ports.
5. Determine which leads (pins) are provided by each device.
6. Determine which leads are required to be on by each device.
7. Design the cable.
8. Build the cable.
9. Test the cable for continuity.
10. Cable the two systems together with the cable.
11. From step 2, measure success.

1. Determine compatibility

Prior to attempting this feat, determine whether this connection is possible. When connecting a terminal to a computer, the two ports must allow for the same communication parameters. Consult the documentation to see if they indeed are compatible. We can use our SCS port profile analysis worksheets to aid in this determination. If the AT is running the UNIX operating system, and it has a serial port, then more than likely it will be compatible. Let's review our ports, starting with the Wyse terminal (Table 4–13).

TABLE 4–13. SCS PORT PROFILE FOR WYSE WY-85 TERMINAL AND PC/AT

Terminal Port Profile

Underline if supported; circle if selected.

Model: WY-85 _____ Vendor: Wyse _____ Port: COMM_____
Port type: DB25 9-pin 5-pin 8-pin/modular 20mA Centronics

Gender: male female

Pin #	Function	Direction	Pin #	Function	Direction
1	Shield Ground	to from n/a	14		to from n/a
2	Transmit Data	to from n/a	15		to from n/a
3	Receive Data	to from n/a	16		to from n/a
4	Request to Send	to from n/a	17		to from n/a
5	Clear to Send	to from n/a	18		to from n/a
6	Data Set Ready	to from n/a	19		to from n/a
7	Signal Ground	to from n/a	20	Data Terminal Ready	to from n/a
8	Data Carrier Detect	to from n/a	21		to from n/a
9		to from n/a	22		to from n/a
10		to from n/a	23	Speed Selector	to from n/a
11		to from n/a	24		to from n/a
12	Speed Indicator	to from n/a	25		to from n/a
13		to from n/a			

Complete the next section only with 36-pin cinch connector.

26		to from n/a	27		to from n/a
28		to from n/a	29		to from n/a
30		to from n/a	31		to from n/a
32		to from n/a	33		to from n/a
34		to from n/a	35		to from n/a
36		to from n/a			

Flow control technique: (XON/XOFF) Hardware _____
Flow control lead(s): 4 11 19 20 __ __ __
Leads that must be on: 5 6 8 __ __ __ __

Printer port: serial   parallel
    Flow control: XON/XOFF hardware _____
    FC lead(s):   4 11 19 20 __ __ __   Connector DB25 Centronics

TABLE 4–13. (Continued)

Options:

    Speeds: 110 300 600 1200 1800 2400 4800 (9600) 19.2 56k _____
    Parity: (even) odd space mark none
    Char-length: (7) 8 _____
    # stop bits: (1) 1.5 2
    Line-ending sequence: cr lf cr/lf cr/lf/lf

    Mode: async sync isoch

	#	Function	Direction
		sync timing leads:	
	15	_____	to from
	17	_____	to from
	24	_____	to from

    Terminal compatibility: ANSI X3.64, VT100, VT220, VT52, _____

The IBM PC/AT documentation should be reviewed next, to fill in the blanks of the computer port profile worksheet. The PC/AT, as we will see, is much the same as a serial port on a standard PC or XT. The main difference will be in the size of the port. For now, let's fill in the worksheet as best we can, based on known information.

Computer Port Profile

Underline if supported; circle if selected.

Model: PC/AT _____ Vendor: IBM _____ Port: COMM _____
Port type: serial parallel
Port: DB25 9-pin 5-pin 8-pin/modular 20mA Centronics

Gender: male female

Pin #	Function	Direction	Pin #	Function	Direction
1	Carrier Detect	to from n/a	14	_____	to from n/a
2	Receive Data	to from n/a	15	_____	to from n/a
3	Transmit Data	to from n/a	16	_____	to from n/a
4	Data Terminal Ready	to from n/a	17	_____	to from n/a
5	Signal Ground	to from n/a	18	_____	to from n/a
6	Data Set Ready	to from n/a	19	_____	to from n/a
7	Request to Send	to from n/a	20	_____	to from n/a
8	Clear to Send	to from n/a	21	_____	to from n/a
9	Ring Indicator	to from n/a	22	_____	to from n/a
10	_____	to from n/a	23	_____	to from n/a
11	_____	to from n/a	24	_____	to from n/a
12	_____	to from n/a	25	_____	to from n/a
13	_____	to from n/a			

Complete the next section only with 36-pin cinch connector.

26	_____	to from n/a	27	_____	to from n/a
28	_____	to from n/a	29	_____	to from n/a
30	_____	to from n/a	31	_____	to from n/a
32	_____	to from n/a	33	_____	to from n/a
34	_____	to from n/a	35	_____	to from n/a
36	_____	to from n/a			

Flow control technique: XON/XOFF ENQ/ACK STX/ETX Hardware _____
Leads that must be on: 8 6 1 _____

TABLE 4–13. *(Continued)*

Options:

Speeds: 110 300 600 1200 1800 2400 4800 ⑨600 19.2 56k____

Parity: ⓔven odd space mark none

Char-length: ⑦ 8 ____

stop bits: ① 1.5 2 ‾‾

Line-ending sequence: cr lf cr/lf cr/lf/lf

Disconnect sequence: EOT DEL ~. _____

Mode: async sync isoch   sync timing leads:

#	Function	Direction
15	_____	to from
17	_____	to from
24	_____	to from

Notes: _____
_____
_____

From the foregoing information, taken directly from the user's documentation for each device, the terminal appears to be compatible with the AT. The common parameters will be 9600 bps, even parity, 1 stop bit, 7 data bits per character, and asynchronous mode. In a UNIX to terminal environment, these are common parameters, with XON/XOFF being used for flow control.

2. Determine signs of success

Now that you have determined that the two devices are compatible, how will you know when you have successfully connected the two systems together? Because this is a direct connection of a terminal to a computer, and the UNIX system on the AT supports multiuser operation, a "login" is involved. A "login" is required to allow a user access to the UNIX system. Upon successful connection of the terminal to the AT port, and proper setup, we will rejoice once we get the "login:" prompt and are able to send and receive data characters successfully. If UNIX is not yet loaded, then you can probably test out the system by using the Mode command. By redirecting the output and input to the Con: address, the terminal connection can be tested. Depending you whether UNIX is loaded, or merely MS-DOS, your signs of success will vary.

3. Determine type of connector

What type of connectors are used on each device? Consulting the documentation is a good way to know the types of connectors on each device. However, it is often just as easy to look at the ports themselves. Only if there are multiple ports on the back of a device is there potential confusion.

Taking a look at the back of the Wyse terminal, you find more than one port. Starting from left, there is a DB25 port labeled COMM, a 9-pin port labeled PR, a flat 8-pin port labeled 20mA, an 8-pin port labeled TEST, and a modular port for the KYBD. By the process of elimination, we can determine which port to use for connection to the AT. The 20 mA port was used prior to the advent of RS232 interface's rise to popularity; hence we will exclude it. The KYBD port is for the keyboard, and the TEST port is for testing purposes. This leaves two ports, COMM and PR. If we look at the AT, it also has a 9-pin port similar to the PR port on the back of the Wyse terminal. You would think that these two are the ports. NOT SO FAST! The COMM tag is an abbreviation for communication, with PR standing for printer. This is highlighted in the documentation, but can be surmised somewhat from the labeling. The COMM port will be used and is a DB25P-size connector. The 9-pin port, PR, is for connecting a local printer. Consult Tutorial Module 1-4 for the connection of a serial printer to these types of printer ports.

4. Determine gender of ports

Viewing the port just selected on the Wyse, the 25 pins indicate that the gender of the terminal port is male. Looking at an AT port, it is a male 9-pin connector. The AT computers also support boards that provide DB25-size ports. This tutorial module assumes that the RS232 interface on the AT is a 9-pin connector. Should your AT have a male DB25 port, consult the tutorial modules involving a PC/XT, as the PC/XTs also have a DB25 connector. The principles of connections will be the same.

5. Determine leads (pins) provided by each device

A port has four categories of leads: ground, data, control, and timing. Ignore the timing category of leads, as we are building a cable to function in an asynchronous environment. The ground leads are usually pins 1 and 7 in a DB25-size connector. However, since a 9-pin AT connector is involved, we cannot make this assumption. So we are interested in determining which ground, data, and control leads are provided by the computer and terminal. "Provided by the computer or terminal" implies that the device is the source of the lead. The direction of the lead is "from" the device, or "out."

The best possible method to determine the direction of the RS232 leads that are used is to consult the documentation. Usually, the manuals or application programmers' guides give the RS232 port pinout descriptions and directions. If the user does not have the information, a BOB or VOM can be used to determine this on the Wyse terminal. Because the AT has a 9-pin connector, and most BOBs have only DB25 connectors, we will use a VOM to check for leads that are "from" the AT. The BOB will be used to perform port analysis on the Wyse Wy-85 terminal port.

Because the Wyse port is a DB25 RS232 port, more than likely the ground leads will be found on leads 1 and 7. Consulting the documentation, this is confirmed. As always, the ground leads have no direction.

Connect a BOB to the COMM port on the back of the Wyse terminal. Power the BOB on as well as the terminal. If a tristate BOB is used, then three leads will be present: Transmit Data, Request to Send, and Data Terminal Ready. If a regular BOB is used, only Request to Send (4) and Data Terminal Ready (20) will be on. Transmit data lamp indicator will register a negative DC voltage indicating that it is "from" the terminal. The tristate shows this as a green light, while a standard BOB only shows this lead on when data are actually being transmitted. Pins 4 and 20 are on whenever the terminal is powered on and in Online mode. These lamps on either type of BOB will be illuminated.

How can we ascertain which leads are provided on the AT port? A BOB cannot be used as previously cited by connecting it to the port. The DB25 connectors on the BOB cannot be connected to the 9-pin AT port. However, using a VOM, or similar technique with a BOB, we can detect which leads are provided in the AT port. The port of a PC must be activated. The following command sequences may be used to enable the port.

"MODE LPT1:=COM1"
"Shift Key & PrtSc Key"

This sequence sets up the 9-pin port to be where the printer output goes, and the Shift/PrtSc sequence actually outputs a copy of the screen contents on the AT. The port should now be enabled.

Consult Tutorial Module 1-1 for the actual technique of using a VOM to determine which leads are present in the interface. Set the scale to be able to read from 0–15 volts DC. With one of the VOM probes touching a ground, touch each of the pins in the AT port. Note the VOM scale with each touching. You are interested in any measurement whatsoever. Pins 1, 2, 5, 6, 8, and 9 register no reading. This means that these leads are either input leads or ground leads. However, pins 3, 4, and 7 do register readings. Pins 4 and 7 should register a positive reading on the scale, normally around 12 volts. These leads, because they are on all the time when the port is enabled, are output control leads. On the other hand, pin 3 registered a reading, but a negative one. The needle on the VOM attempted to register a negative reading. This implies that the lead is off in RS232 terms, although it is present as an output lead. Sound vaguely familiar? Our tristate BOB detected a similar reading on the Wyse terminal lead 2. This turned out to be an output data lead. This is exactly what lead 3 of the AT port is, Transmit Data. We now know all the leads that are provided by both ports. Update the port profiles with this information for later reference. Table 4–14 summarizes the findings thus far.

Consulting the documentation for the AT, you can determine the function of pins 4 and 7. Pin 4 is Data Terminal Ready, normally found on pin 20 of a DB25 connector. Pin 7 is Request to Send, normally pin 4 on a DB25 connector. However, for this exercise, this is not important.

TABLE 4–14. PORT ANALYSIS FINDINGS FOR AT AND WY-85 TERMINAL

	Wyse WY-85		IBM PC/AT
2	Transmit Data (from)	3	Transmit Data (from)
4	Request to Send (from)	4	?? Control Lead (from)
20	Data Terminal Ready (from)	7	?? Control Lead (from)

Furthermore, it is important to find out which leads in the AT port are used for grounds. There is no easy way of determining this using a VOM. Pin 5 in the interface is used as a signal ground. This equates to pin 7 in the RS232 standard. Protective ground is not present, indicating that it is an isolated ground.

6. Determine which leads must be on

We will now proceed to the Wyse terminal to ascertain which control leads must be on for the terminal to communicate. With the BOB connected to the DB25 port labeled COMM, type on the terminal keyboard to see if data will be transmitted. Note the Transmit Data lead, pin 2, on the BOB. If the terminal has the default options set, this lamp should turn on and off to indicate that data are actually sent. It may be hard to notice the lamp being on, as the data you type are traveling at a face pace. You probably don't see any characters on the screen. If this is the case, the duplex option is probably set to full duplex. This is the option we desire once we connect the terminal to the AT, yet does not allow us to view the typed characters during this port analysis. There is an easy way to fix this without actually changing the option in the terminal.

From the findings, Transmit Data, pin 2, is "out" relative to the terminal. This means that data are output on this lead. Hence, the characters that we are typing on the keyboard should be going out on this lead. If pin 2 is out, then more than likely pin 3 is the input data lead, based on the RS232 standard. If we take pin 2 and loop it back to pin 3, then the terminal will receive every character that is output on pin 2. This is the same as optioning the terminal for half duplex. The half duplex option will locally echo all typed characters. We are doing the same thing using the RS232 interface. Now all typed characters should be viewable on the screen as we type them. Indeed, pin 2 is an output data lead, with pin 3 the input data lead. The fact that we are transmitting characters without having connected any modem, computer, or other device tells us a lot. This means that the terminal does not need any of the input control leads to be on prior to data transmission. This is not normal, as most DTE, such as terminal, require certain input control leads to be on prior to outputting data. Consulting the documentation, you will find that the port is optionable as either "EIA Data" or "EIA Modem." The "EIA Data" option does not need the modem control leads, pins 5, 6, and 8, to be on. The terminal in this mode ignores those leads. This is why we are actually transmitting characters. However, if the terminal is set to "EIA Modem," these three input control leads are monitored by the terminal and must be on for data transmission. Definitely have this option set to "EIA Modem" when a modem is being connected to the terminal. In our tutorial module, either way is all right, but could impact how we build our cable. This tutorial module will assume that the option is set to "EIA Modem" and build a cable that includes these input control leads. In your actual cable, the three input leads are not needed if the option is set to "EIA Data."

We now know the important leads in the interface within the Wyse terminal port. The AT must now be reviewed for input leads that are required to be on prior to data transmission. We know from our earlier assessment that pins 3, 4, and 7 are output leads. Pin 5 is the Signal Ground lead. This leaves pins 1, 2, 6, 8, and 9 as possible input leads. The pins are laid out as depicted in Table 4–15.

Ring Indicator is used only when a modem is involved. Pin 2 is Receive Data, an input signal. This is confusing as normally pin 2 is Transmit Data with an "out" direction. Pin 6 is the same as in a DB25 connector. Pins 1 and 8 are not. However, earlier it was pointed out that the 9-pin port functions similar to the PC/XT DB25 ports. We can test this out using the screen print routine.

In a standard XT port, leads 5, 6, and 8 should be on prior to the screen dump successfully completing. The pin numbers are not as important here as the functions/descriptions for each. Clear to Send, Data Set Ready, and Data Carrier Detect had to be on before this exercise would work. In our AT port, these leads equate as laid out in Table 4–16.

If we connect one of the output control leads of the AT, either pin 4 or 7, to all three of these input leads, then they will be on whenever the output leads are on. Assume pin 4 is looped back temporarily to pins 1, 6, and 8 as depicted in Table 4–17.

TABLE 4–15. INPUT CONTROL LEADS OF AT PORT

1	Carrier Detect (CD)
2	Receive Data (RD)
6	Data Set Ready (DSR)
8	Clear to Send (CTS)
9	Ring Indicator (RI)

TABLE 4-16. INPUT CONTROL LEADS OF XT AND AT

Function	PC/XT lead #	PC/AT lead #	Function
Clear to Send (in)	5	8	Clear to Send (in)
Data Set Ready (in)	6	6	Data Set Ready (in)
Carrier Detect (in)	8	1	Carrier Detect (in)

TABLE 4-17. INPUT LEADS BEING HELD ON (TEMPORARY FOR TESTING PURPOSES ONLY)

Function	Lead #	
Clear to Send	8	⟨-:
Data Set Ready	6	⟨-:
Data Carrier Detect	1	⟨-:
		:
Data Terminal Ready	4	--:

Now, whenever we enable the AT's port, pins 1, 6, and 8 will be held on. Connect the VOM probe to the output data lead, pin 3. Perform the "Shift key/PrtSc" sequence and note the measurement on the VOM. Data are being output on this lead. If you disconnect pin 4, the output should halt. If you reconnect, it will continue, providing that it does not timeout in this attempt. Repeat this until you are convinced that the 9-pin port does indeed function in the same manner as the PC/XT DB25 port. Update the port profile worksheets with your findings. For ease of reference, Table 4-18 provides a cross-reference of the AT and PC/XT RS232 port pinouts.

It is advisable to build a cable that brings the 9-pin connector to a DB25-size connector. This sometimes aids in the connection of other devices to the AT ports. If you do this, then connect the leads of the AT port from Table 4-18 to the leads of the PC/XT port. The 9-pin end of the cable would be a female connector, while the DB25 end would be a male connector. This would allow you to connect devices in the same fashion as you would the PC/XT. However, this also implies that when null modem cables are required, another cable would have to be obtained to connect to this 9-pin to DB25 cord. This would not be needed when connecting a modem to an AT, but more than likely when connecting a printer or terminal. In this immediate exercise, this adapter cord will not be used. But, rather, we will design and build a 9-pin to DB25 null modem cable, as required to connect the Wyse terminal.

7. Design the cable

Now that the pinouts for both ports are known, it is time to design the cable. The easiest way to design any RS232 cable is to separate the leads by the categories ground, data, control, and timing. Timing leads are

TABLE 4-18. CROSS-REFERENCE OF AT AND PC/XT PINOUTS

Lead Function	AT lead #		PC/XT lead #
Transmit Data	3	------⟩	2
Receive Data	2	------⟩	3
Request to Send	7	------⟩	4
Clear to Send	8	------⟩	5
Data Set Ready	6	------⟩	6
Signal Ground	5	------⟩	7
Data Carrier Detect	1	------⟩	8
Data Terminal Ready	4	------⟩	20
Ring Indicator	9	------⟩	22

TABLE 4–19. WYSE-TO-AT GROUND LEAD DESIGN

Shield Ground	1	n/a
Signal Ground	7 -----	5

LEGEND: Pin 7 at the Wyse end of the cable will be connected to pin 5 at the AT end of the cable.

not relevant in this tutorial module; hence, we can ignore them. Reviewing our port profiles, we should separate the leads by category, as this will ease our cable design. Furthermore, the general rules for RS232 cable design should be followed:

CABLE DESIGN: GENERAL RULES

1. Connect like categories of leads together.
2. Always connect an "out" to an "in" and an "in" to an "out."
3. A lead that is input may be connected to another lead that is an input, only if both these are connected to an output lead.
4. In synchronous connections, only use one source of timing. (Because the AT-to-Wyse terminal connection is asynchronous, this point is not applicable.)

First, let's review the ground leads. Protective Ground and Signal Ground are straightforward in that you can merely plan on connecting like ground leads together. Hence, the design should allow for the signal grounds to be connected together at each end of the cable. Protective Ground is not present in the AT port, so we can ignore this lead in our design. Consult Table 4–19 for the ground lead design.

Next we will review the data leads. There are only two possible combinations for these two leads in our cable. Either pin 2 at one end of the cable will be connected to pin 3 at the other end, or pin 2 at one end will be connected to pin 2 at the other end. The same occurs for pin 3. Either 3 is connected across to 2 or across to 3. Our general rule 2 states that we should connect an "out" to an "in." Pin 2 of the terminal is Transmit Data (out). This is the lead on which the data from the terminal will be. The AT needs to receive these data as input on its Receive Data lead 2 (input). Hence, we will connect pin 2 at the Wyse end of the cable over to pin 2. The same will hold true for the Receive Data lead at the Wyse end of the cable. This is the lead that the Wyse looks at for any incoming data. These incoming data are the AT's outgoing data; hence, we can merely connect these two together. Table 4–20 depicts the data category of leads to be built in our cable.

The next category of leads is the control leads. Control leads tend to be more difficult than the other leads, yet are crucial to the success of the installation. These leads are normally used to control and indicate the status of each device.

We should review the input signals initially to determine which leads must be on for communication between the two devices. As long as we maintain these leads, the Wyse terminal should be able to communicate with the AT. The first area to address is flow control. Normally, when connecting a terminal to a device, both methods of flow control—hardware and software—are supported. This is definitely the case with the Wyse WY-85. It supports hardware flow control using pin 20. Pin 20 stays on as long as the terminal can receive data and off if it can't receive anymore. The AT also needed to have pins 1, 6, and 8 on to receive, so there is a means of implementing hardware flow control. (Leads 1, 6, and 8 in the 9-pin connector equate to pins 5, 6, and 8 in a DB25 connector.)

TABLE 4–20. DATA LEADS IN THE WYSE-TO-PC/AT CABLE

	Wyse WY-85		IBM PC/AT	
Transmit Data (out)	2	------)	2	Receive Data (in)
Receive Data (in)	3	(------	3	Transmit Data (out)

LEGEND: The "------)" indicates a straight-through connection. Pin 2 at the Wyse end of the cable will be connected straight through to pin 2 at the PC/AT end of the cable. The same is true for pins 3.

In most terminals, such as the Wyse and other DEC VT100-compatible terminals, XOFF/XON is supported. Depending on the operating system running on the AT, this may be the only flow control supported. UNIX is a good example, in that software flow control is normally the only flow control method supported. Hardware flow control is not. Even though hardware flow control may work between the Wyse and the AT, UNIX would not allow this and would misinterpret the control lead fluctuation as a disconnect, instead of a pause. Hence, XON/XOFF is preferred. We will cable for both in this scenario, but software flow control is highly recommended wherever possible.

Since we have just mentioned leads 1, 6, and 8 in the AT port, we will address them first. The Wyse supported either XON/XOFF or pin 20 for flow control. Let's design the cable to support either by tying pin 20 at the Wyse end of the cable across to leads 1, 6, and 8, at the AT end. This will support hardware flow control, as when pin 20 from the Wyse is on, leads 1, 6, and 8, will be also. When it is off, those leads at the AT end of the cable will be off. Our data leads, previously designed, will support software flow control. Because pin 2 of the Wyse will be connected to pin 2 of the AT, whenever the terminal transmits an XOFF character the AT will receive it and be able to act accordingly.

The only other input lead present in the AT is 9, Ring Indicator. This was the lead used to detect ringing when a modem was connected to the port. Since our connection does not involve data communication equipment, we can ignore this lead. This completes the input control leads of the AT end of the cable, as depicted in Table 4–21.

What are the input control leads in the Wyse port. Review the Wyse Terminal Port Profile. Earlier in the text we noted that, depending on the optioning of the terminal, there may not be any control leads that had to be on prior to transmission. Update the profile to include this notation. If the terminal is optioned for "EIA Data," then leads 5, 6, and 8 DO NOT need to be on. If, however, it is optioned "EIA Modem," then leads 5, 6, and 8 are monitored and need to be on prior to data transmission. We will design the cable to handle either situation.

If leads 5, 6, and 8 need to be on (assumption is EIA Modem option), then how can we keep them on? Because the terminal can monitor these to get the status of the connected device, we need to connect them to a lead from the AT. This lead should be one that is on whenever the AT port is enabled. We have two choices! Pin 7, Request to Send, or pin 4, Data Terminal Ready in the 9-pin port are on whenever the port is enabled. Refer to Table 4–18 to see that these equate to pins 4 and 20 of a standard PC/XT serial port. Take your pick as to which one of these you will use to connect across to the Wyse input control leads. You could even split the connections and use both output control leads from the AT port. Table 4–22 depicts one of many connections that are possible.

This type of control lead design will handle either hardware or software flow control. If we are confident that only software flow control is to be used, the many other variations of the control lead design exist. Table 4–23 highlights an example of such a cable. Because the data leads carry the flow control characters, we merely need to keep the input control leads on, not require them to add the intelligence of hardware flow control. Hence, we merely need to apply rules 2 and 3 to connect an output control lead to input control leads. This allows us to minimize the number of conductors needed in our cable. We can get by with only three conductors in the cable. This reduces the cost of our cable.

As we mentioned, since this is an asynchronous connection, the timing leads can be ignored. Hence, our cable design is complete. We merely combine the ground, data, and control leads for a complete cable design. Depending on the cable you design, the Request to Send or Data Terminal leads may not be used. This is "OK," as they are both output control leads from both devices. Furthermore, lead 9 at the AT end and lead 22 at the Wyse port may be ignored. Table 4–24 lays out a couple of possible cable designs. Choose the one that is easiest for you to construct.

TABLE 4–21. AT INPUT CONTROL LEAD CABLE DESIGN

Function	Wyse lead	AT lead	Function
Data Terminal Ready	20 ---|--〉	8	Clear to Send
	|--〉	6	Data Set Ready
	|--〉	1	Data Carrier Detect

LEGEND: The "------〉" implies that the conductor connected to pin 20 "\|--〉" at the Wyse end of the cable is crossed-over to lead 8 at the AT end of the cable. Lead 8 is then "jumpered" locally to leads 6 and 1 in the AT connector.

TABLE 4–22. VARIOUS INPUT CONTROL LEAD DESIGNS FOR WYSE TERMINAL PORT

Function	Wyse lead	AT lead	Function
Clear to Send (in)	5 ⟨-|-----	4	Data Terminal Ready (out)
Data Set Ready (in)	6 ⟨-|		
Carrier Detect (in)	8 ⟨-|		

or

Function	Wyse lead	AT lead	Function
Clear to Send	5 ⟨------	7	Request to Send
Data Set Ready	6 ⟨--:		
Data Carrier Detect	8 ⟨--:		

LEGEND: Either 4 or 7 or a combination of both should be crossed over to leads 5, 6, and 8 at the Wyse end of the cable. The "⟨--" means that the a conductor in the cable connects these two leads within the connectors. The "⟨------" indicates local jumpering leads within "⟨--:" a connector of one end of the cable.

8. Build the cable

This tutorial module will not describe in detail how to construct the cable physically in a step-by-step manner. However, it will highlight the differences involved due to the 9-pin AT connector. Furthermore, it assumes that the cable being constructed is to be directly connected to the AT and the Wyse. This distinction is offered in case the user has already constructed a cable that breaks out the 9-pin AT connector to a DB25-size connector as previously discussed in this chapter. If the latter is the case, refer to Tutorial Module 4–1, VT100 to Megaframe discussion, for this type of cable, as a standard null modem cable will suffice.

Review the port profiles for the AT and Wyse ports. Note specifically the genders of the ports. Our cable should have the opposite genders. The AT is equipped with a 9-pin male port; hence, this cable end will be a 9-pin female connector. The Wyse terminal has a DB25S (female) connector, requiring the cable end to be male. Obtain these connectors as we proceed to the cable (wire) selection.

Reviewing Table 4–24, the cable to be designed for an AT-Wyse connection, note the number of leads involved in the AT port. Not all 9 pins were used. This allows us to a select a cable that has only five conductors within it. If you choose to construct the second possible cable, then a wire with only three conductors can be used. Many possibilities exist, but have you ever heard the telephony term, 4-pair. This is a cable that has four pairs of wires in it, or eight conductors. How about 2-pair, or four wires. This type of wire is found in many office environments, as may be present in the walls of your office. The point here is that you may not need to purchase any more cable to build this one. It could be widely available in your own shop. The only concern is one of electrical interference. If your cable is going to be laid (run) near heavy machinery such as air conditioners,

TABLE 4–23. CONTROL LEAD DESIGN FOR SOFTWARE-ONLY FLOW CONTROL LEAD

Function	Wyse lead	AT lead	Function
Clear to Send	5 ⟨--:	:--⟩ 8	Clear to Send
Data Set Ready	6 ⟨--:	:--⟩ 6	Data Set Ready
Data Carrier Detect	8 ⟨--:	:--⟩ 1	Data Carrier Detect
Data Terminal Ready	20 ---:	:--- 4	Data Terminal Ready

LEGEND: On the Wyse side of the cable, pin 20 should be locally jumpered to pins 5, 6, and 8 of the connector. These leads should not go through the cable from end to end. They are isolated and limited to the Wyse connector. The AT cable end will have leads 4, 1, 6, and 8, all jumpered together within the 9-pin connector. None of these leads passes through the cable.

TABLE 4–24.   VARIOUS WYSE WY-85-TO-IBM PC/AT CABLE DESIGNS

Function	Wyse WY-85 lead		IBM PC/AT lead	Function
Signal Ground	7	-------	5	
Transmit Data (out)	2	------⟩	2	Receive Data (in)
Receive Data (in)	3	⟨------	3	Transmit Data (out)
Data Terminal Ready	20	------⟩	8	Clear to Send
		:--⟩	6	Data Set Ready
		⏐--⟩	1	Data Carrier Detect
Clear to Send	5	⟨-------	4	Data Terminal Ready
Data Set Ready	6	⟨--:		
Data Carrier Detect	8	⟨--:		

or

Function	Wyse WY-85 lead		IBM PC/AT lead	Function
Signal Ground	7	-------	5	
Transmit Data (out)	2	------⟩	2	Receive Data (in)
Receive Data (in)	3	⟨------	3	Transmit Data (out)
Clear to Send	5	⟨--: :--⟩	8	Clear to Send
Data Set Ready	6	⟨--: :--⟩	6	Data Set Ready
Data Carrier Detect	8	⟨--: :--⟩	1	Data Carrier Detect
Data Terminal Ready	20	--: :--	4	Data Terminal Ready

The "------⟩" implies a cross-over connection between two leads in the cable. The "⟨--:" "⟨--:" indicates some local jumpering within one end of the cable. In the case of the second sample cable design, none of the control leads goes from end to end in the cable. They are all locally jumpered, requiring only three conductors in the actual cable.

coolers, heaters, pumps, and so on, then this type of wire is not recommended. The interference from the equipment may cause you problems with your data as they travel over the wire. Many inexpensive RS232 cables have been made out of this common wire.

Table 4–24 outlined which conductors should be connected for the AT to Wyse cable. Connect the conductors to the back of each connector according to this diagram. The item worth mentioning here is the "jumpering" on the back of the AT plug. Our diagram indicates that pin 20 should be crossed over and connected to leads 8, 6, and 1 at the AT end of the cable. Select a conductor within wire and connect it to lead 20 on the back of the DB25 male connector. At the other end of the cable, connect this same conductor to lead 8 on the back side of the 9-pin connector. This normally would be soldered, or possibly snapped, into place. Then, using another piece of wire, connect both leads 6 and 1 on the back side of this connector to lead 8. The ultimate goal is to have lead 20 of the Wyse terminal drive leads 8, 6, and 1 in the AT port. Once you have made these local "jumperings," it is a good practice to shield them from one another with electrical tape. Complete the rest of the cable, connecting the leads as outlined.

Normally, in a DB25 connector, a casing or hood is provided. Not all 9-pin female connectors have this casing. If your connector does not have a hood, then use electrical tape to enclose the cable and connector for shielding purposes. You do not want any of the leads to touch one another unintentionally or have them touch another piece of metal. This could short circuit one of the ports and possible cause damage to your equipment. This should be normal procedure for cable construction.

9. Test for continuity

Refer to Tutorial Module 1–1 for testing the cable using a VOM. If you want to use a break-out box for this, review Tutorial Module 1–4.

10. Cable the two systems together

If, and only if, the cable tests out to match that of our design, you are ready to connect the AT to the Wyse terminal. It is recommended that the computers be turned off prior to completing this step, although not absolutely required. Our cable may only be connected in one way due to the different-size connectors at each. Match up the 9-pin female connector to the male AT port and the male DB25 connector to the Wyse port. Once connected, fasten them using the small screws that are provided with each connector. You should now be prepared to measure your success.

11. Measure success

If you do not have UNIX operating on the AT, but desire to test out the connection, skip to the next section, "Testing the AT-Wyse connection with MS-DOS Print OnLine feature. If you are running UNIX on the AT, success will be achieved if you get the "login:" prompt and can transmit and receive characters correctly without errors. Look for this login prompt once you have the terminal connected to the AT and both systems are up and running. Prior to the AT with UNIX sending out the login prompt, the port must be set up properly. The systems administrator for the AT should be consulted to ensure that this has been done. Consult *DOSIUNIX Systems: Becoming a Super User* (Martin D. Seyer and William J. Mills, Prentice-Hall, Inc.) for more details on how to set up a terminal port under the UNIX operating system.

Once this port is set up properly, check out the Wyse terminal. It should be in the EIA Terminal mode and be optioned to match the line settings of the AT port. Refer to the manual on optioning the terminal in the communication section. Earlier, in step 1 of this tutorial module, the common settings were assessed to be 9600 bps, even parity, 1 stop bit, 7 data bits per character, and asynchronous mode. Software flow control was to be used.

If you receive the "login:" prompt, go ahead and enter your ID followed by the password, if so prompted. You should receive a "successful" login message. If you cannot successfully login, have unreadable characters, or can't enter anything, refer to Appendix J for possible items to check. If you are successful in logging into the UNIX system, you should check out the flow control. The best means of this is to enter a UNIX command that sends your output to the terminal. While this is being received, the terminal operator should enter a Control-s. This should stop the output of data from the UNIX system. To resume, the operator should type a Control-q. If the data stop once you've hit the Control-s sequence, and resume with a Control-q, you have success. CONGRATU-LATIONS!

If you don't get this flow control functionality, check your Wyse terminal options to ensure that the flow control option is set to be XON/XOFF. Furthermore, have the UNIX systems administrator check your profile so that XON/XOFF is set up properly. Table 4–25 outlines the foregoing steps for testing the flow control.

Testing the AT-Wyse Connection with MS-DOS Only

If you do not have UNIX on the AT, but you need to test out the connection, you can send some output to the serial port. This can be done in two different ways. One is to treat the serial port as the printer port; the other is to load a communication software package on the AT and have a computer-to-terminal conversation using the locally connected Wyse.

The first way involves treating the Wyse terminal as a printer. The WY-85 is connected to one of the serial ports on the AT. We will assume that it is the COM1 port, but you can substitute others as appropriate. Table 4–26 outlines the steps to take for testing the connection between the two devices. We will also test for good flow control. The Wyse terminal should have the following options set under the communication options: EIA Data, 9600, even parity, 7 data bits, 1 stop bit, Handshake=DTR.

TABLE 4–25. TEST PROCEDURE FOR XON/XOFF FLOW CONTROL BETWEEN THE WYSE AND AT

---

1. Login.
2. Issue a UNIX command that sends information to the standard output, your terminal. Try "ls" or "cat filename" command.
3. Enter a Control-s. This is done by holding down the Control key and also the "s" key and then releasing them. The data flow should stop.
4. Enter a Control-q. This should activate the flow of data.

TABLE 4–26. TESTING A LOCALLY ATTACHED TERMINAL (AS A PRINTER) TO AN AT

1. Turn the Wyse terminal on, once it is connected to the AT's serial port.
2. Load MS-DOS in the AT, and get to the prompt, C⟩, or whatever drive you have MS-DOS on. Issue a "DIR/W" command to fill the AT screen with data characters.
3. Issue the command "mode com1:96,n,7,1,p" (the "p" is important).
4. Issue the command "mode 1pt1:=com1."
5. Issue a screen dump by holding down the Shift key and PrtSc key simultaneously. This should begin to send the screen contents out to the COM1 port and ultimately to the attached Wyse terminal. If you see the same characters on the Wyse screen that are on your AT screen, then half your testing is complete. If nothing is being displayed on the terminal, consult Appendix J for a list of items to check for possible malfunction.
6. As the screen is being dumped to the terminal, take the terminal offline. This can be done in a number of ways. One such way is to hit the Function key 3 on the Wyse keyboard. This takes the terminal offline and puts it in Option mode. Hitting it again will put the terminal back online, but save this for after the next step. If the AT screen has already finished dumping to the Wyse, repeat step 5 and quickly take the Wyse offline. If you have a BOB, insert this between the two units and watch what happens to DTR when you hit Function key 3. It should go "off."

Follow the steps in the documentation for changing the options. An easy way is as follows:

1. Hit Function key 3.
2. Use Right arrow to highlight "Comm" options.
3. Hit space bar.
4. Use Down arrow and space bar to change options.
5. Hit Function key 3 a couple of times to exit (you can permanently save).

The AT's serial port must be set up to serve as a printer for this test. Issue the following command sequence to set up the serial port to be the default printer port.

```
MODE COM1:96,E,7,1,P   (the P is important to support flow control)
MODE LPT1:=COM1        (this redirects the printer output to the COM1 port)
```

With this setup, and the AT and Wyse cabled together with the newly constructed cable, you can begin testing. Remember that we are looking for (1) data output to appear on the Wyse screen and (2) flow control to work effectively. As noted, Table 4–26 outlines the complete steps to test for both of these conditions.

This should halt the output of data to the terminal. Make a mental note of the last character on the Wyse screen. If this does not stop the data flow, flow control is not working properly. Consult the terminal options and AT systems administrator to ensure the correct setup. The Wyse terminal should have the Handshake option set to DTR. Hit Function key 3 again on the WY-85 keyboard to resume the flow of data from the AT. The rest of the data should be sent to the terminal. Check to see that none of the data characters were lost. Check to see that the last character you noted is followed by the correct next character. This is hardware flow control in action. CONGRATULATIONS!

To check the cabling for software flow control when UNIX is not yet installed, use a communication software application on the AT. When UNIX is ultimately installed, software flow control (XON/XOFF) should be used. We are going to run a communication software package and dump an ASCII file to the COM1 port to see if the Wyse terminal operator can stop the flow of data from the keyboard. If successful, XON/XOFF is functioning.

The Wyse terminal should be optioned in the same manner as before, except that the Handshake option should be set to "XON/XOFF." Once this is set up, load the communication software on the AT. Depending on the software used, the setting of the options will be different. However, our goal is to have the following options:

Flow control: XON/XOFF.
Carriage Return translation out: carriage return and line feed. This outputs a line feed with every carriage return character to prevent overwriting on the terminal's screen.

Local Echo: Yes. This allows the AT operator to view the ASCII file being dumped.
Speed: 9600 bps.
Character length: 7.
Parity: Even.
Stop bits: 1.
Duplex: Half. This has the AT display the character entered on the keyboard.

With both devices optioned correctly and cabled together, issue the command sequence necessary to send an ASCII file. With Procomm, the following is used:

1. Hit PgUp key. This selects file transfer window.
2. Select 7. This selects ASCII file transfer.
3. Enter filename. Enter fully qualified path and filename (e.g., C:\test.txt).

With Crosstalk, the following is used:

1. Hit the Esc key (or Attention key if default is altered).
2. "Send filename" (make sure you are in the correct directory).

Once the file is being transferred, you should see the characters on the Wyse terminal's screen. If not refer to Appendix J to isolate the trouble. Otherwise, test software flow control by entering a Control-s from the terminal's keyboard. This is done by holding down the Control key and hitting the "s" key. This should halt the flow of data from the AT. Hitting Control-q should restart the flow of the data. If neither of these is working right, software flow control is not functioning. Check the options to see if they are correct. Otherwise, CONGRATU-LATIONS! You are experiencing software flow control in action.

If a BOB is used, you can monitor this activity. Connect the BOB to the terminal and the terminal cable to watch the interaction. Once the ASCII transfer begins, you should see data activity on the receive data lead of the BOB, or lead 3. This is the input data lead to the Wyse terminal. The lamp should be flickering or show a dim color due to rapid data transfer. Watch the Transmit Data lead, lead 2 on the BOB, as you enter a Control-s on the Wyse keyboard and the terminal outputs an XOFF character. The Wyse sends its data out on lead 2, so the BOB should indicate that a character is being transmitted. This will only be for a brief moment as only one character is being output. The receive data should register *no* data flow as the flow is suspended. When you wish to continue, issue a Control-q and watch the data flow resume on lead 3, Receive Data.

Tutorial Module 4-4: Connecting a Remote Terminal to a Computer System

In this tutorial module, we have a scenario as depicted in Figure 4–2. This environment is the same as that outlined in Tutorial Module 3–4, connecting a modem to a terminal, and one of the modules involving connecting a computer to a modem. Follow the steps in these modules and test out your connection by dialing into the desired remote system. The remote system could be another computer, a message system, a remote printer, a news system, or a host of other things.

Tutorial Module 4-5: Connecting a Terminal to a Protocol Converter

Often it is necessary to use asynchronous equipment and synchronous equipment together in the same configuration. This can pose problems as equipment using synchronous and asynchronous protocols cannot communicate with each other. This is definitely true when IBM mainframe systems are involved. IBM uses synchronous equipment in its 3270 environments whereas most printers, terminals, and PCs emulating terminals support asynchronous only. How do you then use an asynchronous device in these networks?

The answer is a device known as a protocol converter. The protocol converter featured in this tutorial module is WALLDATA's DCF II, a high-powered converter offering more than mere protocol conversion utilities. This tutorial module will focus on the protocol conversion function only. A protocol converter's role is to allow dissimilar devices to communicate to one another. In this tutorial module, the dissimilar devices are a Wyse WY-85 terminal and an IBM 3270 network. Your scenario may even include a PC emulating a terminal. Whatever the hardware involved, the rationale for such a connection, as depicted in Figure 4–3, is access to the synchronous network applications. Specifically, there may be order entry systems, inquiry to database applications, or generic

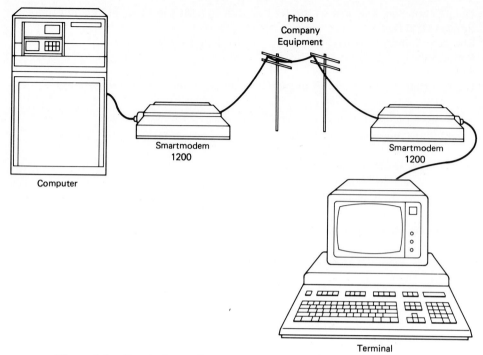

Figure 4–2. Terminal accessing a remote computer system or computer service.

data entry applications that reside on a mainframe. It is not always feasible to use synchronous equipment at a location, even though access to these applications is a must. The protocol converter aids us by allowing these less expensive, or otherwise incompatible, devices to communicate with and access the mainframe applications.

Note that the terminal is connected locally to the protocol converter. The terminal could be remote from the protocol converter and access it through modems. If this is the case, refer to the tutorial modules involving modem connection to set up and test these connections. Furthermore, the protocol converter could be collocated with the mainframe instead of being remote with modems in between the two. In this case, a synchronous modem eliminator or special cable would be required between the protocol converter and the mainframe front-end processor. Refer to Tutorial Modules 4–7 and 4–8 for a further explanation of synchronous connections.

Before reviewing the steps for connections, you should be aware that there are two connections involved using a protocol converter. First, there is the terminal side, whereby a terminal, or PC emulating a terminal, will be connected to a port on the converter. The other connection is on the "back" side of the converter. The author refers to the back side as the connection between the protocol converter and the mainframe, whether this connection is a modem or actually the mainframe, with the front side being either a terminal or a modem for remote access to the protocol converter. We will deal with the front-side connection in this tutorial module, and refer you to Chapter 4, on synchronous 3270 connections, for the back-side connection.

The steps we will follow for this tutorial module are common to all our reviews:

STEPS FOR CONNECTION

1. Determine compatibility (should it work?).
2. Determine signs of success.
3. Determine the type of connector used.
4. Determine gender of the ports.
5. Determine which leads (pins) are provided by each device.
6. Determine which leads are required to be on by each device.
7. Design the cable.
8. Build the cable.
9. Test the cable for continuity.
10. Cable the two systems together with the cable.
11. From step 2, measure success.

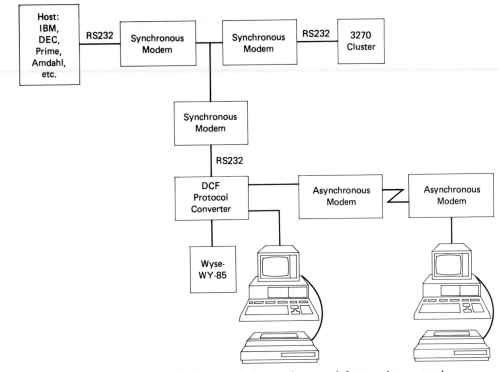

Figure 4–3. Wyse WY-85 terminal accessing a mainframe using protocol converter.

1. Determine compatibility

The purpose of a converter is to allow dissimilar devices to communicate. On the back side is the synchronous environment. In our tutorial module this is a 3270 environment. The term 3270 implies that an IBM 3270 class of device is expected. The 3270 family of terminals and controllers has evolved to include a multitude of different devices. The 3278 is a popular model of terminal that works in the 3270 environment. This terminal attaches to a controller. The controller is normally the interface to the communication link. It handles the inbound and outbound data traffic with usually more than one 3278 terminal attached to it. These terminals have specific characteristics that the controller understands. But more important are the characteristics that the mainframe application understands.

The application, depending on its nature, will put a data entry form on the 3278 screen. This could be an input for a customer's name, address, and phone number. The 3278 device supports certain control sequences that allow the application to position these three fields anywhere on the screen and allows the user to send the information after all fields have been filled in. The control sequences necessary to position these fields on the 3278 are different from those supported on the WY-85 or other VT100-compatible terminals. For example, the sequence to clear a terminal's screen is totally different between the VT100 compatibles and the 3270. This difference in screen handling is handled by the protocol converter.

To make sure that the terminal is compatible with the mainframe application, the protocol converter must know which asynchronous terminal is being used. Normally, most VT100-compatible terminals accept the same "Escape" sequences for screen control. There are other industry-accepted terminal standards, such as the Hewlett-Packard 2600s, Lear-Siegler ADM series, the ADDS Regents, Data General Dashers, Televideo 900s, and others.

The first step in determining compatibility is to ensure that the protocol converter that you are using supports the asynchronous terminal you are connecting on the front side of the converter. Our Wyse WY-85 terminal is a VT100-compatible terminal, meaning that it accepts the same escape sequences as does a DEC VT100 terminal. The WALLDATA DCF II supports the VT100 family of terminals; hence it should be compatible on the front side of the converter. This is an application compatibility, not a physical connectivity question.

The DCF II supports an asynchronous device at multiple speeds, parities, and so on. You should compare the port characteristics in both the DCF II and the Wyse WY-85 terminal to determine compatibility. Upon review, you will find that the common options will be full duplex, 19,200 bps, with even parity, software flow control (XON/XOFF), 7 data bits, and 1 stop bit. The two devices are definitely compatible, with the protocol converter support VT100-compatible escape sequences to offer compatibility with the mainframe application.

2. Determine signs of success

The signs of success may be many in these type connections. The first sign you need to consider is the front side of the converter. The terminal should be able to communicate with the protocol converter. You should get a prompt message from the DCF II converter asking you to enter information. This is obtained upon hitting the Return key a couple of times. This will be your sign of success on the front side of the converter.

On the back side of the converter, the host application connection will dictate the signs of success. There are too many possibilities to attempt to cover in this tutorial module. The author encourages you to consult with analysts responsible or the mainframe system to determine what you should expect on your screen once you connect to the mainframe. The converter will need to be set up to match the characteristics of the network and mainframe. Hence, someone will need to be discussing the specifics of the network and applications. Get together with this person to check on "signs of success." However, a general sign of success is the ability to login to a mainframe application and have the screen appear all right on your terminal's screen, as well as your being able to enter data that are accepted by the host and acted on appropriately. This tutorial module will not test this portion, but advises you to work closely with the mainframe system analysts to test this piece of the connection.

3. Determine type of connector

4. Determine gender of ports

5. Determine leads (pins) provided by each device

6. Determine leads required to be on

The Wyse WY-85 terminal port was analyzed in another tutorial module (4–3). Refer to the specifics of this tutorial module for detailed port analysis of the terminal. In review, the terminal has a male DB25 port labeled "COMM." This is outlined in the SCS port profile depicted in Table 4–27.

The user should now take a detailed look at the WALLDATA DCF II protocol converter and perform in-depth port analysis. Use any of the techniques outlined in the book to find out the port specifics: a VOM, a break-out box, hearsay, or documentation. Table 4–28 summarizes the findings, as pulled from the documentation. Note that the port on the protocol converter is a female DB25 connector.

7. Design the cable

Armed with this port information, the user can design the cable necessary to connect the Wyse WY-85 terminal to a port on the WALLDATA DCF II protocol converter. The easiest method is to separate the leads by category: ground, data, control, and timing. Table 4–29 outlines this, excluding the timing leads. It is worth noting that both terminals provide similar leads, with similar directions. Because of this, a standard null modem cable may be used for connection. We will walk through the design of the standard null modem cable; however, the user could analyze the ports and quickly come to this conclusion.

The following design rules will be followed. They are the same regardless of the connection.

CABLE DESIGN: GENERAL RULES

1. Connect like categories of leads together.
2. Always connect an "out" to an "in" and an "in" to an "out."
3. A lead that is input may be connected to another lead that is an input, only if both these are connected to an output lead.
4. In synchronous connections, only use one source of timing. (Because the DCF-to-terminal connection is asynchronous, this point is not applicable. This will not be the case when the back side of the protocol converter is reviewed.)

First the ground leads! Merely connect the ground leads together from one end to the other. The Protective Ground leads should be connected together. Furthermore, the Signal Grounds should also be connected together.

Next the data leads! There are only two possibilities, either connecting pins 2 and 2 together and pins 3 and 3 together, or crossing them. The directions will dictate the connection. Applying rule 2, the leads will be crossed so outputs will be connected to inputs, and vice versa. Table 4–30 reviews the ground and data lead design.

TABLE 4-27. WYSE WY-85 TERMINAL PORT PROFILE

Terminal Port Profile

Underline if supported; circle if selected.

Model: WY-85 _____ Vendor: Wyse _____ Port: COMM _____

Port type: <u>DB25</u> 9-pin 5-pin 8-pin/modular 20mA Centronics

Gender: <u>male</u> female

Pin #	Function	Direction	Pin #	Function	Direction
1	Shield Ground	to from <u>n/a</u>	14	_____	to from n/a
2	Transmit Data	to <u>from</u> n/a	15	_____	to from n/a
3	Receive Data	<u>to</u> from n/a	16	_____	to from n/a
4	Request to Send	to <u>from</u> n/a	17	_____	to from n/a
5	Clear to Send	<u>to</u> from n/a	18	_____	to from n/a
6	Data Set Ready	<u>to</u> from n/a	19	_____	to from n/a
7	Signal Ground	to from <u>n/a</u>	20	Data Terminal Ready	to <u>from</u> n/a
8	Data Carrier	<u>to</u> from n/a	21	_____	to from n/a
9	_____	to from n/a	22		to from n/a
10	_____	to from n/a	23	Speed Select	to <u>from</u> n/a
11	_____	to from n/a	24	_____	to from n/a
12	Speed Indicator	<u>to</u> from n/a	25	_____	to from n/a
13	_____	to from n/a			

Complete the next section only with 36-pin cinch connector.

26	_____	to from n/a	27	_____	to from n/a
28	_____	to from n/a	29	_____	to from n/a
30	_____	to from n/a	31	_____	to from n/a
32	_____	to from n/a	33	_____	to from n/a
34	_____	to from n/a	35	_____	to from n/a
36	_____	to from n/a			

Flow control technique: (XON/XOFF) hardware _____
Flow control lead(s): 4 11 19 <u>20</u> __ __ __
Leads that must be on: 5 6 8 __ __ __ __
Printer port: serial parallel

Flow control: XON/XOFF Hardware _____
FC lead(s): 4 11 19 20 __ __ __ Connector DB25 Centronics

Options:
    Speeds: 110 300 600 1200 1800 2400 4800 9600 (19.2) 56k _____
    Parity: (even) odd <u>space</u> mark none
    Char-length: (7) 8 __
    # stop bits: (1) 1.5 2
    Line-ending sequence: cr lf cr/lf cr/lf/lf

Mode: async sync isoch

Sync timing leads:

#	Function	Direction
15	_____	to from
17	_____	to from
24	_____	to from

Terminal compatibility: ANSI X3.64, VT100, VT220, VT52, _____

NOTES: The terminal has an option EIA Data that causes the terminal to ignore the presence or absence of leads 5, 6, and 8.

Line-Ending Sequence

TABLE 4–28. WALLDATA DCF II PORT PROFILE

Computer Port Profile

Underline if supported; circle if selected.

Model: DCF II _____ Vendor: WALLDATA _____ Port: _____

Port type: <u>serial</u> parallel

Port: <u>DB25</u> 9-pin 5-pin 8-pin/modular 20mA Centronics

Gender: male <u>female</u>

Pin #	Function	Direction	Pin #	Function	Direction
1	Ground	to <u>from</u> n/a	14	_____	to from n/a
2	Transmit Data	to <u>from</u> n/a	15	_____	to from n/a
3	Receive Data	<u>to</u> from n/a	16	_____	to from n/a
4	Request to Send	<u>to</u> from n/a	17	_____	to from n/a
5	Clear to Send	to <u>from</u> n/a	18	_____	to from n/a
6	Data Set Ready	to <u>from</u> n/a	19	_____	to from n/a
7	Signal Ground	to <u>from</u> n/a	20	Data Terminal Ready	to from n/a
8	Carrier Detect	to <u>from</u> n/a	21	_____	to from n/a
9	_____	to from n/a	22	_____	to from n/a
10	_____	to from n/a	23	_____	to from n/a
11	_____	to from n/a	24	_____	to from n/a
12	_____	to from n/a	25	_____	to from n/a
13	_____	to from n/a			

Complete the next section only with 36-pin cinch connector.

26	_____	to from n/a	27	_____	to from n/a
28	_____	to from n/a	29	_____	to from n/a
30	_____	to from n/a	31	_____	to from n/a
32	_____	to from n/a	33	_____	to from n/a
34	_____	to from n/a	35	_____	to from n/a
36	_____	to from n/a			

Flow control technique: (XON/XOFF) ENQ/ACK STX/ETX <u>Hardware</u> _____

Leads that must be on: <u>5</u> 6 8 __ __ __ __

Options:

    Speeds: <u>110 300 600 1200 1800 2400 4800 9600</u> (19.2) 56k _____

    Parity: (even) odd <u>space</u> <u>mark</u> <u>none</u>

    Char-length: (7) 8 __

    # stop bits: (1) 1.5 2

    Line-ending sequence: cr lf cr/lf cr/lf/lf

    Disconnect sequence: EOT DEL ~. _____

    Mode: async sync isoch

Sync timing leads:

#	Function	Direction
15	_____	to from
17	_____	to from
24	_____	to from

Notes: Pin 5 must be on for the protocol converter to transmit data and can be connected to the attached device's hardware flow control lead.

TABLE 4–29. DCF II AND WY-85 PINOUTS SEPARATED BY CATEGORY

Function	DCF lead #	WY-85 lead #	Function
Ground			
Protective Ground	1	1	Protective Ground
Signal Ground	7	7	Signal Ground
Data			
Transmit Data (out)	2	2	Transmit Data (out)
Receive Data (in)	3	3	Receive Data (in)
Control			
Request to Send (out)	4	4	Request to Send (out)
Clear to Send (in)	5	5	Clear to Send (in)
Data Set Ready (in)	6	6	Data Set Ready (in)
Data Carrier Detect (in)	8	8	Data Carrier Detect (in)
Data Terminal Ready (out)	20	20	Data Terminal Ready (out)

TABLE 4–30. GROUND AND DATA LEAD DESIGN FOR DCF-TO-WY-85 CABLE DESIGN

Function	DCF lead #		WY-85 lead #	Function
Ground				
Protective Ground	1	-------	1	Protective Ground
Signal Ground	7		7	Signal Ground
Data				
Transmit Data (out)	2	------⟩	3	Receive Data (in)
Receive Data (in)	3	⟨------	2	Transmit Data (out)

NOTES: The "-------" indicates a straight-through connection. The "------⟩" indicates a cross-over between the two leads.

Because the cable does not require timing leads, the only remaining category of leads is the control leads. Review Table 4–27 and note the control leads of the WY-85 terminal. A couple of them are not applicable in this cable connection. Specifically, leads 12 and 23 deal with a modem connection where multiple speeds are involved. Ignore them in this design as the terminal is being connected to a computer (protocol converter). This leaves leads 4, 5, 6, 8, and 20. Leads 4 and 20 of each port are output, while 5, 6, and 8 are input leads. The design should allow the output leads to control the input leads. Review Table 4–31 for the completed cable design. Note that whenever lead 4 is on in a port, so will the same port's lead 5 and the other device's lead 8. Furthermore, whenever lead 20 is on at a port, the other device's lead 6 will be on. This termed a standard null modem cable.

8. Build the cable

9. Test for continuity

10. Cable the two systems together

Use any standard cable construction technique outlined in other sections of this book. Recall that the DCF end of the cable is male, while the terminal end is female.

11. Measure success

On the front side of the protocol converter, your success will be measured by your ability to communicate locally with the DCF II. The protocol converter will prompt you for information once you physically connect the terminal and hit a couple of Carriage Returns. Once cabled, hit the Return key several times to get the DCF II to issue you the prompt. If all is functioning properly, you should get a message from the DCF II. CONGRATULATIONS!

TABLE 4–31. COMPLETE CABLE DESIGN FOR WALLDATA DCF II-TO-WYSE WY-85 TERMINAL

Function	DCF lead #		WY-85 lead #	Function
Ground				
Protective Ground	1	-------	1	Protective Ground
Signal Ground	7	-------	7	Signal Ground
Data				
Transmit Data (out	2	------⟩	3	Receive Data (in)
Receive Data (in)	3	⟨------	2	Transmit Data (out)
Control				
Request to Send (out)	4	--|---⟩	8	Data Carrier Detect (in)
Clear to Send (in)	5	⟨-|		
Data Carrier Detect (in)	8	⟨---|--	4	Request to Send (out)
		|-⟩	5	Clear to Send (in)
Data Set Ready (in)	6	⟨------	20	Data Terminal Ready (out)
Data Terminal Ready (out)	20	------⟩	6	Data Set Ready (in)

NOTES: The "-------" indicates a straight-through connection. The "------⟩" indicates a cross-over between the two leads. The jumpering of leads is shown as "--\|---⟩ / ⟨--\|" (e.g., connect lead 4 locally to lead 5 and across to lead 8 on the opposite end of the cable).

Now refer to the back-end discussion for connectivity discussion. This will be found in either Tutorial Module 3–6 for a networked version of the protocol converter or Tutorial Module 4–7 for a locally attached controller to a mainframe using a synchronous interface.

If you get garbled characters, then the speeds, parity, and character lengths are probably not set correctly. Consult Appendix J for standard terminal-to-computer error conditions and areas to check to correct the situation. In these connections, double-vision, or overwriting, may occur. Whatever the conditions, review your setups and options.

Tutorial Module 4-6: Connecting Two Multiuser Micros Together

In this module we will connect a terminal to a multiuser micro. Once this is complete, we will connect this same terminal, through the local MUM, to another MUM by establishing a dial-up connection. This configuration is depicted in Figure 4–4. This module is a combination of Tutorial Modules 4–1 and 3–5. We will not repeat all the steps, as you can break down the connection into the terminal-to-MUM connection and then the MUM-to-modem connection. Consult each of the respective modules for step-by-step approaches. We will, however, zero in the steps for measuring success.

This will be a common scenario in office environments. One of the multiuser computers may run the office accounting system, while the other is used for general-purpose office applications of word processing, spreadsheets, and database applications. Users on the accounting system will need access to the files on the other computer. Be it the data kept in the database, or the need to run a spreadsheet, users will need (remote) access to the other computer. The same rationale for Tutorial Module 5–6 can be applied here, as users of one system need frequently to "login" to another computer system.

The steps we will follow for this tutorial module are common to all our reviews:

STEPS FOR CONNECTION

1. Determine compatibility (should it work?).
2. Determine signs of success.
3. Determine the type of connector used.
4. Determine gender of the ports.
5. Determine which leads (pins) are provided by each device.
6. Determine which leads are required to be on by each device.

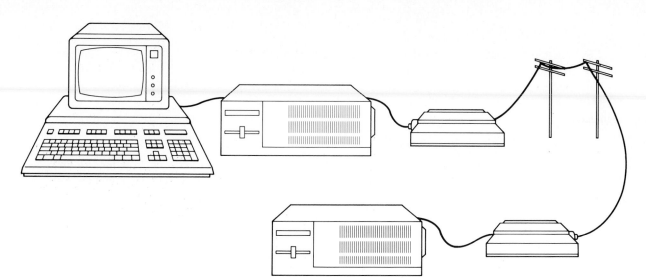

Figure 4-4. Terminal to MUM, calling another MUM through the local computer.

7. Design the cable.
8. Build the cable.
9. Test the cable for continuity.
10. Cable the two systems together with the cable.
11. From step 2, measure success.

1. Determine compatibility

Because the UNIX operating system is running the MUM to which we are locally connected, outbound communications are supported in an asynchronous mode. The speed of communication will be determined by the modem that is attached; assume 1200 bps. The other parameters of character length, parity, number of stop bits, and duplex will be 8, *N*, 1, and full duplex, respectively. As long as the "to be dialed" system accepts incoming calls in a port that has a 212A-compatible modem and is set up to match our local options, then the two systems will be compatible. Check to see if the remote system can automatically answer an incoming call with 1200 bps, 8 data bits, no parity, 1 stop bits, full duplex (echoplex), and asynchronous mode operation. If one of the options needs to be changed, such as character length or parity, adjust accordingly.

2. Determine signs of success

Once connected, there are many ways of testing our success between the systems. Perhaps the easiest is to be on a terminal at one multiuser microsystem, or MUM. At this terminal, the user should be able to call the other MUM and login. Once logged in, a large file should be displayed on his or her terminal to check out the flow control piece. Figure 4-4 depicts conceptually the scenario for measuring our success. The UNIX "cu" command allows a terminal user to "call UNIX" or call another computer system. We will assume that a UNIX systems administrator is involved to set up both ports on the MUMs, as this can be quite complex. For this and other systems administration functions, consult the user's manuals or read *DOSIUNIX Systems: Becoming a Super User*. This tutorial module will hint at where to set up the port, but will not review in-depth administration procedures.

3. Determine type of connector

4. Determine gender of ports

5. Determine leads (pins) provided by each device

6. Determine leads required to be on

7. Design the cables

8. Build the cables

9. Test for continuity

Consult the separate tutorial modules for the details of steps 3–9. The reason for this is that you have multiple connections. First, there is the terminal to be connected to the MUM (Tutorial Module 4–1 or 4–2). On the same multiuser micro, the connection to the modem is outlined in Tutorial Module 3–5. Repeat this for the MUM that will be called. Hence, the separate modules can serve to ensure success in connecting the different segments.

10. Cable the two systems together

The local cabling is also found in the separate modules. However, the connection between the two multiuser microsystems is a dial-up link. Refer to the next step for the actual connection of the two via a dial-up telephone connection.

11. Measure success

The intent of this type connection was to allow electronic mail access to remote file systems or access to applications that reside on a different computer. This tutorial module will not actually exercise any of these scenarios but, rather, will ensure that the link can be established to the remote system, with successful two-way communication between the systems.

Because the local multiuser system has the UNIX operating system, utilities and commands are provided for easy off-premise communications. In particular, the "cu" command can be used to dial a remote system. The remote system does not need to be a UNIX-based system. It can be a mail service, a bulletin board, a PC with a remote access package such as Carbon Copy, a mainframe, a DEC minicomputer, or just about any other system. With the proper use of "cu," a connection can be made.

An assumption is made that a modem is connected and working on the UNIX system. Consult the systems administrator to be sure that this is true.

The "cu" command is an acronym for "call UNIX." It was originally used to establish communication between UNIX systems. With need to establish sessions between computer systems came the requirement of flexibility. Each user of the UNIX system needed the flexibility to establish connections with different systems, which generally required different speeds, duplex, and parities. Do these options sound familiar? The same options are involved in every connection. Furthermore, communication could be required between this UNIX system and a locally connected UNIX system (without modems). The "cu" command had to be flexible enough to accommodate many different connections.

The "cu" command has several options. The command line is similar to the following:

cu -sspeed -lline -h -t -d -o/-e telno

An explanation of the syntax is in order. The "cu" command is entered once a user is logged into the UNIX system. This command should be used with any of the options listed. The options are (s)peed, (l)ine, half (d)uplex, (t)erminal, (d)iagnostics, (o)dd/(e)ven parity, and telephone number.

The command line should be entered with as many options as appropriate. UNIX allows for systems to be defined so that you can merely refer to them by name instead of having to enter all the options each time. Consult with the systems administrator for this feature.

To connect to a system using a 1200 bps modem, even parity, at 123–4567, the following command line would be entered:

cu -s1200 -e 1234567 (return key).

The execution of this command causes the UNIX system to access a local modem that can transmit at 1200 bps and dial the number 1234567. At this point, the user is dialing out of the system onto the telephone network to reach the destination system. If the far-end computer has been set up for auto answer, then the call should be answered by the computer. Once answered, the terminal operator should hit the Enter key a couple of times to allow the remote system to figure out the speed with which the communication is occurring. Login to the system as appropriate, entering your ID and password.

With UNIX and the "cu" command, software flow control (XON/XOFF) is normally automatically used. Hence, the terminal operator can use the Control-s (XOFF) and Control-q (XON) keys to regulate the flow of data. While logged into the remote system, display a standard ASCII file by entering the appropriate sequence.

TABLE 4–32. TERMINAL-TO-COMPUTER SYMPTOMS AND SOLUTIONS

Symptom	Causes
Garbled characters	Parity, speed, character length, stop bits, phone line
Lost data	Flow control
Double spacing	Translation of received carriage returns or line feeds
Overwriting	Translation of received carriage returns or line feeds
No display of typed characters	Far end is not echoplexing, duplex option
Double characters	Duplex option

If the remote system is UNIX system, "cat" a file. While the data are being output, test out the flow control by entering Control-s and Control-q keys alternately. If this does not regulate the flow, be sure that the remote system supports software flow control.

When two or more systems are involved in a communication session, isolating the reasons for the systems not functioning properly together can be difficult. It is better if you separate the connection into small segments and try to diagnose the problem. If the terminal was able to communicate with the attached computer to issue the "cu" command, note the parity, duplex, and character length. Use these or adjust these to match those of the remote system. Refer to Appendix J for standard errors and their possible causes and remedies. Table 4–32 offers a brief summary of the areas to check for solving any problems.

If any of these symptoms exists, check for the cause to ensure consistency of options between the communicating entities. CONGRATULATIONS!

Tutorial Module 4-7: Connecting a Protocol Converter to a Mainframe Front-end Processor

What if a 3270 controller or protocol converter is to be collocated with the mainframe without modems between the two devices? Can this be done? In the case of the protocol converter, this will be a common practice if the terminals to access the protocol converter are not located in the same vicinity. If multiple terminals are to access the protocol converter, then a modem could be attached to the "front side" to allow remote access to the converter. This could be in addition to the local terminal connection discussed in Tutorial Module 4–5.

In the case of a 3270 controller, this is commonly done when the mainframe is short on ports for channel attached devices. Instead of connecting a controller directly to the mainframe, the controller is run through the FEP to increase the number of terminals having access to the mainframe. These terminals would more than likely be local to the controller.

Either of these connections is possible, with the main issue being one of the timing category of leads. In the case of the 3270 controller, protocol converter, or mainframe front-end processor, one of them should be able to provide the timing. If none of them can provide a timing source, then a separate unit should be acquired to provide the timing source. This device is often referred to as a synchronous modem eliminator. In this tutorial module the protocol converter, a WALLDATA DCF II, will be featured to illustrate the connectivity between a controller and FEP, with the controller providing the timing source. For installations where a timing source cannot be provided by either one of the devices, refer to Tutorial Module 4–8, "Connecting a 3270 Controller to a Mainframe Front-End Processor."

The steps for a controller-to-FEP connection involving synchronous interfaces are exactly the same as our other steps. The steps we will follow for this tutorial module are common to all our reviews:

STEPS FOR CONNECTION

1. Determine compatibility (should it work?).
2. Determine signs of success.
3. Determine the type of connector used.
4. Determine gender of ports.
5. Determine which leads (pins) are provided by each device.
6. Determine which leads are required to be on by each device.

Line-Ending Sequence

7. Design the cable.
8. Build the cable.
9. Test the cable for continuity.
10. Cable the two systems together with the cable.
11. From step 2, measure success.

1. Determine compatibility

This tutorial module will not go into the compatibility issues of a protocol converter with a FEP. The whole purpose of a protocol converter was to allow dissimilar devices to communicate. Hence, we will assume that the two systems are compatible. Consult the systems analysts or the vendors to be assured of compatibility. In a general sense, if the FEP supports the connection of a 3270 series controller, and the protocol converter can emulate one of these 3270 series controllers, then the two will be compatible. This tutorial module will focus on the physical compatibility of the two devices.

2. Determine signs of success

The signs of success in this type connection are varied. The basic goal is to connect a protocol converter to the FEP and allow the attached terminals or PCs to access the applications of the mainframe. There is a lot that goes into a successful installation beyond mere connectivity of the devices. Just as the terminal, PC, and protocol converter have options associated with the port, so do the mainframe and FEP. This book is not large enough to include all the mainframe and FEP parameters that must be set up to support such a connection. Consult with the systems analyst for the proper setup. Later in this tutorial module, some of the key parameters necessary to support the protocol converter are given.

3. Determine type of connector

4. Determine gender of ports

Both devices, the IBM FEP and the DCF II protocol converter, utilize DB25-type connectors. They are, however, different genders. The IBM FEP ports are male, while the protocol converter is female. Hence our cable will require different gender connectors at each end, relieving you of concern over which end to connect to which device.

5. Determine leads (pins) provided by each device

6. Determine leads required to be on

The WALLDATA DCF II protocol converter port was analyzed in Tutorial Module 4–5. Table 4–33 summarizes the port specifics, including the input and output leads of the port. Note that lead 24 is provided as a source of timing. Normally the transmit timing is provided on lead 15, with an input direction to DTE, the protocol converter. Because we are not connecting to a modem (DCE), this is not the case. This tutorial module centers around the protocol converter providing the timing source. Lead 24 is the lead that provides the timing source; hence, the ''out'' direction from the port.

How about the port on the front-end processor? Which leads are input and which are output? Using a VOM or BOB, or consulting the documentation, the port can be analyzed in the usual fashion. Table 4–34 lays out the information as pulled from the 3704/3705 manuals. Note that the transmit and receive timing leads are both input. This is due to the normal connection of such a port to a synchronous modem, covered in Tutorial Module 3–6. The port is set up to get its timing from the network. In our tutorial module, the protocol converter will be providing the timing. The FEP you have may be capable of providing the timing on lead 24; however, this module assumes that the external device will be providing the timing.

Also the duplex of the port is important. The port on the FEP will be set up for full duplex, with continuous Request to Send. This implies that carrier will be transmitted at all times. Refer to the synchronous modem discussion for further information on this aspect of a network.

7. Design the cable

The cable design for this connection is fairly straightforward except for the timing leads. The easiest way to tackle the design is to separate each of the leads by category for the two ports. From this we can begin to design the cable.

TABLE 4–33. WALLDATA DCF II COMPUTER PORT PROFILE

Underline if supported; circle if selected.
Model: DCF II _____ Vendor: WALLDATA _____ Port: serial _____
Port type: <u>serial</u> parallel
Port: <u>DB25</u> 9-pin 5-pin 8-pin/modular 20mA Centronics

Gender: male <u>female</u>

Pin #	Function	Direction	Pin #	Function	Direction
1	Ground	to from <u>n/a</u>	14	_____	to from n/a
2	Transmit Data	to <u>from</u> n/a	15	Transmit Timing	<u>to</u> from n/a
3	Receive Data	<u>to</u> from n/a	16	_____	to from n/a
4	Request to Send	to <u>from</u> n/a	17	Receive Timing	to from n/a
5	Clear to Send	<u>to</u> from n/a	18	_____	to from n/a
6	Data Set Ready	to from n/a	19	_____	to from n/a
7	Signal Ground	to from <u>n/a</u>	20	Data Terminal Ready	to <u>from</u> n/a
8	Carrier Detect	<u>to</u> from n/a	21	_____	to from n/a
9	_____	to from n/a	22	_____	to from n/a
10	_____	to from n/a	23	_____	to from n/a
11	_____	to from n/a	24	Transmit Timing	to <u>from</u> n/a
12	_____	to from n/a		_____	to from n/a
13	_____	to from n/a			

Complete the next section only with 36-pin cinch connector.

26	_____	to from n/a	27	_____	to from n/a
28	_____	to from n/a	29	_____	to from n/a
30	_____	to from n/a	31	_____	to from n/a
32	_____	to from n/a	33	_____	to from n/a
34	_____	to from n/a	35	_____	to from n/a
36	_____	to from n/a			

Flow control technique: <u>XON/XOFF</u> ENQ/ACK STX/ETX <u>Hardware</u> _____ .
Leads that must be on: <u>5</u> 6 8 __ __ __ __

Options:
   Speeds: <u>110 300 600 1200 1800 2400 4800</u> (9600) <u>19.2 56k</u> _____
   Parity: <u>even</u> <u>odd</u> <u>space</u> <u>mark</u> <u>none</u>
   Char-length: <u>7</u> <u>8</u> __
   # stop bits: <u>1</u> <u>1.5</u> <u>2</u>
   Line-ending sequence: cr lf cr/lf cr/lf/lf
   Disconnect sequence: EOT DEL ~. _____

Mode: async sync isoch

sync timing leads:

#	Function	Direction
15	Transmit Timing	to from
17	Receive Timing	to from
24	Transmit Timing	to from

Notes: Pin 5 must be on for the protocol converter to transmit data and can be connected to the attached device's hardware flow control lead.

TABLE 4-34. IBM FEP PORT PROFILE

Computer Port Profile

Underline if supported; circle if selected.

Model: 3704/5 FEP ____ Vendor: IBM ____ Port: RS232 ____
Port type: <u>serial</u> parallel
Port: <u>DB25</u> 9-pin 5-pin 8-pin/modular 20mA Centronics

Gender: <u>male</u> female

Pin #	Function	Direction	Pin #	Function	Direction
1	<u>Frame Ground</u>	to from <u>n/a</u>	14	_____	to from n/a
2	<u>Transmit Data</u>	to <u>from</u> n/a	15	<u>Transmit Timing</u>	<u>to</u> from n/a
3	<u>Receive Data</u>	<u>to</u> from n/a	16	_____	to from n/a
4	<u>Request to Send</u>	to <u>from</u> n/a	17	<u>Receive Timing</u>	<u>to</u> from n/a
5	<u>Clear to Send</u>	to from n/a	18	_____	to from n/a
6	<u>Data Set Ready</u>	to from n/a	19	_____	to from n/a
7	<u>Signal Ground</u>	to from <u>n/a</u>	20	<u>Data Terminal Ready</u>	to <u>from</u> n/a
8	<u>Carrier Detect</u>	<u>to</u> from n/a	21	_____	to from n/a
9	_____	to from n/a	22	<u>Ring Indicator</u>	<u>to</u> from n/a
10	_____	to from n/a	23	_____	to from n/a
11	_____	to from n/a	24	_____	to from n/a
12	_____	to from n/a	25	_____	to from n/a
13	_____	to from n/a			

Complete the next section only with 36-pin cinch connector.

26	_____	to from n/a	27	_____	to from n/a
28	_____	to from n/a	29	_____	to from n/a
30	_____	to from n/a	31	_____	to from n/a
32	_____	to from n/a	33	_____	to from n/a
34	_____	to from n/a	35	_____	to from n/a
36	_____	to from n/a			

Flow control technique: XON/XOFF ENQ/ACK STX/ETX Hardware ____
Leads that must be on: 5 6 8 __ __ __ __

Options:
    Speeds: <u>110 300 600 1200 1800 2400 4800</u> (9600) 19.2 56k ____
    Parity: even odd space mark none
    Char-length: 7 8 __
    # stop bits: 1 1.5 2
    Line-ending sequence: cr lf cr/lf cr/lf/lf
    Disconnect sequence: EOT DEL ~. _____

    Mode: async sync isoch   sync timing leads:

#	Function	Direction
15	_____	to from
17	_____	to from
24	_____	to from

Notes: _____
_____
_____

TABLE 4–35. DCF II AND FEP PINOUTS SEPARATED BY CATEGORY

Function	DCF lead #	FEP lead #	Function
Ground			
Protective Ground	1	1	Protective Ground
Signal Ground	7	7	Signal Ground
Data			
Transmit Data (out)	2	2	Transmit Data (out)
Receive Data (in)	3	3	Receive Data (in)
Control			
Request to Send (out)	4	4	Request to Send (out)
Clear to Send (in)	5	5	Clear to Send (in)
Data Set Ready (in)	6	6	Data Set Ready (in)
Data Carrier Detect (in)	8	8	Data Carrier Detect (in)
Data Terminal Ready (out)	20	20	Data Terminal Ready (out)
Timing			
Transmit Timing (in)	15	15	Transmit Timing (in)
Receive Timing (in)	17	17	Receive Timing (in)
Transmit Timing (out)	24		

The following design rules will be followed. They are the same regardless of the connection.

CABLE DESIGN: GENERAL RULES

1. Connect like categories of leads together.
2. Always connect an ''out'' to an ''in'' and an ''in'' to an ''out.''
3. A lead that is input may be connected to another lead that is an input, only if both these are connected to an output lead.
4. In synchronous connections, only use one source of timing.

First the ground leads! Merely connect the ground leads together from one end to the other. The protective ground leads should be connected together. Furthermore, the signal grounds should also be connected together.

Next the data leads! There are only two possibilities, either connecting pins 2 and 2 together and pins 3 and 3 together, or crossing them. The directions will dictate the connection. Applying rule 2, the leads will be crossed so outputs will be connected to inputs, and vice versa. Table 4–36 reviews the ground and data lead design.

The next category of leads are the control leads. The control lead design can be done in many numerous ways. The control leads in a standard null modem cable design may satisfy this cable requirement. Consult Tutorial Module 4–5 for this design. However, the vendor of the DCF II recommends the control lead design in Table 4–37 for local connection of the DCF II and FEP.

The remaining category of leads are the timing leads. Normally, the FEP is expecting both Transmit Timing

TABLE 4–36. GROUND AND DATA LEAD DESIGN FOR DCF-TO-FEP CABLE DESIGN

Function	DCF lead #	FEP lead #	Function
Ground			
Protective Ground	1 -------	1	Protective Ground
Signal Ground	7 -------	7	Signal Ground
Data			
Transmit Data (out)	2 ------⟩	3	Receive Data (in)
Receive Data (in)	3 ⟨------	2	Transmit Data (out)

NOTES: The ''-------'' indicates a straight-through connection. The ''------)'' indicates a cross-over between the two leads.

TABLE 4–37. CONTROL LEAD DESIGN FOR DCF-to-FEP CABLE DESIGN

Function	DCF lead #		FEP lead #	Function
Request to Send (out)	4	---⟩	8	Data Carrier Detect (in)
Data Carrier Detect (in)	8	⟨---	4	Request to Send (out)
Data Set Ready (in)	6	⟨---|--	20	Data Terminal Ready (out)
		|-⟩	5	Clear to Send (in)
Data Terminal Ready (out)	20	---|--⟩	6	Data Set Ready (in)
Clear to Send (in)	5	⟨---|		

NOTES: The jumpering of leads are shown as   "⟨---\|--"
(e.g., connect lead 20 locally to lead 5 and   "\|-⟩"
across to lead 6 on the opposite end of the cable).

and Receive Timing as input leads found on leads 15 and 17, respectively. The same is true of the DCF II. However, the DCF II is being set up to provide the timing. It does this on lead 24 of its port. The Transmit Timing is an output signal on lead 24 of the DCF port. This will be the timing source of the connection. The cable design should begin with this aspect.

The FEP outputs its data at whatever speed (timing) is provided on lead 15. It also receives its data (input) at whatever rate is found on lead 17. There is nothing special about these leads. The signal will be a clock pulse. This pulse will be the rate used by the FEP to synchronize its transmission and reception of data. If the FEP expects both its transmit and receiving timing signals on pins 15 and 17, these two leads should be connected to the timing source. Once this connection is made in our cable, both leads 15 and 17 at the FEP port will reflect whatever clock pulse is found on lead 24 from the DCF II. Table 4–38 outlines this connection.

Because the DCF II is being optioned to provide the timing on its port, it will derive its timing signals from within. Hence, there are no further timing lead designs required. This completes the DCF II to FEP cable design and it summarized in Table 4–39.

TABLE 4–38. TIMING LEAD DESIGN FOR DCF-TO-FEP CABLE DESIGN

Function	DCF lead #		FEP lead #	Function
Transmit Timing (out)	24	----|-⟩	15	Transmit Timing (in)
		|-⟩	17	Receive Transmit (in)

NOTES: The "----\|-⟩ / \|-⟩" Indicates a cross-over and jumpering of leads.

TABLE 4–39. COMPLETE CABLE DESIGN FOR WALLDATA DCF-TO-IBM FEP CONNECTION

Function	DCF lead #		FEP lead #	Function
Protective Ground	1	-------	1	Protective Ground
Signal Ground	7	-------	7	Signal Ground
Transmit Data (out)	2	------⟩	3	Receive Data (in)
Receive Data (in)	3	⟨------	2	Transmit Data (out)
Request to Send (out)	4	---⟩	8	Data Carrier Detect (in)
Data Carrier Detect (in)	8	⟨---	4	Request to Send (out)
Data Set Ready (in)	6	⟨---|--	20	Data Terminal Ready (out)
		|-⟩	5	Clear to Send (in)
Data Terminal Ready (out)	20	---|--⟩	6	Data Set Ready (in)
Clear to Send (in)	5	⟨--|		
Transmit Timing (out)	24	---|--⟩	15	Transmit Timing (in)
		|-⟩	17	Receive Transmit (in)

8. Build the cable

9. Test for continuity

10. Cable the two systems together

11. Measure success

Complete the next three steps in the normal fashion, with a female connector at the FEP end of the cable and a male connector at the DCF II cable end. Work with the mainframe systems analyst to connect the systems together and "gen" the systems for success. CONGRATULATIONS!!!

Tables 4–40, 4–41, and 4–42 include some recommended system generation parameters for the mainframe side of the connection. Get with the systems analyst to set up the proper parameters.

Tutorial Module 4-8: Connecting a 3270 Series Controller Locally to a Mainframe Front-end Processor Using a Synchronous Modem Eliminator

This tutorial module will be the same type connection as Tutorial Module 4–7, except that an assumption will be made that neither the 3270 controller nor the FEP can provide the timing source. In Module 4–7, the protocol converter could provide this timing source; however, here we assume that an external device will be acquired to provide the timing.

The best way to approach this type configuration is to split the two sides of the synchronous modem eliminator, or SME. Although the two sides will be very similar, for cabling considerations it is worth reviewing each separately. Refer to Figure 4–5 for the connection to be covered in this module. Although this tutorial module will cover all the standard steps for connection, it is worthwhile to note upfront that the SME provides two ports that are set up to emulate modems. Hence, the 3270 controller can connect directly to one of these ports. Similarly, the FEP is expecting to connect directly to a modem and, hence, can be connected using a straight-through cable between it and the SME.

The steps we will follow for this tutorial module are common to all our reviews:

STEPS FOR CONNECTION

1. Determine compatibility (should it work?).
2. Determine signs of success.
3. Determine the type of connector used.
4. Determine gender of the ports.
5. Determine which leads (pins) are provided by each device.
6. Determine which leads are required to be on by each device.
7. Design the cable.
8. Build the cable.
9. Test the cable for continuity.
10. Cable the two systems together with the cable.
11. From step 2, measure success.

1. Determine compatibility

2. Determine signs of success

At this point, compatibility will be assumed, as the two communicating entities—the 3270 controller and IBM mainframe FEP—determine the compatibility. The SME only provides the timing source and a null modem function. The speeds for both devices (the 3270 controller and the FEP) should be the same, probably 9600 bps. The IBM devices use 8-bit EBCDIC code. They should both be optioned for external timing or set up so that an external entity provides the timing. The option within the FEP is normally the "Clocking" option and should be set to "Ext" for external. The 3270 controllers normally don't provide timing, so they need not be optioned. However, if your controller has such an option, set it for "External."

The signs of success will mirror those of a remote 3270 controller connected to a FEP with synchronous modems between them. The standard communication between a device attached to the 3270 controller and the application will determine our success. This tutorial module will not measure the success.

TABLE 4–40. SNA NONSWITCHED DEFINITION

GROUP1		
	GROUP ANS=CONT	THIS IS THE DEFAULT OPERAND
	CLOCKING=EXT,	THIS IS THE DEFAULT OPERAND
	DATMODE=HALF,	3270 CNTRLRS ONLY SUPPORT HALF
	DIAL=NO,	THIS SAMPLE IS FOR DEDICATED
	,	LINES
	DUPLEX=FULL,	MODEM & 3705 HARDWARE
	,	DEPENDENT
	ETRATIO=33,	3.3% ERROR TO TRAFFIC RATION FOR
	,	REPORTING TO NPDA
	INTPRI=2,	SEE APPENDIX J FOR CALCULATION
	,	OF LINE PRIORITIES IN NCP REF. GUIDE
	IRETRY=NO,	DEFAULT
	LNCTL=SDLC,	SDLC LINK
	LPDATS=NO,	SPECIFY YES IF USING LPDA/IBM
	,	MODEMS
	NEWSYNC=YES,	MODEM OPTION *IF USED CAN CUT
	,	DOWN ON TEMPRORARY ERRORS
	NRZI=NO,	MODEM OPTION
	MAXDATA=265,	THIS IS VALUE TO BE USED W/3270'S
	,	256 MAX BYTES OF 3270 DATA + RH +
		TH
	MAXOUT=7,	MAX 7 PIUS SEND TO A PU AT 1 TIME
	,	WITHOUT A RESPONSE FROM THE PU
	NPACALL=YES,	SHOULD BE NO IF YOU DON'T USE NPA
	OWNER=CDRM1,	A NAME TO INDICATE THE HOST
	,	THAT OWN'S THIS GROUP OF
	,	RESOURCES
	PACING=0,	NORMALLY NO PACING USED EXCEPT
	,	
	,	FOR PRINTERS AND RJE
		WORKSTATIONS
	PASSLIM=12,	MAX # OF PIUS TO SEND AT ONE TIME
	,	TO A PU. 12 WILL ALLOW 3072 BYTES
	,	TO BE SENT TO A PU AT ONCE
	PAUSE=2,	CUTS DOWN ON NONPRODUCTIVE
	,	POLLING
	PUTYPE=2,	3270'S ARE PU TYPE 2
	REPLYTO=3,	NO RESPONSE WITHIN .3 THEN
	,	TIMEOUT
	RETRIES=(2,1,2)	1 RETRY PAUSE FOR 1 SEC. TRY 2
	,	MORE
	SERVLIM=10,	10 PASSES OF SERVICE ORDER
	,	BEFORE SPECIAL PASS (SNRM'S)
	SPEED=9600,	MAXIMUM SPEED ALLOWABLE
	SRT=(18000,100)	TRANSMISSION/ERROR RETRY
	TRANSFR=45,	45*BFRS = MAX AMOUNT TO DATA TO
	,	ALLOW TO BE TRANSFERRED TO HOST
	,	AT ONE TIME FROM A SINGLE LINE.
	TEXTO=1,	TIMEOUT ERROR IF IT TAKES MORE
	,	THAN A SECOND BETWEEN ANY
	,	2 DATA CHAR.
	DISCNT=NO,	SSCP-LU SESSIONS NOT TERMINATED
	DLOGMOD=	
	MODENTRY,	BIND PARAMETERS SEE SAMPLE 1
	ISTATUS=ACTIVE,	WHEN NCP ACTIVATED ACTIVATE
	,	THESE RESOURCES ALSO.
	MODETAB=	
	TABLNAME,	TABLE OF BIND PARAMETER ENTRIES
	USSTAB=USSNAME,	TABLE OF SESSION REQUEST
		COMMANDS
	SSCPFM=USSSCS,	USES SCS CHARACTER SET FOR ALL
	,	SSCP SESSION MESSAGES.
	VPACING=0,	NO PACING BETWEEN HOST AND NCP
	TYPE=NCP	

TABLE 4–40. *(Continued)*

```
LINE1 LINE                          ONLY 1 3705 PORT IF HALF DUPLEX
ADDRESS=(020,021),
          MAXPU=8                   DYNAMIC RECONFIGURATION
        ,                           OPERAND

SERVIC 1 SERVICE ORDER=(PU1,PU2,PU3),
          MAXLIST=8                 DYNAMIC RECONFIGURATION
        ,                           OPERAND
     SPACE 2

TERM2101 TERMINAL ADDR=60604040,
          POLL=40404040,
          CONV=YES,                 IF HAVE, SEND MESSAGE INSTEAD OF
        ,                           ACK
          CRITSIT=YES,              WORKS
          DIRECTN=INOUT,            DEFAULT
          SRT=(2500,100)            TRAFFIC AND ERROR MAINT STAT
        ,                           THRESH (SPECIFIED ON "GROUP")
TERM2102 TERMINAL ADDR=6060C1C1,POLL=4040C1C1
TERM2103 TERMINAL ADDR=6060C2C2,POLL=4040C2C2
TERM2104 TERMINAL ADDR=6060C3C3,POLL=4040C3C3
TERM2105 TERMINAL ADDR=6060C4C4,POLL=4040C4C4
TERM2106 TERMINAL ADDR=6060C5C5,POLL=4040C5C5
TERM2107 TERMINAL ADDR=6060C6C6,POLL=4040C6C6
TERM2108 TERMINAL ADDR=6060C7C7,POLL=4040C7C7
```

3. Determine type of connector

4. Determine gender of ports

5. Determine leads (pins) provided by each device

6. Determine leads required to be on

Steps 3–6 have been completed for the 3270 in Tutorial Modules 3–6 and 4–7 for the 3270 controller and FEP, respectively. They are summarized in Table 4–43 in the SCS port profile formats.

This terminal port profile could have just have easily been a computer port profile, as terminals attach to the 3270 controller. Review the pinouts of the 3270 controller and compare them to the FEP pinouts. The two ports are similar in that they are both emulating data terminal equipment. This implies that they are expecting to be connected to piece of DCE, such as a modem. Tutorial Module 3–6 outlines the connections they are both expecting. However, we are going to connect them back to back with a SME between them. Therefore, the pinouts of the SME will determine our cable designs.

Consulting the documentation, or using a VOM, or BOB, you should analyze the SME ports. Refer to the information outlined in Table 4–44, and note that the output signals provided by the SME are Clear to Send, Data Set Ready, and Data Carrier Detect, along with Receive Data. In addition Transmit Timing and Receive Timing signals are provided as output leads from the SME. The SME ports emulate a modem, meaning that the ports are expecting to be directly connected to a piece of DTE, such as the 3270 controller and FEP. Hence, our cable design should be straightforward and should be the same to connect both devices to the SME.

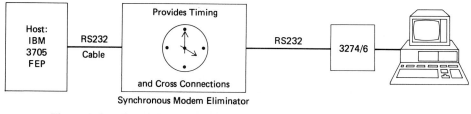

Figure 4–5.   IBM 3270 to synchronous modem eliminator to IBM FEP connection.

TABLE 4–41. GROUP MACRO FOR NCP BSC DEFINITION "ONLY"

```
          SPACE 2
GROUP1
   GROUP CONV=YES,           IF HAVE, SEND MESSAGE INSTEAD OF
         ,                   ACK*
         CRETRY=3,           NUMBER OF ERROR RECOVER
         ,                   ATTEMPTS
         CRITSIT=YES,        SEND MESSAGE IF CPU NO TALKING
         DIAL=NO,
         LNCTL=BSC,
         REPLYTO=.8,         IF NCP DOES NOT RECEIVE A
         ,                   RESPONSE
         SRT=(2500,100),     TRAFFIC AND ERROR MAINT STAT
         ,                   THRESH
         TEXTTO=30,          TIME IN SECONDS BETWEEN
         ,                   CHARACTERS
         TTDCNT=15,          NUMBER OF TIMES ACCEPT BSC
         TYPE=NCP,           NCP ONLY
         WACKCNT=15,         MAX NUMBER TIMES TO ACCEPT BSC
         ISTATUS=INACTIVE    VTAM ONLY
         DLOGMODE=S3270,     VTAM
         PU=YES,             VTAM
         MODETAB=DSILUO,     VTAM
         SSCPFM=USS3270,     VTAM
         USSTAB=USSTBLOC,    VTAM
         VPACING=0           VTAM
         WAKDLAY=2.2
WARNING:
MAX. NUMBER OF "TIMEOUT" INTERVALS SPECIFIABLE IS 16

            >NCP INSTALLATION MANUAL 5–107<

SPACE 3
          SPACE 1
LINE21   LINE ADDRESS=(OCF),3705 PORT ADDRESS
         AVGPB=200,          AVERAGE NUMBER OF BYTES
         ,                   EXPECTED
         CLOCKING=EXT,
         CODE=EBCDIC,
         CUTOFF=1,
         DUPLEX=FULL,
         ETRATIO=30,         ERROR-TO-TRANSMISSION RATIO FOR
         INTPRI=1,
         LPDATS=NO,          SPECIFIES IF MODEMS THAT SUPPORT
         NEGPOLP=2,          PAUSE IN SECONDS AFTER NEGATIVE
         NEWSYNC=NO,
         PAUSE=0,            SECONDS DELAY BETWEEN
         ,                   SUCCESSIVE
         POLIMIT=(1,NOWAIT)  NUMBER OF CONSECUTIVE NEGATIVE
         ,                   POLL
         POLLED=YES,         (DEFAULT IS NO)
         RETRIES=(2,1,2),    ATTEMPTS TO RECOVER FROM
         ,                   ERRORS
         SERVLIM=20,         NUMBER OF SERVICE ORDER TABLE
         SERVPRI=OLD,        PRIORITY SERVICE TO EXISTING
         SESSION=35,         NUMBER OF CONCURRENT SESSIONS
         ,                   ON
         SPEED=9600,
         TRANSFR=45,         NUMBER OF NCP BUFFERS, MAX
         ,                   RECEIV
         TERM=3277,
         TYPE=NCP            ALSO SPECIFIED IN "GROUP"
   SPACE 2
```

TABLE 4–41. (Continued)

```
SRV21 SERVICE
ORDER=(TERM2101,TERM2102,TERM2103,TERM2104,TERM2105,
       TERM2106,TERM2107,TERM2108),
       MAXLIST=35
```

```
CTRL2140 CLUSTER
         BHSET=NONE,          DEFAULT NO BLOCK HANDLERS
         CDATA=NO,            DEFAULT NO CRITICAL DATA
         CUTYPE=3271,         CONTROL UNIT TYPE (DEFAULT)
         GPOLL=40407F7F,      GENERAL POLLING CHARACTERS
         INHIBIT=NONE,        DEFAULT NO FACILITIES INHIBITED
         ITBMODE=(NO,NO),     DEFAULT NO INSERT/DELETE
     LGRAPHS=(REJECT,REJECT),
        ,                     DEFAULT REJECT LEADING GRAPHICS
         XMITLIM=1            TRANSMISSION LIMIT
                              (RECOMMENDED FOR 3270 BSC
                              CLUSTERS)
         SPACE 2
```

```
TERM2101 TERMINAL ADDR=60604040,
         POLL=40404040,
         CONV=YES,           IF HAVE, SEND MESSAGE INSTEAD OF
        ,                     ACK
         CRITSIT=YES,        WORKS
         DIRECTN=INOUT,      DEFAULT
         SRT=(2500,100)      TRAFFIC AND ERROR MAINT STAT
        ,                     THRESH (SPECIFIED ON "GROUP")
TERM2102 TERMINAL ADDR=6060C1C1,POLL=4040C1C1
TERM2103 TERMINAL ADDR=6060C2C2,POLL=4040C2C2
TERM2104 TERMINAL ADDR=6060C3C3,POLL=4040C3C3
TERM2105 TERMINAL ADDR=6060C4C4,POLL=4040C4C4
TERM2106 TERMINAL ADDR=6060C5C5,POLL=4040C5C5
TERM2107 TERMINAL ADDR=6060C6C6,POLL=4040C6C6
TERM2108 TERMINAL ADDR=6060C7C7,POLL=4040C7C7
```

TABLE 4–42. EP BSC DEFINITION

```
             SPACE 2
EPVM GROUP
         DIAL=NO,
         LNCTL=BSC,
         TYPE=EP,            EP ONLY
         CHNPRI=NORMAL,
         CLOCKING=EXT,
         CODE=EBCDIC,
         CU=2701,
         TERM=3277,          DEFAULT
         DISABLE=NO          DEFAULT
         DUPLEX=FULL,
         FEATURE=NODUALCD)
        ,                    DEFAULT FOR 2601 BSC
         INTPRI=1,
         MODEM=OPTION2,
         NEWSYNC=NO,
         SPEED=9600
     SPACE 2

     SPACE 1
EPVMLN1 LINE ADDRESS=(0AE,51),
         DAULCOM=NONE,       DEFAULT
         DUPLEX=FULL,                        SEE GROUP
         INTPRI=1,
         SPEED=9600                          SEE GROUP
```

Line-Ending Sequence

TABLE 4–43. FEP AND 3270 SCS PORT PROFILES

Computer Port Profile

Underline if supported; circle if selected.

Model: 3704/5 FEP _____ Vendor: IBM _____ Port: RS232 _____
Port type: <u>serial</u> parallel
Port: <u>DB25</u> 9-pin 5-pin 8-pin/modular 20mA Centronics

Gender: <u>male</u> female

Pin #	Function	Direction	Pin #	Function	Direction
1	<u>Frame Ground</u>	to from <u>n/a</u>	14	_____	to from n/a
2	<u>Transmit Data</u>	to <u>from</u> n/a	15	<u>Transmit Timing</u>	<u>to</u> from n/a
3	<u>Receive Data</u>	<u>to</u> from n/a	16	_____	to from n/a
4	<u>Request to Send</u>	to <u>from</u> n/a	17	<u>Receive Timing</u>	<u>to</u> from n/a
5	<u>Clear to send</u>	<u>to</u> from n/a	18	_____	to from n/a
6	<u>Data Set Ready</u>	<u>to</u> from n/a	19	_____	to from n/a
7	<u>Signal Ground</u>	<u>to</u> from <u>n/a</u>	20	Data Terminal Ready	to <u>from</u> n/a
8	<u>Carrier Detect</u>	<u>to</u> from n/a	21	_____	to from n/a
9	_____	to from n/a	22	Ring Indicator	<u>to</u> from n/a
10	_____	to from n/a	23	_____	to from n/a
11	_____	to from n/a	24	_____	to from n/a
12	_____	to from n/a	25	_____	to from n/a
13	_____	to from n/a			

Complete the next section only with 36-pin cinch connector.

26	_____	to from n/a	27	_____	to from n/a
28	_____	to from n/a	29	_____	to from n/a
30	_____	to from n/a	31	_____	to from n/a
32	_____	to from n/a	33	_____	to from n/a
34	_____	to from n/a	35	_____	to from n/a
36	_____	to from n/a			

Flow control technique: XON/XOFF ENQ/ACK STX/ETX Hardware _____
Leads that must be on: 5 6 8 __ __ __ __

Options:
   Speeds: <u>110 300 600 1200 1800 2400 4800</u> (9600) 19.2 56k _____
   Parity: even odd space mark none
   Char-length: 7 8 __
   # stop bits: 1 1.5 2
   Line-ending sequence: cr lf cr/lf cr/lf/lf
   Disconnect sequence: EOT DEL ~. _____

Mode: async sync isoch   sync timing leads:

#	Function	Direction
15	_____	to from
17	_____	to from
24	_____	to from

Notes: _____
_____
_____

TABLE 4–43. *(Continued)*

Terminal Port Profile

Underline if supported; circle if selected.

Model: 3270 series _____ Vendor: IBM _____ Port: RS232 _____
Port type: <u>DB25</u> 9-pin 5-pin 8-pin/modular 20mA Centronics

Gender: <u>male</u> female

Pin #	Function	Direction	Pin #	Function	Direction
1	Frame Ground	to from <u>n/a</u>	14	_____	to from n/a
2	Transmit Data	to <u>from</u> n/a	15	Transmit Timing	to from n/a
3	Receive Data	<u>to</u> from n/a	16	_____	to from n/a
4	Request to Send	to <u>from</u> n/a	17	Receive Timing	<u>to</u> from n/a
5	Clear to send	<u>to</u> from n/a	18	_____	to from n/a
6	Data Set Ready	<u>to</u> from n/a	19	_____	to from n/a
7	Signal Ground	to from <u>n/a</u>	20	Data Terminal Ready	to <u>from</u> n/a
8	Carrier Detect	<u>to</u> from n/a	21	_____	to from n/a
9	_____	to from n/a	22	_____	to from n/a
10	_____	to from n/a	23	_____	to from n/a
11	_____	to from n/a	24	_____	to from n/a
12	_____	to from n/a	25	_____	to from n/a
13	_____	to from n/a			

Complete the next section only with 36-pin cinch connector.

26	_____	to from n/a	27	_____	to from n/a
28	_____	to from n/a	29	_____	to from n/a
30	_____	to from n/a	31	_____	to from n/a
32	_____	to from n/a	33	_____	to from n/a
34	_____	to from n/a	35	_____	to from n/a
36	_____	to from n/a			

Flow control technique: XON/XOFF Hardware _____
Flow control lead(s): 4 11 19 20 __ __ __
Leads that must be on: 5 6 8 __ __ __ __
Printer port: serial   parallel
    Flow control: XON/XOFF Hardware _____
                FC lead(s): 4 11 19 20 __ __ __   Connector DB25 Centronics
Options:
    Speeds: <u>110 300 600 1200 1800 2400 4800 9600</u> 19.2 56k _____
    Parity: even odd space mark none
    Char-length: 7 8 __
    # stop bits: 1 1.5 2
    Line-ending sequence: cr lf cr/lf cr/lf/lf

Mode: async sync isoch   sync timing leads:

#	Function	Direction
15	Transmit Timing	to from
17	Receive Timing	to from
24	_____	to from

Terminal compatibility: ANSI X3.64, VT100, VT220, VT52, n/a.
This is a controller that supports various terminals.

Notes: _____
_____
_____

TABLE 4–44. PINOUTS FOR SYNCHRONOUS MODEM ELIMINATOR

SME Function	Lead #
Protective Ground	1
Transmit Data (in)	2
Receive Data (out)	3
Request to Send (in)	4
Clear to Send (out)	5
Data Set Ready (out)	6
Signal Ground	7
Carrier Detect (out)	8
Transmit Timing (out)	15
Receive Timing (out)	17
Data Terminal Ready (in)	20

TABLE 4–45. PINOUTS FOR 3270 AND FEP AND SYNCHRONOUS MODEM ELIMINATOR BY CATEGORY

Function	3270/FEP lead #	SME lead #	Function
Ground			
Protective Ground	1	1	Protective Ground
Signal Ground	7	7	Signal Ground
Data			
Transmit Data (out)	2	2	Transmit Data (in)
Receive Data (in)	3	3	Receive Data (out)
Control			
Request to Send (out)	4	4	Request to Send (in)
Clear to Send (in)	5	5	Clear to Send (out)
Data Set Ready (in)	6	6	Data Set Ready (out)
Carrier Detect (in)	8	8	Carrier Detect (out)
Data Terminal Ready (out)	20	20	Data Terminal Ready (in)
Timing			
Transmit Timing (in)	15	15	Transmit Timing (out)
Receive Timing (in)	17	17	Receive Timing (out)

7. Design the cable

The best way to design the cable is to separate the leads into their individual categories. This will allow for an easier layout of our ultimate cable design. Since both the interfaces are the same, we will depict on one diagram to illustrate both devices, the 3270 and FEP. Table 4–45 summarizes the pinouts for the 3270/FEP and SME ports.

Before actually designing the cable, review the design rules:

CABLE DESIGN: GENERAL RULES

1. Connect like categories of leads together.
2. Always connect an "out" to an "in" and an "in" to an "out."
3. A lead that is input may be connected to another lead that is an input, only if both these are connected to an output lead.
4. In synchronous connections, only use one source of timing.

TABLE 4–46.   CABLE DESIGN FOR 3270 CONTROLLER AND FEP-TO-SME

Function	3270/FEP lead #	SME lead #	Function
Protective Ground	1 -------	1	Protective Ground
Transmit Data (out)	2 -------	2	Transmit Data (in)
Receive Data (in)	3 -------	3	Receive Data (out)
Request to Send (out)	4 -------	4	Request to Send (in)
Clear to Send (in)	5 -------	5	Clear to Send (out)
Data Set Ready (in)	6 -------	6	Data Set Ready (out)
Signal Ground	7 -------	7	Signal Ground
Carrier Detect (in)	8 -------	8	Carrier Detect (out)
Transmit Timing (in)	15 -------	15	Transmit Timing (out)
Receive Timing (in)	17 -------	17	Receive Timing (out)
Data Terminal Ready (out)	20 -------	20	Data Terminal Ready (in)

LEGEND: The ''-------'' implies a straight-through connection. This is a straight-through cable. Be sure that all the pins are provided for in the cable you ultimately build or purchase. If pins 15 and 17 are not present in the cable, the systems will not communicate.

In this particular case due to the synchronous connection, different from most of the other ones in this book, point 4 is applicable. Only use one source of timing. The SME is our single source of timing for both devices, the 3270 controller and the FEP.

The ground leads are straightforward and should be connected from one end of the cable to the other. Looking at the data leads, they are also straightforward. Applying rules 1 and 2, the data leads are straight through from end to end in the cable.

Moving on to the control category of leads, we have a similar situation. Request to Send is an output from the 3270/FEP devices and an input lead for the SME. This implies a straight-through connection. Proceeding through each of the other control leads, Clear to Send, Data Set Ready, Data Carrier Detect, and Data Terminal Ready, the same holds true. Each of these leads should be connected straight through from one end of the cable to the other.

The only category left is timing. The same rules apply, 1 and 2, allowing for straight-through connections of the timing leads. Table 4–46 outlines all the lead designs. Note that they are all straight-through conductors. This means that a straight-through cable has been designed. Any straight-through cable that has all the leads in the table may be used, providing that the genders are considered.

8. Build the cable

9. Test for continuity

10. Cable the two systems together

11. Measure success

Complete the remaining steps as normal. Consult the other tutorial modules for the details of each step. Note that when building the cable to connect the 3270 to the SME, one connector should be female for the 3270 end, with the SME end male. The FEP cable end required a female connector. Hence, both cables will be exactly the same. Measure your success just as you would with a 3270 networked solution. CONGRATULATIONS!

TERMINAL INTERFACING: MOST FREQUENTLY ASKED QUESTIONS

Question 1.   What does it mean when a terminal is ANSI X3.64 compatible?

Answer 1.   The American National Standards Institute (ANSI) produced a standard that defines ''a set of encoded control functions to facilitate data interchange with two-dimensional character-imaging input-output devices.'' The standard outlines guidelines to allow editing functions, formatting, the specification and control of input areas, as well as certain status setting and interrogation functions, mode selection, and typesetting composition functions. The most common use of the standard has been by, but is not limited to, interactive terminal manufacturers.

When a terminal claims ANSI X3.64 compatibility, the implication is that the terminal conforms to the standard. It can handle the escape sequences as outlined in the standard for screen formatting as an example. Hence, any application that uses the appropriate escape sequences can work with the ANSI X3.64 terminal.

Question 2. Is DEC VT100 compatibility the same as ANSI X3.64 compatibility?

Answer 2. NO! The two are very similar, but there are differences. The DEC VT100 terminal is X3.64 compatible, but offers a super-set of features. Some of these features include: double-height characters, 132-column display of characters, etc. These features are not found in the X3.64 standard, but are included in the VT100's capabilities. Hence vendors will indicate that terminals are VT100 compatible, normally with a few exceptions such as the features mentioned above.

Question 3. What is the difference between "print online" and a screen copy?

Answer 3. Print online (POL) refers to the capability of a terminal to simultaneously print the data it receives, as well as display it on the screen. Hence as a terminal displays data received from an attached or remote computer, a hardcopy can be made. The sending computer can control the POL function through escape codes. The computer can cause a terminal to enter POL mode, either displaying or not displaying received data on the screen. Once the data are printed, the computer takes the terminal out of POL mode.

Screen copy, or print local, refers to the capability of a terminal to print a copy of its screen at any given moment. In effect, the printer can produce a picture of the screen contents when the screen copy key is typed. As the data change on the screen, the screen copy key must be typed again to get the new contents.

Question 4. What significance is a terminal's capability to support forms?

Answer 4. If a terminal can support forms, this implies that memory is available for setting up forms for local data entry. The user can fill out a form and transmit it to a remote or local computer, sending only the variable information. The computer can actually send a sequence to request the sending of this variable information. This offloads the computer.

Question 5. Why is it better to have the remote computer echoplex the characters, rather than have the terminal echo them locally?

Answer 5. This feature has to do with data integrity. Echoplexing is enabled (although it is often referred to as full duplex) to have the computer that a terminal is attached to, send back the characters as they are entered on the terminal's keyboard. The terminal displays them only after they are received back through the serial port. If the user sees the same character on the screen that they had typed, they can be assured that the character made it to the computer without error. If however, the displayed character is different, then an error occurred. This allows the user to backspace, and re-enter the character(s). If the terminal was merely locally displaying the characters as they were entered, the user would not be aware of any parity errors, or other problems that might occur.

Question 6. What is wrong when a backspace key is typed on a terminal's keyboard with the cursor on the screen backing up, but the data subsequently entered not appearing correctly in the computer?

Answer 6. Chances are that there are two keys on the terminal's keyboard that perform similar functions. One of them is the backspace key, with the other being the delete key. One of them may be a nondestructive backspace that merely locally backs up one space without altering data, while the other may actually delete a character. Depending on the computer system, either key may be correct. Check which key should be used to back up one space to actually correct a character.

Question 7. What is line wrap?

Answer 7. Line wrap is the ability of a terminal to receive greater than eighty characters (or the maximum line size) of data without losing them. A terminal without line wrap can receive more than eighty characters of data, but will lose the eighty-first through XX character. The cursor will sit in the eightieth position of a line and scroll through the received characters, but the terminal will not display all of them. With line wrap, the cursor advances to the line on the screen automatically and displays the remaining characters.

5

CONNECTING COMPUTERS

In today's environment, the use of personal computers, supermicros, minis, and mainframes is growing by leaps and bounds. This widespread use of all different types of computers dictates the need for users to be able to connect their computer systems to a multitude of other systems. These other systems range from terminals to printers, modems, other PCs, other supermicros, other minis, and mainframes.

The connection of computers to peripherals, such as terminals, printers, and modems, is complex enough. However, when two sophisticated computer systems are to communicate, the level of complexity increases dramatically. This chapter is designed to cover all the various aspects involved when connecting your computer system to a multitude of other devices. The user will find that connecting computers involves many of the same principles as connecting peripherals, with some additional concerns. The sections that follow cover different elements of a computer connection, to prepare the reader for the tutorial modules that feature "how to" connections involving computers.

COMPATIBILITY

Is your computer system compatible with the device you desire to connect it with? This question involves many different elements ranging from the physical connection to the high-level protocol connection. The ports used for the connection must be compatible. However, it is not enough to determine if the two devices can be plugged together. The devices must work together once they are connected. The ports should support common options, including speed, data format, protocol, and operating environment.

OPTIONS

Computer systems offer serial ports for their connection to other devices. This has been the most popular method of connecting systems together. However, the use of local area networks to provide this connection is growing at a rapid rate. Whether a computer is to be connected to a device through a serial port, a local area network (LAN), or other facility, the ports on each device must support the common options. As this text centers on serial and parallel connections, the options associated with LANs will not be covered. However, those found in serial and parallel connections will be highlighted.

The most prevalent options associated with a computer's serial port are the communication mode, speed, character format, stop bits, parity, duplex, flow control, and protocol. The other chapters described the importance of a common operating mode, either asynchronous or synchronous, common speed, and data format. The duplex of a port determines whether or not data can be transmitted in both directions, and if this can be done simultaneously. Half duplex allows two-way transmission, but in only one direction at a time. Full duplex allows for simultaneous transmission of data.

Another term associated with duplex is echoplex. Echoplex is the ability of a port to echo back the characters it receives. When a terminal is connected to a computer port supporting echoplexing, the terminal will not locally display the character until it is received from the line. The computer is actually echoing back every character that it receives. This is "acceptable" when a terminal or PC emulating a terminal is connected to a computer. But what about those instances when two minicomputers are being connected, or when two supermicros are to be connected through a serial port? Then echoplexing may not be desirable. Be aware that echoplexing or full duplex are options that should be checked when connecting computers to other devices.

FLOW CONTROL

When computers are communicating with other devices, this can be one of the most important features/options. If not set correctly, data will be lost! When a computer is outputting information to a terminal user, the data are displayed on the screen as fast as they are received. The user typically cannot read at speeds of 9600 bps; hence, they lose some of the data. If the receiving device is a printer, which is typically slower than a computer's output capability, it will simply print what it can and ignore the rest. The ignored data will drop in the bit bucket.

Suppose two computers are connected with the intention of uploading and downloading data. Whether the connection involves modems, or the computers are connected back to back, at some point one of the computers will need to store the received information to a disk file. What happens to the incoming data while the file is being written?

These examples involving computers clearly define the requirement for "flow control." The tutorial modules highlight this very important element of communication between two systems. Flow control is the ability of a receiving device to regulate the flow of data from the sending device. There are several different types of flow control used between systems. In an asynchronous environment, XON/XOFF, ETX/ACK, ENQ/ACK, and hardware flow control are used. In a parallel connection, hardware flow control is used.

Consult the index for the different sections in this text that detail these types of flow control.

In a synchronous connection, a protocol is involved that is understood by both communicating devices. A protocol is a set of rules governing the exchange of data between two entities. Most protocols stem from a particular device's features or from a vendor's architecture. Prominent protocols in use today are binary synchronous communications (BSC), high-level data link control (HDLC), advanced data communications control procedures (ADCCP), and synchronous data link control (SDLC). Each of these protocols has its own set of rules that is used to exchange information between two devices.

Inherent in the protocol is the flow control mechanism. The synchronous-based protocols break the data into blocks or frames of data. The sending entity will send the information a block or frame at a time. In addition, the sending entity will perform a calculation on the bits of the data in the block. The result of this calculation is a block check character (BCC) or frame check sequence (FCS). The calculation used is not important in our discussion. The important point is that the BCC or FCS is one or two characters that are appended to the block of data. The block and appended character(s) are then sent to the other device. The receiving device then performs the same calculation on the data block that it received and computes a BCC or FCS. A comparison is made between the received BCC and the calculated one. If they are the same, then the block of data was received error free. The receiving entity then notifies the sending device that all was received "OK." If they are different, then the data were received with an error. The protocols allow for asking for a retransmission of one or more blocks of data.

At the time of receipt of a block, the receiving device can respond to the sender, asking for a halting of sending anymore blocks of information until further notice. This flow control would be used for the receiving device to write to disk, display the received information, draw a screen, dump the information to a printer, or clear an error condition. The sending and receiving of blocks of data, with a corresponding acknowledgment of receipt, as well as a message for either continued or suspended transmissions, is the flow control in synchronous communications involving computers.

XMODEM

What about the asynchronous world? Not all computers support synchronous communications, or find it necessary to use this technique with all its inherent overhead. What does the user do when only an asynchronous environment is available? This is very prevalent as most PCs support a serial port that supports only asynchronous connections. PCs need to communicate with other PCs, DEC minicomputers, UNIX systems, and mainframes. It should not be a requirement that more expensive synchronous ports and modems be used when uploading and downloading of files is required. The user needs the ability to send chunks of data in an asynchronous connection with confidence that the receiving device gets them error free. This is desirable when performing file transfers over communication lines with modems or when two computers are connected back to back.

The same concept of blocking data as in synchronous communications is provided by an asynchronous protocol, referred to as XMODEM. XMODEM, and many of its variations, is a set of rules governing the exchange of information between two communicating entities, a protocol. Communication software that supports the uploading and downloading of data typically incorporates this protocol to ensure error-free transmission. Flow control and data retransmission are supported in XMODEM. The user does not need to know the specifics of the protocol; rather he or she must be familiar with how to set up and use this protocol. When analyzing a port, or the communication software that drives the port, assess whether or not a protocol such as XMODEM is supported.

CONNECTOR SIZES

Computer ports come in a variety of sizes including 5-, 8-, 9-, 25-, 36-, and 50-pin connectors. The actual connector may be a "D" subminiature connector, a DB-type connector, a cinch connector, or a modular jack, among others. The DB25-size connector is the most common port on the PC. However, with the introduction of the PC/AT computer, a 9-pin serial interface entered the picture. AT&T's 3B2 computers offer modular jacks for the serial ports. When connecting computers to other devices, the connectors impact the actual interfacing.

DTE/DCE PORT EMULATION

The RS232 port on computers can be one of two types. The serial ports can emulate data terminal equipment, DTE, or data communication equipment, DCE. The RS232 standard supports the interconnection of both DTE and DCE devices for serial communications. As such, the device's ports can take on the characteristics of either DTE or DCE. This means that a port that looks like DTE provides the leads and expects the leads, as laid out in the RS232 standard for DTE equipment. The same is true for DCE ports.

Computers normally have ports that emulate DTE, which allows them to be connected to modems for dial-up access to remote computer systems. If, however, a terminal such as the DEC VT100 were to be locally connected to the computer, a null modem cable (NMC) would be required. An NMC would be required because two devices, both with DTE ports, were to be connected back to back. If a computer port is configured to emulate DCE, or provide the RS232 signals normally provided by a modem, then a terminal (DTE) could be directly connected to the port with a straight-through cable. Hence, a reference is made to what the computer port is emulating or looking like.

From this you can see the importance of understanding the type of port that a device is emulating. You cannot assume that because a computer, terminal, or printer is normally classified as a piece of terminal equipment that it has a DTE-type port.

COMMUNICATION SOFTWARE

When a computer is connected to a printer or terminal, typically no special software is required other than some device driver software. However, if computers are to be connected to other computers, the data exchange will not occur without communication software in each system. If a terminal user of a UNIX system desires to call another system, then networking software must be loaded on the computer to support this. If a minicomputer is to support a connection to a mainframe, then the appropriate communication software must be present on both machines. If a PC is to connect to another computer, communication software is required. The communication software, combined with the appropriate serial ports, allow computers to communicate with other computers.

EMULATION

If a PC or other computer is to connect to a different computer, then the two systems must communicate in a method that both systems understand. Earlier, the discussion of protocols indicated that a device may dictate the protocol. If a PC is to be connected to a mainframe, it can do this with emulation software. A board can be installed to provide synchronous communications. However, software is required to have the PC emulate a terminal that can function in the mainframe environment. Typical terminals emulated are 3278s and 5251s. These operate in a synchronous environment. The emulation software allows the PC to interpret the received mainframe datastreams. Furthermore, the software enables the PC to send information to the mainframe in a format that it can understand.

If a PC is to call another computer, such as a DEC minicomputer, emulation software plays a key role. The bulk of the applications developed on DEC's minis were written to support a DEC VT100 terminal. This terminal supports escape and control characters that allow for screen formatting and terminal setups. The application programs use these capabilities for outputting data to the terminal. When a PC is used instead of one of these terminals, software is available that allows the PC to look like a VT100 to the application. This terminal emulation software translates the received sequences into those understood by the PC. Without terminal emulation software, the PC could not work with the applications.

This need for terminal emulation is not limited to the DEC minicomputers. UNIX-based computer systems support a variety of terminals, yet do not provide direction support for a PC. Emulation software allows the PC to work with a UNIX system in place of a terminal. The terminals emulated, covered in Chapter 4, can be many different varieties, often in the same communication software system. Without emulation, there would be many more incompatible systems than there are today.

From this, the reader can see that the connection of computers to other devices can be more complex than merely connecting terminals, printers, and modems. The tutorial modules that follow are designed to ease the connections involving computers. Each module will highlight a different aspect of connections involving computers. Although not every possible computer connection will be covered, a large number of the more prevalent types of connections are featured.

Tutorial Module 5-1: Connecting a PC to a UNIX System

In this module, we focus on connecting an IBM PC/XT with a serial port to a UNIX computer. The serial port for an IBM may be obtained from a number of sources: dedicated asynchronous communication adapters (ACAs), graphics boards, multifunction boards, and so on. Depending on the IBM PC or compatible, the serial port may be included with the basic system. For purposes of this tutorial module, assume that the RS232 port has been installed on the PC, whether it is built on or has been purchased separately. The IBM PC/XT will be running the communication software package, CROSSTALK XVI, from Microstuf. The software will be set up to emulate a DEC VT100 terminal. This emulation package allows the PC to take on the characteristics of a DEC VT100 terminal. This does not imply that the cable used to connect a DEC terminal to a UNIX system is the same as that required to connect a PC to a UNIX system. This emulation applies to the screen and keyboard characteristics of the terminal.

Figure 5–1 depicts the connection that we will be attempting. The UNIX-based computer is the UNIX PC/3B1.

STEPS FOR CONNECTION

1. Determine compatibility (should it work?).
2. Determine signs of success.
3. Determine the type of connector used.
4. Determine gender of the ports.
5. Determine which leads (pins) are provided by each device.

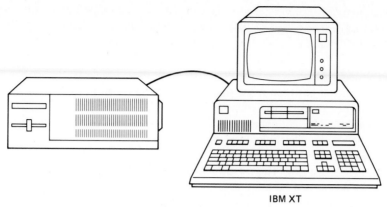

IBM XT

Figure 5–1. PC emulating a terminal, connecting to a UNIX system.

6. Determine which leads are required to be on by each device.
7. Design the cable.
8. Build the cable.
9. Test the cable for continuity.
10. Cable the two systems together with the cable.
11. From step 2, measure success.

1. Determine compatibility

Prior to attempting this feat, the user should make a determination as to whether the connection is possible. The best way of determining compatibility is to check the documentation for both devices. When this is not available, the following procedure is a good method of determining if the two can communicate. If all else fails, ask around to determine if anyone has done the same or a similar connection.

Typically, when connecting a terminal, in this case a PC emulating a terminal, the two ports must allow for the same type of communication parameters. That is, they must support a common communication mode, speed, character format, and protocol. Table 5–1 lists the various options obtained from the user documentation.

From the information in Table 5–1, which was taken directly from the user's manuals, the two systems appear to be compatible. The common options between the two appear to be asynchronous transmission, 9600 bits per second (bps), 7 data bits, 1 stop bit, even parity, full duplex operation, and software flow control.

The user should select the highest port speed common to both devices, except where there is no flow control. If no flow control, be aware that the user could lose some data if one of the devices cannot keep up. In this tutorial module, where a PC is emulating a terminal, more than likely this will not pose a problem. A terminal-to-computer connection commonly is used so the user can log into a different computer. Typing on the keyboard normally poses no threat for loss of data. However, should file transfers be planned, then flow control is a must for the two ports (systems) to be compatible. At 9600 bps and no flow control used while file transfer is occurring, the receiving computer would never be able to halt data transfer long enough to write the information to disk. Consult the discussion on flow control for further explanations and examples of the usefulness of flow control. The reader is encouraged to complete a port profile for each device.

TABLE 5–1. COMMUNICATION PARAMETERS FOR PC AND AT&T UNIX PC/3B1

Parameter	IBM PC/XT	AT&T UNIX PC/3B1
Communication mode	Asynchronous	Asynchronous Synchronous
Speed (bps)	0–9600	0–9600
Character format	7 or 8 bits	7 or 8 bits
Stop bits	1 or 2 bits	1 bit
Parity	Odd/even/none	Odd/even/none
Duplex	Full duplex	Full duplex
Flow control	Hardware (5/6 in) Software (XON/XOFF)	Software (XON/XOFF)

Emulation

The asynchronous mode of operating is used in this type of connection. Consider using synchronous only if a synchronous board and software are available for the PC, with appropriate synchronous software on the UNIX PC/3B1.

2. Determine signs of success

Now that the determination has been made that the two systems can be connected together, the user needs to know, in advance, the signs of a successful connection. Merely connecting the two computers together physically is a milestone, but this usually does not complete the setup. Prior to beginning any connection, be sure that the user knows when he or she has completely and successfully connected the PC/XT to the 3B1.

When connecting a terminal, or PC emulating a terminal to a UNIX system, the UNIX system will prompt the user at the terminal/PC for a login. This is different from a PC that has been booted up. The PC, being a single-user computer, has no need to determine who the user is. As PCs based on the 80386 chip become prevalent, and the 80286-based systems progress, multiuser operating environments will increase in number. The courts are still out on which operating system will win. Regardless, when multiuser systems are involved, normally a login prompt will occur when the two devices are connected properly. Hence, in this connection, we will know when we are successful when the login prompt occurs, and we can type in our ID with the UNIX system receiving it.

As a special note, the two computers may be connected properly physically yet the user may not be able to login successfully. This tutorial module focuses on how to connect the two computers together physically, not on how to perform systems administration to set up UNIX ports. For a good source of information on how to set up computer ports in a UNIX environment, consult *DOS/UNIX Systems: Becoming a Super User* (Martin D. Seyer and William J. Mills, Prentice-Hall). In our discussion, the MS-DOS port on the IBM PC will be set up using the terminal emulation package, Crosstalk XVI, and hence will be included in the discussion. Our goal will be physically to build the cable properly. Hence, look for the ''login:'' prompt to determine when we have been successful.

3. Determine type of connector

The type of connector on each device end will dictate the cable connectors that may be used as well as which ''tools of the trade'' may be used to assist in the building of the cable.

On the IBM PC, there may be multiple connectors (ports) on the back of the PC. They may be many different sizes. Locate the RS232 serial port. It is usually labeled COM1, COM2, RS232, or serial. If the port is not labeled, the user should consult the documentation to determine which port is the RS232. It is important that the correct port is used for this connection.

The standard serial port on most IBM PCs and compatibles is a DB25-size connector. Consult the previous sections for a further explanation of the size of a standard DB25 connector. If a parallel and serial port are present on the PC, there is an easy way to distinguish between the two. The IBM parallel port on a PC is usually a DB25s connector. This is a female port, with 25 sockets for pin insertion. The RS232 port is a DB25P, or male connector. It has a number of pins extruding from the port. Usually all 25 pins are present, but this should not always be assumed. We will later see that not all the pins are required for operation. Some vendors may leave some pins out because they are never used.

The DB25-size connector is the most common port on the PC. However, with the introduction of the PC/AT computer, a 9-pin serial interface entered the picture. Be aware that this 9-pin D-connector could be present on your system to provide the RS232 interface. However, unless a PC/AT is being used, more than likely the interface will be a DB25P-size male connector. The UNIX PC/3B1 provides a standard DB25s connector.

4. Determine gender of ports

At the IBM PC port (ACA), there may be multiple ports, serial and parallel. IBM implemented its parallel port using a DB25 connector. The parallel port is a female port. The serial port is a male connector. The PC end of the cable we will design will be of female gender. We will connect the completed cable to the male DB25 port.

The UNIX PC/3B1 implements its RS232 port using a female DB25 connector. The UNIX system end of the cable to be built will have a male connector on it. We will connect this to the female port on the back of the 3B1.

5. Determine leads (pins) provided by each device

The user should find out the leads and their directions for the PC port as well as the 3B1 port. The task is to determine which leads are provided by the PC port and which should be used in the cable construction.

Connecting Computers   Chap. 5

A port has four categories of leads: ground, data, control, and timing. Ignore the timing category of leads, as we are building a cable to function in an asynchronous environment. The ground leads, usually pins 1 and 7 in a DB25-size connector, have no direction, so they too can be ignored for now. However, these leads must be included in the cable.

Specifically, we are interested in determining which data and control leads are provided by the computers. "Provided by the computer" implies that the computer is the source of the lead. The direction of the lead is "from" the computer. There are multiple methods of determining which leads are provided by a computer.

The simplest method is to consult the documentation for the device/port. Usually, a notation is provided that denotes whether a particular lead's direction is "to" or "from," "in" or "out," or "DTE" or "DCE." Determining whether a port is emulating DTE or DCE can ease the cable design, as we will see further into the tutorial module.

When DTE source is specified, the user should classify the device containing the port as either terminal or communication equipment. DTE is an acronym for data terminal equipment, while DCE stands for data communication equipment. Vendors include this reference as it conforms to the EIA RS232 standard notations. DTE class of equipment usually includes terminals, printers, plotters, front-end processors, and computers. DCE usually represents the modems, line drivers, or multiplexors. In our tutorial module, the PC and 3B1 are considered DTE. The ports are configured to be connected directly to a piece of DCE, or a modem. Hence, if a signal is from the DTE, it is provided by one of the computers and is considered an output signal. The next sections will give the user three different techniques that can be used to determine which leads are provided by each of the computers. The reader is encouraged to take notes when actually working through the analysis of a device's port.

To determine the direction of the RS232 leads that are used, consult the documentation. Usually users' manuals or application programmers' guides give the RS232 port pinout descriptions. The direction is given for each of the signals. The direction notation, as covered previously, was in the format, in/out, to/from, DTE/DCE, or --⟩/⟨--. The arrows are used frequently to indicate from/to, respectively.

If the user does not have the documentation, or is from Missouri (the Show-Me state), as this author is, a break-out box is one of the best means of identifying the leads that are provided by the computers. Many variations of break-out boxes exist today. Some of them allow single signals to be monitored, with others offering the prominent 8 leads. Certain vendors include the capability to monitor the status of all 25 leads.

Another feature is the ability to determine which leads are present, even when they are not on (positive voltage). The RS232 standard outlines the voltage levels of the leads in the interface. A lead is considered on if it has between +3 and +15 volts, while it is interpreted as off when the voltage level is between −3 and −15 volts. Should the leads be present in an interface, but the port not be active, there still could be a relative minus voltage present, to indicate that a lead is provided by the device. Certain break-out boxes indicate only when a lead is on. This is usually denoted by turning on a miniature display light. If the lead is off, or voltage is negative, the light remains off. The more substantial break-out boxes indicate the condition of the leads, regardless of whether they are on or off. Lamps that can have three states can be used to indicate if a lead is on, off, or not present. Usually the lamps are red when the lead is on (positive voltage), while they are green if the lead is off (negative voltage). Should a lead not be used at all, the lamp will remain off. The user should be careful not to misinterpret the lamp indication. Later in the discussion of signals that are "to" a port, this point will be clarified.

For purposes of analyzing the computer ports in this tutorial module, a Black Box Catalog SAM + RS232 V24 tristate break-out box will be used. For ease of reference, we will merely refer to it as either a BOB or a break-out box. This battery-operated break-out box includes the ability to detect whether a lead is on, off, or even included in an interface. Dedicated tristate lamps are included for the leads in Table 5–2.

Ignore the last three indicators in this tutorial module, as they will not be used. A lamp is available to test any of the other leads that does not have a dedicated lamp. The capability to provide cross-overs, or jumpering, is available within the BOB. Furthermore, the user can easily keep certain leads on with the mere flip of a switch. This is not meant to sound like a commercial for the BOB but, rather, to point out features than can be very useful as we progress in this tutorial module. Some of these features will indeed be used to design our cable.

Using the BOB, we can quickly determine which signals are provided by the IBM PC port. Plug the BOB's female DB25 connector into the PC's male RS232 port. Review the section, "Determine the Type of Connector," to ensure that you are connecting the BOB to the correct port. By turning on the tristate break-out box, we are set to identify which leads are provided by the PC. The lamp indicators for the leads Transmit Data, Request to Send, and Data Terminal Ready should be green. This indicates that they are at a relative negative voltage level. Specifically, they are in an "off" state. Because they do show a condition (green/off), we know immediately that these signals are provided by the PC port. In other words, the direction for Transmit Data,

TABLE 5-2. BREAKOUT BOX INDICATOR LAMPS

Lead	Abbreviation	Pin # (RS232 standard)
Transmit Data	TD	2
Receive Data	RD	3
Request to Send	RTS	4
Clear to Send	CTS	5
Data Set Ready	DSR	6
Data Carrier Detect	DCD	8
Transmit Clock	TC	15
Receive Clock	RC	17
Data Terminal Ready	DTR	20
Signal Quality Detect	SQ	21
Ring Indicator	RI	22
Busy	BSY	25

Request to Send, and Data Terminal Ready is "from" the PC. This implies that the port is set up to emulate DTE and is expecting to be directly connected to a modem (DCE). We are not connecting it to a modem, but rather another computer. This hints at the need for a cross-over cable, but let's proceed.

If you are using a break-out box that indicates only when a lead is on (positive voltage), you can use a trick on the PC to determine which leads are provided on the port. The PC has the capability to print to a printer connected to either a parallel port or a serial port. The default printer port is the parallel port. However, the Mode command is provided by the MS-DOS operating system to redirect the output to the serial port. We will use this command to activate some of the control leads. Type the following command and depress the Return/ Enter key:

MODE LPT1:=COM1

This command sets up the serial port, usually denoted as COM1, to be the printer port. Any output destined for a printer will now be routed to the serial port. The user normally holds the shift key and the Prt Sc key simultaneously to dump a picture of the screen to the printer. Do this now to enable the serial (COM1) port. The lamps on the break-out box for the leads Request to Send and Data Terminal Ready, pins 4 and 20, should now be on. (Note: Substitute COM2 for COM1 as appropriate. This will usually be the case when a board-level modem, or even a mouse, is already set up to use COM1. The COM is merely a mnemonic address that identifies the device.)

Pin 2 on the tristate was green, indicating that the Transmit Data lead was present but "off." On other break-out boxes, the lamp will not be on. If the port were properly connected to a printer, with the correct cable, the screen dump would have sent the data out of the serial port. But if you watched the BOB, the Transmit Data lamp never turned "on." Furthermore, when a screen dump is done, the underscore cursor on the PC's screen progresses down the screen, line by line, as the character or images are output through the serial port. The cursor did not advance at all. As a matter of fact, it appears that the system is hung up. Don't fret, as eventually the output routine will timeout and give up, freeing up the system.

Because the transmit data lead did not come on, the requirements of the interface have not been met. Specifically, the port was expecting to be connected to a modem because it is a DTE class port. The modem, or DCE, normally "provides" certain control signals. Because we are lacking these control signals that are input to the PC port, the PC will not transmit data. Until we satisfy these signal requirements, the port will never communicate.

If a device were connected to this port with the proper cable, the Transmit Data lamp on the BOB would have gone on and off at a very rapid pace. This transition of on/off matches the bits of a character. The ones and zeros of a character as it is being output from the port are represented as positive and negative DC voltage levels. Hence the on/off status of the lamp corresponds to the bit makeup of the characters on the screen.

Skip to the next section, "Determine Leads Required to Be on" for the final analysis of the PC port. For those users without a break-out box, yet wanting to use a VOM, consult Chapter 1, Tutorial Module 1–1, as a VOM is used there throughout.

3B1. The same approach should be taken to analyze the 3B1 UNIX system port as we did with the IBM PC or compatible. This next section will not repeat all the same activities as with the PC port, but will note the differences. A BOB will be used in the text, although the documentation and a VOM may be used just as easily. To use a VOM, merely repeat the steps provided in the PC section from Chapter 1.

Locate the serial port to be used on the 3B1 system. Because the 3B1 is a multiuser system, generally more than one serial port will be present. Contact the systems administrator for the UNIX system to determine which port to use. The systems administrator generally keeps a log of the physical layout of the UNIX system and which devices are connected. The next few paragraphs describe the setup required of the systems administrator to enable a port. If this has already been done, skip the sections describing the UNIX software setup and proceed to the section on determining which leads are present.

The one selected will be important because certain software setups have to be in place. Specifically, UNIX needs to have a device definition for the port that you are connecting to. Generally, there is a subdirectory "\dev" that contains all the devices available on a UNIX system. Your UNIX system may vary, but generally the "\dev" directory will contain entries such as the following. The first two statements give the commands necessary to list the directory:

cd \dev   followed by a return

1s −1   followed by a return

```
total 4
crw--w--w-   3 mseyer   users    0,   0 Dec 31 12:24 console
drwxr-xr-x   2 root     sys         592 May  9 1986 dsk
crw-rw-rw-   1 root     sys      8,   0 Dec 29 22:49 1p
drwxr-xr-x   2 root     sys         656 May  9 1986 rdsk
crw--w--w-   3 mseyer   users    0,   0 Dec 31 12:24 syscon
crw--w--w-   3 mseyer   users    0,   0 Dec 31 12:24 systty
crw-rw-rw-   1 root     sys      2,   0 Nov 30 11:24 tty
crw--w--w-   1 uucp     sys      5,   0 Nov 29 23:29 tty1
```

For a complete explanation of this directory listing, the reader is encouraged to consult *DOS/UNIX Systems: Becoming a Super User*. In our discussion it is sufficient to note the rightmost column of data. The last entry in each row of the directory listing is the filename, or device name. We are wanting to connect to the serial port with a name of "tty1." Should more than one serial port be present, the "tty" names will continue with "tty1," "tty2," and so on. Our exercise will assume that the systems administrator wants us to use the "tty1" port.

The systems administrator must also ensure that the port is enabled. Recall from our earlier discussion that we would know we were successful when the "login:" prompt appeared on the PC. The "login:" prompt is originated from the 3B1 UNIX system. For this to occur, the port must be set up to receive the "login:" prompt. This is made possible by having the proper entry in a systems file, commonly tagged "inittab." An entry in this file is necessary for the "login:" prompt to be sent out the "tty1" port. As a user, you need not be concerned with this, providing the systems administrator will set this up for you. Nonetheless, the next section is a listing of a possible entry for enabling the "login:" prompt, as well as the commands to view this.

cd /etc   followed by a return
cat inittab   followed by a return

co:124:respawn:/etc/getty console console
00:2:respawn:/etc/getty ttyl 4800

The last line is the entry that allows us to get a prompt. This entry indicates that a process should be started that puts out the "login:" prompt, on the tty1 port, and at a speed of 4800 bps. Once the system is rebooted, the port should now be enabled.

The purpose for the foregoing software setup discussion was not to attempt to make you UNIX proficient. It was covered to get us to the point where the 3B1 should be enabled. With the port activated, we can now proceed to determine the leads that are provided by the 3B1 UNIX system.

Connect the BOB to the port known as "tty1." We have previously noted that the 3B1 port is of female gender; hence, the male connector on the BOB should be used. This will also be the gender of this end of the cable. Be sure that the 3B1 UNIX system is up and running.

TABLE 5–3. OUTPUT LEADS FOR PC
AND 3B1

Lead #	Function	Direction
2	Transmit Data	from
4	Request to Send	from
20	Data Terminal Ready	from

Turn the BOB on! If a duo-state BOB is used, only two lights should be lit. Pin 4, Request to Send, and pin 20, Data Terminal Ready, should be on. If a tristate BOB is used, pin 2, Transmit Data lamp, will be lit, but green. Hence pins 2, 4, and 20 are provided by the 3B1 port. The port was female, which hinted at being a DCE interface. However, with pins 2, 4, and 20, from the 3B1, the port is set up as a data terminal equipment. This jibes, as the computer is DTE, and it is expecting to be connected to a modem, or DCE device.

We now know which leads (pins) are provided by each computer. The PC and the 3B1 (UNIX system) both provide the same signals. Table 5–3 outlines the leads provided. A cross-over cable is definitely required to connect the 3B1 (DTE) to the PC (DTE). A straight-through cable, 1–1, 2–2, 3–3, 4–4, will not work as the direction of the leads will clash. To complete the cabling requirements, the next section describes how to ascertain which leads are required by each of the ports to function. Once this is known, we can design and construct the cable.

6. Determine leads required to be on

We now have determined which leads are provided by the PC's port. This was done by consulting the documentation or using a break-out box or VOM. The next step is to determine which leads are input signals to the PC port, in other words, which leads should be on for data transmission and reception by the PC.

Recall that we attempted to perform a screen print from the PC keyboard. The port became enabled, yet the output did not actually occur. We were able to detect this, noting that the cursor on the screen did not progress line by line until the screen had been output through the serial port. We also saw no fluctuation on pin 2, Transmit Data, which is the lead used by the PC to send the bits of the character to an attached device. We need to determine the appropriate input signals that must be on for the computer to output data.

The easiest way is to consult the documentation once again. This is the quickest way to note all the input signals for a port. However this can be misleading, as not all the signals may be required prior to data transmission. However, this is a great source to identify the signals "to" the PC port. From this we find that pin 3 (Receive Data), pin 5 (Clear to Send), pin 6 (Data Set Ready), pin 8 (Data Carrier Detect), and pin 22 (Ring Indicator) are input signals to the PC port. As mentioned, not all these leads must be on for output to occur. From previous experience, only pins 5 and 6 are required for a printer connection. When using communication software such as Crosstalk XVI, pin 8 must also be on. Pin 22 is used as an indication that an incoming call is being received. This allows the port to get the modem to answer a call. Pin 22 is not required to be on for data transmission. From these input leads, pins 5, 6, and 8 should be on for our connection.

If the documentation is not available, there are a few generalities that "usually" hold true for guessing which leads are input and which must be on for transmission. Table 5–4 outlines the possibilities. The table assumes conformity to the EIA RS232 standard. Pins 2 and 3 are assumed to be data leads, while 4, 5, 6, 8, and 20 control leads. Pins 1 and 7 are assumed to be ground leads. Based on the experiences of this author, there are no guarantees that the device ports will follow the RS232 standard. However, the PC port does adhere to the standard. As a DTE class of port, the foregoing generality holds true.

BOBs can be used to determine which leads are input and required for communication. Unfortunately, the only way to accomplish this is through trial and error. Since we already know the output signals of the PC's port, pins 2, 4, and 20, we can attempt to determine which of the leads must be on. Refer back to the "general

TABLE 5–4. TYPICAL INPUT AND OUTPUT LEADS FOR DTE/
DCE PRODUCTS

Output leads	Port type	Input leads required
2, 4, 20	data terminal equipment	3, 5, 6, 8
3, 5, 6, 8	data communication equipment	2, 4, 20

rule" chart depicting the DTE input signals. Note that generally if pins 2, 4, and 20 are output signals, then pins 5, 6, and 8 are generally input control signals. Ignore pin 3 for now, as it is a data lead. Using a break-out box, we should keep these pins on somehow. If you are using the tristate BOB, switches are provided for automatically holding Clear to Send, Data Set Ready, and Data Carrier Detect high (on). Flip these switches to "on" and pins 5, 6, and 8 will be turned on. The red light indicates the "on" condition.

If a different break-out box is used, the user can hold these leads "on" by connecting them to another signal. With PC, pins 4 and 20 are on when the port is enabled. Jumper wires are included with the BOB. Connect one end of the jumper wires to pin 4 from the PC port. Connect the other end to pins 5, 6, and 8. Depending on the jumpering wires provided, you may need to wire a couple of them together, so that all three pins can be held on by pin 4. You could just as easily connect the jumper wire to pin 20 and connect it to one or more of the leads to produce the same result. In either case, strapping pin 4 and/or 20 to pins 5, 6, and 8 should turn them on.

If they are not on, then the port is not enabled. In an earlier discussion, the Mode command was covered as a means of enabling the RS232 port. Type "MODE LPT1:=COM1" followed by a Return, and then hold down the Shift key simultaneously with the Prt Sc key. This enables the serial port as the printer port and dumps a copy of the screen contents through that port.

The cursor should scan across the screen while it dumps the screen information out the port. If a break-out box is being used, the Transmit Data lead, pin 2, should be flashing rapidly as the data are being output. Pin 2 was an output signal from the PC for all the data bits, so this is normal. If the light is held on and flashing is almost nonexistent, there is no cause for concern. The important piece of information is that the light has changed. The reason for little or no noticeable fluctuation, corresponding to the on/off condition for the ones and zero bits, is the speed of the port. The data are being output at a high rate of speed, probably 9600 bps. To slow down the output, the user can change the speed of the port with the Mode command. Type the following to reduce the speed of the port to 300 bps.

MODE COM1:300   followed by a return
MODE LPT1:=COM1   followed by a return

This should allow you to see the on/off representation of the ones and zero bits of the characters. You still won't be able to recognize specific characters. At 300 bps, an average of 30 characters is being output each second. This was calculated by dividing the bit rate, 300 bps, by the number of bits per character including start and stop bits, 10, to yield 30 cps. However, the data transmission should be apparent.

If a volt-ohm meter is being used, the user should somehow connect pin 4 and/or 20 to pins 5, 6, and 8. Shielded wire can be used for this. Jumper the ends of four separate wires together and touch-connect them to pins 4, 5, 6, and 8. The tricky part is getting the wires to stay connected to the pins in the PC port. Because we are testing the port only, electrical tape can be used to build a receptable around the end of the wire. This strawlike piece can then be slid onto one of the pins. Repeat this for the other three pins.

Once the connections are made, set up the VOM to monitor pin 2 of the interface. Use the probes to connect to pin 7 and pin 2. Be sure that the proper scale and settings are being used on the VOM to measure up to 15 volts DC. Perform the screen print keystrokes and watch the VOM reflect the data being output on pin 2. Also, check the cursor on the screen to ensure that the screen contents are being output. If not, check the jumpering connections to ensure that they are making contact with the port pins.

The purpose of this exercise was to satisfy the input signals necessary for the PC to output data. From this, the user can assess that pins 5, 6, and 8 are required prior to data transmission. To confirm this, attempt the screen dump routine as before. Monitor the output on the screen, BOB, or VOM. Watch what happens if you disconnect pin 5 or pin 6. In the case of the tristate, merely turn off the switch that keeps pin 5 or 6 on. The screen dump should halt! Reconnect it, or turn it back on. The screen dump should continue. If you halt it too long, the PC will abort the output. But for our purposes, turn it on and off to conclude that pins 5 and 6 must be on for the PC to output data through the RS232 port. Pin 8 does not impact output, but in the case of communication software we are using, it should be on. So we will treat it just like pins 5 and 6.

This is an example of hardware flow control in action. Flow control using the pins of the RS232 interface has been discussed in Chapter 1 of this book. However, the user now knows how to determine which leads are input, and which must be on for data transmission to occur.

3B1. To determine which leads are required to be on, the foregoing steps should be followed to assess which leads must be on for the UNIX system to allow data transmission. As before, the text will assume the use of a BOB, but a VOM and the documentation are just as useful.

Connect the BOB to the "tty1" port, with the 3B1 system up and running. Turn the BOB on. With the port enabled, pins 4 and 20 should be on (high). With the use of a tristate BOB, the pin 2 lamp will indicate that pin 2 is provided by the 3B1. These three leads are the signals provided by the 3B1. If they are not present, reactivate the port.

We now need to attempt to dump information out the "tty1" port from the 3B1. This is necessary to determine which input leads are required. The simplest method in a UNIX system to send something out of a port is redirection—a concept that allows the output of a command or function to be sent to specific devices. Normally, if a user at a terminal, attached to a UNIX computer, issues a command to list the directory, the information is sent back to the terminal that issued the command. Redirection allows the directory listing to be displayed at another terminal, printer, or even put in a file. We will use this concept to redirect the output of a directory command to our "tty1" port. The symbol ")" is used for redirection. Conceptually, we are using another terminal to issue a directory command and sending the listing to another port.

With the 3B1, a console is built into the system. We will use this as our originating point for the directory command. Normally, a window-based environment is provided for each user with the 3B1. Consult with the systems administrator on how to log into UNIX system. Indicate that you need to be at the "$" prompt. The "$" prompt implies that you are successfully logged into UNIX and can issue commands. Should the 3B1 console have the window environment activated, issue the command "/bin/sh," followed by a return. This activates a UNIX session. This is a 3B1-specific function. With most UNIX systems, the systems administrator would provide you a login that would get you to the "$" prompt.

Once you have the "$" prompt, you can begin the redirection routine. At the terminal/console, issue the following command. Watch the BOB, specifically, pin 2. If you are using a VOM, have the black probe grounded, and touch the other probe to pin 2 of the interface. You may have to extend pin 2 out of the DB25 connector by inserting a short piece of wire. Nonetheless, we are interested in the status of pin 2, Transmit Data. This is the lead that the 3B1 will use to transmit the data.

ls) /dev/tty1   followed by a return

The "ls" command is used in UNIX to list the directory. Our command called for a directory listing to be sent out the "tty1" port. If the directory listing is short, pin 2 will not fluctuate much at all. However, it should be noticeable. If you don't see any fluctuation, try a variation of the "ls" command. The 3B1 supports "ls −1," which is a long, detailed, directory listing. Reissue the command as follows to see if data are transmitted.

ls −1) /dev/tty1   followed by a return

Pin 2 should have fluctuated rapidly to match the data bits of the directory listing. The 3B1 should have sent the directory listing out the "tty1" port. We have just learned that no input leads must be on for the 3B1 system to transmit data. We have done nothing to keep any of the input leads turned on (high). We have merely been monitoring up to this point. From this, the standard leads, pin 5, 6, and 8, associated as input with a DTE port are not required to be on.

This is common with UNIX systems, although not always the case. The code in the UNIX operating system that controls the ports relies on what is known as software flow control. Refer to the printer section for a complete understanding of software flow control and its various uses. This implies that the leads of the interface are not monitored by the 3B1. Whereas with the PC, pins 5 and 6 had to be on for the PC output data, the 3B1 requires no input control signals to be present.

If you cannot detect activity on pin 2, there are several items worth checking:

1. Ensure that "tty1" port is the port to which you are connected.
2. Ensure that "/dev/tty1" is the path to the port.
3. Ensure that the "ls" command is supported. Try it from the console without redirecting it.
4. Ensure that your BOB is on, or your VOM is connected to pin 2.

Your computer, not the PC, may require leads to be on. If so, repeat the procedure used with the PC to determine which leads must be present for data transmission.

7. Design the cable

We know what the RS232 hardware requirements are at both ports, the PC and the 3B1 UNIX system. A quick review summarizes our findings (Table 5–5):

TABLE 5–5. PINOUTS FOR PC AND 3B1

	IBM PC			AT&T 3B1 UNIX system	
Pin	Function	Direction	Pin	Function	Direction
			1	Protective Ground	n/a
2	Transmit Data	From	2	Transmit Data	From
3	Receive Data	To	3	Receive Data	To
4	Request to Send	From	4	Request To Send	From
5	Clear to Send	To			
6	Data Set Ready	To			
7	Signal Ground	n/a	7	Signal Ground	n/a
8	Data Carrier Detect	To			
20	Data Terminal Ready	From	20	Data Terminal Ready	From

It is much easier to analyze the cable pinouts if grouped by function. This function is that as outlined in the EIA RS232-C standard document. Once we group the pinouts into the four categories—ground, data, control, and timing—the cable design will be much easier. Table 5–5 should be rearranged as in Table 5–6. We are now ready to design the cable by looking at each category of leads of both ports. A few general rules should be established prior to any cable design. The next section outlines the general cable design rules. Refer to Appendix L for an elaboration on this.

CABLE DESIGN: GENERAL RULES

1. Connect like categories of leads together.
2. Always connect an ''out'' to an ''in'' and an ''in'' to an ''out.''
3. A lead that is input should only be connected to another lead that is an input, if both these are connected to an output lead.
4. In synchronous connections, only use one source of timing. This is not applicable for our tutorial module here, yet it is important when connecting synchronous devices together.

Keeping these general rules in mind, let's design the cable.

Ground leads. First, the ground leads should be dealt with. They are probably the easiest leads to handle. Protective Ground is provided to protect the user from being shocked, in the case of an electrical short of some sort. Pin 1 is generally the Protective Ground lead of most RS232 interfaces. It is also frequently referred to as Chassis Ground, or Frame Ground. In our tutorial module, the PC port documentation does not indicate that a Protective Ground is present. This is not a show stopper because a Protective Ground is provided within the PC itself. It may be isolated from the interface. Nonetheless, we will allow for it in our interface. The 3B1 provides for it. We will merely connect the two protective Ground leads, pins 1 and 1, together.

TABLE 5–6. PINOUTS FOR PC AND 3B1 SEPARATED BY CATEGORY

Ground Leads				
			1	Protective Ground
Signal Ground		7	7	Signal Ground
Data Leads				
Transmit Data (out)		2	2	Transmit Data (out)
Receive Data (in)		3	3	Receive Data (in)
Control Leads				
Request to Send (out)		4	4	Request to Send (out)
Clear to Send (in)		5		
Data Set Ready (in)		6		
Data Carrier Detect (in)		8		
Data Terminal Ready (out)		20	20	Data Terminal Ready (out)
Timing Leads				
n/a				

TABLE 5–7. GROUND LEAD DESIGN FOR PC/3B1
CONNECTION

PC			3B1
Function	Pin #	Pin #	Function
Protective Ground	1 ------- 1		Protective Ground
Signal Ground	7 ------- 7		Signal Ground

LEGEND: The ''-------'' refers to connecting the two leads together.
Pin 1 in the PC end of the cable will be connected to pin 1 at the
3B1 end of the cable by means of a wire between the two pins. This
is commonly referred to as straight through. Pin 7 will be straight
through from end to end.

Signal Ground signals are the key ground leads in the interface. These leads are used as a reference point
for all the other signals in the interface. When the voltage level, as outlined in the RS232-C standard, is to be
±5 volts, this is relative to Signal Ground. Both interfaces provide a Signal Ground lead, found on pin 7 of the
PC and 3B1 ports. These two leads should be connected together to provide a common Signal Ground for the
two interfaces. Table 5–7 summarizes these two connections, completing the design for the ground category of
leads.

Data leads. The next category of leads to tackle is the data leads. There are only two possible connections
for these, so we can quickly lay out the cabling of the data category. The Transmit Data lead, with a direction
of out/from, is the lead on which data will be sent out of a computer. The PC will send all its data on the
Transmit Data lead. Likewise, the 3B1 will send its characters on this lead. Pin 2 is the Transmit Data lead for
both of the computers. General rule 2 indicated to connect an output lead to an input lead. Both pin 2s are
output signals. Hence, we should not connect them straight through.

The Receive Data lead, pin 3 on both ports, is the lead that is used by the computers to receive data. Any
data that the PC wants to receive are expected to arrive on pin 3. Since the 3B1 is sending its data out on pin 2,
destined for the PC, this lead should be connected to the Receive Data lead of the PC. By connecting the 3B1's
pin 2 to the PC's pin 3, the PC will receive whatever information the 3B1 sends it. The converse is true!
Connect the Transmit Data lead of the PC, pin 2, to the Receive Data lead of the 3B1, to allow the 3B1 to get
data from the PC. We now have allowed for data to be output by one device and received (input) by the other.
Table 5–8 depicts the data category portion of the cable design.

Earlier we indicated that there were only two possible connections with the data leads: straight through,
yielding pin 2 connected to pin 2 and pin 3 to pin 3, and crossed over, yielding pin 2 at one end of the cable
connected to pin 3 at the other end, and vice versa. The only other possibility for data lead design appears when
there is only a Receive Data lead on a device's port. This is possible when printers are involved. Consult the
printer chapter for further detail about this.

TABLE 5–8. DATA LEAD DESIGN FOR PC/3B1
CONNECTION

PC			3B1
Function	Pin #	Pin #	Function
Transmit Data	2 ------) 3		Receive Data
Receive Data	3 (------ 2		Transmit Data

LEGEND: The ''------)'' refers to connecting the two leads
together. It differs from the straight-through connection in that
there is a cross-over connection. Pin 2 at the PC end of the
cable is connected to pin 3 at the 3B1 end of the cable, with
a piece of wire between them. The ''------)'' also indicates
that a direction of a lead is involved. This is included for
clarity only, as there are no special wire connections involved.
The same type of connections are made as straight-through
ones. The only difference is that different pins are connected
at each end of the cable.

TABLE 5–9. CONTROL LEADS FOUND IN PC AND 3B1 PORTS

PC			3B1
		Control leads	
Request to Send (out)	4	4	Request to Send (out)
Clear to Send (in)	5		
Data Set Ready (in)	6		
Data Carrier Detect (in)	8		
Data Terminal Ready (out)	20	20	Data Terminal Ready (out)

Control leads. This is generally the toughest category of leads to understand. However, by keeping the general rules for cable design in mind, even the control leads can be easily tackled. Table 5–9 lists the control leads that we have to work with.

Within the control lead category, the direction of the leads is extremely important. Note the directions of the leads, specifically, that pins 5, 6, and 8 in the PC port are input leads. Clear to Send (CTS), Data Set Ready (DSR), and Data Carrier Detect (DCD) are input signals expected by the PC to indicate the status of the connection to the 3B1. In the software that controls the PC's RS232 serial port, a special code is included to monitor the status of these three leads. If they are on, the PC will interpret this as meaning that the connection to the other device is all right. If they are off (low), the PC will assume that the attached device is turned off, or not connected. Because of this monitoring, the cable we design can use this as an advantage. The cable will be designed so that whenever the 3B1 is turned on and its port is enabled, the PC will detect this by watching pins 5, 6, and 8. The completed cable will allow all this to take place without any involvement required by the users of the systems.

Recall that whenever the 3B1's port was enabled, implying that the port parameters had been properly set up in the UNIX operating system environment, pins 4 and 20 were on. These leads were Request to Send (RTS) and Data Terminal Ready (DTR), respectively. If the computer was turned off, or the ports were not active, these leads would be off. Note the direction of these leads as output.

Applying our general rule 2, connect an output to an input lead. If we connect pin 20 at the 3B1 end of the cable, crossed over to pins 5, 6, and 8, at the PC end of the cable, what are the results? As long as the 3B1 port is active, pin 20 will be on. If it is on, and connected to pins 5, 6, and 8, at the PC end, these leads should also be turned on. This is merely a voltage level applied at one end of a wire and conducted across the wire to the other end. Now the PC will be able to know the status of the 3B1 by monitoring pins 5, 6, and 8. When the 3B1 port is enabled, pins 5, 6, and 8 will be on. When the 3B1 port is inactive, pins 5, 6, and 8 will be off. Our communication software program, Crosstalk, can now use this status information to do its thing. Table 5–10 depicts the cross-over connection.

The 3B1 had no input leads that were to be on for data transmission. Our earlier port analysis determined this to be the case when a terminal was to be locally connected. However, chances are that your computer had the same input lead requirements as the PC did. If this is the case, repeat the "cross-over" connection as in

TABLE 5–10. CONTROL LEAD CROSS-OVER FOR PC/3B1 CONNECTION

PC			3B1
Clear to Send (in)	5 ⟨--|---	20	Data Terminal Ready (out)
Data Set Ready	6 ⟨--|		
Data Carrier Detect (in)	8 ⟨--|		

Legend: The "⟨--" indicates a cross-over connection. This implies a connection from pin 20 at the 3B1 end of the cable across to pins 5, 6, and 8 at the PC end of the cable. Pins 5, 6, and 8 are said to be "jumpered" together. Pin 20 should be connected to one of the leads, for example, pin 5. Pins 6 and 8 are then connected together and then to pin 5 to allow pin 20 at one end and pins 5, 6, and 8 to be all "jumpered" together. This daisy chaining allows pin 20 to control the status, on/ off condition, of the PCs pins. DO NOT connect pins 5, 6, and 8 straight through to the other end of the cable. Make only the connections as depicted. Improper connection could cause the status of these leads to be improperly controlled.

Emulation

TABLE 5–11. TWO-WAY CONTROL LEAD CROSS-OVER FOR PC/3B1 CONNECTION

PC				3B1
Clear to Send (in)	5	⟨--|-------	20	Data Terminal Ready (out)
Data Set Ready (in)	6	⟨--|		
Data Carrier Detect (in)	8	⟨--|		
Data Terminal Ready (out)	20	-------|--⟩	5	Clear to Send (in)
		|--⟩	6	Data Set Ready (in)
		|--⟩	8	Data Carrier Detect (in)

Legend: Connect pin 20 from the 3B1 end across to pins 5, 6, and 8 as previously described. Cross over pin 20 from the PC end of the cable to pins 5, 6, and 8 at the 3B1 end of the cable, with a single wire between them in the cable. Then jumper 5, 6, and 8 together at the 3B1 end of the cable. Whenever the PC port is enabled, pins 5, 6, and 8 will be on at the 3B1 end of the cable. It is worth reiterating that the latter cross-over is only required if your computer, instead of the 3B1, has leads that must be on for data transmission.

Table 5–10, but in the reverse direction. Table 5–11 shows how the completed control lead category would be in such a case.

Referring to Table 5–11, note that pins 4 at both ports were not used at all. The signal direction for these leads is out/from. They are provided by each of the computers. We have taken care of all input signal requirements, so these pins serve no purpose in our cable design. However, we could have just as easily used pin 4 instead of pin 20 for our "online" status. Implicit with pin 20's function, Data Terminal Ready, is reference to the readiness of the DTE. Because of this we chose to use pin 20. There will be cases when pin 4 will be used to control the status of input signals. But for now we will ignore these pins.

Timing leads. We will exclude the timing category of leads. Because both ports are asynchronous, we have no timing leads in the RS232 interface to contend with. The nature of asynchronous characters allows them to be individually timed by start and stop bits. Refer back to earlier discussions to review the principles of asynchronous transmission. If we were connecting a high-speed synchronous modem to the 3B1 port, which

TABLE 5–12. IBM PC/XT-TO-AT&T 3B1 COMPLETE CABLE DESIGN

PC		3B1	
Function	Pin #	Pin #	Function
Protective Ground	1 -------	1	Protective Ground
Signal Ground	7 -------	7	Signal Ground
Transmit Data (out)	2 ------⟩	3	Receive Data (in)
Receive Data (in)	3 ⟨------	2	Transmit Data (out)
Clear to Send (in)	5 ⟨--|---	20	Data Terminal Ready (out)
Data Set Ready (in)	6 ⟨--|		
Data Carrier Detect (in)	8 ⟨--|		
{Data Terminal Ready (out)	20 ---|--⟩	5	Clear to Send (in)
	|--⟩	6	Data Set Ready (in)
	|--⟩	8	Data Carrier Detect (in)}

Notes:

1. Pin 1 in the PC end of the cable will be connected to pin 1 at the 3B1 end of the cable by means of a wire between the two pins. Pin 7 will also be straight through from end to end.

2. Pin 2 at the PC end of the cable is connected to pin 3 at the 3B1 end of the cable, with a piece of wire between them. The converse is true with the 3B1's pin 2 crossed over to the PC's pin 3.

3. Cross over pin 20 from the 3B1 end of the cable to pin 5 at the PC end of the cable with single wire between them in the cable. Then jumper 5, 6, and 8 together at the PC end of the cable. Repeat this in the reverse, within the { } braces, if your multiuser computer has input lead requirements as discussed in the text. In our case study, the absence or presence of the reverse cross-over should not impact our connection.

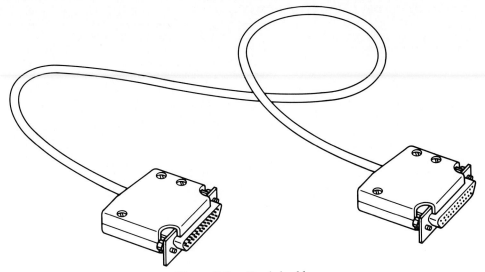

Figure 5–2. Hooded cable.

supports both asynchronous and synchronous operation, or a synchronous network architecture (SNA) board in the PC, this lead category is very important. Refer to Chapter 3, on connecting modems, for further clarity on the timing leads.

The cable has been completely designed. Table 5–12 depicts the final cable design with special notes about the design.

8. Build the Cable

Now that we have a cable design, we are ready to build the cable. We will use standard connector to construct the cable. There are many different options for cable building. Refer to Chapters 1, 2, and 3, on connecting modems and printers, for other cable types that can be made. Substitute the hardware of your choice for this next section.

Cable selection. Knowing the leads that need to be connected is 95 percent of the cable construction. We have just analyzed which leads to connect straight through, cross over, and jumper. We should obtain a cable that has enough leads in it to allow for the cable to be built. Do not use a flat ribbon cable for this, as cross-overs and jumpering are very difficult to accomplish with this. If a cable had all straight-through leads, a flat ribbon cable would do just fine. However, a cable that has DB25 connectors and openable hoods at each end will do. Gender, pins, cable length, and connector type are the considerations that must be taken into account. One such as that in the Figure 5–2 is the basis from which we will build our cable.

Gender. Referring to our checklist, or to the earlier text regarding port analysis, the gender of the port should be checked. This is necessary to ensure that we are working with the right cable. Refer to Table 5–13 for the gender of the ports on the two computers. From this, our cable should have a female DB25 connector at one end, with a male at the other end. When you order a cable, or make it yourself, ensure that these genders are used.

Pins. Before we can actually construct the cable with the cross-over connections, an inventory should be taken of the pins that are present in the cable we are going to use. If you are ordering cable, you should specify

TABLE 5–13. GENDER OF THE PC AND 3B1
COMPUTER PORTS

Computer	Gender of port	Gender of cable end
IBM PC	Male	Female
AT&T 3B1	Female	Male
	Resulting cable	
PC end	Female--------------Male	3B1 end

TABLE 5–14. RS232 CABLE CONDUCTORS

Conductors	Pins provided	Typical use
4	2, 3, 7, 20	Interfacing with few or no input control leads, generally considered a simplified EIA interface
7	2, 3, 4, 6, 7, 8, 20	Computer to computer (asynchronous)
		Computer to Printer/plotter (asynchronous)
		Computer to terminal (asynchronous)
12	1–8, 15, 17, 20, 22	Same as 7 conductor:
		Computer to computer (synchronous)
		Computer to modem (asynchronous)
		Computer to modem (synchronous with DCE timing)
		Terminal to modem (asynchronous)
		Printer to modem
16	1–8, 15, 17, 20–25	Same as 7 and 12 conductor:
		Computer to modem (synchronous with DTE timing)
		Computer to modem with data rate selection and signal quality detection used
25	1–25	All uses; however if a ribbon cable is used, cross-overs and jumpering are difficult

that the correct number of pins are present. Specify pins and how many are required through the cable. When we are connecting a PC to a 3B1, at least five wires should be present in the cable. When ordering cables, vendors need to know the number of conductors in the cable. They are referring to the number of wires that are actually in the cable itself. These conductors go from one end of the cable to the other end. If you are ordering cable from a vendor, be sure that at least five conductors are present. Usually the number of conductors in a cable are 4, 7, 12, 16, or 25. The reason for these numbers is that the common cabling requirements fall within one of these ranges. Any of these cables will provide straight-through conductors unless specifically ordered otherwise with cross-overs and jumpering. Table 5–14 displays the common conductors provided straight through in each of these different cables.

Table 5–14 lays out many possible uses for the different cables. This list is by no means all inclusive or limited by the entries. Consider the example where pin 19 is used for flow control instead of pin 20. A 7 conductor cable could be used even though pin 19 is not present. The user could merely remove pin 20 from the connector and insert it in the pin 19 slot. Later, in the cable construction section, we will deal with how this can actually be done.

The important point is the number of conductors, not necessarily the pin numbers that are there. These can generally be easily changed. For our exercise, we will use a 12 conductor cable, as it can fulfill our requirements of straight-through, cross-overs, and jumpering. This cable provides conductors for leads 1–8, 15, 17, 20, and 22. The 7 conductor cable could have been used, but pin 5 was not present. Recall that we need a lead for this pin number. If a 7 conductor cable is to be used, one of the unused leads from our cable design, specifically, pin 4 or 20, could be extracted and inserted into the pin 5 slot at the PC end of the cable. However, for ease of understanding, we will use the 12 conductor cable.

Continuity check. Whether you purchase a cable or are using a preexisting cable, after the gender and number of conductors are checked, a continuity check should be conducted. If you are confident that the conductors are all straight through in the cable, this step may be skipped. If you are using a cable that has been built for another connection, or if you are from Missouri (the Show-Me state), as this author is, a continuity check should be performed. A continuity check will determine the lead makeup of the cable, specifically, the leads that are straight through, jumpered, or crossed over. Specific test equipment is available for this cable test, but a BOB or a VOM can be used.

The idea of a continuity test is to determine which leads at both ends of the cable are connected together, in any fashion. If we ordered the cable with 12 conductors, our results should be as shown in Table 5–15.

Let's see whether our cable tests out. If you are using a different cable, we will provide some guidance at the end of this discussion that will allow you to complete your testing.

First, let's use a VOM to check our continuity in the cable. This will be a pin-by-pin test. Make notes as you progress to ensure completeness. The author recommends logging them using a chart such as that shown in Table 5–16. Lines will be drawn to identify which conductors are connected, once we identify the connections.

TABLE 5–15. LEADS
IN 12 CONDUCTOR
CABLE

12 conductor cable	
Pin #	Pin #
1	1
2	2
3	3
4	4
5	5
6	6
7	7
8	8
15	15
17	17
20	20
22	22

TABLE 5–16. CHART FOR
CHECKING CONTINUITY

Connector end-A male	Connector end-B female
1	1
2	2
3	3
.	.
.	.
.	.
25	25

Because one of the cable ends is female, getting to each of the sockets may be difficult. It would probably be better if you opened the hoods, commonly referred to as covers, surrounding the connectors at both ends of the cable. This would permit easy access to the leads. This is done by unscrewing the cover screws that hold the connector together. Refer to Figure 5–3. Some connectors may merely pop apart, without screws involved. The connector is put together with two halves. By removing the screws, the hood can be taken apart, thus exposing

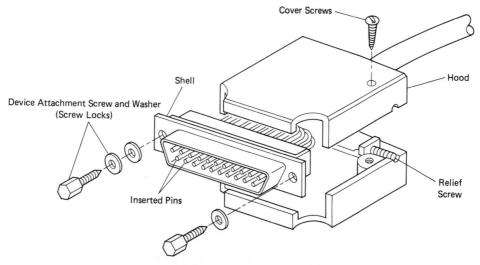

Figure 5–3. DB25 connector assembly.

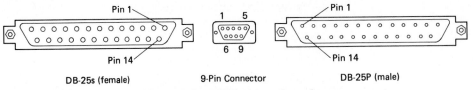

Figure 5–4. DB25 pin number reference.

the leads on the back side of the DB25 connector. Another technique would be to wrap a paper clip around the end of the probe. The end of the opened paper clip can easily fit into the slots of the female connectors. Either way, we need to make contact with the metal slots and pins.

With the hood removed, we can begin our test. Using a VOM, set the meter to the 1 ohm scale. Once set up, touch the two probes together and note the meter reading. We are looking for a similar reading during the continuity check. We will refer to the different probes as read and black, the cable ends as connector A and connector B, and the pins/wires by number. Connector A will be the 3B1 end, while connector B will be the PC end of the cable. The wires in the cable may be different colors. There is inconsistency among the color coding of leads, so we will not reference the colors. Recall the reference number associated with the pin number of the connector. Figure 5–4 is provided for a review of both the male and female numbering schemes.

Follow these steps for a complete checkout of the cable conductors for continuity using a VOM.

1. Insert the probe with the paper clip into pin 1 of connector B. This is the female end of the cable. If you are working with a male/male cable because you are using a computer other than the PC or 3B1, then hold the probe to pin 1 of connector B.
2. Touch each of the pins on connector A with the other probe, one by one, beginning with conductor/pin 1. Note the VOM meter for a continuity reading. This will test for straight-through and cross-over leads. Make a pencil notation on the chart if the VOM indicates there is a connection for a conductor of connector A. Run the probe up and down the rows of connector A to ensure that there are no "jumpered" conductors. More than likely pin 1 of connector B will be straight through to pin 1 of connector A. It is possible that no reading will be detected, indicating that lead 1 does not go through the cable to the other end. Record your findings as in Table 5–17:

TABLE 5–17. LOGGING CONTINUITY TEST RESULTS

Connector end A male		Connector end-B female
1	-------	1
2		2
3		3
.		.
.		.
.		.
25		25

3. Without removing the probe from slot 1 of connector B, test to see if there are any jumpered leads with connector B. This is done by touching each of the slots/pins with the other probe, as you did with connector A. Record your findings! With our cable, no local jumperings are present.

   However, should you find some associated with pin 1 or any other pin, you tag them as shown in Table 5–18. Assume that pin 1 is also jumpered to pin 7 within connector B.
4. Move the probe in connector B to pin 2. Repeat steps 2–3, monitoring the VOM for continuity. Record your findings at each step. Once steps 2–3 have been completed, move the probe in connector B to pin 3, and so on, until all slots in connector B have been tested.
5. Move the probe in connector B over to the other connector A in pin 1. We now must search for any jumpering in the cable that does not go straight through from one end of the cable to the other end. For example, pin 4 in connector A may be **locally jumpered** to pin 5 and not be connected to any conductor

TABLE 5–18. JUMPERED LEADS WITHIN A CABLE

Connector end A male		Connector end B female
1	----|--	1
2	(	2
3	(	3
.	(	.
.	(	.
.	|--	7
.		.
.		.

actually in the cable. Our tests in steps 1–4 would not have detected this. Our cable does not have this connection, but yours may. With the probe touching pin 1, run the other probe up and down the other pins to see if there is any local jumpering. Record the results. Move the probe to pin 2 and repeat this testing until all pins have been checked out.

The end result for our cable should produce a chart such as the following in Table 5–19. Recall that this is exactly what we had ordered with the 12 conductor cable. If you are using a preexisting cable, chances are that

TABLE 5–19. CONTINUITY RESULTS

Connector end A male		Connector end B female
1	--------	1
2	--------	2
3	--------	3
4	--------	4
5	--------	5
6	--------	6
7	--------	7
8	--------	8
9	X	9
10	X	10
11	X	11
12	X	12
13	X	13
14	X	14
15	--------	15
16	X	16
17	--------	17
18	X	18
19	X	19
20	--------	20
21	X	21
22	--------	22
23	X	23
24	X	24
25	X	25

Legend: The ''X'' implies that there is no conductor for that pin number from end to end in the cable.

your findings differ. Don't be alarmed, but merely double check to be sure that you have recorded exactly the way the cable conductors are in the cable. Our ultimate cable will be the same, regardless of what we begin with.

Using BOB for continuity check. The foregoing procedure could have been implemented using a BOB instead of a VOM. Your BOB has a light that can be used to monitor one of the leads of the interface. More than likely, there are multiple ones. We will select pin 20, as a monitoring light for this lead is present on almost all BOBs. This will be our measuring vehicle.

We need a power source, RS232-compatible signal levels, to enable us to drive the light on pin 20 of the BOB. If your BOB has a +V lead, use this as our source. If the BOB does not have a +V lead, use one of the output pins on one of the computer ports that is on. The idea is to connect the pin to be checked to this power source. The other pins, checking for straight through, cross-overs, and jumperings, will be connected to pin 20 on the BOB. Go through the leads one by one as described in the VOM discussion. Record your findings!

We can now build our cable. A very useful tool in building a cable is a pin inserter/extractor. They are only a couple of dollars and are useful when working with the pins of a DB25 connector. If a pin inserter/extractor tool is not available, any small blunt object can be used to extract the pins. Also needle-nosed pliers can be used to insert pins by pulling them. We will use a pin inserter/extractor in this exercise as it is the painless way to construct the cable from the 3B1 to the PC, as in Table 5–20.

Ground leads. Our cable was to have pins 1 and 7 straight through. Since our cable already had these straight through, we don't need to do anything with them. The ground category is taken care of.

Data leads. Our cable was to have the transmit data lead of connector A crossed over to the receive data lead of connector B. The conductor attached to pin 2 in connector A should be connected to pin 3 in connector B. The reverse is also true. Pin 2 in connector B should be crossed over to pin 3 of connector A. The easiest way to do this is to work with one end of the cable to do the cross-overs. We will work with connector B, the PC end of the cable.

Using the pin extractor, remove conductors 2 and 3 from the back of the female DB25 connector. Note the colors of the leads or tag them with a piece of tape so you know which is which. Insert the pin 2 conductor into the pin 3 socket in the back of the connector. Likewise, insert the removed conductor 3 into the 2 slot in the back of the connector as in Table 5–21. You have now effectively crossed over the two data leads to meet our data lead category requirements.

Control leads. The final category of leads in our cable are the control leads. Our cable actually only requires pin 20 of the 3B1 end of the cable to be crossed over to pin 5, with pins 6 and 8 being jumpered together to pin 5 in a daisy chain fashion. However, for completeness, we are going to repeat this in the other direction also. Pin 20 from the PC is to be connected to pins 5, 6, and 8 at the 3B1 end of the cable.

Pin 20 is straight through in the 12 conductor cable. Hence, pin 20 at connector B is connected to pin 20 at connector A. At the B connector, we do not want pin 20 to go straight through. This would break one of our golden rules: DO NOT connect two output signals together. Pins 20 at both ends are output. Hence, we can

TABLE 5–20. CABLE TO BE DESIGNED

PC			3B1
Function	Pin #	Pin #	Function
Protective Ground	1 -------	1	Protective Ground
Signal Ground	7 -------	7	Signal Ground
Transmit Data (out)	2 ------⟩	3	Receive Data (in)
Receive Data (in)	3 ⟨------	2	Transmit Data (out)
Clear to Send (in)	5 ⟨--|---	20	Data Terminal Ready (out)
Data Set Ready (in)	6 ⟨--|		
Data Carrier Detect (in)	8 ⟨--|		
{Data Terminal Ready (out)	20 ---|--⟩	5	Clear to Send (in)
	|--⟩	6	Data Set Ready (in)
	|--⟩	8	Data Carrier Detect (in)}

Note: The connection in the brackets is only for those connections involving a computer other than the 3B1.

TABLE 5–21.
DATA LEAD
CROSS-OVERS
FOR PC/XT-TO-3B1

3B1 A end			PC B end
2	---|	X	2
	|--⟩		3
	|---		2
3	⟨--|	X	3

Legend: The "X" implies
no connection. The "|"
indicates that a cross-over
is present.

extract pin 20 from the back side of connector B. We do, however, want this conductor to be connected to leads 5, 6, and 8 within connector B. The best way to accomplish this is to extract pin 5 from the back side of the connector. In its place, insert the pin 20 conductor. Any reference from here on out to pin 5 will be the pin 20 conductor that is now plugged into the slot 5. Now all we need to do is jumper pins 6 and 8 together and to pin 5.

To jumper pins 5, 6, and 8 together, use a knife to trim a bit of the insulation around the conductor plugged into the pin 5 slot. Go ahead and cut the number 6 and 8 conductors. The conductor, number 5, should not be cut in two. Be sure you leave yourself some slack to work with, on the wire attached to the connector. Trim the end of the conductors left attached to the connector. Connect these bare ends of wire together to the bare piece on the conductor plugged into slot 5 somehow.

Soldering them is a good way. Another means is to use a small piece of wire and wrap the exposed wire of the three conductors together and then insulate this with black electrical tape. Another way is to use the "old" pin 20 (now pin 5). Prior to inserting it into slot 5, trim the insulation a little bit on it, as well as on conductors 6 and 8. Wrap conductor 20 around the other two barren spots, and then insert it into slot 5. Wrap the wound joint with black electrical tape. Any of these methods can be used to perform the cross-over and jumpering. Pin 20 of connector A will control the status of pins 5, 6, and 8 in connector B. Whenever the 3B1 enables its port, this turns on pin 20. Pins 5, 6, and 8 at the PC will be on, as they are connected to pin 20. Table 5–22 depicts the resulting cable conductors.

Repeat this connection in the other direction if your computer, used in place of the 3B1, requires pins 5, 6, and 8 to be controlled by a control lead from the PC. You may substitute pin 4 in place of pin 20, as the output from connector B, because we have already used pin 20.

We have covered all the leads in our cable design except for pins 4 and 22 and the timing leads. The timing leads are to be ignored because this is an asynchronous connection. Hence, pins 15 and 17 should be ignored.

Pin 4 of both computers was an output signal. Our golden rule indicates that no two outputs should be connected together. Our cable offered pin 4 straight through. Hence, unless we remove pin 4 from one of the connectors, we could have a short circuit or cause other electrical problems. It really does not matter which connector this is done in. We will remove conductor 4 from the back side of connector B. It is a good practice to insulate the pin/socket of this pin so it does not accidentally touch another exposed lead. Wrap the metal part of this conductor with black electrical tape to prevent this. Now our cable does not have pin 4 straight through as shown in Table 5–23.

Our final lead that is present in the cable is pin 22. This lead is known as Ring Indicator. Ring Indicator is used whenever a modem is connected to a computer, printer, or terminal (DTE). This does not apply when connecting our two computers together. Lead 22 is normally an input signal at both computers. Two inputs connected together do not pose any problems in our cable. Hence, the user can either leave conductor 22 alone or remove it as you did pin 4.

Table 5–24 shows the resulting cable that we have constructed. It matches the cable that we had designed. If your cable has any other leads in it above what we had set out to include, it is recommended that you remove them. It is not necessary to remove all of them. However, DO NOT allow two outputs to be connected together. This could ground out the interface. If two inputs are connected together, this should pose no problems. If they

TABLE 5–22.
CONTROL
LEADS FOR
3B1 AND PC/XT

3B1 A end		PC B end
X |--〉	5
X |--〉	6
X |--〉	8
20 ---|X	20

Legend: The "X" indicates that there is no connection to pin 20 at connector B. Furthermore, pins 5, 6, and 8 are not connected straight through to the other end of the cable. It is important that they are not. Pins 5, 6, and 8 are jumpered together and are connected to conductor 20 in the cable. At the other end of the cable, connector A, pin 20 is connected straight through.

are, however, connected to an output signal, this could affect the interface. It is recommended that no extraneous conductors are actually connected in the interfaces.

Continuity check. Once the cable has been constructed, it is worthwhile to perform a continuity check. Repeat the procedure as outlined earlier in this chapter for testing continuity of the completed cable. Your results should match those depicted in Table 5–24. If they do not, correct the problem, and recheck the cable. Once the cable is built to your satisfaction, replace the hood/covers around each connector. It is recommended that you label each end of the cable with notations such as "IBM PC end" and "AT&T 3B1 end." Furthermore, a summary of the cross-overs should be kept somewhere, or even attached to the cable with tape. Permanent tagging and logging will save you much time in the future when dealing with the systems or reusing the cable.

Cabling the two systems. With the cable you have just constructed, plug the connectors into the computers. Be sure that connector A is plugged into the 3B1 and connector B is plugged into the PC serial port. Our cable will only allow it to be connected in one manner, due to the differences in gender. However, depending on the systems you are connecting, the gender of both ends of the cable could be the same. If they are labeled, the choice will be easy.

TABLE 5–23.
PIN 4
DISCONNECTED

3B1 A end		PC B end
4 -----X	4
22 -----X	22

Legend: The "X" indicates that there is no connection between the two leads.

TABLE 5–24.
COMPLETELY
CONSTRUCTED
PC/XT-to-3B1
CABLE

3B1 A end		PC B end
1	-------	1
7	-------	7
2	---| X	2
	|--⟩	3
	|--	2
3	⟨--- | X	3
	X |---⟩	5
	X |---⟩	6
	X |---⟩	8
20	----| X	20
4	----- X	4
22	----- X	22
15	-------	15
17	-------	17

Legend: Conductors 15 and 17 are not needed in the cable, but do not cause any problems with their existence. Pin 20 is used to control the status of 5, 6, and 8 at the opposite connector. Pins 5, 6, and 8 are NOT straight through. Pin 4 may have been used in connector B and crossed-over to pins 5, 6, and 8 of connector A, if appropriate. Otherwise, pin 4 should not be straight through. Pin 22 may be straight through, yet may be removed like pin 4.

Screw the connectors onto the ports they are plugged into. As computers are moved slightly, this will prevent the cable from being disconnected. This could be devastating if you are in the middle of a large file transfer and the two systems become unplugged. You are now prepared to attempt to communicate from system to system.

Signs of success. With the cable constructed, and the two systems cabled together, the user can begin to use the two computers. The UNIX system, if properly set up, is waiting for the PC to accept the "login" prompt. The PC can only do this if the communication software is up and running.

At the PC, load Crosstalk or any other communication software package per the instructions provided. Check your chart to see how your communication software should be optioned. From earlier in this chapter, the common options between the two are asynchronous transmission, 9600 bps, 7 data bits, 1 stop bit, even parity, full duplex operation, and software flow control. Set up your parameters to match these. Within the PC, use COM1 or COM2, as appropriate. We will assume COM1. Also, if a terminal emulation is possible, VT100 mode will be fine. UNIX supports any number of different terminals, so select one available in your package.

TABLE 5–25. COMPUTER-TO-COMPUTER SYMPTOMS AND CHECKPOINTS

1. The cable is not securely connected, is connected to the wrong port, or has the wrong ends connected to the wrong port.
2. The far-end computer is not on. Be sure that the 3B1, or equivalent, is up and running.
3. Your port is not enabled for connection to a terminal. Have the systems administrator enable the port.
4. Options are set incorrectly at one or both of the computers. Make sure that the options match at both ports, specifically the speed, character length, parity, and duplex. Also check whether the PC should be set up to use COM1 or COM2, and option accordingly.
5. Reload the communication software on the PC.
6. Recheck the cable design, and continuity.

With these options set up, go to the Online mode of your software. Hit the Break key, or possibly the Return/Enter key a couple of times on the PC. This will allow the far end, 3B1, to determine the speed. You should see the ''login:'' prompt on your screen. This was the sign of success that you noted earlier.

CONGRATULATIONS! You have successfully connected two computers together.

If you do not see the ''login:'' prompt, a couple of possibilities exist. Table 5–25 lays out the steps to be taken if the ''signs of success'' are not evident. Try each of these separately to isolate the problem. One or more of them may be causing the problem.

If you try these steps and you still don't see the ''signs of success,'' consult the systems administrator. You may have a computer hardware or software problem that is beyond the scope of the interfacing discussion in this book.

Tutorial Module 5-2: Connecting a PC/XT to a Toshiba 3100

In this exercise, we will be connecting two IBM PC-compatible computers. The purpose for this type of connection is for file transfer between the two computers. The IBM machine supports $5\frac{1}{4}$-inch disks, while the Toshiba has a built-in $3\frac{1}{2}$-inch disk. By connecting the two computers together, we can transfer data between the two of them, regardless of the media size and format. Several programs are available that allow for easy transfer of files between different computers, including those with incompatible disk formats. Refer to Tutorial Module 5–7 for the discussion of such a program, The Brooklyn Bridge. We will design that cable to connect the two PCs together, taking into account that the PC has a different size connector than the Toshiba. If you want to connect an IBM PC/AT to a Toshiba 3100 for file transfers, refer to Module 5–3, as the connector sizes are the same but the disks sizes are not. In this exercise Figure 5–5 depicts the connection that we are attempting. We have done port analysis for each of these computers. Our discussion will not replicate these, but merely summarize the analyses. Refer to Tutorial Module 1-1 for in-depth analysis of an IBM PC/XT port or Tutorial Module 4–3 to follow the steps in analyzing a 9-pin AT-compatible port.

Figure 5–5. PC/XT to Toshiba 3100 AT connection.

The steps we will follow are common to all our tutorial modules:

STEPS FOR CONNECTION

1. Determine compatibility (should it work?).
2. Determine signs of success.
3. Determine the type of connector used.
4. Determine gender of the ports.
5. Determine which leads (pins) are provided by each device.
6. Determine which leads are required to be on by each device.
7. Design the cable.
8. Build the cable.
9. Test the cable for continuity.
10. Cable the two systems together with the cable.
11. From step 2, measure success.

1. Determine compatibility

Because both these computers are MS-DOS machines, the two should be able to be connected together. Both offer RS232 ports and support the COM1, COM2 address for the serial ports. PC-to-PC connections are prevalent in the business world, so the two should work together. The two computers are compatible.

2. Determine signs of success

How will you know if your connection is successful? Once the two computers are physically cabled together, the two should be able to communicate with each other. We will know that we have a complete and working connection if we can load communication software on each of them and have a "data" conversation between them. This conversation will involve one user entering data on his or her PC keyboard and the user of the AT computer receiving this information. Conversely, the AT user should be able to type information and have it appear on the PC's screen. The ability to send and receive information will be one sign of success. Furthermore, you should be able to send an ASCII file from one machine to the other and have the flow control function. The receiving computer operator should be able to halt the data flow and continue it at his or her leisure. These two items will assure us that we have a successful connection.

3. Determine type of connector

We have, in another tutorial module, determined that the PC/XT is a DB25 connector. The Toshiba 3100 offers an AT-compatible connector. This is a 9-pin male connector. It is still a serial port offering RS232-C-compatible signal levels, but it is of different size and type.

4. Determine gender of ports

The PC/XT offers a DB25P connector. This is a male connector. Do not confuse this with the female connector often found on a PC. The female connector is the parallel port. We will use the male 25-pin connector. Hence, this end of our cable will be a 25-pin female connector.

The Toshiba 3100 (or AT) offers a 9-pin male connector. Be sure that you are using the COMM-labeled 9-pin port and not the RGB monitor port. A female 9-pin connector is required at this end of our cable.

5. Determine leads (pins) provided by each device

6. Determine leads required to be on

Steps 5 and 6 have been summarized in Table 5–26 using the SCS port profile analysis forms. For in-depth, step-by-step port analyses, refer to the respective tutorial modules mentioned earlier.

7. Design the cable

Now that we have a complete understanding of the signals provided and required for both computer devices' serial ports, we can design the cable. We should, as always, keep in mind our rules for connections.

Emulation

TABLE 5–26. IBM PC/XT AND TOSHIBA 3100 PORT PROFILES

Computer Port Profile

Underline if supported; circle if selected.

Model: PC/XT _____ Vendor: IBM _____ Port: ACA _____
Port type: <u>serial</u> parallel
Port: <u>DB25</u> 9-pin 5-pin 8-pin/modular 20mA Centronics ·

Gender: <u>male</u> female

Pin #	Function	Direction	Pin #	Function	Direction
1		to from n/a	14		to from n/a
2	Transmit Data	to from n/a	15		to from n/a
3	Receive Data	to from n/a	16		to from n/a
4	Request to Send	to from n/a	17		to from n/a
5	Clear to Send	to from n/a	18		to from n/a
6	Data Set Ready	to from n/a	19		to from n/a
7	Signal Ground	to from n/a	20	Data Terminal Ready	to from n/a
8	Data Carrier Detect	to from n/a	21		to from n/a
9		to from n/a	22	Ring Indicator	to from n/a
10		to from n/a	23		to from n/a
11		to from n/a	24		to from n/a
12		to from n/a	25		to from n/a
13		to from n/a			

Complete the next section only with 36-pin cinch connector.

#	Function	Direction	#	Function	Direction
26		to from n/a	27		to from n/a
28		to from n/a	29		to from n/a
30		to from n/a	31		to from n/a
32		to from n/a	33		to from n/a
34		to from n/a	35		to from n/a
36		to from n/a			

Flow control technique: XON/XOFF ENQ/ACK STX/ETX (Hardware) _____
Leads that must be on: <u>5</u> <u>6</u> <u>8</u> __ __ __ —

Options:
    Speeds: <u>110 300 600 1200 1800 2400 4800</u> (9600) 19.2 56k _____
    Parity: <u>even</u> <u>odd</u> space mark <u>none</u>
    Char-length: <u>7</u> <u>8</u> __
    # stop bits: <u>1</u> <u>1.5</u> <u>2</u>
    Line-ending sequence: cr lf cr/lf cr/lf/lf
    Disconnect sequence: EOT DEL ~. _____

    Mode: async sync isoch

sync timing leads:

#	Function	Direction
15		to from
17		to from
24		to from

Notes: _____
_____
_____

TABLE 5–26. *(Continued)*

Computer Port Profile

Underline if supported; circle if selected.

Model: 3100 _____ Vendor: Toshiba _____ Port: COMm _____
Port type: <u>serial</u> parallel
Port: DB25 <u>9-pin</u> 5-pin 8-pin/modular 20 mA Centronics

Gender: <u>male</u> female

Pin #	Function	Direction	Pin #	Function	Direction
1	<u>Carrier Detect</u>	to <u>from</u> n/a	14	_____	to from n/a
2	<u>Receive Data</u>	to <u>from</u> n/a	15	_____	to from n/a
3	<u>Transmit Data</u>	<u>to</u> from n/a	16	_____	to from n/a
4	<u>Data Terminal Ready</u>	to <u>from</u> n/a	17	_____	to from n/a
5	<u>Signal Ground</u>	to from n/a	18	_____	to from n/a
6	<u>Data Set Ready</u>	to <u>from</u> n/a	19	_____	to from n/a
7	<u>Request to Send</u>	to <u>from</u> n/a	20	_____	to from n/a
8	<u>Clear to Send</u>	to <u>from</u> n/a	21	_____	to from n/a
9	<u>Ring Indicator</u>	to <u>from</u> n/a	22	_____	to from n/a
10	_____	to from n/a	23	_____	to from n/a
11	_____	to from n/a	24	_____	to from n/a
12	_____	to from n/a	25	_____	to from n/a
13	_____	to from n/a			

Complete the next section only with 36-pin cinch connector.

26	_____	to from n/a	27	_____	to from n/a
28	_____	to from n/a	29	_____	to from n/a
30	_____	to from n/a	31	_____	to from n/a
32	_____	to from n/a	33	_____	to from n/a
34	_____	to from n/a	35	_____	to from n/a
36	_____	to from n/a			

Flow control technique: XON/XOFF ENQ/ACK STX/ETX <u>Hardware</u> _____
Leads that must be on: <u>8</u> <u>6</u> <u>1</u> __ __ __ __

Options:
    Speeds: <u>110 300 600 1200 1800 2400 4800</u> ⃝9600 19.2 56k _____
    Parity: <u>even</u> <u>odd</u> space mark <u>none</u>
    Char-length: <u>7</u> <u>8</u> __
    # stop bits: <u>1</u> <u>1.5</u> <u>2</u>
    Line-ending sequence: cr lf cr/lf cr/lf/lf
    Disconnect sequence: EOT DEL ~. _____

Mode: async sync isoch   sync timing leads:

#	Function	Direction
15	_____	to from
17	_____	to from
24	_____	to from

Notes: The options of this port are set up using the MS-DOS "Mode" command. Your application may do this automatically or through a menu-driven interface.

TABLE 5–27. PC/XT AND TOSHIBA 3100 LEADS SEPARATED BY RS232 CATEGORY

Function	PC/XT lead #	Toshiba 3100 lead #	Function
Ground			
Signal Ground	7	5	Signal Ground
Data			
Transmit Data (out)	2	3	Transmit Data (out)
Receive Data (in)	3	2	Receive Data (in)
Control			
Request to Send (out)	4	7	Request to Send (out)
Clear to Send (in)	5	8	Clear to Send (in)
Data Set Ready (in)	6	6	Data Set Ready (in)
Data Carrier Detect (in)	8	1	Carrier Detect (in)
Data Terminal Ready (out)	20	4	Data Terminal Ready (out)
Ring Indicator (in)	22	9	Ring Indicator (in)
Timing			
n/a			

CABLE DESIGN: GENERAL RULES

1. Connect like categories of leads together.
2. Always connect an "out" to an "in" and an "in" to an "out."
3. A lead that is input may be connected to another lead that is an input, only if both these are connected to an output lead.
4. In synchronous connections, only use one source of timing. (Because the XT-to-Toshiba 3100 connection is asynchronous, this point is not applicable.)

The easiest way to begin our design is to categorize the leads of both ports. By placing the leads into the different categories of ground, data, control, and timing, our design effort will be minimized. Table 5–27 outlines the leads broken out by category.

Both these ports have the same signals, with the same directions. The PC/XT and Toshiba 3100 serial ports have the common output control and output data signals found in devices emulating data terminal equipment. This implies that the ports are expecting to be connected to a piece of data communication equipment such as a modem. The ports also are expecting the same input leads as a piece of DTE, the signals normally provided by a DCE device.

We cannot connect two devices, both emulating DTE, together with a straight-through cable. We must build a null modem cable. We will do this one category at a time for ease of understanding. The user should note that there are many potential variations of this null modem cable. The one we will design represents a common NMC.

The easiest category of leads is the ground category. We only have Signal Grounds, not Protective Grounds, to worry about. Hence our design should allow for merely connecting these two leads together. Specifically, we should connect lead 7 at the XT end of the cable, through the cable to lead 5 at the Toshiba end. The two leads will be connected with a conductor in our wire. Table 5–28 depicts this connection.

The next category is the data leads. These are fairly straightforward, as you want the output data lead from one computer to be connected to the input data lead of the other computer, and vice versa. Applying rules 1 and 2, you would arrive at a design found in Table 5–29.

TABLE 5–28. GROUND LEADS IN PC/XT-TO-TOSHIBA 3100 (or AT)

Function	PC/AT lead #	3100 (AT) lead #	Function
Signal Ground	7 -------	5	Signal Ground

TABLE 5–29. DATA LEADS IN CABLE DESIGN FOR 9-PIN CONNECTORS

Function	PC/AT lead #	3100 (AT) lead #	Function
Transmit Data (out)	2	------⟩ 2	Receive Data (in)
Receive Data (in)	3	⟨------ 3	Transmit Data (out)

LEGEND: The ''------)'' indicates a straight-through connection. Connect the ''out'' data lead from the PC/XT, through the cable, to the ''in'' data lead at the Toshiba end of the cable. Connect the ''in'' data lead across to the ''out'' data lead.

The timing leads are not relative, so we will proceed to the control leads. The important element in a computer-to-computer connection is flow control, and satisfying the input control leads. Flow control between two computers is normally supported by software flow control. XON/XOFF are usually supported by the software that is being run on each system. This implies that the data leads will handle the flow control lead mechanism. We must, however, satisfy the input control leads.

Each of our computers provides a DTE port, as analyzed earlier. This implies that the ports are expecting to be connected to a piece of DCE, such as a modem. Because we are connecting back-to-back computers, or DTE-to-DTE, we must provide for the signals normally given by a modem. Specifically, the control leads—Clear to Send, Data Set Ready, and Data Carrier Detect—must be provided for. The two PCs are expecting these leads to be on before they will transmit or receive data. These input leads are the same on both ports, just different pin numbers used. Note that we are not discussing the Ring Indicator leads. These are used when incoming calls are involved, which is not the case here.

We will use the output signals to satisfy these input leads. We want the opposite device to provide these input leads to the local device. Specifically, we want the Toshiba 3100 output leads to control the PC/XT input control leads.

This reverse is also true. This will allow the computers to know if the other device is turned on or not. Hence, we will connect an output lead from the Toshiba across to input leads on the PC/XT. Output control leads on the PC/XT will be connected to input leads on the 3100 (AT). We have two such leads to deal with, Request to Send and Data Terminal Ready. There are many ways to allow for this. Table 5–30 provides a multitude of possibilities for this cable. Select the one that is easiest for you to build. Note that the number of conductors you have in your cable may dictate which design you use.

Specifically, if you are using 2-pair wire, then only four conductors are available for use. These control leads, along with Signal Ground and the data leads, must not exceed the number of conductors available. Choose the design that will work with the cable you are ultimately going to acquire for cable construction.

Combining all the leads, we have completely designed our IBM PC/XT cable. Table 5–31 outlines the complete cable. Substitute the appropriate control leads based on the number of conductors that you have available.

Steps 8–10. Build the cable, test for continuity, and cable the two systems together as you normally would. Remember that to build the cable, you need a female DB25S for the PC/XT end of the cable and a female 9-pin connector for the Toshiba 3100 (AT) end of the cable.

11. Measure success

We know that we have successfully constructed a cable and connected the two computers together when we can send and receive data between the PC/XT and the Toshiba 3100 (AT) as well as be assured that software flow control functions. At this point, the two computers should be cabled together and turned on.

We will test the systems by loading communication software on each of them. For the purposes of our discussion, Crosstalk XVI will be used. Feel free to use any of your favorite communication software packages on each of them. The setup procedures will vary, but the parameters should be the same. Load the communication software at this time.

The user can load Crosstalk by typing in XTALK followed by a return. This should load the system and offer you a selection of options from which to choose. Follow the normal procedures provided in your Crosstalk documentation. Upon loading, you may select the ''Setup'' option to get you to the status screen. This displays

TABLE 5–30. PC/XT-TO-TOSHIBA 3100 (AT) CONTROL LEAD CROSS-OVERS

For a 7 or more conductor cable

Function	PC/XT lead #	3100 (AT) lead #	Function
Request to Send (out)	4	------⟩ 1	Carrier Detect (in)
Clear to Send (in)	5	⟨--|	
Carrier Detect (in)	8	⟨------ 7	Request to Send (out)
		|--⟩ 8	Clear to Send (in)
Data Terminal Ready (out)	20	------⟩ 6	Data Set Ready (in)
Data Set Ready (in)	6	⟨------ 4	Data Terminal Ready (out)

For 5 or more conductor cable

Function	PC/XT lead #	3100 (AT) lead #	Function
Data Terminal Ready (out)	20	------⟩ 8	Clear to Send (in)
		|--⟩ 6	Data Set Ready (in)
		|--⟩ 1	Carrier Detect (in)
Clear to Send (in)	5	⟨------ 4	Data Terminal Ready (out)
Data Set Ready (in)	6	⟨--|	
Data Carrier Detect (in)	8	⟨--|	

For 3 or more conductor cable

Function	PC/XT lead #	3100 (AT) lead #	Function
Request to Send (out)	4	---- ---- 7	Request to Send (out)
Clear to Send (in)	5	⟨--| |--⟩ 8	Clear to Send (out)
Data Set Ready (in)	6	⟨--| |--⟩ 6	Data Set Ready (in)
Data Carrier Detect (in)	8	⟨--| |--⟩ 1	Data Carrier Detect (in)
Data Terminal Ready	20	---| |--- 4	Data Terminal Ready (out)

LEGEND: Each of these possible cables includes jumpering and cross-overs. The "4------⟩ 1" implies that lead 4 in the PC/XT connector is locally ("5 ⟨--\|") jumpered to lead 5 in the same connector and crossed over to lead 1 in the Toshiba 3100 (AT) connector. The "------⟩" implies that a straight-through connection or a cross-over is involved. If you are using one of the cables that includes "6 ⟨--\|," "8 ⟨--\|," "20 ⟨--\|," this implies that there are no conductors needed that go from end to end in the cable. Local jumpering is all that is used.

TABLE 5–31. IBM PC/XT-TO-TOSHIBA 3100 (AT) CABLE DESIGN

Function	PC/XT lead #	3100 (AT) lead #	Function
Signal Ground	7	------- 5	Signal Ground
Transmit Data (out)	2	------⟩ 2	Receive Data (in)
Receive Data (in)	3	⟨------ 3	Transmit Data (out)
Request to Send (out)	4	---|---⟩ 1	Carrier Detect (in)
Clear to Send (in)	5	⟨--|	
Carrier Detect (in)	8	⟨---|--- 7	Request to Send (out)
		|--⟩ 8	Clear to Send (in)
Data Terminal Ready (out)	20	------⟩ 6	Data Set Ready (in)
Data Set Ready (in)	6	⟨------ 4	Data Terminal Ready (out)

the current settings and allows you to change them for our test. You need to set up the options as defined in our port profile analyses as follows:

port = COM1 (substitute COM2 as appropriate)
speed = 9600
modem type = other
dialing prefix = enter key
dialing suffix = enter key

When prompted, if you want to save these settings, answer "yes." You can save these to any file by entering "save" followed by an Enter key. Enter the filename you want to save these under, such as "pc2at" for later use. Note that the parity is set to none, data length is set to 8, stop bits is 1. You can change these, as long as they are consistent at both ends. Once set up at both ends, hit an Enter key at the "Command?" prompt to go online.

Test your ability to transmit and receive data by typing characters on one of the keyboards. At a minimum, the other computer should display information on its screen. On the other keyboard, repeat the same to be sure that data transmission is occurring. If nothing appears on either screen, recheck your cabling between the two systems, and then the parameters as listed. Both computers should be optioned or set up the same.

More than likely when you are entering data on one computer, the other one will display it, but your local screen will not. This problem has to do with an option known as duplex. Some computers echo back anything that they receive. Back-to-back PCs do not, but Crosstalk can fix this. Note the duplex setting. It is more than likely set to "full." This mode expects the remote computer to echo all characters back. If you change this mode to "half duplex," then Crosstalk will echo back locally anything that you type on the keyboard, as well as send it to the other computer. Do this and repeat the keyboard test to ensure that you can see on your screen everything that is being transmitted to the other computer. Repeat the option setup for both ends (half duplex).

Type enough characters to fill a line, and then hit the Return key. Continue typing and watch the screens. More than likely you will be overwriting the original line of characters. If this is the case, then your computer is outputting only a carriage return when you hit the Return key. It does not add a line feed, necessary to prevent overwriting. Crosstalk can get around this through the "LF" option. Change this option so "LF auto" is set to on. With this setup at both computers, whenever a Return key is typed, both a carriage return and a line feed will occur. Test it to ensure readability at both computers. Save these settings into your file "PC2AT" for later use.

We have now completed 50 percent of our tests to ensure success. The only other piece to test is flow control. Our success here will be determined by the ability to receive large files and temporarily halt the transmission, as well as resume the transmission without any loss of data. The best means of testing this is to use the "Send" command provided by Crosstalk. At the "Command?" prompt, obtained by hitting the Home key, enter "send filename," where filename is a text file that you want to send. This should send the file to other computer. Go over to the other keyboard and enter a Control-s sequence, done by holding down the Ctrl key and typing an "s" key simultaneously. This should halt the reception of data. Wait a few seconds and enter a Control-q sequence to resume transmission. You should not lose any data displayed on your screen. Repeat this at the other computer, sending a filename resident on that computer.

This is software flow control, XON/XOFF, in action. Crosstalk supports this flow control technique automatically. Once you are convinced that both the transmission of data and flow control are functioning, you may now perform file transfers between the two systems. You can use either XMODEM or Crosstalk's file transfer mechanisms to exchange files. This is a very important function, as the two systems, PC/XT and Toshiba 3100, use different disk sizes. This is an easy way to get the files back and forth. The author of this book used a Toshiba 3100 to write while traveling. Upon returning home, he connected the Toshiba back to back with his XT and performed file transfers. This is a life-saving technique that can be performed often.

There are several alternative means of exchanging data between two computers with dissimilar disk sizes. Consult the section on The Brooklyn Bridge in Tutorial Module 5–7 covering laptops for other possible options.

Tutorial Module 5-3: Connecting an IBM PC/AT to a Toshiba 3100

In this exercise, we will be connecting two IBM PC/AT-compatible computers. The purpose of this type of connection is to accomplish file transfer between the two computers. The IBM machine supports $5\frac{1}{4}$-inch disks, while the Toshiba has a built-in $3\frac{1}{2}$-inch disk. By connecting the two computers together, we can transfer data between the two of them, regardless of the media size and format. Several programs are available that allow for easy transfer of files between different computers, including those with incompatible disk formats. Refer to Tutorial Module 5–7 for the discussion of such a program, The Brooklyn Bridge.

In this exercise Figure 5–6 depicts the connection that we are attempting. We have done port analysis for each of these computers in previous exercises. Our discussion will not replicate these, but merely summarize the analyses. Refer to Tutorial Module 4–3 for in-depth analysis of an IBM PC/AT 9-pin AT-compatible port. The Toshiba 3100 is an AT compatible offering the same port. Hence the two ports will be exactly the same. To delineate the two computers, we will refer to the IBM PC/AT as merely the AT, while the Toshiba will be referenced as the 3100, even though they are functionally equivalent ATs.

The steps we will follow are common to all our tutorial modules:

STEPS FOR CONNECTION

1. Determine compatibility (should it work?).
2. Determine signs of success.
3. Determine the type of connector used.
4. Determine gender of the ports.
5. Determine which leads (pins) are provided by each device.
6. Determine which leads are required to be on by each device.
7. Design the cable.
8. Build the cable.
9. Test the cable for continuity.
10. Cable the two systems together with the cable.
11. From step 2, measure success.

Steps 1–2 are the same as in Tutorial Module 5–2.

Compatibility: Yes

Signs of success: Data transmission and flow control

3. Determine type of connector

Both the PC/AT and Toshiba 3100 connectors are 9-pin serial connectors. They are serial ports offering RS232-C-compatible signal levels.

4. Determine gender of ports

The Toshiba 3100 and AT offer a 9-pin male connector. Be sure that you are using the COMM-labeled 9-pin port on the Toshiba and not the RGB monitor port. A female 9-pin connector is required at both ends of our cable.

5. Determine leads (pins) provided by each device

6. Determine leads required to be on

Steps 5 and 6 have been summarized in Table 5–32 using the Software Cabling System (SCS) port profile analysis forms. For in-depth, step-by-step port analyses, refer to Tutorial Module 4–3. Both the PC/AT and Toshiba have the same port specs.

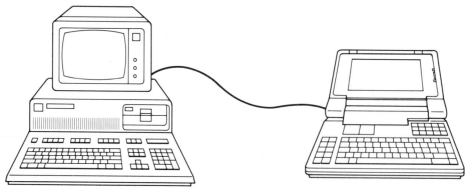

Figure 5–6. PC/AT to Toshiba 3100 connection.

TABLE 5–32. IBM PC/AT AND TOSHIBA 3100 PORT PROFILES

Computer Port Profile

Underline if supported; circle if selected.

Model: PC/AT _____ Vendor: IBM _____ Port: COMM__(ACA)__

Port type: <u>serial</u> parallel

Port: DB25 <u>9-pin</u> 5-pin 8-pin/modular 20mA Centronics

Gender: <u>male</u> female

Pin #	Function	Direction	Pin #	Function	Direction
1	Carrier Detect	to <u>from</u> n/a	14	_____	to from n/a
2	Receive Data	to <u>from</u> n/a	15	_____	to from n/a
3	Transmit Data	<u>to</u> from n/a	16	_____	to from n/a
4	Data Terminal Ready	to <u>from</u> n/a	17	_____	to from n/a
5	Signal Ground	to from n/a	18	_____	to from n/a
6	Data Set Ready	<u>to</u> from n/a	19	_____	to from n/a
7	Request to Send	to <u>from</u> n/a	20	_____	to from n/a
8	Clear to Send	<u>to</u> from n/a	21	_____	to from n/a
9	Ring Indicator	to from n/a	22	_____	to from n/a
10	_____	to from n/a	23	_____	to from n/a
11	_____	to from n/a	24	_____	to from n/a
12	_____	to from n/a	25	_____	to from n/a
13	_____	to from n/a			

Complete the next section only with 36-pin cinch connector.

26	_____	to from n/a	27	_____	to from n/a
28	_____	to from n/a	29	_____	to from n/a
30	_____	to from n/a	31	_____	to from n/a
32	_____	to from n/a	33	_____	to from n/a
34	_____	to from n/a	35	_____	to from n/a
36	_____	to from n/a			

Flow control technique: XON/XOFF ENQ/ACK STX/ETX <u>Hardware</u> _____

Leads that must be on: <u>8</u> <u>6</u> <u>1</u> __ __ __ __

Options:
    Speeds: <u>110 300 600 1200 1800 2400 4800</u> (9600) 19.2 56k _____
    Parity: <u>even</u> <u>odd</u> space mark <u>none</u>
    Char-length: <u>7</u> <u>8</u> ____
    # stop bits: <u>1</u> <u>1.5</u> <u>2</u>
    Line-ending sequence: cr lf cr/lf cr/lf/lf
    Disconnect sequence: EOT   DEL   ~. _____

    Mode: async sync isoch

#	Function	Direction
15	_____	to from
17	_____	to from
24	_____	to from

Notes: The options of this port are set up using the MS-DOS Mode command. Your application may do this automatically or through a menu-driven interface.

7. Design the cable

Now that we have a complete understanding of the signals provided and required for both computer devices' serial ports, we can design the cable. We should, as always, keep in mind our rules for connections.

CABLE DESIGN: GENERAL RULES

1. Connect like categories of leads together.
2. Always connect an "out" to an "in" and an "in" to an "out."
3. A lead that is input may be connected to another lead that is an input, only if both these are connected to an output lead.
4. In synchronous connections, only use one source of timing. (Because the AT-to-Toshiba 3100 connection is asynchronous, this point is not applicable.)

The easiest way to begin our design is to categorize the leads of both ports. By placing the leads into the different categories of ground, data, control, and timing, our design effort will be minimized. Table 5–33 outlines the leads broken out by category.

Both these ports have the same signals, with the same directions. The PC/XT and Toshiba 3100 serial ports have the common output control and output data signals found in devices emulating data terminal equipment. This implies that the ports are expecting to be connected to a piece of data communication equipment, such as a modem. The ports also are expecting the same input leads as a piece of DTE, the signals normally provided by a DCE device.

We cannot connect two devices, both emulating DTE, together with a straight-through cable. We must build a null modem cable. We will do this one category at a time for ease of understanding. The user should note that there are many potential variations of this null modem cable. The one we will design represents a common NMC. This cable design mirrors that found in Tutorial Module 5–2, except that the pin numbers are different between the PC/XT and our PC/AT.

The easiest category of leads is the ground category. We only have Signals Grounds, not Protective Grounds, to worry about. Hence, our design should allow for merely connecting these two leads together. Specifically, we should connect lead 5 at the AT end of the cable, through the cable to lead 5 at the Toshiba end. The two leads will be connected with a conductor in our wire. Table 5–34 depicts this connection.

TABLE 5–33. PC/XT AND TOSHIBA 3100 LEADS SEPARATED BY RS232 CATEGORY

Function	PC/AT lead #	Toshiba 3100 lead #	Function
Ground			
Signal Ground	5	5	Signal Ground
Data			
Transmit Data (out)	3	3	Transmit Data (out)
Receive Data (in)	2	2	Receive Data (in)
Control			
Request to Send (out)	7	7	Request to Send (out)
Clear to Send (in)	8	8	Clear to Send (in)
Data Set Ready (in)	6	6	Data Set Ready (in)
Data Carrier Detect (in)	1	1	Carrier Detect (in)
Data Terminal Ready (out)	4	4	Data Terminal Ready (out)
Ring Indicator (in)	9	9	Ring Indicator (in)
Timing			
n/a			

TABLE 5–34. GROUND LEADS IN PC/AT-TO-TOSHIBA 3100 (OR AT)

Function	PC/AT lead #	3100 (AT) lead #	Function
Signal Ground	5	------- 5	Signal Ground

LEGEND: Merely connect these two leads straight through to one another.

TABLE 5–35.   DATA LEAD DESIGN IN 9-PIN CONNECTORS

Function	PC/AT lead #	3100 (AT) lead #	Function
Transmit Data (out)	3 ------>	2	Receive Data (in)
Receive Data (in)	2 <------	3	Transmit Data (out)

LEGEND: The ''------)'' indicates a cross-over from lead 3 at the AT end connector across to lead 2 at the 3100-end connector. The converse is also true.

The next category is the data leads. These are fairly straightforward, as you want the output data lead from one computer to be connected to the input data lead of the other computer, and vice versa. Applying rules 1 and 2, you would arrive at a design found in Table 5–35.

The timing leads are not relevant, so we will proceed to the control leads. The important element in a computer-to-computer connection is flow control and satisfying the input control leads. Flow control between two computers is normally supported by software flow control. XON/XOFF are usually supported by the software that is being run on each system. This implies that the data leads will handle the flow control lead mechanism. We must, however, satisfy the input control leads.

Each of our computers provides a DTE port, as analyzed earlier. This implies that the ports are expecting to be connected to a piece of DCE, such as a modem. Because we are connecting back-to-back computers, or DTE-to-DTE, we must provide for the signals normally given by a modem. Specifically, the control leads— Clear to Send, Data Set Ready, and Data Carrier Detect—must be provided for. The two PCs are expecting these leads to be on before they will transmit or receive data. These input leads are the same on both ports. Note that we are not discussing the Ring Indicator leads. This is used when incoming calls are involved, which is not the case here.

We will use the output signals to satisfy these input leads. We want the opposite device to provide these input leads to the local device. Specifically, we want the Toshiba 3100 output leads to control the PC/AT input control leads. This reverse is also true. This will allow the computers to know if the other device is turned on or not. Hence, we will connect an output lead from the Toshiba across to input leads on the PC/AT. Output control leads on the PC/AT will be connected to input leads on the 3100 (AT). We have two such leads to consider: Request to Send and Data Terminal Ready. There are many ways to allow for this.

Table 5–36 provides a multitude of possibilities for this cable. Select the one that is easiest for you to build. Note that the number of conductors you have in your cable may dictate which design you use. Specifically, if you are using 2-pair wire, then only four conductors are available for use. These control leads, along with signal ground and the data leads must not exceed the number of conductors available. Choose the design that will work with the cable you are ultimately going to acquire for cable construction. The cross-overs are the same as in Tutorial Module 5–2.

Combining all the leads, we have completely designed our IBM PC/AT cable. Table 5–37 outlines the complete cable. Substitute the appropriate control leads based on the number of conductors that you have available.

Steps 8–10

Build the cable, test for continuity, and cable the two systems together as you normally would. Remember that to build the cable, you need a female 9-pin connector for both ends of the cable.

11. Measure success

We know that we have successfully constructed a cable and connected the two computers together when we can send and receive data between the PC/AT and the Toshiba 3100 (AT), as well as be assured that software flow control functions. We will test the systems with the same procedure used in Tutorial Module 5–2 by loading communication software on each of them. Refer to this module for a complete test of your AT-to-AT connection. For other data exchange applications, refer to the section on laptops in Tutorial Module 5–7.

Tutorial Module 5-4: Connecting Two UNIX Systems Together

In this tutorial module we will connect several UNIX systems together. This will be extremely important for file transfer reasons. Because there is no standard medium between UNIX systems (i.e., floppy or tape layouts),

TABLE 5–36. PC/AT-TO-TOSHIBA 3100 (AT) CONTROL LEAD CROSS-OVERS

For a 7 or More Conductor Cable

Function	PC/AT lead #	3100 (AT) lead #	Function
Request to Send (out)	7	------⟩ 1	Carrier Detect (in)
Clear to Send (in)	8	⟨--|	
Carrier Detect (in)	1	⟨------ 7	Request to Send (out)
		|--⟩ 8	Clear to Send (in)
Data Terminal Ready (out)	4	------⟩ 6	Data Set Ready (in)
Data Set Ready (in)	6	⟨------ 4	Data Terminal Ready (out)

For 5 or More Conductor Cable

Function	PC/AT lead #	3100 (AT) lead #	Function
Data Terminal Ready (out)	4	------⟩ 8	Clear to Send (in)
		|--⟩ 6	Data Set Ready (in)
		|--⟩ 1	Carrier Detect (in)
Clear to Send (in)	8	⟨------ 4	Data Terminal Ready (out)
Data Set Ready (in)	6	⟨--|	
Data Carrier Detect (in)	1	⟨--|	

For 3 or More Conductor Cable

Function	PC/AT lead #	3100 (AT) lead #	Function
Request to Send (out)	7	---- ---- 7	Request to Send (out)
Clear to Send (in)	8	⟨--| |--⟩ 8	Clear to Send (out)
Data Set Ready (in)	6	⟨--| |--⟩ 6	Data Set Ready (in)
Data Carrier Detect (in)	1	⟨--| |--⟩ 1	Data Carrier Detect (in)
Data Terminal Ready	4	---| |--- 4	Data Terminal Ready (out)

LEGEND: Each of these possible cables includes jumpering and cross-overs. The "7 ------⟩ 1" implies that lead 7 in the PC/AT connector is locally ("8 ⟨--\|") jumpered to lead 8 in the same connector and crossed over to lead 1 in the Toshiba 3100 (AT) connector. The "------⟩" implies that a straight-through connection or a cross-over is involved. If you are using one of the cables that includes "6 ⟨--\|," "1 ⟨--\|," "4 ⟨--\|," this implies that there are no conductors needed that go from end to end in the cable. Local jumpering is all that is used.

TABLE 5–37. IBM PC/AT-TO-TOSHIBA 3100 (AT) CABLE DESIGN

Function	PC/AT lead #	3100 (AT) lead #	Function
Signal Ground	5	------- 5	Signal Ground
Transmit Data (out)	3	------⟩ 2	Receive Data (in)
Receive Data (in)	2	⟨------ 3	Transmit Data (out)
Request to Send (out)	7	---|--⟩ 1	Carrier Detect (in)
Clear to Send (in)	8	⟨--|	
Carrier Detect (in)	1	⟨--|-- 7	Request to Send (out)
		|--⟩ 8	Clear to Send (in)
Data Terminal Ready (out)	4	------⟩ 6	Data Set Ready (in)
Data Set Ready (in)	6	⟨------ 4	Data Terminal Ready (out)

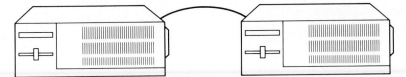

Figure 5–7. Two UNIX systems back to back.

file transfers provide a means of getting data and programs from one system to another. Here we want to illustrate the cable design among DB25, 9-pin, and 8-pin connectors. Hence, we will connect three different computers. The three featured here will be the Pyramid Technology 90 series with ITP, the Plexus P/75 ACP, and the AT&T 3B2 I/O ports. Figure 5–7 outlines the connections to be covered here. For the terminal-to-computer connections, refer to Chapter 4. Note that special cables and adapters are available from the vendors for connecting peripherals, computers, and modems to their ports. This module will not make use of these and design the cable from scratch. An example is the AT&T 8-pin-to-DB25 adapters and black cable. These may be used to connect devices to the 3B2, but will not be discussed here.

Other modules covered the analysis of the different ports on each of the computers. The reader is encouraged to refer to the respective port profiles for summaries of the connectors and pinouts, as well as all the various options available. The steps for the different connections will be the same as in all other tutorial modules, so we will summarize where appropriate.

STEPS FOR CONNECTION

1. Determine compatibility (should it work?).
2. Determine signs of success.
3. Determine the type of connector used.
4. Determine gender of the ports.
5. Determine which leads (pins) are provided by each device.
6. Determine which leads are required to be on by each device.
7. Design the cable.
8. Build the cable.
9. Test the cable for continuity.
10. Cable the two systems together with the cable.
11. From step 2, measure success.

1. Determine compatibility

Should they work? You bet they should. Most UNIX computer systems can communicate with one another easily through communication ports. By connecting the computers together through serial port, the two computer systems can transfer data. The ports should be set up for common options. Our module will assume asynchronous operation, 7 data bits, even parity, 1 stop bit, full duplex, XON/XOFF flow control, and 9600 bps operation. All the computers involved support these setups.

2. Determine signs of success

The connection of the UNIX systems will be considered successful if a terminal at one UNIX system can send and receive data through both UNIX systems to a terminal on the second UNIX system. The UNIX "cu" command or "uucp" facilities can also be used to do the testing for us, once we have the physical connection.

3. Determine type of connector (see Table 5–38)

4. Determine gender of ports (see Table 5–38)

TABLE 5–38. SUMMARY OF CONNECTORS/
GENDERS FOR UNIX COMPUTERS

Computer	Connector	Gender
Pyramid 90x (ICP)	DB25P	Male
Plexus P/75 (ACP)	DB9S (9-pin)	Female
AT&T 3B2	8-Pin receptacle	Female

5. Determine leads (pins) provided by each device

6. Determine leads required to be on

Consult the documentation for each port to get the pinouts. A VOM and BOB can be used to determine which leads are output, as well as determine what the port is emulating (DTE/DCD). Tables 5–39 to 5–41 lay out the pinouts.

TABLE 5–39. PINOUTS FOR PYRAMID TECHNOLOGY 90X (ITP)

Function	Lead #
Frame Ground	1
Transmit Data (out)	2
Received Data (in)	3
Request to Send (out)	4
Clear to Send (in)	5
Data Set Ready (in)	6
Signal Ground	7
Data Carrier Detect (in)	8
Data Terminal Ready (out)	20
Ring Indicator (in)	22

TABLE 5–40. PINOUTS FOR PLEXUS P/75 (ACP)

Function	Lead #
Transmit Data (out)	1
Received Data (in)	6
Request to Send (out)	2
Clear to Send (in)	7
Signal Ground	8
Data Carrier Detect (in)	9
Data Terminal Ready (out)	4
Transmit Clock (in)	5
Received Clock (in)	3

NOTE: Pin 4 is labeled DSR in some of the Plexus documentation, but is an outbound lead. Since the port emulates DTE, this lead is more appropriately labeled DTR.

TABLE 5–41. PINOUTS FOR AT&T 3B2 I/O PORTS (8-PIN MODULAR RECEPTACLE)

Function	Lead #
Protective Ground	1
Transmit Data (out)	3
Received Data (in)	5
Signal Ground	7
Data Carrier Detect (in)	6
Data Terminal Ready (out)	4

Connecting Computers   Chap. 5

7. Design the cable

With the foregoing information, a cable will be built to connect the Pyramid Technology computer to the Plexus, the Pyramid Technology computer to the AT&T 3B2, and the Plexus computer to the AT&T 3B2. The same rules for cable design apply here, regardless of the port size.

CABLE DESIGN: GENERAL RULES

1. Connect like categories of leads together.
2. Always connect an "out" to an "in" and an "in" to an "out."
3. A lead that is input may be connected to another lead that is an input, only if both these are connected to an output lead.
4. In synchronous connections, only use one source of timing. (Because the UNIX connections are asynchronous, this point is not applicable.)

We will not follow a step-by-step approach here, as doing so for the multiple computers in this tutorial module would complicate the text. However, if the user reviews the cable design rules, and reviews Tables 5–39 to 5–41, the cable design should be straightforward. Tables 5–42 to 5–44 summarize the cable designs.

TABLE 5–42. PYRAMID TECHNOLOGY 90X (ITP)-TO-PLEXUS P/75 (ACP) CABLE DESIGN

Function	Pyramid lead #		Plexus lead #	Function
Signal Ground	7	-------	8	Signal Ground
Transmit Data (out)	2	------⟩	6	Received Data (in)
Received Data (in)	3	⟨------	1	Transmit Data (out)
Clear to Send (in)	5	⟨-|----	4	Data Terminal Ready (out)
Data Set Ready (in)	6	⟨-|		
Data Carrier Detect (in)	8	⟨-|		
Data Terminal Ready (out)	20	----|-⟩	7	Clear to Send (in)
		|-⟩	9	Data Carrier Detect (in)

LEGEND: The timing leads of the ACP are not required as this is an asynchronous connection. The "-------" implies a straight-through connection; the "------⟩" indicates a cross-over of leads. The "----\|-⟩ / \|-⟩" indicates there is local jumpering within a connector end.

TABLE 5–43. PYRAMID TECHNOLOGY 90X (ITP)-TO-AT&T 3B2 8-PIN JACK CABLE DESIGN

Function	Pyramid lead #		AT&T lead #	Function
Protective Ground	1	-------	1	Protective Ground
Signal Ground	7	-------	7	Signal Ground
Transmit Data (out)	2	------⟩	5	Received Data (in)
Received Data (in)	3	⟨------	3	Transmit Data (out)
Clear to Send (in)	5	⟨-|----	4	Data Terminal Ready (out)
Data Set Ready (in)	6	⟨-|		
Data Carrier Detect (in)	8	⟨-|		
Data Terminal Ready (out)	20	------⟩	6	Data Carrier Detect (in)

LEGEND: Same as for Table 5–42.

Emulation

TABLE 5–44. PLEXUS P/75 (ACP) 9-PIN-TO-AT&T 3B2 8-PIN JACK CABLE DESIGN

Function	Pyramid lead #		AT&T lead #	Function
Signal Ground	8	--------	7	Signal Ground
Transmit Data (out)	1	------)	5	Received Data (in)
Received Data (in)	6	(------	3	Transmit Data (out)
Clear to Send (in)	7	(-|----	4	Data Terminal Ready (out)
Data Carrier Detect (in)	9	(-|		
Data Terminal Ready (out)	4	------)	6	Data Carrier Detect (in)

LEGEND: Same as for Table 5–42.

8. Build the cable

9. Test for continuity

10. Cable the two systems together

Build the cables as you normally would. Keep in mind the genders that are required. Review steps 3 and 4 to select the connector to use in your cable. Check the cable for continuity once you have built it to the specified design and connect the two computers together.

11. Measure success

The success of any of the connections from Figure 5–7 is determined by the ability to transfer a file from one machine to another. Probably the easiest way to test this is to use a terminal on one computer and to send information from your keyboard to a terminal on the other computer over the direct connection. This will allow you to ensure that data can flow over the connection between the computer.

For ease of reference, assume that you are on a terminal on the Pyramid Technology computer, which is locally connected to an AT&T 3B2 computer. Find out from the systems administrator of the Pyramid computer the port ID that is connected to the 3B2. Repeat the same for the 3B2. The administrator should give you an ID similar to "ttyxxx," where "xxx" is some reference number. This is the port ID that you will use to redirect the terminal's standard input and output for testing. At the Pyramid terminal keyboard, enter the following sequence:

```
cat > /dev/ttyxxx
```

This causes whatever you type to be sent out the port, which is the port on the Pyramid that is connected to the 3B2. At a terminal on the 3B2, issue this command sequence:

```
cat < /dev/ttyxxx
```

Refer to Table 5–57 for this test setup. The data received on port "xxx" of the 3B2, which will arrive from the Pyramid, will be displayed on the terminal on the 3B2. Now proceed to enter information on the keyboard of the terminal on the Pyramid. After you type a line of information and hit the Enter key, the data should appear on the terminal attached to the 3B2. If all is set up properly, CONGRATULATIONS!

If for some reason the data are garbled, consult the options of the ports, speed, parity, character length, and stop bit settings to ensure that they match. If nothing occurs, then recheck your cabling. You should also check with the administrator to ensure that the ports you are using are the proper ports and that the port IDs are consistent with these ports.

Another technique for testing the connection is to set one of the computers (i.e., the 3B2 port) up to issue a login: prompt. This would allow you to use a terminal on the Pyramid, issue a "cu" command to call the 3B2 (even though it is a direct connection), and login to the 3B2. Once logged, you could use the "put" and "take" commands to upload and download files. Prior to your issuing a "cu" command, the port on the 3B2 that is cabled to your Pyramid machine must be properly set up. In particular, it must be set so that it sends you a "login:" prompt. The administrator of the 3B2 can do this for you. As this goes beyond the scope of connection, and into systems administration of UNIX systems, this tutorial module will not cover this piece. However, the systems administrator can assist you in this testing.

The other method is to ''uucp'' a file from one computer to the other over the direct connection. To do this, the systems administrator needs to be involved so that the two UNIX computers know about one another. Refer to *DOSIUNIX Systems*: *Becoming a Super User* for further information about setting up a UNIX machine for ''uucp'' functionality. However, the administrator can set up the appropriate Systems and Devices files so that the two locally connected computers can communicate over the link. As with the use of the ''cu'' command, systems administration is the key to this test of a successful connection. Work with the systems administrator to set this up and test the direct connection. CONGRATULATIONS!

Tutorial Module 5-5: Connecting an IBM PC or PC/AT to an AT&T 3B2

The purpose of this connection is to demonstrate the cable design necessary to connect a DB25 to a modular connector, whereby all input control leads are involved, in particular, Clear to Send, Data Set Ready, and Carrier Detect. This is important, as not all modular ports provided for all these signals, including the adapters used. The AT&T 3B2 is one such animal. Furthermore, the cable design section will show how to construct a modular to 9-pin cable, if an IBM PC/AT or compatible is used instead of a plain PC. This exercise will simply zero in on the cable design piece, not any of the other steps, as the reader can consult the various other tutorial modules to be assured of compatibility, use of terminal emulator to access UNIX, cable construction, SCS port profiles, and how to test this type connection. However, it is important that cable design be understood.

1–6 and 8–11 Refer to separate tutorial modules.

7. Design the cable

Review the SCS port profiles of each device, be it PC, AT, or 3B2. First, this tutorial module will tackle the vanilla PC-to-3B2 connection. This connection can use the terminal/printer adapter discussed at length in Chapter 6. The pinouts for this adapter, provided by AT&T, are as outlined in Table 5–45.

Upon reviewing the port profile for the PC, the reader should note that the PC requires three input leads to be on prior to transmission. They are 5, 6, and 8, or Clear to Send, Data Set Ready, and Data Carrier Detect, respectively. Clear to Send is not provided for in the terminal/printer adapter, which will not allow the PC's communication to function properly. This is the key to this tutorial module. How do we make this adapter support the common terminal emulation software to allow the PC-to-UNIX connection?

Carrier Detect is an output signal provided by the 3B2 whenever the port is active. This lead is an output control signal that should be jumpered to lead 5 to give it life and meaning. On the DB25 side of the terminal printer adapter, the conductor that is crimped to lead 8 should be jumpered to a short piece of insulated wire that can be crimped to lead 5. Note that these leads are inside the adapter on the back side of the DB25 connector. Once this is done, whenever a signal is present on lead 8, the PC will read the same signal on lead 5, allowing

TABLE 5–45. AT&T TERMINAL/ PRINTER ADAPTER (FEMALE DB25 PORT) PINOUTS FROM 3B2

RJ-45 pin		DB25 pin	Function
1	-------	1	Protective Ground
5	⟨------	2	Transmit Data (in)
3	------⟩	3	Received Data (out)
7	-------	7	Signal Ground
4	------⟩	8	Carrier Detect (out)
	|-⟩	6	Data Set Ready (out)
6	⟨---|--	20	Data Terminal Ready (in)

NOTE: The directions are provided as if the other end of the RJ45 cable were attached into a 3B2 I/O port.

TABLE 5–46. MODIFICATION FOR TERMINAL/PRINTER ADAPTER FOR USE WITH PC

RJ-45 pin		DB25 pin	Function
1	-------	1	Protective Ground
5	⟨------	2	Transmit Data (in)
3	------⟩	3	Received Data (out)
7	-------	7	Signal Ground
4	---|-⟩	8	Carrier Detect (out)
	|-⟩	5	Clear to Send (out)
	|-⟩	6	Data Set Ready (out)
6	⟨---|--	20	Data Terminal Ready (in)

the PC's communication software to function accordingly. This is not always an absolute requirement by all communications software, but it should be done for completeness. Table 5–46 outlines this connection.

This completes the design phase of the cable. Proceed with the normal steps 8–11 to check out this connection. We will now proceed with a similar type of connection, without the use of an adapter.

The IBM PC/AT provides its RS232 interface using a 9-pin male connector. The 3B2, as just cited, provides an 8-pin RJ-45-size receptacle. Have you ever tried to get a square peg into a round hole? These two ports are size incompatible. The two ports are signal-level compatible, meaning they conform to the standard but the connectors are different sizes. Furthermore, the pin numbers don't match, requiring much cross over in our design. As before, only the design phase of the steps for connection will be followed.

Reviewing the port profiles for each of the computers, note the pin numbers as summarized in Table 5–47.

There are a number of different ways of designing the cable that will allow these two computers to function together. The standard approach will aid in this design, being with the ground leads. Protective Ground is not supported by the PC/AT, so disregard this lead. However, there are two Signal Ground leads as usual so merely connect these two together, from one end of the cable to the other.

The next category of leads to tackle are the data leads. The rules for cable design advise us to connect "like category" of leads together, as well as connecting "ins" to "outs," and vice versa. Using this logic, we would connect the output data lead from the 3B2, lead 3, to the input data lead at the PC/AT port, lead 2. Repeat the same for the input lead of the 3B2, by connecting it to the AT's output data lead, 3. Table 5–48 summarizes the ground and data lead connections.

The only remaining category of leads are the control leads. These are fairly straightforward in this cable. The best way to design these is to look at the input leads required in the 3B2 port. As it turns out, only one lead, 6, needs to be on for the port to function. Connect this lead through the cable to one of the output control

TABLE 5–47. AT&T 3B2 AND IBM PC/AT SERIAL PORT PINOUTS

Function	3B2 lead #	PC/AT lead #	Function
Protective Ground	1	n/a	
Signal Ground	7	5	Signal Ground
Transmit Data (out)	3	3	Transmit Data (out)
Receive Data (in)	5	2	Receive Data (in)
Data Terminal Ready (out)	4	4	Data Terminal Ready (out)
Data Carrier Detect (in)	6	1	Carrier Detect (in)
		6	Data Set Ready (in)
		7	Request to Send (out)
		8	Clear to Send (in)
		9	Ring Indicator (in)

TABLE 5–48. GROUND AND DATA LEAD DESIGN FOR 3B2-TO-PC/AT CABLE

Function	3B2 lead #	PC/AT lead #	Function
Signal Ground	7 ------- 5		Signal Ground
Transmit Data (out)	3 ------) 2		Receive Data (in)
Receive Data (in)	5 ⟨------ 3		Transmit Data (out)

LEGEND: The "------)" indicates a "cross-over."

leads of the PC/AT port. Pin 4 is a good choice. Hence, when Data Terminal Ready is on in the AT's port, when the port is enabled, then Data Carrier Detect will be on in the 3B2 port.

Next look at the input control leads required at the AT port. First, let's rule out Ring Indicator. This lead is used when a modem is involved to indicate an incoming call. This leaves Clear to Send, Data Set Ready, and Carrier Detect. Somehow the cable should allow for these leads to be turned on. It is most desirable, but not absolutely required, for the remote device to control the status of these leads, so the AT will know if the 3B2 is up and running. Hence, an output control lead from the 3B2 port should be connected to these leads. The 3B2 port only has one output control lead, 4. Connect this through the cable to the AT end. It should be connected to all three AT input control leads as depicted in Table 5–49.

This completes the cable design for the AT&T 3B2-to-IBM PC/AT connection and is summarized in Table 5–50.

The 3B2 end of the cable will be an RJ-45 jack, while the AT end will be a female 9-pin connector. Select a cable that has an RJ-45 jack on one end of it. The cable should be 4-pair cable. If the other end of the cable has another RJ-45 jack on the end of it, cut the jack off. Do all the cross-overs and jumpering at this end of the cable. This will ease the cable construction immensely.

Spend the extra time necessary to know which lead in the cable is lead 1, 2, and so on. Remember that you need to locate lead 1 in the 3B2 port, and then know relative to the portion of the RJ-45 jack at the end of the cable, which conductor aligns with lead 1 of the 3B2 port. Note the color, so you will know this at the other end of the cable. Once lead 1 is found, lay out leads 2–8 with their associated colors. This will be important, after you have cut off the jack at the other end. You will need to the know the lead numbers and associated colors for correct cable construction.

TABLE 5–49. CONTROL LEAD DESIGN FOR 3B2-TO-PC/AT CABLE

Data Carrier Detect (in)	6 ⟨------ 4	Data Terminal Ready (out)
Data Terminal Ready (out)	4 ---:--) 1	Carrier Detect (in)
	:--) 6	Data Set Ready (in)
	:--) 8	Clear to Send (in)

LEGEND: The "⟨------" indicates a cross-over connection from one end of the cable to the other. The "---:--) / :--)" indicates local jumpering of leads on the back side of the connector.

TABLE 5–50. AT&T 3B2-TO-IBM PC/AT COMPLETE CABLE DESIGN

Function	3B2 lead #	PC/AT lead #	Function
Signal Ground	7 ------- 5		Signal Ground
Transmit Data (out)	3 ------) 2		Receive Data (in)
Receive Data (in)	5 ⟨------ 3		Transmit Data (out)
Data Carrier Detect (in)	6 ⟨------ 4		Data Terminal Ready (out)
Data Terminal Ready (out)	4 ---:--) 1		Carrier Detect (in)
	:--) 6		Data Set Ready (in)
	:--) 8		Clear to Send (in)

After you know the colors and lead numbers in the cable, review the female connector to locate pin 1. Once this lead is found, and the other lead numbers are known, construct the cable per the design. Go through steps 8–11 of standard PC connections in the normal fashion to complete this tutorial module. For testing, refer to Tutorial Module 4–2. CONGRATULATIONS!

Tutorial Module 5-6: Connecting an AT&T 3B2 to Another 3B2

In this tutorial module we will connect two multiuser systems together, as depicted in Figure 5–8. This will be a common scenario in office environments. One of the multiuser computers may run the office accounting system, while the other is used for general-purpose office applications of word processing, spreadsheets, and database applications. Users on the accounting system will need access to the files on the other computer. Be it the data kept in the database, or the need to run a spreadsheet, users will need (remote) access to the other computer.

File transfer between two dissimilar computers is another reason for this type of computer. Although the interface may be different between an AT&T 3B2/400 and an Altos, Sperry, or Tandy UNIX system, the concept will be the same. Refer to other tutorial modules for these particulars. However, file transfer can be a solution to media incompatibility for porting programs and files.

Another very important application is electronic mail. This is the computerized ability to send mail between users in a location. Users on both systems need to be able to send information between them. The configuration outlined in Figure 5–8 allows for this mail feature. The other need is resource sharing. An office may have a laser printer attached to the second computer. Users of the first computer should not be restricted from accessing this nice printer. With a connection between the two computer systems, not only can the laser printer be used by all, but also peripherals such as a modem for off-premise communications. Users familiar with the UNIX command "cu" will appreciate this feature. If desired, users accessing one of the computers from a different location with a terminal or PC will be able to access information on the second computer. Security procedures should be put in place to prevent unauthorized access to both systems as well as to individual files.

Tape backup is another justification for this type of connection. Why should you have a tape backup system on both computers? If the users of one computer system need to back up on an occasional basis, then you don't necessarily need a second tape backup unit. With a link between the two systems, however, you can do a file transfer to the machine with the tape unit and then issue the command necessary to perform the backup. If appropriate, this can be done automatically during off-hours. Coordinate the procedures for this with the systems administrator, as this can be a time saver.

The steps we will follow for this tutorial module are common to all our reviews:

STEPS FOR CONNECTION

1. Determine compatibility (should it work?).
2. Determine signs of success.
3. Determine the type of connector used.
4. Determine gender of the ports.
5. Determine which leads (pins) are provided by each device.
6. Determine which leads are required to be on by each device.
7. Design the cable.
8. Build the cable.
9. Test the cable for continuity.
10. Cable the two systems together with the cable.
11. From step 2, measure success.

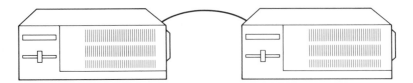

Figure 5–8. Back-to-back multiuser micros.

1. Determine compatibility

The AT&T 3B2 series of computers offers RS232-compatible signals for supporting character-oriented devices. The UNIX operating system governs the 3B2 environment. UNIX was originally designed to support asynchronous terminals. As each of the ports on the two separate 3B2s supports asynchronous devices, they should be compatible. Review and fill in the SCS port profiles with information from the user's manual. With a multiuser system, the pertinent information may be scattered among multiple manuals. However, it is worthwhile to collect it and compile it into a single profile. Table 5–51 outlines a partially complete AT&T 3B2/400 port profile. The common options between the two systems should be either 9600 or 19,200 bps, 7 data bits, 1 stop bit, even parity, full duplex, and asynchronous mode.

2. Determine signs of success

Once connected, there are many ways of testing our success between the systems. Perhaps the easiest means is to be on a terminal at one multiuser microsystem, or MUM. At this terminal, the user should be able to issue some commands to have information go from the local 3B2/400 to the other 3B and be displayed on a terminal attached to the second 3B2/400. Figure 5–8 depicts conceptually the scenario for measuring our success. The UNIX "cu" command allows a terminal user to "call UNIX," or call another computer system. If a systems administrator is involved to set up both the ports on the MUMs, this can be used to test the connection. For this and other systems administration functions, the reader is encouraged to consult the user's manuals or read *DOS/ UNIX Systems: Becoming a Super User*. This tutorial module will hint at where to set up the port, but not do thorough in-depth administration procedures.

There is a very simple approach to measuring our success. it will be used here in this tutorial module. Using simple redirection commands, common to all UNIX systems, our ability to send information entered at one keyboard to a device on the second computer can be tested. If we can output from one device, through both systems, to another device, then success is obtained.

3. Determine type of connector

4. Determine gender of ports

Consulting either the user's documentation or viewing the 3B2 port itself, the reader can surmise that the serial port is not a DB25-size connector. Rather, it is an 8-pin modular port. The port is of female gender. Typically, when dealing with modular connections, gender is not always spoken of. The connections are referred to as sockets or jacks, or RJ cables and connectors. This is due to the telephone company's labeling of RJ-11, RJ-45, and RJ-8 connectors. RJ-11 are 2-pair or four conductor/wire cables. RJ-12 are six conductor (3-pair). RJ-45 are 4-pair connectors and cables and contain eight conductors. We will, however, discuss male as being the jack and female as being the receptacle or socket. The ports on the 3B2 are RJ-45 receptacles. Connecting the two 3B2s will present little concern when actually designing, building, and connecting them with cables. However, when connecting a device, such as a terminal, printer, or modem, that has a DB25-size connector, adapters must be used that convert RJ-45 ports to DB25. Refer to Chapter 6 for a detailed treatment of this discussion. For this tutorial module, modular cables will suffice, as both ports of concern are RJ-45 receptacles. Our cable will need 8-pin jacks on each end of it. Update the port profiles with this information.

5. Determine leads (pins) provided by each device

6. Determine leads required to be on

Consulting the documentation is the easiest method of determining which leads are provided by and required by the 3B2 I/O modular port. Another technique is to use a VOM. The VOM technique is discussed in Tutorial Module 5–1, as it may be applicable to other computer systems and devices. Refer to that section for a step-by-step approach to performing port analysis involving RJ-type ports. A normal break-out box will not work for these types of port, as a BOB needs a DB25 connector. However, BOBs are being offered that do have 8-pin connectors on them instead of, or in conjunction with, DB25 connectors. Regardless of technique, manual or documentation review, Table 5–52 outlines the leads provided by the 3B2 I/O expansion board ports.

7. Design the cable

With the foregoing pinout summary, you can begin to design the cable. The best way to work toward the design is to separate the modular pinouts by category as you would standard DB25 pinouts. Table 5–53 does this for you, including both 3B2s for future design reference.

TABLE 5–51. AT&T 3B2/400 PORT PROFILE

Computer Port Profile

Underline if supported; circle if selected.

Model: 3B2/400 _____ Vendor: AT&T _____ Port: I/O ports __

Port type: <u>serial</u> parallel

Port: DB25   9-pin   5-pin   <u>8-pin/modular</u> 20mA Centronics

Gender: male   <u>female</u>

Pin #	Function	Direction	Pin #	Function	Direction
1	Protective Ground	to from n/a	14	_____	to from n/a
2	_____	to <u>from</u> n/a	15	_____	to from n/a
3	Transmit Data	to <u>from</u> n/a	16	_____	to from n/a
4	Data Terminal Ready	to <u>from</u> n/a	17	_____	to from n/a
5	Receive Data	<u>to</u> from n/a	18	_____	to from n/a
6	Data Carrier Detect	<u>to</u> from n/a	19	_____	to from n/a
7	Signal Ground	to from <u>n/a</u>	20	_____	to from n/a
8	_____	to from n/a	21	_____	to from n/a
9	_____	to from n/a	22	_____	to from n/a
10	_____	to from n/a	23	_____	to from n/a
11	_____	to from n/a	24	_____	to from n/a
12	_____	to from n/a	25	_____	to from n/a
13	_____	to from n/a			

Complete the next section only with 36-pin cinch connector.

26	_____	to from n/a	27	_____	to from n/a
28	_____	to from n/a	29	_____	to from n/a
30	_____	to from n/a	31	_____	to from n/a
32	_____	to from n/a	33	_____	to from n/a
34	_____	to from n/a	35	_____	to from n/a
36	_____	to from n/a			

Flow control technique: <u>XON/XOFF</u> ENQ/ACK STX/ETX Hardware _____

Leads that must be on: 5 6 <u>8</u> 20 __ __ __

Options:
   Speeds: 110 <u>300 600 1200 1800 2400 4800</u> ⬭9600⬭ 19.2 56k _____
   Parity: ⬭even⬭ odd space <u>mark</u> <u>none</u>
   Char-length:⬭7⬭8 ____
   # stop bits: ⬭1⬭ <u>1.5</u> <u>2</u>
   Line-ending sequence: cr lf cr/lf cr/lf/lf
   Disconnect sequence: EOT   DEL   ~. _____

	Mode: async sync isoch		Sync timing leads:	

#	Function		Direction
15	n/a	_____	to from
17	n/a	_____	to from
24	n/a	_____	to from

Notes: This port is a serial port with RS232-compatible signals. Although it is modular, adapters are used to convert it to DB25-size connectors for DTE and DCE connections. Consult a separate port profile sheet for these ports converted to terminal/printer or acu (automatic calling unit)/modem ports with the adapters.

TABLE 5–52. AT&T 3B2 I/O PORT-PROVIDED LEADS (MODULAR PORT)

Function	3B2 lead #	
Protective Ground	1	
Transmit Data (out)	3	
Data Terminal Ready (out)	4	(will be on if the port is enabled)
Receive Data (in)	5	
Data Carrier Detect (in)	6	(should be on for the port to communicate)
Signal Ground	7	

NOTES: It is important to note that these pinouts are those of the port on the computer itself, not those provided by a cable or adapter that may be connected to the 3B2. This is pointed out because AT&T provides different cables and adapters that cross over some of the leads. This is the raw modular receptacle on the computer itself. The direction and functions may appear awkward if you bring into play some of these adapters. This tutorial module will deal with the raw port for now for ease of understanding. A separate section will deal with the various adapters provided by AT&T, TRW, AMP, Black Box, and Misco.

From the foregoing it is worthwhile to note that only six conductors/leads will be required. However, do not assume that an RJ-12 cable, with 3-pair, will work here. The conductors may not align properly with the leads actually in the ports. It is better to work with RJ-45 jacks and cables and do the jumpering within the cable.

Also, note that we have on a single input control lead and output control lead to deal with. This should simplify our design substantially. The rules for cable design are not different, regardless of the size of connector. They are outlined as follows:

CABLE DESIGN: GENERAL RULES

1. Connect like categories of leads together.
2. Always connect an ''out'' to an ''in'' and an ''in'' to an ''out.''
3. A lead that is input may be connected to another lead that is an input only if both of these are connected to an output lead.
4. In synchronous connections, only use one source of timing. (Because the 3B2-to-3B2 connection is asynchronous, this point is not applicable.)

The ground leads should be tackled first, as they are straightforward. The Protective Ground leads should be connected straight through from one end of the cable to the other. The same holds true for Signal Ground leads. We will have a conductor that connects lead 1 at one end of the cable to lead 1 at the other end, repeating this for lead 7.

TABLE 5–53. AT&T 3B2 PINOUTS SEPARATED BY CATEGORY

Function	3B2 lead #	3B2 lead #	Function
Ground			
Protective Ground	1	1	Protective Ground
Signal Ground	7	7	Signal Ground
Data			
Transmit Data (out)	3	3	Transmit Data (out)
Receive Data (in)	5	5	Receive Data (in)
Control			
Data Terminal Ready (out)	4	4	Data Terminal Ready (out)
Data Carrier Detect (in)	6	6	Data Carrier Detect (in)

TABLE 5–54. AT&T 3B2-TO-3B2 MUM CABLE DESIGN FOR MODULAR PORTS

Function	3B2 lead #		3B2 lead #	Function
Ground				
Protective Ground	1	-------	1	Protective Ground
Signal Ground	7	-------	7	Signal Ground
Data				
Transmit Data (out)	3	------⟩	5	Receive Data (in)
Receive Data (in)	5	⟨------	3	Transmit Data (out)
Control				
Data Terminal Ready (out)	4	------⟩	6	Data Carrier Detect (in)
Data Carrier Detect (in)	6	⟨------	4	Data Terminal Ready (out)

LEGEND: The ''-------'' indicates a straight-through connection from one end of the cable to the other. The ''------)'' implies a cross-over. Even though only six conductors are required, an RJ-45-size jack should be used to build this cable.

The data leads are also fairly straightforward. Noting that the two interfaces are the same, and that the output data lead is 3, while the input data lead is 5, the design is simplified. Applying rules 1 and 2, you will connect the output data lead from one computer to the input data lead of the other, repeating this for the other computer's output data lead. Table 5–54 lays out this design.

The control leads are normally the most difficult category of leads to deal with. However, with this interface, the same logic applied to the data leads prevails. Connect the output control lead (pay no attention to the function description) from one computer to the input control lead at the other computer. Repeat this from the other computer's perspective. The functions may be confusing, so ignore them for this tutorial module. The important concept is the direction of the control leads. With this design, a computer will know if the other one is powered on with its port enabled. Table 5–54 outlines the completed 3B2-to-3B2 cable design.

8. Build the cable

With the foregoing design in mind, you are ready to build a cable. The first step is to determine the length of cable necessary to connect the two computers. It is hoped that the two computer systems will be kept in the same general area. The RS232 standard suggests not exceeding 50 feet between the two devices. You should try and adhere to this if at all possible. If not, try to get extended distance cables and ensure that the cable does not get laid near to any heavy machinery that might cause interference. Such equipment includes other computers, air conditioners, heaters, pumps, and compressors.

Note that only six conductors are required. This implies that you can use an RJ-12 ''cord'' but not an RJ-12 jack. An 8-pin jack is required, so you may align the conductors with the leads. This tutorial module will assume that you are using an RJ-45 jack and cable (eight conductors). Just as with the DB25 connectors, it is important that you note the lead/pin number in both the port as well as the cable. The relative pin numbers must match up. Figure 5–9 lays out the pin numbering of the 3B2 receptacle port.

When viewing the port, with the receptacle piece facing you, and the wires of the receptacle on the top side, the pins are numbered 1–8, from right to left. Hence the jack that plugs into the receptacle is just the opposite, with pins 1–8 from left to right when it is facing you and pins on the top.

Review the notes associated with Figure 5–9 as it is important to note the bearing of the pin numbering. Figure 5–10 lays out the corresponding pin number of the cable and jack. With the known relative numbering of the pin numbers, you conceptually want to design the cable with the appropriate cross-over.

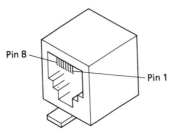

Figure 5–9. AT&T 3B2 receptacle pin number.

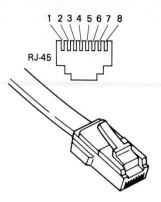

1 2 3 4 5 6 7 8

RJ-45

Figure 5–10.   Pin numbering of an RJ-45 jack with cable.

A couple of different techniques may be used to construct the cable. In this exercise, we will make the cable from scratch using connectors and a crimping tool. One of the easiest methods is to lay out the colors of the wires in the cable. The cable the author used was flat with eight conductors in it. The conductors were as given in Table 5–55.

Not all RJ-45-type cables will have the same color scheme. Lay out the cable per the cable you have. The reason for this is to ease the actual straight-through and cross-over conductors. The goal is to lay out the colors in the correct order at each cable end before crimping on the connector/jack.

Cross-reference the color layout with the actual desired cable design from Table 5–55. If you are holding the cable ends, side by side, with the same color of lead on the right, then you can prepare the cable ends. Table 5–56 lays out the order in which to put the conductors prior to crimping the jack on the cable.

The RJ-45 male jacks must be put on in a certain fashion. Because we have laid out the colored conductors in a certain order, the first color, blue, or pin 1 must be inserted into the jack so that this conductor aligns with the appropriate pin 1 in the jack. This is imperative so that when we finally plug the jack into the receptacle of the 3B2, the pins align properly. Figure 5–11 shows which way to position the jack onto the cable for proper crimping. Once aligned, crimp the jack onto the cable using a modular jack crimping tool. Do the same for the other end of the cable. Once completed, it is worthwhile to document the layout of this cable and somehow fasten it to the modular cord itself for future reference.

TABLE 5–55.   RJ-45 CABLE

Wire #	Color
1	Blue
2	Orange
3	Black
4	Red
5	Green
6	Yellow
7	Brown
8	Silver/gray

TABLE 5–56.   COLOR-CODED LAYOUT OF THE TWO ENDS OF THE CABLE

	Cable end A	Cable end B
COLOR	S BN Y G R BK OR BL	S BN R BK Y G OR BL

LEGEND: s = silver, bn = brown, y = yellow, g = green, r = red, bk = black, or = orange, bl = blue. Your colors will probably differ, so lay them out in a similar fashion. The viewing of the cable ends is from right to left, to align with our pin numbers. Once laid out in this fashion, you can crimp on the connectors.

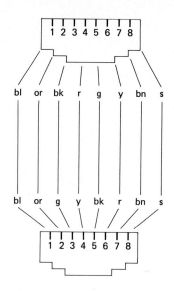

Figure 5–11. Jack and pin layout for modular cable construction.

9. Test for continuity

Use a VOM or other standard technique to test for continuity within the newly constructed cable. Your findings should match those of Table 5–54 and Figure 5–11. If not, cut off the connector from the problem end of the cable, repeat the layout step, and recrimp.

10. Cable the two systems together

Once you have the the correct cable constructed, the two computers should be cabled together. Each end of this cable is a mirror image of the other end, so you may connect either end into either computer system.

11. Measure success

For the more sophisticated user, success could be tested using the "cu" command. With the ports set up properly, a user at one computer could "call UNIX," establishing a session with the second UNIX computer. This requires the proper entries to set up such files as the "inittab," "Systems," and "Devices" files. Consult the UNIX computer's systems administrator before attempting to test the connection in this fashion.

The simplest method is to attempt a conversation between two terminals, each connected to one of the 3B2s. Figure 5–12 depicts the arrangement.

If our connection is complete, then this should be a fairly straightforward test. Within the UNIX environment, ports are defined on a system in some directory of the computer. Most standard UNIX systems have the ports

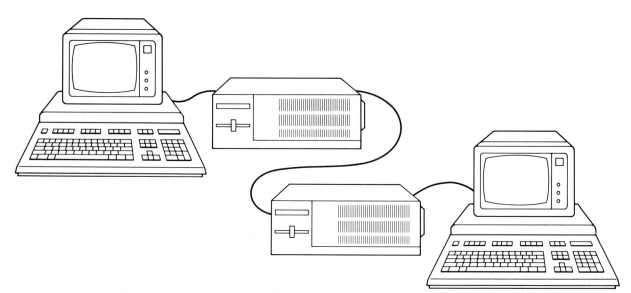

Figure 5–12. Terminal-to-terminal communication through two UNIX computers.

listed in the "/dev" directory. Normally, terminals are listed under this directory as "ttyxxx," with the "xxx" being a specific number. The best way to confirm this is to display that directory to get a feel for the ports/devices on the system.

At the terminal keyboard attached to 3B2 A, login. Issue the following commands to get a listing of the "/dev" directory of devices.

ls −l /dev   followed by a return

This should list the contents of the "/dev" directory. If it does not, then be sure that this is a valid directory on your system. If not, ask the administrator where the "devices" are listed, and issue the "ls" command for that directory. Note the "ttyxxx" devices listed. To find out the port to which you are connected, a UNIX command in normally used. Enter the command "who am i" or "who," followed by a return. These commands will provide you a listing of the port that you are logged into, or a listing of all users that are logged in at the current time, respectively. Locate your login in the listing, and note the "tty" devices that you are using. Make a mental notation of this.

Repeat this exercise at a terminal on the second UNIX system. You now know which specific ports that you want to communicate between. The only missing pieces are the ports that contain the cable between the two computers. The systems administrator will normally assign the ports for connecting the two computers together. Ask him or her for this information, and make a notation of the "tty" device. You should now have four different "tty" ports that you know of. We will refer to these as terminal A port, 3B2 A port, 3B2 B port, and terminal B port. An assumption will be made that the corresponding "tty" port numbers will be as follows: tty001, tty002, tty003, tty004. Your system will more than likely differ from this, so adjust accordingly.

If you are not familiar with the redirection commands ")" and "⟨," consult any of a host of UNIX books. When you are logged into a UNIX system, there are a couple of concepts with which you should be familiar. Two of the most prominent are "standard input" and "standard output." Standard input is a term applied to the normal source of input for a UNIX process or activity. Standard output is the normal place to put the output from a UNIX process or activity. Bringing this close to home, when you are logged into a UNIX system on a terminal, your keyboard provides the standard input to the UNIX system. Your display/CRT is the standard output for your login session. When you input a command, such as a sort, UNIX will send the results of the sort to the standard output, your display, unless you specify otherwise. The sort routine will sort information provided from the standard input, unless you tell it to get the data to sort from a file or elsewhere.

If you understand these concepts, then be aware that UNIX provides the ability to "redirect" the output or input to something other than the standard input and output devices. For example, the sorted data will probably need to be saved in a file. Using the ")" symbol, you can send the results of the Sort command to a file instead of the standard output, your terminal. You could also send the results to another device, such as a printer, or another computer attached to a port.

Just as you redirect the output from a process to a device attached to one of the ports on 3B2 A, you can also redirect the input to a terminal on either of the computers. Using the "⟨" symbol with the appropriate commands, input can be redirected. Redirection will allow us to test our 3B2-to-3B2 connection. We will redirect the input to allow communication between two terminals attached to the connected 3B2s.

Login to the 3B2 A computer using terminal A as you normally would. Once successfully logged in, skip over to terminal B and login to 3B2 B (see Table 5–57). Armed with the port names, we can now test out our computer-to-computer connection or perhaps terminals-through-computers connection. The next section outlines the steps for testing the systems.

You could have just as easily redirected the information from a terminal on computer A across to a printer on computer B. The important point is that you are to communicate across the 3B2-to-3B2 connection. If you are successful with this, you should try the "cu" between machines, as this will be useful for day-to-day operations. Get the systems administrator involved for this aspect of testing.

If the information does not show up on terminal B, recheck your cabling. First, recheck your cable construction for proper design and good continuity. If the two computers are cabled together correctly, be sure that you are able to login successfully to each respective computer. You should first be convinced that your terminal A-to-3B2 A and terminal B-to-3B2 B connections work properly. If you still cannot perform the sequence, consult your systems administrator. It is possible that ports tty002 and tty003 are not set up properly. They need to be set up with the common options outlined in step 1 of this tutorial module. Ensure that the ports have been properly set up on both UNIX systems. After repeated unsuccessful attempts to redirect data, and thorough checking and rechecking of options and UNIX system entries, consult your vendors.

TABLE 5–57. TESTING TWO BACK-TO-BACK UNIX SYSTEMS

Terminal A input	Terminal B input	Results (not on screen)
cat ⟩ /dev/tty002		Data input at this keyboard will be output to 3B2 A's port tty002, which is the port that we cabled to the other 3B2.
	cat ⟨ /dev/tty003	Output destined for this terminal will come from tty003 or 3B2 B's port cabled to 3B2 A.
Now is the time for good men and women to come to the aid of this connection.		The information input on terminal A's keyboard, "Now is . . . connection," should appear on terminal B's screen. CONGRATULATIONS!

Tutorial Module 5-7: Connecting Laptop Computers

This tutorial module will be different from most of the others in that the use of laptops will be featured. One of the benefits of laptops is their portability. This portability affords the user opportunities to connect his or her portable computer to many different systems, including both computer systems and phone systems. This tutorial module will highlight various cables and connectors that make it easier for the laptop user to connect a system and communicate with others.

The steps and rules of connections will not be covered here, as the reader can simply refer to a similar tutorial module where a PC or XT is involved. For example, the NEC MultiSpeed laptop is IBM PC compatible and provides a DB25 port just like those used in a PC/XT. To connect the NEC to other devices, refer to modules that feature the connection of an IBM PC or XT to other devices. The connection of the NEC will be the same as the PC or XT proceedings.

Due to incompatible floppy disk sizes between some laptops and desktops, laptops will be connected frequently "back to back" for file transfers. The cables used for this can be constructed in a number of different ways as discussed in the other tutorial modules. Depending on how completely you want to be equipped, you could end up having many different cables to do simple tasks. These tasks include connecting the laptop to another desktop or laptop, modem, or hotel telephone jack.

To this author, portable computers, or laptops, are heavy enough without the extra equipment that may need to be kept with the laptop to make it complete. The user should be able to travel with a minimal amount of equipment beyond the laptop itself. The author has some recommendations that will allow for a minimal amount of cabling hardware to be lugged around with the laptop. The laptops discussed here are the NEC MultiSpeed (with a DB25P serial port) and the Toshiba 3100 (with a 9-pin male serial port). You will learn how to use a single cable for computer-to-computer connections, computer-to-modem connections, and telephone connections using a single modular cord.

First, let's consider connecting the laptop to a desktop. Assume that a laptop has a DB25S female connector just as an IBM PC/XT does. The NEC MultiSpeed will be featured here. This laptop has $3\frac{1}{2}$-inch floppies, compared with the $5\frac{1}{4}$-inch floppies on the user's desktop that sits at home or office. The need to exchange data is immense and increasing. The best way to allow this data exchange is through a "back-to-back" connection between the laptop and the desktop using the serial ports. A standard null modem cable will work here, but it can be bulky. Refer to other tutorial modules for some standard null modem cables. The next section covers cable building using minimal materials for light weight and compactness.

Many adapters available today have a DB25 connector on one side and an 8-pin modular receptacle on the other side. AT&T uses them on its 3B2 series computers. TRW, Black Box, and AMP, to name just a few, offer such adapters. By using these adapters along with a standard telephone modular cord like that in your house, you can connect the two computer systems. Acquire two such adapters with a female DB25s connector on one side and the 8-pin receptacle on the other. It really does not matter what the adapters' internal connections are, as you will be modifying them.

The normal PC-to-PC cable can be constructed in a number of different manners. The key is to ensure that

TABLE 5–58. PC AND LAPTOP
PINOUTS

Lead	Function
2	Transmit Data (out)
3	Receive Data (in)
4	Request to Send (out)
5	Clear to Send (in)
6	Data Set Ready (in)
7	Signal Ground (n/a)
8	Data Carrier Detect (in)
20	Data Terminal Ready (out)

NOTE: Leads 5, 6, and 8 should be on
for data transmission to occur.

the ground, data, and control leads of both computer ports are taken care of. Table 5–58 lays out the pinouts of the IBM PC and NEC ports. Both computers offer the same interface.

Armed with this information, many different null modem cables can be built. Our goal is to optimize the cable requirements. Hence, we will lay out a cable design that uses the minimal number of leads, yet allows for maximum functionality. The simplest null modem cable requires only three leads: Signal Ground, and the two data leads. Hence, a simple cable design only requires three conductors in the cable from end to end. A standard modular cord, the same as that found in your home to connect a telephone to a wall outlet, has four conductors. We will use this type cord, as it will also serve as the cable to connect a laptop modem to a wall outlet in the home, office, or hotel room.

How can we use a 2-pair (four-wire) cord to connect our 4-pair (eight-wire) adapters? The four-wire cord snaps right into the eight-wire modular jack on the adapter. It does, however, only make contact with the inside four leads in the jack of the adapter. Make note of this as you can modify the modular-to-DB25S adapter to use only these leads. The easiest way to work with these leads is to note their colors. Pick the wires on the inside of the adapter and log their colors. Refer to these colors when the modifications are made to the adapters.

The simplest cable design required only three leads. This exercise will allow for four leads as the adapters will be designed to work with a stand-alone modem as well as back-to-back computers. Refer to the other tutorial modules to discover how actually to design cables. Table 5–59 summarizes the cable design that we need to achieve using two DB25s modular adapters and a single 2-pair telephone cord.

TABLE 5–59. BACK-TO-BACK CABLE DESIGN FOR DESKTOP PC-
TO-LAPTOP (OR ANOTHER PC)

Computer 1			Computer 2
Function	Lead	Lead	Function
Transmit Data (out)	2 ------⟩	3	Receive Data (in)
Receive Data (in)	3 ⟨------	2	Transmit Data (out)
Signal Ground (n/a)	7 -------	7	Signal Ground (n/a)
Data Carrier Detect (in)	8 ⟨------	4	Request to Send (out)
Clear to Send (in)	5⟨-|	|-⟩ 5	Clear to Send (in)
Data Set Ready (in)	6⟨-|	|-⟩ 6	Data Set Ready (in)
Data Terminal Ready (out)	20 --|	|-⟩ 8	Data Carrier Detect (in)
		|-- 20	Data Terminal Ready (out)

NOTE: If you don't need a cable for a modem, remove the connection between lead 8 of computer 1 and lead 4 of computer 2, and duplicate the connection of leads 20, 5, 6, and 8 for computer 1, as in computer 2. The purpose for this design will become clearer when an adapter is made to use the same adapter for computer 1, the 2-pair modular cord, and a different adapter to connect a modem. If you need a PC-to-stand-alone modem (not an internal modem), then use this design.

TABLE 5–60. MODULAR JACK
ADAPTER LEADS

Leads	Important leads (note colors)	
X X X X	X X	(red green)
X X X X	X X	(blue black)

NOTE: For our purposes, we will label the leads red, green, blue, black. Your lead colors will more than likely vary, so make a notation for cross-reference.

To build the cable to utilize only four wires, remove the cover from the DB25s-to-modular adapters. We will work with the adapter for computer 1 first. Look at the back, or inside, of the modular jack outlet. Locate the innermost four wires. This could be difficult, as the leads are staggered atop one another. Table 5–60 highlights the leads that interest you. Label this adapter for easy reference, such as "Main Computer."

Disconnect the leads that go to the DB25 side of the adapter, as you will be modifying the cross-overs and jumperings. Using the color of leads cited in the Table 5–60 notes, connect the red wire to lead 2 of the DB25 connector, the green wire to lead 3, the blue wire to lead 8, and the black wire to lead 7. Now use a piece of insulated wire to connect leads 5, 6, and 20 together to product a resulting adapter as depicted in Table 5–61. Label this adapter for easy reference, such as "Main Computer."

Repeat this for the other side to match the layout. Table 5–62 highlights the resulting adapter that should be labeled "Secondary Computer."

TABLE 5–61. MODULAR-TO-DB25
ADAPTER CABLING FOR MAIN PC

DB25 lead		Modular lead	
2	----	X X	(red) (green)
3	------	|	
8	----	X X	(blue) (black)
7	-------	|	
5	--|		
6	--|		
20	--|		

TABLE 5–62. MODULAR-TO-
DB25 ADAPTER CABLING FOR
SECONDARY PC

DB25 lead		Modular lead	
3	----	X X	(red) (green)
2	------	|	
4	----	X X	(blue) (black)
7	------	|	
5	--|		
6	--|		
8	--|		
20	--|		

NOTE: Leads 2 and 3 are switched as compared to the other adapter. Furthermore, lead 4 is connected to the blue conductor. Also, 5, 6, 8, and 20 are connected together versus only 5, 6, and 20 in the main adapter.

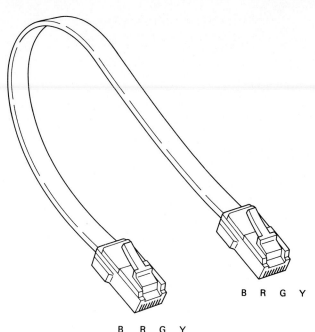

Figure 5–13. 2-pair straight-through conductors.

Check the adapters for continuity to ensure that you have constructed them to produce the lead layouts as in Table 5–62. Once you have achieved the proper cabling, replace the covers back onto the adapters. Now locate a 2-pair modular cord that offers four wires that are straight-through, from end to end. Some have the conductors crossed within them. The easiest way to check these cables to ensure straight-through conductors is to look at both ends, side by side. The colors of the leads should be in the same order from left to right, if the cord ends are held in the exact same positions. Figure 5–13 depicts how to hold the cables to ensure straight-through conductors. If the two cable ends are held in the same positions, the colors should match from left to right.

Should the conductor layout not match from left to right, with the jacks held in the same positions, then you do not have a straight-through cord. A different cord should be used that is straight through. If all the conductors are the same color, not allowing for a comparison, it is a good idea to perform a continuity check with a VOM (or other tool). The same correlation of leads, from left to right, should be produced if it is a straight-through cord.

Now the cable construction is complete. The reader has the cable necessary to connect two PCs, either two desktop PCs or a laptop and a desktop. Different-length 2-pair modular cords can be used as required. However, Figure 5–14 depicts the resulting cable. Three lightweight and compact pieces were required. The laptop user will appreciate these as they take up less space in their carrying case.

The other connection typically required of a laptop owner is one of connecting the laptop to a stand-alone modem. Our intent here is to maximize the cabling by reducing the size and numbers of cables required. Because

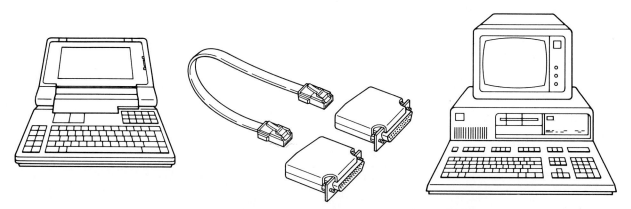

Figure 5–14. DB25-to-modular adapters for PC-to-PC connection.

Emulation

TABLE 5–63. MODEM DB25P-
TO-MODULAR ADAPTER FOR
LAPTOP

DB25 lead		Modular lead		
2	----	X X		(red) (green)
3	------			
8	----	X X		(blue) (black)
7	------	|		
4	--|			
6	--|			
20	--|			

NOTE: Leads 2, 3, 8, and 7 are connected
to the same-color conductors as are those
in the "Main Computer" adapter. This will
allow a straight-through connection of these
leads. Also, pin 6 from the modem will
keep its own leads 4 and 20 on by these
jumperings.

most modems are equipped with a female DB25s port, we need a DB25P to modular adapter. If this adapter is properly constructed, we can use it in conjunction with the "Main Computer" adapter and modular cord. This will allow us to have a PC-to-modem cord without forcing us to carry a dedicated cord.

The reader should acquire a DB25P (male)-to-modular adapter. Remove the cover, disconnect the wires from the back of the DB25 port, and note the colors of the innermost four conductors. Assuming that the colors are the same as before in the other adapters, build the adapter to match the layout of Table 5–63.

Whenever lead 6 is on from the modem, leads 4 and 20 will also be on. If your modem does not provide, as an output signal, lead 6, then locate another outbound control lead. Usually, either lead 5 or 6 will be outbound control leads. If leads 4 and 20 are not required to be on by the modem, such as with the Hayes Smartmodem 1200, then you can ignore the 4, 6, 20 jumpering. Once these jumperings are in place, check the adapter for continuity. Replace the adapter cover and label this adapter as "Modem Adapter."

You now have a complete cable set up to connect the laptop, or other PC, to a stand-alone modem. Figure 5–15 depicts the connection.

With the three adapters, "Main," Secondary," and "Modem," along with the 2-pair modular telephone cord, the reader has obtained a multitude of cabling options with a single cord. Furthermore, this same 2-pair cord is the same type used to connect a modem to a modular phone outlet. A second modular cord can be carried if a stand-alone modem will be used frequently. For those laptop owners with built-in modems, a single modular phone cord can be carried for those back-to-back PC connections, as well as to connect your internal modem to the wall outlet.

What about those connections involving DB25-to-DB9 (AT-type) ports? You can acquire an 8-pin to 9-pin adapter, much like the DB25 to modular one. Merely repeat the jumperings and cross-overs to accommodate the

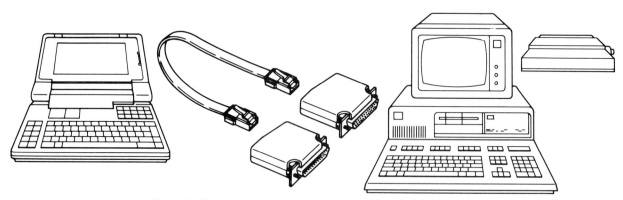

Figure 5–15. Laptop-to-modem connection using modular adapters.

9-pin layout of an AT port. Table 4–18 lists this as it was covered in Tutorial Module 4–3. You now have ultimate flexibility between laptops and desktops.

Brooklyn Bridge

The Brooklyn Bridge from White Crane Systems is a set of programs that lets you smoothly integrate your laptop computers into your normal IBM-PC office environment. It accomplishes this by hooking together a laptop and desktop computer through their serial ports and letting you use the disk drives of one machine from the other. You have learned how to build a cable to connect two such computers together. A cable does, however, come with this software package. You can sit at your desktop PC and copy files to the laptop disks. Or you can type on your laptop and access both the floppy disks and the hard disk on the desktop PC.

More than that, the Bridge allows you to read and write all the DOS devices. Besides the floppy drive, hard disks, and RAM disks, this includes printers, plotters, a clock/calendar, or any other DOS device. For example, you can use the Bridge to print a file from your laptop computer on a printer to your desktop PC.

TABLE 5–64. DISK DRIVE DESIGNATIONS FOR LAPTOP-TO-DESKTOP CONNECTIONS

Laptop disk	Desktop disk
A: B: C:	D: E: F:

NOTE: From the laptop keyboard, the user would access drives A–F. The Brooklyn Bridge would access all of them, as if they were on your laptop. Drives A and B would be the laptop floppies, and the C drive could be a RAM disk. Drive D would be the desktop's floppy drive A, with drive E being floppy drive B. The hard disk would be accessed by denoting drive F:. The reverse, using a desktop keyboard, can also be set up.

Because the Bridge operates as a device driver under MS-DOS, its operations are transparent to the user. The remote drives, as depicted in Table 5–64, simply appear as the next available drive letters on the machine you are using. You can use standard DOS commands with the remote drives just like your regular drives. The command ''COPY A:AUTOEXEC.BAT F:'' will copy the autoexec.bat file on the laptop's floppy drive A: onto the desktop's hard disk drive. You can COPY, DEL, DIR, CHKDSK, TYPE, or use a file in any program. The hardcopy devices can also be accessed.

This author uses The Brooklyn Bridge frequently on the NEC MultiSpeed laptop computer. A lot of this text was prepared on an airplane, in a hotel room, and under a shade tree. Upon return to the stable environment of an office, the cable was placed between the two systems, and the files transferred onto the hard disk of the desktop, and also to the desktop's floppy for backup. The Brooklyn Bridge can replace communication software programs for file transfer purposes. Some of the Comm software has problems transferring files with ''nulls'' embedded in the file, causing file lengths to be different between files. The Brooklyn Bridge transfers them with ease to create an exact copy of the file.

If you have a desktop and laptop system, you will need to pay special attention to the files and the latest version of them. The connection is so easy between the two systems that you may accidentally copy an older-version file and wipe out the latest edition. An easy means of circumventing this is to do a directory listing of the file system on both systems, sorting them alphabetically by the date of the file. A command line that accomplishes this is ''dir | sort /+24.'' This command will list the standard MS-DOS directory sorted by the date field. The user can then visually compare the files to determine which ones need to be copied.

COMPUTER INTERFACING: MOST FREQUENTLY ASKED QUESTIONS

Question 1.   The manufacturer of a computer states that the RS232 cables can only be run up to 50 feet. Is there a way to extend this distance without losing any data?

Answer 1.   The manufacturer is indicating that its port conforms to the RS232-C standard, which recommends a maximum distance of 50 feet of cable between devices. The reason for limited distance is signal levels, which fade over distance due to loss of signal strength, interference, etc. Vendors offer extended distance cables that support distances much greater than 50 feet. These cables have extra shielding that reduces signal loss. Hence greater distance is possible.

Question 2.   Is there a single cable that will allow a PC to work with any other device? Why won't one cable work?

Answer 2.   The RS232 standard was established for the connection of DTE and DCE devices. Normally modems were connected to a computer or terminals using RS232 interfaces. With the advent of minicomputers and microcomputers, devices such as terminals and printers were locally connected to computers using the RS232 interface. The cable necessary to connect two local devices depends on whether a device's port emulates DTE or DCE.

Also, printers using hardware flow control with serial interfaces, don't all use the same lead for flow control. One, four, eleven, nineteen, or twenty of the leads could be used. Hence no one cable can meet all the possibilities.

Question 3.   When an IBM PC or compatible has both a serial and a parallel port, how can a user know the difference?

Answer 3.   The serial port on a PC or compatible board is always male. The parallel port is female. In the case of an IBM PC/AT or compatible, the serial port is a 9-pin male connector, while the parallel port is a 25-pin parallel port.

Question 4.   What is systems administration or systems generation?

Answer 4.   These are techniques for defining the parameters necessary to make a computer support attached devices. Systems administration is the term predominantly used for minicomputers or PCs running UNIX systems. System generation refers to the similar setup that occurs in mainframes.

Question 5.   Most back-to-back connections require a null modem cable. How can a computer-to-terminal connection use a straight-through cable?

Answer 5.   A straight-through cable is used to connect a computer to a modem, or a DTE device to a DCE device. Hence, the computer is emulating DTE and the terminal emulating DCE, or vice versa. Many computer manufacturers define their ports to emulate DCE ports so terminal connections can use ribbon cables for connections.

Question 6.   When do I need a protocol converter?

Answer 6.   Devices communicate with a set of rules, just as humans do: during a conversation, one party listens, while the other talks. If one party didn't hear what was said, he or she would ask the other party to repeat it. If the other party doesn't, that part of the conversation is lost. The words and characters between each party must be the same; otherwise an interpreter is required. The same is true of devices. If two devices with different communication rules (protocols) or different characters/words (ASCII/EBCDIC) need to communicate, an interpreter (protocol converter) is used. The protocol converter allows dissimilar devices to communicate. Also the converter maps each device's capabilities to the others.

Question 7.   What is a sex changer?

Answer 7.   When two devices are being connected together and the cable to be used has the wrong genders, a sex changer can be used to swap the gender of one of the cable ends. The sex changer is a small unit that has the same gender connector on both sides, normally about the size of a matchbook. If the cable end is male, with a female connector required, an F/F (female/female) sex changer would be used to convert the cable end to female.

Question 8.   When a user disconnects from a remote computer, how does the computer know?

Answer 8.   Most computers accept the "Control-D" sequence, EOT, as the end of transmission character. Receipt of this character is interpreted to mean that the connection should be broken. The computer then uses the RS232 leads to disconnect the dial-up connection. By lowering pin 20, DTR, the modem will disconnect the attached line. Hence the connection is broken by the computer upon receipt of a Control D. Depending on the system, different characters may be used, but the concept is the same.

Question 9.   In the middle of downloading a file from an online computer service onto a local PC, what happens to cause the download to abort?

Answer 9.   Many things could happen. The most prominent reason for an abnormal ending to a download is the receipt of a character that closes the file you are receiving into. Several computer service bureaus embed control characters in their data to prevent such downloading. Upon receipt of these control sequences, the terminal emulation or communication software will act on the received control sequences. Check the emulation package to see if an option exists to receive, but not interpret, the received control sequences to get around this problem.

6

SPECIAL TOOLS FOR CONNECTIONS: SOFTWARE, HARDWARE, AND CABLE DESIGNS

Several software and hardware tools are available to aid the user with the installation and connection of computers, printers, terminals, and modems. The hardware tools were used in the step-by-step approaches of the tutorial modules; refer to the appropriate modules for a detailed explanation of how to use each of these. This chapter introduces some special cabling systems used by some vendors, specifically, the use of modular-to-DB25 adapters, as well as a couple of software products that aid the user in connections.

Cable builders can save considerable time and energy in producing a wider variety of cabling solutions by using a cabling program as a tool or as an aid. Vendors can expand their markets by making products more easily attached to both existing and available products. Connectivity is perhaps the major obstacle to product success in today's marketplace.

SCS RS232 CABLE DESIGNER

This is a software tool designed for interfacing computer and peripherals. It runs on any IBM PC or compatible. It provides an easy-to-use, menu-driven interface for reviewing device pinouts and designing custom cables, with capability of keeping a large database of devices and their pinouts.

You've all experienced it! You must connect two devices together that use an RS232 interface. The tutorial modules in this book covered the various aspects of interfacing devices, yet you know there has to be an easier way. You know there is nothing complicated about connecting a printer to a computer, a terminal to a computer, a computer to a computer, or a modem to any of these devices. Merely cross the data leads and provide a signal ground. Right?!

Well, maybe, in 10 percent of the connections this might work as the tutorial modules highlight. But what about those items such as flow control, control leads, and other null modem cables? Soon the simple task of connecting two devices becomes complex. Is a null modem cable, a straight-through cable, needed, or is the connection even possible?

How Does it Work?

To start the program from either a floppy disk– or a hard disk–based PC, the user merely types in the command "SCS." The main menu appears offering the user a friendly interface to an otherwise complex subject, RS232 cabling.

```
RS-232 Cable Designer V1.04
(C) Copyright 1985, 1986, 1987
Significant Systems


                    MAIN MENU


         F1   1.  PRODUCT INTERFACES
         F2   2.  ADD A NEW COMPUTER OR PERIPHERAL
         F3   3.  CABLE DESIGN
         F4   4.  ASYNCHRONOUS NULL-MODEM CABLES
         F5   5.  RS232 STANDARD
         F6   6.  CENTRONICS PARALLEL STANDARD
         F7   7.  IBM PARALLEL CABLE
         F8   8.  MODULAR TO DB25 ADAPTER
         F9   9.  PRODUCT BLURBS
         ESC      EXIT PROGRAM
```

The RS232 Cable Designer has a database of over 200 devices with all the information necessary to allow many cables to be designed. If the user wants to see the cable necessary to connect an IBM PC to an HP LaserJet printer, select "CABLE DESIGN" by pressing Function key 3 or the "3" digit. The names of the devices will appear in alphabetical order. The user selects the IBM PC entry, or whatever other computer for which the user is designing a cable, by using the cursor keys or an attached mouse, or by entering the first letter of the vendor's name. In this example the user would enter an "i" for the IBM PC. Either of these methods allows you to scroll up and down the database of devices quickly. Once you have highlighted the correct entry, such as the IBM PC, select it by hitting the Enter key.

Repeat this sequence for any device that is to be connected to the IBM PC, such as an HP LaserJet printer. Once the printer is highlighted, hitting the Enter key will select it. That's all there is to designing a cable. This is much simpler than even using a break-out device on a port to perform port analysis. The RS232 Cable Designer will then draw on the screen the cable necessary to connect the PC to an HP LaserJet printer. Factors, including flow control, are taken into account automatically to give you a complete cable design.

Are you ready to design the cable necessary to connect an Okidata 2410 to an Apple Computer, or a Hayes modem to a DEC VT100, or two computers back to back, or a terminal to a supermicro? This program has hundreds of computers, printers, plotters, terminals, and modems in the database from which to choose.

But what if the device you have is not listed? A facility is provided within the RS232 Cable Designer to add any number of different devices to the database. Information from the port profiles used in this textbook can be used to complete the form offered by this software program. This allows the program to keep up to data and include the latest products. Once a device is added, the user can produce cable designs to connect it to any other device in the database. This program has a very complex set of logic and algorithms to allow the thousands of cables that it is capable of designing.

Often, the user needs to know which leads are present in a port, which may be used for flow control, and what is the gender of the port. The "product interfaces" function shows the pins of a port and any special information available about the interface.

Built-in, context-sensitive help screens are provided in this software to aid both the novice and experienced user. The RS232 Cable Designer also provides online access to information about the RS232 interface, the parallel standard, the IBM parallel cabling, standard null modem cables, and modular to DB232 adapters. If a user wants to see the actual pinouts of a port, the software will display this information on the screen, allowing the user to produce a hardcopy of this on an attached printer.

As a strong proponent of easing the connection of a diverse set of devices, the author highly recommends this software program to anyone who has to get involved in the cable design or cable selection necessary to connect computers, printers, terminals, and modems. The software from Significant Systems, with a list price of $125, is distributed by Market Central, Inc., 15 N. Jefferson Avenue, Canonsburg, PA 15317, (412) 746–6000. Several mail-order catalogs, such as Black Box (412–746–5530) and Misco (1–800–631–2227), also carry this product.

SCS QUICK CABLER

Many cable builders and vendors would be aided by the use of a cable building program. For those instances when standard-sized connectors are used, and common serial interfaces, the RS232 Cable Designer will work great. But what about those computer vendors that are offering 3-pin ports, 5-pin ports, 8-pin ports, and 9-pin ports that are not PC/AT compatible? For that matter, even when the DB25 connectors are used with odd-ball pin number assignments, the user is often left troubled on cable designing. Cable builders often have the need to connect equipment that does not have known cabling available. Building custom cables should not be a shot-in-the-dark proposition.

The Quick Cabler is another software product produced by Significant Systems. QC software that runs on a PC or compatible provides the ability to design cables, regardless of the connector sizes on devices. The Quick Cabler is not restricted to configuring cables for RS232 DB25 interfaced devices only. Synchronous and asynchronous cables for serial devices utilizing DB25, 9-pin, 8-pin modular, 5-pin "D" connectors, and other connectors may be constructed. The devices for which cables may be designed include computers, printers, modems, and terminals. The cables, such as those in the tutorial modules, could easily and quickly have been designed with the Quick Cabler software package.

A session with the Quick Cabler might follow this order:

1. Three lines of user input are allowed for specifying items such as a full product description, port gender, and device interface.

2. The user is prompted to describe a device port, including

Name the device

Grounding information

Data leads

Timing leads

Control leads

The name of the device is used for reference purposes. The four categories of leads are input by the user directly from the product documentation. This textbook's tutorial modules referred to leads by pin numbers. This is not always practical when dealing with odd-sized connectors, or even DB25 connectors. Hence, values for the leads may be pin numbers, wire colors, or any special codes that the user desires. Quick Cabler can adapt to any of these, or mixtures of them. Hence, one port could reference pins and colors, while the other one referenced colors only. The ultimate cable design would retain the user's nomenclature.

3. Once input, Quick Cabler designs the cable necessary to connect the two devices described. The connection could be a 5-pin Apple computer port and a DB25 Hayes Smartmodem. A 9-pin AT to 8-pin modular AT&T 3B2 could be easily designed. The old standby DB25-to-DB25 is a cinch with the Quick Cabler.

4. The user then has an option to store the completed cable design. For future reference, the user can name the cable so it is easily recognized for later retrieval. The AT-to-Hayes cable design could be called the "ATHAYES" cable, while the Apple-to-Hayes cable could be called "cpumodem," and the AT-to-AT&T could be a "9-pin, 8-pin" cable. The user determines the name of the cable to be used for subsequent viewing of the designed cable.

From the tutorial modules presented in this textbook, the reader can see how confusing these connections can be. The interactive session presents options for the user in a clear format. All questions are specific and carefully worded to help with any misunderstanding due to vocabulary. The logic that gathers lead information flows and changes with the user's input.

The Quick Cabler is simple and easy to use, and is a great aid in solving connectivity problems. The Quick Cabler is a must for every cable builder. Contact your cable distributor for the availability of this software design tool. The software from Significant Systems is also distributed by Market Central, Inc., 15 N. Jefferson Avenue, Canonsburg, PA 15317, (412) 746–6000.

BREAKOUT

The tutorial modules referenced a break-out box as a hardware tool that aids in the analysis of product ports, as well as in debugging problems. Black Box (412–746–5530) offers a software version of this same tool that runs on any PC or compatible.

BREAKOUT runs on your IBM PC, or compatible, and gives you the same capabilities that a break-out box offers. With this software, you can monitor, raise, and lower the leads of the RS232 interface. The monitoring of leads 2, 3, 5, 6, and 8 is provided. Furthermore, the user can raise and lower leads 4, 20, and 22 from the keyboard.

The user can send data to the interface directly from the keyboard. For example, the author tested this product by connecting a Hayes Smartmodem 2400 to the RS232 port on an AT&T PC 6300. Using this tool, the dialing sequence "ATDT5551212" was sent out the serial port to the attached modem, with the modem responding and dialing the number. Once the far-end computer system answered the call, the PC display showed all the data, both incoming and outgoing.

The ability to display data in the buffer in both hex and ASCII provides the user with a great debugging tool. BREAKOUT provides this feature, even though this is not something the user gets with a standard hardware break-out box. Test sequences can be stored in the buffer and sent out the port. This can aid in the diagnosing and debugging of local and remote systems.

BREAK-OUT BOX

Commonly referred to as a BOB, this tool is very useful for performing port analyses. It can show the status of individual RS232 leads. Specifically, LEDs (light-emitting diodes) are provided to show if the lead is on or off, high or low, present or not present. Cross-connections are possible, allowing for a cable to be tested prior to actual construction. Refer to Tutorial Module 5–1 for a step-by-step layout of the use of a BOB.

PIN INSERTER/EXTRACTOR

This tool allows the user to insert and remove the individual pins of an RS232 interface connector. When building a cable, the inserter/extractor allows the user easily to place the pins in their proper sockets. As custom cables are constructed, this tool can save countless hours.

SEX CHANGER

This appliance allows you to use cables with the wrong-gendered connectors. If a terminal and modem are being connected and have male and female ports, respectively, a cable that has female connectors at each will not work. However, with a sex changer that converts one end of the cable to a male connector, the cable can be used.

AT&T MODULAR-TO-DB25 ADAPTERS

In the past few years, it has become increasingly more popular to cable between asynchronous systems using modular cords. The idea is to reduce cabling costs by using standard 4-pair wires between the systems. In most asynchronous, not synchronous, environments, it is possible to utilize no more than eight leads from the RS232 interface standard. This allows the use of standard 4-pair cabling, modular jacks, and RJ-type connectors.

However, the bulk of DTE and DCE products on the market today still are equipped with male and female DB25 connectors. To marry these two techniques, adapters are used to convert the RJ-45 type jacks to 25-pin type connectors to plug into the various modems, computer, terminals, and printers. This discussion will center on the various adapters and 4-pair cables used in the industry today. Discussion on each adapter will include the number of leads supported as well as the layout of cross-connections between the RJ-45 receptacle and the DB25 connector that actually connects to the device.

First, the common leads that would be included in a 4-pair modular-type jack should be listed. These are the most common leads encountered when interfacing asynchronous devices. Table 6–1 outlines the nine most common leads used, with normally one of them being excluded. Typically, the Protective Ground is omitted. This is due to the isolated ground concept allowing for protection from electrical shock to occur within each separate device to be connected. Nonetheless, it may be included in some cables.

TABLE 6–1.
MOST COMMON
LEADS FOUND IN
4-PAIR CABLES

Protective Ground
Transmit Data
Receive Data
Request to Send
Clear to Send
Data Set Ready
Signal Ground
Data Carrier Detect
Data Terminal Ready

The lead numbers have been omitted purposely as the conductor numbers of the cable rarely match the actual pin numbers of a DB25 connector as outlined in the RS232 interface.

The first group of modular connectors to be covered will be the AT&T modular-to-DB25 adapters. The AT&T 3B2 series computers utilize these adapters to connect terminals, printers, and modems to the computers. Beyond the cabling costs cited earlier, a rationale for using these sizes of ports on a computer is space. The 8-pin modular receptacles take up far less room than does a comparable DB25 connector, hence allowing the over size of a computer to shrink. This is a very key consideration when multiuser computers are involved, such as UNIX systems. If a computer is to support from 1 to 100 users, the size of the computer should be dictated by the devices supported within, such as disk drives, tape drives, memory, and so on not simply the number of ports to be provided. Hence, the smaller the port, the better.

The AT&T 3B2 computer systems provide an 8-pin modular receptacle for each I/O port. The pinouts of this port are outlined in Table 6–2 from Tutorial Modules 5–6 and 4–6. Refer to each of these modules for further insight into connections using step-by-step procedures.

What if a terminal is to be connected to this size port? What about a printer with an RS232 port? Modems are common devices attached to UNIX systems. How do you connect these devices with DB25 ports? Adapters are the answer. Many firms offer many different adapters, such as AT&T, Black Box, Misco, AMP, TRW, and telephone companies, to name just a few. It is important to know what the pinouts are for each of these prior to attempting to connect two devices together. Specifically, if you are using preconstructed adapters, it is imperative that you specify to the cable manufacturer the devices that you are connecting. The AT&T 3B2 connections will be dealt with first, followed by a discussion of the pinouts of some of these vendor's adapters.

Dealing with the AT&T 3B2 computer system will allow us to highlight the connection of terminals, printers, and modems. First, we will focus on the specific adapters provided for use by AT&T with the 3B2, their pinouts, cables, and finally a chart easing the selection of adapters.

There are two basic adapters associated with a 3B2 computer. These adapters convert the RJ-45-size connections to DB25, as depicted in Figure 6–1. One of them, a terminal/printer adapter, comes with either a male or female

TABLE 6–2. AT&T 3B2 I/O PORT-PROVIDED LEADS (MODULAR PORT)

Function	3B2 lead #	
Protective Ground	1	
Transmit Data (out)	3	
Data Terminal Ready (out)	4	(will be on if the port is enabled)
Receive Data (in)	5	
Data Carrier Detect (in)	6	(should be on for the port to communicate)
Signal Ground	7	

NOTES: It is important to note that these pinouts are those of the port on the computer itself, not those provided by a cable or adapter that may be connected to the 3B2. The next section will discuss the adapters themselves. Pins 2 and 8 are reserved, meaning not used at this time.

AT&T Modular-to-DB25 Adapters

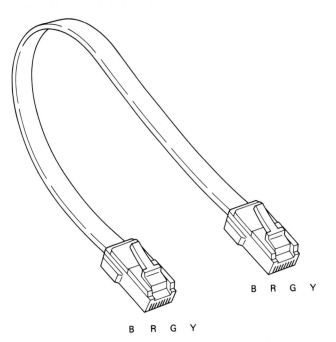

B   R   G   Y

B   R   G   Y

Figure 6–1. RJ-45-to-DB25 adapters.

DB25 connector. The other is labeled an ACU/modem connector and is normally of male gender. The reason for this gender is that most modems or pieces of DCE are interfaced by female ports.

The terminal/printer adapter used in this exercise was part no. 232 21 25 010. This may or not be consistent with the parts available at the time of this book's publication. However, you should know that this discussion involves the adapter that is used to connect a piece of equipment emulating DTE. This means that the port on the device provides the common signals that data terminal equipment provides, as outlined in the RS232 standard. Common leads are Transmit Data, Request to Send, and Data Terminal Ready. Further, this device expects signals normally provided by DCE, such as Receive Data, Clear to Send, Data Set Ready, and Data Carrier Detect. This is cited as some piece of DTE, such as AT&T's 510A terminal, that has a port that emulates DCE. However, in our example, assume that a terminal, such as the Wyse WY-85 or AT&T 610, is to be connected. Both devices have ports that emulate DTE.

Another important element of the AT&T cabling system provided for the 3B2 computers is the cable used to connect the computer port to the RJ-45 receptacle of the adapter. This cable DOES NOT provide straight-through conductors. The leads are inverted. The actual cable conductor layout is outlined in Table 6–3. This can be misleading if the adapters are being used with common 4-pair wiring, without the AT&T cable. The AT&T cable that has these reversed leads is normally black. The best way to tell if the leads are reversed is to hold the jacks at the ends of the cable, side by side, both in the exact relative position, and look at the colors of the leads. The order of the leads (colors) should be exactly the opposite. If they are exactly the same, this is not the intended cable to use with the AT&T-provided adapters. Later in this section we will point out the adapters to use if your cable has straight-through conductors. We will assume that your cable matches that of Figure 6–2.

The end of the cable that has a free-hanging prong is the end that plugs into the 3B2 port. The prong is used to connect to a ground strap. The cable plugs into the 3B2 port with the snap piece of the jack on the

TABLE 6–3. AT&T 3B2 BLACK MODULAR CABLE (REVERSED LEADS)

Color	Color
or si rd gr ye bl bk	xx bk bl ye gr rd si or

NOTE: Holding the jacks in the same relative position (snaps on bottom or snaps on top), the colors are depicted from left to right. The "XX" indicates a ground wire with no specific color; or = orange, si = silver/gray, rd = red, gr = green, ye = yellow, bl = blue, bk = black.

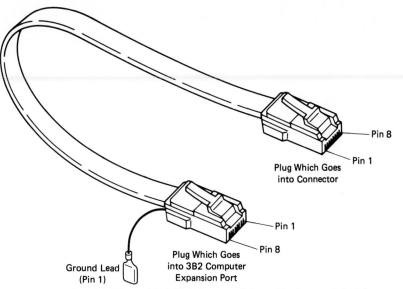

Figure 6–2. AT&T-provided 3B2 black modular cable (reversed leads).

bottom. Review Table 6–2 for the pin numbers and assignment of the 3B2 port. When looking at the port itself on the 3B2, the pin numbers are read and ascend from left to right as depicted in Figure 6–3. This would mean that, when viewing the black AT&T cable (reversed), looking at the jack with the snap on the bottom, and viewing the end that is plugged into a receptacle, pin 1 is on the left. Pin 1 in the 3B2 end of the cable would then not have a conductor in it. Pin 2 would be the black conductor, with the orange conductor aligning with pin 8 of the 3B2 port. If this sounds confusing, you should try to write about it to make it clear. Plug this cable end into the 3B2 I/O port.

The terminal/printer adapter attaches to the other end of this black cable. Select either a male or female adapter to fit on your particular piece of DTE. In the case of the Wyse WY-85 terminal, a female adapter is required, while an AT&T 610 terminal requires a male adapter. Consult the device's port profile to make this determination.

Before you actually connect the cable end into the adapter, let's review the pinouts. Because the black cable reversed the leads, note the conductor colors. At this end of the cable, viewing the RJ-45 jack with the snap locking piece on the bottom and the part of the jack that plugs into a receptacle facing you, pin 1 is now on the right side of the jack, with pin 8 being the orange conductor on the far left. The pin numbering has been reversed. This is done to match that of the adapter pin numbering.

Figure 6–4 shows the RJ-45-size receptacle found on the AT&T terminal/printer adapters. Note that, when facing the port, with the snap locking receptacle on the bottom side, pin 8 is on the right, while pin 1 is on the left. This is directly the opposite of the 3B2 port and, hence, is the reversing cable. The important point is how the adapter actually connects these pins to the leads of the DB25 connector on the other side of the adapter.

The actual functions and directions of the DB25 side of the adapter are laid out in Table 6–4. Note that the data leads and control signals seem to be reversed. Pay no attention to the function name, but rather note the direction of the data and control signals. Refer to them as "control in," "control out," "data in," and "data out," for ease of reference.

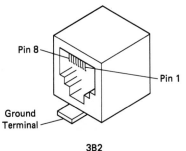

3B2
Expansion Port

Figure 6–3. Modular jack expansions port for 3B2.

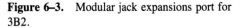

AT&T Modular-to-DB25 Adapters·

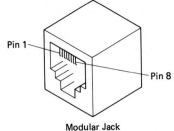

Pin 1

Pin 8

Modular Jack
in 8-Pin-to-25-Pin Connector

8-Pin Modular Jack	25-Pin RS-232-C Jack or Plug for Printer or Terminal
1 PROT GRD	1 FRAME GROUND
2 RESERVED	4 RESERVED
3 TXDO	3 TRANSMIT DATA
4 DTRO	8 DATA TERMINAL READY
5 RXDO	2 RECEIVE DATA
6 DCDO	20 DATA CARRIER DET
7 SIG GRD	7 SIGNAL GROUND
8 RESERVED	5 RESERVED

Figure 6–4. Modular jack pinout of a terminal/printer adapter.

TABLE 6–4. DB25 PINOUTS OF TERMINAL/ PRINTER ADAPTER

DB25 pin #	Function	Category
1	Frame Ground	Ground
2	Receive Data (in)	Data
3	Transmit Data (out)	Data
7	Signal Ground	Ground
8	Data Terminal Ready (out)	Control
20	Data Carrier Detect (in)	Control

NOTES: Pins 4 and 5 are reserved, or not used at this time in the adapter.

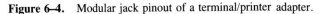

    Connecting the Wyse WY-85 or AT&T 610 to this terminal/printer adapter presents little problem. The Wyse WY-85 can be optioned to ignore the DCE-provided signals normally found on leads 5, 6, and 8, as the AT&T 610 terminal does. What if your terminal cannot function without a couple of the key leads, mainly 5 and 6? Fret not! Open up the adapter and connect the same lead that runs to lead 8 at the back of the DB25 connector to leads 5 and 6. This is called jumpering, as discussed in normal cable design and construction. This can usually be accomplished with a short piece of wire being crimped into slots 5 and 6 on the back of the connector, as well as soldering or connecting the leads 5, 6, and 8 together. With this done, as long as lead 8 is on (from the 3B2), leads 5 and 6 will also be on. Some connectors already provide this type of jumpering, but check to be sure that yours does. Some of them strap lead 20 to this lead to accomplish the same end result. Since the adapter used for this exercise used pin 20 to keep 6 high, our figures will depict this.

    Now let's follow the pin numbers from end to end in this type of connection without our special 5 and 8 jumpering (see Table 6–5).

    The final cross-connections in the terminal/printer adapter accomplish that outlined in Table 6–6.

    What does the ACU/modem adapter look like? The connections involved in connecting a modem to an AT&T 3B2 utilize the same cables and ports, but with a different adapter. It is not worth repeating the cable layout and cross-overs, as they have been outlined in the terminal/printer section. However, it is worthwhile to note the layout of the ACU/modem adapter between the RJ-45 receptacle and the DB25 connector. Table 6–7 lists the actual pinouts of the ACU/modem adapter.

TABLE 6–5. PIN NUMBERS FOR 3B2-TO-TERMINAL CONNECTIONS

3B2 port	3B2 cable end	Adapter cable end	RJ-45	DB25	Terminal port
1 -------	1 -------	1 -------	1 -------	1 -------	1
5 -------	5 -------	5 -------	5 -------	2 -------	2
3 -------	3 -------	3 -------	3 -------	3 -------	3
7 -------	7 -------	7 -------	7 -------	7 -------	7
4 -------	4 -------	4 -------	4 -------	8 -------	8
6 -------	6 -------	6 -------	6 ---:--	20 -------	20
				:-- 6 -------	6
2 -------	2 -------	2 -------	2 -------	4 -------	4 (reserved)
8 -------	8 -------	8 -------	8 -------	5 -------	5 (reserved)

NOTES: Each end of the connection has the relative reference to the pin numbers reversed. The black cable reverses it to match the reversed notations at the RJ-45 receptacle of the adapter as compared to the 3B2 port. Because the 3B2 does not use its pins 2 and 8, they are classified as reserved.

TABLE 6–6. TERMINAL/PRINTER RJ-45 ADAPTER MODIFICATIONS FOR DTE

RJ-45	DB25	RJ-45	DB25
1 -------	1	1 -------	1
5 ⟨------	2	5 ⟨------	2
3 ------⟩	3	3 ------⟩	3
7 -------	7	7 -------	7
4 ---:--⟩	8	4 ---:--⟩	8
:--⟩	5	:--⟩	5
		:--⟩	6
:--⟩	6		
6 ⟨--:---	20	6 -------	20

TABLE 6–7. AT&T ACU/MODEM MODULAR-TO-DB25 ADAPTER PINOUTS

RJ-45	DB25
1 -------	1
3 ------⟩	2
5 ⟨------	3
7 -------	7
6 ⟨------	8
4 ------⟩	20
2 -------	5 (reserved)
8 -------	4 (reserved)

NOTES: If your modem requires pin 4 to be on, then open the adapter, strap a lead into pin 4's socket, and jumper it to the wire on pin 20. Whenever the 3B2 has pin 20 turned on, pin 4 will be on. In most cases, this should work fine.

AT&T Modular-to-DB25 Adapters

Now that you have a good understanding of connectors used to connect peripherals to the 3B2, how can these same connectors be used to connect non-3B2 computers and peripherals together? This next discussion will highlight the use of the terminal/printer and ACU/modem connector, with both straight-through and black "reversing" cable, as both these cable types may be available. If you are using adapters provided by companies other than AT&T, skip to the next section, where a discussion focuses on these.

The best way to approach the use of adapters and straight-through or reversing cables is to categorize device ports. The two types of port, DTE and DCE, give us four possible connections. Hence, we should allow for a DTE-to-DTE, DTE-to-DCE, DCE-to-DTE, or DCE-to-DCE connection.

Recall that DTE and DCE ports refer to devices emulating those pieces of equipment, not necessarily that category of equipment. The example cited earlier was the 510A terminal that is DTE, but the port emulates DCE. Other examples are a Zilog 8000 computer, the early Microdata Reality computers, and most auxiliary ports on terminals used to connect local printers. These ports all emulate DCE and expect to be connected to a DTE-type port.

Some computers, such as the IBM PC, AT&T 3B5, and MUMs, are set up to connect to modems. This implies that they are emulating DTE ports and are to be connected to DCE ports. If you are going to connect a terminal, such as the Wyse WY-85 (DTE port) to the port, then a null modem cable is required. The point here is that it is important as to what the device port is emulating, or looking like, rather that what the device actually is.

The easiest way to approach this is to summarize the connection in a table. This will allow a quick determination of the combinations to use (see Table 6–8).

When connecting two pieces of DTE, software flow control should be supported, as these adapters, without other modifications, will not support hardware flow control. This is because the hardware flow control leads 4, 20, 11, 19, or whatever will not control the proper leads. Furthermore, no "reversing" cables are used, as they provide no function when not involving the 3B2 computer modular port. The resulting cables are as follows (see Table 6–9).

These should aid you in using the AT&T-provided modular-to-DB25 adapters to connect different devices together. Consult the other sections involving different vendors' adapters to get more ideas on how to ease the cabling between devices.

TRW MODULAR-TO-DB25 ADAPTERS

Because of the widespread use of 4-pair twisted pair in building today, and the ability for serial connection using this medium, many vendors are providing solutions to interconnections using adapters. These adapters provide for connection to a standard DB25 port, either male or female, and the ability to use modular cords between two adapters. This allows the use of 4-pair wire and modular jacks as the cable between devices. An adapter is required at each end of the 4-pair cable. Figure 6–5 depicts the idea behind these connections.

TABLE 6–8. USING AT&T TERMINAL/PRINTER AND ACU/MODEM ADAPTERS

Device A	Adapter	Cabling	Adapter	Device B
1. DTE	ACU/modem	Straight through	Terminal/printer	DTE
2. DTE	ACU/modem	Straight through	ACU/modem	DCE
3. DCE	ACU/modem	Straight through	ACU/modem	DTE
4. DCE	ACU/modem	Straight through	Terminal/printer	DCE

NOTES:
1. Using the adapters for DTE-to-DTE connections, the ACU/modem connector should be modified so that lead 20 is strapped to lead 6 on the DB25 side of the connector. Otherwise, lead 6 will be missing.
2. For DTE-to-DCE connections, using the ACU/modem adapters, lead 6 is not supported. If lead 6 is required, then on the ACU/modem adapter to be used at the DTE port, strap lead 6 to lead 8 on the DB25 side of the adapter. Thus, when 8 is on, lead 6 will also be on.
3. The same holds true as in note 2.
4. For DCE-to-DCE connections, the terminal/printer adapter may cause a problem. On the DB25 side, lead 20 should be disconnected from lead 6. Once cabled to the ACU/modem adapter, then lead 20 will be controlled by lead 8 of the ACU/modem adapter and not have two output leads connected to a single input lead.

TABLE 6–9. LEAD CONNECTIONS FOR MODULAR ADAPTERS

ACU/Modem adapter DB25 pin		Terminal/Printer adapter DB25 pin	ACU/Modem adapter DB25 pin		ACU/Modem adapter DB25 pin
1	-------	1	1	-------	1
2	-------	3	2	-------	2
3	-------	2	3	-------	3
4	-------	5	4	-------	4
5	-------	4	5	-------	5
7	-------	7	7	-------	7
			8	-------	8
			20	-------	20
8	----:--	6			
	:--	20			
20	-------	8			

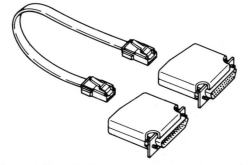

Figure 6–5. RS232-to-modular adapters for cabling.

TRW is a major supplier of these adapters. There are a variety different pinouts in the adapters. The equipment that you are connecting dictates which adapter is required. These adapters have different pinouts. The 4-pair (eight-wire) cable that connects two adapters together can be of varying distances. A tool is available that allows the user to build custom-length 4-pair cable. This crimping tool also lets the user connect a modular jack onto the twisted-pair cabling found in most buildings.

One such adapter is Part No. 002–00035–6, or TRW Reference number FM-001, which provides the pinouts shown in Table 6–10 on the DB25 side of the adapter. On the modular side of the adapter these leads are cross-referenced as shown.

TABLE 6–10. TRW MODULAR ADAPTER PINOUTS

RS232 signal	DB25 lead #		Modular lead #
Signal Ground	7	-------	1
Request to Send	4	-------	2
Transmit Data	2	-------	3
Data Terminal Ready	20	-------	4
Receive Data	3	-------	5
Data Carrier Detect	8	-------	6
Ground	7	-------	7
Clear to Send	5	-------	8

The user can take two of these adapters, match them, and place a standard modular cable between them. Modifications are possible to the adapters to allow for all cross-connections, such as those featured in the tutorial modules. Using a software program, such as the Quick Cabler, makes connections with these adapters really simple. Instead of designing a cable by the numbers, the colors of the conductors within the adapters can be used by the Quick Cabler. The user can build custom cables with maximum flexibility using these modular to DB25 adapters.

Appendix F lists some of the adapters available from TRW, along with their associated pinouts.

APPENDIX A. RS232 CIRCUIT SUMMARY WITH CCITT EQUIVALENTS*

Figure A-1 is a summary of the RS232 interface pin assignments. For ease of reference, each signal is grouped into one of the categories of ground, data, control, or timing. For explanations of each, refer to the text. Both the EIA and CCITT nomenclatures are given for cross-reference between the U.S. and international versions of the standard.

FIGURE A-1. RS-232 CIRCUIT SUMMARY WITH CCITT EQUIVALENTS

Pin	Interchange Circuit	CCITT Equivalent	Description	Gnd	Data From DCE	Data To DCE	Control From DCE	Control To DCE	Timing From DCE	Timing To DCE
1	AA	101	Protective ground	X						
7	AB	102	Signal ground common return	X						
2	BA	103	Transmitted data			X				
3	BB	104	Received data		X					
4	CA	105	Request to send					X		
5	CB	106	Clear to send				X			
6	CC	107	Data set ready				X			
20	CD	108.2	Data terminal ready					X		
22	CE	125	Ring indicator				X			
8	CF	109	Received line signal detector				X			
21	CG	110	Signal quality detector				X			
23	CH	111	Data signal rate selector (DTE)					X		
23	CI	112	Data signal rate selector (DCE)				X			
24	DA	113	Transmitter signal element timing (DTE)							X
15	DB	114	Transmitter signal element timing (DCE)						X	
17	DD	115	Receiver signal element timing (DCE)						X	
14	SBA	118	Secondary transmitted data			X				
16	SBB	119	Secondary received data		X					
19	SCA	120	Secondary request to send					X		
13	SCB	121	Secondary clear to send				X			
12	SCF	122	Secondary received line signal detector				X			

* Martin D. Seyer and William J. Mills, *DOS UNIX Systems: Becoming a Super User*, © 1986, pp. 232–36. Reprinted by permission of Prentice-Hall, Inc., Englewood Cliffs, New Jersey.

APPENDIX B. CENTRONICS STANDARD*

Signal Name	Pin(s)	Source	Category	Description
Data strobe	1, 19	IBM	Timing	A 1-microsecond pulse used to clock data from the IBM to the printer.
Data 1	2, 20	IBM	Data	Each one of these leads provides for a single bit of a data character. A high represents a 1; a low represents a 0.
Data 2	3, 21	IBM	Data	
Data 3	4, 22	IBM	Data	
Data 4	5, 23	IBM	Data	
Data 5	6, 24	IBM	Data	
Data 6	7, 25	IBM	Data	
Data 7	8, 26	IBM	Data	
Data 8	8, 27	IBM	Data	
Acknowledge	10, 28	Ptr	Control	This pulse indicates either the reception of a character or the end of a functional operation.
Busy	11, 29	Ptr	Control	A signal level indicating that the printer cannot receive any more data. This is caused by a paper-out or other fault condition. Consult the manual for a list of the conditions affecting this control lead.
PE	12	Ptr	Control	A control lead indicating that the printer is out of paper.
Select	13	Ptr	Control	A control lead indicating that the printer is selected by the IBM.
0 volts	14	Ptr	Ground	A signal ground reference for other signals.
OSCXT	15	Ptr	—	A 100/200-kHz signal, varying among printers.
0 volts	16	N/A	Ground	A signal ground reference.
Chassis ground	17	Ptr	Ground	A frame ground for electrical protection.
+5 volts	18	Ptr	—	Positive voltage.
Input prime	31, 30	IBM	Control	A signal that clears the printer buffer and reinitializes the control logic.
Fault	32	Ptr	Control	A signal that indicates a printer fault condition.

Notes: (a) The second pin number indicates the twisted-pair return or signal reference lead. The IBM interface uses pins 18 to 25 on the DB25 connector for this purpose. See the following table for crossovers between the two types of connectors. (b) Pins 1, 10, 31, and 32 are active or on when they are low. All others are high to indicate an on condition.

* Martin D. Seyer and William J. Mills, *DOS UNIX Systems: Becoming a Super User*, © 1986, pp. 232–36. Reprinted by permission of Prentice-Hall, Inc., Englewood Cliffs, New Jersey.

TYPICAL PIN CROSSOVERS BETWEEN THE PC AND THE CENTRONICS PARALLEL CONNECTORS

IBM DB25S		Amphenol
1	←——————→	1
2	←——————→	2
3	←——————→	3
4	←——————→	4
5	←——————→	5
6	←——————→	6
7	←——————→	7
8	←——————→	8
9	←——————→	9
10	←——————→	10
11	←——————→	11
12	←——————→	12
13	←——————→	13
14	←——————→	14
15	←——————→	32
16	←——————→	31
17	←——————→	36
18	←——————→	33
19	←——————→	19
20	←——————→	21
21	←——————→	23
22	←——————→	25
23	←——————→	27
24	←——————→	29
25	←——————→	30

APPENDIX C. PINOUTS FOR SERIAL COMPUTERS AND PERIPHERALS

Included in this appendix are charts displaying RS232-C pin assignments, together with their functions and directions, available for ports offered on various devices. The devices are separated by category (computers, modems, printers, and terminals) and alphabetized within each category. In addition, pertinent facts relating to items such as flow control are included. These items are extremely important when connecting combinations of computers, modems, and peripherals.

From these lists, a determination can be made for the construction of an RS232 cable for connecting equipment. Once the devices have been selected, note the corresponding PIN CONFIGURATION. Use this PIN CONFIGURA-TION in conjunction with Appendix D to build the appropriate cable.

This text carries the pinning process a step further than previous texts. It provides an orderly approach to analyzing a port. The chapters are full of examples on this process. A key ingredient to this is the logging of the features of a port. A standard form is included to record the information about a port, its pinouts, pin configuration, gender, required leads, expected leads, flow control, compatibility, and other useful details. The goal is to provide the user an easy method of summarizing information about a port for easy connection of different devices. The charts in this appendix provide the pinouts as well as flow control information. The user may fill in the other information as connections are attempted. It is the hope of this author that the vendors of these and future products will provide a single sheet in their documentation containing the information contained in the port profiles used in this handbook.

The standard form for data collection is borrowed from Significant Systems cabling products. The form is the Software Cabling System Port Profile. There are separate forms for computers, modems, printers, and terminals. Figure C-1 provides a blank Printer Port Profile.

Note the information contained in the profile form. The user should use the Printer Port Profile form to record the results of a port analysis on a printer's port. There are similar forms for the other classes of devices, computers, modems, and terminals at the back of this appendix. Using the form is fairly straightforward. A number of fields are provided with some suggested values. The user should underline all "supported items" that a device provides. The options actually selected for interfacing to a given device should be circled. This will allow the user a future reference for two devices that are connected.

An example is "Flow Control". From the Printer Port Profile form there are 3 lines that are to be filled in with this information:

FLOW CONTROL TECHNIQUE: XON/XOFF ENQ/ACK STX/ETX Hardware

FLOW CONTROL LEAD(S): 4 11 19 20 __ __ __

LEADS THAT MUST BE ON: 5 6 8 __ __ __ __

If the printer port being analyzed supports both hardware and software flow control, then the user should underline both "XON/XOFF & Hardware" (assuming XON/XOFF is the technique). Because hardware flow control is supported, the next line should be filled in by underlining the lead(s) that can be used for hardware flow control (assume leads 11 & 20 here). Furthermore, if the printer must have lead 5 on before it can send or receive data, this should also be underlined.

Once the supported features are underlined, the user should determine the common options to be used with the device to be connected. If both devices have a completed port profile form, the user can merely circle the common items that will actually be used. In this example, even though both hardware and software flow control are supported, the attached computer may only support software flow control (XON/XOFF). Hence the common option would be software flow control. The user would circle "XON/XOFF". The completed section of the Printer Port Profile form would be as follows:

FLOW CONTROL TECHNIQUE: XON/XOFF ENQ/ACK STX/ETX Hardware

FLOW CONTROL LEAD(s): 4 11 19 20

LEADS THAT MUST BE ON: 5 6 8

FIGURE C-1. SOFTWARE CABLING SYSTEM PRINTER PORT PROFILE

PRINTER PORT PROFILE (Underline if supported, circle if selected)
COMPANY: _____
PRODUCT: _____
PORT: _____   PORT TYPE: serial parallel ____
CONNECTOR: DB25 9-pin 5-pin 8-pin Centronics GENDER: male female
PIN CONFIGURATION: ____

Pin #	Function	Direction	Pin #	Function	Direction
1	_____	to from n/a	14	_____	to from n/a
2	_____	to from n/a	15	_____	to from n/a
3	_____	to from n/a	16	_____	to from n/a
4	_____	to from n/a	17	_____	to from n/a
5	_____	to from n/a	18	_____	to from n/a
6	_____	to from n/a	19	_____	to from n/a
7	_____	to from n/a	20	_____	to from n/a
8	_____	to from n/a	21	_____	to from n/a
9	_____	to from n/a	22	_____	to from n/a
10	_____	to from n/a	23	_____	to from n/a
11	_____	to from n/a	24	_____	to from n/a
12	_____	to from n/a	25	_____	to from n/a
13	_____	to from n/a			

(complete the next section only with 36-pin cinch connectors)

Pin #	Function	Direction	Pin #	Function	Direction
26	_____	to from n/a	27	_____	to from n/a
28	_____	to from n/a	29	_____	to from n/a
30	_____	to from n/a	31	_____	to from n/a
32	_____	to from n/a	33	_____	to from n/a
34	_____	to from n/a	35	_____	to from n/a
36	_____	to from n/a			

FLOW CONTROL TECHNIQUE: XON/XOFF ENQ/ACK STX/ETX Hardware
FLOW CONTROL LEAD(s): 4 11 19 20 ___ ___ ___
LEADS THAT MUST BE ON: 5 6 8 ___ ___ ___
SPEEDS: 110 300 600 1200 1800 2400 4800 9600 19.2 56k _____
PARITY: even odd space mark none   CHARACTER LENGTH: 7 8 _____
STOP BITS: 1 1.5 2   LINE ENDING SEQUENCE: cr 1f cr/1f
PRINTER COMPATIBILITY MODES: EpsonMX/FX/RX Diablo630 HPLaserJet
    NEC3500 IMBgraphics Printronix TI-810 _____
MODE: async sync isoch
PAGE DESCRIPTION LANGUAGE: PostScript DDL _____
NOTE 1: _____
NOTE: 2: _____

The pin configuration for new devices can be acquired by comparing an existing port in this appendix to the new device's port. Once an exact replication is found, note the Pin Configuration and fill in the "Pin Config:" field. Another method is using the Software Cabling System's RS232 Cable Designer software package. This was discussed in Chapter 6. Either way will allow the user to use Appendix D to design the cable required to connect the two devices together.

The other fields should be completed with as much information as possible. The profiles in this appendix contain a substantial amount of information about ports. Included are the pinouts, flow control techniques, and in some cases the port genders. As further information about a port is discovered, the user will be able to use this appendix and the port profile forms as an ongoing reference for connecting computers, modems, printers, and terminals. Blank forms are included at the end of each appendix section to allow the readers to add their own devices.

Every attempt was made to include as many different devices and accurate pin configurations as possible. As this book is a sequel to the initial text, *RS232 Made Easy,* these configurations can be used in conjunction with the pin configurations found in the original textbook. Feel free to mix and match! Happy Connections!!!!

COMPUTER PORT PROFILE (Underline if supported, circle if selected)
COMPANY: Action Computer Enterprise Inc
PRODUCT: Discovery X3 computer

PORT female (Modem port)   PORT TYPE: serial _____
CONNECTOR: DB25 9-PIN 8-PIN(modular) _____   GENDER: male female
PIN CONFIGURATION: C01

PIN	FUNCTION	DIRECTION
1:FG	Frame Ground	N/A
2:TD	Transmit Data	FROM
3:RD	Receive Data	TO
4:RTS	Request to Send	FROM
5:CTS	Clear to Send	TO
6:DSR	Data Set Ready	TO
7:SG	Signal Ground	N/A
8:DCD	Data Carrier Detect	TO
12:CI		TO
13:SCTS	Secondary Cl'r to Send	TO
20:DTR	Data Terminal Ready	FROM
22:RI	Ring Indicator	TO

FLOW CONTROL: 5   XON: YES ACK: LEADS THAT MUST BE ON: _ _ _
SPEEDS: 110 300 600 1200 1800 2400 4800 9600 19.2 56k _____
PARITY: even odd space mark none   CHARACTER LENGTH: 7 8 ___
STOP BITS: 1 1.5 2   LINE-ENDING CHARS: cr lf cr/lf
DISCONNECT SEQUENCE: EOT DEL ~. _____ MODE: async sync isoch
NOTE 1:
NOTE 2:

COMPUTER PORT PROFILE (Underline if supported, circle if selected)
COMPANY: Action Computer Enterprise Inc
PRODUCT: Discovery X3 computer

PORT female (User #1-16)   PORT TYPE: serial _____
CONNECTOR: DB25 9-PIN 8-PIN(modular) _____   GENDER: male female
PIN CONFIGURATION: C09

PIN	FUNCTION	DIRECTION
1:PG	Protective Ground	N/A
2:RD	Receive Data	TO
3:TD	Transmit Data	FROM
5:CTS	Clear to Send	FROM
6:DSR	Data Set Ready	FROM
7:SG	Signal Ground	N/A
8:RLSD	Rec.Line Signal Detect	FROM
19:SRTS	Secondary Req.to Send	TO
20:DTR	Data Terminal Ready	TO

FLOW CONTROL: 20   XON: YES ACK: LEADS THAT MUST BE ON: _ _ _
SPEEDS: 110 300 600 1200 1800 2400 4800 9600 19.2 56k _____
PARITY: even odd space mark none   CHARACTER LENGTH: 7 8 ___
STOP BITS: 1 1.5 2   LINE-ENDING CHARS: cr lf cr/lf
DISCONNECT SEQUENCE: EOT DEL ~. _____ MODE: async sync isoch
NOTE 1:
NOTE 2:

COMPUTER PORT PROFILE **(Underline if supported, circle if selected)**
COMPANY: Action Computer Enterprise Inc
PRODUCT: Discovery X3 computer

```
PORT  female-service port              PORT TYPE: serial _____
CONNECTOR: DB25  9-PIN  8-PIN(modular) _____  GENDER: male  female
PIN CONFIGURATION: C09
```

PIN	FUNCTION	DIRECTION
1:PG	Protective Ground	N/A
2:RD	Receive Data	TO
3:TD	Transmit Data	FROM
5:CTS	Clear to Send	FROM
6:DSR	Data Set Ready	FROM
7:SG	Signal Ground	N/A
8:RLSD	Rec.Line Signal Detect	FROM
19:SRTS	Secondary Req.to Send	TO
20:DTR	Data Terminal Ready	TO

```
FLOW CONTROL: 20          XON: YES  ACK:     LEADS THAT MUST BE ON: _ _ _
SPEEDS:  110 300 600 1200 1800 2400 4800 9600 19.2 56k _____
PARITY: even odd space mark none          CHARACTER LENGTH:  7 8 ___
# STOP BITS:  1 1.5 2                      LINE-ENDING CHARS: cr lf cr/lf
DISCONNECT SEQUENCE:  EOT  DEL  ~. _____ MODE: async sync isoch
NOTE 1:
NOTE 2:
```

COMPUTER PORT PROFILE **(Underline if supported, circle if selected)**
COMPANY: Altos Computer Systems
PRODUCT: 586 computer

```
PORT  female                           PORT TYPE: serial _____
CONNECTOR: DB25  9-PIN  8-PIN(modular) _____  GENDER: male  female
PIN CONFIGURATION: C14
```

PIN	FUNCTION	DIRECTION
1:PG	Protective Ground	N/A
2:TD	Transmit Data	TO
3:RD	Receive Data	FROM
4:RTS	Request to Send	TO
5:CTS	Clear to Send	FROM
6:DSR	Data Set Ready	FROM
7:SG	Signal Ground	N/A
8:DCD	Data Carrier Detect	FROM
20:DTR	Data Terminal Ready	TO

```
FLOW CONTROL:             XON: YES  ACK:     LEADS THAT MUST BE ON: _ _ _
SPEEDS:  110 300 600 1200 1800 2400 4800 9600 19.2 56k _____
PARITY: even odd space mark none          CHARACTER LENGTH:  7 8 ___
# STOP BITS:  1 1.5 2                      LINE-ENDING CHARS: cr lf cr/lf
DISCONNECT SEQUENCE:  EOT  DEL  ~. _____ MODE: async sync isoch
NOTE 1:
NOTE 2:
```

COMPUTER PORT PROFILE (Underline if supported, circle if selected)
COMPANY: Anafaze Inc.
PRODUCT: 8 PID controller

PORT RS-232   PORT TYPE: serial _____
CONNECTOR: DB25 9-PIN 8-PIN(modular) _____   GENDER: male female
PIN CONFIGURATION: C06

PIN	FUNCTION	DIRECTION
2:RD	Receive Data	TO
3:TD	Transmit Data	FROM
7:SG	Signal Ground	N/A

FLOW CONTROL: XON: YES ACK: LEADS THAT MUST BE ON: _ _ _
SPEEDS: 110 300 600 1200 1800 2400 4800 9600 19.2 56k _____
PARITY: even odd space mark none   CHARACTER LENGTH: 7 8 ___
STOP BITS: 1 1.5 2   LINE-ENDING CHARS: cr lf cr/lf
DISCONNECT SEQUENCE: EOT DEL ~. _____   MODE: async sync isoch
NOTE 1:
NOTE 2:

COMPUTER PORT PROFILE (Underline if supported, circle if selected)
COMPANY: Apparat, Inc.
PRODUCT: 7950 Short Slot Parallel/Serial Card

PORT 9-port male   PORT TYPE: serial _____
CONNECTOR: DB25 9-PIN 8-PIN(modular) _____   GENDER: male female
PIN CONFIGURATION: C16

PIN	FUNCTION	DIRECTION
1:CD	Carrier Detect	TO
2:RD	Receive Data	TO
3:TD	Transmit Data	FROM
4:DTR	Data Terminal Ready	FROM
5:SG	Signal Ground	N/A
6:DSR	Data Set Ready	TO
7:RTS	Request to Send	FROM
8:CTS	Clear to Send	TO
9:RI	Ring Indicator	TO

FLOW CONTROL: 5 6 8   XON: ACK: LEADS THAT MUST BE ON: _ _ _
SPEEDS: 110 300 600 1200 1800 2400 4800 9600 19.2 56k _____
PARITY: even odd space mark none   CHARACTER LENGTH: 7 8 ___
STOP BITS: 1 1.5 2   LINE-ENDING CHARS: cr lf cr/lf
DISCONNECT SEQUENCE: EOT DEL ~. _____   MODE: async sync isoch
NOTE 1:
NOTE 2:

COMPUTER PORT PROFILE (Underline if supported, circle if selected)
COMPANY: Apparat, Inc.
PRODUCT: Crambo II & Limbo II boards

PORT 9-PIN male   PORT TYPE: serial _____
CONNECTOR: DB25 9-PIN 8-PIN(modular) _____   GENDER: male female
PIN CONFIGURATION: C16

PIN	FUNCTION	DIRECTION
1:CD	Carrier Detect	TO
2:RD	Receive Data	TO
3:TD	Transmit Data	FROM
4:DTR	Data Terminal Ready	FROM
5:SG	Signal Ground	N/A
6:DSR	Data Set Ready	TO
7:RTS	Request to Send	FROM
8:CTS	Clear to Send	TO
9:RI	Ring Indicator	TO

FLOW CONTROL: 5 6 8   XON: ACK: LEADS THAT MUST BE ON: _ _ _
SPEEDS: 110 300 600 1200 1800 2400 4800 9600 19.2 56k _____
PARITY: even odd space mark none   CHARACTER LENGTH: 7 8 ___
STOP BITS: 1 1.5 2   LINE-ENDING CHARS: cr lf cr/lf
DISCONNECT SEQUENCE: EOT DEL ~. _____   MODE: async sync isoch
NOTE 1:
NOTE 2:

COMPUTER PORT PROFILE (Underline if supported, circle if selected)
COMPANY: Applied Engineering
PRODUCT: Serial Pro board (for Apple)

PORT female-modem port   PORT TYPE: serial _____
CONNECTOR: DB25 9-PIN 8-PIN(modular) _____   GENDER: male female
PIN CONFIGURATION: C07

PIN	FUNCTION	DIRECTION
1:CG	Chassis Ground	N/A
2:TD	Transmit Data	FROM
3:RD	Receive Data	TO
6:DSR	Data Set Ready	TO
7:SG	Signal Ground	N/A
8:DCD	Data Carrier Detect	TO
20:DTR	Data Terminal Ready	FROM

FLOW CONTROL: XON: ACK: LEADS THAT MUST BE ON: _ _ _
SPEEDS: 110 300 600 1200 1800 2400 4800 9600 19.2 56k _____
PARITY: even odd space mark none   CHARACTER LENGTH: 7 8 ___
STOP BITS: 1 1.5 2   LINE-ENDING CHARS: cr lf cr/lf
DISCONNECT SEQUENCE: EOT DEL ~. _____   MODE: async sync isoch
NOTE 1:
NOTE 2:

COMPUTER PORT PROFILE (Underline if supported, circle if selected)
COMPANY: Applied Engineering
PRODUCT: Serial Pro board (for Apple)

PORT female-printer port   PORT TYPE: serial _____
CONNECTOR: DB25 9-PIN 8-PIN(modular) _____ GENDER: male female
PIN CONFIGURATION: C09

PIN	FUNCTION	DIRECTION
1:CG	Chassis Ground	N/A
2:RD	Receive Data	TO
3:TD	Transmit Data	FROM
4:DCD	Data Carrier Detect	TO
6:DTR	Data Terminal Ready	FROM
7:SG	Signal Ground	N/A
8:DTR	Data Terminal Ready	FROM
11:DCD	Data Carrier Detect	TO
19:DCD	Data Carrier Detect	TO
20:DSR	Data Set Ready	TO

FLOW CONTROL: 4 11 19 20 XON: YES ACK: LEADS THAT MUST BE ON: _ _ _
SPEEDS: 110 300 600 1200 1800 2400 4800 9600 19.2 56k _____
PARITY: even odd space mark none   CHARACTER LENGTH: 7 8 ___
STOP BITS: 1 1.5 2   LINE-ENDING CHARS: cr lf cr/lf
DISCONNECT SEQUENCE: EOT DEL ~. _____   MODE: async sync isoch
NOTE 1: Select one of the "DCD" leads as the input flow
NOTE 2: control lead to be connected to the printer lead.

COMPUTER PORT PROFILE (Underline if supported, circle if selected)
COMPANY: Aprotek Microcomputer Periph.
PRODUCT: 1000 Eprom Programmer

PORT female   PORT TYPE: serial _____
CONNECTOR: DB25 9-PIN 8-PIN(modular) _____ GENDER: male female
PIN CONFIGURATION: C06

PIN	FUNCTION	DIRECTION
2:RD	Receive Data	TO
3:TD	Transmit Data	FROM
7:SG	Signal Ground	N/A

FLOW CONTROL: XON: ACK: LEADS THAT MUST BE ON: _ _ _
SPEEDS: 110 300 600 1200 1800 2400 4800 9600 19.2 56k _____
PARITY: even odd space mark none   CHARACTER LENGTH: 7 8 ___
STOP BITS: 1 1.5 2   LINE-ENDING CHARS: cr lf cr/lf
DISCONNECT SEQUENCE: EOT DEL ~. _____   MODE: async sync isoch
NOTE 1: Leads 4 & 5 are internally jumpered together.
NOTE 2: Leads 20 & 6 are also jumpered together

COMPUTER PORT PROFILE (Underline if supported, circle if selected)
COMPANY: Basic Time
PRODUCT: AT4X4 board

PORT male(9-PIN)   PORT TYPE: serial _____
CONNECTOR: DB25 9-PIN 8-PIN(modular) _____   GENDER: male female
PIN CONFIGURATION: C16

PIN	FUNCTION	DIRECTION
1:DCD	Data Carrier Detect	TO
2:RD	Receive Data	TO
3:TD	Transmit Data	FROM
4:DTR	Data Terminal Ready	FROM
5:SG	Signal Ground	N/A
6:DSR	Data Set Ready	TO
7:RTS	Request to Send	FROM
8:CTS	Clear to Send	TO
9:RI	Ring Indicator	TO

FLOW CONTROL: 1 6 8   XON: ACK: LEADS THAT MUST BE ON: _ _ _
SPEEDS: 110 300 600 1200 1800 2400 4800 9600 19.2 56k _____
PARITY: even odd space mark none   CHARACTER LENGTH: 7 8 ___
STOP BITS: 1 1.5 2   LINE-ENDING CHARS: cr lf cr/lf
DISCONNECT SEQUENCE: EOT DEL ~. _____ MODE: async sync isoch
NOTE 1: Leads 1/6/8 should be on for data transmission.
NOTE 2:

COMPUTER PORT PROFILE (Underline if supported, circle if selected)
COMPANY: Basic Time
PRODUCT: AT4X4 boards

PORT male(25-PIN)   PORT TYPE: serial _____
CONNECTOR: DB25 9-PIN 8-PIN(modular) _____   GENDER: male female
PIN CONFIGURATION: C01

PIN	FUNCTION	DIRECTION
2:TD	Transmit Data	FROM
3:RD	Receive Data	TO
4:RTS	Request to Send	FROM
5:CTS	Clear to Send	TO
6:DSR	Data Set Ready	TO
7:SG	Signal Ground	N/A
8:CD	Carrier Detect	TO
20:DTR	Data Terminal Ready	FROM
22:RI	Ring Indicator	TO

FLOW CONTROL: 5 6 8   XON: ACK: LEADS THAT MUST BE ON: _ _ _
SPEEDS: 110 300 600 1200 1800 2400 4800 9600 19.2 56k _____
PARITY: even odd space mark none   CHARACTER LENGTH: 7 8 ___
STOP BITS: 1 1.5 2   LINE-ENDING CHARS: cr lf cr/lf
DISCONNECT SEQUENCE: EOT DEL ~. _____ MODE: async sync isoch
NOTE 1: Leads 5/6/8 should be on for data transmission.
NOTE 2:

COMPUTER PORT PROFILE (Underline if supported, circle if selected)
COMPANY: Basic Time
PRODUCT: B-250 I/O Card

PORT male   PORT TYPE: serial _____
CONNECTOR: DB25 9-PIN 8-PIN(modular) _____   GENDER: male female
PIN CONFIGURATION: C01

PIN	FUNCTION	DIRECTION
2:TD	Transmit Data	FROM
3:RD	Receive Data	TO
4:RTS	Request to Send	FROM
5:CS		TO
6:DSR	Data Set Ready	TO
7:SG	Signal Ground	N/A
8:CD	Carrier Detect	TO
20:DTR	Data Terminal Ready	FROM
22:RI	Ring Indicator	TO

FLOW CONTROL: 5 6 8   XON: ACK: LEADS THAT MUST BE ON: _ _ _
SPEEDS: 110 300 600 1200 1800 2400 4800 9600 19.2 56k _____
PARITY: even odd space mark none   CHARACTER LENGTH: 7 8 ___
STOP BITS: 1 1.5 2   LINE-ENDING CHARS: cr lf cr/lf
DISCONNECT SEQUENCE: EOT DEL ~. _____ MODE: async sync isoch
NOTE 1: Leads 5/6/8 should be on for data transmission
NOTE 2:

COMPUTER PORT PROFILE (Underline if supported, circle if selected)
COMPANY: Basic Time
PRODUCT: BTurbo 286 computer

PORT male(25-PIN)   PORT TYPE: serial _____
CONNECTOR: DB25 9-PIN 8-PIN(modular) _____   GENDER: male female
PIN CONFIGURATION: C01

PIN	FUNCTION	DIRECTION
2:TD	Transmit Data	FROM
3:RD	Receive Data	TO
4:RTS	Request to Send	FROM
5:CTS	Clear to Send	TO
6:DSR	Data Set Ready	TO
7:SG	Signal Ground	N/A
8:CD	Carrier Detect	TO
20:DTR	Data Terminal Ready	FROM
22:RI	Ring Indicator	TO

FLOW CONTROL: 5 6 8   XON: ACK: LEADS THAT MUST BE ON: _ _ _
SPEEDS: 110 300 600 1200 1800 2400 4800 9600 19.2 56k _____
PARITY: even odd space mark none   CHARACTER LENGTH: 7 8 ___
STOP BITS: 1 1.5 2   LINE-ENDING CHARS: cr lf cr/lf
DISCONNECT SEQUENCE: EOT DEL ~. _____ MODE: async sync isoch
NOTE 1: Leads 5/6/8 should be on for data transmission.
NOTE 2:

COMPUTER PORT PROFILE (Underline if supported, circle if selected)
COMPANY: Boca Research, Inc.
PRODUCT: BOCA I/O board

PORT male(9-PIN)   PORT TYPE: serial _____
CONNECTOR: DB25 9-PIN 8-PIN(modular) ____   GENDER: male female
PIN CONFIGURATION: C16

PIN	FUNCTION	DIRECTION
1:CD	Carrier Detect	TO
2:RD	Receive Data	TO
3:TD	Transmit Data	FROM
4:DTR	Data Terminal Ready	FROM
5:SG	Signal Ground	N/A
6:DSR	Data Set Ready	TO
7:RTS	Request to Send	FROM
8:CTS	Clear to Send	TO
9:RI	Ring Indicator	TO

FLOW CONTROL: 1 6 8   XON: ACK: LEADS THAT MUST BE ON: _ _ _
SPEEDS: 110 300 600 1200 1800 2400 4800 9600 19.2 56k _____
PARITY: even odd space mark none   CHARACTER LENGTH: 7 8 ___
STOP BITS: 1 1.5 2   LINE-ENDING CHARS: cr lf cr/lf
DISCONNECT SEQUENCE: EOT DEL ~. _____   MODE: async sync isoch
NOTE 1: Leads 1/6/8 should be on for data transmission
NOTE 2:

COMPUTER PORT PROFILE (Underline if supported, circle if selected)
COMPANY: Boca Research, Inc.
PRODUCT: MEMEK board

PORT male(DB-25P)   PORT TYPE: serial _____
CONNECTOR: DB25 9-PIN 8-PIN(modular) ____   GENDER: male female
PIN CONFIGURATION: C01

PIN	FUNCTION	DIRECTION
1:CG	Chassis Ground	N/A
2:TD	Transmit Data	FROM
3:RD	Receive Data	TO
4:RTS	Request to Send	FROM
5:CTS	Clear to Send	TO
6:DSR	Data Set Ready	TO
7:SG	Signal Ground	N/A
8:DCD	Data Carrier Detect	TO
20:DTR	Data Terminal Ready	FROM
22:RI	Ring Indicator	TO

FLOW CONTROL: 5 6 8   XON: ACK: LEADS THAT MUST BE ON: _ _ _
SPEEDS: 110 300 600 1200 1800 2400 4800 9600 19.2 56k _____
PARITY: even odd space mark none   CHARACTER LENGTH: 7 8 ___
STOP BITS: 1 1.5 2   LINE-ENDING CHARS: cr lf cr/lf
DISCONNECT SEQUENCE: EOT DEL ~. _____   MODE: async sync isoch
NOTE 1: Leads 5/6/8 should be on for transmission.
NOTE 2:

COMPUTER PORT PROFILE (Underline if supported, circle if selected)
COMPANY: BTI Computer Systems
PRODUCT: 5000 computer

PORT female   PORT TYPE: serial _____
CONNECTOR: DB25 9-PIN 8-PIN(modular) _____   GENDER: male female
PIN CONFIGURATION: C17

PIN	FUNCTION	DIRECTION
1:G	Ground	N/A
2:RD	Receive Data	TO
3:TD	Transmit Data	FROM
7:SG	Signal Ground	N/A
8:DTR	Data Terminal Ready	FROM
9:+12V		FROM
10:-12V		FROM
20:CD	Carrier Detect	TO
22:RI	Ring Indicator	TO

FLOW CONTROL: XON: YES ACK: LEADS THAT MUST BE ON: _ _ _
SPEEDS: 110 300 600 1200 1800 2400 4800 9600 19.2 56k _____
PARITY: even odd space mark none   CHARACTER LENGTH: 7 8 ___
STOP BITS: 1 1.5 2   LINE-ENDING CHARS: cr lf cr/lf
DISCONNECT SEQUENCE: EOT DEL ~. _____ MODE: async sync isoch
NOTE 1:
NOTE 2:

COMPUTER PORT PROFILE (Underline if supported, circle if selected)
COMPANY: BTI Computer Systems
PRODUCT: BTI 8000 computer

PORT female   PORT TYPE: serial _____
CONNECTOR: DB25 9-PIN 8-PIN(modular) _____   GENDER: male female
PIN CONFIGURATION: C14

PIN	FUNCTION	DIRECTION	PIN	FUNCTION	DIRECTION
1:FG	Frame Ground	N/A	7:SG	Signal Ground	N/A
2:TD	Transmit Data	TO	8:DCD	Data Carrier Detect	FROM
3:RD	Receive Data	FROM	9:+12V		FROM
4:RTS	Request to Send	TO	10:-12V		FROM
5:CTS	Clear to Send	FROM	20:DTR	Data Terminal Ready	TO
6:DSR	Data Set Ready	TO	22:RI	Ring Indicator	FROM

FLOW CONTROL: 4   XON: YES ACK: LEADS THAT MUST BE ON: _ _ _
SPEEDS: 110 300 600 1200 1800 2400 4800 9600 19.2 56k _____
PARITY: even odd space mark none   CHARACTER LENGTH: 7 8 ___
STOP BITS: 1 1.5 2   LINE-ENDING CHARS: cr lf cr/lf
DISCONNECT SEQUENCE: EOT DEL ~. _____ MODE: async sync isoch
NOTE 1: The jumper plug should be in the "TERM" position
NOTE 2: so the port emulates DCE.

COMPUTER PORT PROFILE (Underline if supported, circle if selected)
COMPANY: BTI Computer Systems
PRODUCT: BTI 8000 computer

PORT female   PORT TYPE: serial _____
CONNECTOR: DB25 9-PIN 8-PIN(modular) _____   GENDER: male female
PIN CONFIGURATION: C01

PIN	FUNCTION	DIRECTION	PIN	FUNCTION	DIRECTION
1:FG	Frame Ground	N/A	7:SG	Signal Ground	N/A
2:TD	Transmit Data	FROM	8:DCD	Data Carrier Detect	TO
3:RD	Receive Data	TO	9:+12V		FROM
4:RTS	Request to Send	FROM	10:-12V		FROM
5:CTS	Clear to Send	TO	20:DTR	Data Terminal Ready	FROM
6:DSR	Data Set Ready	TO	22:RI	Ring Indicator	TO

FLOW CONTROL: 5   XON: YES ACK: LEADS THAT MUST BE ON: _ _ _
SPEEDS: 110 300 600 1200 1800 2400 4800 9600 19.2 56k _____
PARITY: even odd space mark none   CHARACTER LENGTH: 7 8 ___
STOP BITS: 1 1.5 2   LINE-ENDING CHARS: cr lf cr/lf
DISCONNECT SEQUENCE: EOT DEL ~. _____   MODE: async sync isoch
NOTE 1: The jumper plug should be in the "MOD" position to
NOTE 2: have the port emulate DTE

COMPUTER PORT PROFILE (Underline if supported, circle if selected)
COMPANY: CH Products
PRODUCT: Microstick

PORT female (DB-25)   PORT TYPE: serial _____
CONNECTOR: DB25 9-PIN 8-PIN(modular) _____   GENDER: male female
PIN CONFIGURATION: C06

PIN	FUNCTION	DIRECTION
2:RD	Receive Data	TO
3:TD	Transmit Data	FROM
7:SG	Signal Ground	N/A
11:+V		

FLOW CONTROL: XON: ACK: LEADS THAT MUST BE ON: _ _ _
SPEEDS: 110 300 600 1200 1800 2400 4800 9600 19.2 56k _____
PARITY: even odd space mark none   CHARACTER LENGTH: 7 8 ___
STOP BITS: 1 1.5 2   LINE-ENDING CHARS: cr lf cr/lf
DISCONNECT SEQUENCE: EOT DEL ~. _____   MODE: async sync isoch
NOTE 1:
NOTE 2:

COMPUTER PORT PROFILE (Underline if supported, circle if selected)
COMPANY: CompuPro
PRODUCT: Interfacer 3

PORT port 7   PORT TYPE: serial _____
CONNECTOR: DB25 9-PIN 8-PIN(modular) _____   GENDER: male female
PIN CONFIGURATION: C01

PIN	FUNCTION	DIRECTION
2:TD	Transmit Data	FROM
3:RD	Receive Data	TO
4:		FROM
5:		TO
6:		TO
7:SG	Signal Ground	N/A
8:CD	Carrier Detect	TO
20:		FROM

FLOW CONTROL: 5   XON: YES ACK: LEADS THAT MUST BE ON: _ _ _
SPEEDS: 110 300 600 1200 1800 2400 4800 9600 19.2 56k _____
PARITY: even odd space mark none   CHARACTER LENGTH: 7 8 ___
STOP BITS: 1 1.5 2   LINE-ENDING CHARS: cr lf cr/lf
DISCONNECT SEQUENCE: EOT DEL ~. _____ MODE: async sync isoch
NOTE 1: PIN 5 must be high to transmit data.
NOTE 2: PIN 6 must be high to receive data.

COMPUTER PORT PROFILE (Underline if supported, circle if selected)
COMPANY: CompuPro
PRODUCT: Interfacer 3

PORT ports 0-6   PORT TYPE: serial _____
CONNECTOR: DB25 9-PIN 8-PIN(modular) _____   GENDER: male female
PIN CONFIGURATION: C03

PIN	FUNCTION	DIRECTION
2:RD	Receive Data	TO
3:TD	Transmit Data	FROM
4:		TO
5:		FROM
6:		FROM
7:SG	Signal Ground	N/A
8:		TO
20:		TO

FLOW CONTROL: XON: YES ACK: LEADS THAT MUST BE ON: _ _ _
SPEEDS: 110 300 600 1200 1800 2400 4800 9600 19.2 56k _____
PARITY: even odd space mark none   CHARACTER LENGTH: 7 8 ___
STOP BITS: 1 1.5 2   LINE-ENDING CHARS: cr lf cr/lf
DISCONNECT SEQUENCE: EOT DEL ~. _____ MODE: async sync isoch
NOTE 1:
NOTE 2:

COMPUTER PORT PROFILE (Underline if supported, circle if selected)
COMPANY: CompuPro
PRODUCT: Interfacer 4

PORT port 3   PORT TYPE: serial _____
CONNECTOR: DB25 9-PIN 8-PIN(modular) _____   GENDER: male female
PIN CONFIGURATION: C01

PIN	FUNCTION	DIRECTION
2:TD	Transmit Data	FROM
3:RD	Receive Data	TO
4:		FROM
5:		TO
6:		TO
7:SG	Signal Ground	N/A
8:CD	Carrier Detect	TO
20:		FROM

FLOW CONTROL: 5   XON: YES ACK: LEADS THAT MUST BE ON: _ _ _
SPEEDS: 110 300 600 1200 1800 2400 4800 9600 19.2 56k _____
PARITY: even odd space mark none   CHARACTER LENGTH: 7 8 ___
STOP BITS: 1 1.5 2   LINE-ENDING CHARS: cr lf cr/lf
DISCONNECT SEQUENCE: EOT DEL ~. _____   MODE: async sync isoch
NOTE 1: PIN 5 must be high to transmit data.
NOTE 2: PIN 6 must be high to receive data.

COMPUTER PORT PROFILE (Underline if supported, circle if selected)
COMPANY: CompuPro
PRODUCT: Interfacer 4 board

PORT ports 1 & 2   PORT TYPE: serial _____
CONNECTOR: DB25 9-PIN 8-PIN(modular) _____   GENDER: male female
PIN CONFIGURATION: C03

PIN	FUNCTION	DIRECTION
2:RD	Receive Data	TO
3:TD	Transmit Data	FROM
4:		TO
5:		FROM
6:		FROM
7:SG	Signal Ground	N/A
8:		TO
20:		TO

FLOW CONTROL: XON: YES ACK: LEADS THAT MUST BE ON: _ _ _
SPEEDS: 110 300 600 1200 1800 2400 4800 9600 19.2 56k _____
PARITY: even odd space mark none   CHARACTER LENGTH: 7 8 ___
STOP BITS: 1 1.5 2   LINE-ENDING CHARS: cr lf cr/lf
DISCONNECT SEQUENCE: EOT DEL ~. _____   MODE: async sync isoch
NOTE 1:
NOTE 2:

COMPUTER PORT PROFILE **(Underline if supported, circle if selected)**
COMPANY: CompuPro
PRODUCT: SPIO & Interfacer 3A boards

PORT port 7   PORT TYPE: serial _____
CONNECTOR: DB25 9-PIN 8-PIN(modular) _____   GENDER: male female
PIN CONFIGURATION: C07

PIN	FUNCTION	DIRECTION
2:TD	Transmit Data	FROM
3:RD	Receive Data	TO
5:		TO
7:SG	Signal Ground	N/A
8:CD	Carrier Detect	TO
20:		FROM

FLOW CONTROL: 5   XON: YES ACK: LEADS THAT MUST BE ON: _ _ _
SPEEDS: 110 300 600 1200 1800 2400 4800 9600 19.2 56k _____
PARITY: even odd space mark none   CHARACTER LENGTH: 7 8 ___
STOP BITS: 1 1.5 2   LINE-ENDING CHARS: cr lf cr/lf
DISCONNECT SEQUENCE: EOT DEL ~. _____   MODE: async sync isoch
NOTE 1: PIN 5 must be high to transmit data.
NOTE 2:

COMPUTER PORT PROFILE **(Underline if supported, circle if selected)**
COMPANY: CompuPro
PRODUCT: SPIO, Interfacer 3A boards

PORT ports 0-6   PORT TYPE: serial _____
CONNECTOR: DB25 9-PIN 8-PIN(modular) _____   GENDER: male female
PIN CONFIGURATION: C03

PIN	FUNCTION	DIRECTION
2:RD	Receive Data	TO
3:TD	Transmit Data	FROM
5:		FROM
7:SG	Signal Ground	N/A
8:		TO
20:		TO

FLOW CONTROL: 20   XON: YES ACK: LEADS THAT MUST BE ON: _ _ _
SPEEDS: 110 300 600 1200 1800 2400 4800 9600 19.2 56k _____
PARITY: even odd space mark none   CHARACTER LENGTH: 7 8 ___
STOP BITS: 1 1.5 2   LINE-ENDING CHARS: cr lf cr/lf
DISCONNECT SEQUENCE: EOT DEL ~. _____   MODE: async sync isoch
NOTE 1: PIN 20 must be high to transmit data
NOTE 2:

COMPUTER PORT PROFILE (Underline if supported, circle if selected)
COMPANY: CompuPro
PRODUCT: System Support 1 boards

PORT ports 1 & 2   PORT TYPE: serial _____
CONNECTOR: DB25 9-PIN 8-PIN(modular) _____   GENDER: male female
PIN CONFIGURATION: C03

PIN	FUNCTION	DIRECTION
2:TD	Transmit Data	TO
3:RD	Receive Data	FROM
4:		TO
5:		FROM
6:		FROM
7:SG	Signal Ground	N/A
8:		TO
20:		TO

FLOW CONTROL: XON: YES ACK: LEADS THAT MUST BE ON: _ _ _
SPEEDS: 110 300 600 1200 1800 2400 4800 9600 19.2 56k _____
PARITY: even odd space mark none   CHARACTER LENGTH: 7 8 ___
STOP BITS: 1 1.5 2   LINE-ENDING CHARS: cr lf cr/lf
DISCONNECT SEQUENCE: EOT DEL ~. _____   MODE: async sync isoch
NOTE 1:
NOTE 2:

COMPUTER PORT PROFILE (Underline if supported, circle if selected)
COMPANY: CompuPro
PRODUCT: System Support 2, SP186, & SPUZ boards

PORT DCE   PORT TYPE: serial _____
CONNECTOR: DB25 9-PIN 8-PIN(modular) _____   GENDER: male female
PIN CONFIGURATION: C03

PIN	FUNCTION	DIRECTION
2:RD	Receive Data	TO
3:TD	Transmit Data	FROM
5:		FROM
7:SG	Signal Ground	N/A
8:		TO
20:		TO

FLOW CONTROL: 20   XON: YES ACK: LEADS THAT MUST BE ON: _ _ _
SPEEDS: 110 300 600 1200 1800 2400 4800 9600 19.2 56k _____
PARITY: even odd space mark none   CHARACTER LENGTH: 7 8 ___
STOP BITS: 1 1.5 2   LINE-ENDING CHARS: cr lf cr/lf
DISCONNECT SEQUENCE: EOT DEL ~. _____   MODE: async sync isoch
NOTE 1: PIN 20 must be on to transmit data
NOTE 2:

COMPUTER PORT PROFILE (Underline if supported, circle if selected)
COMPANY: Computer Friends
PRODUCT: Mac Master (Serial)

PORT female (J1)   PORT TYPE: serial _____
CONNECTOR: DB25 9-PIN 8-PIN(modular) _____   GENDER: male female
PIN CONFIGURATION: C01

PIN	FUNCTION	DIRECTION
1:FG	Frame Ground	N/A
2:TD	Transmit Data	FROM
3:RD	Receive Data	TO
4:RTS	Request to Send	FROM
5:CTS	Clear to Send	TO
6:DSR	Data Set Ready	TO
7:SG	Signal Ground	N/A
8:DCD	Data Carrier Detect	TO
20:DTR	Data Terminal Ready	FROM

FLOW CONTROL: 20   XON: YES ACK: LEADS THAT MUST BE ON: _ _ _
SPEEDS: 110 300 600 1200 1800 2400 4800 9600 19.2 56k _____
PARITY: even odd space mark none   CHARACTER LENGTH: 7 8 ___
STOP BITS: 1 1.5 2   LINE-ENDING CHARS: cr lf cr/lf
DISCONNECT SEQUENCE: EOT DEL ~. _____ MODE: async sync isoch
NOTE 1: Leads 5/6/8 must be on.
NOTE 2:

COMPUTER PORT PROFILE (Underline if supported, circle if selected)
COMPANY: Computer Friends
PRODUCT: Mac Master (Serial)

PORT female (J2)   PORT TYPE: serial _____
CONNECTOR: DB25 9-PIN 8-PIN(modular) _____   GENDER: male female
PIN CONFIGURATION: C14

PIN	FUNCTION	DIRECTION
1:FG	Frame Ground	N/A
2:TD	Transmit Data	TO
3:RD	Receive Data	FROM
5:CTS	Clear to Send	FROM
6:DSR	Data Set Ready	FROM
7:SG	Signal Ground	N/A
8:DCD	Data Carrier Detect	FROM
20:DTR	Data Terminal Ready	TO

FLOW CONTROL: 20   XON: YES ACK: LEADS THAT MUST BE ON: _ _ _
SPEEDS: 110 300 600 1200 1800 2400 4800 9600 19.2 56k _____
PARITY: even odd space mark none   CHARACTER LENGTH: 7 8 ___
STOP BITS: 1 1.5 2   LINE-ENDING CHARS: cr lf cr/lf
DISCONNECT SEQUENCE: EOT DEL ~. _____ MODE: async sync isoch
NOTE 1: Lead 20 should be connected to flow control lead
NOTE 2: of attached device

COMPUTER PORT PROFILE (Underline if supported, circle if selected)
COMPANY: Connecticut microComputer, Inc
PRODUCT: A64R, B64R, C64R, MAR, N16R controllers

PORT female   PORT TYPE: serial _____
CONNECTOR: DB25 9-PIN 8-PIN(modular) _____   GENDER: male female
PIN CONFIGURATION: C14

PIN	FUNCTION	DIRECTION
1:PG	Protective Ground	N/A
2:TD	Transmit Data	TO
3:RD	Receive Data	FROM
4:RTS	Request to Send	TO
5:CTS	Clear to Send	FROM
6:DSR	Data Set Ready	FROM
7:SG	Signal Ground	N/A
8:RLSD	Rec.Line Signal Detect	FROM
20:DTR	Data Terminal Ready	TO

FLOW CONTROL: 20 4   XON: YES ACK: LEADS THAT MUST BE ON: _ _ _
SPEEDS: 110 300 600 1200 1800 2400 4800 9600 19.2 56k _____
PARITY: even odd space mark none   CHARACTER LENGTH: 7 8 ___
STOP BITS: 1 1.5 2   LINE-ENDING CHARS: cr lf cr/lf
DISCONNECT SEQUENCE: EOT DEL ~. _____   MODE: async sync isoch
NOTE 1: Leads 6 & 8 are always on
NOTE 2:

COMPUTER PORT PROFILE (Underline if supported, circle if selected)
COMPANY: Connecticut microComputer Inc.
PRODUCT: BUSSter modules

PORT female   PORT TYPE: serial _____
CONNECTOR: DB25 9-PIN 8-PIN(modular) _____   GENDER: male female
PIN CONFIGURATION: C14

PIN	FUNCTION	DIRECTION
1:PG	Protective Ground	N/A
2:TD	Transmit Data	TO
3:RD	Receive Data	FROM
4:RTS	Request to Send	TO
5:CTS	Clear to Send	FROM
6:DSR	Data Set Ready	FROM
7:SG	Signal Ground	N/A
8:RLSD	Rec.Line Signal Detect	FROM
20:DTR	Data Terminal Ready	TO

FLOW CONTROL: 20   XON: ACK: LEADS THAT MUST BE ON: _ _ _
SPEEDS: 110 300 600 1200 1800 2400 4800 9600 19.2 56k _____
PARITY: even odd space mark none   CHARACTER LENGTH: 7 8 ___
STOP BITS: 1 1.5 2   LINE-ENDING CHARS: cr lf cr/lf
DISCONNECT SEQUENCE: EOT DEL ~. _____   MODE: async sync isoch
NOTE 1: Lead 20 & 4 are the input busy leads. Leasd 6 & 8
NOTE 2: are always +12V. Lead 5 is the ready output lead

COMPUTER PORT PROFILE (Underline if supported, circle if selected)
COMPANY: Connecticut microComputer, Inc
PRODUCT: GPAD-R interface

PORT male or female   PORT TYPE: serial _____
CONNECTOR: DB25 9-PIN 8-PIN(modular) _____   GENDER: male female
PIN CONFIGURATION: C14

PIN	FUNCTION	DIRECTION
1:PG	Protective Ground	N/A
2:TD	Transmit Data	TO
3:RD	Receive Data	FROM
4:RTS	Request to Send	TO
5:CTS	Clear to Send	FROM
6:DSR	Data Set Ready	FROM
7:SG	Signal Ground	N/A
8:RLSD	Rec.Line Signal Detect	FROM
20:DTR	Data Terminal Ready	TO

FLOW CONTROL: 20 4   XON: YES   ACK: LEADS THAT MUST BE ON: _ _ _
SPEEDS: 110 300 600 1200 1800 2400 4800 9600 19.2 56k _____
PARITY: even odd space mark none   CHARACTER LENGTH: 7 8 ___
STOP BITS: 1 1.5 2   LINE-ENDING CHARS: cr lf cr/lf
DISCONNECT SEQUENCE: EOT DEL ~. _____   MODE: async sync isoch
NOTE 1: Leads 6 & 8 are always on.
NOTE 2:

COMPUTER PORT PROFILE (Underline if supported, circle if selected)
COMPANY: Consolink Corporation
PRODUCT: Micro Spooler

PORT female (serial in)   PORT TYPE: serial _____
CONNECTOR: DB25 9-PIN 8-PIN(modular) _____   GENDER: male female
PIN CONFIGURATION: C14

PIN	FUNCTION	DIRECTION
1:FG	Frame Ground	N/A
2:TD	Transmit Data	TO
3:RD	Receive Data	FROM
5:CTS	Clear to Send	FROM
6:DSR	Data Set Ready	FROM
7:SG	Signal Ground	N/A
20:DTR	Data Terminal Ready	TO

FLOW CONTROL: 20   XON: YES   ACK: YES   LEADS THAT MUST BE ON: _ _ _
SPEEDS: 110 300 600 1200 1800 2400 4800 9600 19.2 56k _____
PARITY: even odd space mark none   CHARACTER LENGTH: 7 8 ___
STOP BITS: 1 1.5 2   LINE-ENDING CHARS: cr lf cr/lf
DISCONNECT SEQUENCE: EOT DEL ~. _____   MODE: async sync isoch
NOTE 1: Lead 20 should be connected to the attached
NOTE 2: printer's flow control lead

COMPUTER PORT PROFILE   (Underline if supported, circle if selected)
COMPANY: Consolink Corporation
PRODUCT: SooperSpooler

PORT female (serial out)   PORT TYPE: serial _____
CONNECTOR: DB25 9-PIN 8-PIN(modular) _____   GENDER: male female
PIN CONFIGURATION: C14

PIN	FUNCTION	DIRECTION
1:CG	Chassis Ground	N/A
2:TD	Transmit Data	TO
3:RD	Receive Data	FROM
5:CTS	Clear to Send	FROM
6:DSR	Data Set Ready	FROM
7:SG	Signal Ground	N/A
20:DTR	Data Terminal Ready	TO

FLOW CONTROL: XON: YES ACK: YES LEADS THAT MUST BE ON: _ _ _
SPEEDS: 110 300 600 1200 1800 2400 4800 9600 19.2 56k _____
PARITY: even odd space mark none   CHARACTER LENGTH: 7 8 ___
STOP BITS: 1 1.5 2   LINE-ENDING CHARS: cr lf cr/lf
DISCONNECT SEQUENCE: EOT DEL ~. _____   MODE: async sync isoch
NOTE 1: Lead 20 should be connected to the hardware flow
NOTE 2: control lead of the attached printer

COMPUTER PORT PROFILE   (Underline if supported, circle if selected)
COMPANY: Convergent Technologies
PRODUCT: MegaFrame s/1280 computer

PORT female   PORT TYPE: serial _____
CONNECTOR: DB25 9-PIN 8-PIN(modular) _____   GENDER: male female
PIN CONFIGURATION: C01

PIN	FUNCTION	DIRECTION
1:PG	Protective Ground	N/A
2:TD	Transmit Data	FROM
3:RD	Receive Data	TO
4:RTS	Request to Send	FROM
5:CTS	Clear to Send	TO
6:DSR	Data Set Ready	TO
7:SG	Signal Ground	N/A
8:CD	Carrier Detect	TO
20:DTR	Data Terminal Ready	FROM

FLOW CONTROL: 5 6 8   XON: YES ACK: LEADS THAT MUST BE ON: _ _ _
SPEEDS: 110 300 600 1200 1800 2400 4800 9600 19.2 56k _____
PARITY: even odd space mark none   CHARACTER LENGTH: 7 8 ___
STOP BITS: 1 1.5 2   LINE-ENDING CHARS: cr lf cr/lf
DISCONNECT SEQUENCE: EOT DEL ~. _____   MODE: async sync isoch
NOTE 1:
NOTE 2:

COMPUTER PORT PROFILE (Underline if supported, circle if selected)
COMPANY: Convergent Technologies
PRODUCT: MightyFrame S/320 computer

PORT female   PORT TYPE: serial _____
CONNECTOR: DB25 9-PIN 8-PIN(modular) _____ GENDER: male female
PIN CONFIGURATION: C01

PIN	FUNCTION	DIRECTION
1:PG	Protective Ground	N/A
2:TD	Transmit Data	FROM
3:RD	Receive Data	TO
4:RTS	Request to Send	FROM
5:CTS	Clear to Send	TO
6:DSR	Data Set Ready	TO
7:SG	Signal Ground	N/A
8:CD	Carrier Detect	TO
20:DTR	Data Terminal Ready	FROM

FLOW CONTROL: 5 6 8   XON: YES ACK: LEADS THAT MUST BE ON: _ _ _
SPEEDS: 110 300 600 1200 1800 2400 4800 9600 19.2 56k _____
PARITY: even odd space mark none   CHARACTER LENGTH: 7 8 ___
STOP BITS: 1 1.5 2   LINE-ENDING CHARS: cr lf cr/lf
DISCONNECT SEQUENCE: EOT DEL ~. _____ MODE: async sync isoch
NOTE 1:
NOTE 2:

COMPUTER PORT PROFILE (Underline if supported, circle if selected)
COMPANY: Data World Products
PRODUCT: Sensatrol controller

PORT male & female   PORT TYPE: serial _____
CONNECTOR: DB25 9-PIN 8-PIN(modular) _____ GENDER: male female
PIN CONFIGURATION: C14

PIN	FUNCTION	DIRECTION
1:PG	Protective Ground	N/A
2:TD	Transmit Data	TO
3:RD	Receive Data	FROM
4:RTS	Request to Send	TO
5:CTS	Clear to Send	FROM
6:DSR	Data Set Ready	FROM
7:SG	Signal Ground	N/A
20:DTR	Data Terminal Ready	TO

FLOW CONTROL: XON: ACK: LEADS THAT MUST BE ON: _ _ _
SPEEDS: 110 300 600 1200 1800 2400 4800 9600 19.2 56k _____
PARITY: even odd space mark none   CHARACTER LENGTH: 7 8 ___
STOP BITS: 1 1.5 2   LINE-ENDING CHARS: cr lf cr/lf
DISCONNECT SEQUENCE: EOT DEL ~. _____ MODE: async sync isoch
NOTE 1:
NOTE 2:

COMPUTER PORT PROFILE (Underline if supported, circle if selected)
COMPANY: Datacom Northwest, Inc.
PRODUCT: Printer Sharing Unit

PORT female (J1-J8)   PORT TYPE: serial _____
CONNECTOR: DB25 9-PIN 8-PIN(modular) _____ GENDER: male female
PIN CONFIGURATION: C14

PIN	FUNCTION	DIRECTION
1:FG	Frame Ground	N/A
2:TD	Transmit Data	TO
3:RD	Receive Data	FROM
4:RTS	Request to Send	TO
5:CTS	Clear to Send	FROM
6:DSR	Data Set Ready	FROM
7:SG	Signal Ground	N/A
8:DCD	Data Carrier Detect	FROM
20:		TO

FLOW CONTROL: 5   XON: YES ACK: LEADS THAT MUST BE ON: _ _ _
SPEEDS: 110 300 600 1200 1800 2400 4800 9600 19.2 56k _____
PARITY: even odd space mark none   CHARACTER LENGTH: 7 8 ___
STOP BITS: 1 1.5 2   LINE-ENDING CHARS: cr lf cr/lf
DISCONNECT SEQUENCE: EOT DEL ~. _____ MODE: async sync isoch
NOTE 1: Lead 5 will be on when the PSU can receive data.
NOTE 2:

COMPUTER PORT PROFILE (Underline if supported, circle if selected)
COMPANY: Datacom Northwest, Inc.
PRODUCT: Printer Sharing Unit

PORT female (JM-printer)   PORT TYPE: serial _____
CONNECTOR: DB25 9-PIN 8-PIN(modular) _____ GENDER: male female
PIN CONFIGURATION: C09

PIN	FUNCTION	DIRECTION	PIN	FUNCTION	DIRECTION
1:FG	Frame Ground	N/A	8:DCD	Data Carrier Detect	FROM
2:TD	Transmit Data	TO	11:B	Busy	TO
3:RD	Receive Data	FROM	12:SDCD	Secondary DCD	TO
4:RTS	Request to Send	TO	19:SRTS	Secondary Req.to Send	TO
5:CTS	Clear to Send	FROM	20:DTR	Data Terminal Ready	TO
6:DSR	Data Set Ready	FROM	25:B	Busy	TO
7:SG	Signal Ground	N/A			

FLOW CONTROL: 20   XON: YES ACK: LEADS THAT MUST BE ON: _ _ _
SPEEDS: 110 300 600 1200 1800 2400 4800 9600 19.2 56k _____
PARITY: even odd space mark none   CHARACTER LENGTH: 7 8 ___
STOP BITS: 1 1.5 2   LINE-ENDING CHARS: cr lf cr/lf
DISCONNECT SEQUENCE: EOT DEL ~. _____ MODE: async sync isoch
NOTE 1: Either of the leads 11/12/19/20/25 may be used
NOTE 2: for flow control from the attached printer.

COMPUTER PORT PROFILE (Underline if supported, circle if selected)
COMPANY: Digital Products, Inc.
PRODUCT: PrintDirector MultiSpool

PORT female(printer port)   PORT TYPE: serial _____
CONNECTOR: DB25 9-PIN 8-PIN(modular) _____ GENDER: male female
PIN CONFIGURATION: C14

PIN	FUNCTION	DIRECTION
1:CG	Chassis Ground	N/A
2:TD	Transmit Data	TO
3:RD	Receive Data	FROM
5:B	Busy	FROM
6:B	Busy	FROM
7:SG	Signal Ground	N/A
8:B	Busy	FROM
20:B	Busy	TO

FLOW CONTROL: 20   XON: YES ACK: LEADS THAT MUST BE ON: _ _ _
SPEEDS: 110 300 600 1200 1800 2400 4800 9600 19.2 56k _____
PARITY: even odd space mark none   CHARACTER LENGTH: 7 8 ___
STOP BITS: 1 1.5 2   LINE-ENDING CHARS: cr lf cr/lf
DISCONNECT SEQUENCE: EOT DEL ~. _____ MODE: async sync isoch
NOTE 1: These PINouts are when the "DCE" mode is used.
NOTE 2:

COMPUTER PORT PROFILE (Underline if supported, circle if selected)
COMPANY: Digital Products, Inc.
PRODUCT: PrintDirector MultiSpool

PORT female(printer port)   PORT TYPE: serial _____
CONNECTOR: DB25 9-PIN 8-PIN(modular) _____ GENDER: male female
PIN CONFIGURATION: C07

PIN	FUNCTION	DIRECTION
1:CG	Chassis Ground	N/A
2:TD	Transmit Data	FROM
3:RD	Receive Data	TO
5:B	Busy	TO
6:B	Busy	TO
7:SG	Signal Ground	N/A
8:B	Busy	TO
20:B	Busy	FROM

FLOW CONTROL: 20   XON: YES ACK: LEADS THAT MUST BE ON: _ _ _
SPEEDS: 110 300 600 1200 1800 2400 4800 9600 19.2 56k _____
PARITY: even odd space mark none   CHARACTER LENGTH: 7 8 ___
STOP BITS: 1 1.5 2   LINE-ENDING CHARS: cr lf cr/lf
DISCONNECT SEQUENCE: EOT DEL ~. _____ MODE: async sync isoch
NOTE 1: These PINouts describe the DTE mode.
NOTE 2:

COMPUTER PORT PROFILE (Underline if supported, circle if selected)
COMPANY: Dual Systems Corporation
PRODUCT: 83/80 & 83/500 systems

PORT female   PORT TYPE: serial _____
CONNECTOR: DB25 9-PIN 8-PIN(modular) _____   GENDER: male female
PIN CONFIGURATION: C14

PIN	FUNCTION	DIRECTION
2:TD	Transmit Data	TO
3:RD	Receive Data	FROM
4:RTS	Request to Send	TO
5:CTS	Clear to Send	FROM
6:DSR	Data Set Ready	FROM
7:SG	Signal Ground	N/A
8:RLSD	Rec.Line Signal Detect	FROM
17:RC	Rec. Clk/Reverse Chann	FROM
20:DTR	Data Terminal Ready	TO
24:TC	Transmit Clock	TO

FLOW CONTROL: 20   XON: YES ACK: LEADS THAT MUST BE ON: _ _ _
SPEEDS: 110 300 600 1200 1800 2400 4800 9600 19.2 56k _____
PARITY: even odd space mark none   CHARACTER LENGTH: 7 8 ___
STOP BITS: 1 1.5 2   LINE-ENDING CHARS: cr lf cr/lf
DISCONNECT SEQUENCE: EOT DEL ~. _____   MODE: async sync isoch
NOTE 1: These ports can be optioned to emulate DTE instead
NOTE 2: of DCE.

COMPUTER PORT PROFILE (Underline if supported, circle if selected)
COMPANY: Dual Systems Corporation
PRODUCT: IOS8 & IOSP boards(Chapperal computer)

PORT female   PORT TYPE: serial _____
CONNECTOR: DB25 9-PIN 8-PIN(modular) _____   GENDER: male female
PIN CONFIGURATION: C14

PIN	FUNCTION	DIRECTION
1:FG	Frame Ground	N/A
2:TD	Transmit Data	TO
3:RD	Receive Data	FROM
5:CTS	Clear to Send	FROM
6:DSR	Data Set Ready	FROM
7:SG	Signal Ground	N/A
8:RLSD	Rec.Line Signal Detect	FROM
20:DTR	Data Terminal Ready	TO

FLOW CONTROL: 20   XON: YES ACK: LEADS THAT MUST BE ON: _ _ _
SPEEDS: 110 300 600 1200 1800 2400 4800 9600 19.2 56k _____
PARITY: even odd space mark none   CHARACTER LENGTH: 7 8 ___
STOP BITS: 1 1.5 2   LINE-ENDING CHARS: cr lf cr/lf
DISCONNECT SEQUENCE: EOT DEL ~. _____   MODE: async sync isoch
NOTE 1: PIN 8 is always on.
NOTE 2:

COMPUTER PORT PROFILE (Underline if supported, circle if selected)
COMPANY: General Robotics Corporation
PRODUCT: DLV11 async port

```
PORT  male or female                    PORT TYPE: serial _____
CONNECTOR: DB25  9-PIN  8-PIN(modular) _____  GENDER: male  female
PIN CONFIGURATION: C06
```

PIN	FUNCTION	DIRECTION
1:PG	Protective Ground	N/A
2:RD	Receive Data	TO
3:TD	Transmit Data	FROM
7:SG	Signal Ground	N/A

```
FLOW CONTROL:          XON: YES  ACK:     LEADS THAT MUST BE ON: _ _ _
SPEEDS:  110 300 600 1200 1800 2400 4800 9600 19.2 56k _____
PARITY: even odd space mark none          CHARACTER LENGTH:  7 8 ___
# STOP BITS:  1 1.5 2                      LINE-ENDING CHARS: cr lf cr/lf
DISCONNECT SEQUENCE:  EOT  DEL  ~. _____ MODE: async sync isoch
NOTE 1:
NOTE 2:
```

COMPUTER PORT PROFILE (Underline if supported, circle if selected)
COMPANY: General Robotics Corporation
PRODUCT: MLV11 dual port async interface

```
PORT  male or female                    PORT TYPE: serial _____
CONNECTOR: DB25  9-PIN  8-PIN(modular) _____  GENDER: male  female
PIN CONFIGURATION: C06
```

PIN	FUNCTION	DIRECTION
1:PG	Protective Ground	N/A
2:RD	Receive Data	TO
3:TD	Transmit Data	FROM
7:SG	Signal Ground	N/A

```
FLOW CONTROL:          XON: YES  ACK:     LEADS THAT MUST BE ON: _ _ _
SPEEDS:  110 300 600 1200 1800 2400 4800 9600 19.2 56k _____
PARITY: even odd space mark none          CHARACTER LENGTH:  7 8 ___
# STOP BITS:  1 1.5 2                      LINE-ENDING CHARS: cr lf cr/lf
DISCONNECT SEQUENCE:  EOT  DEL  ~. _____ MODE: async sync isoch
NOTE 1:
NOTE 2:
```

COMPUTER PORT PROFILE (Underline if supported, circle if selected)
COMPANY: General Robotics Corporation
PRODUCT: QLV11 quad serial async interface

PORT male or female   PORT TYPE: serial _____
CONNECTOR: DB25 9-PIN 8-PIN(modular) _____   GENDER: male female
PIN CONFIGURATION: C15

PIN	FUNCTION	DIRECTION	PIN	FUNCTION	DIRECTION
1:PG	Protective Ground	N/A	8:DCD	Data Carrier Detect	TO
2:RD	Receive Data	TO	14:SRD	Supervisory Rec. Data	TO
3:TD	Transmit Data	FROM	16:STD	Supervisory Trans.Data	FROM
4:RTS	Request to Send	FROM	20:DTR	Data Terminal Ready	FROM
5:CTS	Clear to Send	TO	22:RI	Ring Indicator	TO
7:SG	Signal Ground	N/A			

FLOW CONTROL: 5   XON: YES ACK: LEADS THAT MUST BE ON: _ _ _
SPEEDS: 110 300 600 1200 1800 2400 4800 9600 19.2 56k _____
PARITY: even odd space mark none   CHARACTER LENGTH: 7 8 ___
STOP BITS: 1 1.5 2   LINE-ENDING CHARS: cr lf cr/lf
DISCONNECT SEQUENCE: EOT DEL ~. _____ MODE: async sync isoch
NOTE 1:
NOTE 2:

COMPUTER PORT PROFILE (Underline if supported, circle if selected)
COMPANY: Gould Inc.
PRODUCT: 8512-2(8-line async controller)

PORT male   PORT TYPE: serial _____
CONNECTOR: DB25 9-PIN 8-PIN(modular) _____   GENDER: male female
PIN CONFIGURATION: C01

PIN	FUNCTION	DIRECTION	PIN	FUNCTION	DIRECTION
1:PG	Protective Ground	N/A	8:RLSD	Rec.Line Signal Detect	TO
2:TD	Transmit Data	FROM	15:TC	Transmit Clock	TO
3:RD	Receive Data	TO	17:RC	Rec. Clk/Reverse Chann	TO
4:RTS	Request to Send	FROM	20:DTR	Data Terminal Ready	FROM
5:CTS	Clear to Send	TO	22:RI	Ring Indicator	TO
6:DSR	Data Set Ready	TO	24:TC	Transmit Clock	FROM
7:SG	Signal Ground	N/A			

FLOW CONTROL: 5   XON: YES ACK: LEADS THAT MUST BE ON: _ _ _
SPEEDS: 110 300 600 1200 1800 2400 4800 9600 19.2 56k _____
PARITY: even odd space mark none   CHARACTER LENGTH: 7 8 ___
STOP BITS: 1 1.5 2   LINE-ENDING CHARS: cr lf cr/lf
DISCONNECT SEQUENCE: EOT DEL ~. _____ MODE: async sync isoch
NOTE 1:
NOTE 2:

COMPUTER PORT PROFILE (Underline if supported, circle if selected)
COMPANY: Hewlett Packard
PRODUCT: Portable PLUS

PORT HP 92221P cable
CONNECTOR: DB25 9-PIN 8-PIN(modular) _____
PIN CONFIGURATION: C14

PORT TYPE: serial _____
GENDER: male female

PIN	FUNCTION	DIRECTION
2:TD	Transmit Data	TO
3:RD	Receive Data	FROM
4:RTS	Request to Send	TO
5:CTS	Clear to Send	FROM
6:DSR	Data Set Ready	FROM
7:SG	Signal Ground	N/A
8:RLSD	Rec.Line Signal Detect	FROM
20:DTR	Data Terminal Ready	TO

FLOW CONTROL: XON: ACK: LEADS THAT MUST BE ON: _ _ _
SPEEDS: 110 300 600 1200 1800 2400 4800 9600 19.2 56k _____
PARITY: even odd space mark none   CHARACTER LENGTH: 7 8 ___
STOP BITS: 1 1.5 2   LINE-ENDING CHARS: cr lf cr/lf
DISCONNECT SEQUENCE: EOT DEL ~. _____ MODE: async sync isoch
NOTE 1: The HP Portable PLUS has a 9-PIN female port that
NOTE 2: the cable above converts to the above DB25 port

COMPUTER PORT PROFILE (Underline if supported, circle if selected)
COMPANY: Hewlett Packard
PRODUCT: Portable PLUS computer

PORT HP 92221P cable
CONNECTOR: DB25 9-PIN 8-PIN(modular) _____
PIN CONFIGURATION: C01

PORT TYPE: serial _____
GENDER: male female

PIN	FUNCTION	DIRECTION
2:TD	Transmit Data	FROM
3:RD	Receive Data	TO
4:RTS	Request to Send	FROM
5:CTS	Clear to Send	TO
6:DSR	Data Set Ready	TO
7:SG	Signal Ground	N/A
8:RLSD	Rec.Line Signal Detect	TO
20:DTR	Data Terminal Ready	FROM
22:RI	Ring Indicator	TO

FLOW CONTROL: XON: ACK: LEADS THAT MUST BE ON: _ _ _
SPEEDS: 110 300 600 1200 1800 2400 4800 9600 19.2 56k _____
PARITY: even odd space mark none   CHARACTER LENGTH: 7 8 ___
STOP BITS: 1 1.5 2   LINE-ENDING CHARS: cr lf cr/lf
DISCONNECT SEQUENCE: EOT DEL ~. _____ MODE: async sync isoch
NOTE 1: The HP Portable PLUS is equipped with a 9-PIN port
NOTE 2: that the above cable converts to DB-25

COMPUTER PORT PROFILE (Underline if supported, circle if selected)
COMPANY: HiTech International, Inc.
PRODUCT: RS-232C Adapter

PORT male   PORT TYPE: serial _____
CONNECTOR: DB25 9-PIN 8-PIN(modular) _____   GENDER: male female
PIN CONFIGURATION: C01

PIN	FUNCTION	DIRECTION
1:PG	Protective Ground	N/A
2:TD	Transmit Data	FROM
3:RD	Receive Data	TO
4:RTS	Request to Send	FROM
5:CTS	Clear to Send	TO
6:DSR	Data Set Ready	TO
7:SG	Signal Ground	N/A
8:DCD	Data Carrier Detect	TO
20:DTR	Data Terminal Ready	FROM
22:RI	Ring Indicator	TO

FLOW CONTROL: 5 6 8   XON: ACK: LEADS THAT MUST BE ON: _ _ _
SPEEDS: 110 300 600 1200 1800 2400 4800 9600 19.2 56k _____
PARITY: even odd space mark none   CHARACTER LENGTH: 7 8 ___
STOP BITS: 1 1.5 2   LINE-ENDING CHARS: cr lf cr/lf
DISCONNECT SEQUENCE: EOT DEL ~. _____   MODE: async sync isoch
NOTE 1:
NOTE 2:

COMPUTER PORT PROFILE (Underline if supported, circle if selected)
COMPANY: Husky Computers, Inc.
PRODUCT: Hunter computer

PORT EIA   PORT TYPE: serial _____
CONNECTOR: DB25 9-PIN 8-PIN(modular) _____   GENDER: male female
PIN CONFIGURATION: C01

PIN	FUNCTION	DIRECTION	PIN	FUNCTION	DIRECTION
1:PG	Protective Ground	N/A	8:DCD	Data Carrier Detect	TO
2:TD	Transmit Data	FROM	10:+5V		FROM
3:RD	Receive Data	TO	15:TC	Transmit Clock	TO
4:RTS	Request to Send	FROM	17:RC	Rec. Clk/Reverse Chann	TO
5:CTS	Clear to Send	TO	20:DTR	Data Terminal Ready	FROM
6:DSR	Data Set Ready	TO	22:RI	Ring Indicator	TO
7:SG	Signal Ground	N/A			

FLOW CONTROL: 5 6 8   XON: YES ACK: YES LEADS THAT MUST BE ON: _ _ _
SPEEDS: 110 300 600 1200 1800 2400 4800 9600 19.2 56k _____
PARITY: even odd space mark none   CHARACTER LENGTH: 7 8 ___
STOP BITS: 1 1.5 2   LINE-ENDING CHARS: cr lf cr/lf
DISCONNECT SEQUENCE: EOT DEL ~. _____   MODE: async sync isoch
NOTE 1:
NOTE 2:

COMPUTER PORT PROFILE (Underline if supported, circle if selected)
COMPANY: IBC (Integrated Business Comp)
PRODUCT: Ensign II computer

PORT   PORT TYPE: serial _____
CONNECTOR: DB25 9-PIN 8-PIN(modular) _____   GENDER: male female
PIN CONFIGURATION: C13

PIN	FUNCTION	DIRECTION
1:CG	Chassis Ground	N/A
2:RD	Receive Data	TO
3:TD	Transmit Data	FROM
4:RTS	Request to Send	FROM
5:CTS	Clear to Send	TO
7:SG	Signal Ground	N/A

FLOW CONTROL: XON: YES ACK: LEADS THAT MUST BE ON: _ _ _
SPEEDS: 110 300 600 1200 1800 2400 4800 9600 19.2 56k _____
PARITY: even odd space mark none   CHARACTER LENGTH: 7 8 ___
STOP BITS: 1 1.5 2   LINE-ENDING CHARS: cr lf cr/lf
DISCONNECT SEQUENCE: EOT DEL ~. _____   MODE: async sync isoch
NOTE 1:
NOTE 2:

COMPUTER PORT PROFILE (Underline if supported, circle if selected)
COMPANY: IBC (Integrated Business Comp)
PRODUCT: Mega-Star Desk Top computer

PORT   PORT TYPE: serial _____
CONNECTOR: DB25 9-PIN 8-PIN(modular) _____   GENDER: male female
PIN CONFIGURATION: C13

PIN	FUNCTION	DIRECTION
1:CG	Chassis Ground	N/A
2:RD	Receive Data	TO
3:TD	Transmit Data	FROM
5:CTS	Clear to Send	TO
7:SG	Signal Ground	N/A

FLOW CONTROL: XON: YES ACK: LEADS THAT MUST BE ON: _ _ _
SPEEDS: 110 300 600 1200 1800 2400 4800 9600 19.2 56k _____
PARITY: even odd space mark none   CHARACTER LENGTH: 7 8 ___
STOP BITS: 1 1.5 2   LINE-ENDING CHARS: cr lf cr/lf
DISCONNECT SEQUENCE: EOT DEL ~. _____   MODE: async sync isoch
NOTE 1:
NOTE 2:

COMPUTER PORT PROFILE (Underline if supported, circle if selected)
COMPANY: IBM Corporation
PRODUCT: 3704/5 FEP

PORT male
CONNECTOR: DB25 9-PIN 8-PIN(modular) _____
PIN CONFIGURATION: C01

PORT TYPE: serial _____
GENDER: male female

PIN	FUNCTION	DIRECTION	PIN	FUNCTION	DIRECTION
1:PG	Protective Ground	N/A	7:SG	Signal Ground	N/A
2:TD	Transmit Data	FROM	8:DCD	Data Carrier Detect	TO
3:RD	Receive Data	TO	15:TC	Transmit Clock	TO
4:RTS	Request to Send	FROM	17:RC	Rec. Clk/Reverse Chann	TO
5:CTS	Clear to Send	TO	20:DTR	Data Terminal Ready	FROM
6:DSR	Data Set Ready	TO	22:RI	Ring Indicator	TO

FLOW CONTROL: XON: ACK: LEADS THAT MUST BE ON: _ _ _
SPEEDS: 110 300 600 1200 1800 2400 4800 9600 19.2 56k _____
PARITY: even odd space mark none   CHARACTER LENGTH: 7 8 ___
STOP BITS: 1 1.5 2   LINE-ENDING CHARS: cr lf cr/lf
DISCONNECT SEQUENCE: EOT DEL ~. _____ MODE: async sync isoch
NOTE 1:
NOTE 2:

COMPUTER PORT PROFILE (Underline if supported, circle if selected)
COMPANY: IBM Corportion
PRODUCT: PS/2, PC/XT(ACA or equivalent)

PORT male (25-PIN)
CONNECTOR: DB25 9-PIN 8-PIN(modular) _____
PIN CONFIGURATION: C01

PORT TYPE: serial _____
GENDER: male female

PIN	FUNCTION	DIRECTION
1:PG	Protective Ground	N/A
2:TD	Transmit Data	FROM
3:RD	Receive Data	TO
4:RTS	Request to Send	FROM
5:CTS	Clear to Send	TO
6:DSR	Data Set Ready	TO
7:SG	Signal Ground	N/A
8:DCD	Data Carrier Detect	TO
20:DTR	Data Terminal Ready	FROM
22:RI	Ring Indicator	TO

FLOW CONTROL: XON: ACK: LEADS THAT MUST BE ON: _ _ _
SPEEDS: 110 300 600 1200 1800 2400 4800 9600 19.2 56k _____
PARITY: even odd space mark none   CHARACTER LENGTH: 7 8 ___
STOP BITS: 1 1.5 2   LINE-ENDING CHARS: cr lf cr/lf
DISCONNECT SEQUENCE: EOT DEL ~. _____ MODE: async sync isoch
NOTE 1: Leads 5/6/8 should be on for data flow.
NOTE 2:

COMPUTER PORT PROFILE (Underline if supported, circle if selected)
COMPANY: Icon Systems & Software
PRODUCT: MPS020-2 computer

PORT female   PORT TYPE: serial _____
CONNECTOR: DB25 9-PIN 8-PIN(modular) _____   GENDER: male female
PIN CONFIGURATION: C01

PIN	FUNCTION	DIRECTION	PIN	FUNCTION	DIRECTION
1:G	Ground	N/A	7:SG	Signal Ground	N/A
2:TD	Transmit Data	FROM	8:DCD	Data Carrier Detect	TO
3:RD	Receive Data	TO	15:TC	Transmit Clock	TO
4:RTS	Request to Send	FROM	17:RC	Rec. Clk/Reverse Chann	TO
5:CTS	Clear to Send	TO	20:DTR	Data Terminal Ready	FROM
6:DSR	Data Set Ready	TO	24:ETC	External Transmit Cloc	FROM

FLOW CONTROL: XON: YES ACK: LEADS THAT MUST BE ON: _ _ _
SPEEDS: 110 300 600 1200 1800 2400 4800 9600 19.2 56k _____
PARITY: even odd space mark none   CHARACTER LENGTH: 7 8 ___
STOP BITS: 1 1.5 2   LINE-ENDING CHARS: cr lf cr/lf
DISCONNECT SEQUENCE: EOT DEL ~. _____ MODE: async sync isoch
NOTE 1:
NOTE 2:

COMPUTER PORT PROFILE (Underline if supported, circle if selected)
COMPANY: IDEAssociates
PRODUCT: All aboard

PORT male   PORT TYPE: serial _____
CONNECTOR: DB25 9-PIN 8-PIN(modular) _____   GENDER: male female
PIN CONFIGURATION: C07

PIN	FUNCTION	DIRECTION
2:TD	Transmit Data	FROM
3:RD	Receive Data	TO
5:CTS	Clear to Send	FROM
6:DSR	Data Set Ready	FROM
7:SG	Signal Ground	N/A
8:CD	Carrier Detect	FROM
20:DTR	Data Terminal Ready	FROM
22:RI	Ring Indicator	TO

FLOW CONTROL: 5 6 8   XON: ACK: LEADS THAT MUST BE ON: _ _ _
SPEEDS: 110 300 600 1200 1800 2400 4800 9600 19.2 56k _____
PARITY: even odd space mark none   CHARACTER LENGTH: 7 8 ___
STOP BITS: 1 1.5 2   LINE-ENDING CHARS: cr lf cr/lf
DISCONNECT SEQUENCE: EOT DEL ~. _____ MODE: async sync isoch
NOTE 1: Leads 5/6/8 should be on to transmit data
NOTE 2:

COMPUTER PORT PROFILE (Underline if supported, circle if selected)
COMPANY: IDEAssociates
PRODUCT: Minicomm board

PORT male   PORT TYPE: serial _____
CONNECTOR: DB25 9-PIN 8-PIN(modular) _____ GENDER: male female
PIN CONFIGURATION: C01

PIN	FUNCTION	DIRECTION
2:TD	Transmit Data	FROM
3:RD	Receive Data	TO
4:RTS	Request to Send	FROM
5:CTS	Clear to Send	TO
6:DSR	Data Set Ready	TO
7:SG	Signal Ground	N/A
8:CD	Carrier Detect	TO
20:DTR	Data Terminal Ready	FROM

FLOW CONTROL: XON: ACK: LEADS THAT MUST BE ON: _ _ _
SPEEDS: 110 300 600 1200 1800 2400 4800 9600 19.2 56k _____
PARITY: even odd space mark none   CHARACTER LENGTH: 7 8 ___
STOP BITS: 1 1.5 2   LINE-ENDING CHARS: cr lf cr/lf
DISCONNECT SEQUENCE: EOT DEL ~. _____   MODE: async sync isoch
NOTE 1:
NOTE 2:

COMPUTER PORT PROFILE (Underline if supported, circle if selected)
COMPANY: Int'l Parallel Machines
PRODUCT: IP-1 series

PORT female   PORT TYPE: serial _____
CONNECTOR: DB25 9-PIN 8-PIN(modular) _____ GENDER: male female
PIN CONFIGURATION: C14

PIN	FUNCTION	DIRECTION
2:TD	Transmit Data	TO
3:RD	Receive Data	FROM
4:RTS	Request to Send	TO
5:CTS	Clear to Send	FROM
6:DSR	Data Set Ready	FROM
7:SG	Signal Ground	N/A
20:DTR	Data Terminal Ready	TO

FLOW CONTROL: XON: YES ACK: LEADS THAT MUST BE ON: _ _ _
SPEEDS: 110 300 600 1200 1800 2400 4800 9600 19.2 56k _____
PARITY: even odd space mark none   CHARACTER LENGTH: 7 8 ___
STOP BITS: 1 1.5 2   LINE-ENDING CHARS: cr lf cr/lf
DISCONNECT SEQUENCE: EOT DEL ~. _____   MODE: async sync isoch
NOTE 1:
NOTE 2:

COMPUTER PORT PROFILE (Underline if supported, circle if selected)
COMPANY: Integrated Marketing Corp.
PRODUCT: Data Manager print sharing device

PORT female (1 of 2 out)   PORT TYPE: serial _____
CONNECTOR: DB25 9-PIN 8-PIN(modular) _____   GENDER: male female
PIN CONFIGURATION: C01

PIN	FUNCTION	DIRECTION
1:CG	Chassis Ground	N/A
2:TD	Transmit Data	FROM
3:RD	Receive Data	TO
4:RTS	Request to Send	FROM
5:CTS	Clear to Send	TO
6:DSR	Data Set Ready	TO
7:SG	Signal Ground	N/A
8:CD	Carrier Detect	TO
20:DTR	Data Terminal Ready	FROM

FLOW CONTROL: 20   XON: YES ACK: LEADS THAT MUST BE ON: _ _ _
SPEEDS: 110 300 600 1200 1800 2400 4800 9600 19.2 56k _____
PARITY: even odd space mark none   CHARACTER LENGTH: 7 8 ___
STOP BITS: 1 1.5 2   LINE-ENDING CHARS: cr lf cr/lf
DISCONNECT SEQUENCE: EOT DEL ~. _____   MODE: async sync isoch
NOTE 1: Leads 5/6/8 should be tied to the flow control of
NOTE 2: the attached printers

COMPUTER PORT PROFILE (Underline if supported, circle if selected)
COMPANY: L/F Technologies, Inc.
PRODUCT: 1600/800 computers

PORT female(DB25)   PORT TYPE: serial _____
CONNECTOR: DB25 9-PIN 8-PIN(modular) _____   GENDER: male female
PIN CONFIGURATION: C11

PIN	FUNCTION	DIRECTION
1:PG	Protective Ground	N/A
2:TD	Transmit Data	FROM
3:RD	Receive Data	TO
4:RTS	Request to Send	FROM
5:CTS	Clear to Send	TO
7:SG	Signal Ground	N/A
8:DSR	Data Set Ready	TO
17:RC	Rec. Clk/Reverse Chann	TO
20:DTR	Data Terminal Ready	FROM
24:TC	Transmit Clock	TO

FLOW CONTROL: 5   XON: YES ACK: LEADS THAT MUST BE ON: _ _ _
SPEEDS: 110 300 600 1200 1800 2400 4800 9600 19.2 56k _____
PARITY: even odd space mark none   CHARACTER LENGTH: 7 8 ___
STOP BITS: 1 1.5 2   LINE-ENDING CHARS: cr lf cr/lf
DISCONNECT SEQUENCE: EOT DEL ~. _____   MODE: async sync isoch
NOTE 1:
NOTE 2:

COMPUTER PORT PROFILE   (Underline if supported, circle if selected)
COMPANY: Mouse Systems Corporation
PRODUCT: PC Mouse, FieldMouse

PORT   female(DB-25)   PORT TYPE: serial _____
CONNECTOR: DB25 9-PIN 8-PIN(modular) _____   GENDER: male female
PIN CONFIGURATION: C06

PIN	FUNCTION	DIRECTION
3:TD	Transmit Data	FROM
7:SG	Signal Ground	N/A

FLOW CONTROL: XON: ACK: LEADS THAT MUST BE ON: _ _ _
SPEEDS: 110 300 600 1200 1800 2400 4800 9600 19.2 56k _____
PARITY: even odd space mark none   CHARACTER LENGTH: 7 8 ___
STOP BITS: 1 1.5 2   LINE-ENDING CHARS: cr lf cr/lf
DISCONNECT SEQUENCE: EOT DEL ~. _____   MODE: async sync isoch
NOTE 1:
NOTE 2:

COMPUTER PORT PROFILE   (Underline if supported, circle if selected)
COMPANY: NBI, Inc.
PRODUCT: 5000S Integrated WorkStation(ONE IWS)

PORT   female   PORT TYPE: serial _____
CONNECTOR: DB25 9-PIN 8-PIN(modular) _____   GENDER: male female
PIN CONFIGURATION: C01

PIN	FUNCTION	DIRECTION
1:FG	Frame Ground	N/A
2:TD	Transmit Data	FROM
3:RD	Receive Data	TO
4:RTS	Request to Send	FROM
5:CTS	Clear to Send	TO
6:DSR	Data Set Ready	TO
7:SG	Signal Ground	N/A
8:DCD	Data Carrier Detect	TO
20:DTR	Data Terminal Ready	FROM

FLOW CONTROL: XON: YES ACK: LEADS THAT MUST BE ON: _ _ _
SPEEDS: 110 300 600 1200 1800 2400 4800 9600 19.2 56k _____
PARITY: even odd space mark none   CHARACTER LENGTH: 7 8 ___
STOP BITS: 1 1.5 2   LINE-ENDING CHARS: cr lf cr/lf
DISCONNECT SEQUENCE: EOT DEL ~. _____   MODE: async sync isoch
NOTE 1: Hardware flow control is not supported. DropPINg
NOTE 2: leads 6 & 8 will cause a disconnect status

COMPUTER PORT PROFILE (Underline if supported, circle if selected)
COMPANY: NEC
PRODUCT: PC-8201A computer

PORT female
CONNECTOR: DB25 9-PIN 8-PIN(modular) _____
PIN CONFIGURATION: C01

PORT TYPE: serial _____
GENDER: male female

PIN	FUNCTION	DIRECTION
1:PG	Protective Ground	N/A
2:TD	Transmit Data	FROM
3:RD	Receive Data	TO
4:RTS	Request to Send	FROM
5:CTS	Clear to Send	TO
6:DSR	Data Set Ready	TO
7:SG	Signal Ground	N/A
8:DCD	Data Carrier Detect	TO
20:DTR	Data Terminal Ready	FROM
22:RI	Ring Indicator	TO

FLOW CONTROL: 5   XON: ACK: LEADS THAT MUST BE ON: _ _ _
SPEEDS: 110 300 600 1200 1800 2400 4800 9600 19.2 56k _____
PARITY: even odd space mark none   CHARACTER LENGTH: 7 8 ___
STOP BITS: 1 1.5 2   LINE-ENDING CHARS: cr lf cr/lf
DISCONNECT SEQUENCE: EOT DEL ~. _____   MODE: async sync isoch
NOTE 1:
NOTE 2:

COMPUTER PORT PROFILE (Underline if supported, circle if selected)
COMPANY: Personal Micro Computers, Inc.
PRODUCT: MicroMate

PORT female (terminal)
CONNECTOR: DB25 9-PIN 8-PIN(modular) _____
PIN CONFIGURATION: C14

PORT TYPE: serial _____
GENDER: male female

PIN	FUNCTION	DIRECTION
1:G	Ground	N/A
2:RD	Receive Data	TO
3:TD	Transmit Data	FROM
4:CTS	Clear to Send	TO
5:RTS	Request to Send	FROM
6:DTR	Data Terminal Ready	FROM
7:SG	Signal Ground	N/A
8:DCD	Data Carrier Detect	FROM
20:DTR	Data Terminal Ready	TO

FLOW CONTROL: XON: YES ACK: LEADS THAT MUST BE ON: _ _ _
SPEEDS: 110 300 600 1200 1800 2400 4800 9600 19.2 56k _____
PARITY: even odd space mark none   CHARACTER LENGTH: 7 8 ___
STOP BITS: 1 1.5 2   LINE-ENDING CHARS: cr lf cr/lf
DISCONNECT SEQUENCE: EOT DEL ~. _____   MODE: async sync isoch
NOTE 1:
NOTE 2:

COMPUTER PORT PROFILE   (Underline if supported, circle if selected)
COMPANY: Personal Micro Computers, Inc.
PRODUCT: MicroMate computer

PORT female (modem port)   PORT TYPE: serial _____
CONNECTOR: DB25 9-PIN 8-PIN(modular) _____   GENDER: male female
PIN CONFIGURATION: C01

PIN	FUNCTION	DIRECTION
1:G	Ground	N/A
2:TD	Transmit Data	FROM
3:RD	Receive Data	TO
4:RTS	Request to Send	FROM
5:CTS	Clear to Send	TO
6:DSR	Data Set Ready	TO
7:SG	Signal Ground	N/A
8:DCD	Data Carrier Detect	TO
20:DTR	Data Terminal Ready	FROM

FLOW CONTROL: XON: YES ACK: LEADS THAT MUST BE ON: _ _ _
SPEEDS: 110 300 600 1200 1800 2400 4800 9600 19.2 56k _____
PARITY: even odd space mark none   CHARACTER LENGTH: 7 8 ___
STOP BITS: 1 1.5 2   LINE-ENDING CHARS: cr lf cr/lf
DISCONNECT SEQUENCE: EOT DEL ~. _____   MODE: async sync isoch
NOTE 1:
NOTE 2:

COMPUTER PORT PROFILE   (Underline if supported, circle if selected)
COMPANY: Pertec Computer Company
PRODUCT: 3200 & 4200 computers

PORT male   PORT TYPE: serial _____
CONNECTOR: DB25 9-PIN 8-PIN(modular) _____   GENDER: male female
PIN CONFIGURATION: C01

PIN	FUNCTION	DIRECTION
1:PG	Protective Ground	N/A
2:TD	Transmit Data	FROM
3:RD	Receive Data	TO
4:RTS	Request to Send	FROM
5:CTS	Clear to Send	TO
6:DSR	Data Set Ready	TO
7:SG	Signal Ground	N/A
8:DCD	Data Carrier Detect	TO
20:DTR	Data Terminal Ready	FROM

FLOW CONTROL: 5   XON: YES ACK: LEADS THAT MUST BE ON: _ _ _
SPEEDS: 110 300 600 1200 1800 2400 4800 9600 19.2 56k _____
PARITY: even odd space mark none   CHARACTER LENGTH: 7 8 ___
STOP BITS: 1 1.5 2   LINE-ENDING CHARS: cr lf cr/lf
DISCONNECT SEQUENCE: EOT DEL ~. _____   MODE: async sync isoch
NOTE 1: Lead 5 should be tied to the attached device's
NOTE 2: flow control lead

COMPUTER PORT PROFILE (Underline if supported, circle if selected)
COMPANY: Plexus Computers, Inc.
PRODUCT: ICP board

PORT female   PORT TYPE: serial _____
CONNECTOR: DB25 9-PIN 8-PIN(modular) _____   GENDER: male female
PIN CONFIGURATION: C01

PIN	FUNCTION	DIRECTION	PIN	FUNCTION	DIRECTION
2:TD	Transmit Data	FROM	8:DCD	Data Carrier Detect	TO
3:RD	Receive Data	TO	11:SS	Speed Select	FROM
4:RTS	Request to Send	FROM	15:TC	Transmit Clock	TO
5:CTS	Clear to Send	TO	17:RC	Rec. Clk/Reverse Chann	TO
6:DSR	Data Set Ready	TO	20:DTR	Data Terminal Ready	FROM
7:SG	Signal Ground	N/A			

FLOW CONTROL: XON: YES ACK: LEADS THAT MUST BE ON: _ _ _
SPEEDS: 110 300 600 1200 1800 2400 4800 9600 19.2 56k _____
PARITY: even odd space mark none   CHARACTER LENGTH: 7 8 ___
STOP BITS: 1 1.5 2   LINE-ENDING CHARS: cr lf cr/lf
DISCONNECT SEQUENCE: EOT DEL ~. _____   MODE: async sync isoch
NOTE 1:
NOTE 2:

COMPUTER PORT PROFILE (Underline if supported, circle if selected)
COMPANY: Plexus Computers, Inc.
PRODUCT: P/15 & P/20 computer

PORT female (ports 6 & 7)   PORT TYPE: serial _____
CONNECTOR: DB25 9-PIN 8-PIN(modular) _____   GENDER: male female
PIN CONFIGURATION: C01

PIN	FUNCTION	DIRECTION	PIN	FUNCTION	DIRECTION
1:FG	Frame Ground	N/A	7:DCD	Data Carrier Detect	TO
2:TD	Transmit Data	FROM	15:TC	Transmit Clock	TO
3:RD	Receive Data	TO	17:RC	Rec. Clk/Reverse Chann	TO
4:RTS	Request to Send	FROM	20:DTR	Data Terminal Ready	FROM
5:CTS	Clear to Send	TO	22:RI	Ring Indicator	TO
6:SG	Signal Ground	N/A			

FLOW CONTROL: XON: YES ACK: LEADS THAT MUST BE ON: _ _ _
SPEEDS: 110 300 600 1200 1800 2400 4800 9600 19.2 56k _____
PARITY: even odd space mark none   CHARACTER LENGTH: 7 8 ___
STOP BITS: 1 1.5 2   LINE-ENDING CHARS: cr lf cr/lf
DISCONNECT SEQUENCE: EOT DEL ~. _____   MODE: async sync isoch
NOTE 1:
NOTE 2:

COMPUTER PORT PROFILE   (Underline if supported, circle if selected)
COMPANY: Practical Peripherals
PRODUCT: SeriALL card

PORT female   PORT TYPE: serial _____
CONNECTOR: DB25 9-PIN 8-PIN(modular) _____   GENDER: male female
PIN CONFIGURATION: C01

PIN	FUNCTION	DIRECTION
1:PG	Protective Ground	N/A
2:TD	Transmit Data	FROM
3:RD	Receive Data	TO
4:RTS	Request to Send	FROM
5:CTS	Clear to Send	TO
6:DSR	Data Set Ready	TO
7:SG	Signal Ground	N/A
8:DCD	Data Carrier Detect	TO
20:DTR	Data Terminal Ready	FROM

FLOW CONTROL: XON: YES ACK: LEADS THAT MUST BE ON: _ _ _
SPEEDS: 110 300 600 1200 1800 2400 4800 9600 19.2 56k _____
PARITY: even odd space mark none   CHARACTER LENGTH: 7 8 ___
STOP BITS: 1 1.5 2   LINE-ENDING CHARS: cr lf cr/lf
DISCONNECT SEQUENCE: EOT DEL ~. _____ MODE: async sync isoch
NOTE 1:
NOTE 2:

COMPUTER PORT PROFILE   (Underline if supported, circle if selected)
COMPANY: Prime Computer, Inc.
PRODUCT: 2350/2450/2655/9655/9755/9955II computers

PORT female (9-PIN async)   PORT TYPE: serial _____
CONNECTOR: DB25 9-PIN 8-PIN(modular) _____   GENDER: male female
PIN CONFIGURATION: C05

PIN	FUNCTION	DIRECTION
2:TD	Transmit Data	FROM
3:RD	Receive Data	TO
4:RTS	Request to Send	FROM
5:CTS	Clear to Send	TO
7:SG	Signal Ground	N/A
8:DCD	Data Carrier Detect	TO
9:DTR	Data Terminal Ready	FROM

FLOW CONTROL: XON: ACK: LEADS THAT MUST BE ON: _ _ _
SPEEDS: 110 300 600 1200 1800 2400 4800 9600 19.2 56k _____
PARITY: even odd space mark none   CHARACTER LENGTH: 7 8 ___
STOP BITS: 1 1.5 2   LINE-ENDING CHARS: cr lf cr/lf
DISCONNECT SEQUENCE: EOT DEL ~. _____ MODE: async sync isoch
NOTE 1:
NOTE 2:

COMPUTER PORT PROFILE (Underline if supported, circle if selected)
COMPANY: Prime Computer, Inc.
PRODUCT: 2350/2450/2655/9655/9755/9955II computers

PORT female (synchronous)   PORT TYPE: serial _____
CONNECTOR: DB25 9-PIN 8-PIN(modular) _____   GENDER: male female
PIN CONFIGURATION: C01

2:TD	Transmit Data	FROM
3:RD	Receive Data	TO
4:RTS	Request to Send	FROM
5:CTS	Clear to Send	TO
6:DSR	Data Set Ready	TO
7:SG	Signal Ground	N/A
8:DCD	Data Carrier Detect	TO
15:TC	Transmit Clock	TO
17:RC	Rec. Clk/Reverse Chann	TO
20:DTR	Data Terminal Ready	FROM
22:RI	Ring Indicator	TO
24:TC	Transmit Clock	FROM

FLOW CONTROL: XON: YES ACK: LEADS THAT MUST BE ON: _ _ _
SPEEDS: 110 300 600 1200 1800 2400 4800 9600 19.2 56k _____
PARITY: even odd space mark none   CHARACTER LENGTH: 7 8 ___
STOP BITS: 1 1.5 2   LINE-ENDING CHARS: cr lf cr/lf
DISCONNECT SEQUENCE: EOT DEL ~. _____   MODE: async sync isoch
NOTE 1:
NOTE 2:

COMPUTER PORT PROFILE (Underline if supported, circle if selected)
COMPANY: Pyramid Technology
PRODUCT: 90mx, 90x, 98x computers (ITP ports)

PORT male   PORT TYPE: serial _____
CONNECTOR: DB25 9-PIN 8-PIN(modular) _____   GENDER: male female
PIN CONFIGURATION: C01

PIN	FUNCTION	DIRECTION
1:FG	Frame Ground	N/A
2:TD	Transmit Data	FROM
3:RD	Receive Data	TO
4:RTS	Request to Send	FROM
5:CTS	Clear to Send	TO
6:DSR	Data Set Ready	TO
7:SG	Signal Ground	N/A
8:DCD	Data Carrier Detect	TO
20:DTR	Data Terminal Ready	FROM
22:RI	Ring Indicator	TO

FLOW CONTROL: 8   XON: YES ACK: LEADS THAT MUST BE ON: _ _ _
SPEEDS: 110 300 600 1200 1800 2400 4800 9600 19.2 56k _____
PARITY: even odd space mark none   CHARACTER LENGTH: 7 8 ___
STOP BITS: 1 1.5 2   LINE-ENDING CHARS: cr lf cr/lf
DISCONNECT SEQUENCE: EOT DEL ~. _____   MODE: async sync isoch
NOTE 1: Lead 8 must be on for data flow
NOTE 2:

COMPUTER PORT PROFILE (Underline if supported, circle if selected)
COMPANY: QDP Computer Systems, Inc.
PRODUCT: QDP-16 computer

PORT male (DB-25)   PORT TYPE: serial _____
CONNECTOR: DB25 9-PIN 8-PIN(modular) _____   GENDER: male female
PIN CONFIGURATION: C01

PIN	FUNCTION	DIRECTION
2:TD	Transmit Data	FROM
3:RD	Receive Data	TO
4:RTS	Request to Send	FROM
5:CTS	Clear to Send	TO
6:DSR	Data Set Ready	TO
7:SG	Signal Ground	N/A
8:CD	Carrier Detect	TO
20:DTR	Data Terminal Ready	FROM
22:RI	Ring Indicator	TO

FLOW CONTROL: 5 6 8   XON: ACK: LEADS THAT MUST BE ON: _ _ _
SPEEDS: 110 300 600 1200 1800 2400 4800 9600 19.2 56k _____
PARITY: even odd space mark none   CHARACTER LENGTH: 7 8 __
STOP BITS: 1 1.5 2   LINE-ENDING CHARS: cr lf cr/lf
DISCONNECT SEQUENCE: EOT DEL ~. _____   MODE: async sync isoch
NOTE 1: Leads 5/6/8/ should be on for data flow.
NOTE 2:

COMPUTER PORT PROFILE (Underline if supported, circle if selected)
COMPANY: QDP Computer Systems, Inc.
PRODUCT: 100/200/300/400/500 computers

PORT female (DB-25)   PORT TYPE: serial _____
CONNECTOR: DB25 9-PIN 8-PIN(modular) _____   GENDER: male female
PIN CONFIGURATION: C14

PIN	FUNCTION	DIRECTION
2:RD	Receive Data	TO
3:TD	Transmit Data	FROM
4:RTS	Request to Send	TO
5:CTS	Clear to Send	FROM
6:DSR	Data Set Ready	FROM
7:SG	Signal Ground	N/A
20:DTR	Data Terminal Ready	TO

FLOW CONTROL: 20   XON: YES ACK: LEADS THAT MUST BE ON: _ _ _
SPEEDS: 110 300 600 1200 1800 2400 4800 9600 19.2 56k _____
PARITY: even odd space mark none   CHARACTER LENGTH: 7 8 __
STOP BITS: 1 1.5 2   LINE-ENDING CHARS: cr lf cr/lf
DISCONNECT SEQUENCE: EOT DEL ~. _____   MODE: async sync isoch
NOTE 1:
NOTE 2:

COMPUTER PORT PROFILE (Underline if supported, circle if selected)
COMPANY: Quadram Corporation
PRODUCT: Async Adapter, Silver Quadboard

PORT   PORT TYPE: serial _____
CONNECTOR: DB25 9-PIN 8-PIN(modular) _____   GENDER: male female
PIN CONFIGURATION: C01

PIN	FUNCTION	DIRECTION
2:TD	Transmit Data	FROM
3:RD	Receive Data	TO
4:RTS	Request to Send	FROM
5:CTS	Clear to Send	TO
6:DSR	Data Set Ready	TO
7:SG	Signal Ground	N/A
8:CD	Carrier Detect	TO
20:DTR	Data Terminal Ready	FROM
22:RI	Ring Indicator	TO

FLOW CONTROL: 5 6 8   XON: ACK: LEADS THAT MUST BE ON: _ _ _
SPEEDS: 110 300 600 1200 1800 2400 4800 9600 19.2 56k _____
PARITY: even odd space mark none   CHARACTER LENGTH: 7 8 ___
STOP BITS: 1 1.5 2   LINE-ENDING CHARS: cr lf cr/lf
DISCONNECT SEQUENCE: EOT DEL ~. _____   MODE: async sync isoch
NOTE 1: Leads 5/6/8 should be on for data transmission.
NOTE 2:

COMPUTER PORT PROFILE (Underline if supported, circle if selected)
COMPANY: Quadram Corporation
PRODUCT: Quad 512+, QuadPort-XT,QuadEMS+ I/O boards

PORT   PORT TYPE: serial _____
CONNECTOR: DB25 9-PIN 8-PIN(modular) _____   GENDER: male female
PIN CONFIGURATION: C01

PIN	FUNCTION	DIRECTION
1:PG	Protective Ground	N/A
2:TD	Transmit Data	FROM
3:RD	Receive Data	TO
4:RTS	Request to Send	FROM
5:CTS	Clear to Send	TO
6:DSR	Data Set Ready	TO
7:SG	Signal Ground	N/A
8:CD	Carrier Detect	TO
20:DTR	Data Terminal Ready	FROM
22:RI	Ring Indicator	TO

FLOW CONTROL: 5 6 8   XON: ACK: LEADS THAT MUST BE ON: _ _ _
SPEEDS: 110 300 600 1200 1800 2400 4800 9600 19.2 56k _____
PARITY: even odd space mark none   CHARACTER LENGTH: 7 8 ___
STOP BITS: 1 1.5 2   LINE-ENDING CHARS: cr lf cr/lf
DISCONNECT SEQUENCE: EOT DEL ~. _____   MODE: async sync isoch
NOTE 1: Leads 5/6/8 should be on for data transmission
NOTE 2:

COMPUTER PORT PROFILE (Underline if supported, circle if selected)
COMPANY: Quadram Corporation
PRODUCT: Quadboard-AT

PORT 9-PIN   PORT TYPE: serial _____
CONNECTOR: DB25 9-PIN 8-PIN(modular) _____   GENDER: male female
PIN CONFIGURATION: C16

PIN	FUNCTION	DIRECTION
1:CD	Carrier Detect	TO
2:RD	Receive Data	TO
3:TD	Transmit Data	FROM
4:DTR	Data Terminal Ready	FROM
5:SG	Signal Ground	N/A
6:DSR	Data Set Ready	TO
7:RTS	Request to Send	FROM
8:CTS	Clear to Send	TO
9:RI	Ring Indicator	TO

FLOW CONTROL: 1 6 8   XON: ACK: LEADS THAT MUST BE ON: _ _ _
SPEEDS: 110 300 600 1200 1800 2400 4800 9600 19.2 56k _____
PARITY: even odd space mark none   CHARACTER LENGTH: 7 8 ___
STOP BITS: 1 1.5 2   LINE-ENDING CHARS: cr lf cr/lf
DISCONNECT SEQUENCE: EOT DEL ~. _____   MODE: async sync isoch
NOTE 1: Leads 1/6/8 should be on for data transmission.
NOTE 2:

COMPUTER PORT PROFILE (Underline if supported, circle if selected)
COMPANY: SBE, Inc.
PRODUCT: 300 computers

PORT Ch 0/1   PORT TYPE: serial _____
CONNECTOR: DB25 9-PIN 8-PIN(modular) _____   GENDER: male female
PIN CONFIGURATION: C14

PIN	FUNCTION	DIRECTION
1:G	Ground	N/A
2:RD	Receive Data	TO
3:TD	Transmit Data	FROM
4:CTS	Clear to Send	TO
5:RTS	Request to Send	FROM
7:SG	Signal Ground	N/A
8:RTS	Request to Send	FROM
15:TC	Transmit Clock	FROM
17:RC	Rec. Clk/Reverse Chann	FROM
20:DTR	Data Terminal Ready	TO

FLOW CONTROL: 20   XON: YES ACK: LEADS THAT MUST BE ON: _ _ _
SPEEDS: 110 300 600 1200 1800 2400 4800 9600 19.2 56k _____
PARITY: even odd space mark none   CHARACTER LENGTH: 7 8 ___
STOP BITS: 1 1.5 2   LINE-ENDING CHARS: cr lf cr/lf
DISCONNECT SEQUENCE: EOT DEL ~. _____   MODE: async sync isoch
NOTE 1: The timing lead directions can be altered.
NOTE 2:

COMPUTER PORT PROFILE (Underline if supported, circle if selected)
COMPANY: Sigma Designs, Inc.
PRODUCT: Maximizer board

PORT male (DB-25)   PORT TYPE: serial _____
CONNECTOR: DB25 9-PIN 8-PIN(modular) _____ GENDER: male female
PIN CONFIGURATION: C01

PIN	FUNCTION	DIRECTION
1:CG	Chassis Ground	N/A
2:TD	Transmit Data	FROM
3:RD	Receive Data	TO
4:RTS	Request to Send	FROM
5:CTS	Clear to Send	TO
6:DSR	Data Set Ready	TO
7:SG	Signal Ground	N/A
8:DCD	Data Carrier Detect	TO
20:DTR	Data Terminal Ready	FROM
22:RI	Ring Indicator	TO

FLOW CONTROL: 5 6 8   XON: ACK: LEADS THAT MUST BE ON: _ _ _
SPEEDS: 110 300 600 1200 1800 2400 4800 9600 19.2 56k _____
PARITY: even odd space mark none   CHARACTER LENGTH: 7 8 ___
STOP BITS: 1 1.5 2   LINE-ENDING CHARS: cr lf cr/lf
DISCONNECT SEQUENCE: EOT DEL ~. _____ MODE: async sync isoch
NOTE 1: Leads 5/6/8 should be on for data flow.
NOTE 2:

COMPUTER PORT PROFILE (Underline if supported, circle if selected)
COMPANY: Sperry
PRODUCT: PC-HT

PORT male (DB-25)   PORT TYPE: serial _____
CONNECTOR: DB25 9-PIN 8-PIN(modular) _____ GENDER: male female
PIN CONFIGURATION: C01

PIN	FUNCTION	DIRECTION
1:FG	Frame Ground	N/A
2:TD	Transmit Data	FROM
3:RD	Receive Data	TO
4:RTS	Request to Send	FROM
5:CTS	Clear to Send	TO
6:DSR	Data Set Ready	TO
7:SG	Signal Ground	N/A
8:CD	Carrier Detect	TO
20:DTR	Data Terminal Ready	FROM
22:RI	Ring Indicator	TO

FLOW CONTROL: XON: ACK: LEADS THAT MUST BE ON: _ _ _
SPEEDS: 110 300 600 1200 1800 2400 4800 9600 19.2 56k _____
PARITY: even odd space mark none   CHARACTER LENGTH: 7 8 ___
STOP BITS: 1 1.5 2   LINE-ENDING CHARS: cr lf cr/lf
DISCONNECT SEQUENCE: EOT DEL ~. _____ MODE: async sync isoch
NOTE 1: Leads 5/6/8 should be on for data flow.
NOTE 2:

COMPUTER PORT PROFILE (Underline if supported, circle if selected)
COMPANY: Sperry
PRODUCT: PC-IT

PORT male (DB-9)   PORT TYPE: serial _____
CONNECTOR: DB25 9-PIN 8-PIN(modular) _____   GENDER: male female
PIN CONFIGURATION: C16

PIN	FUNCTION	DIRECTION
1:CD	Carrier Detect	TO
2:RD	Receive Data	TO
3:TD	Transmit Data	FROM
4:DTR	Data Terminal Ready	FROM
5:SG	Signal Ground	N/A
6:DSR	Data Set Ready	TO
7:RTS	Request to Send	FROM
8:CTS	Clear to Send	TO
9:RI	Ring Indicator	TO

FLOW CONTROL: XON: ACK: LEADS THAT MUST BE ON: _ _ _
SPEEDS: 110 300 600 1200 1800 2400 4800 9600 19.2 56k _____
PARITY: even odd space mark none   CHARACTER LENGTH: 7 8 ___
STOP BITS: 1 1.5 2   LINE-ENDING CHARS: cr lf cr/lf
DISCONNECT SEQUENCE: EOT DEL ~. _____ MODE: async sync isoch
NOTE 1: Leads 1/6/8 should be on for data flow.
NOTE 2:

COMPUTER PORT PROFILE (Underline if supported, circle if selected)
COMPANY: Sperry
PRODUCT: SVT 12XX terminal

PORT (DB-25)   PORT TYPE: serial _____
CONNECTOR: DB25 9-PIN 8-PIN(modular) _____   GENDER: male female
PIN CONFIGURATION: P10

PIN	FUNCTION	DIRECTION
2:TD	Transmit Data	FROM
3:RD	Receive Data	TO
4:RTS	Request to Send	FROM
5:CTS	Clear to Send	TO
6:DSR	Data Set Ready	TO
7:SG	Signal Ground	N/A
8:CD	Carrier Detect	TO
20:DTR	Data Terminal Ready	FROM

FLOW CONTROL: XON: ACK: LEADS THAT MUST BE ON: _ _ _
SPEEDS: 110 300 600 1200 1800 2400 4800 9600 19.2 56k _____
PARITY: even odd space mark none   CHARACTER LENGTH: 7 8 ___
STOP BITS: 1 1.5 2   LINE-ENDING CHARS: cr lf cr/lf
DISCONNECT SEQUENCE: EOT DEL ~. _____ MODE: async sync isoch
NOTE 1:
NOTE 2:

COMPUTER PORT PROFILE (Underline if supported, circle if selected)
COMPANY: STB Systems, Inc.
PRODUCT: Rio Grande board

PORT male (9-PIN serial)   PORT TYPE: serial _____
CONNECTOR: DB25 9-PIN 8-PIN(modular) _____ GENDER: male female
PIN CONFIGURATION: C16

PIN	FUNCTION	DIRECTION
1:CD	Carrier Detect	TO
2:RD	Receive Data	TO
3:TD	Transmit Data	FROM
4:DTR	Data Terminal Ready	FROM
5:SG	Signal Ground	N/A
6:DSR	Data Set Ready	TO
7:RTS	Request to Send	FROM
8:CTS	Clear to Send	TO
9:RI	Ring Indicator	TO

FLOW CONTROL: XON: ACK: LEADS THAT MUST BE ON: _ _ _
SPEEDS: 110 300 600 1200 1800 2400 4800 9600 19.2 56k _____
PARITY: even odd space mark none   CHARACTER LENGTH: 7 8 ___
STOP BITS: 1 1.5 2   LINE-ENDING CHARS: cr lf cr/lf
DISCONNECT SEQUENCE: EOT DEL ~. _____ MODE: async sync isoch
NOTE 1: Leads 1/6/8 must be on for data flow.
NOTE 2:

COMPUTER PORT PROFILE (Underline if supported, circle if selected)
COMPANY: Suncoast/Easycom
PRODUCT: BF-64MD

PORT female(Printer-NOR)   PORT TYPE: serial _____
CONNECTOR: DB25 9-PIN 8-PIN(modular) _____ GENDER: male female
PIN CONFIGURATION: C01

PIN	FUNCTION	DIRECTION
1:FG	Frame Ground	N/A
2:TD	Transmit Data	FROM
3:RD	Receive Data	TO
4:RTS	Request to Send	FROM
6:DSR	Data Set Ready	TO
7:SG	Signal Ground	N/A
20:DTR	Data Terminal Ready	FROM

FLOW CONTROL: 6   XON: YES ACK: LEADS THAT MUST BE ON: _ _ _
SPEEDS: 110 300 600 1200 1800 2400 4800 9600 19.2 56k _____
PARITY: even odd space mark none   CHARACTER LENGTH: 7 8 ___
STOP BITS: 1 1.5 2   LINE-ENDING CHARS: cr lf cr/lf
DISCONNECT SEQUENCE: EOT DEL ~. _____ MODE: async sync isoch
NOTE 1: The "cable connector" should be in the "NOR"
NOTE 2: position for these PINouts--check "REV" entry.

COMPUTER PORT PROFILE (Underline if supported, circle if selected)
COMPANY: Suncoast/Easycom
PRODUCT: BF-64MD buffer

PORT female (computer)   PORT TYPE: serial _____
CONNECTOR: DB25 9-PIN 8-PIN(modular) _____   GENDER: male female
PIN CONFIGURATION: P08

PIN	FUNCTION	DIRECTION
1:FG	Frame Ground	N/A
2:TD	Transmit Data	FROM
3:RD	Receive Data	TO
4:RTS	Request to Send	FROM
5:CTS	Clear to Send	TO
6:DSR	Data Set Ready	TO
7:SG	Signal Ground	N/A
20:DTR	Data Terminal Ready	FROM

FLOW CONTROL: 20   XON: YES ACK: LEADS THAT MUST BE ON: _ _ _
SPEEDS: 110 300 600 1200 1800 2400 4800 9600 19.2 56k _____
PARITY: even odd space mark none   CHARACTER LENGTH: 7 8 ___
STOP BITS: 1 1.5 2   LINE-ENDING CHARS: cr lf cr/lf
DISCONNECT SEQUENCE: EOT DEL ~. _____   MODE: async sync isoch
NOTE 1: The "cable connector" should be plugged into the
NOTE 2: position marked "normal" for this PINout.

COMPUTER PORT PROFILE (Underline if supported, circle if selected)
COMPANY: Suncoast/Easycom
PRODUCT: BF-64MD buffer

PORT female(computer-REV)   PORT TYPE: serial _____
CONNECTOR: DB25 9-PIN 8-PIN(modular) _____   GENDER: male female
PIN CONFIGURATION: C14

PIN	FUNCTION	DIRECTION
1:FG	Frame Ground	N/A
2:RD	Receive Data	TO
3:TD	Transmit Data	FROM
4:CTS	Clear to Send	TO
5:RTS	Request to Send	FROM
6:DTR	Data Terminal Ready	FROM
7:SG	Signal Ground	N/A
8:DCD	Data Carrier Detect	FROM
20:DSR	Data Set Ready	TO

FLOW CONTROL: 6   XON: YES ACK: LEADS THAT MUST BE ON: _ _ _
SPEEDS: 110 300 600 1200 1800 2400 4800 9600 19.2 56k _____
PARITY: even odd space mark none   CHARACTER LENGTH: 7 8 ___
STOP BITS: 1 1.5 2   LINE-ENDING CHARS: cr lf cr/lf
DISCONNECT SEQUENCE: EOT DEL ~. _____   MODE: async sync isoch
NOTE 1: The position of the "cable connector" should be
NOTE 2: in the "REV" mode, so the port emulates DCE

COMPUTER PORT PROFILE (Underline if supported, circle if selected)
COMPANY: Suncoast/Easycom
PRODUCT: BF-64MD buffer

PORT female(printer-REV)   PORT TYPE: serial _____
CONNECTOR: DB25 9-PIN 8-PIN(modular) _____   GENDER: male female
PIN CONFIGURATION: C14

PIN	FUNCTION	DIRECTION
1:FG	Frame Ground	N/A
2:RD	Receive Data	TO
3:TD	Transmit Data	FROM
5:RTS	Request to Send	FROM
6:DTR	Data Terminal Ready	FROM
7:SG	Signal Ground	N/A
8:DCD	Data Carrier Detect	FROM
20:DTR	Data Terminal Ready	TO

FLOW CONTROL: 20   XON: YES ACK: LEADS THAT MUST BE ON: _ _ _
SPEEDS: 110 300 600 1200 1800 2400 4800 9600 19.2 56k _____
PARITY: even odd space mark none   CHARACTER LENGTH: 7 8 ___
STOP BITS: 1 1.5 2   LINE-ENDING CHARS: cr lf cr/lf
DISCONNECT SEQUENCE: EOT DEL ~. _____ MODE: async sync isoch
NOTE 1: The "cable connector" should be in the "REV"
NOTE 2: position for these PINouts--check the "NOR" entry.

COMPUTER PORT PROFILE (Underline if supported, circle if selected)
COMPANY: Suncoast/Easycom
PRODUCT: BF-64U buffer

PORT female (computer)   PORT TYPE: serial _____
CONNECTOR: DB25 9-PIN 8-PIN(modular) _____   GENDER: male female
PIN CONFIGURATION: P03

PIN	FUNCTION	DIRECTION
1:FG	Frame Ground	N/A
2:TD	Transmit Data	FROM
3:RD	Receive Data	TO
4:RTS	Request to Send	FROM
5:CTS	Clear to Send	TO
6:DSR	Data Set Ready	TO
7:SG	Signal Ground	N/A
8:DCD	Data Carrier Detect	TO
20:DTR	Data Terminal Ready	FROM

FLOW CONTROL: 20   XON: YES ACK: LEADS THAT MUST BE ON: _ _ _
SPEEDS: 110 300 600 1200 1800 2400 4800 9600 19.2 56k _____
PARITY: even odd space mark none   CHARACTER LENGTH: 7 8 ___
STOP BITS: 1 1.5 2   LINE-ENDING CHARS: cr lf cr/lf
DISCONNECT SEQUENCE: EOT DEL ~. _____ MODE: async sync isoch
NOTE 1:
NOTE 2:

COMPUTER PORT PROFILE   (Underline if supported, circle if selected)
COMPANY: Suncoast/Easycom
PRODUCT: BF-64U buffer

PORT   female(printer)   PORT TYPE: serial _____
CONNECTOR: DB25 9-PIN 8-PIN(modular) _____   GENDER: male female
PIN CONFIGURATION: C01

PIN	FUNCTION	DIRECTION
1:FG	Frame Ground	N/A
2:TD	Transmit Data	FROM
3:RD	Receive Data	TO
4:RTS	Request to Send	FROM
5:CTS	Clear to Send	TO
6:DSR	Data Set Ready	TO
7:SG	Signal Ground	N/A
8:DCD	Data Carrier Detect	TO
20:DTR	Data Terminal Ready	FROM

FLOW CONTROL: 5 6 8   XON: YES ACK: LEADS THAT MUST BE ON: _ _ _
SPEEDS: 110 300 600 1200 1800 2400 4800 9600 19.2 56k _____
PARITY: even odd space mark none   CHARACTER LENGTH: 7 8 ___
STOP BITS: 1 1.5 2   LINE-ENDING CHARS: cr lf cr/lf
DISCONNECT SEQUENCE: EOT DEL ~. _____   MODE: async sync isoch
NOTE 1: Leads 5/6/8 should be on for normal output
NOTE 2:

COMPUTER PORT PROFILE   (Underline if supported, circle if selected)
COMPANY: Tecmar Inc.
PRODUCT: Maestro AT board

PORT   male(DTE--25-PIN)   PORT TYPE: serial _____
CONNECTOR: DB25 9-PIN 8-PIN(modular) _____   GENDER: male female
PIN CONFIGURATION: C01

PIN	FUNCTION	DIRECTION
2:TD	Transmit Data	FROM
3:RD	Receive Data	TO
4:RTS	Request to Send	FROM
5:CTS	Clear to Send	TO
6:DSR	Data Set Ready	TO
7:SG	Signal Ground	N/A
8:DCD	Data Carrier Detect	TO
20:DTR	Data Terminal Ready	FROM
22:RI	Ring Indicator	TO

FLOW CONTROL: 5 6 8   XON: ACK: LEADS THAT MUST BE ON: _ _ _
SPEEDS: 110 300 600 1200 1800 2400 4800 9600 19.2 56k _____
PARITY: even odd space mark none   CHARACTER LENGTH: 7 8 ___
STOP BITS: 1 1.5 2   LINE-ENDING CHARS: cr lf cr/lf
DISCONNECT SEQUENCE: EOT DEL ~. _____   MODE: async sync isoch
NOTE 1: This PINout is when the JPR3: port is configured
NOTE 2: as "DTE"(25-PIN). It can be "DCE, or a 9-PIN port

COMPUTER PORT PROFILE (Underline if supported, circle if selected)
COMPANY: Tecmar, Inc.
PRODUCT: Captain & MegaFunction boards

PORT male(25-PIN)   PORT TYPE: serial _____
CONNECTOR: DB25 9-PIN 8-PIN(modular) _____   GENDER: male female
PIN CONFIGURATION: C01

PIN	FUNCTION	DIRECTION
2:TD	Transmit Data	FROM
3:RD	Receive Data	TO
4:RTS	Request to Send	FROM
5:CTS	Clear to Send	TO
6:DSR	Data Set Ready	TO
7:SG	Signal Ground	N/A
8:DCD	Data Carrier Detect	TO
20:DTR	Data Terminal Ready	FROM
22:RI	Ring Indicator	TO

FLOW CONTROL: 5 6 8   XON: ACK: LEADS THAT MUST BE ON: _ _ _
SPEEDS: 110 300 600 1200 1800 2400 4800 9600 19.2 56k _____
PARITY: even odd space mark none   CHARACTER LENGTH: 7 8 ___
STOP BITS: 1 1.5 2   LINE-ENDING CHARS: cr lf cr/lf
DISCONNECT SEQUENCE: EOT DEL ~. _____ MODE: async sync isoch
NOTE 1: Leasds 5/6/8 should be on for data transmission.
NOTE 2:

COMPUTER PORT PROFILE (Underline if supported, circle if selected)
COMPANY: Tecmar, Inc.
PRODUCT: Maestro AT board

PORT male(9-PIN)   PORT TYPE: serial _____
CONNECTOR: DB25 9-PIN 8-PIN(modular) _____   GENDER: male female
PIN CONFIGURATION: C16

PIN	FUNCTION	DIRECTION
1:RLSD	Rec.Line Signal Detect	TO
2:RD	Receive Data	TO
3:TD	Transmit Data	FROM
4:DTR	Data Terminal Ready	FROM
5:SG	Signal Ground	N/A
6:DSR	Data Set Ready	TO
7:RTS	Request to Send	FROM
8:CTS	Clear to Send	TO
9:RI	Ring Indicator	TO

FLOW CONTROL: XON: ACK: LEADS THAT MUST BE ON: _ _ _
SPEEDS: 110 300 600 1200 1800 2400 4800 9600 19.2 56k _____
PARITY: even odd space mark none   CHARACTER LENGTH: 7 8 ___
STOP BITS: 1 1.5 2   LINE-ENDING CHARS: cr lf cr/lf
DISCONNECT SEQUENCE: EOT DEL ~. _____ MODE: async sync isoch
NOTE 1:
NOTE 2:

COMPUTER PORT PROFILE (Underline if supported, circle if selected)
COMPANY: U.S.DATA
PRODUCT: REACT Ind. Graphics Control System

PORT female (COMM1)   PORT TYPE: serial _____
CONNECTOR: DB25 9-PIN 8-PIN(modular) _____ GENDER: male female
PIN CONFIGURATION: C05

PIN	FUNCTION	DIRECTION
1:PG	Protective Ground	N/A
2:TD	Transmit Data	FROM
3:RD	Receive Data	TO
4:RTS	Request to Send	FROM
5:CTS	Clear to Send	TO
7:SG	Signal Ground	N/A

FLOW CONTROL: 5   XON: YES ACK: LEADS THAT MUST BE ON: _ _ _
SPEEDS: 110 300 600 1200 1800 2400 4800 9600 19.2 56k _____
PARITY: even odd space mark none   CHARACTER LENGTH: 7 8 ___
STOP BITS: 1 1.5 2   LINE-ENDING CHARS: cr lf cr/lf
DISCONNECT SEQUENCE: EOT DEL ~. _____ MODE: async sync isoch
NOTE 1: Lead 5 must be on to send data.
NOTE 2:

COMPUTER PORT PROFILE (Underline if supported, circle if selected)
COMPANY: Wall Data, Inc.
PRODUCT: DCF II

PORT female   PORT TYPE: serial _____
CONNECTOR: DB25 9-PIN 8-PIN(modular) _____ GENDER: male female
PIN CONFIGURATION: C01

PIN	FUNCTION	DIRECTION	PIN	FUNCTION	DIRECTION
1:PG	Protective Ground	N/A	7:SG	Signal Ground	N/A
2:TD	Transmit Data	FROM	8:DCD	Data Carrier Detect	TO
3:RD	Receive Data	TO	15:TC	Transmit Clock	TO
4:RTS	Request to Send	FROM	17:RC	Rec. Clk/Reverse Chann	TO
5:CTS	Clear to Send	TO	20:DTR	Data Terminal Ready	FROM
6:DSR	Data Set Ready	TO	24:TC	Transmit Clock	FROM

FLOW CONTROL: 5   XON: YES ACK: LEADS THAT MUST BE ON: _ _ _
SPEEDS: 110 300 600 1200 1800 2400 4800 9600 19.2 56k _____
PARITY: even odd space mark none   CHARACTER LENGTH: 7 8 ___
STOP BITS: 1 1.5 2   LINE-ENDING CHARS: cr lf cr/lf
DISCONNECT SEQUENCE: EOT DEL ~. _____ MODE: async sync isoch
NOTE 1:
NOTE 2:

COMPUTER PORT PROFILE (Underline if supported, circle if selected)
COMPANY: Wang Laboratories, Inc.
PRODUCT: Laptop Computer

PORT RS-232   PORT TYPE: serial _____
CONNECTOR: DB25 9-PIN 8-PIN(modular) _____   GENDER: male female
PIN CONFIGURATION: C01

PIN	FUNCTION	DIRECTION		PIN	FUNCTION	DIRECTION
1:PG	Protective Ground	N/A		8:DCD	Data Carrier Detect	TO
2:TD	Transmit Data	FROM		15:TT	Transmit Timing	TO
3:RD	Receive Data	TO		17:RT	Receive Timing	TO
4:RTS	Request to Send	FROM		20:DTR	Data Terminal Ready	FROM
5:CTS	Clear to Send	TO		22:RI	Ring Indicator	TO
6:DSR	Data Set Ready	TO		24:TT	Transmit Timing	FROM
7:SG	Signal Ground	N/A				

FLOW CONTROL: XON: ACK: LEADS THAT MUST BE ON: _ _ _
SPEEDS: 110 300 600 1200 1800 2400 4800 9600 19.2 56k _____
PARITY: even odd space mark none   CHARACTER LENGTH: 7 8 ___
STOP BITS: 1 1.5 2   LINE-ENDING CHARS: cr lf cr/lf
DISCONNECT SEQUENCE: EOT DEL ~. _____ MODE: async sync isoch
NOTE 1:
NOTE 2:

COMPUTER PORT PROFILE (Underline if supported, circle if selected)
COMPANY: Wang Laboratories, Inc.
PRODUCT: PC & APC computers

PORT male (9-PIN serial)   PORT TYPE: serial _____
CONNECTOR: DB25 9-PIN 8-PIN(modular) _____   GENDER: male female
PIN CONFIGURATION: C16

PIN	FUNCTION	DIRECTION
1:DCD	Data Carrier Detect	TO
2:RD	Receive Data	TO
3:TD	Transmit Data	FROM
4:DTR	Data Terminal Ready	FROM
5:SG	Signal Ground	N/A
6:DSR	Data Set Ready	TO
7:RTS	Request to Send	FROM
8:CTS	Clear to Send	TO
9:RI	Ring Indicator	TO

FLOW CONTROL: XON: ACK: LEADS THAT MUST BE ON: _ _ _
SPEEDS: 110 300 600 1200 1800 2400 4800 9600 19.2 56k _____
PARITY: even odd space mark none   CHARACTER LENGTH: 7 8 ___
STOP BITS: 1 1.5 2   LINE-ENDING CHARS: cr lf cr/lf
DISCONNECT SEQUENCE: EOT DEL ~. _____ MODE: async sync isoch
NOTE 1: Leads 1/6/8 should be on for data flow.
NOTE 2:

COMPUTER PORT PROFILE (Underline if supported, circle if selected)
COMPANY: Wang Laboratories, Inc.
PRODUCT: PC & APC computers

PORT male (DB-25)   PORT TYPE: serial _____
CONNECTOR: DB25 9-PIN 8-PIN(modular) _____   GENDER: male female
PIN CONFIGURATION: C01

PIN   FUNCTION   DIRECTION
1:PG   Protective Ground   N/A
2:TD   Transmit Data   FROM
3:RD   Receive Data   TO
4:RTS   Request to Send   FROM
5:CTS   Clear to Send   TO
6:DSR   Data Set Ready   TO
7:SG   Signal Ground   N/A
8:DCD   Data Carrier Detect   TO
20:DTR Data Terminal Ready   FROM

FLOW CONTROL: XON: ACK: LEADS THAT MUST BE ON: _ _ _
SPEEDS: 110 300 600 1200 1800 2400 4800 9600 19.2 56k _____
PARITY: even odd space mark none   CHARACTER LENGTH: 7 8 ___
STOP BITS: 1 1.5 2   LINE-ENDING CHARS: cr lf cr/lf
DISCONNECT SEQUENCE: EOT DEL ~. _____ MODE: async sync isoch
NOTE 1: Leads 5/6/8 should be on for data flow.
NOTE 2:

COMPUTER PORT PROFILE (Underline if supported, circle if selected)
COMPANY: xePIX, Inc.
PRODUCT: Gator/L, Gator/S computers

PORT female   PORT TYPE: serial _____
CONNECTOR: DB25 9-PIN 8-PIN(modular) _____ GENDER: male female
PIN CONFIGURATION: C01

PIN   FUNCTION   DIRECTION
1:PG   Protective Ground   N/A
2:TD   Transmit Data   FROM
3:RD   Receive Data   TO
4:RTS   Request to Send   FROM
5:CTS   Clear to Send   TO
6:DSR   Data Set Ready   TO
7:SG   Signal Ground   N/A
8:DCD   Data Carrier Detect   TO
20:DTR Data Terminal Ready   FROM

FLOW CONTROL: 5 6 8   XON: YES ACK: LEADS THAT MUST BE ON: _ _ _
SPEEDS: 110 300 600 1200 1800 2400 4800 9600 19.2 56k _____
PARITY: even odd space mark none   CHARACTER LENGTH: 7 8 ___
STOP BITS: 1 1.5 2   LINE-ENDING CHARS: cr lf cr/lf
DISCONNECT SEQUENCE: EOT DEL ~. _____ MODE: async sync isoch
NOTE 1: Leads 5/6/8 should be on for data flow.
NOTE 2:

COMPUTER PORT PROFILE (Underline if supported, circle if selected)
COMPANY: _____
PRODUCT: _____

PORT: _____   Port Type: serial parallel __
CONNECTOR: DB25 9-pin 5-pin 8-pin Centronics Gender: male   female
Pin Configuration: ___

Pin #	Function	Direction	Pin #	Function	Direction
1	_____	to from n/a	14	_____	to from n/a
2	_____	to from n/a	15	_____	to from n/a
3	_____	to from n/a	16	_____	to from n/a
4	_____	to from n/a	17	_____	to from n/a
5	_____	to from n/a	18	_____	to from n/a
6	_____	to from n/a	19	_____	to from n/a
7	_____	to from n/a	20	_____	to from n/a
8	_____	to from n/a	21	_____	to from n/a
9	_____	to from n/a	22	_____	to from n/a
10	_____	to from n/a	23	_____	to from n/a
11	_____	to from n/a	24	_____	to from n/a
12	_____	to from n/a	25	_____	to from n/a
13	_____	to from n/a			

(complete the next section only with 36-pin cinch connectors)

Pin #	Function	Direction	Pin #	Function	Direction
26	_____	to from n/a	27	_____	to from n/a
28	_____	to from n/a	29	_____	to from n/a
30	_____	to from n/a	31	_____	to from n/a
32	_____	to from n/a	33	_____	to from n/a
34	_____	to from n/a	35	_____	to from n/a
36	_____	to from n/a			

Flow Control Technique: XON/XOFF ENQ/ACK STX/ETX Hardware
Flow Control lead(s):   4 11 19 20 __ __ __
Leads that must be on: 5   6   8 __ __ __ __
Speeds: 110 300 600 1200 1800 2400 4800 9600 19.2 56k _____
Parity: even odd space mark none   CHARACTER LENGTH: 7 8 ___
Stop Bits: 1 1.5 2   Line Ending Sequence: cr lf cr/lf
DISCONNECT SEQUENCE: EOT DEL ~. _____Mode: async sync isoch
NOTE 1:_____
NOTE 2:_____

COMPUTER PORT PROFILE (Underline if supported, circle if selected)
COMPANY: _____
PRODUCT: _____

PORT: _____   Port Type: serial parallel __
CONNECTOR: DB25 9-pin 5-pin 8-pin Centronics Gender: male female
Pin Configuration: ___

Pin #	Function	Direction	Pin #	Function	Direction
1	_____	to from n/a	14	_____	to from n/a
2	_____	to from n/a	15	_____	to from n/a
3	_____	to from n/a	16	_____	to from n/a
4	_____	to from n/a	17	_____	to from n/a
5	_____	to from n/a	18	_____	to from n/a
6	_____	to from n/a	19	_____	to from n/a
7	_____	to from n/a	20	_____	to from n/a
8	_____	to from n/a	21	_____	to from n/a
9	_____	to from n/a	22	_____	to from n/a
10	_____	to from n/a	23	_____	to from n/a
11	_____	to from n/a	24	_____	to from n/a
12	_____	to from n/a	25	_____	to from n/a
13	_____	to from n/a			

(complete the next section only with 36-pin cinch connectors)

26	_____	to from n/a	27	_____	to from n/a
28	_____	to from n/a	29	_____	to from n/a
30	_____	to from n/a	31	_____	to from n/a
32	_____	to from n/a	33	_____	to from n/a
34	_____	to from n/a	35	_____	to from n/a
36	_____	to from n/a			

Flow Control Technique: XON/XOFF ENQ/ACK STX/ETX Hardware
Flow Control lead(s):   4 11 19 20 __ __ __
Leads that must be on: 5 6 8 __ __ __
Speeds: 110 300 600 1200 1800 2400 4800 9600 19.2 56k _____
Parity: even odd space mark none   CHARACTER LENGTH: 7 8 ___
Stop Bits: 1 1.5 2   Line Ending Sequence: cr lf cr/lf
DISCONNECT SEQUENCE: EOT DEL ~. _____ Mode: async sync isoch
NOTE 1:_____
NOTE 2:_____

COMPUTER PORT PROFILE (Underline if supported, circle if selected)

COMPANY: _____

PRODUCT: _____

PORT: _____   Port Type: serial parallel __

CONNECTOR: DB25 9-pin 5-pin 8-pin Centronics Gender: male female

Pin Configuration: ___

Pin #	Function	Direction	Pin #	Function	Direction
1	_____	to from n/a	14	_____	to from n/a
2	_____	to from n/a	15	_____	to from n/a
3	_____	to from n/a	16	_____	to from n/a
4	_____	to from n/a	17	_____	to from n/a
5	_____	to from n/a	18	_____	to from n/a
6	_____	to from n/a	19	_____	to from n/a
7	_____	to from n/a	20	_____	to from n/a
8	_____	to from n/a	21	_____	to from n/a
9	_____	to from n/a	22	_____	to from n/a
10	_____	to from n/a	23	_____	to from n/a
11	_____	to from n/a	24	_____	to from n/a
12	_____	to from n/a	25	_____	to from n/a
13	_____	to from n/a			

(complete the next section only with 36-pin cinch connectors)

Pin #	Function	Direction	Pin #	Function	Direction
26	_____	to from n/a	27	_____	to from n/a
28	_____	to from n/a	29	_____	to from n/a
30	_____	to from n/a	31	_____	to from n/a
32	_____	to from n/a	33	_____	to from n/a
34	_____	to from n/a	35	_____	to from n/a
36	_____	to from n/a			

Flow Control Technique: XON/XOFF ENQ/ACK STX/ETX Hardware

Flow Control lead(s):   4 11 19 20 __ __ __

Leads that must be on: 5   6   8 __ __ __ __

Speeds: 110 300 600 1200 1800 2400 4800 9600 19.2 56k _____

Parity: even odd space mark none   CHARACTER LENGTH: 7 8 ___

Stop Bits: 1 1.5 2   Line Ending Sequence: cr lf cr/lf

DISCONNECT SEQUENCE: EOT DEL ~. _____Mode: async sync isoch

NOTE 1:_____

NOTE 2:_____

COMPUTER PORT PROFILE (Underline if supported, circle if selected)
COMPANY: _____
PRODUCT: _____

PORT: _____   Port Type: serial parallel __
CONNECTOR: DB25 9-pin 5-pin 8-pin Centronics Gender: male female
Pin Configuration: ___

Pin #	Function	Direction	Pin #	Function	Direction
1	_____	to from n/a	14	_____	to from n/a
2	_____	to from n/a	15	_____	to from n/a
3	_____	to from n/a	16	_____	to from n/a
4	_____	to from n/a	17	_____	to from n/a
5	_____	to from n/a	18	_____	to from n/a
6	_____	to from n/a	19	_____	to from n/a
7	_____	to from n/a	20	_____	to from n/a
8	_____	to from n/a	21	_____	to from n/a
9	_____	to from n/a	22	_____	to from n/a
10	_____	to from n/a	23	_____	to from n/a
11	_____	to from n/a	24	_____	to from n/a
12	_____	to from n/a	25	_____	to from n/a
13	_____	to from n/a			

(complete the next section only with 36-pin cinch connectors)

Pin #	Function	Direction	Pin #	Function	Direction
26	_____	to from n/a	27	_____	to from n/a
28	_____	to from n/a	29	_____	to from n/a
30	_____	to from n/a	31	_____	to from n/a
32	_____	to from n/a	33	_____	to from n/a
34	_____	to from n/a	35	_____	to from n/a
36	_____	to from n/a			

Flow Control Technique: XON/XOFF ENQ/ACK STX/ETX Hardware
Flow Control lead(s):   4 11 19 20 __ __ __
Leads that must be on: 5   6   8 __ __ __ __
Speeds: 110 300 600 1200 1800 2400 4800 9600 19.2 56k _____
Parity: even odd space mark none   CHARACTER LENGTH: 7 8 ___
Stop Bits: 1 1.5 2   Line Ending Sequence: cr lf cr/lf
DISCONNECT SEQUENCE: EOT   DEL   ~. _____Mode: async sync isoch
NOTE 1:_____
NOTE 2:_____

MODEM PORT PROFILE **(Underline if supported, circle if selected)**
COMPANY: Anchor Automation, Inc.
PRODUCT: VM520 modem

PORT: female   PORT TYPE: serial _____ ___
CONNECTOR: DB25 9-pin 8-pin(modular)   GENDER: male female
PIN CONFIGURATION: C14

PIN	FUNCTION	DIRECTION
1:FG	Frame Ground	N/A
2:TD	Transmit Data	TO
3:RD	Receive Data	FROM
5:CTS	Clear to Send	FROM
7:SG	Signal Ground	N/A
8:DCD	Data Carrier Detect	FROM
20:DTR	Data Terminal Ready	TO
22:RI	Ring Indicator	FROM

FLOW CONTROL   XON: ACK: LEADS THAT MUST BE ON: _____
SPEEDS: 110 300 600 1200 1800 2400 4800 9600 19.2 56k _____
COMPATIBILITY: 103 212 V.22bis _____
PARITY: even odd space mark none   CHARACTER LENGTH: 7 8 ___
STOP BITS: 1 1.5 2   LINE-ENDING CHARs: cr lf cr/lf
AUTO-ANSWER: yes no   RTS/CTS delay: _____
DISCONNECT SEQUENCE: EOT DEL _____
INTELLIGENT MODEMS....
  Dialing Technique: Touch-tone Pulse
  Compatibility: Hayes _____
  Command Line Prefix: AT _____   Dial command: D _____
  Touch-tone dial: T ___   Pulse Dial: P ___ Pause: , ___
  Wait for dial tone: W ___   Wait for quiet answer: @ ___
  Flash: ! ___   Dial stored number: S ___
  Return to command state after dialing: ; ___
  Escape sequence: +++ ___   Switch-Hook control: H ___
  Store Phone#: &Z ___
MODE: async sync isoch
NOTE 1: _____
NOTE 2: _____

MODEM PORT PROFILE   (Underline if supported, circle if selected)
COMPANY: AT&T
PRODUCT: 103JR modem

PORT: female (DTE port)   PORT TYPE: serial _____

CONNECTOR: DB25 9-pin 8-pin(modular)   GENDER: male female

PIN CONFIGURATION: C14

PIN	FUNCTION	DIRECTION
2:TD	Transmit Data	TO
3:RD	Receive Data	FROM
5:CTS	Clear to Send	FROM
6:MR	Modem Ready	FROM
7:SG	Signal Ground	N/A
8:DCD	Data Carrier Detect	FROM
9:+12V		FROM
10:-12V		FROM
20:DTR	Data Terminal Ready	TO
22:RI	Ring Indicator	FROM
25:B	Busy	TO

FLOW CONTROL   XON: ACK: LEADS THAT MUST BE ON: _____

SPEEDS: 110 300 600 1200 1800 2400 4800 9600 19.2 56k _____

COMPATIBILITY: 103 212 V.22bis _____

PARITY: even odd space mark none   CHARACTER LENGTH: 7 8 ___

STOP BITS: 1 1.5 2   LINE-ENDING CHARs: cr lf cr/lf

AUTO-ANSWER: yes no   RTS/CTS delay: _____

DISCONNECT SEQUENCE: EOT DEL _____

INTELLIGENT MODEMS....

  Dialing Technique: Touch-tone Pulse

  Compatibility: Hayes _____

  Command Line Prefix: AT _____   Dial command: D _____

  Touch-tone dial: T ___   Pulse Dial: P ___ Pause: , ___

  Wait for dial tone: W ___   Wait for quiet answer: @ ___

  Flash: ! ___   Dial stored number: S ___

  Return to command state after dialing: ; ___

  Escape sequence: +++ ___   Switch-Hook control: H ___

  Store Phone#: &Z ___

MODE: async sync isoch

NOTE 1: _____

NOTE 2: _____

MODEM PORT PROFILE (Underline if supported, circle if selected)
COMPANY: AT&T
PRODUCT: 201C modem

PORT: female   PORT TYPE: serial _____
CONNECTOR: DB25 9-pin 8-pin(modular)   GENDER: male female
PIN CONFIGURATION: C14

PIN	FUNCTION	DIRECTION
2:TD	Transmit Data	TO
3:RD	Receive Data	FROM
4:RTS	Request to Send	TO
5:CTS	Clear to Send	FROM
6:DSR	Data Set Ready	FROM
7:SG	Signal Ground	N/A
8:RLSD	Rec.Line Signal Detect	FROM
9:+12V		FROM
10:-12V		FROM
14:SYNC		TO
15:TC	Transmit Clock	FROM
17:RC	Rec. Clk/Reverse Chann	FROM
19:+5V		FROM
20:DTR	Data Terminal Ready	TO
24:TC	Transmit Clock	TO

FLOW CONTROL   XON: ACK: LEADS THAT MUST BE ON: _____
SPEEDS: 110 300 600 1200 1800 2400 4800 9600 19.2 56k _____
COMPATIBILITY: 103 212 V.22bis _____
PARITY: even odd space mark none   CHARACTER LENGTH: 7 8 ___
STOP BITS: 1 1.5 2   LINE-ENDING CHARs: cr lf cr/lf
AUTO-ANSWER: yes no   RTS/CTS delay: _____
DISCONNECT SEQUENCE: EOT DEL _____
INTELLIGENT MODEMS....
  Dialing Technique: Touch-tone Pulse
  Compatibility: Hayes _____
  Command Line Prefix: AT _____   Dial command: D _____
  Touch-tone dial: T ___ Pulse Dial: P ___ Pause: , ___
  Wait for dial tone: W ___   Wait for quiet answer: @ ___
  Flash: ! ___   Dial stored number: S ___
  Return to command state after dialing: ; ___
  Escape sequence: +++ ___   Switch-Hook control: H ___
  Store Phone#: &Z ___
MODE: async sync isoch
NOTE 1: _____
NOTE 2: _____

MODEM PORT PROFILE   (Underline if supported, circle if selected)
COMPANY: AT&T
PRODUCT: 2024/2048/2096 modems (Dataphone II)

PORT: RS-232 (from RS-449)   PORT TYPE: serial _____

CONNECTOR: DB25 9-pin 8-pin(modular)   GENDER: male female

PIN CONFIGURATION: C14

PIN	FUNCTION	DIRECTION
2:TD	Transmit Data	TO
3:RD	Receive Data	FROM
4:RTS	Request to Send	TO
5:CTS	Clear to Send	FROM
6:DSR	Data Set Ready	FROM
7:SG	Signal Ground	N/A
8:RLSD	Rec.Line Signal Detect	FROM
15:TT	Transmit Timing	FROM
17:RT	Receive Timing	FROM
20:DTR	Data Terminal Ready	TO
22:RI	Ring Indicator	FROM
23:DRS	Data Rate Select	TO
24:TT	Transmit Timing	TO

FLOW CONTROL   XON: ACK: LEADS THAT MUST BE ON: _____

SPEEDS: 110 300 600 1200 1800 2400 4800 9600 19.2 56k _____

COMPATIBILITY: 103 212 V.22bis _____

PARITY: even odd space mark none   CHARACTER LENGTH: 7 8 ___

\# STOP BITS: 1 1.5 2   LINE-ENDING CHARs: cr lf cr/lf

AUTO-ANSWER: yes no   RTS/CTS delay: _____

DISCONNECT SEQUENCE: EOT DEL _____

INTELLIGENT MODEMS....

  Dialing Technique: Touch-tone Pulse

  Compatibility: Hayes _____

  Command Line Prefix: AT _____   Dial command: D _____

  Touch-tone dial: T ___ Pulse Dial: P ___ Pause: , ___

  Wait for dial tone: W ___   Wait for quiet answer: @ ___

  Flash: ! ___   Dial stored number: S ___

  Return to command state after dialing: ; ___

  Escape sequence: +++ ___   Switch-Hook control: H ___

  Store Phone#: &Z ___

MODE: async sync isoch

NOTE 1: _____

NOTE 2: _____

MODEM PORT PROFILE (Underline if supported, circle if selected)
COMPANY: AT&T
PRODUCT: 2028 modem

PORT: female (customer)   PORT TYPE: serial _____
CONNECTOR: DB25 9-pin 8-pin(modular)   GENDER: male female
PIN CONFIGURATION: C14

PIN	FUNCTION	DIRECTION
1:PG	Protective Ground	N/A
2:TD	Transmit Data	TO
3:RD	Receive Data	FROM
4:RTS	Request to Send	TO
5:CTS	Clear to Send	FROM
6:DSR	Data Set Ready	FROM
7:SG	Signal Ground	N/A
8:RLSD	Rec.Line Signal Detect	FROM
9:+14V		FROM
10:-14V		FROM
12:SDCD	Secondary DCD	FROM
20:DTR	Data Terminal Ready	TO
22:RI	Ring Indicator	FROM

FLOW CONTROL   XON: ACK: LEADS THAT MUST BE ON: _____
SPEEDS: 110 300 600 1200 1800 2400 4800 9600 19.2 56k _____
COMPATIBILITY: 103 212 V.22bis _____
PARITY: even odd space mark none   CHARACTER LENGTH: 7 8 ___
STOP BITS: 1 1.5 2   LINE-ENDING CHARs: cr lf cr/lf
AUTO-ANSWER: yes no   RTS/CTS delay: _____
DISCONNECT SEQUENCE: EOT DEL _____
INTELLIGENT MODEMS....
  Dialing Technique: Touch-tone Pulse
  Compatibility: Hayes _____
  Command Line Prefix: AT _____   Dial command: D _____
  Touch-tone dial: T ___ Pulse Dial: P ___ Pause: , ___
  Wait for dial tone: W ___   Wait for quiet answer: @ ___
  Flash: ! ___   Dial stored number: S ___
  Return to command state after dialing: ; ___
  Escape sequence: +++ ___   Switch-Hook control: H ___
  Store Phone#: &Z ___
MODE: async sync isoch
NOTE 1: _____
NOTE 2: _____

MODEM PORT PROFILE   (Underline if supported, circle if selected)
COMPANY: AT&T
PRODUCT: 208A modem

PORT: female   PORT TYPE: serial _____

CONNECTOR: DB25 9-pin 8-pin(modular)   GENDER: male female

PIN CONFIGURATION: C14

PIN	FUNCTION	DIRECTION
2:TD	Transmit Data	TO
3:RD	Receive Data	FROM
4:RTS	Request to Send	TO
5:CTS	Clear to Send	FROM
6:DSR	Data Set Ready	FROM
7:SG	Signal Ground	N/A
8:CD	Carrier Detect	FROM
9:+12V		FROM
10:-12V		FROM
11:EM		
14:SYNC		TO
15:TC	Transmit Clock	FROM
17:RC	Rec. Clk/Reverse Chann	FROM
20:		TO
24:ETC	External Transmit Cloc	TO
25:+5V		FROM

FLOW CONTROL   XON: ACK: LEADS THAT MUST BE ON: _____

SPEEDS: 110 300 600 1200 1800 2400 4800 9600 19.2 56k _____

COMPATIBILITY: 103 212 V.22bis _____

PARITY: even odd space mark none   CHARACTER LENGTH: 7 8 ___

STOP BITS: 1 1.5 2   LINE-ENDING CHARs: cr lf cr/lf

AUTO-ANSWER: yes no   RTS/CTS delay: _____

DISCONNECT SEQUENCE: EOT DEL _____

INTELLIGENT MODEMS....

   Dialing Technique: Touch-tone Pulse

   Compatibility: Hayes _____

   Command Line Prefix: AT _____   Dial command: D _____

   Touch-tone dial: T ___   Pulse Dial: P ___   Pause: , ___

   Wait for dial tone: W ___   Wait for quiet answer: @ ___

   Flash: ! ___   Dial stored number: S ___

   Return to command state after dialing: ; ___

   Escape sequence: +++ ___   Switch-Hook control: H ___

   Store Phone#: &Z ___

MODE: async sync isoch

NOTE 1: _____

NOTE 2: _____

MODEM PORT PROFILE (Underline if supported, circle if selected)
COMPANY: AT&T
PRODUCT: 212A modem

PORT: female
CONNECTOR: DB25 9-pin 8-pin(modular)
PIN CONFIGURATION: C14

PORT TYPE: serial _____
GENDER: male female

PIN	FUNCTION	DIRECTION
2:TD	Transmit Data	TO
3:RD	Receive Data	FROM
5:CTS	Clear to Send	FROM
6:DSR	Data Set Ready	FROM
7:SG	Signal Ground	N/A
8:RLSD	Rec.Line Signal Detect	FROM
9:+V		FROM
10:-V		FROM
12:SS	Speed Select	FROM
15:TC	Transmit Clock	FROM
17:RC	Rec. Clk/Reverse Chann	FROM
18:AL		FROM
20:DTR	Data Terminal Ready	TO
21:RDL		FROM
22:RI	Ring Indicator	FROM
23:SS	Speed Select	FROM
24:ETC	External Transmit Cloc	TO
25:AL		TO

FLOW CONTROL   XON: ACK: LEADS THAT MUST BE ON: _____
SPEEDS: 110 300 600 1200 1800 2400 4800 9600 19.2 56k _____
COMPATIBILITY: 103 212 V.22bis _____
PARITY: even odd space mark none   CHARACTER LENGTH: 7 8 ___
STOP BITS: 1 1.5 2   LINE-ENDING CHARs: cr lf cr/lf
AUTO-ANSWER: yes no   RTS/CTS delay: _____
DISCONNECT SEQUENCE: EOT DEL _____
INTELLIGENT MODEMS....
  Dialing Technique: Touch-tone Pulse
  Compatibility: Hayes _____
  Command Line Prefix: AT _____   Dial command: D _____
  Touch-tone dial: T ___ Pulse Dial: P ___ Pause: , ___
  Wait for dial tone: W ___   Wait for quiet answer: @ ___
  Flash: ! ___   Dial stored number: S ___
  Return to command state after dialing: ; ___
  Escape sequence: +++ ___   Switch-Hook control: H ___
  Store Phone#: &Z ___
MODE: async sync isoch
NOTE 1: _____
NOTE 2: _____

MODEM PORT PROFILE   **(Underline if supported, circle if selected)**
COMPANY: AT&T
PRODUCT: 2212C modem

PORT: female   PORT TYPE: serial _____

CONNECTOR: DB25 9-pin 8-pin(modular)   GENDER: male female

PIN CONFIGURATION: C14

PIN	FUNCTION	DIRECTION
2:TD	Transmit Data	TO
3:RD	Receive Data	FROM
5:CTS	Clear to Send	FROM
6:DSR	Data Set Ready	FROM
7:SG	Signal Ground	N/A
8:CD	Carrier Detect	FROM
9:+12V		FROM
20:DTR	Data Terminal Ready	TO
22:RI	Ring Indicator	FROM

FLOW CONTROL   XON: ACK: LEADS THAT MUST BE ON: _____

SPEEDS: 110 300 600 1200 1800 2400 4800 9600 19.2 56k _____

COMPATIBILITY: 103 212 V.22bis _____

PARITY: even odd space mark none   CHARACTER LENGTH: 7 8 ___

\# STOP BITS: 1 1.5 2   LINE-ENDING CHARs: cr lf cr/lf

AUTO-ANSWER: yes no   RTS/CTS delay: _____

DISCONNECT SEQUENCE: EOT DEL _____

INTELLIGENT MODEMS....

   Dialing Technique: Touch-tone Pulse

   Compatibility: Hayes _____

   Command Line Prefix: AT _____   Dial command: D _____

   Touch-tone dial: T ___   Pulse Dial: P ___   Pause: , ___

   Wait for dial tone: W ___   Wait for quiet answer: @ ___

   Flash: ! ___   Dial stored number: S ___

   Return to command state after dialing: ; ___

   Escape sequence: +++ ___   Switch-Hook control: H ___

   Store Phone#: &Z ___

MODE: async sync isoch

NOTE 1: _____

NOTE 2: _____

MODEM PORT PROFILE (Underline if supported, circle if selected)
COMPANY: AT&T
PRODUCT: 2400 bps modem (Dataphone I)

PORT: DTE   PORT TYPE: serial _____
CONNECTOR: DB25 9-pin 8-pin(modular)   GENDER: male female
PIN CONFIGURATION: C14

PIN	FUNCTION	DIRECTION
2:TD	Transmit Data	TO
3:RD	Receive Data	FROM
4:RTS	Request to Send	TO
5:CTS	Clear to Send	FROM
6:DSR	Data Set Ready	FROM
7:SG	Signal Ground	N/A
8:CD	Carrier Detect	FROM
15:TT	Transmit Timing	FROM
17:RT	Receive Timing	FROM
20:DTR	Data Terminal Ready	TO
24:TT	Transmit Timing	TO

FLOW CONTROL   XON: ACK: LEADS THAT MUST BE ON: _____
SPEEDS: 110 300 600 1200 1800 2400 4800 9600 19.2 56k _____
COMPATIBILITY: 103 212 V.22bis _____
PARITY: even odd space mark none   CHARACTER LENGTH: 7 8 ___
STOP BITS: 1 1.5 2   LINE-ENDING CHARs: cr lf cr/lf
AUTO-ANSWER: yes no   RTS/CTS delay: _____
DISCONNECT SEQUENCE: EOT DEL _____
INTELLIGENT MODEMS....
   Dialing Technique: Touch-tone Pulse
   Compatibility: Hayes _____
   Command Line Prefix: AT _____   Dial command: D _____
   Touch-tone dial: T ___ Pulse Dial: P ___ Pause: , ___
   Wait for dial tone: W ___   Wait for quiet answer: @ ___
   Flash: ! ___   Dial stored number: S ___
   Return to command state after dialing: ; ___
   Escape sequence: +++ ___   Switch-Hook control: H ___
   Store Phone#: &Z ___
MODE: async sync isoch
NOTE 1: Lead 6 is always on when power is applied.
NOTE 2: _____If DTE is to provide timing, option=ext. timing.

MODEM PORT PROFILE (Underline if supported, circle if selected)
COMPANY: AT&T
PRODUCT: 719 Networker

PORT: RS-232(for DCE conn)   PORT TYPE: serial _____
CONNECTOR: DB25 9-pin 8-pin(modular)   GENDER: male female
PIN CONFIGURATION: C08

PIN	FUNCTION	DIRECTION
1:G	Ground	N/A
2:TD	Transmit Data	FROM
3:RD	Receive Data	TO
4:+12V		FROM
7:SG	Signal Ground	N/A
20:+12V		FROM

FLOW CONTROL   XON: ACK: LEADS THAT MUST BE ON: _____
SPEEDS: 110 300 600 1200 1800 2400 4800 9600 19.2 56k _____
COMPATIBILITY: 103 212 V.22bis _____
PARITY: even odd space mark none   CHARACTER LENGTH: 7 8 ___
STOP BITS: 1 1.5 2   LINE-ENDING CHARs: cr lf cr/lf
AUTO-ANSWER: yes no   RTS/CTS delay: _____
DISCONNECT SEQUENCE: EOT DEL _____
INTELLIGENT MODEMS....
  Dialing Technique: Touch-tone Pulse
  Compatibility: Hayes _____
  Command Line Prefix: AT _____   Dial command: D _____
  Touch-tone dial: T ___ Pulse Dial: P ___ Pause: , ___
  Wait for dial tone: W ___   Wait for quiet answer: @ ___
  Flash: ! ___   Dial stored number: S ___
  Return to command state after dialing: ; ___
  Escape sequence: +++ ___   Switch-Hook control: H ___
  Store Phone#: &Z ___
MODE: async sync isoch
NOTE 1: _____
NOTE 2: _____

MODEM PORT PROFILE (Underline if supported, circle if selected)
COMPANY: AT&T
PRODUCT: 719 Networker

PORT: RS-232(for DTE conn)   PORT TYPE: serial _____
CONNECTOR: DB25 9-pin 8-pin(modular)   GENDER: male female
PIN CONFIGURATION: C10

PIN	FUNCTION	DIRECTION
1:G	Ground	N/A
2:TD	Transmit Data	TO
3:RD	Receive Data	FROM
6:+12V		FROM
7:SG	Signal Ground	N/A
8:+12V		FROM

FLOW CONTROL   XON: ACK: LEADS THAT MUST BE ON: _____
SPEEDS: 110 300 600 1200 1800 2400 4800 9600 19.2 56k _____
COMPATIBILITY: 103 212 V.22bis _____
PARITY: even odd space mark none   CHARACTER LENGTH: 7 8 ___
STOP BITS: 1 1.5 2   LINE-ENDING CHARs: cr lf cr/lf
AUTO-ANSWER: yes no   RTS/CTS delay: _____
DISCONNECT SEQUENCE: EOT DEL _____
INTELLIGENT MODEMS....
  Dialing Technique: Touch-tone Pulse
  Compatibility: Hayes _____
  Command Line Prefix: AT _____   Dial command: D _____
  Touch-tone dial: T ___   Pulse Dial: P ___ Pause: , ___
  Wait for dial tone: W ___   Wait for quiet answer: @ ___
  Flash: ! ___   Dial stored number: S ___
  Return to command state after dialing: ; ___
  Escape sequence: +++ ___   Switch-Hook control: H ___
  Store Phone#: &Z ___
MODE: async sync isoch
NOTE 1: _____
NOTE 2: _____

MODEM PORT PROFILE (Underline if supported, circle if selected)
COMPANY: AT&T
PRODUCT: 9600 bps modem (Dataphone I)

PORT: DTE interface   PORT TYPE: serial _____
CONNECTOR: DB25 9-pin 8-pin(modular)   GENDER: male female
PIN CONFIGURATION: C14

PIN	FUNCTION	DIRECTION
2:TD	Transmit Data	TO
3:RD	Receive Data	FROM
4:RTS	Request to Send	TO
5:CTS	Clear to Send	FROM
6:DSR	Data Set Ready	FROM
7:SG	Signal Ground	N/A
8:CD	Carrier Detect	FROM
15:TT	Transmit Timing	FROM
17:RT	Receive Timing	FROM
20:DTR	Data Terminal Ready	TO
24:TT	Transmit Timing	TO

FLOW CONTROL   XON: ACK: LEADS THAT MUST BE ON: _____
SPEEDS: 110 300 600 1200 1800 2400 4800 9600 19.2 56k _____
COMPATIBILITY: 103 212 V.22bis _____
PARITY: even odd space mark none   CHARACTER LENGTH: 7 8 ___
STOP BITS: 1 1.5 2   LINE-ENDING CHARs: cr lf cr/lf
AUTO-ANSWER: yes no   RTS/CTS delay: _____
DISCONNECT SEQUENCE: EOT DEL _____
INTELLIGENT MODEMS....
   Dialing Technique: Touch-tone Pulse
   Compatibility: Hayes _____
   Command Line Prefix: AT _____   Dial command: D _____
   Touch-tone dial: T ___   Pulse Dial: P ___   Pause: , ___
   Wait for dial tone: W ___   Wait for quiet answer: @ ___
   Flash: ! ___   Dial stored number: S ___
   Return to command state after dialing: ; ___
   Escape sequence: +++ ___   Switch-Hook control: H ___
   Store Phone#: &Z ___
MODE: async sync isoch
NOTE 1: _____
NOTE 2: _____

MODEM PORT PROFILE (Underline if supported, circle if selected)
COMPANY: AT&T
PRODUCT: ADU

PORT: RS-232   PORT TYPE: serial _____
CONNECTOR: DB25 9-pin 8-pin(modular)   GENDER: male female
PIN CONFIGURATION: C14

PIN	FUNCTION	DIRECTION
1:PG	Protective Ground	N/A
2:TD	Transmit Data	TO
3:RD	Receive Data	FROM
5:CTS	Clear to Send	FROM
6:DSR	Data Set Ready	FROM
7:SG	Signal Ground	N/A
8:DCD	Data Carrier Detect	FROM
20:DTR	Data Terminal Ready	TO

FLOW CONTROL   XON: ACK: LEADS THAT MUST BE ON: _____
SPEEDS: 110 300 600 1200 1800 2400 4800 9600 19.2 56k _____
COMPATIBILITY: 103 212 V.22bis _____
PARITY: even odd space mark none   CHARACTER LENGTH: 7 8 ___
STOP BITS: 1 1.5 2   LINE-ENDING CHARs: cr lf cr/lf
AUTO-ANSWER: yes no   RTS/CTS delay: _____
DISCONNECT SEQUENCE: EOT DEL _____
INTELLIGENT MODEMS....
  Dialing Technique: Touch-tone Pulse
  Compatibility: Hayes _____
  Command Line Prefix: AT _____   Dial command: D _____
  Touch-tone dial: T ___ Pulse Dial: P ___ Pause: , ___
  Wait for dial tone: W ___   Wait for quiet answer: @ ___
  Flash: ! ___   Dial stored number: S ___
  Return to command state after dialing: ; ___
  Escape sequence: +++ ___   Switch-Hook control: H ___
  Store Phone#: &Z ___
MODE: async sync isoch
NOTE 1: _____
NOTE 2: _____

MODEM PORT PROFILE   (Underline if supported, circle if selected)
COMPANY: AT&T
PRODUCT: DTDM(7404D) data module

PORT: PORT TYPE: serial _____
CONNECTOR: DB25 9-pin 8-pin(modular)   GENDER: male female
PIN CONFIGURATION: C14

PIN	FUNCTION	DIRECTION
1:PG	Protective Ground	N/A
2:TD	Transmit Data	TO
3:RD	Receive Data	FROM
4:RTS	Request to Send	TO
5:CTS	Clear to Send	FROM
6:DSR	Data Set Ready	FROM
7:SG	Signal Ground	N/A
8:DCD	Data Carrier Detect	FROM
15:TT	Transmit Timing	FROM
17:RT	Receive Timing	FROM
20:DTR	Data Terminal Ready	TO

FLOW CONTROL   XON: YES ACK: LEADS THAT MUST BE ON: _____
SPEEDS: 110 300 600 1200 1800 2400 4800 9600 19.2 56k _____
COMPATIBILITY: 103 212 V.22bis _____
PARITY: even odd space mark none   CHARACTER LENGTH: 7 8 ___
STOP BITS: 1 1.5 2   LINE-ENDING CHARs: cr lf cr/lf
AUTO-ANSWER: yes no   RTS/CTS delay: _____
DISCONNECT SEQUENCE: EOT DEL _____
INTELLIGENT MODEMS....
  Dialing Technique: Touch-tone Pulse
  Compatibility: Hayes _____
  Command Line Prefix: AT _____   Dial command: D _____
  Touch-tone dial: T ___ Pulse Dial: P ___ Pause: , ___
  Wait for dial tone: W ___   Wait for quiet answer: @ ___
  Flash: ! ___   Dial stored number: S ___
  Return to command state after dialing: ; ___
  Escape sequence: +++ ___   Switch-Hook control: H ___
  Store Phone#: &Z ___
MODE: async sync isoch
NOTE 1: This is a data module for a PBX.
NOTE 2: _____

MODEM PORT PROFILE (Underline if supported, circle if selected)
COMPANY: AT&T
PRODUCT: ISN (AIM 8 interface)

PORT: RS-232(DCE mode)   PORT TYPE: serial _____
CONNECTOR: DB25 9-pin 8-pin(modular)   GENDER: male female
PIN CONFIGURATION: C17

PIN	FUNCTION	DIRECTION
2:DTD		TO
3:RD	Receive Data	FROM
7:SG	Signal Ground	N/A
8:DCD	Data Carrier Detect	FROM
20:DTR	Data Terminal Ready	TO
22:RI	Ring Indicator	FROM

FLOW CONTROL   XON: YES ACK: LEADS THAT MUST BE ON: _____
SPEEDS: 110 300 600 1200 1800 2400 4800 9600 19.2 56k _____
COMPATIBILITY: 103 212 V.22bis _____
PARITY: even odd space mark none   CHARACTER LENGTH: 7 8 ___
STOP BITS: 1 1.5 2   LINE-ENDING CHARs: cr lf cr/lf
AUTO-ANSWER: yes no   RTS/CTS delay: _____
DISCONNECT SEQUENCE: EOT DEL _____
INTELLIGENT MODEMS....
   Dialing Technique: Touch-tone Pulse
   Compatibility: Hayes _____
   Command Line Prefix: AT _____   Dial command: D _____
   Touch-tone dial: T ___ Pulse Dial: P ___ Pause: , ___
   Wait for dial tone: W ___   Wait for quiet answer: @ ___
   Flash: ! ___   Dial stored number: S ___
   Return to command state after dialing: ; ___
   Escape sequence: +++ ___   Switch-Hook control: H ___
   Store Phone#: &Z ___
MODE: async sync isoch
NOTE 1: Normally the leads 5/6 should be connected to
NOTE 2: _____lead 8 at the attached device's connector

MODEM PORT PROFILE   (Underline if supported, circle if selected)
COMPANY: AT&T
PRODUCT: ISN (AIM4 interface)

PORT: RS-232(DCE mode)   PORT TYPE: serial _____
CONNECTOR: DB25 9-pin 8-pin(modular)   GENDER: male female
PIN CONFIGURATION: C14

PIN	FUNCTION	DIRECTION
2:TD	Transmit Data	TO
3:RD	Receive Data	FROM
4:RTS	Request to Send	TO
5:CTS	Clear to Send	FROM
6:DSR	Data Set Ready	FROM
7:SG	Signal Ground	N/A
8:DCD	Data Carrier Detect	FROM
20:DTR	Data Terminal Ready	TO
22:RI	Ring Indicator	FROM

FLOW CONTROL: 4   XON: ACK: LEADS THAT MUST BE ON: _____
SPEEDS: 110 300 600 1200 1800 2400 4800 9600 19.2 56k _____
COMPATIBILITY: 103 212 V.22bis _____
PARITY: even odd space mark none   CHARACTER LENGTH: 7 8 ___
STOP BITS: 1 1.5 2   LINE-ENDING CHARs: cr lf cr/lf
AUTO-ANSWER: yes no   RTS/CTS delay: _____
DISCONNECT SEQUENCE: EOT DEL _____
INTELLIGENT MODEMS....
  Dialing Technique: Touch-tone Pulse
  Compatibility: Hayes _____
  Command Line Prefix: AT _____   Dial command: D _____
  Touch-tone dial: T ___ Pulse Dial: P ___ Pause: , ___
  Wait for dial tone: W ___   Wait for quiet answer: @ ___
  Flash: ! ___   Dial stored number: S ___
  Return to command state after dialing: ; ___
  Escape sequence: +++ ___   Switch-Hook control: H ___
  Store Phone#: &Z ___
MODE: async sync isoch
NOTE 1: _____
NOTE 2: _____

MODEM PORT PROFILE **(Underline if supported, circle if selected)**
COMPANY: AT&T
PRODUCT: LADS modems

PORT: female (DB-25)   PORT TYPE: serial _____
CONNECTOR: DB25 9-pin 8-pin(modular) GENDER: male female
PIN CONFIGURATION: C14

PIN	FUNCTION	DIRECTION
1:PG	Protective Ground	N/A
2:TD	Transmit Data	TO
3:RD	Receive Data	FROM
4:RTS	Request to Send	TO
5:CTS	Clear to Send	FROM
6:DSR	Data Set Ready	FROM
7:SG	Signal Ground	N/A
8:RLSD	Rec.Line Signal Detect	FROM
9:+6V		FROM
10:-6V		FROM
15:TT	Transmit Timing	FROM
17:RT	Receive Timing	FROM
20:		TO
24:ETC	External Transmit Cloc	TO

FLOW CONTROL   XON: ACK: LEADS THAT MUST BE ON: _____
SPEEDS: 110 300 600 1200 1800 2400 4800 9600 19.2 56k _____
COMPATIBILITY: 103 212 V.22bis _____
PARITY: even odd space mark none   CHARACTER LENGTH: 7 8 ___
STOP BITS: 1 1.5 2   LINE-ENDING CHARs: cr lf cr/lf
AUTO-ANSWER: yes no   RTS/CTS delay: _____
DISCONNECT SEQUENCE: EOT DEL _____
INTELLIGENT MODEMS....
  Dialing Technique: Touch-tone Pulse
  Compatibility: Hayes _____
  Command Line Prefix: AT _____   Dial command: D _____
  Touch-tone dial: T ___   Pulse Dial: P ___ Pause: , ___
  Wait for dial tone: W ___   Wait for quiet answer: @ ___
  Flash: ! ___   Dial stored number: S ___
  Return to command state after dialing: ; ___
  Escape sequence: +++ ___   Switch-Hook control: H ___
  Store Phone#: &Z ___
MODE: async sync isoch
NOTE 1: _____
NOTE 2: _____

MODEM PORT PROFILE (Underline if supported, circle if selected)
COMPANY: AT&T
PRODUCT: Model 4000 modem

PORT: female   PORT TYPE: serial _____
CONNECTOR: DB25   9-pin   8-pin(modular)   GENDER: male   female
PIN CONFIGURATION: C14

PIN	FUNCTION	DIRECTION
2:TD	Transmit Data	TO
3:RD	Receive Data	FROM
5:CTS	Clear to Send	FROM
6:DSR	Data Set Ready	FROM
7:SG	Signal Ground	N/A
8:DCD	Data Carrier Detect	FROM
20:DTR	Data Terminal Ready	TO
22:RI	Ring Indicator	FROM

FLOW CONTROL   XON: ACK: LEADS THAT MUST BE ON: _____
SPEEDS: 110 300 600 1200 1800 2400 4800 9600 19.2 56k _____
COMPATIBILITY: 103 212 V.22bis _____
PARITY: even odd space mark none   CHARACTER LENGTH: 7 8 ___
STOP BITS: 1 1.5 2   LINE-ENDING CHARs: cr lf cr/lf
AUTO-ANSWER: yes no   RTS/CTS delay: _____
DISCONNECT SEQUENCE: EOT   DEL _____
INTELLIGENT MODEMS....
   Dialing Technique: Touch-tone   Pulse
   Compatibility: Hayes _____
   Command Line Prefix: AT _____   Dial command: D _____
   Touch-tone dial: T ___   Pulse Dial: P ___   Pause: ,   ___
   Wait for dial tone: W   ___   Wait for quiet answer: @ ___
   Flash: ! ___   Dial stored number: S ___
   Return to command state after dialing: ; ___
   Escape sequence: +++   ___   Switch-Hook control: H ___
   Store Phone#:   &Z ___
MODE: async sync isoch
NOTE 1: Lead 8 follows the condition of the line carrier.
NOTE 2: _____Leads 5/6 are always held high.

MODEM PORT PROFILE (Underline if supported, circle if selected)
COMPANY: AT&T
PRODUCT: ODS RS232-1 optic modem

PORT: female or male   PORT TYPE: serial _____
CONNECTOR: DB25 9-pin 8-pin(modular)   GENDER: male female
PIN CONFIGURATION: C14

PIN	FUNCTION	DIRECTION
1:CG	Chassis Ground	N/A
2:TD	Transmit Data	TO
3:RD	Receive Data	FROM
4:RTS	Request to Send	TO
5:CTS	Clear to Send	FROM
6:DSR	Data Set Ready	FROM
7:SG	Signal Ground	N/A
8:CD	Carrier Detect	FROM
15:TT	Transmit Timing	FROM
17:RT	Receive Timing	FROM
20:DTR	Data Terminal Ready	TO
22:RI	Ring Indicator	FROM
24:ETC	External Transmit Cloc	TO

FLOW CONTROL   XON: ACK: LEADS THAT MUST BE ON: _____
SPEEDS: 110 300 600 1200 1800 2400 4800 9600 19.2 56k _____
COMPATIBILITY: 103 212 V.22bis _____
PARITY: even odd space mark none   CHARACTER LENGTH: 7 8 ___
STOP BITS: 1 1.5 2   LINE-ENDING CHARs: cr lf cr/lf
AUTO-ANSWER: yes no   RTS/CTS delay: _____
DISCONNECT SEQUENCE: EOT DEL _____
INTELLIGENT MODEMS....
  Dialing Technique: Touch-tone Pulse
  Compatibility: Hayes _____
  Command Line Prefix: AT _____   Dial command: D _____
  Touch-tone dial: T ___ Pulse Dial: P ___ Pause: , ___
  Wait for dial tone: W ___   Wait for quiet answer: @ ___
  Flash: ! ___   Dial stored number: S ___
  Return to command state after dialing: ; ___
  Escape sequence: +++ ___   Switch-Hook control: H ___
  Store Phone#: &Z ___
MODE: async sync isoch
NOTE 1: _____
NOTE 2: _____

MODEM PORT PROFILE   (Underline if supported, circle if selected)
COMPANY: AT&T
PRODUCT: RS232-2 optic modem

PORT: female or male   PORT TYPE: serial _____
CONNECTOR: DB25 9-pin 8-pin(modular) GENDER: male female
PIN CONFIGURATION: C14

PIN	FUNCTION	DIRECTION
2:TD	Transmit Data	TO
3:RD	Receive Data	FROM
6:DSR	Data Set Ready	FROM
7:SG	Signal Ground	N/A
20:DTR	Data Terminal Ready	TO

FLOW CONTROL   XON: ACK: LEADS THAT MUST BE ON: _____
SPEEDS: 110 300 600 1200 1800 2400 4800 9600 19.2 56k _____
COMPATIBILITY: 103 212 V.22bis _____
PARITY: even odd space mark none   CHARACTER LENGTH: 7 8 ___
STOP BITS: 1 1.5 2   LINE-ENDING CHARs: cr lf cr/lf
AUTO-ANSWER: yes no   RTS/CTS delay: _____
DISCONNECT SEQUENCE: EOT DEL _____
INTELLIGENT MODEMS....
  Dialing Technique: Touch-tone Pulse
  Compatibility: Hayes _____
  Command Line Prefix: AT _____   Dial command: D _____
  Touch-tone dial: T ___ Pulse Dial: P ___ Pause: , ___
  Wait for dial tone: W ___   Wait for quiet answer: a ___
  Flash: ! ___   Dial stored number: S ___
  Return to command state after dialing: ; ___
  Escape sequence: +++ ___   Switch-Hook control: H ___
  Store Phone#: &Z ___
MODE: async sync isoch
NOTE 1: _____
NOTE 2: _____

MODEM PORT PROFILE (Underline if supported, circle if selected)
COMPANY: AT&T'
PRODUCT: 202T modem

PORT: female (customer)   PORT TYPE: serial _____
CONNECTOR: DB25 9-pin 8-pin(modular)   GENDER: male female
PIN CONFIGURATION: C02

PIN	FUNCTION	DIRECTION
1:PG	Protective Ground	N/A
2:TD	Transmit Data	TO
3:RD	Receive Data	FROM
4:RTS	Request to Send	TO
5:CTS	Clear to Send	FROM
6:DSR	Data Set Ready	FROM
7:SG	Signal Ground	N/A
8:DCD	Data Carrier Detect	FROM
9:+14V		FROM
10:-14V		FROM
11:SRTS	Secondary Req.to Send	TO
12:SDCD	Secondary DCD	FROM
20:		TO

FLOW CONTROL   XON: ACK: LEADS THAT MUST BE ON: _____
SPEEDS: 110 300 600 1200 1800 2400 4800 9600 19.2 56k _____
COMPATIBILITY: 103 212 V.22bis _____
PARITY: even odd space mark none   CHARACTER LENGTH: 7 8 ___
STOP BITS: 1 1.5 2   LINE-ENDING CHARs: cr lf cr/lf
AUTO-ANSWER: yes no   RTS/CTS delay: _____
DISCONNECT SEQUENCE: EOT DEL _____
INTELLIGENT MODEMS....
  Dialing Technique: Touch-tone Pulse
  Compatibility: Hayes _____
  Command Line Prefix: AT _____   Dial command: D _____
  Touch-tone dial: T ___ Pulse Dial: P ___ Pause: , ___
  Wait for dial tone: W ___   Wait for quiet answer: @ ___
  Flash: ! ___   Dial stored number: S ___
  Return to command state after dialing: ; ___
  Escape sequence: +++ ___   Switch-Hook control: H ___
  Store Phone#: &Z ___
MODE: async sync isoch
NOTE 1: _____
NOTE 2: _____

MODEM PORT PROFILE (Underline if supported, circle if selected)
COMPANY: Datacom Northwest, Inc.
PRODUCT: Data Broadcase Device (DBF400 & DBF800)

PORT: female (J1-J8)   PORT TYPE: serial _____
CONNECTOR: DB25 9-pin 8-pin(modular) GENDER: male female
PIN CONFIGURATION: C14

PIN	FUNCTION	DIRECTION
2:TD	Transmit Data	TO
3:RD	Receive Data	FROM
4:RTS	Request to Send	TO
5:CTS	Clear to Send	FROM
6:DSR	Data Set Ready	FROM
7:SG	Signal Ground	N/A
8:DCD	Data Carrier Detect	FROM
15:TC	Transmit Clock	FROM
17:RC	Rec. Clk/Reverse Chann	FROM
20:DTR	Data Terminal Ready	TO

FLOW CONTROL   XON: ACK: LEADS THAT MUST BE ON: _____
SPEEDS: 110 300 600 1200 1800 2400 4800 9600 19.2 56k _____
COMPATIBILITY: 103 212 V.22bis _____
PARITY: even odd space mark none   CHARACTER LENGTH: 7 8 ___
STOP BITS: 1 1.5 2   LINE-ENDING CHARs: cr lf cr/lf
AUTO-ANSWER: yes no   RTS/CTS delay: _____
DISCONNECT SEQUENCE: EOT DEL _____
INTELLIGENT MODEMS....
  Dialing Technique: Touch-tone Pulse
  Compatibility: Hayes _____
  Command Line Prefix: AT _____   Dial command: D _____
  Touch-tone dial: T ___ Pulse Dial: P ___ Pause: , ___
  Wait for dial tone: W ___   Wait for quiet answer: a ___
  Flash: ! ___   Dial stored number: S ___
  Return to command state after dialing: ; ___
  Escape sequence: +++ ___   Switch-Hook control: H ___
  Store Phone#: &Z ___
MODE: async sync isoch
NOTE 1: Omit leads 15 & 17 with asynchronous connections.
NOTE 2: _____

MODEM PORT PROFILE   (Underline if supported, circle if selected)
COMPANY: Datacom Northwest, Inc.
PRODUCT: Data Broadcast Device (DBF400 & DBF800)

PORT: female (JM)   PORT TYPE: serial _____

CONNECTOR: DB25 9-pin 8-pin(modular)   GENDER: male female

PIN CONFIGURATION: C01

PIN	FUNCTION	DIRECTION
2:TD	Transmit Data	FROM
3:RD	Receive Data	TO
4:RTS	Request to Send	FROM
5:CTS	Clear to Send	TO
6:DSR	Data Set Ready	TO
7:SG	Signal Ground	N/A
8:DCD	Data Carrier Detect	TO
15:TC	Transmit Clock	TO
17:RC	Rec. Clk/Reverse Chann	TO
20:DTR	Data Terminal Ready	FROM

FLOW CONTROL   XON: ACK: LEADS THAT MUST BE ON: _____

SPEEDS: 110 300 600 1200 1800 2400 4800 9600 19.2 56k _____

COMPATIBILITY: 103 212 V.22bis _____

PARITY: even odd space mark none   CHARACTER LENGTH: 7 8 ___

STOP BITS: 1 1.5 2   LINE-ENDING CHARs: cr lf cr/lf

AUTO-ANSWER: yes no   RTS/CTS delay: _____

DISCONNECT SEQUENCE: EOT DEL _____

INTELLIGENT MODEMS....

  Dialing Technique: Touch-tone Pulse

  Compatibility: Hayes _____

  Command Line Prefix: AT _____   Dial command: D _____

  Touch-tone dial: T ___   Pulse Dial: P ___   Pause: , ___

  Wait for dial tone: W ___   Wait for quiet answer: @ ___

  Flash: ! ___   Dial stored number: S ___

  Return to command state after dialing: ; ___

  Escape sequence: +++ ___   Switch-Hook control: H ___

  Store Phone#: &Z ___

MODE: async sync isoch

NOTE 1: Omit leads 15 & 17 for asynchronous connections.

NOTE 2: _____

MODEM PORT PROFILE (Underline if supported, circle if selected)
COMPANY: Datacom Northwest, Inc.
PRODUCT: Modem/Terminal Sharing Unit

PORT: female (J1-J8)   PORT TYPE: serial _____
CONNECTOR: DB25 9-pin 8-pin(modular)   GENDER: male female
PIN CONFIGURATION: C14

PIN	FUNCTION	DIRECTION
2:TD	Transmit Data	TO
3:RD	Receive Data	FROM
4:RTS	Request to Send	TO
5:CTS	Clear to Send	FROM
6:DSR	Data Set Ready	FROM
7:SG	Signal Ground	N/A
8:DCD	Data Carrier Detect	FROM
15:TC	Transmit Clock	FROM
17:RC	Rec. Clk/Reverse Chann	FROM
20:DTR	Data Terminal Ready	TO

FLOW CONTROL   XON: ACK: LEADS THAT MUST BE ON: _____
SPEEDS: 110 300 600 1200 1800 2400 4800 9600 19.2 56k _____
COMPATIBILITY: 103 212 V.22bis _____
PARITY: even odd space mark none   CHARACTER LENGTH: 7 8 ___
STOP BITS: 1 1.5 2   LINE-ENDING CHARs: cr lf cr/lf
AUTO-ANSWER: yes no   RTS/CTS delay: _____
DISCONNECT SEQUENCE: EOT DEL _____
INTELLIGENT MODEMS....
   Dialing Technique: Touch-tone Pulse
   Compatibility: Hayes _____
   Command Line Prefix: AT _____   Dial command: D _____
   Touch-tone dial: T ___ Pulse Dial: P ___ Pause: , ___
   Wait for dial tone: W ___   Wait for quiet answer: @ ___
   Flash: ! ___   Dial stored number: S ___
   Return to command state after dialing: ; ___
   Escape sequence: +++ ___   Switch-Hook control: H ___
   Store Phone#: &Z ___
MODE: async sync isoch
NOTE 1: Omit leads 15 & 17 if asynchronous devices are
NOTE 2: _____to be connected

MODEM PORT PROFILE (Underline if supported, circle if selected)
COMPANY: Datacom Northwest, Inc.
PRODUCT: Modem/Terminal Sharing Unit

PORT: female(JM) port   PORT TYPE: serial _____
CONNECTOR: DB25 9-pin 8-pin(modular)   GENDER: male female
PIN CONFIGURATION: C01

PIN	FUNCTION	DIRECTION
2:TD	Transmit Data	FROM
3:RD	Receive Data	TO
4:RTS	Request to Send	FROM
5:CTS	Clear to Send	TO
6:DSR	Data Set Ready	TO
7:SG	Signal Ground	N/A
8:DCD	Data Carrier Detect	TO
15:TC	Transmit Clock	TO
17:RC	Rec. Clk/Reverse Chann	TO
20:DTR	Data Terminal Ready	FROM

FLOW CONTROL   XON: ACK: LEADS THAT MUST BE ON: _____
SPEEDS: 110 300 600 1200 1800 2400 4800 9600 19.2 56k _____
COMPATIBILITY: 103 212 V.22bis _____
PARITY: even odd space mark none   CHARACTER LENGTH: 7 8 ___
STOP BITS: 1 1.5 2   LINE-ENDING CHARs: cr lf cr/lf
AUTO-ANSWER: yes no   RTS/CTS delay: _____
DISCONNECT SEQUENCE: EOT DEL _____
INTELLIGENT MODEMS....
   Dialing Technique: Touch-tone Pulse
   Compatibility: Hayes _____
   Command Line Prefix: AT _____   Dial command: D _____
   Touch-tone dial: T ___   Pulse Dial: P ___   Pause: , ___
   Wait for dial tone: W ___   Wait for quiet answer: @ ___
   Flash: ! ___   Dial stored number: S ___
   Return to command state after dialing: ; ___
   Escape sequence: +++ ___   Switch-Hook control: H ___
   Store Phone#: &Z ___
MODE: async sync isoch
NOTE 1: Omit leads 15 & 17 if asynchronous devices is
NOTE 2: _____to be connected to the unit.

MODEM PORT PROFILE (Underline if supported, circle if selected)
COMPANY: Datacom Northwest, Inc.
PRODUCT: SHM modem

PORT: female   PORT TYPE: serial _____
CONNECTOR: DB25 9-pin 8-pin(modular)   GENDER: male female
PIN CONFIGURATION: C14

PIN	FUNCTION	DIRECTION
1:PG	Protective Ground	N/A
2:TD	Transmit Data	TO
3:RD	Receive Data	FROM
4:RTS	Request to Send	TO
5:CTS	Clear to Send	FROM
6:DSR	Data Set Ready	FROM
7:SG	Signal Ground	N/A
8:DCD	Data Carrier Detect	FROM
20:DTR	Data Terminal Ready	TO

FLOW CONTROL: 4 20   XON: YES ACK: LEADS THAT MUST BE ON: _____
SPEEDS: 110 300 600 1200 1800 2400 4800 9600 19.2 56k _____
COMPATIBILITY: 103 212 V.22bis _____
PARITY: even odd space mark none   CHARACTER LENGTH: 7 8 ___
STOP BITS: 1 1.5 2   LINE-ENDING CHARs: cr lf cr/lf
AUTO-ANSWER: yes no   RTS/CTS delay: _____
DISCONNECT SEQUENCE: EOT DEL _____
INTELLIGENT MODEMS....
  Dialing Technique: Touch-tone Pulse
  Compatibility: Hayes _____
  Command Line Prefix: AT _____   Dial command: D _____
  Touch-tone dial: T ___ Pulse Dial: P ___ Pause: , ___
  Wait for dial tone: W ___   Wait for quiet answer: @ ___
  Flash: ! ___   Dial stored number: S ___
  Return to command state after dialing: ; ___
  Escape sequence: +++ ___   Switch-Hook control: H ___
  Store Phone#: &Z ___
MODE: async sync isoch
NOTE 1: Leads 4/20 control the state of lead 8 at the
NOTE 2: other end modem. The S1 switch should be "DCE".

MODEM PORT PROFILE (Underline if supported, circle if selected)
COMPANY: Datacomm Northwest, Inc.
PRODUCT: Modem Eliminator

PORT: female(both)
CONNECTOR: DB25 9-pin 8-pin(modular)
PIN CONFIGURATION: C14

PORT TYPE: serial _____
GENDER: male female

PIN	FUNCTION	DIRECTION
1:PG	Protective Ground	N/A
2:TD	Transmit Data	TO
3:RD	Receive Data	FROM
4:RTS	Request to Send	TO
5:CTS	Clear to Send	FROM
6:DSR	Data Set Ready	FROM
7:SG	Signal Ground	N/A
8:DCD	Data Carrier Detect	FROM
12:SDCD	Secondary DCD	FROM
13:SCTS	Secondary Cl'r to Send	FROM
14:STD	Supervisory Trans.Data	TO
15:TC	Transmit Clock	FROM
16:SRD	Supervisory Rec. Data	FROM
17:RC	Rec. Clk/Reverse Chann	FROM
18:DCR		FROM
20:DTR	Data Terminal Ready	TO
22:RI	Ring Indicator	FROM
24:ETC	External Transmit Cloc	TO

FLOW CONTROL   XON: ACK: LEADS THAT MUST BE ON: _____
SPEEDS: 110 300 600 1200 1800 2400 4800 9600 19.2 56k _____
COMPATIBILITY: 103 212 V.22bis _____
PARITY: even odd space mark none   CHARACTER LENGTH: 7 8 ___
STOP BITS: 1 1.5 2   LINE-ENDING CHARs: cr lf cr/lf
AUTO-ANSWER: yes no   RTS/CTS delay: _____
DISCONNECT SEQUENCE: EOT DEL _____
INTELLIGENT MODEMS....
   Dialing Technique: Touch-tone Pulse
   Compatibility: Hayes _____
   Command Line Prefix: AT _____   Dial command: D _____
   Touch-tone dial: T ___ Pulse Dial: P ___ Pause: , ___
   Wait for dial tone: W ___   Wait for quiet answer: @ ___
   Flash: ! ___   Dial stored number: S ___
   Return to command state after dialing: ; ___
   Escape sequence: +++ ___   Switch-Hook control: H ___
   Store Phone#: &Z ___
MODE: async sync isoch
NOTE 1: This device sets between two pieces of DTE.
NOTE 2: _____

Appendix C

MODEM PORT PROFILE (Underline if supported, circle if selected)
COMPANY: Datacomm Northwest, Inc.
PRODUCT: Synchronous SHM modem

PORT: female   PORT TYPE: serial _____
CONNECTOR: DB25 9-pin 8-pin(modular)   GENDER: male female
PIN CONFIGURATION: C14

PIN	FUNCTION	DIRECTION
2:TD	Transmit Data	TO
3:RD	Receive Data	FROM
4:RTS	Request to Send	TO
5:CTS	Clear to Send	FROM
6:DSR	Data Set Ready	FROM
7:SG	Signal Ground	N/A
8:DCD	Data Carrier Detect	FROM
15:TC	Transmit Clock	FROM
17:RC	Rec. Clk/Reverse Chann	FROM
20:DTR	Data Terminal Ready	TO

FLOW CONTROL   XON: ACK: LEADS THAT MUST BE ON: _____
SPEEDS: 110 300 600 1200 1800 2400 4800 9600 19.2 56k _____
COMPATIBILITY: 103 212 V.22bis _____
PARITY: even odd space mark none   CHARACTER LENGTH: 7 8 ___
STOP BITS: 1 1.5 2   LINE-ENDING CHARs: cr lf cr/lf
AUTO-ANSWER: yes no   RTS/CTS delay: _____
DISCONNECT SEQUENCE: EOT DEL _____
INTELLIGENT MODEMS....
  Dialing Technique: Touch-tone Pulse
  Compatibility: Hayes _____
  Command Line Prefix: AT _____   Dial command: D _____
  Touch-tone dial: T ___ Pulse Dial: P ___ Pause: , ___
  Wait for dial tone: W ___   Wait for quiet answer: @ ___
  Flash: ! ___   Dial stored number: S ___
  Return to command state after dialing: ; ___
  Escape sequence: +++ ___   Switch-Hook control: H ___
  Store Phone#: &Z ___
MODE: async sync isoch
NOTE 1: Include timing leads in cable design.
NOTE 2: _____

MODEM PORT PROFILE (Underline if supported, circle if selected)
COMPANY: Fastcomm Data Corporation
PRODUCT: 2400/2496/9600 series modems

PORT: female   PORT TYPE: serial _____
CONNECTOR: DB25 9-pin 8-pin(modular)   GENDER: male female
PIN CONFIGURATION: C14

PIN	FUNCTION	DIRECTION
1:PG	Protective Ground	N/A
2:TD	Transmit Data	TO
3:RD	Receive Data	FROM
4:RTS	Request to Send	TO
5:CTS	Clear to Send	FROM
6:DSR	Data Set Ready	FROM
7:SG	Signal Ground	N/A
8:DCD	Data Carrier Detect	FROM
20:DTR	Data Terminal Ready	TO
22:RI	Ring Indicator	FROM

FLOW CONTROL   XON: ACK: LEADS THAT MUST BE ON: _____
SPEEDS: 110 300 600 1200 1800 2400 4800 9600 19.2 56k _____
COMPATIBILITY: 103 212 V.22bis _____
PARITY: even odd space mark none   CHARACTER LENGTH: 7 8 ___
STOP BITS: 1 1.5 2   LINE-ENDING CHARs: cr lf cr/lf
AUTO-ANSWER: yes no   RTS/CTS delay: _____
DISCONNECT SEQUENCE: EOT DEL _____
INTELLIGENT MODEMS....
   Dialing Technique: Touch-tone Pulse
   Compatibility: Hayes _____
   Command Line Prefix: AT _____   Dial command: D _____
   Touch-tone dial: T ___   Pulse Dial: P ___   Pause: , ___
   Wait for dial tone: W ___   Wait for quiet answer: @ ___
   Flash: ! ___   Dial stored number: S ___
   Return to command state after dialing: ; ___
   Escape sequence: +++ ___   Switch-Hook control: H ___
   Store Phone#: &Z ___
MODE: async sync isoch
NOTE 1: _____
NOTE 2: _____

MODEM PORT PROFILE (Underline if supported, circle if selected)
COMPANY: General Datacom, Inc.
PRODUCT: 208B+/SD modem

PORT: EIA   PORT TYPE: serial _____
CONNECTOR: DB25 9-pin 8-pin(modular)   GENDER: male female
PIN CONFIGURATION: C14

PIN	FUNCTION	DIRECTION
1:PG	Protective Ground	N/A
2:TD	Transmit Data	TO
3:RD	Receive Data	FROM
4:RTS	Request to Send	TO
5:CTS	Clear to Send	FROM
6:DSR	Data Set Ready	FROM
7:SG	Signal Ground	N/A
8:DCD	Data Carrier Detect	FROM
9:+12V		FROM
10:-12V		FROM
15:TC	Transmit Clock	FROM
17:RC	Rec. Clk/Reverse Chann	FROM
20:DTR	Data Terminal Ready	TO
24:ETC	External Transmit Cloc	TO

FLOW CONTROL   XON: ACK: LEADS THAT MUST BE ON: _____
SPEEDS: 110 300 600 1200 1800 2400 4800 9600 19.2 56k _____
COMPATIBILITY: 103 212 V.22bis _____
PARITY: even odd space mark none   CHARACTER LENGTH: 7 8 ___
STOP BITS: 1 1.5 2   LINE-ENDING CHARs: cr lf cr/lf
AUTO-ANSWER: yes no   RTS/CTS delay: _____
DISCONNECT SEQUENCE: EOT DEL _____
INTELLIGENT MODEMS....
  Dialing Technique: Touch-tone Pulse
  Compatibility: Hayes _____
  Command Line Prefix: AT _____   Dial command: D _____
  Touch-tone dial: T ___ Pulse Dial: P ___ Pause: , ___
  Wait for dial tone: W ___   Wait for quiet answer: @ ___
  Flash: ! ___   Dial stored number: S ___
  Return to command state after dialing: ; ___
  Escape sequence: +++ ___   Switch-Hook control: H ___
  Store Phone#: &Z ___
MODE: async sync isoch
NOTE 1: Remember to add the timing leads in your cable
NOTE 2: _____design for this synchronous modem.

MODEM PORT PROFILE (Underline if supported, circle if selected)
COMPANY: General DataCom, Inc.
PRODUCT: Acculine 2400 modem

PORT: RS232   PORT TYPE: serial _____
CONNECTOR: DB25 9-pin 8-pin(modular)   GENDER: male female
PIN CONFIGURATION: C14

PIN	FUNCTION	DIRECTION
1:FG	Frame Ground	N/A
2:TD	Transmit Data	TO
3:RD	Receive Data	FROM
5:CTS	Clear to Send	FROM
6:DSR	Data Set Ready	FROM
7:SG	Signal Ground	N/A
8:RLSD	Rec.Line Signal Detect	FROM
9:+12V		FROM
10:-12V		
13:SCTS	Secondary Cl'r to Send	FROM
14:STD	Supervisory Trans.Data	TO
15:TT	Transmit Timing	FROM
16:SRD	Supervisory Rec. Data	FROM
17:RT	Receive Timing	FROM
20:DTR	Data Terminal Ready	TO
22:RI	Ring Indicator	FROM

FLOW CONTROL: 5 6   XON: ACK: LEADS THAT MUST BE ON: _____
SPEEDS: 110 300 600 1200 1800 2400 4800 9600 19.2 56k _____
COMPATIBILITY: 103 212 V.22bis _____
PARITY: even odd space mark none   CHARACTER LENGTH: 7 8 ___
STOP BITS: 1 1.5 2   LINE-ENDING CHARs: cr lf cr/lf
AUTO-ANSWER: yes no   RTS/CTS delay: _____
DISCONNECT SEQUENCE: EOT DEL _____
INTELLIGENT MODEMS....
  Dialing Technique: Touch-tone Pulse
  Compatibility: Hayes _____
  Command Line Prefix: AT _____   Dial command: D _____
  Touch-tone dial: T ___ Pulse Dial: P ___ Pause: , ___
  Wait for dial tone: W ___   Wait for quiet answer: @ ___
  Flash: ! ___   Dial stored number: S ___
  Return to command state after dialing: ; ___
  Escape sequence: +++ ___   Switch-Hook control: H ___
  Store Phone#: &Z ___
MODE: async sync isoch
NOTE 1: Leads 13-17 are used only in synchronous modes.
NOTE 2: _____A Y-Cable is available for connections.

MODEM PORT PROFILE (Underline if supported, circle if selected)
COMPANY: General Robotics Corporation
PRODUCT: DHV11 multiplexor

PORT: male   PORT TYPE: serial _____
CONNECTOR: DB25 9-pin 8-pin(modular) GENDER: male female
PIN CONFIGURATION: C01

PIN	FUNCTION	DIRECTION
1:PG	Protective Ground	N/A
2:TD	Transmit Data	FROM
3:RD	Receive Data	TO
4:RTS	Request to Send	FROM
5:CTS	Clear to Send	TO
6:DSR	Data Set Ready	TO
7:SG	Signal Ground	N/A
8:DCD	Data Carrier Detect	TO
14:STD	Supervisory Trans.Data	FROM
15:TC	Transmit Clock	TO
16:SRD	Supervisory Rec. Data	TO
20:DTR	Data Terminal Ready	FROM
22:RI	Ring Indicator	TO

FLOW CONTROL: 5 6 8   XON: YES ACK: LEADS THAT MUST BE ON: _____
SPEEDS: 110 300 600 1200 1800 2400 4800 9600 19.2 56k _____
COMPATIBILITY: 103 212 V.22bis _____
PARITY: even odd space mark none   CHARACTER LENGTH: 7 8 ___
STOP BITS: 1 1.5 2   LINE-ENDING CHARs: cr lf cr/lf
AUTO-ANSWER: yes no   RTS/CTS delay: _____
DISCONNECT SEQUENCE: EOT DEL _____
INTELLIGENT MODEMS....
  Dialing Technique: Touch-tone Pulse
  Compatibility: Hayes _____
  Command Line Prefix: AT _____   Dial command: D _____
  Touch-tone dial: T ___   Pulse Dial: P ___ Pause: , ___
  Wait for dial tone: W ___   Wait for quiet answer: @ ___
  Flash: ! ___   Dial stored number: S ___
  Return to command state after dialing: ; ___
  Escape sequence: +++ ___   Switch-Hook control: H ___
  Store Phone#: &Z ___
MODE: async sync isoch
NOTE 1: Leads 5/6/8 should be on for the unit to transmit.
NOTE 2: _____

MODEM PORT PROFILE (Underline if supported, circle if selected)
COMPANY: Hayes Microcomputer Products
PRODUCT: Smartmodem 1200 modem

PORT: female   PORT TYPE: serial _____
CONNECTOR: DB25 9-pin 8-pin(modular)   GENDER: male female
PIN CONFIGURATION: C14

PIN	FUNCTION	DIRECTION
1:PG	Protective Ground	N/A
2:TD	Transmit Data	TO
3:RD	Receive Data	FROM
5:CTS	Clear to Send	FROM
6:DSR	Data Set Ready	FROM
7:SG	Signal Ground	N/A
8:CD	Carrier Detect	FROM
12:SS	Speed Select	FROM
20:DTR	Data Terminal Ready	TO
22:RI	Ring Indicator	FROM

FLOW CONTROL   XON: ACK: LEADS THAT MUST BE ON: _____
SPEEDS: 110 300 600 1200 1800 2400 4800 9600 19.2 56k _____
COMPATIBILITY: 103 212 V.22bis _____
PARITY: even odd space mark none   CHARACTER LENGTH: 7 8 ___
STOP BITS: 1 1.5 2   LINE-ENDING CHARs: cr lf cr/lf
AUTO-ANSWER: yes no   RTS/CTS delay: _____
DISCONNECT SEQUENCE: EOT DEL _____
INTELLIGENT MODEMS....
  Dialing Technique: Touch-tone Pulse
  Compatibility: Hayes _____
  Command Line Prefix: AT _____   Dial command: D _____
  Touch-tone dial: T ___ Pulse Dial: P ___ Pause: , ___
  Wait for dial tone: W ___   Wait for quiet answer: @ ___
  Flash: ! ___   Dial stored number: S ___
  Return to command state after dialing: ; ___
  Escape sequence: +++ ___   Switch-Hook control: H ___
  Store Phone#: &Z ___
MODE: async sync isoch
NOTE 1: _____
NOTE 2: _____

MODEM PORT PROFILE   (Underline if supported, circle if selected)
COMPANY: Hayes Microcomputer Products
PRODUCT: Smartmodem 2400 modem

PORT: female   PORT TYPE: serial _____
CONNECTOR: DB25 9-pin 8-pin(modular) GENDER: male female
PIN CONFIGURATION: C14

PIN	FUNCTION	DIRECTION
1:PG	Protective Ground	N/A
2:TD	Transmit Data	TO
3:RD	Receive Data	FROM
4:RTS	Request to Send	TO
5:CTS	Clear to Send	FROM
6:DSR	Data Set Ready	FROM
7:SG	Signal Ground	N/A
8:DCD	Data Carrier Detect	FROM
12:SS	Speed Select	FROM
15:TC	Transmit Clock	FROM
17:RC	Rec. Clk/Reverse Chann	FROM
20:DTR	Data Terminal Ready	TO
22:RI	Ring Indicator	FROM
23:SS	Speed Select	FROM
24:TC	Transmit Clock	TO

FLOW CONTROL   XON: ACK: LEADS THAT MUST BE ON: _____
SPEEDS: 110 300 600 1200 1800 2400 4800 9600 19.2 56k _____
COMPATIBILITY: 103 212 V.22bis _____
PARITY: even odd space mark none   CHARACTER LENGTH: 7 8 ___
STOP BITS: 1 1.5 2   LINE-ENDING CHARs: cr lf cr/lf
AUTO-ANSWER: yes no   RTS/CTS delay: _____
DISCONNECT SEQUENCE: EOT DEL _____
INTELLIGENT MODEMS....
   Dialing Technique: Touch-tone Pulse
   Compatibility: Hayes _____
   Command Line Prefix: AT _____   Dial command: D _____
   Touch-tone dial: T ___ Pulse Dial: P ___ Pause: , ___
   Wait for dial tone: W ___   Wait for quiet answer: @ ___
   Flash: ! ___   Dial stored number: S ___
   Return to command state after dialing: ; ___
   Escape sequence: +++ ___   Switch-Hook control: H ___
   Store Phone#: &Z ___
MODE: async sync isoch
NOTE 1: This modem supports both async and sync operation
NOTE 2: _____

MODEM PORT PROFILE   (Underline if supported, circle if selected)
COMPANY: Hayes Microcomputer Products
PRODUCT: Smartmodem 300 modem

PORT: female   PORT TYPE: serial _____

CONNECTOR: DB25 9-pin 8-pin(modular)   GENDER: male female

PIN CONFIGURATION: C14

PIN	FUNCTION	DIRECTION
1:PG	Protective Ground	N/A
2:TD	Transmit Data	TO
3:RD	Receive Data	FROM
5:CTS	Clear to Send	FROM
6:DSR	Data Set Ready	FROM
7:SG	Signal Ground	N/A
8:CD	Carrier Detect	FROM
20:DTR	Data Terminal Ready	TO
22:RI	Ring Indicator	FROM

FLOW CONTROL   XON: ACK: LEADS THAT MUST BE ON: _____

SPEEDS: 110 300 600 1200 1800 2400 4800 9600 19.2 56k _____

COMPATIBILITY: 103 212 V.22bis _____

PARITY: even odd space mark none   CHARACTER LENGTH: 7 8 ___

STOP BITS: 1 1.5 2   LINE-ENDING CHARs: cr lf cr/lf

AUTO-ANSWER: yes no   RTS/CTS delay: _____

DISCONNECT SEQUENCE: EOT DEL _____

INTELLIGENT MODEMS....

  Dialing Technique: Touch-tone Pulse

  Compatibility: Hayes _____

  Command Line Prefix: AT _____   Dial command: D _____

  Touch-tone dial: T ___   Pulse Dial: P ___   Pause: , ___

  Wait for dial tone: W ___   Wait for quiet answer: @ ___

  Flash: ! ___   Dial stored number: S ___

  Return to command state after dialing: ; ___

  Escape sequence: +++ ___   Switch-Hook control: H ___

  Store Phone#: &Z ___

MODE: async sync isoch

NOTE 1: _____

NOTE 2: _____

MODEM PORT PROFILE (Underline if supported, circle if selected)
COMPANY: Infotron Systems
PRODUCT: LD210/SA line driver

PORT: female   PORT TYPE: serial _____
CONNECTOR: DB25 9-pin 8-pin(modular)   GENDER: male female
PIN CONFIGURATION: C14

PIN	FUNCTION	DIRECTION
1:PG	Protective Ground	N/A
2:TD	Transmit Data	TO
3:RD	Receive Data	FROM
4:RTS	Request to Send	TO
5:CTS	Clear to Send	FROM
6:DSR	Data Set Ready	FROM
7:SG	Signal Ground	N/A
8:RLSD	Rec.Line Signal Detect	FROM
15:TC	Transmit Clock	FROM
17:RC	Rec. Clk/Reverse Chann	FROM
20:DTR	Data Terminal Ready	TO

FLOW CONTROL   XON: ACK: LEADS THAT MUST BE ON: _____
SPEEDS: 110 300 600 1200 1800 2400 4800 9600 19.2 56k _____
COMPATIBILITY: 103 212 V.22bis _____
PARITY: even odd space mark none   CHARACTER LENGTH: 7 8 ___
STOP BITS: 1 1.5 2   LINE-ENDING CHARs: cr lf cr/lf
AUTO-ANSWER: yes no   RTS/CTS delay: _____
DISCONNECT SEQUENCE: EOT DEL _____
INTELLIGENT MODEMS....
  Dialing Technique: Touch-tone Pulse
  Compatibility: Hayes _____
  Command Line Prefix: AT _____   Dial command: D _____
  Touch-tone dial: T ___ Pulse Dial: P ___ Pause: , ___
  Wait for dial tone: W ___   Wait for quiet answer: @ ___
  Flash: ! ___   Dial stored number: S ___
  Return to command state after dialing: ; ___
  Escape sequence: +++ ___   Switch-Hook control: H ___
  Store Phone#: &Z ___
MODE: async sync isoch
NOTE 1: _____
NOTE 2: _____

MODEM PORT PROFILE (Underline if supported, circle if selected)
COMPANY: International Daata Sciences
PRODUCT: 6220 limited distance modem

PORT: female   PORT TYPE: serial _____
CONNECTOR: DB25 9-pin 8-pin(modular)   GENDER: male female
PIN CONFIGURATION: C14

PIN	FUNCTION	DIRECTION
1:FG	Frame Ground	N/A
2:TD	Transmit Data	TO
3:RD	Receive Data	FROM
4:RTS	Request to Send	TO
5:CTS	Clear to Send	FROM
6:DSR	Data Set Ready	FROM
7:SG	Signal Ground	N/A
8:DCD	Data Carrier Detect	FROM
20:		TO

FLOW CONTROL   XON: ACK: LEADS THAT MUST BE ON: _____
SPEEDS: 110 300 600 1200 1800 2400 4800 9600 19.2 56k _____
COMPATIBILITY: 103 212 V.22bis _____
PARITY: even odd space mark none   CHARACTER LENGTH: 7 8 ___
STOP BITS: 1 1.5 2   LINE-ENDING CHARs: cr lf cr/lf
AUTO-ANSWER: yes no   RTS/CTS delay: _____
DISCONNECT SEQUENCE: EOT DEL _____
INTELLIGENT MODEMS....
  Dialing Technique: Touch-tone Pulse
  Compatibility: Hayes _____
  Command Line Prefix: AT _____   Dial command: D _____
  Touch-tone dial: T ___ Pulse Dial: P ___ Pause: , ___
  Wait for dial tone: W ___   Wait for quiet answer: @ ___
  Flash: ! ___   Dial stored number: S ___
  Return to command state after dialing: ; ___
  Escape sequence: +++ ___   Switch-Hook control: H ___
  Store Phone#: &Z ___
MODE: async sync isoch
NOTE 1: _____
NOTE 2: _____

MODEM PORT PROFILE (Underline if supported, circle if selected)
COMPANY: International Data Sciences
PRODUCT: 6000 limited distance modem

PORT: female   PORT TYPE: serial _____
CONNECTOR: DB25 9-pin 8-pin(modular)   GENDER: male female
PIN CONFIGURATION: C14

PIN	FUNCTION	DIRECTION
1:FG	Frame Ground	N/A
2:TD	Transmit Data	TO
3:RD	Receive Data	FROM
4:RTS	Request to Send	TO
5:CTS	Clear to Send	FROM
6:DSR	Data Set Ready	FROM
7:SG	Signal Ground	N/A
8:DCD	Data Carrier Detect	FROM
9:+V		FROM
10:-V		FROM
15:TC	Transmit Clock	FROM
17:RC	Rec. Clk/Reverse Chann	FROM
20:		TO
24:ETC	External Transmit Cloc	TO

FLOW CONTROL   XON: ACK: LEADS THAT MUST BE ON: _____
SPEEDS: 110 300 600 1200 1800 2400 4800 9600 19.2 56k _____
COMPATIBILITY: 103 212 V.22bis _____
PARITY: even odd space mark none   CHARACTER LENGTH: 7 8 ___
STOP BITS: 1 1.5 2   LINE-ENDING CHARs: cr lf cr/lf
AUTO-ANSWER: yes no   RTS/CTS delay: _____
DISCONNECT SEQUENCE: EOT DEL _____
INTELLIGENT MODEMS....
  Dialing Technique: Touch-tone Pulse
  Compatibility: Hayes _____
  Command Line Prefix: AT _____   Dial command: D _____
  Touch-tone dial: T ___ Pulse Dial: P ___ Pause: , ___
  Wait for dial tone: W ___   Wait for quiet answer: @ ___
  Flash: ! ___   Dial stored number: S ___
  Return to command state after dialing: ; ___
  Escape sequence: +++ ___   Switch-Hook control: H ___
  Store Phone#: &Z ___
MODE: async sync isoch
NOTE 1: _____
NOTE 2: _____

MODEM PORT PROFILE (Underline if supported, circle if selected)
COMPANY: Microcom, Inc.
PRODUCT: AX/1200, AX/2400 modems

PORT: female   PORT TYPE: serial _____
CONNECTOR: DB25 9-pin 8-pin(modular)   GENDER: male female
PIN CONFIGURATION: C14

PIN	FUNCTION	DIRECTION
1:PG	Protective Ground	N/A
2:TD	Transmit Data	TO
3:RD	Receive Data	FROM
4:RTS	Request to Send	TO
5:CTS	Clear to Send	FROM
6:DSR	Data Set Ready	FROM
7:SG	Signal Ground	N/A
8:CD	Carrier Detect	FROM
12:SS	Speed Select	FROM
15:TC	Transmit Clock	FROM
17:RC	Rec. Clk/Reverse Chann	FROM
20:DTR	Data Terminal Ready	TO
22:RI	Ring Indicator	FROM
23:SS	Speed Select	FROM
25:B	Busy	TO

FLOW CONTROL   XON: ACK: LEADS THAT MUST BE ON: _____
SPEEDS: 110 300 600 1200 1800 2400 4800 9600 19.2 56k _____
COMPATIBILITY: 103 212 V.22bis _____
PARITY: even odd space mark none   CHARACTER LENGTH: 7 8 ___
STOP BITS: 1 1.5 2   LINE-ENDING CHARs: cr lf cr/lf
AUTO-ANSWER: yes no   RTS/CTS delay: _____
DISCONNECT SEQUENCE: EOT DEL _____
INTELLIGENT MODEMS....
  Dialing Technique: Touch-tone Pulse
  Compatibility: Hayes _____
  Command Line Prefix: AT _____   Dial command: D _____
  Touch-tone dial: T ___ Pulse Dial: P ___ Pause: , ___
  Wait for dial tone: W ___   Wait for quiet answer: @ ___
  Flash: ! ___   Dial stored number: S ___
  Return to command state after dialing: ; ___
  Escape sequence: +++ ___   Switch-Hook control: H ___
  Store Phone#: &Z ___
MODE: async sync isoch
NOTE 1: _____
NOTE 2: _____

MODEM PORT PROFILE (Underline if supported, circle if selected)
COMPANY: MultiTech Systems
PRODUCT: MultiModem 224 modem

PORT: female   PORT TYPE: serial _____
CONNECTOR: DB25 9-pin 8-pin(modular)   GENDER: male female
PIN CONFIGURATION: C14

PIN	FUNCTION	DIRECTION
2:TD	Transmit Data	TO
3:RD	Receive Data	FROM
4:RTS	Request to Send	TO
5:CTS	Clear to Send	FROM
6:DSR	Data Set Ready	FROM
7:SG	Signal Ground	N/A
8:DCD	Data Carrier Detect	FROM
9:+V		FROM
15:TC	Transmit Clock	FROM
17:RC	Rec. Clk/Reverse Chann	FROM
20:DTR	Data Terminal Ready	TO
22:RI	Ring Indicator	FROM

FLOW CONTROL   XON: ACK: LEADS THAT MUST BE ON: _____
SPEEDS: 110 300 600 1200 1800 2400 4800 9600 19.2 56k _____
COMPATIBILITY: 103 212 V.22bis _____
PARITY: even odd space mark none   CHARACTER LENGTH: 7 8 ___
STOP BITS: 1 1.5 2   LINE-ENDING CHARs: cr lf cr/lf
AUTO-ANSWER: yes no   RTS/CTS delay: _____
DISCONNECT SEQUENCE: EOT DEL _____
INTELLIGENT MODEMS....
  Dialing Technique: Touch-tone Pulse
  Compatibility: Hayes _____
  Command Line Prefix: AT _____   Dial command: D _____
  Touch-tone dial: T ___ Pulse Dial: P ___ Pause: , ___
  Wait for dial tone: W ___   Wait for quiet answer: @ ___
  Flash: ! ___   Dial stored number: S ___
  Return to command state after dialing: ; ___
  Escape sequence: +++ ___   Switch-Hook control: H ___
  Store Phone#: &Z ___
MODE: async sync isoch
NOTE 1: This modem supports both async and synch operation
NOTE 2: _____

MODEM PORT PROFILE (Underline if supported, circle if selected)
COMPANY: MultiTech Systems, Inc.
PRODUCT: MultiModem 1200/300

PORT: female   PORT TYPE: serial _____
CONNECTOR: DB25 9-pin 8-pin(modular)   GENDER: male female
PIN CONFIGURATION: C14

PIN	FUNCTION	DIRECTION
2:TD	Transmit Data	TO
3:RD	Receive Data	FROM
5:CTS	Clear to Send	FROM
6:DSR	Data Set Ready	FROM
7:SG	Signal Ground	N/A
8:DCD	Data Carrier Detect	FROM
9:+V		FROM
12:HS		FROM
20:DTR	Data Terminal Ready	TO
22:RI	Ring Indicator	FROM

FLOW CONTROL   XON: ACK: LEADS THAT MUST BE ON: _____
SPEEDS: 110 300 600 1200 1800 2400 4800 9600 19.2 56k _____
COMPATIBILITY: 103 212 V.22bis _____
PARITY: even odd space mark none   CHARACTER LENGTH: 7 8 ___
STOP BITS: 1 1.5 2   LINE-ENDING CHARs: cr lf cr/lf
AUTO-ANSWER: yes no   RTS/CTS delay: _____
DISCONNECT SEQUENCE: EOT DEL _____
INTELLIGENT MODEMS....
   Dialing Technique: Touch-tone Pulse
   Compatibility: Hayes _____
   Command Line Prefix: AT _____   Dial command: D _____
   Touch-tone dial: T ___   Pulse Dial: P ___ Pause: , ___
   Wait for dial tone: W ___   Wait for quiet answer: @ ___
   Flash: ! ___   Dial stored number: S ___
   Return to command state after dialing: ; ___
   Escape sequence: +++ ___   Switch-Hook control: H ___
   Store Phone#: &Z ___
MODE: async sync isoch
NOTE 1: _____
NOTE 2: _____

MODEM PORT PROFILE (Underline if supported, circle if selected)
COMPANY: NEC America, Inc.
PRODUCT: 1220/30HN modem

PORT: female   PORT TYPE: serial _____
CONNECTOR: DB25 9-pin 8-pin(modular)   GENDER: male female
CONFIGURATION: C14

PIN	FUNCTION	DIRECTION
1:FG	Frame Ground	N/A
2:TD	Transmit Data	TO
3:RD	Receive Data	FROM
5:CTS	Clear to Send	FROM
6:DSR	Data Set Ready	FROM
7:SG	Signal Ground	N/A
8:CD	Carrier Detect	FROM
9:+V		FROM
10:-V		FROM
12:SS	Speed Select	FROM
20:DTR	Data Terminal Ready	TO
22:RI	Ring Indicator	FROM
23:SS	Speed Select	TO

FLOW CONTROL   XON: ACK: LEADS THAT MUST BE ON: _____
SPEEDS: 110 300 600 1200 1800 2400 4800 9600 19.2 56k _____
COMPATIBILITY: 103 212 V.22bis _____
PARITY: even odd space mark none   CHARACTER LENGTH: 7 8 ___
STOP BITS: 1 1.5 2   LINE-ENDING CHARs: cr lf cr/lf
AUTO-ANSWER: yes no   RTS/CTS delay: ___
DISCONNECT SEQUENCE: EOT DEL _____
INTELLIGENT MODEMS....
    Dialing Technique: Touch-tone Pulse
    Compatibility: Hayes _____
    Command Line Prefix: AT _____   Dial command: D _____
    Touch-tone dial: T ___   Pulse Dial: P ___ Pause: , ___
    Wait for dial tone: W ___   Wait for quiet answer: @ ___
    Flash: ! ___   Dial stored number: S ___
    Return to command state after dialing: ; ___
    Escape sequence: +++ ___   Switch-Hook control: H ___
    Store Phone#: &Z ___
Mode: async sync isoch
NOTE 1:
NOTE 2:

MODEM PORT PROFILE (Underline if supported, circle if selected)
COMPANY: NEC America, Inc.
PRODUCT: 2420/30HN modem

PORT: female   PORT TYPE: serial _____
CONNECTOR: DB25 9-pin 8-pin(modular)   GENDER: male female
CONFIGURATION: C14

PIN	FUNCTION	DIRECTION
1:FG	Frame Ground	N/A
2:TD	Transmit Data	TO
3:RD	Receive Data	FROM
4:RTS	Request to Send	TO
5:CTS	Clear to Send	FROM
6:MR	Modem Ready	FROM
7:SG	Signal Ground	N/A
8:CD	Carrier Detect	FROM
9:+V		FROM
10:-V		FROM
11:SS	Speed Select	FROM
12:SS	Speed Select	FROM
15:TC	Transmit Clock	FROM
17:RC	Rec. Clk/Reverse Chann	FROM
18:LL		TO
20:DTR	Data Terminal Ready	TO
21:RDL		TO
22:RI	Ring Indicator	FROM
23:SS	Speed Select	TO
24:ETC	External Transmit Cloc	TO
25:TM		FROM

FLOW CONTROL   XON: ACK: LEADS THAT MUST BE ON: _____
SPEEDS: 110 300 600 1200 1800 2400 4800 9600 19.2 56k _____
COMPATIBILITY: 103 212 V.22bis _____
PARITY: even odd space mark none   CHARACTER LENGTH: 7 8 ___
STOP BITS: 1 1.5 2   LINE-ENDING CHARs: cr lf cr/lf
AUTO-ANSWER: yes no   RTS/CTS delay: ___
DISCONNECT SEQUENCE: EOT DEL _____
INTELLIGENT MODEMS....
   Dialing Technique: Touch-tone Pulse
   Compatibility: Hayes _____
   Command Line Prefix: AT _____   Dial command: D _____
   Touch-tone dial: T ___   Pulse dial: P ___ Pause: , ___
   Wait for dial tone: W ___   Wait for quiet answer: @ ___
   Flash: ! ___   Dial stored number: S ___
   Return to command state after dialing: ; ___
   Escape sequence: +++ ___   Switch-Hook control: H ___
   Store Phone#: &Z ___
Mode: async sync isoch
NOTE 1:
NOTE 2:

MODEM PORT PROFILE (Underline if supported, circle if selected)
COMPANY: NEC America, Inc.
PRODUCT: N500A DSU

PORT: female   PORT TYPE: serial _____
CONNECTOR: DB25 9-pin 8-pin(modular)   GENDER: male female
CONFIGURATION: C14

PIN	FUNCTION	DIRECTION
1:G	Ground	N/A
2:TD	Transmit Data	TO
3:RD	Receive Data	FROM
4:RTS	Request to Send	TO
5:CTS	Clear to Send	FROM
6:DSR	Data Set Ready	FROM
7:SG	Signal Ground	N/A
8:RLSD	Rec.Line Signal Detect	FROM
9:+12V		FROM
12:RT	Receive Timing	
15:TT	Transmit Timing	FROM
17:RT	Receive Timing	FROM
18:LL		TO
20:		TO
24:TT	Transmit Timing	TO
25:TM		FROM

FLOW CONTROL   XON: ACK: LEADS THAT MUST BE ON: _____
SPEEDS: 110 300 600 1200 1800 2400 4800 9600 19.2 56k _____
COMPATIBILITY: 103 212 V.22bis
_____
PARITY: even odd space mark none   CHARACTER LENGTH: 7 8 ___
STOP BITS: 1 1.5 2   LINE-ENDING CHARs: cr lf cr/lf
AUTO-ANSWER: yes no   RTS/CTS delay: ___
DISCONNECT SEQUENCE: EOT DEL _____
INTELLIGENT MODEMS....
    Dialing Technique: Touch-tone Pulse
    Compatibility: Hayes _____
    Command Line Prefix: AT _____   Dial command: D _____
    Touch-tone dial: T ___   Pulse dial: P ___ Pause: , ___
    Wait for dial tone: W ___   Wait for quiet answer: @ ___
    Flash: ! ___   Dial stored number: S ___
    Return to command state after dialing: ; ___
    Escape sequence: +++ ___   Switch-Hook control: H ___
    Store Phone#: &Z ___
Mode: async sync isoch
NOTE 1:
NOTE 2:

MODEM PORT PROFILE (Underline if supported, circle if selected)
COMPANY: Novation, Inc.
PRODUCT: P1200 series modems

PORT: female   PORT TYPE: serial _____
CONNECTOR: DB25 9-pin 8-pin(modular)   GENDER: male female
CONFIGURATION: C14

PIN	FUNCTION	DIRECTION
1:G	Ground	N/A
2:TD	Transmit Data	TO
3:RD	Receive Data	FROM
5:CTS	Clear to Send	FROM
6:DSR	Data Set Ready	FROM
7:SG	Signal Ground	N/A
8:DCD	Data Carrier Detect	FROM
12:SS	Speed Select	FROM
20:DTR	Data Terminal Ready	TO
22:RI	Ring Indicator	FROM

FLOW CONTROL   XON: ACK: LEADS THAT MUST BE ON: _____
SPEEDS: 110 300 600 1200 1800 2400 4800 9600 19.2 56k _____
COMPATIBILITY: 103 212 V.22bis

_____

PARITY: even odd space mark none   CHARACTER LENGTH: 7 8 ___
STOP BITS: 1 1.5 2   LINE-ENDING CHARs: cr lf cr/lf
AUTO-ANSWER: yes no   RTS/CTS delay: ___
DISCONNECT SEQUENCE: EOT DEL _____
INTELLIGENT MODEMS....
    Dialing Technique: Touch-tone Pulse
    Compatibility: Hayes _____
    Command Line Prefix: AT _____   Dial command: D _____
    Touch-tone dial: T ___   Pulse dial: P ___   Pause: , ___
    Wait for dial tone: W ___   Wait for quiet answer: @ ___
    Flash: ! ___   Dial stored number: S ___
    Return to command state after dialing: ; ___
    Escape sequence: +++ ___   Switch-Hook control: H ___
    Store Phone#: &Z ___
Mode: async sync isoch
NOTE 1:
NOTE 2:

MODEM PORT PROFILE (Underline if supported, circle if selected)
COMPANY: Novation, Inc.
PRODUCT: P2400 series modems

PORT: female   PORT TYPE: serial _____
CONNECTOR: DB25 9-pin 8-pin(modular)   GENDER: male female
CONFIGURATION: C14

PIN	FUNCTION	DIRECTION
1:G	Ground	N/A
2:TD	Transmit Data	TO
3:RD	Receive Data	FROM
4:RTS	Request to Send	TO
5:CTS	Clear to Send	FROM
6:DSR	Data Set Ready	FROM
7:SG	Signal Ground	N/A
8:DCD	Data Carrier Detect	FROM
9:+12V		FROM
10:-12V		FROM
12:SS	Speed Select	FROM
15:TT	Transmit Timing	FROM
17:RT	Receive Timing	FROM
20:DTR	Data Terminal Ready	TO
22:RI	Ring Indicator	FROM
24:ETC	External Transmit Cloc	TO

FLOW CONTROL   XON: ACK: LEADS THAT MUST BE ON: _____
SPEEDS: 110 300 600 1200 1800 2400 4800 9600 19.2 56k _____
COMPATIBILITY: 103 212 V.22bis
_____

PARITY: even odd space mark none   CHARACTER LENGTH: 7 8 ___
STOP BITS: 1 1.5 2   LINE-ENDING CHARs: cr lf cr/lf
AUTO-ANSWER: yes no   RTS/CTS delay: ___
DISCONNECT SEQUENCE: EOT DEL _____
INTELLIGENT MODEMS....
    Dialing Technique: Touch-tone Pulse
    Compatibility: Hayes _____
    Command Line Prefix: AT _____   Dial command: D _____
    Touch-tone dial: T ___   Pulse dial: P ___ Pause: , ___
    Wait for dial tone: W ___   Wait for quiet answer: @ ___
    Flash: ! ___   Dial stored number: S ___
    Return to command state after dialing: ; ___
    Escape sequence: +++ ___   Switch-Hook control: H ___
    Store Phone#: &Z ___
Mode: async sync isoch
NOTE 1:
NOTE 2:

MODEM PORT PROFILE (Underline if supported, circle if selected)
COMPANY: Patton Electronics, Co.
PRODUCT: 100 series short range modems

PORT: female or male   PORT TYPE: serial _____
CONNECTOR: DB25 9-pin 8-pin(modular)   GENDER: male female
CONFIGURATION: C14

PIN	FUNCTION	DIRECTION
1:FG	Frame Ground	N/A
2:TD	Transmit Data	TO
3:RD	Receive Data	FROM
4:RTS	Request to Send	TO
5:CTS	Clear to Send	FROM
6:DSR	Data Set Ready	FROM
7:SG	Signal Ground	N/A
8:DCD	Data Carrier Detect	FROM
20:DTR	Data Terminal Ready	TO

FLOW CONTROL   XON: ACK: LEADS THAT MUST BE ON: _____
SPEEDS: 110 300 600 1200 1800 2400 4800 9600 19.2 56k _____
COMPATIBILITY: 103 212 V.22bis

_____
PARITY: even odd space mark none   CHARACTER LENGTH: 7 8 ___
STOP BITS: 1 1.5 2   LINE-ENDING CHARs: cr lf cr/lf
AUTO-ANSWER: yes no   RTS/CTS delay: ___
DISCONNECT SEQUENCE: EOT DEL _____
INTELLIGENT MODEMS....
     Dialing Technique: Touch-tone Pulse
    Compatibility: Hayes _____
    Command Line Prefix: AT _____   Dial command: D _____
    Touch-tone dial: T ___   Pulse dial: P ___   Pause: , ___
    Wait for dial tone: W ___   Wait for quiet answer: @ ___
    Flash: ! ___   Dial stored number: S ___
    Return to command state after dialing: ; ___
    Escape sequence: +++ ___   Switch-Hook control: H ___
    Store Phone#: &Z ___
Mode: async sync isoch
NOTE 1: The gender can be either when ordering modems.
NOTE 2: The pins in the model 100/101 can be reversed

MODEM PORT PROFILE (Underline if supported, circle if selected)
COMPANY: Penril DataComm
PRODUCT: 8192 modem

PORT: female   PORT TYPE: serial _____
CONNECTOR: DB25 9-pin 8-pin(modular) GENDER: male female
CONFIGURATION: C14

PIN	FUNCTION	DIRECTION
1:PG	Protective Ground	N/A
2:TD	Transmit Data	TO
3:RD	Receive Data	FROM
4:RTS	Request to Send	TO
5:CTS	Clear to Send	FROM
6:DSR	Data Set Ready	FROM
7:SG	Signal Ground	N/A
8:RLSD	Rec.Line Signal Detect	FROM
15:TC	Transmit Clock	FROM
17:RC	Rec. Clk/Reverse Chann	FROM
20:		TO
24:TC	Transmit Clock	TO

FLOW CONTROL   XON: ACK: LEADS THAT MUST BE ON: _____
SPEEDS: 110 300 600 1200 1800 2400 4800 9600 19.2 56k _____
COMPATIBILITY: 103 212 V.22bis

_____

PARITY: even odd space mark none   CHARACTER LENGTH: 7 8 ___
STOP BITS: 1 1.5 2   LINE-ENDING CHARs: cr lf cr/lf
AUTO-ANSWER: yes no   RTS/CTS delay: ___
DISCONNECT SEQUENCE: EOT DEL _____
INTELLIGENT MODEMS....
    Dialing Technique: Touch-tone Pulse
    Compatibility: Hayes _____
    Command Line Prefix: AT _____   Dial command: D _____
    Touch-tone dial: T ___   Pulse dial: P ___   Pause: , ___
    Wait for dial tone: W ___   Wait for quiet answer: @ ___
    Flash: ! ___   Dial stored number: S ___
    Return to command state after dialing: ; ___
    Escape sequence: +++ ___   Switch-Hook control: H ___
    Store Phone#: &Z ___
Mode: async sync isoch
NOTE 1:
NOTE 2:

MODEM PORT PROFILE (Underline if supported, circle if selected)
COMPANY: Penril DataComm
PRODUCT: CADET 1200 modem

PORT: female   PORT TYPE: serial _____
CONNECTOR: DB25 9-pin 8-pin(modular) GENDER: male female
CONFIGURATION: C14

PIN	FUNCTION	DIRECTION
1:G	Ground	N/A
2:TD	Transmit Data	TO
3:RD	Receive Data	FROM
5:CTS	Clear to Send	FROM
6:DSR	Data Set Ready	FROM
7:SG	Signal Ground	N/A
8:CD	Carrier Detect	FROM
9:+V		FROM
10:-V		FROM
12:SS	Speed Select	FROM
20:DTR	Data Terminal Ready	TO
22:RI	Ring Indicator	FROM

FLOW CONTROL   XON: ACK: LEADS THAT MUST BE ON: _____
SPEEDS: 110 300 600 1200 1800 2400 4800 9600 19.2 56k _____
COMPATIBILITY: 103 212 V.22bis

_____
PARITY: even odd space mark none   CHARACTER LENGTH: 7 8 ___
STOP BITS: 1 1.5 2   LINE-ENDING CHARs: cr lf cr/lf
AUTO-ANSWER: yes no   RTS/CTS delay: ___
DISCONNECT SEQUENCE: EOT DEL _____
INTELLIGENT MODEMS....
     Dialing Technique: Touch-tone Pulse
     Compatibility: Hayes _____
     Command Line Prefix: AT _____   Dial command: D _____
     Touch-tone dial: T ___   Pulse dial: P ___ Pause: , ___
     Wait for dial tone: W ___   Wait for quiet answer: @ ___
     Flash: ! ___   Dial stored number: S ___
     Return to command state after dialing: ; ___
     Escape sequence: +++ ___   Switch-Hook control: H ___
     Store Phone#: &Z ___
Mode: async sync isoch
NOTE 1:
NOTE 2:

MODEM PORT PROFILE (Underline if supported, circle if selected)
COMPANY: Penril DataComm
PRODUCT: CADET 2400 modem

PORT: female   PORT TYPE: serial _____
CONNECTOR: DB25 9-pin 8-pin(modular) GENDER: male female
CONFIGURATION: C14

PIN	FUNCTION	DIRECTION
1:G	Ground	N/A
2:TD	Transmit Data	TO
3:RD	Receive Data	FROM
5:CTS	Clear to Send	FROM
6:DSR	Data Set Ready	FROM
7:SG	Signal Ground	N/A
8:CD	Carrier Detect	FROM
9:+V		FROM
10:-V		FROM
12:SS	Speed Select	FROM
20:DTR	Data Terminal Ready	TO
22:RI	Ring Indicator	FROM

FLOW CONTROL   XON: ACK: LEADS THAT MUST BE ON: _____
SPEEDS: 110 300 600 1200 1800 2400 4800 9600 19.2 56k _____
COMPATIBILITY: 103 212 V.22bis

_____
PARITY: even odd space mark none   CHARACTER LENGTH: 7 8 ___
STOP BITS: 1 1.5 2   LINE-ENDING CHARs: cr lf cr/lf
AUTO-ANSWER: yes no   RTS/CTS delay: ___
DISCONNECT SEQUENCE: EOT DEL _____
INTELLIGENT MODEMS....
     Dialing Technique: Touch-tone Pulse
    Compatibility: Hayes _____
    Command Line Prefix: AT _____   Dial command: D _____
    Touch-tone dial: T ___   Pulse dial: P ___ Pause: , ___
    Wait for dial tone: W ___   Wait for quiet answer: @ ___
    Flash: ! ___   Dial stored number: S ___
    Return to command state after dialing: ; ___
    Escape sequence: +++ ___   Switch-Hook control: H ___
    Store Phone#: &Z ___
Mode: async sync isoch
NOTE 1:
NOTE 2:

MODEM PORT PROFILE (Underline if supported, circle if selected)
COMPANY: Penril DataComm
PRODUCT: Datalink 2400/4800/9600 modems

PORT: female   PORT TYPE: serial _____
CONNECTOR: DB25 9-pin 8-pin(modular)   GENDER: male female
CONFIGURATION: C14

PIN	FUNCTION	DIRECTION
1:FG	Frame Ground	N/A
2:TD	Transmit Data	TO
3:RD	Receive Data	FROM
4:RTS	Request to Send	TO
5:CTS	Clear to Send	FROM
6:DSR	Data Set Ready	FROM
7:SG	Signal Ground	N/A
8:CD	Carrier Detect	FROM
9:+V		FROM
10:-V		FROM
15:TC	Transmit Clock	FROM
17:RC	Rec. Clk/Reverse Chann	FROM
18:AL		TO
20:DTR	Data Terminal Ready	TO
21:RL		TO
22:RI	Ring Indicator	FROM
23:SS	Speed Select	TO
24:ETC	External Transmit Cloc	TO
25:TM		FROM

FLOW CONTROL   XON: ACK: LEADS THAT MUST BE ON: _____
SPEEDS: 110 300 600 1200 1800 2400 4800 9600 19.2 56k _____
COMPATIBILITY: 103 212 V.22bis
_____

PARITY: even odd space mark none   CHARACTER LENGTH: 7 8 ___
STOP BITS: 1 1.5 2   LINE-ENDING CHARs: cr lf cr/lf
AUTO-ANSWER: yes no   RTS/CTS delay: ___
DISCONNECT SEQUENCE: EOT DEL _____
INTELLIGENT MODEMS....
    Dialing Technique: Touch-tone Pulse
   Compatibility: Hayes _____
   Command Line Prefix: AT _____   Dial command: D _____
   Touch-tone dial: T ___   Pulse dial: P ___ Pause: , ___
   Wait for dial tone: W ___   Wait for quiet answer: @ ___
   Flash: ! ___   Dial stored number: S ___
   Return to command state after dialing: ; ___
   Escape sequence: +++ ___   Switch-Hook control: H ___
   Store Phone#: &Z ___
Mode: async sync isoch
NOTE 1:
NOTE 2:

MODEM PORT PROFILE (Underline if supported, circle if selected)
COMPANY: Penril DataComm
PRODUCT: PSH 96A modem

PORT: female   PORT TYPE: serial _____
CONNECTOR: DB25 9-pin 8-pin(modular)   GENDER: male female
CONFIGURATION: C14

PIN	FUNCTION	DIRECTION
1:FG	Frame Ground	N/A
2:TD	Transmit Data	TO
3:RD	Receive Data	FROM
4:RTS	Request to Send	TO
5:CTS	Clear to Send	FROM
6:DSR	Data Set Ready	FROM
7:SG	Signal Ground	N/A
8:CD	Carrier Detect	FROM
9:+15V		FROM
10:-15V		FROM
20:DTR	Data Terminal Ready	TO
22:RI	Ring Indicator	FROM

FLOW CONTROL   XON: ACK: LEADS THAT MUST BE ON: _____
SPEEDS: 110 300 600 1200 1800 2400 4800 9600 19.2 56k _____
COMPATIBILITY: 103 212 V.22bis

_____
PARITY: even odd space mark none   CHARACTER LENGTH: 7 8 ___
STOP BITS: 1 1.5 2   LINE-ENDING CHARs: cr lf cr/lf
AUTO-ANSWER: yes no   RTS/CTS delay: ___
DISCONNECT SEQUENCE: EOT DEL _____
INTELLIGENT MODEMS....
    Dialing Technique: Touch-tone Pulse
    Compatibility: Hayes _____
    Command Line Prefix: AT _____   Dial command: D _____
    Touch-tone dial: T ___   Pulse dial: P ___   Pause: , ___
    Wait for dial tone: W ___   Wait for quiet answer: @ ___
    Flash: ! ___   Dial stored number: S ___
    Return to command state after dialing: ; ___
    Escape sequence: +++ ___   Switch-Hook control: H ___
    Store Phone#: &Z ___
Mode: async sync isoch
NOTE 1:
NOTE 2:

MODEM PORT PROFILE (Underline if supported, circle if selected)
COMPANY: Prentice Corporation
PRODUCT: 1100/1200 statistical multiplexers

PORT: female   PORT TYPE: serial _____
CONNECTOR: DB25 9-pin 8-pin(modular) GENDER: male female
CONFIGURATION: C14

PIN	FUNCTION	DIRECTION
1:CG	Chassis Ground	N/A
2:TD	Transmit Data	TO
3:RD	Receive Data	FROM
4:RTS	Request to Send	TO
5:CTS	Clear to Send	FROM
6:DSR	Data Set Ready	FROM
7:SG	Signal Ground	N/A
8:RLSD	Rec.Line Signal Detect	FROM
15:TC	Transmit Clock	FROM
17:RC	Rec. Clk/Reverse Chann	FROM
20:DTR	Data Terminal Ready	TO
24:ETC	External Transmit Cloc	TO

FLOW CONTROL   XON: ACK: LEADS THAT MUST BE ON: _____
SPEEDS: 110 300 600 1200 1800 2400 4800 9600 19.2 56k _____
COMPATIBILITY: 103 212 V.22bis

_____
PARITY: even odd space mark none   CHARACTER LENGTH: 7 8 ___
STOP BITS: 1 1.5 2   LINE-ENDING CHARs: cr lf cr/lf
AUTO-ANSWER: yes no   RTS/CTS delay: ___
DISCONNECT SEQUENCE: EOT DEL _____
INTELLIGENT MODEMS....
    Dialing Technique: Touch-tone Pulse
   Compatibility: Hayes _____
   Command Line Prefix: AT _____   Dial command: D _____
   Touch-tone dial: T ___   Pulse dial: P ___ Pause: , ___
   Wait for dial tone: W ___   Wait for quiet answer: @ ___
   Flash: ! ___   Dial stored number: S ___
   Return to command state after dialing: ; ___
   Escape sequence: +++ ___   Switch-Hook control: H ___
   Store Phone#: &Z ___
Mode: async sync isoch
NOTE 1:
NOTE 2:

MODEM PORT PROFILE (Underline if supported, circle if selected)
COMPANY: Prentice Corporation
PRODUCT: 212 TCM modem

PORT: female   PORT TYPE: serial _____
CONNECTOR: DB25 9-pin 8-pin(modular)   GENDER: male female
CONFIGURATION: C14

PIN	FUNCTION	DIRECTION
1:CG	Chassis Ground	N/A
2:TD	Transmit Data	TO
3:RD	Receive Data	FROM
5:CTS	Clear to Send	FROM
6:DSR	Data Set Ready	FROM
7:SG	Signal Ground	N/A
8:RLSD	Rec.Line Signal Detect	FROM
9:+12V		FROM
10:-12V		FROM
20:DTR	Data Terminal Ready	TO
22:RI	Ring Indicator	FROM

FLOW CONTROL   XON: ACK: LEADS THAT MUST BE ON: _____
SPEEDS: 110 300 600 1200 1800 2400 4800 9600 19.2 56k _____
COMPATIBILITY: 103 212 V.22bis

_____
PARITY: even odd space mark none   CHARACTER LENGTH: 7 8 ___
STOP BITS: 1 1.5 2   LINE-ENDING CHARs: cr lf cr/lf
AUTO-ANSWER: yes no   RTS/CTS delay: ___
DISCONNECT SEQUENCE: EOT DEL _____
INTELLIGENT MODEMS....
     Dialing Technique: Touch-tone Pulse
     Compatibility: Hayes _____
     Command Line Prefix: AT _____   Dial command: D _____
     Touch-tone dial: T ___   Pulse dial: P ___ Pause: , ___
     Wait for dial tone: W ___   Wait for quiet answer: @ ___
     Flash: ! ___   Dial stored number: S ___
     Return to command state after dialing: ; ___
     Escape sequence: +++ ___   Switch-Hook control: H ___
     Store Phone#: &Z ___
Mode: async sync isoch
NOTE 1:
NOTE 2:

MODEM PORT PROFILE (Underline if supported, circle if selected)
COMPANY: Prentice Corporation
PRODUCT: 9629 modem

PORT: female   PORT TYPE: serial _____
CONNECTOR: DB25 9-pin 8-pin(modular)   GENDER: male female
CONFIGURATION: C14

PIN	FUNCTION	DIRECTION
1:PG	Protective Ground	N/A
2:TD	Transmit Data	TO
3:RD	Receive Data	FROM
4:RTS	Request to Send	TO
5:CTS	Clear to Send	FROM
6:DSR	Data Set Ready	FROM
7:SG	Signal Ground	N/A
8:RLSD	Rec.Line Signal Detect	FROM
9:+12V		FROM
10:-12V		FROM
14:AL		TO
15:TT	Transmit Timing	FROM
17:RT	Receive Timing	FROM
20:DTR	Data Terminal Ready	TO
23:DRS	Data Rate Select	TO
24:TT	Transmit Timing	TO

FLOW CONTROL   XON: ACK: LEADS THAT MUST BE ON: _____
SPEEDS: 110 300 600 1200 1800 2400 4800 9600 19.2 56k _____
COMPATIBILITY: 103 212 V.22bis

_____
PARITY: even odd space mark none   CHARACTER LENGTH: 7 8 ___
STOP BITS: 1 1.5 2   LINE-ENDING CHARs: cr lf cr/lf
AUTO-ANSWER: yes no   RTS/CTS delay: ___
DISCONNECT SEQUENCE: EOT DEL _____
INTELLIGENT MODEMS....
     Dialing Technique: Touch-tone Pulse
   Compatibility: Hayes _____
   Command Line Prefix: AT _____   Dial command: D _____
   Touch-tone dial: T ___   Pulse dial: P ___   Pause: , ___
   Wait for dial tone: W ___   Wait for quiet answer: @ ___
   Flash: ! ___   Dial stored number: S ___
   Return to command state after dialing: ; ___
   Escape sequence: +++ ___   Switch-Hook control: H ___
   Store Phone#: &Z ___
Mode: async sync isoch
NOTE 1:
NOTE 2:

MODEM PORT PROFILE (Underline if supported, circle if selected)
COMPANY: Prentice Corporation
PRODUCT: ALD/2 modem

PORT: female   PORT TYPE: serial _____
CONNECTOR: DB25 9-pin 8-pin(modular)   GENDER: male female
CONFIGURATION: C14

PIN	FUNCTION	DIRECTION
1:PG	Protective Ground	N/A
2:TD	Transmit Data	TO
3:RD	Receive Data	FROM
4:RTS	Request to Send	TO
5:CTS	Clear to Send	FROM
6:DSR	Data Set Ready	FROM
7:SG	Signal Ground	N/A
8:RLSD	Rec.Line Signal Detect	FROM
9:+12V		FROM
10:-12V		FROM
20:DTR	Data Terminal Ready	TO

FLOW CONTROL   XON: ACK: LEADS THAT MUST BE ON: _____
SPEEDS: 110 300 600 1200 1800 2400 4800 9600 19.2 56k _____
COMPATIBILITY: 103 212 V.22bis

_____
PARITY: even odd space mark none   CHARACTER LENGTH: 7 8 ___
STOP BITS: 1 1.5 2   LINE-ENDING CHARs: cr lf cr/lf
AUTO-ANSWER: yes no   RTS/CTS delay: ___
DISCONNECT SEQUENCE: EOT DEL _____
INTELLIGENT MODEMS....
     Dialing Technique: Touch-tone Pulse
     Compatibility: Hayes _____
     Command Line Prefix: AT _____   Dial command: D _____
     Touch-tone dial: T ___   Pulse dial: P ___ Pause: , ___
     Wait for dial tone: W ___   Wait for quiet answer: @ ___
     Flash: ! ___   Dial stored number: S ___
     Return to command state after dialing: ; ___
     Escape sequence: +++ ___   Switch-Hook control: H ___
     Store Phone#: &Z ___
Mode: async sync isoch
NOTE 1:
NOTE 2:

MODEM PORT PROFILE (Underline if supported, circle if selected)
COMPANY: Prentice Corporation
PRODUCT: HSLD modems

PORT: female   PORT TYPE: serial _____
CONNECTOR: DB25 9-pin 8-pin(modular) GENDER: male female
CONFIGURATION: C14

PIN	FUNCTION	DIRECTION
1:PG	Protective Ground	N/A
2:TD	Transmit Data	TO
3:RD	Receive Data	FROM
4:RTS	Request to Send	TO
5:CTS	Clear to Send	FROM
6:DSR	Data Set Ready	FROM
7:SG	Signal Ground	N/A
8:RLSD	Rec.Line Signal Detect	FROM
9:+12V		FROM
10:-12V		FROM
15:TC	Transmit Clock	FROM
17:RC	Rec. Clk/Reverse Chann	FROM
20:DTR	Data Terminal Ready	TO
21:SQ		FROM
24:ETC	External Transmit Cloc	TO
25:RDS		TO

FLOW CONTROL   XON: ACK: LEADS THAT MUST BE ON: _____
SPEEDS: 110 300 600 1200 1800 2400 4800 9600 19.2 56k _____
COMPATIBILITY: 103 212 V.22bis
_____

PARITY: even odd space mark none   CHARACTER LENGTH: 7 8 ___
STOP BITS: 1 1.5 2   LINE-ENDING CHARs: cr lf cr/lf
AUTO-ANSWER: yes no   RTS/CTS delay: ___
DISCONNECT SEQUENCE: EOT DEL _____
INTELLIGENT MODEMS....
    Dialing Technique: Touch-tone Pulse
    Compatibility: Hayes _____
    Command Line Prefix: AT _____   Dial command: D _____
    Touch-tone dial: T ___   Pulse dial: P ___ Pause: , ___
    Wait for dial tone: W ___   Wait for quiet answer: @ ___
    Flash: ! ___   Dial stored number: S ___
    Return to command state after dialing: ; ___
    Escape sequence: +++ ___   Switch-Hook control: H ___
    Store Phone#: &Z ___
Mode: async sync isoch
NOTE 1:
NOTE 2:

MODEM PORT PROFILE   (Underline if supported, circle if selected)
COMPANY: Prentice Corporation
PRODUCT: P-201C modem

PORT: female   PORT TYPE: serial _____
CONNECTOR: DB25 9-pin 8-pin(modular) GENDER: male female
CONFIGURATION: C14

PIN	FUNCTION	DIRECTION
1:PG	Protective Ground	N/A
2:TD	Transmit Data	TO
3:RD	Receive Data	FROM
4:RTS	Request to Send	TO
5:CTS	Clear to Send	FROM
6:DSR	Data Set Ready	FROM
7:SG	Signal Ground	N/A
8:DCD	Data Carrier Detect	FROM
9:+12V		FROM
10:-12V		FROM
15:TT	Transmit Timing	FROM
17:RT	Receive Timing	FROM
18:DCR		
20:DTR	Data Terminal Ready	TO
22:RI	Ring Indicator	FROM
24:ETC	External Transmit Cloc	TO

FLOW CONTROL   XON: ACK: LEADS THAT MUST BE ON: _____
SPEEDS: 110 300 600 1200 1800 2400 4800 9600 19.2 56k _____
COMPATIBILITY: 103 212 V.22bis
_____
PARITY: even odd space mark none   CHARACTER LENGTH: 7 8 ___
STOP BITS: 1 1.5 2   LINE-ENDING CHARs: cr lf cr/lf
AUTO-ANSWER: yes no   RTS/CTS delay: ___
DISCONNECT SEQUENCE: EOT DEL _____
INTELLIGENT MODEMS....
    Dialing Technique: Touch-tone Pulse
    Compatibility: Hayes _____
    Command Line Prefix: AT _____   Dial command: D _____
    Touch-tone dial: T ___   Pulse dial: P ___ Pause: , ___
    Wait for dial tone: W ___   Wait for quiet answer: @ ___
    Flash: ! ___   Dial stored number: S ___
    Return to command state after dialing: ; ___
    Escape sequence: +++ ___   Switch-Hook control: H ___
    Store Phone#: &Z ___
Mode: async sync isoch
NOTE 1:
NOTE 2:

MODEM PORT PROFILE (Underline if supported, circle if selected)
COMPANY: Prentice Corporation
PRODUCT: P-208 A/B modems

PORT: female   PORT TYPE: serial _____
CONNECTOR: DB25 9-pin 8-pin(modular)   GENDER: male female
CONFIGURATION: C14

PIN	FUNCTION	DIRECTION
1:PG	Protective Ground	N/A
2:TD	Transmit Data	TO
3:RD	Receive Data	FROM
4:RTS	Request to Send	TO
5:CTS	Clear to Send	FROM
6:DSR	Data Set Ready	FROM
7:SG	Signal Ground	N/A
8:RLSD	Rec.Line Signal Detect	FROM
9:+12V		FROM
10:-12V		FROM
11:QM		FROM
14:NS		TO
15:TT	Transmit Timing	FROM
17:RT	Receive Timing	FROM
20:DTR	Data Terminal Ready	TO
22:RI	Ring Indicator	FROM
24:TT	Transmit Timing	TO
25:B	Busy	TO

FLOW CONTROL   XON: ACK: LEADS THAT MUST BE ON: _____
SPEEDS: 110 300 600 1200 1800 2400 4800 9600 19.2 56k _____
COMPATIBILITY: 103 212 V.22bis
_____

PARITY: even odd space mark none   CHARACTER LENGTH: 7 8 ___
STOP BITS: 1 1.5 2   LINE-ENDING CHARs: cr lf cr/lf
AUTO-ANSWER: yes no   RTS/CTS delay: ___
DISCONNECT SEQUENCE: EOT DEL _____
INTELLIGENT MODEMS....
    Dialing Technique: Touch-tone Pulse
    Compatibility: Hayes _____
    Command Line Prefix: AT _____   Dial command: D _____
    Touch-tone dial: T ___   Pulse dial: P ___ Pause: , ___
    Wait for dial tone: W ___   Wait for quiet answer: @ ___
    Flash: ! ___   Dial stored number: S ___
    Return to command state after dialing: ; ___
    Escape sequence: +++ ___   Switch-Hook control: H ___
    Store Phone#: &Z ___
Mode: async sync isoch
NOTE 1:
NOTE 2:

MODEM PORT PROFILE (Underline if supported, circle if selected)
COMPANY: Prentice Corporation
PRODUCT: P-212AD modem

PORT: female   PORT TYPE: serial _____
CONNECTOR: DB25 9-pin 8-pin(modular)   GENDER: male female
CONFIGURATION: C14

PIN	FUNCTION	DIRECTION
1:CG	Chassis Ground	N/A
2:TD	Transmit Data	TO
3:RD	Receive Data	FROM
5:CTS	Clear to Send	FROM
6:DSR	Data Set Ready	FROM
7:SG	Signal Ground	N/A
8:CD	Carrier Detect	FROM
9:+12V		FROM
10:-12V		FROM
12:SS	Speed Select	FROM
20:DTR	Data Terminal Ready	TO
22:RI	Ring Indicator	FROM
25:B	Busy	TO

FLOW CONTROL   XON: ACK: LEADS THAT MUST BE ON: _____
SPEEDS: 110 300 600 1200 1800 2400 4800 9600 19.2 56k _____
COMPATIBILITY: 103 212 V.22bis

_____
PARITY: even odd space mark none   CHARACTER LENGTH: 7 8 ___
STOP BITS: 1 1.5 2   LINE-ENDING CHARs: cr lf cr/lf
AUTO-ANSWER: yes no   RTS/CTS delay: ___
DISCONNECT SEQUENCE: EOT DEL _____
INTELLIGENT MODEMS....
    Dialing Technique: Touch-tone Pulse
    Compatibility: Hayes _____
    Command Line Prefix: AT _____   Dial command: D _____
    Touch-tone dial: T ___   Pulse dial: P ___   Pause: , ___
    Wait for dial tone: W ___   Wait for quiet answer: @ ___
    Flash: ! ___   Dial stored number: S ___
    Return to command state after dialing: ; ___
    Escape sequence: +++ ___   Switch-Hook control: H ___
    Store Phone#: &Z ___
Mode: async sync isoch
NOTE 1:
NOTE 2:

MODEM PORT PROFILE (Underline if supported, circle if selected)
COMPANY: Prentice Corporation
PRODUCT: P-212ZX modem

PORT: female   PORT TYPE: serial _____
CONNECTOR: DB25 9-pin 8-pin(modular)   GENDER: male female
CONFIGURATION: C14

PIN	FUNCTION	DIRECTION
2:TD	Transmit Data	TO
3:RD	Receive Data	FROM
5:CTS	Clear to Send	FROM
6:DSR	Data Set Ready	FROM
7:SG	Signal Ground	N/A
8:CD	Carrier Detect	FROM
12:SS	Speed Select	FROM
20:DTR	Data Terminal Ready	TO
22:RI	Ring Indicator	FROM

FLOW CONTROL   XON: ACK: LEADS THAT MUST BE ON: _____
SPEEDS: 110 300 600 1200 1800 2400 4800 9600 19.2 56k _____
COMPATIBILITY: 103 212 V.22bis

_____
PARITY: even odd space mark none   CHARACTER LENGTH: 7 8 ___
STOP BITS: 1 1.5 2   LINE-ENDING CHARs: cr lf cr/lf
AUTO-ANSWER: yes no   RTS/CTS delay: ___
DISCONNECT SEQUENCE: EOT DEL _____
INTELLIGENT MODEMS....
     Dialing Technique: Touch-tone Pulse
   Compatibility: Hayes _____
   Command Line Prefix: AT _____   Dial command: D _____
   Touch-tone dial: T ___   Pulse dial: P ___   Pause: , ___
   Wait for dial tone: W ___   Wait for quiet answer: @ ___
   Flash: ! ___   Dial stored number: S ___
   Return to command state after dialing: ; ___
   Escape sequence: +++ ___   Switch-Hook control: H ___
   Store Phone#: &Z ___
Mode: async sync isoch
NOTE 1:
NOTE 2:

MODEM PORT PROFILE (Underline if supported, circle if selected)
COMPANY: Prentice Corporation
PRODUCT: P224 modem

PORT: female   PORT TYPE: serial _____
CONNECTOR: DB25 9-pin 8-pin(modular)   GENDER: male female
CONFIGURATION: C14

PIN	FUNCTION	DIRECTION
1:FG	Frame Ground	N/A
2:TD	Transmit Data	TO
3:RD	Receive Data	FROM
4:RTS	Request to Send	TO
5:CTS	Clear to Send	FROM
6:DSR	Data Set Ready	FROM
7:SG	Signal Ground	N/A
8:CD	Carrier Detect	FROM
12:SS	Speed Select	TO
15:TC	Transmit Clock	FROM
17:RC	Rec. Clk/Reverse Chann	FROM
18:TM		TO
20:DTR	Data Terminal Ready	TO
21:TM		TO
22:RI	Ring Indicator	FROM
24:ETC	External Transmit Cloc	TO

FLOW CONTROL   XON: ACK: LEADS THAT MUST BE ON: _____
SPEEDS: 110 300 600 1200 1800 2400 4800 9600 19.2 56k _____
COMPATIBILITY: 103 212 V.22bis
_____

PARITY: even odd space mark none   CHARACTER LENGTH: 7 8 ___
STOP BITS: 1 1.5 2   LINE-ENDING CHARs: cr lf cr/lf
AUTO-ANSWER: yes no   RTS/CTS delay: ___
DISCONNECT SEQUENCE: EOT DEL _____
INTELLIGENT MODEMS....
     Dialing Technique: Touch-tone Pulse
    Compatibility: Hayes _____
    Command Line Prefix: AT _____   Dial command: D _____
    Touch-tone dial: T ___   Pulse dial: P ___   Pause: , ___
    Wait for dial tone: W ___   Wait for quiet answer: @ ___
    Flash: ! ___   Dial stored number: S ___
    Return to command state after dialing: ; ___
    Escape sequence: +++ ___   Switch-Hook control: H ___
    Store Phone#: &Z ___
Mode: async sync isoch
NOTE 1:
NOTE 2:

MODEM PORT PROFILE   (Underline if supported, circle if selected)
COMPANY: Prentice Corporation
PRODUCT: POPCOM X100 modem

PORT: female   PORT TYPE: serial _____
CONNECTOR: DB25 9-pin 8-pin(modular)   GENDER: male female
CONFIGURATION: C14

PIN	FUNCTION	DIRECTION
2:TD	Transmit Data	TO
3:RD	Receive Data	FROM
5:CTS	Clear to Send	FROM
6:DSR	Data Set Ready	FROM
7:SG	Signal Ground	N/A
8:CD	Carrier Detect	FROM
12:SS	Speed Select	FROM
20:DTR	Data Terminal Ready	TO
22:RI	Ring Indicator	FROM

FLOW CONTROL   XON: ACK: LEADS THAT MUST BE ON: _____
SPEEDS: 110 300 600 1200 1800 2400 4800 9600 19.2 56k _____
COMPATIBILITY: 103 212 V.22bis

_____
PARITY: even odd space mark none   CHARACTER LENGTH: 7 8 ___
STOP BITS: 1 1.5 2   LINE-ENDING CHARs: cr lf cr/lf
AUTO-ANSWER: yes no   RTS/CTS delay: ___
DISCONNECT SEQUENCE: EOT DEL _____
INTELLIGENT MODEMS....
    Dialing Technique: Touch-tone Pulse
    Compatibility: Hayes _____
    Command Line Prefix: AT _____   Dial command: D _____
    Touch-tone dial: T ___   Pulse dial: P ___ Pause: , ___
    Wait for dial tone: W ___   Wait for quiet answer: @ ___
    Flash: ! ___   Dial stored number: S ___
    Return to command state after dialing: ; ___
    Escape sequence: +++ ___   Switch-Hook control: H ___
    Store Phone#: &Z ___
Mode: async sync isoch
NOTE 1: If the modem senses data to it on lead 3, it will
NOTE 2: change the direction of the leads 2/3/4/6/20

MODEM PORT PROFILE (Underline if supported, circle if selected)
COMPANY: Prentice Corporation
PRODUCT: TriModem

PORT: female   PORT TYPE: serial _____
CONNECTOR: DB25 9-pin 8-pin(modular)   GENDER: male female
CONFIGURATION: C14

PIN	FUNCTION	DIRECTION
1:CG	Chassis Ground	N/A
2:TD	Transmit Data	TO
3:RD	Receive Data	FROM
5:CTS	Clear to Send	FROM
6:DSR	Data Set Ready	FROM
7:SG	Signal Ground	N/A
8:RLSD	Rec.Line Signal Detect	FROM
9:+12V		FROM
10:-12V		FROM
11:AS		FROM
12:SS	Speed Select	FROM
15:TC	Transmit Clock	FROM
17:RC	Rec. Clk/Reverse Chann	FROM
18:TM		FROM
20:DTR	Data Terminal Ready	TO
22:RI	Ring Indicator	FROM
24:TC	Transmit Clock	TO
25:B	Busy	TO

FLOW CONTROL   XON: ACK: LEADS THAT MUST BE ON: _____
SPEEDS: 110 300 600 1200 1800 2400 4800 9600 19.2 56k _____
COMPATIBILITY: 103 212 V.22bis
_____

PARITY: even odd space mark none   CHARACTER LENGTH: 7 8 ___
STOP BITS: 1 1.5 2   LINE-ENDING CHARs: cr lf cr/lf
AUTO-ANSWER: yes no   RTS/CTS delay: ___
DISCONNECT SEQUENCE: EOT DEL _____
INTELLIGENT MODEMS....
    Dialing Technique: Touch-tone Pulse
    Compatibility: Hayes _____
    Command Line Prefix: AT _____   Dial command: D _____
    Touch-tone dial: T ___   Pulse dial: P ___ Pause: , ___
    Wait for dial tone: W ___   Wait for quiet answer: @ ___
    Flash: ! ___   Dial stored number: S ___
    Return to command state after dialing: ; ___
    Escape sequence: +++ ___   Switch-Hook control: H ___
    Store Phone#: &Z ___
Mode: async sync isoch
NOTE 1:
NOTE 2:

MODEM PORT PROFILE (Underline if supported, circle if selected)
COMPANY: Qubie'
PRODUCT: 212A/1200E modems

PORT: female   PORT TYPE: serial _____
CONNECTOR: DB25 9-pin 8-pin(modular) GENDER: male female
CONFIGURATION: C14

PIN	FUNCTION	DIRECTION
1:CG	Chassis Ground	N/A
2:TD	Transmit Data	TO
3:RD	Receive Data	FROM
4:RTS	Request to Send	TO
5:CTS	Clear to Send	FROM
6:DSR	Data Set Ready	FROM
7:SG	Signal Ground	N/A
8:DCD	Data Carrier Detect	FROM
20:DTR	Data Terminal Ready	TO
22:RI	Ring Indicator	FROM

FLOW CONTROL   XON: ACK: LEADS THAT MUST BE ON: _____
SPEEDS: 110 300 600 1200 1800 2400 4800 9600 19.2 56k _____
COMPATIBILITY: 103 212 V.22bis
_____

PARITY: even odd space mark none   CHARACTER LENGTH: 7 8 ___
STOP BITS: 1 1.5 2   LINE-ENDING CHARs: cr lf cr/lf
AUTO-ANSWER: yes no   RTS/CTS delay: ___
DISCONNECT SEQUENCE: EOT DEL _____
INTELLIGENT MODEMS....
     Dialing Technique: Touch-tone Pulse
   Compatibility: Hayes _____
   Command Line Prefix: AT _____   Dial command: D _____
   Touch-tone dial: T ___   Pulse dial: P ___   Pause: , ___
   Wait for dial tone: W ___   Wait for quiet answer: @ ___
   Flash: ! ___   Dial stored number: S ___
   Return to command state after dialing: ; ___
   Escape sequence: +++ ___   Switch-Hook control: H ___
   Store Phone#: &Z ___
Mode: async sync isoch
NOTE 1:
NOTE 2:

MODEM PORT PROFILE (Underline if supported, circle if selected)
COMPANY: Racal-Vadic
PRODUCT: 1200VP modem

PORT: female   PORT TYPE: serial _____
CONNECTOR: DB25 9-pin 8-pin(modular)   GENDER: male female
CONFIGURATION: C14

PIN	FUNCTION	DIRECTION
2:TD	Transmit Data	TO
3:RD	Receive Data	FROM
4:RTS	Request to Send	TO
5:CTS	Clear to Send	FROM
6:DSR	Data Set Ready	FROM
7:SG	Signal Ground	N/A
8:DCD	Data Carrier Detect	FROM
20:DTR	Data Terminal Ready	TO
22:RI	Ring Indicator	FROM

FLOW CONTROL   XON: ACK: LEADS THAT MUST BE ON: _____
SPEEDS: 110 300 600 1200 1800 2400 4800 9600 19.2 56k _____
COMPATIBILITY: 103 212 V.22bis

_____
PARITY: even odd space mark none   CHARACTER LENGTH: 7 8 ___
STOP BITS: 1 1.5 2   LINE-ENDING CHARs: cr lf cr/lf
AUTO-ANSWER: yes no   RTS/CTS delay: ___
DISCONNECT SEQUENCE: EOT DEL _____
INTELLIGENT MODEMS....
    Dialing Technique: Touch-tone Pulse
    Compatibility: Hayes _____
    Command Line Prefix: AT _____   Dial command: D _____
    Touch-tone dial: T ___   Pulse dial: P ___ Pause: , ___
    Wait for dial tone: W ___   Wait for quiet answer: @ ___
    Flash: ! ___   Dial stored number: S ___
    Return to command state after dialing: ; ___
    Escape sequence: +++ ___   Switch-Hook control: H ___
    Store Phone#: &Z ___
Mode: async sync isoch
NOTE 1:
NOTE 2:

MODEM PORT PROFILE (Underline if supported, circle if selected)
COMPANY: Racal-Vadic
PRODUCT: 2400PA/1200PA modems

PORT: female   PORT TYPE: serial _____
CONNECTOR: DB25 9-pin 8-pin(modular) GENDER: male female
CONFIGURATION: C14

PIN	FUNCTION	DIRECTION
1:PG	Protective Ground	N/A
2:TD	Transmit Data	TO
3:RD	Receive Data	FROM
4:RTS	Request to Send	TO
5:CTS	Clear to Send	FROM
6:DSR	Data Set Ready	FROM
7:SG	Signal Ground	N/A
8:CD	Carrier Detect	FROM
9:+V		FROM
10:-V		FROM
12:SS	Speed Select	FROM
15:TC	Transmit Clock	FROM
17:RC	Rec. Clk/Reverse Chann	FROM
20:DTR	Data Terminal Ready	TO
22:RI	Ring Indicator	FROM
24:ETC	External Transmit Cloc	TO

FLOW CONTROL   XON: ACK: LEADS THAT MUST BE ON: _____
SPEEDS: 110 300 600 1200 1800 2400 4800 9600 19.2 56k _____
COMPATIBILITY: 103 212 V.22bis

_____
PARITY: even odd space mark none   CHARACTER LENGTH: 7 8 ___
STOP BITS: 1 1.5 2   LINE-ENDING CHARs: cr lf cr/lf
AUTO-ANSWER: yes no   RTS/CTS delay: ___
DISCONNECT SEQUENCE: EOT DEL _____
INTELLIGENT MODEMS....
      Dialing Technique: Touch-tone Pulse
     Compatibility: Hayes _____
     Command Line Prefix: AT _____   Dial command: D _____
     Touch-tone dial: T ___   Pulse dial: P ___   Pause: , ___
     Wait for dial tone: W ___   Wait for quiet answer: @ ___
     Flash: ! ___   Dial stored number: S ___
     Return to command state after dialing: ; ___
     Escape sequence: +++ ___   Switch-Hook control: H ___
     Store Phone#: &Z ___
Mode: async sync isoch
NOTE 1:
NOTE 2:

MODEM PORT PROFILE (Underline if supported, circle if selected)
COMPANY: Racal-Vadic
PRODUCT: 2400V modem

PORT: female   PORT TYPE: serial _____
CONNECTOR: DB25 9-pin 8-pin(modular)   GENDER: male female
CONFIGURATION: C14

PIN	FUNCTION	DIRECTION
1:FG	Frame Ground	N/A
2:TD	Transmit Data	TO
3:RD	Receive Data	FROM
4:RTS	Request to Send	TO
5:CTS	Clear to Send	FROM
6:DSR	Data Set Ready	FROM
7:SG	Signal Ground	N/A
8:CD	Carrier Detect	FROM
9:+V		FROM
10:-V		FROM
15:TC	Transmit Clock	FROM
17:RC	Rec. Clk/Reverse Chann	FROM
20:DTR	Data Terminal Ready	TO
22:RI	Ring Indicator	FROM

FLOW CONTROL   XON: ACK: LEADS THAT MUST BE ON: _____
SPEEDS: 110 300 600 1200 1800 2400 4800 9600 19.2 56k _____
COMPATIBILITY: 103 212 V.22bis

_____
PARITY: even odd space mark none   CHARACTER LENGTH: 7 8 ___
STOP BITS: 1 1.5 2   LINE-ENDING CHARs: cr lf cr/lf
AUTO-ANSWER: yes no   RTS/CTS delay: ___
DISCONNECT SEQUENCE: EOT DEL _____
INTELLIGENT MODEMS....
    Dialing Technique: Touch-tone Pulse
    Compatibility: Hayes _____
    Command Line Prefix: AT _____   Dial command: D _____
    Touch-tone dial: T ___   Pulse dial: P ___ Pause: , ___
    Wait for dial tone: W ___   Wait for quiet answer: @ ___
    Flash: ! ___   Dial stored number: S ___
    Return to command state after dialing: ; ___
    Escape sequence: +++ ___   Switch-Hook control: H ___
    Store Phone#: &Z ___
Mode: async sync isoch
NOTE 1: Leads 20 & 4 must be on to send data.
NOTE 2:

MODEM PORT PROFILE (Underline if supported, circle if selected)
COMPANY: Racal-Vadic
PRODUCT: 9600VP modem

PORT: female   PORT TYPE: serial _____
CONNECTOR: DB25 9-pin 8-pin(modular) GENDER: male female
CONFIGURATION: C14

PIN	FUNCTION	DIRECTION
1:PG	Protective Ground	N/A
2:TD	Transmit Data	TO
3:RD	Receive Data	FROM
4:RTS	Request to Send	TO
5:CTS	Clear to Send	FROM
6:DSR	Data Set Ready	FROM
7:SG	Signal Ground	N/A
8:CD	Carrier Detect	FROM
9:+V		FROM
10:-V		FROM
12:SS	Speed Select	FROM
15:TC	Transmit Clock	FROM
17:RC	Rec. Clk/Reverse Chann	FROM
20:DTR	Data Terminal Ready	TO
22:RI	Ring Indicator	FROM
24:ETC	External Transmit Cloc	TO

FLOW CONTROL   XON: ACK: LEADS THAT MUST BE ON: _____
SPEEDS: 110 300 600 1200 1800 2400 4800 9600 19.2 56k _____
COMPATIBILITY: 103 212 V.22bis

_____
PARITY: even odd space mark none   CHARACTER LENGTH: 7 8 ___
STOP BITS: 1 1.5 2   LINE-ENDING CHARs: cr lf cr/lf
AUTO-ANSWER: yes no   RTS/CTS delay: ___
DISCONNECT SEQUENCE: EOT DEL _____
INTELLIGENT MODEMS....
     Dialing Technique: Touch-tone Pulse
     Compatibility: Hayes _____
     Command Line Prefix: AT _____   Dial command: D _____
     Touch-tone dial: T ___   Pulse dial: P ___   Pause: , ___
     Wait for dial tone: W ___   Wait for quiet answer: @ ___
     Flash: ! ___   Dial stored number: S ___
     Return to command state after dialing: ; ___
     Escape sequence: +++ ___   Switch-Hook control: H ___
     Store Phone#: &Z ___
Mode: async sync isoch
NOTE 1:
NOTE 2:

MODEM PORT PROFILE (Underline if supported, circle if selected)
COMPANY: Racal-Vadic
PRODUCT: VA2450,55P/S/G/K modems

PORT: female   PORT TYPE: serial _____
CONNECTOR: DB25 9-pin 8-pin(modular) GENDER: male female
CONFIGURATION: C09

PIN	FUNCTION	DIRECTION
1:CG	Chassis Ground	N/A
2:TD	Transmit Data	TO
3:RD	Receive Data	FROM
4:RTS	Request to Send	TO
5:CTS	Clear to Send	FROM
6:DSR	Data Set Ready	FROM
7:SG	Signal Ground	N/A
8:CD	Carrier Detect	FROM
9:+12V		FROM
10:-12V		FROM
12:SCD		FROM
13:SCTS	Secondary Cl'r to Send	FROM
14:STD	Supervisory Trans.Data	TO
15:TC	Transmit Clock	FROM
16:SRD	Supervisory Rec. Data	FROM
17:RC	Rec. Clk/Reverse Chann	FROM
18:B	Busy	TO
19:SRTS	Secondary Req.to Send	TO
20:DTR	Data Terminal Ready	TO
22:RI	Ring Indicator	FROM
24:ETC	External Transmit Cloc	TO
25:B	Busy	TO

FLOW CONTROL   XON: ACK: LEADS THAT MUST BE ON: _____
SPEEDS: 110 300 600 1200 1800 2400 4800 9600 19.2 56k _____
COMPATIBILITY: 103 212 V.22bis

_____
PARITY: even odd space mark none   CHARACTER LENGTH: 7 8 ___
STOP BITS: 1 1.5 2   LINE-ENDING CHARs: cr lf cr/lf
AUTO-ANSWER: yes no   RTS/CTS delay: ___
DISCONNECT SEQUENCE: EOT DEL _____
INTELLIGENT MODEMS....
     Dialing Technique: Touch-tone Pulse
     Compatibility: Hayes _____
     Command Line Prefix: AT _____   Dial command: D _____
     Touch-tone dial: T ___   Pulse dial: P ___ Pause: , ___
     Wait for dial tone: W ___   Wait for quiet answer: @ ___
     Flash: ! ___   Dial stored number: S ___
     Return to command state after dialing: ; ___
     Escape sequence: +++ ___   Switch-Hook control: H ___
     Store Phone#: &Z ___
Mode: async sync isoch
NOTE 1:
NOTE 2:

MODEM PORT PROFILE (Underline if supported, circle if selected)
COMPANY: Sony
PRODUCT: MDM-1200 modem

PORT: female   PORT TYPE: serial _____
CONNECTOR: DB25 9-pin 8-pin(modular)   GENDER: male female
CONFIGURATION: C14

PIN	FUNCTION	DIRECTION
1:PG	Protective Ground	N/A
2:TD	Transmit Data	TO
3:RD	Receive Data	FROM
5:CTS	Clear to Send	FROM
6:DSR	Data Set Ready	FROM
7:SG	Signal Ground	N/A
8:CD	Carrier Detect	FROM
12:SS	Speed Select	FROM
20:DTR	Data Terminal Ready	TO
22:RI	Ring Indicator	FROM
25:TM		FROM

FLOW CONTROL   XON: ACK: LEADS THAT MUST BE ON: _____
SPEEDS: 110 300 600 1200 1800 2400 4800 9600 19.2 56k _____
COMPATIBILITY: 103 212 V.22bis

_____
PARITY: even odd space mark none   CHARACTER LENGTH: 7 8 ___
STOP BITS: 1 1.5 2   LINE-ENDING CHARs: cr lf cr/lf
AUTO-ANSWER: yes no   RTS/CTS delay: ___
DISCONNECT SEQUENCE: EOT DEL _____
INTELLIGENT MODEMS....
     Dialing Technique: Touch-tone Pulse
     Compatibility: Hayes _____
     Command Line Prefix: AT _____   Dial command: D _____
     Touch-tone dial: T ___   Pulse dial: P ___ Pause: , ___
     Wait for dial tone: W ___   Wait for quiet answer: @ ___
     Flash: ! ___   Dial stored number: S ___
     Return to command state after dialing: ; ___
     Escape sequence: +++ ___   Switch-Hook control: H ___
     Store Phone#: &Z ___
Mode: async sync isoch
NOTE 1:
NOTE 2:

MODEM PORT PROFILE (Underline if supported, circle if selected)
COMPANY: Teltone Corporation
PRODUCT: DCS-2B (M-822)

PORT: female   PORT TYPE: serial _____
CONNECTOR: DB25 9-pin 8-pin(modular)   GENDER: male female
CONFIGURATION: C14

PIN	FUNCTION	DIRECTION
2:TD	Transmit Data	TO
3:RD	Receive Data	FROM
4:RTS	Request to Send	TO
5:CTS	Clear to Send	FROM
6:DSR	Data Set Ready	FROM
7:SG	Signal Ground	N/A
8:RLSD	Rec.Line Signal Detect	FROM
20:DTR	Data Terminal Ready	TO

FLOW CONTROL   XON: ACK: LEADS THAT MUST BE ON: _____
SPEEDS: 110 300 600 1200 1800 2400 4800 9600 19.2 56k _____
COMPATIBILITY: 103 212 V.22bis

_____
PARITY: even odd space mark none   CHARACTER LENGTH: 7 8 ___
STOP BITS: 1 1.5 2   LINE-ENDING CHARs: cr lf cr/lf
AUTO-ANSWER: yes no   RTS/CTS delay: ___
DISCONNECT SEQUENCE: EOT DEL _____
INTELLIGENT MODEMS....
     Dialing Technique: Touch-tone Pulse
     Compatibility: Hayes _____
     Command Line Prefix: AT _____   Dial command: D _____
     Touch-tone dial: T ___   Pulse dial: P ___   Pause: , ___
     Wait for dial tone: W ___   Wait for quiet answer: @ ___
     Flash: ! ___   Dial stored number: S ___
     Return to command state after dialing: ; ___
     Escape sequence: +++ ___   Switch-Hook control: H ___
     Store Phone#: &Z ___
Mode: async sync isoch
NOTE 1:
NOTE 2:

MODEM PORT PROFILE (Underline if supported, circle if selected)
COMPANY: USRobotics, Inc.
PRODUCT: Auto Dial 212A modem

PORT: female   PORT TYPE: serial _____
CONNECTOR: DB25 9-pin 8-pin(modular)   GENDER: male female
CONFIGURATION: C14

PIN	FUNCTION	DIRECTION
2:TD	Transmit Data	TO
3:RD	Receive Data	FROM
5:CTS	Clear to Send	FROM
6:DSR	Data Set Ready	FROM
7:SG	Signal Ground	N/A
8:CD	Carrier Detect	FROM
12:SS	Speed Select	FROM
20:DTR	Data Terminal Ready	TO
22:RI	Ring Indicator	FROM

FLOW CONTROL   XON: ACK: LEADS THAT MUST BE ON: _____
SPEEDS: 110 300 600 1200 1800 2400 4800 9600 19.2 56k _____
COMPATIBILITY: 103 212 V.22bis

_____

PARITY: even odd space mark none   CHARACTER LENGTH: 7 8 ___
STOP BITS: 1 1.5 2   LINE-ENDING CHARs: cr lf cr/lf
AUTO-ANSWER: yes no   RTS/CTS delay: ___
DISCONNECT SEQUENCE: EOT DEL _____
INTELLIGENT MODEMS....
    Dialing Technique: Touch-tone Pulse
    Compatibility: Hayes _____
    Command Line Prefix: AT _____   Dial command: D _____
    Touch-tone dial: T ___   Pulse dial: P ___ Pause: , ___
    Wait for dial tone: W ___   Wait for quiet answer: @ ___
    Flash: ! ___   Dial stored number: S ___
    Return to command state after dialing: ; ___
    Escape sequence: +++ ___   Switch-Hook control: H ___
    Store Phone#: &Z ___
Mode: async sync isoch
NOTE 1:
NOTE 2:

MODEM PORT PROFILE   (Underline if supported, circle if selected)
COMPANY: USRobotics, Inc.
PRODUCT: Courier 1200 & 2400

PORT: female   PORT TYPE: serial _____

CONNECTOR: DB25 9-pin 8-pin(modular)   GENDER: male female

CONFIGURATION: C14

PIN	FUNCTION	DIRECTION
2:TD	Transmit Data	TO
3:RD	Receive Data	FROM
5:CTS	Clear to Send	FROM
6:DSR	Data Set Ready	FROM
7:SG	Signal Ground	N/A
8:CD	Carrier Detect	FROM
12:SS	Speed Select	FROM
20:DTR	Data Terminal Ready	TO
22:RI	Ring Indicator	FROM

FLOW CONTROL   XON: ACK: LEADS THAT MUST BE ON: _____

SPEEDS: 110 300 600 1200 1800 2400 4800 9600 19.2 56k _____

COMPATIBILITY: 103 212 V.22bis

_____

PARITY: even odd space mark none   CHARACTER LENGTH: 7 8 ___

STOP BITS: 1 1.5 2   LINE-ENDING CHARs: cr lf cr/lf

AUTO-ANSWER: yes no   RTS/CTS delay: ___

DISCONNECT SEQUENCE: EOT DEL _____

INTELLIGENT MODEMS....

    Dialing Technique: Touch-tone Pulse

  Compatibility: Hayes _____

  Command Line Prefix: AT _____   Dial command: D _____

  Touch-tone dial: T ___   Pulse dial: P ___   Pause: , ___

  Wait for dial tone: W ___   Wait for quiet answer: @ ___

  Flash: ! ___   Dial stored number: S ___

  Return to command state after dialing: ; ___

  Escape sequence: +++ ___   Switch-Hook control: H ___

  Store Phone#: &Z ___

Mode: async sync isoch

NOTE 1:

NOTE 2:

MODEM PORT PROFILE   (Underline if supported, circle if selected)
COMPANY: USRobotics, Inc.
PRODUCT: Microlink 1200 & 2400 modem

PORT: female   PORT TYPE: serial _____
CONNECTOR: DB25 9-pin 8-pin(modular)   GENDER: male female
CONFIGURATION: C14

PIN	FUNCTION	DIRECTION
2:TD	Transmit Data	TO
3:RD	Receive Data	FROM
5:CTS	Clear to Send	FROM
6:DSR	Data Set Ready	FROM
7:SG	Signal Ground	N/A
8:CD	Carrier Detect	FROM
12:SS	Speed Select	FROM
20:DTR	Data Terminal Ready	TO
22:RI	Ring Indicator	FROM

FLOW CONTROL   XON: ACK: LEADS THAT MUST BE ON: _____
SPEEDS: 110 300 600 1200 1800 2400 4800 9600 19.2 56k _____
COMPATIBILITY: 103 212 V.22bis

_____

PARITY: even odd space mark none   CHARACTER LENGTH: 7 8 ___
STOP BITS: 1 1.5 2   LINE-ENDING CHARs: cr lf cr/lf
AUTO-ANSWER: yes no   RTS/CTS delay: ___
DISCONNECT SEQUENCE: EOT DEL _____
INTELLIGENT MODEMS....
     Dialing Technique: Touch-tone Pulse
  Compatibility: Hayes _____
  Command Line Prefix: AT _____   Dial command: D _____
  Touch-tone dial: T ___   Pulse dial: P ___ Pause: , ___
  Wait for dial tone: W ___   Wait for quiet answer: @ ___
  Flash: ! ___   Dial stored number: S ___
  Return to command state after dialing: ; ___
  Escape sequence: +++ ___   Switch-Hook control: H ___
  Store Phone#: &Z ___
Mode: async sync isoch
NOTE 1:
NOTE 2:

MODEM PORT PROFILE (Underline if supported, circle if selected)
COMPANY: USRobotics, Inc.
PRODUCT: Password modem

PORT: female   PORT TYPE: serial _____
CONNECTOR: DB25 9-pin 8-pin(modular)   GENDER: male female
CONFIGURATION: C14

PIN	FUNCTION	DIRECTION
2:TD	Transmit Data	TO
3:RD	Receive Data	FROM
5:CTS	Clear to Send	FROM
6:DSR	Data Set Ready	FROM
7:SG	Signal Ground	N/A
8:CD	Carrier Detect	FROM
12:SS	Speed Select	FROM
20:DTR	Data Terminal Ready	TO
22:RI	Ring Indicator	FROM

FLOW CONTROL   XON: ACK: LEADS THAT MUST BE ON: _____
SPEEDS: 110 300 600 1200 1800 2400 4800 9600 19.2 56k _____
COMPATIBILITY: 103 212 V.22bis

_____
PARITY: even odd space mark none   CHARACTER LENGTH: 7 8 ___
STOP BITS: 1 1.5 2   LINE-ENDING CHARs: cr lf cr/lf
AUTO-ANSWER: yes no   RTS/CTS delay: ___
DISCONNECT SEQUENCE: EOT DEL _____
INTELLIGENT MODEMS....
     Dialing Technique: Touch-tone Pulse
    Compatibility: Hayes _____
    Command Line Prefix: AT _____   Dial command: D _____
    Touch-tone dial: T ___   Pulse dial: P ___ Pause: , ___
    Wait for dial tone: W ___   Wait for quiet answer: @ ___
    Flash: ! ___   Dial stored number: S ___
    Return to command state after dialing: ; ___
    Escape sequence: +++ ___   Switch-Hook control: H ___
    Store Phone#: &Z ___
Mode: async sync isoch
NOTE 1:
NOTE 2:

MODEM PORT PROFILE (Underline if supported, circle if selected)
COMPANY: _____
PRODUCT: _____

PORT: _____   Port Type: serial
CONNECTOR: DB25 9-pin 8-pin(modular)   Gender: male female
Pin Configuration: ___

Pin #	Function	Direction	Pin #	Function	Direction
1	_____	to from n/a	14	_____	to from n/a
2	_____	to from n/a	15	_____	to from n/a
3	_____	to from n/a	16	_____	to from n/a
4	_____	to from n/a	17	_____	to from n/a
5	_____	to from n/a	18	_____	to from n/a
6	_____	to from n/a	19	_____	to from n/a
7	_____	to from n/a	20	_____	to from n/a
8	_____	to from n/a	21	_____	to from n/a
9	_____	to from n/a	22	_____	to from n/a
10	_____	to from n/a	23	_____	to from n/a
11	_____	to from n/a	24	_____	to from n/a
12	_____	to from n/a	25	_____	to from n/a
13	_____	to from n/a			

(complete the next section only with 36-pin cinch connectors)

Pin #	Function	Direction	Pin #	Function	Direction
26	_____	to from n/a	27	_____	to from n/a
28	_____	to from n/a	29	_____	to from n/a
30	_____	to from n/a	31	_____	to from n/a
32	_____	to from n/a	33	_____	to from n/a
34	_____	to from n/a	35	_____	to from n/a
36	_____	to from n/a			

Flow Control Technique: XON/XOFF ENQ/ACK STX/ETX
Leads that must be on: 5 6 8 __ __ __
Speeds: 110 300 600 1200 1800 2400 4800 9600 19.2 56k _____
COMPATIBILITY: 103 212 V.22bis _____
Parity: even odd space mark none   CHARACTER LENGTH: 7 8 ___
Stop Bits: 1 1.5 2   Line Ending Sequence: cr lf cr/lf
AUTO-ANSWER: yes no   RTS/CTS delay: ____
DISCONNECT SEQUENCE: EOT DEL _____
INTELLIGENT MODEMS....
  Dialing Technique: Touch-tone   Pulse
  Compatibility: Hayes _____
  Command Line Prefix: AT _____   Dial Command: D ____
  Touch-tone Dial: T _____   Pulse Dial: P ___ Pause: , __
  Wait for Dial Tone: W _____   Wait for Quiet Answer: @ __
  Flash: ! _____   Dial Stored Number: S _____
  Return to Command State After Dialing:
  Escape Sequence: +++ _____   Switch-Hook Control: H _____
  Store Phone#: &Z _____
Mode: async sync isoch
NOTE 1:_____
NOTE 2:_____

MODEM PORT PROFILE (Underline if supported, circle if selected)
COMPANY: _____
PRODUCT: _____

PORT: _____   Port Type: serial
CONNECTOR: DB25 9-pin 8-pin(modular)   Gender: male female
Pin Configuration: ___

Pin #	Function	Direction	Pin #	Function	Direction
1	_____	to from n/a	14	_____	to from n/a
2	_____	to from n/a	15	_____	to from n/a
3	_____	to from n/a	16	_____	to from n/a
4	_____	to from n/a	17	_____	to from n/a
5	_____	to from n/a	18	_____	to from n/a
6	_____	to from n/a	19	_____	to from n/a
7	_____	to from n/a	20	_____	to from n/a
8	_____	to from n/a	21	_____	to from n/a
9	_____	to from n/a	22	_____	to from n/a
10	_____	to from n/a	23	_____	to from n/a
11	_____	to from n/a	24	_____	to from n/a
12	_____	to from n/a	25	_____	to from n/a
13	_____	to from n/a			

(complete the next section only with 36-pin cinch connectors)

Pin #	Function	Direction	Pin #	Function	Direction
26	_____	to from n/a	27	_____	to from n/a
28	_____	to from n/a	29	_____	to from n/a
30	_____	to from n/a	31	_____	to from n/a
32	_____	to from n/a	33	_____	to from n/a
34	_____	to from n/a	35	_____	to from n/a
36	_____	to from n/a			

Flow Control Technique: XON/XOFF ENQ/ACK STX/ETX
Leads that must be on: 5 6 8 ___ ___ ___
Speeds: 110 300 600 1200 1800 2400 4800 9600 19.2 56k _____
COMPATIBILITY: 103 212 V.22bis _____
Parity: even odd space mark none _____   CHARACTER LENGTH: 7 8 ___
Stop Bits: 1 1.5 2   Line Ending Sequence: cr lf cr/lf
AUTO-ANSWER: yes no   RTS/CTS delay: ____
DISCONNECT SEQUENCE: EOT DEL _____
INTELLIGENT MODEMS....
  Dialing Technique: Touch-tone   Pulse
  Compatibility: Hayes _____
  Command Line Prefix: AT _____   Dial Command: D ____
  Touch-tone Dial: T _____   Pulse Dial: P ___ Pause: , __
  Wait for Dial Tone: W _____   Wait for Quiet Answer: @ __
  Flash: ! _____   Dial Stored Number: S _____
  Return to Command State After Dialing: ; _____
  Escape Sequence: +++ _____   Switch-Hook Control: H _____
  Store Phone#: &Z _____
Mode: async sync isoch
NOTE 1:_____
NOTE 2:_____

MODEM PORT PROFILE (Underline if supported, circle if selected)
COMPANY: _____
PRODUCT: _____

PORT: _____   Port Type: serial
CONNECTOR: DB25 9-pin 8-pin(modular)   Gender: male female
Pin Configuration: ___

Pin #	Function	Direction	Pin #	Function	Direction
1	_____	to from n/a	14	_____	to from n/a
2	_____	to from n/a	15	_____	to from n/a
3	_____	to from n/a	16	_____	to from n/a
4	_____	to from n/a	17	_____	to from n/a
5	_____	to from n/a	18	_____	to from n/a
6	_____	to from n/a	19	_____	to from n/a
7	_____	to from n/a	20	_____	to from n/a
8	_____	to from n/a	21	_____	to from n/a
9	_____	to from n/a	22	_____	to from n/a
10	_____	to from n/a	23	_____	to from n/a
11	_____	to from n/a	24	_____	to from n/a
12	_____	to from n/a	25	_____	to from n/a
13	_____	to from n/a			

(complete the next section only with 36-pin cinch connectors)

Pin #	Function	Direction	Pin #	Function	Direction
26	_____	to from n/a	27	_____	to from n/a
28	_____	to from n/a	29	_____	to from n/a
30	_____	to from n/a	31	_____	to from n/a
32	_____	to from n/a	33	_____	to from n/a
34	_____	to from n/a	35	_____	to from n/a
36	_____	to from n/a			

Flow Control Technique: XON/XOFF ENQ/ACK STX/ETX
Leads that must be on: 5 6 8 __ __ __ __
Speeds: 110 300 600 1200 1800 2400 4800 9600 19.2 56k _____
COMPATIBILITY: 103 212 V.22bis _____
Parity: even odd space mark none _____   CHARACTER LENGTH: 7 8 ___
Stop Bits: 1 1.5 2   Line Ending Sequence: cr lf cr/lf
AUTO-ANSWER: yes no   RTS/CTS delay: ____
DISCONNECT SEQUENCE: EOT DEL _____
INTELLIGENT MODEMS....
  Dialing Technique: Touch-tone   Pulse
  Compatibility: Hayes _____
  Command Line Prefix: AT _____   Dial Command: D ____
  Touch-tone Dial: T _____   Pulse Dial: P ___ Pause: , __
  Wait for Dial Tone: W _____   Wait for Quiet Answer: @ __
  Flash: ! _____   Dial Stored Number: S _____
  Return to Command State After Dialing: ; _____
  Escape Sequence: +++ _____   Switch-Hook Control: H _____
  Store Phone#: &Z _____
Mode: async sync isoch
NOTE 1:_____
NOTE 2:_____

MODEM PORT PROFILE (Underline if supported, circle if selected)
COMPANY: _____
PRODUCT: _____

PORT: _____   Port Type: serial
CONNECTOR: DB25 9-pin 8-pin(modular)   Gender: male female
Pin Configuration: ___

Pin #	Function	Direction	Pin #	Function	Direction
1	_____	to from n/a	14	_____	to from n/a
2	_____	to from n/a	15	_____	to from n/a
3	_____	to from n/a	16	_____	to from n/a
4	_____	to from n/a	17	_____	to from n/a
5	_____	to from n/a	18	_____	to from n/a
6	_____	to from n/a	19	_____	to from n/a
7	_____	to from n/a	20	_____	to from n/a
8	_____	to from n/a	21	_____	to from n/a
9	_____	to from n/a	22	_____	to from n/a
10	_____	to from n/a	23	_____	to from n/a
11	_____	to from n/a	24	_____	to from n/a
12	_____	to from n/a	25	_____	to from n/a
13	_____	to from n/a			

(complete the next section only with 36-pin cinch connectors)

Pin #	Function	Direction	Pin #	Function	Direction
26	_____	to from n/a	27	_____	to from n/a
28	_____	to from n/a	29	_____	to from n/a
30	_____	to from n/a	31	_____	to from n/a
32	_____	to from n/a	33	_____	to from n/a
34	_____	to from n/a	35	_____	to from n/a
36	_____	to from n/a			

Flow Control Technique: XON/XOFF ENQ/ACK STX/ETX
Leads that must be on: 5   6   8 __ __ __ __
Speeds: 110 300 600 1200 1800 2400 4800 9600 19.2 56k _____
COMPATIBILITY: 103 212 V.22bis _____
Parity: even odd space mark none   CHARACTER LENGTH: 7 8 ___
Stop Bits: 1 1.5 2   Line Ending Sequence: cr lf cr/lf
AUTO-ANSWER: yes no   RTS/CTS delay: ____
DISCONNECT SEQUENCE: EOT DEL _____
INTELLIGENT MODEMS....
  Dialing Technique: Touch-tone   Pulse
  Compatibility: Hayes _____
  Command Line Prefix: AT _____   Dial Command: D ____
  Touch-tone Dial: T _____   Pulse Dial: P ___ Pause: , __
  Wait for Dial Tone: W _____   Wait for Quiet Answer: @ __
  Flash: ! _____   Dial Stored Number: S _____
  Return to Command State After Dialing: ; _____
  Escape Sequence: +++ _____   Switch-Hook Control: H _____
  Store Phone#: &Z _____
Mode: async sync isoch
NOTE 1:_____
NOTE 2:_____

PRINTER PORT PROFILE (Underline if supported, circle if selected)
COMPANY: Applied Computer Sciences, Inc
PRODUCT: ACS/HP Laser Printer

PORT: female   PORT TYPE: serial
CONNECTOR: DB25 DB9 5-PIN 8-PIN Centronics   GENDER: male female
PIN CONFIGURATION: P11

PIN	FUNCTION	DIRECTION
1:CG	Chassis Ground	N/A
2:TD	Transmit Data	FROM
3:RD	Receive Data	TO
7:SG	Signal Ground	N/A
20:DTR	Data Terminal Ready	FROM

FLOW CONTROL: 20   XON: YES ACK: LEADS THAT MUST BE ON:_____
SPEEDS: 110 300 600 1200 1800 2400 4800 9600 19.2 56k _____
PARITY: even odd space mark none   CHARACTER LENGTH: 7 8 ___
STOP BITS: 1 1.5 2   LINE-ENDING SEQUENCE: cr lf cr/lf
PRINTER COMPATIBILITY MODES: EpsonMX/FX/RX Diablo630 HPLaserJet NEC3500
  IBMgraphics Printronix TI-810_____   MODE: async sync isoch
PAGE DESCRIPTION LANGUAGE: PostScript DDL _____
NOTE 1:
NOTE 2:

PRINTER PORT PROFILE (Underline if supported, circle if selected)
COMPANY: Applied Computer Sciences, Inc
PRODUCT: Primage 90 printer

PORT: PORT TYPE: serial
CONNECTOR: DB25 DB9 5-PIN 8-PIN Centronics   GENDER: male female
PIN CONFIGURATION: P04

PIN	FUNCTION	DIRECTION
1:G	Ground	N/A
2:TD	Transmit Data	FROM
3:RD	Receive Data	TO
4:RTS	Request to Send	FROM
7:SG	Signal Ground	N/A
11:PB	Printer Busy	FROM
20:DTR	Data Terminal Ready	FROM

FLOW CONTROL: 11 20   XON: YES ACK: LEADS THAT MUST BE ON:_____
SPEEDS: 110 300 600 1200 1800 2400 4800 9600 19.2 56k _____
PARITY: even odd space mark none   CHARACTER LENGTH: 7 8 ___
STOP BITS: 1 1.5 2   LINE-ENDING SEQUENCE: cr lf cr/lf
PRINTER COMPATIBILITY MODES: EpsonMX/FX/RX Diablo630 HPLaserJet NEC3500
  IBMgraphics Printronix TI-810_____   MODE: async sync isoch
PAGE DESCRIPTION LANGUAGE: PostScript DDL _____
NOTE 1:
NOTE 2:

PRINTER PORT PROFILE (Underline if supported, circle if selected)
COMPANY: Applied Engineering
PRODUCT: Serial Pro board

PORT: female (modem port)   PORT TYPE: serial
CONNECTOR: DB25 DB9 5-PIN 8-PIN Centronics   GENDER: male female
PIN CONFIGURATION: C07

PIN	FUNCTION	DIRECTION
1:CG	Chassis Ground	N/A
2:TD	Transmit Data	FROM
3:RD	Receive Data	TO
6:DSR	Data Set Ready	TO
7:SG	Signal Ground	N/A
8:DCD	Data Carrier Detect	TO
20:DTR	Data Terminal Ready	FROM

FLOW CONTROL: XON: ACK: LEADS THAT MUST BE ON:_____
SPEEDS: 110 300 600 1200 1800 2400 4800 9600 19.2 56k _____
PARITY: even odd space mark none   CHARACTER LENGTH: 7 8 ___
STOP BITS: 1 1.5 2   LINE-ENDING SEQUENCE: cr lf cr/lf
PRINTER COMPATIBILITY MODES: EpsonMX/FX/RX Diablo630 HPLaserJet NEC3500
  IBMgraphics Printronix TI-810_____ MODE: async sync isoch
PAGE DESCRIPTION LANGUAGE: PostScript DDL _____
NOTE 1:
NOTE 2:

PRINTER PORT PROFILE (Underline if supported, circle if selected)
COMPANY: Applied Engineering
PRODUCT: Serial Pro board

PORT: female-printer port   PORT TYPE: serial
CONNECTOR: DB25 DB9 5-PIN 8-PIN Centronics   GENDER: male female
PIN CONFIGURATION: C09

PIN	FUNCTION	DIRECTION	PIN	FUNCTION	DIRECTION
1:CG	Chassis Ground	N/A	7:SG	Signal Ground	N/A
2:RD	Receive Data	TO	8:DTR	Data Terminal Ready	FROM
3:TD	Transmit Data	FROM	11:DCD	Data Carrier Detect	TO
4:DCD	Data Carrier Detect	TO	19:DCD	Data Carrier Detect	TO
6:DTR	Data Terminal Ready	FROM	20:DCD	Data Carrier Detect	TO

FLOW CONTROL: 20 4 11 19 XON: YES ACK: LEADS THAT MUST BE ON:_____
SPEEDS: 110 300 600 1200 1800 2400 4800 9600 19.2 56k _____
PARITY: even odd space mark none   CHARACTER LENGTH: 7 8 ___
STOP BITS: 1 1.5 2   LINE-ENDING SEQUENCE: cr lf cr/lf
PRINTER COMPATIBILITY MODES: EpsonMX/FX/RX Diablo630 HPLaserJet NEC3500
  IBMgraphics Printronix TI-810_____ MODE: async sync isoch
PAGE DESCRIPTION LANGUAGE: PostScript DDL _____
NOTE 1:
NOTE 2:

PRINTER PORT PROFILE   (Underline if supported, circle if selected)
COMPANY: AT&T
PRODUCT: 5310/5320 teleprinter

PORT: EIA   PORT TYPE: serial
CONNECTOR: DB25 DB9 5-PIN 8-PIN Centronics   GENDER: male female
PIN CONFIGURATION: P05

PIN	FUNCTION	DIRECTION	PIN	FUNCTION	DIRECTION
1:PG	Protective Ground	N/A	8:DCD	Data Carrier Detect	TO
2:TD	Transmit Data	FROM	11:SRTS	Secondary Req.to Send	FROM
3:RD	Receive Data	TO	12:SS	Speed Select	TO
4:RTS	Request to Send	FROM	19:SRTS	Secondary Req.to Send	FROM
6:DSR	Data Set Ready	TO	20:DTR	Data Terminal Ready	FROM
7:SG	Signal Ground	N/A	22:RI	Ring Indicator	TO

FLOW CONTROL: 11   XON: YES ACK: LEADS THAT MUST BE ON:_____
SPEEDS: 110 300 600 1200 1800 2400 4800 9600 19.2 56k _____
PARITY: even odd space mark none   CHARACTER LENGTH: 7 8 ___
STOP BITS: 1 1.5 2   LINE-ENDING SEQUENCE: cr lf cr/lf
PRINTER COMPATIBILITY MODES: EpsonMX/FX/RX Diablo630 HPLaserJet NEC3500
   IBMgraphics Printronix TI-810_____ MODE: async sync isoch
PAGE DESCRIPTION LANGUAGE: PostScript DDL _____
NOTE 1: male port
NOTE 2: rts is tied active

PRINTER PORT PROFILE   (Underline if supported, circle if selected)
COMPANY: Blue Chip Electronics
PRODUCT: 256X line printers (26067A/B interface)

PORT: serial   PORT TYPE: serial
CONNECTOR: DB25 DB9 5-PIN 8-PIN Centronics   GENDER: male female
PIN CONFIGURATION: P03

PIN	FUNCTION	DIRECTION
1:FG	Frame Ground	N/A
2:TD	Transmit Data	FROM
3:RD	Receive Data	TO
4:RTS	Request to Send	FROM
5:CTS	Clear to Send	TO
6:DSR	Data Set Ready	TO
7:SG	Signal Ground	N/A
8:CD	Carrier Detect	TO
20:DTR	Data Terminal Ready	FROM

FLOW CONTROL: 20   XON: YES ACK: YES LEADS THAT MUST BE ON:_____
SPEEDS: 110 300 600 1200 1800 2400 4800 9600 19.2 56k _____
PARITY: even odd space mark none   CHARACTER LENGTH: 7 8 ___
STOP BITS: 1 1.5 2   LINE-ENDING SEQUENCE: cr lf cr/lf
PRINTER COMPATIBILITY MODES: EpsonMX/FX/RX Diablo630 HPLaserJet NEC3500
   IBMgraphics Printronix TI-810_____ MODE: async sync isoch
PAGE DESCRIPTION LANGUAGE: PostScript DDL _____
NOTE 1:
NOTE 2:

PRINTER PORT PROFILE   (Underline if supported, circle if selected)
COMPANY: brother
PRODUCT: M-1009 printer

PORT: female   PORT TYPE: serial
CONNECTOR: DB25 DB9 5-PIN 8-PIN Centronics   GENDER: male female
PIN CONFIGURATION: P11

PIN	FUNCTION	DIRECTION
1:FG	Frame Ground	N/A
2:TD	Transmit Data	FROM
3:RD	Receive Data	TO
6:DSR	Data Set Ready	TO
7:SG	Signal Ground	N/A
11:B	Busy	FROM
20:DTR	Data Terminal Ready	FROM

FLOW CONTROL: 20 11   XON: ACK: LEADS THAT MUST BE ON:_____
SPEEDS: 110 300 600 1200 1800 2400 4800 9600 19.2 56k _____
PARITY: even odd space mark none   CHARACTER LENGTH: 7 8 ___
STOP BITS: 1 1.5 2   LINE-ENDING SEQUENCE: cr lf cr/lf
PRINTER COMPATIBILITY MODES: EpsonMX/FX/RX Diablo630 HPLaserJet NEC3500
  IBMgraphics Printronix TI-810_____ MODE: async sync isoch
PAGE DESCRIPTION LANGUAGE: PostScript DDL _____
NOTE 1:
NOTE 2:

PRINTER PORT PROFILE   (Underline if supported, circle if selected)
COMPANY: brother
PRODUCT: M-1109 printer

PORT: female   PORT TYPE: serial
CONNECTOR: DB25 DB9 5-PIN 8-PIN Centronics   GENDER: male female
PIN CONFIGURATION: P03

PIN	FUNCTION	DIRECTION
1:FG	Frame Ground	N/A
2:TD	Transmit Data	FROM
3:RD	Receive Data	TO
4:RTS	Request to Send	FROM
6:DSR	Data Set Ready	TO
7:SG	Signal Ground	N/A
11:SRTS	Secondary Req.to Send	FROM
20:DTR	Data Terminal Ready	FROM

FLOW CONTROL: 20   XON: YES ACK: LEADS THAT MUST BE ON:_____
SPEEDS: 110 300 600 1200 1800 2400 4800 9600 19.2 56k _____
PARITY: even odd space mark none   CHARACTER LENGTH: 7 8 ___
STOP BITS: 1 1.5 2   LINE-ENDING SEQUENCE: cr lf cr/lf
PRINTER COMPATIBILITY MODES: EpsonMX/FX/RX Diablo630 HPLaserJet NEC3500
  IBMgraphics Printronix TI-810_____ MODE: async sync isoch
PAGE DESCRIPTION LANGUAGE: PostScript DDL _____
NOTE 1: PIN 11 is high when the printer is busy
NOTE 2:

PRINTER PORT PROFILE (Underline if supported, circle if selected)
COMPANY: brother
PRODUCT: M-1509 printer

PORT: female   PORT TYPE: serial
CONNECTOR: DB25 DB9 5-PIN 8-PIN Centronics   GENDER: male female
PIN CONFIGURATION: P03

PIN	FUNCTION	DIRECTION	PIN	FUNCTION	DIRECTION
1:FG	Frame Ground	N/A	6:DSR	Data Set Ready	TO
2:SD	Send Data	FROM	7:SG	Signal Ground	N/A
3:RD	Receive Data	TO	8:CD	Carrier Detect	TO
4:RTS	Request to Send	FROM	14:SCA		FROM
5:CTS	Clear to Send	TO	20:DTR	Data Terminal Ready	FROM

FLOW CONTROL: 20   XON: YES ACK: LEADS THAT MUST BE ON:_____
SPEEDS: 110 300 600 1200 1800 2400 4800 9600 19.2 56k _____
PARITY: even odd space mark none   CHARACTER LENGTH: 7 8 ___
STOP BITS: 1 1.5 2   LINE-ENDING SEQUENCE: cr lf cr/lf
PRINTER COMPATIBILITY MODES: EpsonMX/FX/RX Diablo630 HPLaserJet NEC3500
   IBMgraphics Printronix TI-810_____   MODE: async sync isoch
PAGE DESCRIPTION LANGUAGE: PostScript DDL _____
NOTE 1:
NOTE 2:

PRINTER PORT PROFILE (Underline if supported, circle if selected)
COMPANY: C.Itoh
PRODUCT: 8510/1550/NLQ Prowriter printers

PORT: female   PORT TYPE: serial
CONNECTOR: DB25 DB9 5-PIN 8-PIN Centronics   GENDER: male female
PIN CONFIGURATION: P03

PIN	FUNCTION	DIRECTION	PIN	FUNCTION	DIRECTION
1:FG	Frame Ground	N/A	6:DSR	Data Set Ready	TO
2:TD	Transmit Data	FROM	7:SG	Signal Ground	N/A
3:RD	Receive Data	TO	8:CD	Carrier Detect	TO
4:RTS	Request to Send	FROM	14:F	Fault	FROM
5:CTS	Clear to Send	TO	20:DTR	Data Terminal Ready	FROM

FLOW CONTROL: 20 14   XON: YES ACK: YES LEADS THAT MUST BE ON:_____
SPEEDS: 110 300 600 1200 1800 2400 4800 9600 19.2 56k _____
PARITY: even odd space mark none   CHARACTER LENGTH: 7 8 ___
STOP BITS: 1 1.5 2   LINE-ENDING SEQUENCE: cr lf cr/lf
PRINTER COMPATIBILITY MODES: EpsonMX/FX/RX Diablo630 HPLaserJet NEC3500
   IBMgraphics Printronix TI-810_____   MODE: async sync isoch
PAGE DESCRIPTION LANGUAGE: PostScript DDL _____
NOTE 1: Leads 5/6/8 are not required if hardware flow
NOTE 2: control is used

PRINTER PORT PROFILE   (Underline if supported, circle if selected)
COMPANY: C.Itoh
PRODUCT: C-310/15 printers

PORT: PORT TYPE: serial
CONNECTOR: DB25 DB9 5-PIN 8-PIN Centronics   GENDER: male female
PIN CONFIGURATION: P08

PIN	FUNCTION	DIRECTION
1:FG	Frame Ground	N/A
2:TD	Transmit Data	FROM
3:RD	Receive Data	TO
4:RTS	Request to Send	FROM
5:CTS	Clear to Send	TO
6:DSR	Data Set Ready	TO
7:SG	Signal Ground	N/A
14:F	Fault	FROM
20:DTR	Data Terminal Ready	FROM

FLOW CONTROL: 20 14   XON: YES ACK: YES LEADS THAT MUST BE ON:_____
SPEEDS: 110 300 600 1200 1800 2400 4800 9600 19.2 56k _____
PARITY: even odd space mark none   CHARACTER LENGTH: 7 8 ___
STOP BITS: 1 1.5 2   LINE-ENDING SEQUENCE: cr lf cr/lf
PRINTER COMPATIBILITY MODES: EpsonMX/FX/RX Diablo630 HPLaserJet NEC3500
   IBMgraphics Printronix TI-810_____   MODE: async sync isoch
PAGE DESCRIPTION LANGUAGE: PostScript DDL _____
NOTE 1:
NOTE 2:

PRINTER PORT PROFILE   (Underline if supported, circle if selected)
COMPANY: Canon Inc.
PRODUCT: LBP-8 A1/A2 Laser printer

PORT: serial   PORT TYPE: serial
CONNECTOR: DB25 DB9 5-PIN 8-PIN Centronics   GENDER: male female
PIN CONFIGURATION: P08

PIN	FUNCTION	DIRECTION
1:FG	Frame Ground	N/A
2:TD	Transmit Data	FROM
3:RD	Receive Data	TO
4:RTS	Request to Send	FROM
6:DSR	Data Set Ready	TO
7:SG	Signal Ground	N/A
20:DTR	Data Terminal Ready	FROM

FLOW CONTROL: 20   XON: YES ACK: YES LEADS THAT MUST BE ON:_____
SPEEDS: 110 300 600 1200 1800 2400 4800 9600 19.2 56k _____
PARITY: even odd space mark none   CHARACTER LENGTH: 7 8 ___
STOP BITS: 1 1.5 2   LINE-ENDING SEQUENCE: cr lf cr/lf
PRINTER COMPATIBILITY MODES: EpsonMX/FX/RX Diablo630 HPLaserJet NEC3500
   IBMgraphics Printronix TI-810_____   MODE: async sync isoch
PAGE DESCRIPTION LANGUAGE: PostScript DDL _____
NOTE 1:
NOTE 2:

PRINTER PORT PROFILE   (Underline if supported, circle if selected)
COMPANY: Canon, Inc.
PRODUCT: BJ series bubble printers

PORT: female   PORT TYPE: serial
CONNECTOR: DB25 DB9 5-PIN 8-PIN Centronics   GENDER: male female
PIN CONFIGURATION: PO9

PIN	FUNCTION	DIRECTION	PIN	FUNCTION	DIRECTION
1:FG	Frame Ground	N/A	6:DSR	Data Set Ready	TO
2:TD	Transmit Data	FROM	7:SG	Signal Ground	N/A
3:RD	Receive Data	TO	8:DCD	Data Carrier Detect	TO
4:RTS	Request to Send	FROM	11:RC	Rec. Clk/Reverse Chann	FROM
5:CTS	Clear to Send	TO	20:DTR	Data Terminal Ready	FROM

FLOW CONTROL: 4   XON: YES ACK: LEADS THAT MUST BE ON:_____
SPEEDS: 110 300 600 1200 1800 2400 4800 9600 19.2 56k _____
PARITY: even odd space mark none   CHARACTER LENGTH: 7 8 ___
STOP BITS: 1 1.5 2   LINE-ENDING SEQUENCE: cr lf cr/lf
PRINTER COMPATIBILITY MODES: EpsonMX/FX/RX Diablo630 HPLaserJet NEC3500
   IBMgraphics Printronix TI-810_____   MODE: async sync isoch
PAGE DESCRIPTION LANGUAGE: PostScript DDL _____
NOTE 1:
NOTE 2:

PRINTER PORT PROFILE   (Underline if supported, circle if selected)
COMPANY: Centronics Data Computer Corp.
PRODUCT: 351 printer

PORT: serial   PORT TYPE: serial
CONNECTOR: DB25 DB9 5-PIN 8-PIN Centronics   GENDER: male female
PIN CONFIGURATION: PO5

PIN	FUNCTION	DIRECTION	PIN	FUNCTION	DIRECTION
1:PG	Protective Ground	N/A	6:DSR	Data Set Ready	TO
2:TD	Transmit Data	FROM	7:SG	Signal Ground	N/A
3:RD	Receive Data	TO	8:CD	Carrier Detect	TO
4:RTS	Request to Send	FROM	11:RC	Rec. Clk/Reverse Chann	FROM
5:CTS	Clear to Send	TO	20:DTR	Data Terminal Ready	FROM

FLOW CONTROL: 11 20   XON: YES ACK: LEADS THAT MUST BE ON:_____
SPEEDS: 110 300 600 1200 1800 2400 4800 9600 19.2 56k _____
PARITY: even odd space mark none   CHARACTER LENGTH: 7 8 ___
STOP BITS: 1 1.5 2   LINE-ENDING SEQUENCE: cr lf cr/lf
PRINTER COMPATIBILITY MODES: EpsonMX/FX/RX Diablo630 HPLaserJet NEC3500
   IBMgraphics Printronix TI-810_____   MODE: async sync isoch
PAGE DESCRIPTION LANGUAGE: PostScript DDL _____
NOTE 1: Leads 5/6/8 must be on to receive data.
NOTE 2: PIN 11's polarity for hardware flow control

PRINTER PORT PROFILE   (Underline if supported, circle if selected)
COMPANY: Citizen America Corporation
PRODUCT: MSP-20/25, MSP-10/15, 120-D printers

PORT: female   PORT TYPE: serial
CONNECTOR: DB25 DB9 5-PIN 8-PIN Centronics   GENDER: male female
PIN CONFIGURATION: P03

PIN	FUNCTION	DIRECTION	PIN	FUNCTION	DIRECTION
1:FG	Frame Ground	N/A	7:SG	Signal Ground	N/A
2:TD	Transmit Data	FROM	11:RC	Rec. Clk/Reverse Chann	FROM
3:RD	Receive Data	TO	20:DTR	Data Terminal Ready	FROM
4:RTS	Request to Send	FROM	25:+5V		FROM
6:DSR	Data Set Ready	TO			

FLOW CONTROL: 20   XON: YES   ACK: LEADS THAT MUST BE ON:_____
SPEEDS: 110 300 600 1200 1800 2400 4800 9600 19.2 56k _____
PARITY: even odd space mark none   CHARACTER LENGTH: 7 8 ___
STOP BITS: 1 1.5 2   LINE-ENDING SEQUENCE: cr lf cr/lf
PRINTER COMPATIBILITY MODES: EpsonMX/FX/RX Diablo630 HPLaserJet NEC3500
    IBMgraphics Printronix TI-810_____   MODE: async sync isoch
PAGE DESCRIPTION LANGUAGE: PostScript DDL _____
NOTE 1:
NOTE 2:

PRINTER PORT PROFILE   (Underline if supported, circle if selected)
COMPANY: Citizen America Corporation
PRODUCT: Tribute 224

PORT: PORT TYPE: serial
CONNECTOR: DB25 DB9 5-PIN 8-PIN Centronics   GENDER: male female
PIN CONFIGURATION: P03

PIN	FUNCTION	DIRECTION
1:FG	Frame Ground	N/A
2:TD	Transmit Data	FROM
3:RD	Receive Data	TO
4:RTS	Request to Send	FROM
5:CTS	Clear to Send	TO
6:DSR	Data Set Ready	TO
7:SG	Signal Ground	N/A
8:CD	Carrier Detect	TO
14:F	Fault	FROM
20:DTR	Data Terminal Ready	FROM

FLOW CONTROL: 20 14   XON: YES   ACK: YES LEADS THAT MUST BE ON:_____
SPEEDS: 110 300 600 1200 1800 2400 4800 9600 19.2 56k _____
PARITY: even odd space mark none   CHARACTER LENGTH: 7 8 ___
STOP BITS: 1 1.5 2   LINE-ENDING SEQUENCE: cr lf cr/lf
PRINTER COMPATIBILITY MODES: EpsonMX/FX/RX Diablo630 HPLaserJet NEC3500
    IBMgraphics Printronix TI-810_____   MODE: async sync isoch
PAGE DESCRIPTION LANGUAGE: PostScript DDL _____
NOTE 1: Lead 25 can provide +5V
NOTE 2:

PRINTER PORT PROFILE (Underline if supported, circle if selected)
COMPANY: Computer Products(Memodyne)
PRODUCT: MP 401 Thermal Printer

PORT: female   PORT TYPE: serial
CONNECTOR: DB25 DB9 5-PIN 8-PIN Centronics   GENDER: male female
PIN CONFIGURATION: P11

PIN	FUNCTION	DIRECTION
1:CG	Chassis Ground	N/A
3:RD	Receive Data	TO
7:SG	Signal Ground	N/A
20:DTR	Data Terminal Ready	FROM

FLOW CONTROL: 20   XON: YES ACK: LEADS THAT MUST BE ON:_____
SPEEDS: 110 300 600 1200 1800 2400 4800 9600 19.2 56k _____
PARITY: even odd space mark none   CHARACTER LENGTH: 7 8 ___
STOP BITS: 1 1.5 2   LINE-ENDING SEQUENCE: cr lf cr/lf
PRINTER COMPATIBILITY MODES: EpsonMX/FX/RX Diablo630 HPLaserJet NEC3500
   IBMgraphics Printronix TI-810_____   MODE: async sync isoch
PAGE DESCRIPTION LANGUAGE: PostScript DDL _____
NOTE 1:
NOTE 2:

PRINTER PORT PROFILE (Underline if supported, circle if selected)
COMPANY: Consolink Corporation
PRODUCT: Micro Spooler

PORT: female (serial in)   PORT TYPE: serial
CONNECTOR: DB25 DB9 5-PIN 8-PIN Centronics   GENDER: male female
PIN CONFIGURATION: P08

PIN	FUNCTION	DIRECTION
1:FG	Frame Ground	N/A
2:TD	Transmit Data	FROM
3:RD	Receive Data	TO
4:RTS	Request to Send	FROM
6:DSR	Data Set Ready	TO
7:SG	Signal Ground	N/A
20:DTR	Data Terminal Ready	FROM

FLOW CONTROL: 20   XON: YES ACK: YES LEADS THAT MUST BE ON:_____
SPEEDS: 110 300 600 1200 1800 2400 4800 9600 19.2 56k _____
PARITY: even odd space mark none   CHARACTER LENGTH: 7 8 ___
STOP BITS: 1 1.5 2   LINE-ENDING SEQUENCE: cr lf cr/lf
PRINTER COMPATIBILITY MODES: EpsonMX/FX/RX Diablo630 HPLaserJet NEC3500
   IBMgraphics Printronix TI-810_____   MODE: async sync isoch
PAGE DESCRIPTION LANGUAGE: PostScript DDL _____
NOTE 1:
NOTE 2:

PRINTER PORT PROFILE (Underline if supported, circle if selected)
COMPANY: Consolink Corporation
PRODUCT: SooperSpooler

PORT: female (serial in)   PORT TYPE: serial
CONNECTOR: DB25 DB9 5-PIN 8-PIN Centronics   GENDER: male female
PIN CONFIGURATION: P08

PIN	FUNCTION	DIRECTION
1:FG	Frame Ground	N/A
2:TD	Transmit Data	FROM
3:RD	Receive Data	TO
4:RTS	Request to Send	FROM
6:DSR	Data Set Ready	TO
7:SG	Signal Ground	N/A
20:DTR	Data Terminal Ready	FROM

FLOW CONTROL: 20   XON: YES ACK: YES LEADS THAT MUST BE ON:_____
SPEEDS: 110 300 600 1200 1800 2400 4800 9600 19.2 56k _____
PARITY: even odd space mark none   CHARACTER LENGTH: 7 8 ___
STOP BITS: 1 1.5 2   LINE-ENDING SEQUENCE: cr lf cr/lf
PRINTER COMPATIBILITY MODES: EpsonMX/FX/RX Diablo630 HPLaserJet NEC3500
   IBMgraphics Printronix TI-810_____ MODE: async sync isoch
PAGE DESCRIPTION LANGUAGE: PostScript DDL _____
NOTE 1:
NOTE 2:

PRINTER PORT PROFILE (Underline if supported, circle if selected)
COMPANY: Craden Peripherals Corp.
PRODUCT: DP4 printer

PORT: male   PORT TYPE: serial
CONNECTOR: DB25 DB9 5-PIN 8-PIN Centronics   GENDER: male female
PIN CONFIGURATION: P08

PIN	FUNCTION	DIRECTION
1:PG	Protective Ground	N/A
2:TD	Transmit Data	FROM
3:RD	Receive Data	TO
4:RTS	Request to Send	FROM
5:CTS	Clear to Send	TO
6:DSR	Data Set Ready	TO
7:SG	Signal Ground	N/A
20:DTR	Data Terminal Ready	FROM

FLOW CONTROL: 20   XON: YES ACK: LEADS THAT MUST BE ON:_____
SPEEDS: 110 300 600 1200 1800 2400 4800 9600 19.2 56k _____
PARITY: even odd space mark none   CHARACTER LENGTH: 7 8 ___
STOP BITS: 1 1.5 2   LINE-ENDING SEQUENCE: cr lf cr/lf
PRINTER COMPATIBILITY MODES: EpsonMX/FX/RX Diablo630 HPLaserJet NEC3500
   IBMgraphics Printronix TI-810_____ MODE: async sync isoch
PAGE DESCRIPTION LANGUAGE: PostScript DDL _____
NOTE 1:
NOTE 2:

PRINTER PORT PROFILE (Underline if supported, circle if selected)
COMPANY: Datapoint Corporation
PRODUCT: 9611 printer

PORT: serial   PORT TYPE: serial
CONNECTOR: DB25 DB9 5-PIN 8-PIN Centronics   GENDER: male female
PIN CONFIGURATION: P08

PIN	FUNCTION	DIRECTION
1:PG	Protective Ground	N/A
2:TD	Transmit Data	FROM
3:RD	Receive Data	TO
4:OL		FROM
6:DSR	Data Set Ready	TO
7:SG	Signal Ground	N/A
20:PB	Printer Busy	FROM

FLOW CONTROL: 20   XON: ACK: LEADS THAT MUST BE ON:_____
SPEEDS: 110 300 600 1200 1800 2400 4800 9600 19.2 56k _____
PARITY: even odd space mark none   CHARACTER LENGTH: 7 8 ___
STOP BITS: 1 1.5 2   LINE-ENDING SEQUENCE: cr lf cr/lf
PRINTER COMPATIBILITY MODES: EpsonMX/FX/RX Diablo630 HPLaserJet NEC3500
    IBMgraphics Printronix TI-810_____ MODE: async sync isoch
PAGE DESCRIPTION LANGUAGE: PostScript DDL _____
NOTE 1: "ol" stands for online and will be on with power.
NOTE 2:

PRINTER PORT PROFILE (Underline if supported, circle if selected)
COMPANY: Datapoint Corporation
PRODUCT: 9623 printer

PORT: female   PORT TYPE: serial
CONNECTOR: DB25 DB9 5-PIN 8-PIN Centronics   GENDER: male female
PIN CONFIGURATION: P08

PIN	FUNCTION	DIRECTION
1:CG	Chassis Ground	N/A
2:TD	Transmit Data	FROM
3:RD	Receive Data	TO
4:RTS	Request to Send	FROM
7:SG	Signal Ground	N/A
20:DTR	Data Terminal Ready	FROM

FLOW CONTROL: 20   XON: ACK: LEADS THAT MUST BE ON:_____
SPEEDS: 110 300 600 1200 1800 2400 4800 9600 19.2 56k _____
PARITY: even odd space mark none   CHARACTER LENGTH: 7 8 ___
STOP BITS: 1 1.5 2   LINE-ENDING SEQUENCE: cr lf cr/lf
PRINTER COMPATIBILITY MODES: EpsonMX/FX/RX Diablo630 HPLaserJet NEC3500
    IBMgraphics Printronix TI-810_____ MODE: async sync isoch
PAGE DESCRIPTION LANGUAGE: PostScript DDL _____
NOTE 1:
NOTE 2:

PRINTER PORT PROFILE   (Underline if supported, circle if selected)
COMPANY: Datapoint Corporation
PRODUCT: 9628 printer

PORT: female   PORT TYPE: serial
CONNECTOR: DB25 DB9 5-PIN 8-PIN Centronics   GENDER: male female
PIN CONFIGURATION: P07

PIN	FUNCTION	DIRECTION
1:PG	Protective Ground	N/A
2:TD	Transmit Data	FROM
3:RD	Receive Data	TO
6:DSR	Data Set Ready	TO
7:SG	Signal Ground	N/A
11:PB	Printer Busy	FROM
20:DTR	Data Terminal Ready	FROM

FLOW CONTROL: 11   XON: ACK: LEADS THAT MUST BE ON:_____
SPEEDS: 110 300 600 1200 1800 2400 4800 9600 19.2 56k _____
PARITY: even odd space mark none   CHARACTER LENGTH: 7 8 ___
STOP BITS: 1 1.5 2   LINE-ENDING SEQUENCE: cr lf cr/lf
PRINTER COMPATIBILITY MODES: EpsonMX/FX/RX Diablo630 HPLaserJet NEC3500
   IBMgraphics Printronix TI-810_____   MODE: async sync isoch
PAGE DESCRIPTION LANGUAGE: PostScript DDL _____
NOTE 1:
NOTE 2:

PRINTER PORT PROFILE   (Underline if supported, circle if selected)
COMPANY: Datasouth Computer Corporation
PRODUCT: DS-180/DS-220 printers

PORT: female   PORT TYPE: serial
CONNECTOR: DB25 DB9 5-PIN 8-PIN Centronics   GENDER: male female
PIN CONFIGURATION: P07

PIN	FUNCTION	DIRECTION
1:CG	Chassis Ground	N/A
2:TD	Transmit Data	FROM
3:RD	Receive Data	TO
7:SG	Signal Ground	N/A
11:DTR	Data Terminal Ready	FROM
20:DTR	Data Terminal Ready	FROM

FLOW CONTROL: 11 20   XON: YES ACK: LEADS THAT MUST BE ON:_____
SPEEDS: 110 300 600 1200 1800 2400 4800 9600 19.2 56k _____
PARITY: even odd space mark none   CHARACTER LENGTH: 7 8 ___
STOP BITS: 1 1.5 2   LINE-ENDING SEQUENCE: cr lf cr/lf
PRINTER COMPATIBILITY MODES: EpsonMX/FX/RX Diablo630 HPLaserJet NEC3500
   IBMgraphics Printronix TI-810_____   MODE: async sync isoch
PAGE DESCRIPTION LANGUAGE: PostScript DDL _____
NOTE 1:
NOTE 2:

PRINTER PORT PROFILE (Underline if supported, circle if selected)
COMPANY: Datasouth Computer Corporation
PRODUCT: Pagewriter 8 printer

PORT: female   PORT TYPE: serial
CONNECTOR: DB25 DB9 5-PIN 8-PIN Centronics   GENDER: male female
PIN CONFIGURATION: P01

PIN	FUNCTION	DIRECTION	PIN	FUNCTION	DIRECTION
1:FG	Frame Ground	N/A	6:DSR	Data Set Ready	
2:TD	Transmit Data	FROM	7:SG	Signal Ground	N/A
3:RD	Receive Data	TO	8:CD	Carrier Detect	TO
4:RTS	Request to Send	FROM	19:RC	Rec. Clk/Reverse Chann	FROM
5:CTS	Clear to Send	TO	20:DTR	Data Terminal Ready	FROM

FLOW CONTROL: 19   XON: ACK: LEADS THAT MUST BE ON:_____
SPEEDS: 110 300 600 1200 1800 2400 4800 9600 19.2 56k _____
PARITY: even odd space mark none   CHARACTER LENGTH: 7 8 ___
STOP BITS: 1 1.5 2   LINE-ENDING SEQUENCE: cr lf cr/lf
PRINTER COMPATIBILITY MODES: EpsonMX/FX/RX Diablo630 HPLaserJet NEC3500
   IBMgraphics Printronix TI-810_____   MODE: async sync isoch
PAGE DESCRIPTION LANGUAGE: PostScript DDL _____
NOTE 1:
NOTE 2:

PRINTER PORT PROFILE (Underline if supported, circle if selected)
COMPANY: Digital Matrix Corporation
PRODUCT: Durawriter 9/80, 9/132 & Formwriter printers

PORT: female   PORT TYPE: serial
CONNECTOR: DB25 DB9 5-PIN 8-PIN Centronics   GENDER: male female
PIN CONFIGURATION: P10

PIN	FUNCTION	DIRECTION
1:FG	Frame Ground	N/A
2:TD	Transmit Data	FROM
3:RD	Receive Data	TO
4:RTS	Request to Send	FROM
7:SG	Signal Ground	N/A
11:AB	Auxiliary Busy	FROM
20:DTR	Data Terminal Ready	FROM
22:+5V		

FLOW CONTROL: XON: YES ACK: LEADS THAT MUST BE ON:_____
SPEEDS: 110 300 600 1200 1800 2400 4800 9600 19.2 56k _____
PARITY: even odd space mark none   CHARACTER LENGTH: 7 8 ___
STOP BITS: 1 1.5 2   LINE-ENDING SEQUENCE: cr lf cr/lf
PRINTER COMPATIBILITY MODES: EpsonMX/FX/RX Diablo630 HPLaserJet NEC3500
   IBMgraphics Printronix TI-810_____   MODE: async sync isoch
PAGE DESCRIPTION LANGUAGE: PostScript DDL _____
NOTE 1: The printer should be optioned for XON/XOFF, as
NOTE 2: the busy lead(11) is positive with busy condition.

PRINTER PORT PROFILE   (Underline if supported, circle if selected)
COMPANY: Digital Products, Inc.
PRODUCT: PrintDirector MultiSpool

PORT: female-computer port   PORT TYPE: serial
CONNECTOR: DB25 DB9 5-PIN 8-PIN Centronics   GENDER: male female
PIN CONFIGURATION: P11

PIN	FUNCTION	DIRECTION
1:CG	Chassis Ground	N/A
2:TD	Transmit Data	FROM
3:RD	Receive Data	TO
5:B	Busy	TO
6:B	Busy	TO
7:SG	Signal Ground	N/A
8:B	Busy	TO
20:B	Busy	FROM

FLOW CONTROL: 20   XON: YES ACK: LEADS THAT MUST BE ON:_____
SPEEDS: 110 300 600 1200 1800 2400 4800 9600 19.2 56k _____
PARITY: even odd space mark none   CHARACTER LENGTH: 7 8 ___
STOP BITS: 1 1.5 2   LINE-ENDING SEQUENCE: cr lf cr/lf
PRINTER COMPATIBILITY MODES: EpsonMX/FX/RX Diablo630 HPLaserJet NEC3500
   IBMgraphics Printronix TI-810_____ MODE: async sync isoch
PAGE DESCRIPTION LANGUAGE: PostScript DDL _____
NOTE 1: These PINouts are while in the "DTE" mode.
NOTE 2:

PRINTER PORT PROFILE   (Underline if supported, circle if selected)
COMPANY: Dynax, Inc.
PRODUCT: DX/DM/HR/DH series printers

PORT: female   PORT TYPE: serial
CONNECTOR: DB25 DB9 5-PIN 8-PIN Centronics   GENDER: male female
PIN CONFIGURATION: P03

PIN	FUNCTION	DIRECTION
1:S	Shield	N/A
2:TD	Transmit Data	FROM
3:RD	Receive Data	TO
4:RTS	Request to Send	FROM
5:CTS	Clear to Send	TO
6:DSR	Data Set Ready	TO
7:SG	Signal Ground	N/A
8:DCD	Data Carrier Detect	TO
20:DTR	Data Terminal Ready	FROM

FLOW CONTROL: 20   XON: YES ACK: LEADS THAT MUST BE ON:_____
SPEEDS: 110 300 600 1200 1800 2400 4800 9600 19.2 56k _____
PARITY: even odd space mark none   CHARACTER LENGTH: 7 8 ___
STOP BITS: 1 1.5 2   LINE-ENDING SEQUENCE: cr lf cr/lf
PRINTER COMPATIBILITY MODES: EpsonMX/FX/RX Diablo630 HPLaserJet NEC3500
   IBMgraphics Printronix TI-810_____ MODE: async sync isoch
PAGE DESCRIPTION LANGUAGE: PostScript DDL _____
NOTE 1: PIN 5 must be on for XON/XOFF to function.
NOTE 2:

PRINTER PORT PROFILE   (Underline if supported, circle if selected)
COMPANY: Epson America, Inc.
PRODUCT: 8148/8149/8143 interface for EX/RX/FX & LQ ptrs.

PORT: female (DB-25)   PORT TYPE: serial
CONNECTOR: DB25 DB9 5-PIN 8-PIN Centronics   GENDER: male female
PIN CONFIGURATION: P07

PIN	FUNCTION	DIRECTION
1:CG	Chassis Ground	N/A
2:TD	Transmit Data	FROM
3:RD	Receive Data	TO
6:DSR	Data Set Ready	TO
7:SG	Signal Ground	N/A
8:DCD	Data Carrier Detect	TO
11:RC	Rec. Clk/Reverse Chann	FROM
20:DTR	Data Terminal Ready	FROM

FLOW CONTROL: 11   XON: YES ACK: LEADS THAT MUST BE ON:_____
SPEEDS: 110 300 600 1200 1800 2400 4800 9600 19.2 56k _____
PARITY: even odd space mark none   CHARACTER LENGTH: 7 8 ___
STOP BITS: 1 1.5 2   LINE-ENDING SEQUENCE: cr lf cr/lf
PRINTER COMPATIBILITY MODES: EpsonMX/FX/RX Diablo630 HPLaserJet NEC3500
  IBMgraphics Printronix TI-810_____   MODE: async sync isoch
PAGE DESCRIPTION LANGUAGE: PostScript DDL _____
NOTE 1:
NOTE 2:

PRINTER PORT PROFILE   (Underline if supported, circle if selected)
COMPANY: Epson America, Inc.
PRODUCT: FX/EX/RX/LQ printers with 8100 serial interface

PORT: female   PORT TYPE: serial
CONNECTOR: DB25 DB9 5-PIN 8-PIN Centronics   GENDER: male female
PIN CONFIGURATION: P07

PIN	FUNCTION	DIRECTION
1:CG	Chassis Ground	N/A
2:TD	Transmit Data	FROM
3:RD	Receive Data	TO
6:DSR	Data Set Ready	TO
7:SG	Signal Ground	N/A
8:DCD	Data Carrier Detect	TO
11:RC	Rec. Clk/Reverse Chann	FROM
20:DTR	Data Terminal Ready	FROM

FLOW CONTROL: 11   XON: YES ACK: LEADS THAT MUST BE ON:_____
SPEEDS: 110 300 600 1200 1800 2400 4800 9600 19.2 56k _____
PARITY: even odd space mark none   CHARACTER LENGTH: 7 8 ___
STOP BITS: 1 1.5 2   LINE-ENDING SEQUENCE: cr lf cr/lf
PRINTER COMPATIBILITY MODES: EpsonMX/FX/RX Diablo630 HPLaserJet NEC3500
  IBMgraphics Printronix TI-810_____   MODE: async sync isoch
PAGE DESCRIPTION LANGUAGE: PostScript DDL _____
NOTE 1:
NOTE 2:

PRINTER PORT PROFILE   **(Underline if supported, circle if selected)**
COMPANY: Ergo Systems, Inc.
PRODUCT: HUSH 80 printer

PORT: female (DB25)   PORT TYPE: serial
CONNECTOR: DB25 DB9 5-PIN 8-PIN Centronics   GENDER: male female
PIN CONFIGURATION: P11

PIN	FUNCTION	DIRECTION
1:TD	Transmit Data	FROM
3:RD	Receive Data	TO
5:DSR	Data Set Ready	TO
6:DSR	Data Set Ready	TO
7:SG	Signal Ground	N/A
8:DSR	Data Set Ready	TO
20:DTR	Data Terminal Ready	FROM

FLOW CONTROL: 20   XON: YES ACK: LEADS THAT MUST BE ON:_____
SPEEDS: 110 300 600 1200 1800 2400 4800 9600 19.2 56k _____
PARITY: even odd space mark none   CHARACTER LENGTH: 7 8 ___
STOP BITS: 1 1.5 2   LINE-ENDING SEQUENCE: cr lf cr/lf
PRINTER COMPATIBILITY MODES: EpsonMX/FX/RX Diablo630 HPLaserJet NEC3500
   IBMgraphics Printronix TI-810_____   MODE: async sync isoch
PAGE DESCRIPTION LANGUAGE: PostScript DDL _____
NOTE 1: This port can be optioned to emulate DCE
NOTE 2:

PRINTER PORT PROFILE   **(Underline if supported, circle if selected)**
COMPANY: Facit, Inc.
PRODUCT: 4514/4511/4510/4512/4513 printers

PORT: female   PORT TYPE: serial
CONNECTOR: DB25 DB9 5-PIN 8-PIN Centronics   GENDER: male female
PIN CONFIGURATION: P04

PIN	FUNCTION	DIRECTION
1:CG	Chassis Ground	N/A
2:TD	Transmit Data	FROM
3:RD	Receive Data	TO
4:RTS	Request to Send	FROM
7:SG	Signal Ground	N/A
11:B	Busy	FROM
19:B	Busy	FROM
20:DTR	Data Terminal Ready	FROM

FLOW CONTROL: 11 19   XON: YES ACK: YES LEADS THAT MUST BE ON:_____
SPEEDS: 110 300 600 1200 1800 2400 4800 9600 19.2 56k _____
PARITY: even odd space mark none   CHARACTER LENGTH: 7 8 ___
STOP BITS: 1 1.5 2   LINE-ENDING SEQUENCE: cr lf cr/lf
PRINTER COMPATIBILITY MODES: EpsonMX/FX/RX Diablo630 HPLaserJet NEC3500
   IBMgraphics Printronix TI-810_____   MODE: async sync isoch
PAGE DESCRIPTION LANGUAGE: PostScript DDL _____
NOTE 1: This PINout classification assumes that PIN 11 is
NOTE 2: being used for flow control

PRINTER PORT PROFILE (Underline if supported, circle if selected)
COMPANY: Facit, Inc.
PRODUCT: 4550/51 plotters

PORT: female   PORT TYPE: serial
CONNECTOR: DB25 DB9 5-PIN 8-PIN Centronics   GENDER: male female
PIN CONFIGURATION: P01

PIN	FUNCTION	DIRECTION
1:CG	Chassis Ground	N/A
2:TD	Transmit Data	FROM
3:RD	Receive Data	TO
4:RTS	Request to Send	FROM
5:CTS	Clear to Send	TO
6:DSR	Data Set Ready	TO
7:SG	Signal Ground	N/A
11:B	Busy	FROM
19:B	Busy	FROM
20:DTR	Data Terminal Ready	FROM

FLOW CONTROL: 19 11   XON: YES ACK: YES LEADS THAT MUST BE ON:_____
SPEEDS: 110 300 600 1200 1800 2400 4800 9600 19.2 56k _____
PARITY: even odd space mark none   CHARACTER LENGTH: 7 8 ___
STOP BITS: 1 1.5 2   LINE-ENDING SEQUENCE: cr lf cr/lf
PRINTER COMPATIBILITY MODES: EpsonMX/FX/RX Diablo630 HPLaserJet NEC3500
   IBMgraphics Printronix TI-810_____   MODE: async sync isoch
PAGE DESCRIPTION LANGUAGE: PostScript DDL _____
NOTE 1: a +5V signal can be provided on lead 18
NOTE 2:

PRINTER PORT PROFILE (Underline if supported, circle if selected)
COMPANY: Facit, Inc.
PRODUCT: 4580/C5500 printers

PORT: female   PORT TYPE: serial
CONNECTOR: DB25 DB9 5-PIN 8-PIN Centronics   GENDER: male female
PIN CONFIGURATION: P01

PIN	FUNCTION	DIRECTION	PIN	FUNCTION	DIRECTION
1:CG	Chassis Ground	N/A	7:SG	Signal Ground	N/A
2:TD	Transmit Data	FROM	8:DCD	Data Carrier Detect	TO
3:RD	Receive Data	TO	11:B	Busy	FROM
4:RTS	Request to Send	FROM	19:B	Busy	FROM
5:CTS	Clear to Send	TO	20:DTR	Data Terminal Ready	FROM
6:DSR	Data Set Ready	TO			

FLOW CONTROL: 19 11   XON: YES ACK: YES LEADS THAT MUST BE ON:_____
SPEEDS: 110 300 600 1200 1800 2400 4800 9600 19.2 56k _____
PARITY: even odd space mark none   CHARACTER LENGTH: 7 8 ___
STOP BITS: 1 1.5 2   LINE-ENDING SEQUENCE: cr lf cr/lf
PRINTER COMPATIBILITY MODES: EpsonMX/FX/RX Diablo630 HPLaserJet NEC3500
   IBMgraphics Printronix TI-810_____   MODE: async sync isoch
PAGE DESCRIPTION LANGUAGE: PostScript DDL _____
NOTE 1: The C5500 can provide +-12 volts on PINs 9/10.
NOTE 2: The 4580 & C5500s can provide +5V on PIN 18

PRINTER PORT PROFILE   (Underline if supported, circle if selected)
COMPANY: Facit, Inc.
PRODUCT: C5500 printer

PORT: female   PORT TYPE: serial
CONNECTOR: DB25 DB9 5-PIN 8-PIN Centronics   GENDER: male female
PIN CONFIGURATION: PO4

PIN	FUNCTION	DIRECTION
1:FG	Frame Ground	N/A
2:TD	Transmit Data	FROM
3:RD	Receive Data	TO
4:RTS	Request to Send	FROM
7:SG	Signal Ground	N/A
11:PB	Printer Busy	FROM
19:PB	Printer Busy	FROM
20:DTR	Data Terminal Ready	FROM

FLOW CONTROL: 11 19 20   XON: YES ACK: LEADS THAT MUST BE ON:_____
SPEEDS: 110 300 600 1200 1800 2400 4800 9600 19.2 56k _____
PARITY: even odd space mark none   CHARACTER LENGTH: 7 8 ___
STOP BITS: 1 1.5 2   LINE-ENDING SEQUENCE: cr lf cr/lf
PRINTER COMPATIBILITY MODES: EpsonMX/FX/RX Diablo630 HPLaserJet NEC3500
   IBMgraphics Printronix TI-810_____ MODE: async sync isoch
PAGE DESCRIPTION LANGUAGE: PostScript DDL _____
NOTE 1:Check the polarity of the flow control leads
NOTE 2:

PRINTER PORT PROFILE   (Underline if supported, circle if selected)
COMPANY: Genicom Corporation
PRODUCT: 3210/3014/3024 printers

PORT: female   PORT TYPE: serial
CONNECTOR: DB25 DB9 5-PIN 8-PIN Centronics   GENDER: male female
PIN CONFIGURATION: PO9

PIN	FUNCTION	DIRECTION
1:CG	Chassis Ground	N/A
2:TD	Transmit Data	FROM
3:RD	Receive Data	TO
4:RTS	Request to Send	FROM
5:CTS	Clear to Send	TO
7:SG	Signal Ground	N/A
20:DTR	Data Terminal Ready	FROM

FLOW CONTROL: 4 20   XON: YES ACK: LEADS THAT MUST BE ON:_____
SPEEDS: 110 300 600 1200 1800 2400 4800 9600 19.2 56k _____
PARITY: even odd space mark none   CHARACTER LENGTH: 7 8 ___
STOP BITS: 1 1.5 2   LINE-ENDING SEQUENCE: cr lf cr/lf
PRINTER COMPATIBILITY MODES: EpsonMX/FX/RX Diablo630 HPLaserJet NEC3500
   IBMgraphics Printronix TI-810_____ MODE: async sync isoch
PAGE DESCRIPTION LANGUAGE: PostScript DDL _____
NOTE 1:PIN 20 is optionable as either flow control or
NOTE 2: power on condition status

PRINTER PORT PROFILE (Underline if supported, circle if selected)
COMPANY: Genicom Corporation
PRODUCT: 3310/3320/3410 printers

PORT: female   PORT TYPE: serial
CONNECTOR: DB25 DB9 5-PIN 8-PIN Centronics   GENDER: male female
PIN CONFIGURATION: P01

PIN	FUNCTION	DIRECTION	PIN	FUNCTION	DIRECTION
1:PG	Protective Ground	N/A	7:SG	Signal Ground	N/A
2:TD	Transmit Data	FROM	9:+V		
3:RD	Receive Data	TO	10:-V		
4:RTS	Request to Send	FROM	19:SRTS	Secondary Req.to Send	FROM
5:CTS	Clear to Send	TO	20:DTR	Data Terminal Ready	FROM
6:DSR	Data Set Ready	TO			

FLOW CONTROL: 19 4 20   XON: YES ACK: LEADS THAT MUST BE ON:_____
SPEEDS: 110 300 600 1200 1800 2400 4800 9600 19.2 56k _____
PARITY: even odd space mark none   CHARACTER LENGTH: 7 8 ___
STOP BITS: 1 1.5 2   LINE-ENDING SEQUENCE: cr lf cr/lf
PRINTER COMPATIBILITY MODES: EpsonMX/FX/RX Diablo630 HPLaserJet NEC3500
   IBMgraphics Printronix TI-810_____ MODE: async sync isoch
PAGE DESCRIPTION LANGUAGE: PostScript DDL _____
NOTE 1:
NOTE 2:

PRINTER PORT PROFILE (Underline if supported, circle if selected)
COMPANY: Genicom Corporation
PRODUCT: 4400 printers

PORT: female   PORT TYPE: serial
CONNECTOR: DB25 DB9 5-PIN 8-PIN Centronics   GENDER: male female
PIN CONFIGURATION: P03

PIN	FUNCTION	DIRECTION	PIN	FUNCTION	DIRECTION
1:CG	Chassis Ground	N/A	6:DSR	Data Set Ready	TO
2:TD	Transmit Data	FROM	7:SG	Signal Ground	N/A
3:RD	Receive Data	TO	11:SRTS	Secondary Req.to Send	FROM
4:RTS	Request to Send	FROM	19:SRTS	Secondary Req.to Send	FROM
5:CTS	Clear to Send	TO	20:DTR	Data Terminal Ready	FROM

FLOW CONTROL: 20 4 11 19 XON: YES ACK: LEADS THAT MUST BE ON:_____
SPEEDS: 110 300 600 1200 1800 2400 4800 9600 19.2 56k _____
PARITY: even odd space mark none   CHARACTER LENGTH: 7 8 ___
STOP BITS: 1 1.5 2   LINE-ENDING SEQUENCE: cr lf cr/lf
PRINTER COMPATIBILITY MODES: EpsonMX/FX/RX Diablo630 HPLaserJet NEC3500
   IBMgraphics Printronix TI-810_____ MODE: async sync isoch
PAGE DESCRIPTION LANGUAGE: PostScript DDL _____
NOTE 1:
NOTE 2:

PRINTER PORT PROFILE   (Underline if supported, circle if selected)
COMPANY: HanZon Data Inc.
PRODUCT: LP3000 printer

PORT: female   PORT TYPE: serial
CONNECTOR: DB25 DB9 5-PIN 8-PIN Centronics   GENDER: male female
PIN CONFIGURATION: P11

PIN	FUNCTION	DIRECTION
1:FG	Frame Ground	N/A
2:TD	Transmit Data	FROM
3:RD	Receive Data	TO
7:SG	Signal Ground	N/A
20:DTR	Data Terminal Ready	FROM

FLOW CONTROL: 20   XON: ACK: LEADS THAT MUST BE ON:_____
SPEEDS: 110 300 600 1200 1800 2400 4800 9600 19.2 56k _____
PARITY: even odd space mark none   CHARACTER LENGTH: 7 8 ___
STOP BITS: 1 1.5 2   LINE-ENDING SEQUENCE: cr lf cr/lf
PRINTER COMPATIBILITY MODES: EpsonMX/FX/RX Diablo630 HPLaserJet NEC3500
  IBMgraphics Printronix TI-810_____   MODE: async sync isoch
PAGE DESCRIPTION LANGUAGE: PostScript DDL _____
NOTE 1:
NOTE 2:

PRINTER PORT PROFILE   (Underline if supported, circle if selected)
COMPANY: HanZon Data Inc.
PRODUCT: Universal Serial Interface card

PORT: female   PORT TYPE: serial
CONNECTOR: DB25 DB9 5-PIN 8-PIN Centronics   GENDER: male female
PIN CONFIGURATION: P11

PIN	FUNCTION	DIRECTION
1:FG	Frame Ground	N/A
2:RD	Receive Data	FROM
3:RD	Receive Data	TO
7:SG	Signal Ground	N/A
20:DTR	Data Terminal Ready	FROM

FLOW CONTROL: 20   XON: YES ACK: YES LEADS THAT MUST BE ON:_____
SPEEDS: 110 300 600 1200 1800 2400 4800 9600 19.2 56k _____
PARITY: even odd space mark none   CHARACTER LENGTH: 7 8 ___
STOP BITS: 1 1.5 2   LINE-ENDING SEQUENCE: cr lf cr/lf
PRINTER COMPATIBILITY MODES: EpsonMX/FX/RX Diablo630 HPLaserJet NEC3500
  IBMgraphics Printronix TI-810_____   MODE: async sync isoch
PAGE DESCRIPTION LANGUAGE: PostScript DDL _____
NOTE 1:
NOTE 2:

PRINTER PORT PROFILE (Underline if supported, circle if selected)
COMPANY: Hewlett-Packard
PRODUCT: LaserJet 500+ printer

PORT: serial (female)   PORT TYPE: serial
CONNECTOR: DB25 DB9 5-PIN 8-PIN Centronics   GENDER: male female
PIN CONFIGURATION: P11

PIN	FUNCTION	DIRECTION
1:FG	Frame Ground	N/A
2:TD	Transmit Data	FROM
3:RD	Receive Data	TO
7:SG	Signal Ground	N/A
20:DTR	Data Terminal Ready	FROM

FLOW CONTROL: 20   XON: YES ACK: LEADS THAT MUST BE ON:_____
SPEEDS: 110 300 600 1200 1800 2400 4800 9600 19.2 56k _____
PARITY: even odd space mark none   CHARACTER LENGTH: 7 8 ___
STOP BITS: 1 1.5 2   LINE-ENDING SEQUENCE: cr lf cr/lf
PRINTER COMPATIBILITY MODES: EpsonMX/FX/RX Diablo630 HPLaserJet NEC3500
   IBMgraphics Printronix TI-810_____ MODE: async sync isoch
PAGE DESCRIPTION LANGUAGE: PostScript DDL _____
NOTE 1:also supports RS-422
NOTE 2:

PRINTER PORT PROFILE (Underline if supported, circle if selected)
COMPANY: Holoscan Corporation
PRODUCT: 20 Laser Printer (w/ WP-300 controller)

PORT: female   PORT TYPE: serial
CONNECTOR: DB25 DB9 5-PIN 8-PIN Centronics   GENDER: male female
PIN CONFIGURATION: P08

PIN	FUNCTION	DIRECTION
1:PG	Protective Ground	N/A
2:TD	Transmit Data	FROM
3:RD	Receive Data	TO
4:RTS	Request to Send	FROM
7:SG	Signal Ground	N/A
20:DTR	Data Terminal Ready	FROM

FLOW CONTROL: 20   XON: YES ACK: YES LEADS THAT MUST BE ON:_____
SPEEDS: 110 300 600 1200 1800 2400 4800 9600 19.2 56k _____
PARITY: even odd space mark none   CHARACTER LENGTH: 7 8 ___
STOP BITS: 1 1.5 2   LINE-ENDING SEQUENCE: cr lf cr/lf
PRINTER COMPATIBILITY MODES: EpsonMX/FX/RX Diablo630 HPLaserJet NEC3500
   IBMgraphics Printronix TI-810_____ MODE: async sync isoch
PAGE DESCRIPTION LANGUAGE: PostScript DDL _____
NOTE 1:PIN 4 is high whenever power is applied
NOTE 2:

PRINTER PORT PROFILE   (Underline if supported, circle if selected)
COMPANY: ICS Computer Products
PRODUCT: SP-2010 printer

PORT: female(connector-A)   PORT TYPE: serial
CONNECTOR: DB25 DB9 5-PIN 8-PIN Centronics   GENDER: male female
PIN CONFIGURATION: C05

PIN	FUNCTION	DIRECTION
1:PG	Protective Ground	N/A
2:TD	Transmit Data	FROM
3:RD	Receive Data	TO
4:RTS	Request to Send	FROM
5:CTS	Clear to Send	TO
6:DSR	Data Set Ready	TO
7:SG	Signal Ground	N/A
11:B	Busy	FROM

FLOW CONTROL: 11   XON: YES ACK: LEADS THAT MUST BE ON:_____
SPEEDS: 110 300 600 1200 1800 2400 4800 9600 19.2 56k _____
PARITY: even odd space mark none   CHARACTER LENGTH: 7 8 ___
\# STOP BITS: 1 1.5 2   LINE-ENDING SEQUENCE: cr lf cr/lf
PRINTER COMPATIBILITY MODES: EpsonMX/FX/RX Diablo630 HPLaserJet NEC3500
   IBMgraphics Printronix TI-810_____   MODE: async sync isoch
PAGE DESCRIPTION LANGUAGE: PostScript DDL _____
NOTE 1:
NOTE 2:

PRINTER PORT PROFILE   (Underline if supported, circle if selected)
COMPANY: Imagen Corporation
PRODUCT: Image Processor

PORT: PORT TYPE: serial
CONNECTOR: DB25 DB9 5-PIN 8-PIN Centronics   GENDER: male female
PIN CONFIGURATION: P09

PIN	FUNCTION	DIRECTION
1:TD	Transmit Data	FROM
3:RD	Receive Data	TO
4:RTS	Request to Send	FROM
5:CTS	Clear to Send	TO
7:SG	Signal Ground	N/A
20:DTR	Data Terminal Ready	FROM

FLOW CONTROL: 4   XON: YES ACK: LEADS THAT MUST BE ON:_____
SPEEDS: 110 300 600 1200 1800 2400 4800 9600 19.2 56k _____
PARITY: even odd space mark none   CHARACTER LENGTH: 7 8 ___
\# STOP BITS: 1 1.5 2   LINE-ENDING SEQUENCE: cr lf cr/lf
PRINTER COMPATIBILITY MODES: EpsonMX/FX/RX Diablo630 HPLaserJet NEC3500
   IBMgraphics Printronix TI-810_____   MODE: async sync isoch
PAGE DESCRIPTION LANGUAGE: PostScript DDL _____
NOTE 1:
NOTE 2:

PRINTER PORT PROFILE (Underline if supported, circle if selected)
COMPANY: Imagen Corporation
PRODUCT: ImageServer XP

PORT: male   PORT TYPE: serial
CONNECTOR: DB25 DB9 5-PIN 8-PIN Centronics   GENDER: male female
PIN CONFIGURATION: P09

PIN	FUNCTION	DIRECTION
1:CG	Chassis Ground	N/A
2:TD	Transmit Data	FROM
3:RD	Receive Data	TO
4:RTS	Request to Send	FROM
5:CTS	Clear to Send	TO
7:SG	Signal Ground	N/A
20:DTR	Data Terminal Ready	FROM

FLOW CONTROL: 4   XON: YES ACK: LEADS THAT MUST BE ON:_____
SPEEDS: 110 300 600 1200 1800 2400 4800 9600 19.2 56k _____
PARITY: even odd space mark none   CHARACTER LENGTH: 7 8 ___
STOP BITS: 1 1.5 2   LINE-ENDING SEQUENCE: cr lf cr/lf
PRINTER COMPATIBILITY MODES: EpsonMX/FX/RX Diablo630 HPLaserJet NEC3500
    IBMgraphics Printronix TI-810_____   MODE: async sync isoch
PAGE DESCRIPTION LANGUAGE: PostScript DDL _____
NOTE 1:
NOTE 2:

PRINTER PORT PROFILE (Underline if supported, circle if selected)
COMPANY: Integrated Marketing Corp.
PRODUCT: Data Manager print sharing device

PORT: female (serial in)   PORT TYPE: serial
CONNECTOR: DB25 DB9 5-PIN 8-PIN Centronics   GENDER: male female
PIN CONFIGURATION: P03

PIN	FUNCTION	DIRECTION
1:CG	Chassis Ground	N/A
2:TD	Transmit Data	FROM
3:RD	Receive Data	TO
4:RTS	Request to Send	FROM
5:CTS	Clear to Send	TO
6:DSR	Data Set Ready	TO
7:SG	Signal Ground	N/A
8:CD	Carrier Detect	TO
20:DTR	Data Terminal Ready	FROM

FLOW CONTROL: 20   XON: YES ACK: LEADS THAT MUST BE ON:_____
SPEEDS: 110 300 600 1200 1800 2400 4800 9600 19.2 56k _____
PARITY: even odd space mark none   CHARACTER LENGTH: 7 8 ___
STOP BITS: 1 1.5 2   LINE-ENDING SEQUENCE: cr lf cr/lf
PRINTER COMPATIBILITY MODES: EpsonMX/FX/RX Diablo630 HPLaserJet NEC3500
    IBMgraphics Printronix TI-810_____   MODE: async sync isoch
PAGE DESCRIPTION LANGUAGE: PostScript DDL _____
NOTE 1:
NOTE 2:

PRINTER PORT PROFILE   (Underline if supported, circle if selected)
COMPANY: Leading Edge Products, Inc.
PRODUCT: F10 printers

PORT: female   PORT TYPE: serial
CONNECTOR: DB25 DB9 5-PIN 8-PIN Centronics   GENDER: male female
PIN CONFIGURATION: P03

PIN	FUNCTION	DIRECTION
1:FG	Frame Ground	N/A
2:TD	Transmit Data	FROM
3:RD	Receive Data	TO
4:RTS	Request to Send	FROM
5:CTS	Clear to Send	TO
6:DSR	Data Set Ready	TO
7:SG	Signal Ground	N/A
8:CD	Carrier Detect	TO
20:DTR	Data Terminal Ready	FROM

FLOW CONTROL: 20   XON: YES ACK: LEADS THAT MUST BE ON:_____
SPEEDS: 110 300 600 1200 1800 2400 4800 9600 19.2 56k _____
PARITY: even odd space mark none   CHARACTER LENGTH: 7 8 ___
STOP BITS: 1 1.5 2   LINE-ENDING SEQUENCE: cr lf cr/lf
PRINTER COMPATIBILITY MODES: EpsonMX/FX/RX Diablo630 HPLaserJet NEC3500
   IBMgraphics Printronix TI-810_____ MODE: async sync isoch
PAGE DESCRIPTION LANGUAGE: PostScript DDL _____
NOTE 1:
NOTE 2:

PRINTER PORT PROFILE   (Underline if supported, circle if selected)
COMPANY: LOVESHAW Corporation
PRODUCT: Little David(JET Jr.) printer

PORT: female   PORT TYPE: serial
CONNECTOR: DB25 DB9 5-PIN 8-PIN Centronics   GENDER: male female
PIN CONFIGURATION: C06

PIN	FUNCTION	DIRECTION
1:TD	Transmit Data	TO
3:RD	Receive Data	FROM
7:SG	Signal Ground	N/A

FLOW CONTROL: XON: ACK: LEADS THAT MUST BE ON:_____
SPEEDS: 110 300 600 1200 1800 2400 4800 9600 19.2 56k _____
PARITY: even odd space mark none   CHARACTER LENGTH: 7 8 ___
STOP BITS: 1 1.5 2   LINE-ENDING SEQUENCE: cr lf cr/lf
PRINTER COMPATIBILITY MODES: EpsonMX/FX/RX Diablo630 HPLaserJet NEC3500
   IBMgraphics Printronix TI-810_____ MODE: async sync isoch
PAGE DESCRIPTION LANGUAGE: PostScript DDL _____
NOTE 1:
NOTE 2:

PRINTER PORT PROFILE (Underline if supported, circle if selected)
COMPANY: Memodyne Corporation
PRODUCT: MP401 thermal printer

PORT: female

PORT TYPE: serial

CONNECTOR: DB25 DB9 5-PIN 8-PIN Centronics

GENDER: male female

PIN CONFIGURATION: P11

PIN	FUNCTION	DIRECTION
1:CG	Chassis Ground	N/A
2:TD	Transmit Data	FROM
3:RD	Receive Data	TO
7:SG	Signal Ground	N/A
20:DTR	Data Terminal Ready	FROM

FLOW CONTROL: 20   XON: YES ACK: LEADS THAT MUST BE ON:_____

SPEEDS: 110 300 600 1200 1800 2400 4800 9600 19.2 56k _____

PARITY: even odd space mark none   CHARACTER LENGTH: 7 8 ___

\# STOP BITS: 1 1.5 2   LINE-ENDING SEQUENCE: cr lf cr/lf

PRINTER COMPATIBILITY MODES: EpsonMX/FX/RX Diablo630 HPLaserJet NEC3500

  IBMgraphics Printronix TI-810_____   MODE: async sync isoch

PAGE DESCRIPTION LANGUAGE: PostScript DDL _____

NOTE 1:

NOTE 2:

PRINTER PORT PROFILE (Underline if supported, circle if selected)
COMPANY: Monarch Marking
PRODUCT: 6042 printer

PORT: female

PORT TYPE: serial

CONNECTOR: DB25 DB9 5-PIN 8-PIN Centronics

GENDER: male female

PIN CONFIGURATION: C06

PIN	FUNCTION	DIRECTION
1:PG	Protective Ground	N/A
2:RD	Receive Data	TO
3:TD	Transmit Data	FROM
7:SG	Signal Ground	N/A
20:DTR	Data Terminal Ready	FROM

FLOW CONTROL: 20   XON: ACK: LEADS THAT MUST BE ON:_____

SPEEDS: 110 300 600 1200 1800 2400 4800 9600 19.2 56k _____

PARITY: even odd space mark none   CHARACTER LENGTH: 7 8 ___

\# STOP BITS: 1 1.5 2   LINE-ENDING SEQUENCE: cr lf cr/lf

PRINTER COMPATIBILITY MODES: EpsonMX/FX/RX Diablo630 HPLaserJet NEC3500

  IBMgraphics Printronix TI-810_____   MODE: async sync isoch

PAGE DESCRIPTION LANGUAGE: PostScript DDL _____

NOTE 1:

NOTE 2:

PRINTER PORT PROFILE   (Underline if supported, circle if selected)
COMPANY: Monarch Marking
PRODUCT: 6070 printer/labeller

PORT: female   PORT TYPE: serial
CONNECTOR: DB25 DB9 5-PIN 8-PIN Centronics   GENDER: male female
PIN CONFIGURATION: C14

PIN	FUNCTION	DIRECTION
1:G	Ground	N/A
2:RD	Receive Data	TO
3:TD	Transmit Data	FROM
4:CTS	Clear to Send	TO
5:RTS	Request to Send	FROM
6:DTR	Data Terminal Ready	FROM
7:SG	Signal Ground	N/A
20:DTR	Data Terminal Ready	TO

FLOW CONTROL: XON: YES   ACK: LEADS THAT MUST BE ON:_____
SPEEDS: 110 300 600 1200 1800 2400 4800 9600 19.2 56k _____
PARITY: even odd space mark none   CHARACTER LENGTH: 7 8 ___
STOP BITS: 1 1.5 2   LINE-ENDING SEQUENCE: cr lf cr/lf
PRINTER COMPATIBILITY MODES: EpsonMX/FX/RX Diablo630 HPLaserJet NEC3500
   IBMgraphics Printronix TI-810_____   MODE: async sync isoch
PAGE DESCRIPTION LANGUAGE: PostScript DDL _____
NOTE 1:
NOTE 2:

PRINTER PORT PROFILE   (Underline if supported, circle if selected)
COMPANY: NEC Corporation
PRODUCT: PINwriter printers (P series)

PORT: serial   PORT TYPE: serial
CONNECTOR: DB25 DB9 5-PIN 8-PIN Centronics   GENDER: male female
PIN CONFIGURATION: P01

PIN	FUNCTION	DIRECTION
1:TD	Transmit Data	FROM
3:RD	Receive Data	TO
4:RTS	Request to Send	FROM
5:CTS	Clear to Send	TO
6:DSR	Data Set Ready	TO
7:SG	Signal Ground	N/A
8:CD	Carrier Detect	TO
19:RC	Rec. Clk/Reverse Chann	FROM
20:DTR	Data Terminal Ready	FROM

FLOW CONTROL: 19   XON: YES   ACK: YES LEADS THAT MUST BE ON:_____
SPEEDS: 110 300 600 1200 1800 2400 4800 9600 19.2 56k _____
PARITY: even odd space mark none   CHARACTER LENGTH: 7 8 ___
STOP BITS: 1 1.5 2   LINE-ENDING SEQUENCE: cr lf cr/lf
PRINTER COMPATIBILITY MODES: EpsonMX/FX/RX Diablo630 HPLaserJet NEC3500
   IBMgraphics Printronix TI-810_____   MODE: async sync isoch
PAGE DESCRIPTION LANGUAGE: PostScript DDL _____
NOTE 1:leads 5/6/8 must be on for printer to function
NOTE 2:

PRINTER PORT PROFILE (Underline if supported, circle if selected)
COMPANY: Norcom Electronics Corp.
PRODUCT: DP-80 printer

PORT: female   PORT TYPE: serial
CONNECTOR: DB25 DB9 5-PIN 8-PIN Centronics   GENDER: male female
PIN CONFIGURATION: P12

PIN	FUNCTION	DIRECTION
1:TD	Transmit Data	FROM
3:RD	Receive Data	TO
4:RTS	Request to Send	FROM
5:CTS	Clear to Send	TO
7:SG	Signal Ground	N/A

FLOW CONTROL: 4   XON: YES ACK: LEADS THAT MUST BE ON:_____
SPEEDS: 110 300 600 1200 1800 2400 4800 9600 19.2 56k _____
PARITY: even odd space mark none   CHARACTER LENGTH: 7 8 ___
STOP BITS: 1 1.5 2   LINE-ENDING SEQUENCE: cr lf cr/lf
PRINTER COMPATIBILITY MODES: EpsonMX/FX/RX Diablo630 HPLaserJet NEC3500
   IBMgraphics Printronix TI-810_____   MODE: async sync isoch
PAGE DESCRIPTION LANGUAGE: PostScript DDL _____
NOTE 1:
NOTE 2:

PRINTER PORT PROFILE (Underline if supported, circle if selected)
COMPANY: OASYS, Inc.
PRODUCT: LaserPro EXPRESS/810/1510 printers

PORT: female   PORT TYPE: serial
CONNECTOR: DB25 DB9 5-PIN 8-PIN Centronics   GENDER: male female
PIN CONFIGURATION: P11

PIN	FUNCTION	DIRECTION
1:G	Ground	N/A
2:TD	Transmit Data	FROM
3:RD	Receive Data	TO
7:SG	Signal Ground	N/A
20:DTR	Data Terminal Ready	FROM

FLOW CONTROL: 20   XON: YES ACK: YES LEADS THAT MUST BE ON:_____
SPEEDS: 110 300 600 1200 1800 2400 4800 9600 19.2 56k _____
PARITY: even odd space mark none   CHARACTER LENGTH: 7 8 ___
STOP BITS: 1 1.5 2   LINE-ENDING SEQUENCE: cr lf cr/lf
PRINTER COMPATIBILITY MODES: EpsonMX/FX/RX Diablo630 HPLaserJet NEC3500
   IBMgraphics Printronix TI-810_____   MODE: async sync isoch
PAGE DESCRIPTION LANGUAGE: PostScript DDL _____
NOTE 1:Insure that the polarity of DTR lead is positive
NOTE 2:

PRINTER PORT PROFILE   (Underline if supported, circle if selected)
COMPANY: Okidata
PRODUCT: ML182 (w/ SS RS-232C)

PORT: female   PORT TYPE: serial
CONNECTOR: DB25 DB9 5-PIN 8-PIN Centronics   GENDER: male female
PIN CONFIGURATION: P05

PIN	FUNCTION	DIRECTION
1:PG	Protective Ground	N/A
2:TD	Transmit Data	FROM
3:RD	Receive Data	TO
4:RTS	Request to Send	FROM
6:DSR	Data Set Ready	TO
7:SG	Signal Ground	N/A
11:STD	Supervisory Trans.Data	FROM
20:DTR	Data Terminal Ready	FROM

FLOW CONTROL: 11 20 4   XON: YES ACK: LEADS THAT MUST BE ON:_____
SPEEDS: 110 300 600 1200 1800 2400 4800 9600 19.2 56k _____
PARITY: even odd space mark none   CHARACTER LENGTH: 7 8 ___
STOP BITS: 1 1.5 2   LINE-ENDING SEQUENCE: cr lf cr/lf
PRINTER COMPATIBILITY MODES: EpsonMX/FX/RX Diablo630 HPLaserJet NEC3500
   IBMgraphics Printronix TI-810_____ MODE: async sync isoch
PAGE DESCRIPTION LANGUAGE: PostScript DDL _____
NOTE 1:
NOTE 2:

PRINTER PORT PROFILE   (Underline if supported, circle if selected)
COMPANY: Okidata
PRODUCT: ML182 printer (w/ HS RS-232C)

PORT: female   PORT TYPE: serial
CONNECTOR: DB25 DB9 5-PIN 8-PIN Centronics   GENDER: male female
PIN CONFIGURATION: P07

PIN	FUNCTION	DIRECTION
1:PG	Protective Ground	N/A
3:RD	Receive Data	TO
7:SG	Signal Ground	N/A
11:STD	Supervisory Trans.Data	FROM
20:DTR	Data Terminal Ready	FROM

FLOW CONTROL: 11   XON: ACK: LEADS THAT MUST BE ON:_____
SPEEDS: 110 300 600 1200 1800 2400 4800 9600 19.2 56k _____
PARITY: even odd space mark none   CHARACTER LENGTH: 7 8 ___
STOP BITS: 1 1.5 2   LINE-ENDING SEQUENCE: cr lf cr/lf
PRINTER COMPATIBILITY MODES: EpsonMX/FX/RX Diablo630 HPLaserJet NEC3500
   IBMgraphics Printronix TI-810_____ MODE: async sync isoch
PAGE DESCRIPTION LANGUAGE: PostScript DDL _____
NOTE 1:
NOTE 2:

PRINTER PORT PROFILE (Underline if supported, circle if selected)
COMPANY: Olympia
PRODUCT: ESW series printers

PORT: male   PORT TYPE: serial
CONNECTOR: DB25 DB9 5-PIN 8-PIN Centronics   GENDER: male female
PIN CONFIGURATION: P09

PIN	FUNCTION	DIRECTION
1:CG	Chassis Ground	N/A
2:TD	Transmit Data	FROM
3:RD	Receive Data	TO
4:RTS	Request to Send	FROM
5:CTS	Clear to Send	TO
7:SG	Signal Ground	N/A
8:DCD	Data Carrier Detect	TO
20:DTR	Data Terminal Ready	FROM

FLOW CONTROL: 4   XON: YES ACK: LEADS THAT MUST BE ON:_____
SPEEDS: 110 300 600 1200 1800 2400 4800 9600 19.2 56k _____
PARITY: even odd space mark none   CHARACTER LENGTH: 7 8 ___
STOP BITS: 1 1.5 2   LINE-ENDING SEQUENCE: cr lf cr/lf
PRINTER COMPATIBILITY MODES: EpsonMX/FX/RX Diablo630 HPLaserJet NEC3500
    IBMgraphics Printronix TI-810_____ MODE: async sync isoch
PAGE DESCRIPTION LANGUAGE: PostScript DDL _____
NOTE 1:
NOTE 2:

PRINTER PORT PROFILE (Underline if supported, circle if selected)
COMPANY: Olympia USA Inc.
PRODUCT: NP 80/136 printers

PORT: female   PORT TYPE: serial
CONNECTOR: DB25 DB9 5-PIN 8-PIN Centronics   GENDER: male female
PIN CONFIGURATION: P05

PIN	FUNCTION	DIRECTION
1:FG	Frame Ground	N/A
2:TD	Transmit Data	FROM
3:RD	Receive Data	TO
4:RTS	Request to Send	FROM
5:CTS	Clear to Send	TO
6:DSR	Data Set Ready	TO
7:SG	Signal Ground	N/A
8:DCD	Data Carrier Detect	TO
11:RC	Rec. Clk/Reverse Chann	FROM
20:DTR	Data Terminal Ready	FROM

FLOW CONTROL: 11   XON: YES ACK: LEADS THAT MUST BE ON:_____
SPEEDS: 110 300 600 1200 1800 2400 4800 9600 19.2 56k _____
PARITY: even odd space mark none   CHARACTER LENGTH: 7 8 ___
STOP BITS: 1 1.5 2   LINE-ENDING SEQUENCE: cr lf cr/lf
PRINTER COMPATIBILITY MODES: EpsonMX/FX/RX Diablo630 HPLaserJet NEC3500
    IBMgraphics Printronix TI-810_____ MODE: async sync isoch
PAGE DESCRIPTION LANGUAGE: PostScript DDL _____
NOTE 1:
NOTE 2:

PRINTER PORT PROFILE (Underline if supported, circle if selected)
COMPANY: Output Technology Corporation
PRODUCT: OT-700 printer

PORT: female   PORT TYPE: serial
CONNECTOR: DB25 DB9 5-PIN 8-PIN Centronics   GENDER: male female
PIN CONFIGURATION: P03

PIN	FUNCTION	DIRECTION
1:FG	Frame Ground	N/A
2:TD	Transmit Data	FROM
3:RD	Receive Data	TO
4:RTS	Request to Send	FROM
7:SG	Signal Ground	N/A
11:B	Busy	FROM
19:B	Busy	FROM
20:DTR	Data Terminal Ready	FROM

FLOW CONTROL: 20 11 19   XON: YES ACK: YES LEADS THAT MUST BE ON:_____
SPEEDS: 110 300 600 1200 1800 2400 4800 9600 19.2 56k _____
PARITY: even odd space mark none   CHARACTER LENGTH: 7 8 ___
STOP BITS: 1 1.5 2   LINE-ENDING SEQUENCE: cr lf cr/lf
PRINTER COMPATIBILITY MODES: EpsonMX/FX/RX Diablo630 HPLaserJet NEC3500
  IBMgraphics Printronix TI-810_____ MODE: async sync isoch
PAGE DESCRIPTION LANGUAGE: PostScript DDL _____
NOTE 1:
NOTE 2:

PRINTER PORT PROFILE (Underline if supported, circle if selected)
COMPANY: Perry Data Systems, Inc.
PRODUCT: 2014/2042 printers

PORT: female   PORT TYPE: serial
CONNECTOR: DB25 DB9 5-PIN 8-PIN Centronics   GENDER: male female
PIN CONFIGURATION: P07

PIN	FUNCTION	DIRECTION
1:FG	Frame Ground	N/A
2:TD	Transmit Data	FROM
3:RD	Receive Data	TO
7:SG	Signal Ground	N/A
11:RTS	Request to Send	FROM
20:DTR	Data Terminal Ready	FROM

FLOW CONTROL: 11   XON: YES ACK: LEADS THAT MUST BE ON:_____
SPEEDS: 110 300 600 1200 1800 2400 4800 9600 19.2 56k _____
PARITY: even odd space mark none   CHARACTER LENGTH: 7 8 ___
STOP BITS: 1 1.5 2   LINE-ENDING SEQUENCE: cr lf cr/lf
PRINTER COMPATIBILITY MODES: EpsonMX/FX/RX Diablo630 HPLaserJet NEC3500
  IBMgraphics Printronix TI-810_____ MODE: async sync isoch
PAGE DESCRIPTION LANGUAGE: PostScript DDL _____
NOTE 1:
NOTE 2:

PRINTER PORT PROFILE   (Underline if supported, circle if selected)
COMPANY: Primages, Inc.
PRODUCT: 90/100 printers

PORT: female   PORT TYPE: serial
CONNECTOR: DB25 DB9 5-PIN 8-PIN Centronics   GENDER: male female
PIN CONFIGURATION: P04

PIN	FUNCTION	DIRECTION
1:CG	Chassis Ground	N/A
2:TD	Transmit Data	FROM
3:RD	Receive Data	TO
4:RTS	Request to Send	FROM
7:SG	Signal Ground	N/A
11:PB	Printer Busy	FROM
20:DTR	Data Terminal Ready	FROM

FLOW CONTROL: 11 20   XON: YES ACK: LEADS THAT MUST BE ON:_____
SPEEDS: 110 300 600 1200 1800 2400 4800 9600 19.2 56k _____
PARITY: even odd space mark none   CHARACTER LENGTH: 7 8 ___
STOP BITS: 1 1.5 2   LINE-ENDING SEQUENCE: cr lf cr/lf
PRINTER COMPATIBILITY MODES: EpsonMX/FX/RX Diablo630 HPLaserJet NEC3500
   IBMgraphics Printronix TI-810_____   MODE: async sync isoch
PAGE DESCRIPTION LANGUAGE: PostScript DDL _____
NOTE 1:
NOTE 2:

PRINTER PORT PROFILE   (Underline if supported, circle if selected)
COMPANY: Printer Products
PRODUCT: S100/S200/S400/S500/S600/S700/S800 series printers

PORT: female   PORT TYPE: serial
CONNECTOR: DB25 DB9 5-PIN 8-PIN Centronics   GENDER: male female
PIN CONFIGURATION: P05

PIN	FUNCTION	DIRECTION
1:CG	Chassis Ground	N/A
2:TD	Transmit Data	FROM
3:RD	Receive Data	TO
4:RTS	Request to Send	FROM
5:CTS	Clear to Send	TO
7:SG	Signal Ground	N/A
11:PB	Printer Busy	FROM
20:DTR	Data Terminal Ready	FROM
22:R		TO
23:F	Fault	FROM

FLOW CONTROL: 11   XON: ACK: LEADS THAT MUST BE ON:_____
SPEEDS: 110 300 600 1200 1800 2400 4800 9600 19.2 56k _____
PARITY: even odd space mark none   CHARACTER LENGTH: 7 8 ___
STOP BITS: 1 1.5 2   LINE-ENDING SEQUENCE: cr lf cr/lf
PRINTER COMPATIBILITY MODES: EpsonMX/FX/RX Diablo630 HPLaserJet NEC3500
   IBMgraphics Printronix TI-810_____   MODE: async sync isoch
PAGE DESCRIPTION LANGUAGE: PostScript DDL _____
NOTE 1:
NOTE 2:

PRINTER PORT PROFILE   (Underline if supported, circle if selected)
COMPANY: QMS, Inc.
PRODUCT: KISS printer

PORT: female   PORT TYPE: serial
CONNECTOR: DB25 DB9 5-PIN 8-PIN Centronics   GENDER: male female
PIN CONFIGURATION: P08

PIN	FUNCTION	DIRECTION
1:CG	Chassis Ground	N/A
2:TD	Transmit Data	FROM
3:RD	Receive Data	TO
4:RTS	Request to Send	FROM
6:DSR	Data Set Ready	TO
7:LG	Logic Ground	N/A
20:DTR	Data Terminal Ready	FROM

FLOW CONTROL: 20 4   XON: YES ACK: LEADS THAT MUST BE ON:_____
SPEEDS: 110 300 600 1200 1800 2400 4800 9600 19.2 56k _____
PARITY: even odd space mark none   CHARACTER LENGTH: 7 8 ___
STOP BITS: 1 1.5 2   LINE-ENDING SEQUENCE: cr lf cr/lf
PRINTER COMPATIBILITY MODES: EpsonMX/FX/RX Diablo630 HPLaserJet NEC3500
   IBMgraphics Printronix TI-810_____   MODE: async sync isoch
PAGE DESCRIPTION LANGUAGE: PostScript DDL _____
NOTE 1:
NOTE 2:

PRINTER PORT PROFILE   (Underline if supported, circle if selected)
COMPANY: Quadram Corporation
PRODUCT: Quadlaser printer

PORT: female   PORT TYPE: serial
CONNECTOR: DB25 DB9 5-PIN 8-PIN Centronics   GENDER: male female
PIN CONFIGURATION: P08

PIN	FUNCTION	DIRECTION
1:PG	Protective Ground	N/A
2:TD	Transmit Data	FROM
3:RD	Receive Data	TO
4:RTS	Request to Send	FROM
5:CTS	Clear to Send	TO
6:DSR	Data Set Ready	TO
7:SG	Signal Ground	N/A
20:DTR	Data Terminal Ready	FROM

FLOW CONTROL: 20   XON: YES ACK: LEADS THAT MUST BE ON:_____
SPEEDS: 110 300 600 1200 1800 2400 4800 9600 19.2 56k _____
PARITY: even odd space mark none   CHARACTER LENGTH: 7 8 ___
STOP BITS: 1 1.5 2   LINE-ENDING SEQUENCE: cr lf cr/lf
PRINTER COMPATIBILITY MODES: EpsonMX/FX/RX Diablo630 HPLaserJet NEC3500
   IBMgraphics Printronix TI-810_____   MODE: async sync isoch
PAGE DESCRIPTION LANGUAGE: PostScript DDL _____
NOTE 1:
NOTE 2:

PRINTER PORT PROFILE   (Underline if supported, circle if selected)
COMPANY: Qume Corporation
PRODUCT: LaserTEN printer

PORT: serial   PORT TYPE: serial
CONNECTOR: DB25 DB9 5-PIN 8-PIN Centronics   GENDER: male female
PIN CONFIGURATION: P03

PIN	FUNCTION	DIRECTION
1:CG	Chassis Ground	N/A
2:TD	Transmit Data	FROM
3:RD	Receive Data	TO
4:RTS	Request to Send	FROM
5:CTS	Clear to Send	TO
6:DSR	Data Set Ready	TO
7:SG	Signal Ground	N/A
8:CD	Carrier Detect	TO
20:DTR	Data Terminal Ready	FROM

FLOW CONTROL: 20   XON: YES ACK: YES LEADS THAT MUST BE ON:_____
SPEEDS: 110 300 600 1200 1800 2400 4800 9600 19.2 56k _____
PARITY: even odd space mark none   CHARACTER LENGTH: 7 8 ___
STOP BITS: 1 1.5 2   LINE-ENDING SEQUENCE: cr lf cr/lf
PRINTER COMPATIBILITY MODES: EpsonMX/FX/RX Diablo630 HPLaserJet NEC3500
   IBMgraphics Printronix TI-810_____ MODE: async sync isoch
PAGE DESCRIPTION LANGUAGE: PostScript DDL _____
NOTE 1:
NOTE 2:

PRINTER PORT PROFILE   (Underline if supported, circle if selected)
COMPANY: RCA
PRODUCT: VP2100 printer

PORT: female   PORT TYPE: serial
CONNECTOR: DB25 DB9 5-PIN 8-PIN Centronics   GENDER: male female
PIN CONFIGURATION: P03

PIN	FUNCTION	DIRECTION
1:FG	Frame Ground	N/A
2:TD	Transmit Data	FROM
3:RD	Receive Data	TO
4:RTS	Request to Send	FROM
6:DSR	Data Set Ready	TO
7:SG	Signal Ground	N/A
11:SRTS	Secondary Req.to Send	FROM
20:DTR	Data Terminal Ready	FROM

FLOW CONTROL: 20   XON: YES ACK: LEADS THAT MUST BE ON:_____
SPEEDS: 110 300 600 1200 1800 2400 4800 9600 19.2 56k _____
PARITY: even odd space mark none   CHARACTER LENGTH: 7 8 ___
STOP BITS: 1 1.5 2   LINE-ENDING SEQUENCE: cr lf cr/lf
PRINTER COMPATIBILITY MODES: EpsonMX/FX/RX Diablo630 HPLaserJet NEC3500
   IBMgraphics Printronix TI-810_____ MODE: async sync isoch
PAGE DESCRIPTION LANGUAGE: PostScript DDL _____
NOTE 1:Lead 11 is reverse polarity FROM   lead 20
NOTE 2:

PRINTER PORT PROFILE   (Underline if supported, circle if selected)
COMPANY: Ricoh
PRODUCT: LP4080R Laser printer

PORT: female   PORT TYPE: serial
CONNECTOR: DB25 DB9 5-PIN 8-PIN Centronics   GENDER: male female
PIN CONFIGURATION: P03

PIN	FUNCTION	DIRECTION
1:FG	Frame Ground	N/A
2:TD	Transmit Data	FROM
3:RD	Receive Data	TO
4:RTS	Request to Send	FROM
5:CTS	Clear to Send	TO
6:DSR	Data Set Ready	TO
7:SG	Signal Ground	N/A
8:CD	Carrier Detect	TO
20:DTR	Data Terminal Ready	FROM

FLOW CONTROL: 20   XON: YES ACK: YES LEADS THAT MUST BE ON:_____
SPEEDS: 110 300 600 1200 1800 2400 4800 9600 19.2 56k _____
PARITY: even odd space mark none   CHARACTER LENGTH: 7 8 ___
STOP BITS: 1 1.5 2   LINE-ENDING SEQUENCE: cr lf cr/lf
PRINTER COMPATIBILITY MODES: EpsonMX/FX/RX Diablo630 HPLaserJet NEC3500
   IBMgraphics Printronix TI-810_____ MODE: async sync isoch
PAGE DESCRIPTION LANGUAGE: PostScript DDL _____
NOTE 1:
NOTE 2:

PRINTER PORT PROFILE   (Underline if supported, circle if selected)
COMPANY: Ricoh
PRODUCT: RP3400Q printer

PORT: female   PORT TYPE: serial
CONNECTOR: DB25 DB9 5-PIN 8-PIN Centronics   GENDER: male female
PIN CONFIGURATION: P08

PIN	FUNCTION	DIRECTION
1:FG	Frame Ground	N/A
2:TD	Transmit Data	FROM
3:RD	Receive Data	TO
4:RTS	Request to Send	FROM
7:SG	Signal Ground	N/A
20:DTR	Data Terminal Ready	FROM

FLOW CONTROL: 20   XON: YES ACK: LEADS THAT MUST BE ON:_____
SPEEDS: 110 300 600 1200 1800 2400 4800 9600 19.2 56k _____
PARITY: even odd space mark none   CHARACTER LENGTH: 7 8 ___
STOP BITS: 1 1.5 2   LINE-ENDING SEQUENCE: cr lf cr/lf
PRINTER COMPATIBILITY MODES: EpsonMX/FX/RX Diablo630 HPLaserJet NEC3500
   IBMgraphics Printronix TI-810_____ MODE: async sync isoch
PAGE DESCRIPTION LANGUAGE: PostScript DDL _____
NOTE 1:
NOTE 2:

PRINTER PORT PROFILE (Underline if supported, circle if selected)
COMPANY: Sato Corporation
PRODUCT: M4500 thermal printer

PORT: female   PORT TYPE: serial
CONNECTOR: DB25 DB9 5-PIN 8-PIN Centronics   GENDER: male female
PIN CONFIGURATION: P08

PIN	FUNCTION	DIRECTION
1:FG	Frame Ground	N/A
2:TD	Transmit Data	FROM
3:RD	Receive Data	TO
4:RTS	Request to Send	FROM
5:CTS	Clear to Send	TO
6:DSR	Data Set Ready	TO
7:SG	Signal Ground	N/A
20:DTR	Data Terminal Ready	FROM

FLOW CONTROL: 20   XON: ACK: YES LEADS THAT MUST BE ON:_____
SPEEDS: 110 300 600 1200 1800 2400 4800 9600 19.2 56k _____
PARITY: even odd space mark none   CHARACTER LENGTH: 7 8 ___
STOP BITS: 1 1.5 2   LINE-ENDING SEQUENCE: cr lf cr/lf
PRINTER COMPATIBILITY MODES: EpsonMX/FX/RX Diablo630 HPLaserJet NEC3500
   IBMgraphics Printronix TI-810_____ MODE: async sync isoch
PAGE DESCRIPTION LANGUAGE: PostScript DDL _____
NOTE 1:
NOTE 2:

PRINTER PORT PROFILE (Underline if supported, circle if selected)
COMPANY: Sato Corporation
PRODUCT: M4600 thermal printer

PORT: female   PORT TYPE: serial
CONNECTOR: DB25 DB9 5-PIN 8-PIN Centronics   GENDER: male female
PIN CONFIGURATION: P11

PIN	FUNCTION	DIRECTION
1:FG	Frame Ground	N/A
3:RD	Receive Data	TO
7:SG	Signal Ground	N/A
20:DTR	Data Terminal Ready	FROM

FLOW CONTROL: 20   XON: ACK: LEADS THAT MUST BE ON:_____
SPEEDS: 110 300 600 1200 1800 2400 4800 9600 19.2 56k _____
PARITY: even odd space mark none   CHARACTER LENGTH: 7 8 ___
STOP BITS: 1 1.5 2   LINE-ENDING SEQUENCE: cr lf cr/lf
PRINTER COMPATIBILITY MODES: EpsonMX/FX/RX Diablo630 HPLaserJet NEC3500
   IBMgraphics Printronix TI-810_____ MODE: async sync isoch
PAGE DESCRIPTION LANGUAGE: PostScript DDL _____
NOTE 1:
NOTE 2:

PRINTER PORT PROFILE   (Underline if supported, circle if selected)
COMPANY: Service Concepts, Int.
PRODUCT: Adeus 2000 printers

PORT: serial   PORT TYPE: serial
CONNECTOR: DB25 DB9 5-PIN 8-PIN Centronics   GENDER: male female
PIN CONFIGURATION: P08

PIN	FUNCTION	DIRECTION
1:FG	Frame Ground	N/A
2:TD	Transmit Data	FROM
3:RD	Receive Data	TO
4:RTS	Request to Send	FROM
5:CTS	Clear to Send	TO
6:DSR	Data Set Ready	TO
7:SG	Signal Ground	N/A
20:DTR	Data Terminal Ready	FROM

FLOW CONTROL: 20   XON: YES ACK: YES LEADS THAT MUST BE ON:_____
SPEEDS: 110 300 600 1200 1800 2400 4800 9600 19.2 56k _____
PARITY: even odd space mark none   CHARACTER LENGTH: 7 8 ___
STOP BITS: 1 1.5 2   LINE-ENDING SEQUENCE: cr lf cr/lf
PRINTER COMPATIBILITY MODES: EpsonMX/FX/RX Diablo630 HPLaserJet NEC3500
   IBMgraphics Printronix TI-810_____ MODE: async sync isoch
PAGE DESCRIPTION LANGUAGE: PostScript DDL _____
NOTE 1:this printers also equipped with a parallel port
NOTE 2:

PRINTER PORT PROFILE   (Underline if supported, circle if selected)
COMPANY: Shinwa of America, Inc.
PRODUCT: VP & LP printers

PORT: female   PORT TYPE: serial
CONNECTOR: DB25 DB9 5-PIN 8-PIN Centronics   GENDER: male female
PIN CONFIGURATION: P10

PIN	FUNCTION	DIRECTION
1:G	Ground	N/A
2:TD	Transmit Data	FROM
3:RD	Receive Data	TO
4:RTS	Request to Send	FROM
6:DSR	Data Set Ready	TO
7:SG	Signal Ground	N/A
8:CD	Carrier Detect	TO
14:AF		TO
20:DTR	Data Terminal Ready	FROM

FLOW CONTROL: XON: YES ACK: LEADS THAT MUST BE ON:_____
SPEEDS: 110 300 600 1200 1800 2400 4800 9600 19.2 56k _____
PARITY: even odd space mark none   CHARACTER LENGTH: 7 8 ___
STOP BITS: 1 1.5 2   LINE-ENDING SEQUENCE: cr lf cr/lf
PRINTER COMPATIBILITY MODES: EpsonMX/FX/RX Diablo630 HPLaserJet NEC3500
   IBMgraphics Printronix TI-810_____ MODE: async sync isoch
PAGE DESCRIPTION LANGUAGE: PostScript DDL _____
NOTE 1:
NOTE 2:

PRINTER PORT PROFILE   (Underline if supported, circle if selected)
COMPANY: Siemens
PRODUCT: PT88/PT89 printers

PORT: female   PORT TYPE: serial
CONNECTOR: DB25 DB9 5-PIN 8-PIN Centronics   GENDER: male female
PIN CONFIGURATION: P15

PIN	FUNCTION	DIRECTION
1:PG	Protective Ground	N/A
2:TD	Transmit Data	FROM
3:RD	Receive Data	TO
4:RTS	Request to Send	FROM
5:CTS	Clear to Send	TO
6:DSR	Data Set Ready	TO
7:SG	Signal Ground	N/A
8:DCD	Data Carrier Detect	TO
20:DTR	Data Terminal Ready	FROM
25:B	Busy	FROM

FLOW CONTROL: 25 20   XON: YES ACK: YES LEADS THAT MUST BE ON:_____
SPEEDS: 110 300 600 1200 1800 2400 4800 9600 19.2 56k _____
PARITY: even odd space mark none   CHARACTER LENGTH: 7 8 ___
STOP BITS: 1 1.5 2   LINE-ENDING SEQUENCE: cr lf cr/lf
PRINTER COMPATIBILITY MODES: EpsonMX/FX/RX Diablo630 HPLaserJet NEC3500
   IBMgraphics Printronix TI-810_____   MODE: async sync isoch
PAGE DESCRIPTION LANGUAGE: PostScript DDL _____
NOTE 1:
NOTE 2:

PRINTER PORT PROFILE   (Underline if supported, circle if selected)
COMPANY: Singer Data Products, Inc.
PRODUCT: PC-200/PC-4 (HR) printers

PORT: male or female   PORT TYPE: serial
CONNECTOR: DB25 DB9 5-PIN 8-PIN Centronics   GENDER: male female
PIN CONFIGURATION: P08

PIN	FUNCTION	DIRECTION
2:TD	Transmit Data	FROM
3:RD	Receive Data	TO
4:RTS	Request to Send	FROM
6:DSR	Data Set Ready	TO
7:SG	Signal Ground	N/A
20:DTR	Data Terminal Ready	FROM

FLOW CONTROL: 20 11 14   XON: YES ACK: LEADS THAT MUST BE ON:_____
SPEEDS: 110 300 600 1200 1800 2400 4800 9600 19.2 56k _____
PARITY: even odd space mark none   CHARACTER LENGTH: 7 8 ___
STOP BITS: 1 1.5 2   LINE-ENDING SEQUENCE: cr lf cr/lf
PRINTER COMPATIBILITY MODES: EpsonMX/FX/RX Diablo630 HPLaserJet NEC3500
   IBMgraphics Printronix TI-810_____   MODE: async sync isoch
PAGE DESCRIPTION LANGUAGE: PostScript DDL _____
NOTE 1: These PINouts apply to boards HRE-2006A-M6 or
NOTE 2: higher, and HRE-2006B-M0 or higher

PRINTER PORT PROFILE   (Underline if supported, circle if selected)
COMPANY: Singer Data Products
PRODUCT: PC-200/Hermes PC-4 (HR) printers

PORT: male   PORT TYPE: serial
CONNECTOR: DB25 DB9 5-PIN 8-PIN Centronics   GENDER: male female
PIN CONFIGURATION: P08

PIN	FUNCTION	DIRECTION
2:TD	Transmit Data	FROM
3:RD	Receive Data	TO
4:RTS	Request to Send	FROM
7:SG	Signal Ground	N/A
20:DTR	Data Terminal Ready	FROM

FLOW CONTROL: 20 11 14   XON: YES ACK: LEADS THAT MUST BE ON:_____
SPEEDS: 110 300 600 1200 1800 2400 4800 9600 19.2 56k _____
PARITY: even odd space mark none   CHARACTER LENGTH: 7 8 ___
STOP BITS: 1 1.5 2   LINE-ENDING SEQUENCE: cr lf cr/lf
PRINTER COMPATIBILITY MODES: EpsonMX/FX/RX Diablo630 HPLaserJet NEC3500
   IBMgraphics Printronix TI-810_____   MODE: async sync isoch
PAGE DESCRIPTION LANGUAGE: PostScript DDL _____
NOTE 1: The above PINouts apply to serial numbered boards
NOTE 2: lower than HRE-2006A-M6 or lower than HRE-2006B-M0

PRINTER PORT PROFILE   (Underline if supported, circle if selected)
COMPANY: Star Micronics
PRODUCT: NB-15 printer

PORT: female(serial)   PORT TYPE: serial
CONNECTOR: DB25 DB9 5-PIN 8-PIN Centronics   GENDER: male female
PIN CONFIGURATION: P05

PIN	FUNCTION	DIRECTION
1:G	Ground	N/A
2:TD	Transmit Data	FROM
3:RD	Receive Data	TO
4:RTS	Request to Send	FROM
5:CTS	Clear to Send	TO
6:DSR	Data Set Ready	TO
7:SG	Signal Ground	N/A
8:DCD	Data Carrier Detect	TO
11:B	Busy	FROM
20:DTR	Data Terminal Ready	FROM

FLOW CONTROL: 11 20   XON: YES ACK: YES LEADS THAT MUST BE ON:_____
SPEEDS: 110 300 600 1200 1800 2400 4800 9600 19.2 56k _____
PARITY: even odd space mark none   CHARACTER LENGTH: 7 8 ___
STOP BITS: 1 1.5 2   LINE-ENDING SEQUENCE: cr lf cr/lf
PRINTER COMPATIBILITY MODES: EpsonMX/FX/RX Diablo630 HPLaserJet NEC3500
   IBMgraphics Printronix TI-810_____ MODE: async sync isoch
PAGE DESCRIPTION LANGUAGE: PostScript DDL _____
NOTE 1:This port is an option on this printer
NOTE 2:

PRINTER PORT PROFILE   (Underline if supported, circle if selected)
COMPANY: Star Micronics
PRODUCT: SD/SB printers

PORT: serial   PORT TYPE: serial
CONNECTOR: DB25 DB9 5-PIN 8-PIN Centronics   GENDER: male female
PIN CONFIGURATION: PO5

PIN	FUNCTION	DIRECTION
1:G	Ground	N/A
2:TD	Transmit Data	FROM
3:RD	Receive Data	TO
4:RTS	Request to Send	FROM
5:CTS	Clear to Send	TO
7:SG	Signal Ground	N/A
11:RC	Rec. Clk/Reverse Chann	FROM
20:DTR	Data Terminal Ready	FROM

FLOW CONTROL: 11 20   XON: YES   ACK: YES LEADS THAT MUST BE ON:_____
SPEEDS: 110 300 600 1200 1800 2400 4800 9600 19.2 56k _____
PARITY: even odd space mark none   CHARACTER LENGTH: 7 8 ___
STOP BITS: 1 1.5 2   LINE-ENDING SEQUENCE: cr lf cr/lf
PRINTER COMPATIBILITY MODES: EpsonMX/FX/RX Diablo630 HPLaserJet NEC3500
   IBMgraphics Printronix TI-810_____   MODE: async sync isoch
PAGE DESCRIPTION LANGUAGE: PostScript DDL _____
NOTE 1:
NOTE 2:

PRINTER PORT PROFILE   (Underline if supported, circle if selected)
COMPANY: Swintec
PRODUCT: 8011/8012/8014/8016 typewriters (printers)

PORT: female   PORT TYPE: serial
CONNECTOR: DB25 DB9 5-PIN 8-PIN Centronics   GENDER: male female
PIN CONFIGURATION: C14

PIN	FUNCTION	DIRECTION
1:FG	Frame Ground	N/A
2:RD	Receive Data	TO
3:TD	Transmit Data	FROM
5:CTS	Clear to Send	TO
6:DTR	Data Terminal Ready	FROM
7:SG	Signal Ground	N/A
8:DTR	Data Terminal Ready	FROM
20:DSR	Data Set Ready	TO

FLOW CONTROL: 6   XON: YES   ACK: LEADS THAT MUST BE ON:_____
SPEEDS: 110 300 600 1200 1800 2400 4800 9600 19.2 56k _____
PARITY: even odd space mark none   CHARACTER LENGTH: 7 8 ___
STOP BITS: 1 1.5 2   LINE-ENDING SEQUENCE: cr lf cr/lf
PRINTER COMPATIBILITY MODES: EpsonMX/FX/RX Diablo630 HPLaserJet NEC3500
   IBMgraphics Printronix TI-810_____   MODE: async sync isoch
PAGE DESCRIPTION LANGUAGE: PostScript DDL _____
NOTE 1: This port emulates DCE.
NOTE 2: speed is limited to 300, 1200, or 4800 baud

PRINTER PORT PROFILE   (Underline if supported, circle if selected)
COMPANY: Swintec
PRODUCT: Computermate 2100 printer

PORT: female   PORT TYPE: serial
CONNECTOR: DB25 DB9 5-PIN 8-PIN Centronics   GENDER: male female
PIN CONFIGURATION: P11

PIN	FUNCTION	DIRECTION
1:FG	Frame Ground	N/A
2:TD	Transmit Data	FROM
3:RD	Receive Data	TO
7:SG	Signal Ground	N/A
20:DTR	Data Terminal Ready	FROM

FLOW CONTROL: 20   XON: YES ACK: LEADS THAT MUST BE ON:_____
SPEEDS: 110 300 600 1200 1800 2400 4800 9600 19.2 56k _____
PARITY: even odd space mark none   CHARACTER LENGTH: 7 8 ___
STOP BITS: 1 1.5 2   LINE-ENDING SEQUENCE: cr lf cr/lf
PRINTER COMPATIBILITY MODES: EpsonMX/FX/RX Diablo630 HPLaserJet NEC3500
   IBMgraphics Printronix TI-810_____   MODE: async sync isoch
PAGE DESCRIPTION LANGUAGE: PostScript DDL _____
NOTE 1:
NOTE 2:

PRINTER PORT PROFILE   (Underline if supported, circle if selected)
COMPANY: Syntest Corporation
PRODUCT: SP-309 alphanumeric ticket printer

PORT: female   PORT TYPE: serial
CONNECTOR: DB25 DB9 5-PIN 8-PIN Centronics   GENDER: male female
PIN CONFIGURATION: P07

PIN	FUNCTION	DIRECTION
1:G	Ground	N/A
3:RD	Receive Data	TO
7:SG	Signal Ground	N/A
11:B	Busy	FROM
20:DTR	Data Terminal Ready	FROM

FLOW CONTROL: 11   XON: YES ACK: LEADS THAT MUST BE ON:_____
SPEEDS: 110 300 600 1200 1800 2400 4800 9600 19.2 56k _____
PARITY: even odd space mark none   CHARACTER LENGTH: 7 8 ___
STOP BITS: 1 1.5 2   LINE-ENDING SEQUENCE: cr lf cr/lf
PRINTER COMPATIBILITY MODES: EpsonMX/FX/RX Diablo630 HPLaserJet NEC3500
   IBMgraphics Printronix TI-810_____   MODE: async sync isoch
PAGE DESCRIPTION LANGUAGE: PostScript DDL _____
NOTE 1:
NOTE 2:

PRINTER PORT PROFILE   (Underline if supported, circle if selected)
COMPANY: TAB Products Co.
PRODUCT: M-184 M-21 M-23 & M-25 printers

PORT: female   PORT TYPE: serial
CONNECTOR: DB25 DB9 5-PIN 8-PIN Centronics   GENDER: male female
PIN CONFIGURATION: P05

PIN	FUNCTION	DIRECTION
1:PG	Protective Ground	N/A
2:TD	Transmit Data	FROM
3:RD	Receive Data	TO
4:RTS	Request to Send	FROM
6:DSR	Data Set Ready	TO
7:SG	Signal Ground	N/A
11:STD	Supervisory Trans.Data	FROM
20:DTR	Data Terminal Ready	FROM

FLOW CONTROL: 11 20   XON: YES ACK: LEADS THAT MUST BE ON:_____
SPEEDS: 110 300 600 1200 1800 2400 4800 9600 19.2 56k _____
PARITY: even odd space mark none   CHARACTER LENGTH: 7 8 ___
STOP BITS: 1 1.5 2   LINE-ENDING SEQUENCE: cr lf cr/lf
PRINTER COMPATIBILITY MODES: EpsonMX/FX/RX Diablo630 HPLaserJet NEC3500
  IBMgraphics Printronix TI-810_____ MODE: async sync isoch
PAGE DESCRIPTION LANGUAGE: PostScript DDL _____
NOTE 1:
NOTE 2:

PRINTER PORT PROFILE   (Underline if supported, circle if selected)
COMPANY: Talaris Systems Inc.
PRODUCT: 800/1200/2400 Laser printers

PORT: female   PORT TYPE: serial
CONNECTOR: DB25 DB9 5-PIN 8-PIN Centronics   GENDER: male female
PIN CONFIGURATION: P08

PIN	FUNCTION	DIRECTION	PIN	FUNCTION	DIRECTION
1:G	Ground	N/A	7:SG	Signal Ground	N/A
2:TD	Transmit Data	FROM	15:TC	Transmit Clock	TO
3:RD	Receive Data	TO	17:RC	Rec. Clk/Reverse Chann	TO
4:RTS	Request to Send	FROM	20:DTR	Data Terminal Ready	FROM
5:CTS	Clear to Send	TO			

FLOW CONTROL: 20   XON: YES ACK: LEADS THAT MUST BE ON:_____
SPEEDS: 110 300 600 1200 1800 2400 4800 9600 19.2 56k _____
PARITY: even odd space mark none   CHARACTER LENGTH: 7 8 ___
STOP BITS: 1 1.5 2   LINE-ENDING SEQUENCE: cr lf cr/lf
PRINTER COMPATIBILITY MODES: EpsonMX/FX/RX Diablo630 HPLaserJet NEC3500
  IBMgraphics Printronix TI-810_____ MODE: async sync isoch
PAGE DESCRIPTION LANGUAGE: PostScript DDL _____
NOTE 1:
NOTE 2:

PRINTER PORT PROFILE   **(Underline if supported, circle if selected)**
COMPANY: Talaris Systems, Inc.
PRODUCT: 810/610 Laser printers

PORT: female   PORT TYPE: serial
CONNECTOR: DB25 DB9 5-PIN 8-PIN Centronics   GENDER: male female
PIN CONFIGURATION: PO9

PIN	FUNCTION	DIRECTION
1:CG	Chassis Ground	N/A
2:TD	Transmit Data	FROM
3:RD	Receive Data	TO
4:RTS	Request to Send	FROM
6:DSR	Data Set Ready	TO
7:SG	Signal Ground	N/A
20:DTR	Data Terminal Ready	FROM

FLOW CONTROL: 4 20   XON: YES ACK: LEADS THAT MUST BE ON:_____
SPEEDS: 110 300 600 1200 1800 2400 4800 9600 19.2 56k _____
PARITY: even odd space mark none   CHARACTER LENGTH: 7 8 ___
STOP BITS: 1 1.5 2   LINE-ENDING SEQUENCE: cr lf cr/lf
PRINTER COMPATIBILITY MODES: EpsonMX/FX/RX Diablo630 HPLaserJet NEC3500
  IBMgraphics Printronix TI-810_____   MODE: async sync isoch
PAGE DESCRIPTION LANGUAGE: PostScript DDL _____
NOTE 1:
NOTE 2:

PRINTER PORT PROFILE   **(Underline if supported, circle if selected)**
COMPANY: Toshiba America - IS Division
PRODUCT: P13xx & P3xx & PageLaser12 printers

PORT: female serial   PORT TYPE: serial
CONNECTOR: DB25 DB9 5-PIN 8-PIN Centronics   GENDER: male female
PIN CONFIGURATION: PO1

PIN	FUNCTION	DIRECTION
1:FG	Frame Ground	N/A
2:SD		FROM
3:RD	Receive Data	TO
4:RTS	Request to Send	FROM
5:CTS	Clear to Send	TO
6:DSR	Data Set Ready	TO
7:SG	Signal Ground	N/A
8:CD	Carrier Detect	TO
19:DTR	Data Terminal Ready	FROM
20:DTR	Data Terminal Ready	FROM

FLOW CONTROL: 19 14 20   XON: YES ACK: YES LEADS THAT MUST BE ON:_____
SPEEDS: 110 300 600 1200 1800 2400 4800 9600 19.2 56k _____
PARITY: even odd space mark none   CHARACTER LENGTH: 7 8 ___
STOP BITS: 1 1.5 2   LINE-ENDING SEQUENCE: cr lf cr/lf
PRINTER COMPATIBILITY MODES: EpsonMX/FX/RX Diablo630 HPLaserJet NEC3500
  IBMgraphics Printronix TI-810_____   MODE: async sync isoch
PAGE DESCRIPTION LANGUAGE: PostScript DDL _____
NOTE 1:
NOTE 2:

PRINTER PORT PROFILE   (Underline if supported, circle if selected)
COMPANY: Versatec(Xerox)
PRODUCT: V-80 printer/plotter

PORT: serial   PORT TYPE: serial

CONNECTOR: DB25 DB9 5-PIN 8-PIN Centronics   GENDER: male female

PIN CONFIGURATION: P06

PIN	FUNCTION	DIRECTION
1:PG	Protective Ground	N/A
3:RD	Receive Data	TO
7:SG	Signal Ground	N/A
18:+5V		FROM
20:DTR	Data Terminal Ready	FROM
25:PB	Printer Busy	FROM

FLOW CONTROL: 25 20   XON: ACK: LEADS THAT MUST BE ON:_____

SPEEDS: 110 300 600 1200 1800 2400 4800 9600 19.2 56k _____

PARITY: even odd space mark none   CHARACTER LENGTH: 7 8 ___

STOP BITS: 1 1.5 2   LINE-ENDING SEQUENCE: cr lf cr/lf

PRINTER COMPATIBILITY MODES: EpsonMX/FX/RX Diablo630 HPLaserJet NEC3500

  IBMgraphics Printronix TI-810_____ MODE: async sync isoch

PAGE DESCRIPTION LANGUAGE: PostScript DDL _____

NOTE 1:

NOTE 2:

PRINTER PORT PROFILE (Underline if supported, circle if selected)
COMPANY: _____
PRODUCT: _____

PORT: _____   Port Type: serial parallel __
CONNECTOR: DB25 9-pin 5-pin 8-pin Centronics Gender: male female
Pin Configuration: ___

Pin #	Function	Direction	Pin #	Function	Direction
1	_____	to from n/a	14	_____	to from n/a
2	_____	to from n/a	15	_____	to from n/a
3	_____	to from n/a	16	_____	to from n/a
4	_____	to from n/a	17	_____	to from n/a
5	_____	to from n/a	18	_____	to from n/a
6	_____	to from n/a	19	_____	to from n/a
7	_____	to from n/a	20	_____	to from n/a
8	_____	to from n/a	21	_____	to from n/a
9	_____	to from n/a	22	_____	to from n/a
10	_____	to from n/a	23	_____	to from n/a
11	_____	to from n/a	24	_____	to from n/a
12	_____	to from n/a	25	_____	to from n/a
13	_____	to from n/a			

(complete the next section only with 36-pin cinch connectors)

Pin #	Function	Direction	Pin #	Function	Direction
26	_____	to from n/a	27	_____	to from n/a
28	_____	to from n/a	29	_____	to from n/a
30	_____	to from n/a	31	_____	to from n/a
32	_____	to from n/a	33	_____	to from n/a
34	_____	to from n/a	35	_____	to from n/a
36	_____	to from n/a			

Flow Control Technique: XON/XOFF ENQ/ACK STX/ETX Hardware
Flow Control lead(s):   4 11 19 20 __ __ __
Leads that must be on: 5 6 8 __ __ __ __
Speeds: 110 300 600 1200 1800 2400 4800 9600 19.2 56k _____
Parity: even odd space mark none   CHARACTER LENGTH: 7 8 ___
Stop Bits: 1 1.5 2   Line Ending Sequence: cr lf cr/lf
Printer Compatibility Modes: EpsonMX/FX/RX Diablo630 HPLaserJet NEC3500
  IBMgraphics Printronix TI-810 _____Mode: async sync isoch
Page Description Language: PostScript DDL _____

NOTE 1:_____
NOTE 2:_____

PRINTER PORT PROFILE (Underline if supported, circle if selected)
COMPANY: _____
PRODUCT: _____

PORT: _____   Port Type: serial parallel __
CONNECTOR: DB25 9-pin 5-pin 8-pin Centronics Gender: male female
Pin Configuration: ___

Pin #	Function	Direction	Pin #	Function	Direction
1	_____	to from n/a	14	_____	to from n/a
2	_____	to from n/a	15	_____	to from n/a
3	_____	to from n/a	16	_____	to from n/a
4	_____	to from n/a	17	_____	to from n/a
5	_____	to from n/a	18	_____	to from n/a
6	_____	to from n/a	19	_____	to from n/a
7	_____	to from n/a	20	_____	to from n/a
8	_____	to from n/a	21	_____	to from n/a
9	_____	to from n/a	22	_____	to from n/a
10	_____	to from n/a	23	_____	to from n/a
11	_____	to from n/a	24	_____	to from n/a
12	_____	to from n/a	25	_____	to from n/a
13	_____	to from n/a			

(complete the next section only with 36-pin cinch connectors)

Pin #	Function	Direction	Pin #	Function	Direction
26	_____	to from n/a	27	_____	to from n/a
28	_____	to from n/a	29	_____	to from n/a
30	_____	to from n/a	31	_____	to from n/a
32	_____	to from n/a	33	_____	to from n/a
34	_____	to from n/a	35	_____	to from n/a
36	_____	to from n/a			

Flow Control Technique: XON/XOFF ENQ/ACK STX/ETX Hardware
Flow Control lead(s):   4 11 19 20 __ __ __
Leads that must be on: 5   6   8 __ __ __ __
Speeds: 110 300 600 1200 1800 2400 4800 9600 19.2 56k _____
Parity: even odd space mark none   CHARACTER LENGTH: 7 8 ___
Stop Bits: 1 1.5 2   Line Ending Sequence: cr lf cr/lf
Printer Compatibility Modes: EpsonMX/FX/RX Diablo630 HPLaserJet NEC3500
  IBMgraphics Printronix TI-810 _____Mode: async sync isoch
Page Description Language: PostScript DDL _____

NOTE 1:_____
NOTE 2:_____

PRINTER PORT PROFILE (Underline if supported, circle if selected)
COMPANY: _____
PRODUCT: _____

PORT: _____   Port Type: serial parallel __
CONNECTOR: DB25 9-pin 5-pin 8-pin Centronics Gender: male female
Pin Configuration: ___

Pin #	Function	Direction	Pin #	Function	Direction
1	_____	to from n/a	14	_____	to from n/a
2	_____	to from n/a	15	_____	to from n/a
3	_____	to from n/a	16	_____	to from n/a
4	_____	to from n/a	17	_____	to from n/a
5	_____	to from n/a	18	_____	to from n/a
6	_____	to from n/a	19	_____	to from n/a
7	_____	to from n/a	20	_____	to from n/a
8	_____	to from n/a	21	_____	to from n/a
9	_____	to from n/a	22	_____	to from n/a
10	_____	to from n/a	23	_____	to from n/a
11	_____	to from n/a	24	_____	to from n/a
12	_____	to from n/a	25	_____	to from n/a
13	_____	to from n/a			

(complete the next section only with 36-pin cinch connectors)

Pin #	Function	Direction	Pin #	Function	Direction
26	_____	to from n/a	27	_____	to from n/a
28	_____	to from n/a	29	_____	to from n/a
30	_____	to from n/a	31	_____	to from n/a
32	_____	to from n/a	33	_____	to from n/a
34	_____	to from n/a	35	_____	to from n/a
36	_____	to from n/a			

Flow Control Technique: XON/XOFF ENQ/ACK STX/ETX Hardware
Flow Control lead(s):   4 11 19 20 __ __ __
Leads that must be on: 5   6   8 __ __ __ __
Speeds: 110 300 600 1200 1800 2400 4800 9600 19.2 56k _____
Parity: even odd space mark none   CHARACTER LENGTH: 7 8 ___
Stop Bits: 1 1.5 2   Line Ending Sequence: cr lf cr/lf
Printer Compatibility Modes: EpsonMX/FX/RX Diablo630 HPLaserJet NEC3500
   IBMgraphics Printronix TI-810 _____Mode: async sync isoch
Page Description Language: PostScript DDL _____

NOTE 1:_____
NOTE 2:_____

PRINTER PORT PROFILE (Underline if supported, circle if selected)
COMPANY: _____
PRODUCT: _____

PORT: _____   Port Type: serial parallel ___
CONNECTOR: DB25 9-pin 5-pin 8-pin Centronics Gender: male female
Pin Configuration: ___

Pin #	Function	Direction	Pin #	Function	Direction
1	_____	to from n/a	14	_____	to from n/a
2	_____	to from n/a	15	_____	to from n/a
3	_____	to from n/a	16	_____	to from n/a
4	_____	to from n/a	17	_____	to from n/a
5	_____	to from n/a	18	_____	to from n/a
6	_____	to from n/a	19	_____	to from n/a
7	_____	to from n/a	20	_____	to from n/a
8	_____	to from n/a	21	_____	to from n/a
9	_____	to from n/a	22	_____	to from n/a
10	_____	to from n/a	23	_____	to from n/a
11	_____	to from n/a	24	_____	to from n/a
12	_____	to from n/a	25	_____	to from n/a
13	_____	to from n/a			

(complete the next section only with 36-pin cinch connectors)

Pin #	Function	Direction	Pin #	Function	Direction
26	_____	to from n/a	27	_____	to from n/a
28	_____	to from n/a	29	_____	to from n/a
30	_____	to from n/a	31	_____	to from n/a
32	_____	to from n/a	33	_____	to from n/a
34	_____	to from n/a	35	_____	to from n/a
36	_____	to from n/a			

Flow Control Technique: XON/XOFF ENQ/ACK STX/ETX Hardware
Flow Control lead(s):   4 11 19 20 ___ ___ ___
Leads that must be on: 5   6   8 ___ ___ ___ ___
Speeds: 110 300 600 1200 1800 2400 4800 9600 19.2 56k _____
Parity: even odd space mark none   CHARACTER LENGTH: 7 8 ___
Stop Bits: 1 1.5 2   Line Ending Sequence: cr lf cr/lf
Printer Compatibility Modes: EpsonMX/FX/RX Diablo630 HPLaserJet NEC3500
   IBMgraphics Printronix TI-810 _____Mode: async sync isoch
Page Description Language: PostScript DDL _____

NOTE 1:_____
NOTE 2:_____

TERMINAL PORT PROFILE   (Underline if supported, circle if selected)
COMPANY: AT&T
PRODUCT: 4425 terminal

PORT: RS-232   PORT TYPE: serial
CONNECTOR: DB25 9-PIN 8-PIN(modular)   GENDER: male female
PIN CONFIGURATION: P10

PIN	FUNCTION	DIRECTION	PIN	FUNCTION	DIRECTION
1:PG	Protective Ground	N/A	10:-12V		FROM
2:TD	Transmit Data	FROM	11:STD	Supervisory Trans.Data	FROM
3:RD	Receive Data	TO	14:+5V		FROM
4:RTS	Request to Send	FROM	15:TC	Transmit Clock	TO
5:CTS	Clear to Send	TO	17:RC	Rec. Clk/Reverse Chann	TO
6:DSR	Data Set Ready	TO	19:SRTS	Secondary Req.to Send	FROM
7:SG	Signal Ground	N/A	20:DTR	Data Terminal Ready	FROM
8:DCD	Data Carrier Detect	TO	23:SS	Speed Select	FROM
9:+12V		FROM			

FLOW CONTROL: XON: YES ACK: LEADS THAT MUST BE ON: __ __ __
PRINTER PORT: serial   parallel   FLOW CONTROL: XON/XOFF Hardware
  FLOW CONTROL LEAD(s):   4 11 19 20 __ __   CONNECTOR: DB25 Centronics
SPEEDS: 110 300 600 1200 1800 2400 4800 9600 19.2 56k _____
PARITY: even odd space mark none   CHARACTER LENGTH: 7 8 ___
STOP BITS: 1 1.5 2   LINE-ENDING SEQUENCE: cr lf cr/lf
MODE: async sync isoch   EMULATION/COMPATIBLE: ANSI X3.64
    VT100, Televideo 925, ADM-3A, DG100, Hazeltine 1420, HP2621, Regent 25/30
NOTE 1: Leads 19 & 20 are always on.
NOTE 2:

TERMINAL PORT PROFILE   (Underline if supported, circle if selected)
COMPANY: AT&T
PRODUCT: 510A terminal

PORT: female   PORT TYPE: serial
CONNECTOR: DB25 9-PIN 8-PIN(modular)   GENDER: male female
PIN CONFIGURATION: C14

PIN	FUNCTION	DIRECTION	PIN	FUNCTION	DIRECTION
2:TD	Transmit Data	TO	6:DSR	Data Set Ready	FROM
3:RD	Receive Data	FROM	7:SG	Signal Ground	N/A
4:RTS	Request to Send	TO	8:DCD	Data Carrier Detect	FROM
5:CTS	Clear to Send	FROM	20:DTR	Data Terminal Ready	TO

FLOW CONTROL: XON: YES ACK: LEADS THAT MUST BE ON: __ __ __
PRINTER PORT: SERIAL   PARALLEL   FLOW CONTROL: XON/XOFF Hardware
  FLOW CONTROL LEAD(s):   4 11 19 20 __ __   CONNECTOR: DB25 Centronics
SPEEDS: 110 300 600 1200 1800 2400 4800 9600 19.2 56k _____
PARITY: even odd space mark none   CHARACTER LENGTH: 7 8 ___
STOP BITS: 1 1.5 2   LINE-ENDING SEQUENCE: cr lf cr/lf
MODE: async sync isoch   EMULATION/COMPATIBLE: ANSI X3.64
    VT100, Televideo 925, ADM-3A, DG100, Hazeltine 1420, HP2621, Regent 25/30
NOTE 1:
NOTE 2:

TERMINAL PORT PROFILE   (Underline if supported, circle if selected)
COMPANY: AT&T
PRODUCT: 5410/4410 terminal

PORT: female(modem)   PORT TYPE: serial
CONNECTOR: DB25 9-PIN 8-PIN(modular)   GENDER: male female
PIN CONFIGURATION: P10

PIN	FUNCTION	DIRECTION
1:PG	Protective Ground	N/A
2:TD	Transmit Data	FROM
3:RD	Receive Data	TO
4:RTS	Request to Send	FROM
5:CTS	Clear to Send	TO
6:DSR	Data Set Ready	TO
7:SG	Signal Ground	N/A
8:DCD	Data Carrier Detect	TO
20:DTR	Data Terminal Ready	FROM

FLOW CONTROL: XON: YES ACK: LEADS THAT MUST BE ON: __ __ __
PRINTER PORT: SERIAL   PARALLEL   FLOW CONTROL: XON/XOFF Hardware
  FLOW CONTROL LEAD(s):   4 11 19 20 __ __   CONNECTOR: DB25 Centronics
SPEEDS: 110 300 600 1200 1800 2400 4800 9600 19.2 56k _____
PARITY: even odd space mark none   CHARACTER LENGTH: 7 8 ___
STOP BITS: 1 1.5 2   LINE-ENDING SEQUENCE: cr lf cr/lf
MODE: async sync isoch   EMULATION/COMPATIBLE: ANSI X3.64
   VT100, Televideo 925, ADM-3A, DG100, Hazeltine 1420, HP2621, Regent 25/30
NOTE 1:
NOTE 2:

TERMINAL PORT PROFILE   (Underline if supported, circle if selected)
COMPANY: AT&T
PRODUCT: 610 terminal

PORT: female(AUX PORT)   PORT TYPE: serial
CONNECTOR: DB25 9-PIN 8-PIN(modular)   GENDER: male female
PIN CONFIGURATION: C14

PIN	FUNCTION	DIRECTION
1:PG	Protective Ground	N/A
2:TD	Transmit Data	TO
3:RD	Receive Data	FROM
6:DSR	Data Set Ready	FROM
7:SG	Signal Ground	N/A
8:DCD	Data Carrier Detect	FROM
20:DTR	Data Terminal Ready	TO

FLOW CONTROL: XON: YES ACK: LEADS THAT MUST BE ON: __ __ __
PRINTER PORT: SERIAL   PARALLEL   FLOW CONTROL: XON/XOFF Hardware
  FLOW CONTROL LEAD(s):   4 11 19 20 __ __   CONNECTOR: DB25 Centronics
SPEEDS: 110 300 600 1200 1800 2400 4800 9600 19.2 56k _____
PARITY: even odd space mark none   CHARACTER LENGTH: 7 8 ___
STOP BITS: 1 1.5 2   LINE-ENDING SEQUENCE: cr lf cr/lf
MODE: async sync isoch   EMULATION/COMPATIBLE: ANSI X3.64
   VT100, Televideo 925, ADM-3A, DG100, Hazeltine 1420, HP2621, Regent 25/30
NOTE 1:
NOTE 2:

TERMINAL PORT PROFILE (Underline if supported, circle if selected)
COMPANY: AT&T
PRODUCT: 610 terminal

PORT: female(MAIN PORT)   PORT TYPE: serial
CONNECTOR: DB25 9-PIN 8-PIN(modular)   GENDER: male female
PIN CONFIGURATION: P10

PIN	FUNCTION	DIRECTION
1:PG	Protective Ground	N/A
2:TD	Transmit Data	FROM
3:RD	Receive Data	TO
4:RTS	Request to Send	FROM
6:DSR	Data Set Ready	TO
7:SG	Signal Ground	N/A
20:DTR	Data Terminal Ready	FROM
23:SS	Speed Select	FROM

FLOW CONTROL: XON: YES ACK: LEADS THAT MUST BE ON: __ __ __
PRINTER PORT: SERIAL   PARALLEL   FLOW CONTROL: XON/XOFF Hardware
   FLOW CONTROL LEAD(s):   4 11 19 20 __ __   CONNECTOR: DB25 Centronics
SPEEDS: 110 300 600 1200 1800 2400 4800 9600 19.2 56k _____
PARITY: even odd space mark none   CHARACTER LENGTH: 7 8 ___
STOP BITS: 1 1.5 2   LINE-ENDING SEQUENCE: cr lf cr/lf
MODE: async sync isoch   EMULATION/COMPATIBLE: ANSI X3.64
   VT100, Televideo 925, ADM-3A, DG100, Hazeltine 1420, HP2621, Regent 25/30
NOTE 1:
NOTE 2:

TERMINAL PORT PROFILE (Underline if supported, circle if selected)
COMPANY: Beehive International
PRODUCT: ATL-004 terminal

PORT: female(AUX 25 PIN)   PORT TYPE: serial
CONNECTOR: DB25 9-PIN 8-PIN(modular)   GENDER: male female
PIN CONFIGURATION: C02

PIN	FUNCTION	DIRECTION	PIN	FUNCTION	DIRECTION
1:CG	Chassis Ground	N/A	6:DSR	Data Set Ready	FROM
2:TD	Transmit Data	TO	7:SG	Signal Ground	N/A
3:RD	Receive Data	FROM	8:DCD	Data Carrier Detect	FROM
4:RTS	Request to Send	TO	11:PB	Printer Busy	TO
5:CTS	Clear to Send	FROM	20:DTR	Data Terminal Ready	TO

FLOW CONTROL: 11 20   XON: YES ACK: LEADS THAT MUST BE ON: __ __ __
PRINTER PORT: SERIAL   PARALLEL   FLOW CONTROL: XON/XOFF Hardware
   FLOW CONTROL LEAD(s):   4 11 19 20 __ __   CONNECTOR: DB25 Centronics
SPEEDS: 110 300 600 1200 1800 2400 4800 9600 19.2 56k _____
PARITY: even odd space mark none   CHARACTER LENGTH: 7 8 ___
STOP BITS: 1 1.5 2   LINE-ENDING SEQUENCE: cr lf cr/lf
MODE: async sync isoch   EMULATION/COMPATIBLE: ANSI X3.64
   VT100, Televideo 925, ADM-3A, DG100, Hazeltine 1420, HP2621, Regent 25/30
NOTE 1:
NOTE 2:

TERMINAL PORT PROFILE (Underline if supported, circle if selected)
COMPANY: Beehive International
PRODUCT: ATL-004/ATL-008 terminals

PORT: female(main 25-PIN)   PORT TYPE: serial
CONNECTOR: DB25 9-PIN 8-PIN(modular)   GENDER: male female
PIN CONFIGURATION: P03

PIN	FUNCTION	DIRECTION	PIN	FUNCTION	DIRECTION
1:PG	Protective Ground	N/A	7:SG	Signal Ground	N/A
2:TD	Transmit Data	FROM	8:RLSD	Rec.Line Signal Detect	TO
3:RD	Receive Data	TO	15:TC	Transmit Clock	TO
4:RTS	Request to Send	FROM	17:RC	Rec. Clk/Reverse Chann	TO
5:CTS	Clear to Send	TO	20:DTR	Data Terminal Ready	FROM
6:DSR	Data Set Ready	TO			

FLOW CONTROL: 20   XON: YES ACK: LEADS THAT MUST BE ON: __ __ __
PRINTER PORT: SERIAL   PARALLEL   FLOW CONTROL: XON/XOFF Hardware
  FLOW CONTROL LEAD(s):   4 11 19 20 __ __   CONNECTOR: DB25 Centronics
SPEEDS: 110 300 600 1200 1800 2400 4800 9600 19.2 56k _____
PARITY: even odd space mark none   CHARACTER LENGTH: 7 8 ___
STOP BITS: 1 1.5 2   LINE-ENDING SEQUENCE: cr lf cr/lf
MODE: async sync isoch   EMULATION/COMPATIBLE: ANSI X3.64
    VT100, Televideo 925, ADM-3A, DG100, Hazeltine 1420, HP2621, Regent 25/30
NOTE 1:
NOTE 2:

TERMINAL PORT PROFILE (Underline if supported, circle if selected)
COMPANY: Beehive International
PRODUCT: ATL-220 terminal

PORT: male(main 25-PIN)   PORT TYPE: serial
CONNECTOR: DB25 9-PIN 8-PIN(modular)   GENDER: male female
PIN CONFIGURATION: P03

PIN	FUNCTION	DIRECTION	PIN	FUNCTION	DIRECTION
1:FG	Frame Ground	N/A	7:SG	Signal Ground	N/A
2:TD	Transmit Data	FROM	8:RLSD	Rec.Line Signal Detect	TO
3:RD	Receive Data	TO	12:SI	Serial In	TO
4:RTS	Request to Send	FROM	20:DTR	Data Terminal Ready	FROM
5:CTS	Clear to Send	TO	23:SS	Speed Select	FROM
6:DSR	Data Set Ready	TO			

FLOW CONTROL: 20   XON: YES ACK: LEADS THAT MUST BE ON: __ __ __
PRINTER PORT: SERIAL   PARALLEL   FLOW CONTROL: XON/XOFF Hardware
  FLOW CONTROL LEAD(s):   4 11 19 20 __ __   CONNECTOR: DB25 Centronics
SPEEDS: 110 300 600 1200 1800 2400 4800 9600 19.2 56k _____
PARITY: even odd space mark none   CHARACTER LENGTH: 7 8 ___
STOP BITS: 1 1.5 2   LINE-ENDING SEQUENCE: cr lf cr/lf
MODE: async sync isoch   EMULATION/COMPATIBLE: ANSI X3.64
    VT100, Televideo 925, ADM-3A, DG100, Hazeltine 1420, HP2621, Regent 25/30
NOTE 1:
NOTE 2:

TERMINAL PORT PROFILE   (Underline if supported, circle if selected)
COMPANY: Beehive International
PRODUCT: ATL-220/ATL-008/DM5 terminals

PORT: female(AUX 25 PIN)   PORT TYPE: serial
CONNECTOR: DB25 9-PIN 8-PIN(modular)   GENDER: male female
PIN CONFIGURATION: C09

PIN	FUNCTION	DIRECTION	PIN	FUNCTION	DIRECTION
1:FG	Frame Ground	N/A	7:SG	Signal Ground	N/A
2:TD	Transmit Data	TO	8:DCD	Data Carrier Detect	FROM
3:RD	Receive Data	FROM	11:PB	Printer Busy	TO
4:RTS	Request to Send	TO	19:PB	Printer Busy	TO
5:CTS	Clear to Send	FROM	20:DTR	Data Terminal Ready	TO
6:DSR	Data Set Ready	FROM			

FLOW CONTROL: 19 20 11   XON: YES ACK: LEADS THAT MUST BE ON: __ __ __
PRINTER PORT: SERIAL   PARALLEL   FLOW CONTROL: XON/XOFF Hardware
  FLOW CONTROL LEAD(s):   4 11 19 20 __ __   CONNECTOR: DB25 Centronics
SPEEDS: 110 300 600 1200 1800 2400 4800 9600 19.2 56k _____
PARITY: even odd space mark none   CHARACTER LENGTH: 7 8 ___
STOP BITS: 1 1.5 2   LINE-ENDING SEQUENCE: cr lf cr/lf
MODE: async sync isoch   EMULATION/COMPATIBLE: ANSI X3.64
    VT100, Televideo 925, ADM-3A, DG100, Hazeltine 1420, HP2621, Regent 25/30
NOTE 1:
NOTE 2:

TERMINAL PORT PROFILE   (Underline if supported, circle if selected)
COMPANY: Beehive International
PRODUCT: DM5 terminal

PORT: female(Main)   PORT TYPE: serial
CONNECTOR: DB25 9-PIN 8-PIN(modular)   GENDER: male female
PIN CONFIGURATION: P08

PIN	FUNCTION	DIRECTION
1:CG	Chassis Ground	N/A
2:TD	Transmit Data	FROM
3:RD	Receive Data	TO
4:RTS	Request to Send	FROM
5:CTS	Clear to Send	TO
6:DSR	Data Set Ready	TO
7:SG	Signal Ground	N/A
20:DTR	Data Terminal Ready	FROM

FLOW CONTROL: 20   XON: YES ACK: LEADS THAT MUST BE ON: __ __ __
PRINTER PORT: SERIAL   PARALLEL   FLOW CONTROL: XON/XOFF Hardware
  FLOW CONTROL LEAD(s):   4 11 19 20 __ __   CONNECTOR: DB25 Centronics
SPEEDS: 110 300 600 1200 1800 2400 4800 9600 19.2 56k _____
PARITY: even odd space mark none   CHARACTER LENGTH: 7 8 ___
STOP BITS: 1 1.5 2   LINE-ENDING SEQUENCE: cr lf cr/lf
MODE: async sync isoch   EMULATION/COMPATIBLE: ANSI X3.64
    VT100, Televideo 925, ADM-3A, DG100, Hazeltine 1420, HP2621, Regent 25/30
NOTE 1:
NOTE 2:

TERMINAL PORT PROFILE (Underline if supported, circle if selected)
COMPANY: Computerwise, Inc.
PRODUCT: TransTerm 3

PORT: female   PORT TYPE: serial
CONNECTOR: DB25 9-PIN 8-PIN(modular)   GENDER: male female
PIN CONFIGURATION: P10

PIN	FUNCTION	DIRECTION	PIN	FUNCTION	DIRECTION
1:FG	Frame Ground	N/A	5:CTS	Clear to Send	TO
2:TD	Transmit Data	FROM	6:DSR	Data Set Ready	TO
3:RD	Receive Data	TO	7:SG	Signal Ground	N/A
4:RTS	Request to Send	FROM	20:DTR	Data Terminal Ready	FROM

FLOW CONTROL: XON: YES ACK: LEADS THAT MUST BE ON: __ __ __
PRINTER PORT: SERIAL   PARALLEL   FLOW CONTROL: XON/XOFF Hardware
   FLOW CONTROL LEAD(s): 4 11 19 20 __ __   CONNECTOR: DB25 Centronics
SPEEDS: 110 300 600 1200 1800 2400 4800 9600 19.2 56k _____
PARITY: even odd space mark none   CHARACTER LENGTH: 7 8 ___
STOP BITS: 1 1.5 2   LINE-ENDING SEQUENCE: cr lf cr/lf
MODE: async sync isoch   EMULATION/COMPATIBLE: ANSI X3.64
   VT100, Televideo 925, ADM-3A, DG100, Hazeltine 1420, HP2621, Regent 25/30
NOTE 1:
NOTE 2:

TERMINAL PORT PROFILE (Underline if supported, circle if selected)
COMPANY: Computerwise, Inc.
PRODUCT: TransTerm 5/6 terminals

PORT: female   PORT TYPE: serial
CONNECTOR: DB25 9-PIN 8-PIN(modular)   GENDER: male female
PIN CONFIGURATION: P10

PIN	FUNCTION	DIRECTION
1:FG	Frame Ground	N/A
2:TD	Transmit Data	FROM
3:RD	Receive Data	TO
4:RTS	Request to Send	FROM
5:CTS	Clear to Send	TO
7:SG	Signal Ground	N/A
20:DTR	Data Terminal Ready	FROM

FLOW CONTROL: XON: YES ACK: LEADS THAT MUST BE ON: __ __ __
PRINTER PORT: SERIAL   PARALLEL   FLOW CONTROL: XON/XOFF Hardware
   FLOW CONTROL LEAD(s): 4 11 19 20 __ __   CONNECTOR: DB25 Centronics
SPEEDS: 110 300 600 1200 1800 2400 4800 9600 19.2 56k _____
PARITY: even odd space mark none   CHARACTER LENGTH: 7 8 ___
STOP BITS: 1 1.5 2   LINE-ENDING SEQUENCE: cr lf cr/lf
MODE: async sync isoch   EMULATION/COMPATIBLE: ANSI X3.64
   VT100, Televideo 925, ADM-3A, DG100, Hazeltine 1420, HP2621, Regent 25/30
NOTE 1:
NOTE 2:

TERMINAL PORT PROFILE (Underline if supported, circle if selected)
COMPANY: Computerwise, Inc.
PRODUCT: TransTerm 7 terminal

PORT: female (9-PIN)   PORT TYPE: serial
CONNECTOR: DB25 9-PIN 8-PIN(modular)   GENDER: male female
PIN CONFIGURATION: C05

PIN	FUNCTION	DIRECTION
1:G	Ground	N/A
2:TD	Transmit Data	FROM
3:RD	Receive Data	TO
4:RTS	Request to Send	FROM
7:SG	Signal Ground	N/A

FLOW CONTROL: XON: YES ACK: LEADS THAT MUST BE ON: __ __ __
PRINTER PORT: SERIAL PARALLEL   FLOW CONTROL: XON/XOFF Hardware
   FLOW CONTROL LEAD(s):   4 11 19 20 __ __   CONNECTOR: DB25 Centronics
SPEEDS: 110 300 600 1200 1800 2400 4800 9600 19.2 56k _____
PARITY: even odd space mark none   CHARACTER LENGTH: 7 8 ___
STOP BITS: 1 1.5 2   LINE-ENDING SEQUENCE: cr lf cr/lf
MODE: async sync isoch   EMULATION/COMPATIBLE: ANSI X3.64
   VT100, Televideo 925, ADM-3A, DG100, Hazeltine 1420, HP2621, Regent 25/30
NOTE 1:
NOTE 2:

TERMINAL PORT PROFILE (Underline if supported, circle if selected)
COMPANY: Datapoint Corporation
PRODUCT: 8242 Workstation

PORT: HOST (female)   PORT TYPE: serial
CONNECTOR: DB25 9-PIN 8-PIN(modular)   GENDER: male female
PIN CONFIGURATION: P10

PIN	FUNCTION	DIRECTION	PIN	FUNCTION	DIRECTION
1:CG	Chassis Ground	N/A	8:DCD	Data Carrier Detect	TO
2:TD	Transmit Data	FROM	12:+5V		FROM
3:RD	Receive Data	TO	13:SG	Signal Ground	N/A
4:RTS	Request to Send	FROM	20:DTR	Data Terminal Ready	FROM
5:CTS	Clear to Send	TO	24:-12V		FROM
6:DSR	Data Set Ready	TO	25:+12V		FROM
7:SG	Signal Ground	N/A			

FLOW CONTROL: XON: ACK: LEADS THAT MUST BE ON: __ __ __
PRINTER PORT: SERIAL PARALLEL   FLOW CONTROL: XON/XOFF Hardware
   FLOW CONTROL LEAD(s):   4 11 19 20 __ __   CONNECTOR: DB25 Centronics
SPEEDS: 110 300 600 1200 1800 2400 4800 9600 19.2 56k _____
PARITY: even odd space mark none   CHARACTER LENGTH: 7 8 ___
STOP BITS: 1 1.5 2   LINE-ENDING SEQUENCE: cr lf cr/lf
MODE: async sync isoch   EMULATION/COMPATIBLE: ANSI X3.64
   VT100, Televideo 925, ADM-3A, DG100, Hazeltine 1420, HP2621, Regent 25/30
NOTE 1:
NOTE 2:

TERMINAL PORT PROFILE (Underline if supported, circle if selected)
COMPANY: Digital Equipment Corp.
PRODUCT: VT100 terminal

PORT: EIA   PORT TYPE: serial
CONNECTOR: DB25 9-PIN 8-PIN(modular)   GENDER: male female
PIN CONFIGURATION: P10

PIN	FUNCTION	DIRECTION	PIN	FUNCTION	DIRECTION
1:PG	Protective Ground	N/A	7:SG	Signal Ground	N/A
2:TD	Transmit Data	FROM	11:SRTS	Secondary Req.to Send	FROM
3:RD	Receive Data	TO	19:SRTS	Secondary Req.to Send	FROM
4:RTS	Request to Send	FROM	20:DTR	Data Terminal Ready	FROM

FLOW CONTROL: XON: YES ACK: LEADS THAT MUST BE ON: __ __ __
PRINTER PORT: SERIAL   PARALLEL   FLOW CONTROL: XON/XOFF Hardware
   FLOW CONTROL LEAD(s):   4 11 19 20 __ __   CONNECTOR: DB25 Centronics
SPEEDS: 110 300 600 1200 1800 2400 4800 9600 19.2 56k _____
PARITY: even odd space mark none   CHARACTER LENGTH: 7 8 __
STOP BITS: 1 1.5 2   LINE-ENDING SEQUENCE: cr lf cr/lf
MODE: async sync isoch   EMULATION/COMPATIBLE: ANSI X3.64
    VT100, Televideo 925, ADM-3A, DG100, Hazeltine 1420, HP2621, Regent 25/30
NOTE 1:
NOTE 2:

TERMINAL PORT PROFILE (Underline if supported, circle if selected)
COMPANY: Esprit Systems, Inc.
PRODUCT: ESP 6110+ terminal

PORT: AUX port   PORT TYPE: serial
CONNECTOR: DB25 9-PIN 8-PIN(modular)   GENDER: male female
PIN CONFIGURATION: C02

PIN	FUNCTION	DIRECTION	PIN	FUNCTION	DIRECTION
1:PG	Protective Ground	N/A	6:DSR	Data Set Ready	FROM
2:DI	Data In	TO	7:SG	Signal Ground	N/A
3:DO	Data Out	FROM	8:DCD	Data Carrier Detect	FROM
4:RTS	Request to Send	TO	11:PB	Printer Busy	TO
5:CTS	Clear to Send	FROM	20:		TO

FLOW CONTROL: 11   XON: YES ACK: LEADS THAT MUST BE ON: __ __ __
PRINTER PORT: SERIAL   PARALLEL   FLOW CONTROL: XON/XOFF Hardware
   FLOW CONTROL LEAD(s):   4 11 19 20 __ __   CONNECTOR: DB25 Centronics
SPEEDS: 110 300 600 1200 1800 2400 4800 9600 19.2 56k _____
PARITY: even odd space mark none   CHARACTER LENGTH: 7 8 __
STOP BITS: 1 1.5 2   LINE-ENDING SEQUENCE: cr lf cr/lf
MODE: async sync isoch   EMULATION/COMPATIBLE: ANSI X3.64
    VT100, Televideo 925, ADM-3A, DG100, Hazeltine 1420, HP2621, Regent 25/30
NOTE 1:
NOTE 2:

TERMINAL PORT PROFILE   (Underline if supported, circle if selected)
COMPANY: Esprit Systems, Inc.
PRODUCT: ESP 6110+ terminal

PORT: main   PORT TYPE: serial
CONNECTOR: DB25 9-PIN 8-PIN(modular)   GENDER: male female
PIN CONFIGURATION: P05

PIN	FUNCTION	DIRECTION	PIN	FUNCTION	DIRECTION
1:PG	Protective Ground	N/A	6:DSR	Data Set Ready	TO
2:TD	Transmit Data	FROM	7:SG	Signal Ground	N/A
3:RD	Receive Data	TO	8:DCD	Data Carrier Detect	TO
4:RTS	Request to Send	FROM	11:PB	Printer Busy	FROM
5:CTS	Clear to Send	TO	20:DTR	Data Terminal Ready	FROM

FLOW CONTROL: 11   XON: YES ACK: LEADS THAT MUST BE ON: __ __ __
PRINTER PORT: SERIAL   PARALLEL   FLOW CONTROL: XON/XOFF Hardware
   FLOW CONTROL LEAD(s):   4 11 19 20 __ __   CONNECTOR: DB25 Centronics
SPEEDS: 110 300 600 1200 1800 2400 4800 9600 19.2 56k _____
PARITY: even odd space mark none   CHARACTER LENGTH: 7 8 __
STOP BITS: 1 1.5 2   LINE-ENDING SEQUENCE: cr lf cr/lf
MODE: async sync isoch   EMULATION/COMPATIBLE: ANSI X3.64
   VT100, Televideo 925, ADM-3A, DG100, Hazeltine 1420, HP2621, Regent 25/30
NOTE 1: PIN 11 relays the status provided by an attached
NOTE 2: printer to the terminal's aux port

TERMINAL PORT PROFILE   (Underline if supported, circle if selected)
COMPANY: Esprit Systems, Inc.
PRODUCT: ESP 6310 terminal

PORT: AUX port   PORT TYPE: serial
CONNECTOR: DB25 9-PIN 8-PIN(modular)   GENDER: male female
PIN CONFIGURATION: C02

PIN	FUNCTION	DIRECTION	PIN	FUNCTION	DIRECTION
1:PG	Protective Ground	N/A	6:DSR	Data Set Ready	FROM
2:DI	Data In	TO	7:SG	Signal Ground	N/A
3:DO	Data Out	FROM	8:DCD	Data Carrier Detect	FROM
4:RTS	Request to Send	TO	11:PB	Printer Busy	TO
5:CTS	Clear to Send	FROM	20:DTR	Data Terminal Ready	TO

FLOW CONTROL: 11   XON: YES ACK: LEADS THAT MUST BE ON: __ __ __
PRINTER PORT: SERIAL   PARALLEL   FLOW CONTROL: XON/XOFF Hardware
   FLOW CONTROL LEAD(s):   4 11 19 20 __ __   CONNECTOR: DB25 Centronics
SPEEDS: 110 300 600 1200 1800 2400 4800 9600 19.2 56k _____
PARITY: even odd space mark none   CHARACTER LENGTH: 7 8 __
STOP BITS: 1 1.5 2   LINE-ENDING SEQUENCE: cr lf cr/lf
MODE: async sync isoch   EMULATION/COMPATIBLE: ANSI X3.64
   VT100, Televideo 925, ADM-3A, DG100, Hazeltine 1420, HP2621, Regent 25/30
NOTE 1:
NOTE 2:

TERMINAL PORT PROFILE (Underline if supported, circle if selected)
COMPANY: Esprit Systems, Inc.
PRODUCT: ESP 6310 terminal

PORT: main   PORT TYPE: serial
CONNECTOR: DB25 9-PIN 8-PIN(modular)   GENDER: male female
PIN CONFIGURATION: P10

PIN	FUNCTION	DIRECTION	PIN	FUNCTION	DIRECTION
1:PG	Protective Ground	N/A	6:DSR	Data Set Ready	TO
2:TD	Transmit Data	FROM	7:SG	Signal Ground	N/A
3:RD	Receive Data	TO	8:DCD	Data Carrier Detect	TO
4:RTS	Request to Send	FROM	20:DTR	Data Terminal Ready	FROM
5:CTS	Clear to Send	TO			

FLOW CONTROL: XON: YES ACK: LEADS THAT MUST BE ON: __ __ __
PRINTER PORT: SERIAL   PARALLEL   FLOW CONTROL: XON/XOFF Hardware
  FLOW CONTROL LEAD(s):   4 11 19 20 __ __   CONNECTOR: DB25 Centronics
SPEEDS: 110 300 600 1200 1800 2400 4800 9600 19.2 56k _____
PARITY: even odd space mark none   CHARACTER LENGTH: 7 8 ___
STOP BITS: 1 1.5 2   LINE-ENDING SEQUENCE: cr lf cr/lf
MODE: async sync isoch   EMULATION/COMPATIBLE: ANSI X3.64
   VT100, Televideo 925, ADM-3A, DG100, Hazeltine 1420, HP2621, Regent 25/30
NOTE 1:
NOTE 2:

TERMINAL PORT PROFILE (Underline if supported, circle if selected)
COMPANY: Esprit Systems, Inc.
PRODUCT: ESP 6515 terminal

PORT: AUX   PORT TYPE: serial
CONNECTOR: DB25 9-PIN 8-PIN(modular)   GENDER: male female
PIN CONFIGURATION: C01

PIN	FUNCTION	DIRECTION
1:PG	Protective Ground	N/A
2:TD	Transmit Data	FROM
3:RD	Receive Data	TO
4:RTS	Request to Send	FROM
6:DSR	Data Set Ready	TO
7:SG	Signal Ground	N/A
20:DTR	Data Terminal Ready	FROM

FLOW CONTROL: 6   XON: YES ACK: LEADS THAT MUST BE ON: __ __ __
PRINTER PORT: SERIAL   PARALLEL   FLOW CONTROL: XON/XOFF Hardware
  FLOW CONTROL LEAD(s):   4 11 19 20 __ __   CONNECTOR: DB25 Centronics
SPEEDS: 110 300 600 1200 1800 2400 4800 9600 19.2 56k _____
PARITY: even odd space mark none   CHARACTER LENGTH: 7 8 ___
STOP BITS: 1 1.5 2   LINE-ENDING SEQUENCE: cr lf cr/lf
MODE: async sync isoch   EMULATION/COMPATIBLE: ANSI X3.64
   VT100, Televideo 925, ADM-3A, DG100, Hazeltine 1420, HP2621, Regent 25/30
NOTE 1:
NOTE 2:

TERMINAL PORT PROFILE (Underline if supported, circle if selected)
COMPANY: Esprit Systems, Inc.
PRODUCT: ESP 6515 terminal

PORT: main   PORT TYPE: serial
CONNECTOR: DB25 9-PIN 8-PIN(modular)   GENDER: male female
PIN CONFIGURATION: P10

PIN	FUNCTION	DIRECTION	PIN	FUNCTION	DIRECTION
1:PG	Protective Ground	N/A	7:SG	Signal Ground	N/A
2:TD	Transmit Data	FROM	8:CD	Carrier Detect	TO
3:RD	Receive Data	TO	12:SS	Speed Select	TO
4:RTS	Request to Send	FROM	20:DTR	Data Terminal Ready	FROM
5:CTS	Clear to Send	TO	23:SS	Speed Select	FROM
6:DSR	Data Set Ready	TO			

FLOW CONTROL: XON: YES ACK: LEADS THAT MUST BE ON: __ __ __
PRINTER PORT: SERIAL   PARALLEL   FLOW CONTROL: XON/XOFF Hardware
   FLOW CONTROL LEAD(s): 4 11 19 20 __ __   CONNECTOR: DB25 Centronics
SPEEDS: 110 300 600 1200 1800 2400 4800 9600 19.2 56k _____
PARITY: even odd space mark none   CHARACTER LENGTH: 7 8 ___
STOP BITS: 1 1.5 2   LINE-ENDING SEQUENCE: cr lf cr/lf
MODE: async sync isoch   EMULATION/COMPATIBLE: ANSI X3.64
   VT100, Televideo 925, ADM-3A, DG100, Hazeltine 1420, HP2621, Regent 25/30
NOTE 1:
NOTE 2:

TERMINAL PORT PROFILE (Underline if supported, circle if selected)
COMPANY: Esprit Systems, Inc.
PRODUCT: Esprit III Color terminal

PORT: EIA   PORT TYPE: serial
CONNECTOR: DB25 9-PIN 8-PIN(modular)   GENDER: male female
PIN CONFIGURATION: P10

PIN	FUNCTION	DIRECTION	PIN	FUNCTION	DIRECTION
1:PG	Protective Ground	N/A	6:DSR	Data Set Ready	TO
2:TD	Transmit Data	FROM	7:SG	Signal Ground	N/A
3:RD	Receive Data	TO	8:DCD	Data Carrier Detect	TO
4:RTS	Request to Send	FROM	20:DTR	Data Terminal Ready	FROM
5:CTS	Clear to Send	TO			

FLOW CONTROL: XON: YES ACK: LEADS THAT MUST BE ON: __ __ __
PRINTER PORT: SERIAL   PARALLEL   FLOW CONTROL: XON/XOFF Hardware
   FLOW CONTROL LEAD(s): 4 11 19 20 __ __   CONNECTOR: DB25 Centronics
SPEEDS: 110 300 600 1200 1800 2400 4800 9600 19.2 56k _____
PARITY: even odd space mark none   CHARACTER LENGTH: 7 8 ___
STOP BITS: 1 1.5 2   LINE-ENDING SEQUENCE: cr lf cr/lf
MODE: async sync isoch   EMULATION/COMPATIBLE: ANSI X3.64
   VT100, Televideo 925, ADM-3A, DG100, Hazeltine 1420, HP2621, Regent 25/30
NOTE 1:
NOTE 2:

TERMINAL PORT PROFILE (Underline if supported, circle if selected)
COMPANY: Esprit Systems, Inc.
PRODUCT: Esprit III Color terminal

PORT: Printer EIA   PORT TYPE: serial
CONNECTOR: DB25 9-PIN 8-PIN(modular)   GENDER: male female
PIN CONFIGURATION: C14

PIN	FUNCTION	DIRECTION	PIN	FUNCTION	DIRECTION
1:PG	Protective Ground	N/A	6:DSR	Data Set Ready	FROM
2:DI	Data In	TO	7:SG	Signal Ground	N/A
3:DO	Data Out	FROM	8:DCD	Data Carrier Detect	FROM
4:RTS	Request to Send	TO	20:DTR	Data Terminal Ready	TO
5:CTS	Clear to Send	FROM			

FLOW CONTROL: 4 20   XON: YES ACK: LEADS THAT MUST BE ON: __ __ __
PRINTER PORT: SERIAL   PARALLEL   FLOW CONTROL: XON/XOFF Hardware
   FLOW CONTROL LEAD(s):   4 11 19 20 __ __   CONNECTOR: DB25 Centronics
SPEEDS: 110 300 600 1200 1800 2400 4800 9600 19.2 56k _____
PARITY: even odd space mark none   CHARACTER LENGTH: 7 8 ___
STOP BITS: 1 1.5 2   LINE-ENDING SEQUENCE: cr lf cr/lf
MODE: async sync isoch   EMULATION/COMPATIBLE: ANSI X3.64
     VT100, Televideo 925, ADM-3A, DG100, Hazeltine 1420, HP2621, Regent 25/30
NOTE 1:
NOTE 2:

TERMINAL PORT PROFILE (Underline if supported, circle if selected)
COMPANY: Esprit Systems, Inc.
PRODUCT: OPUS2 terminal

PORT: aux   PORT TYPE: serial
CONNECTOR: DB25 9-PIN 8-PIN(modular)   GENDER: male female
PIN CONFIGURATION: C14

PIN	FUNCTION	DIRECTION
1:PG	Protective Ground	N/A
2:DI	Data In	TO
3:DO	Data Out	FROM
4:RTS	Request to Send	TO
5:CTS	Clear to Send	FROM
6:DSR	Data Set Ready	FROM
7:SG	Signal Ground	N/A
20:DTR	Data Terminal Ready	TO

FLOW CONTROL: 20   XON: YES ACK: LEADS THAT MUST BE ON: __ __ __
PRINTER PORT: SERIAL   PARALLEL   FLOW CONTROL: XON/XOFF Hardware
   FLOW CONTROL LEAD(s):   4 11 19 20 __ __   CONNECTOR: DB25 Centronics
SPEEDS: 110 300 600 1200 1800 2400 4800 9600 19.2 56k _____
PARITY: even odd space mark none   CHARACTER LENGTH: 7 8 ___
STOP BITS: 1 1.5 2   LINE-ENDING SEQUENCE: cr lf cr/lf
MODE: async sync isoch   EMULATION/COMPATIBLE: ANSI X3.64
     VT100, Televideo 925, ADM-3A, DG100, Hazeltine 1420, HP2621, Regent 25/30
NOTE 1:
NOTE 2:

TERMINAL PORT PROFILE (Underline if supported, circle if selected)
COMPANY: Esprit Systems, Inc.
PRODUCT: OPUS2 terminal

PORT: main   PORT TYPE: serial
CONNECTOR: DB25 9-PIN 8-PIN(modular)   GENDER: male female
PIN CONFIGURATION: P03

PIN	FUNCTION	DIRECTION
1:PG	Protective Ground	N/A
2:TD	Transmit Data	FROM
3:RD	Receive Data	TO
4:RTS	Request to Send	FROM
5:CTS	Clear to Send	TO
6:DSR	Data Set Ready	TO
7:SG	Signal Ground	N/A
8:DCD	Data Carrier Detect	TO
20:DTR	Data Terminal Ready	FROM

FLOW CONTROL: 20   XON: YES ACK: LEADS THAT MUST BE ON: __ __ __
PRINTER PORT: SERIAL   PARALLEL   FLOW CONTROL: XON/XOFF Hardware
   FLOW CONTROL LEAD(s):   4 11 19 20 __ __ CONNECTOR: DB25 Centronics
SPEEDS: 110 300 600 1200 1800 2400 4800 9600 19.2 56k _____
PARITY: even odd space mark none   CHARACTER LENGTH: 7 8 __
STOP BITS: 1 1.5 2   LINE-ENDING SEQUENCE: cr lf cr/lf
MODE: async sync isoch   EMULATION/COMPATIBLE: ANSI X3.64
    VT100, Televideo 925, ADM-3A, DG100, Hazeltine 1420, HP2621, Regent 25/30
NOTE 1:
NOTE 2:

TERMINAL PORT PROFILE (Underline if supported, circle if selected)
COMPANY: G. R. Electronics, Ltd.
PRODUCT: Oyster 80/16S terminal

PORT: host   PORT TYPE: serial
CONNECTOR: DB25 9-PIN 8-PIN(modular)   GENDER: male female
PIN CONFIGURATION: P08

PIN	FUNCTION	DIRECTION	PIN	FUNCTION	DIRECTION
1:CG	Chassis Ground	N/A	7:SG	Signal Ground	N/A
2:TD	Transmit Data	FROM	9:+5V		
3:RD	Receive Data	TO	15:TT	Transmit Timing	TO
4:RTS	Request to Send	FROM	17:RT	Receive Timing	TO
5:CTS	Clear to Send	TO	20:DTR	Data Terminal Ready	FROM
6:DSR	Data Set Ready	TO	24:T/X		FROM

FLOW CONTROL: 20   XON: YES ACK: LEADS THAT MUST BE ON: __ __ __
PRINTER PORT: SERIAL   PARALLEL   FLOW CONTROL: XON/XOFF Hardware
   FLOW CONTROL LEAD(s):   4 11 19 20 __ __ CONNECTOR: DB25 Centronics
SPEEDS: 110 300 600 1200 1800 2400 4800 9600 19.2 56k _____
PARITY: even odd space mark none   CHARACTER LENGTH: 7 8 __
STOP BITS: 1 1.5 2   LINE-ENDING SEQUENCE: cr lf cr/lf
MODE: async sync isoch   EMULATION/COMPATIBLE: ANSI X3.64
    VT100, Televideo 925, ADM-3A, DG100, Hazeltine 1420, HP2621, Regent 25/30
NOTE 1:
NOTE 2:

TERMINAL PORT PROFILE (Underline if supported, circle if selected)
COMPANY: Hewlett-Packard
PRODUCT: 2392A/2393A/2304A/2397A terminals

PORT: female(port1)   PORT TYPE: serial
CONNECTOR: DB25 9-PIN 8-PIN(modular)   GENDER: male female
PIN CONFIGURATION: P01

PIN	FUNCTION	DIRECTION	PIN	FUNCTION	DIRECTION
1:PG	Protective Ground	N/A	8:DCD	Data Carrier Detect	TO
2:TD	Transmit Data	FROM	12:SDCD	Secondary DCD	
3:RD	Receive Data	TO	19:SRTS	Secondary Req.to Send	FROM
4:RTS	Request to Send	FROM	20:DTR	Data Terminal Ready	FROM
5:CTS	Clear to Send	TO	22:RI	Ring Indicator	TO
6:DM		TO	23:DRS	Data Rate Select	FROM
7:SG	Signal Ground	N/A			

FLOW CONTROL: 19   XON: YES ACK: LEADS THAT MUST BE ON: __ __ __
PRINTER PORT: SERIAL PARALLEL   FLOW CONTROL: XON/XOFF Hardware
FLOW CONTROL LEAD(s): 4 11 19 20 __ __   CONNECTOR: DB25 Centronics
SPEEDS: 110 300 600 1200 1800 2400 4800 9600 19.2 56k _____
PARITY: even odd space mark none   CHARACTER LENGTH: 7 8 ___
STOP BITS: 1 1.5 2   LINE-ENDING SEQUENCE: cr lf cr/lf
MODE: async sync isoch   EMULATION/COMPATIBLE: ANSI X3.64
    VT100, Televideo 925, ADM-3A, DG100, Hazeltine 1420, HP2621, Regent 25/30
NOTE 1:
NOTE 2:

TERMINAL PORT PROFILE (Underline if supported, circle if selected)
COMPANY: Hewlett-Packard
PRODUCT: 2392A/2393A/2394A/2397A terminals

PORT: female(port 2)   PORT TYPE: serial
CONNECTOR: DB25 9-PIN 8-PIN(modular)   GENDER: male female
PIN CONFIGURATION: C01

PIN	FUNCTION	DIRECTION	PIN	FUNCTION	DIRECTION
1:G	Ground	N/A	7:SG	Signal Ground	N/A
2:TD	Transmit Data	FROM	11:SDCD	Secondary DCD	TO
3:RD	Receive Data	TO	19:SRTS	Secondary Req.to Send	FROM
4:RTS	Request to Send	FROM	20:DTR	Data Terminal Ready	FROM
5:CTS	Clear to Send	TO	22:RI	Ring Indicator	TO
6:DSR	Data Set Ready	TO	23:DRS	Data Rate Select	FROM

FLOW CONTROL: XON: YES ACK: LEADS THAT MUST BE ON: __ __ __
PRINTER PORT: SERIAL PARALLEL   FLOW CONTROL: XON/XOFF Hardware
  FLOW CONTROL LEAD(s): 4 11 19 20 __ __   CONNECTOR: DB25 Centronics
SPEEDS: 110 300 600 1200 1800 2400 4800 9600 19.2 56k _____
PARITY: even odd space mark none   CHARACTER LENGTH: 7 8 ___
STOP BITS: 1 1.5 2   LINE-ENDING SEQUENCE: cr lf cr/lf
MODE: async sync isoch   EMULATION/COMPATIBLE: ANSI X3.64
    VT100, Televideo 925, ADM-3A, DG100, Hazeltine 1420, HP2621, Regent 25/30
NOTE 1:
NOTE 2:

TERMINAL PORT PROFILE (Underline if supported, circle if selected)
COMPANY: Houston Computer Services
PRODUCT: Plus 10 terminal

PORT: female(DCE-printer)   PORT TYPE: serial
CONNECTOR: DB25 9-PIN 8-PIN(modular) GENDER: male female
PIN CONFIGURATION: C14

PIN	FUNCTION	DIRECTION	PIN	FUNCTION	DIRECTION
1:FG	Frame Ground	N/A	6:DSR	Data Set Ready	FROM
2:TD	Transmit Data	TO	7:SG	Signal Ground	N/A
3:RD	Receive Data	FROM	8:DCD	Data Carrier Detect	FROM
4:RTS	Request to Send	TO	20:DTR	Data Terminal Ready	TO
5:CTS	Clear to Send	FROM			

FLOW CONTROL: 20   XON: YES ACK: LEADS THAT MUST BE ON: __ __ __
PRINTER PORT: SERIAL   PARALLEL   FLOW CONTROL: XON/XOFF Hardware
   FLOW CONTROL LEAD(s):   4 11 19 20 __ __   CONNECTOR: DB25 Centronics
SPEEDS: 110 300 600 1200 1800 2400 4800 9600 19.2 56k _____
PARITY: even odd space mark none   CHARACTER LENGTH: 7 8 ___
STOP BITS: 1 1.5 2   LINE-ENDING SEQUENCE: cr lf cr/lf
MODE: async sync isoch   EMULATION/COMPATIBLE: ANSI X3.64
     VT100, Televideo 925, ADM-3A, DG100, Hazeltine 1420, HP2621, Regent 25/30
NOTE 1:
NOTE 2:

TERMINAL PORT PROFILE (Underline if supported, circle if selected)
COMPANY: Houston Computer Services
PRODUCT: Plus 10 terminal

PORT: female(DTE-computer)   PORT TYPE: serial
CONNECTOR: DB25 9-PIN 8-PIN(modular) GENDER: male female
PIN CONFIGURATION: P03

PIN	FUNCTION	DIRECTION
1:FG	Frame Ground	N/A
2:TD	Transmit Data	FROM
3:RD	Receive Data	TO
4:RTS	Request to Send	FROM
5:CTS	Clear to Send	TO
6:DSR	Data Set Ready	TO
7:SG	Signal Ground	N/A
8:DCD	Data Carrier Detect	TO
20:DTR	Data Terminal Ready	FROM

FLOW CONTROL: 20   XON: YES ACK: LEADS THAT MUST BE ON: __ __ __
PRINTER PORT: SERIAL   PARALLEL   FLOW CONTROL: XON/XOFF Hardware
   FLOW CONTROL LEAD(s):   4 11 19 20 __ __   CONNECTOR: DB25 Centronics
SPEEDS: 110 300 600 1200 1800 2400 4800 9600 19.2 56k _____
PARITY: even odd space mark none   CHARACTER LENGTH: 7 8 ___
STOP BITS: 1 1.5 2   LINE-ENDING SEQUENCE: cr lf cr/lf
MODE: async sync isoch   EMULATION/COMPATIBLE: ANSI X3.64
     VT100, Televideo 925, ADM-3A, DG100, Hazeltine 1420, HP2621, Regent 25/30
NOTE 1:
NOTE 2:

TERMINAL PORT PROFILE (Underline if supported, circle if selected)
COMPANY: Human Designed Systems, Inc.
PRODUCT: HDS 200 terminal

PORT: male(Lines 1 & 3)   PORT TYPE: serial
CONNECTOR: DB25 9-PIN 8-PIN(modular)   GENDER: male female
PIN CONFIGURATION: P10

PIN	FUNCTION	DIRECTION
1:G	Ground	N/A
2:TD	Transmit Data	FROM
3:RD	Receive Data	TO
4:RTS	Request to Send	FROM
5:CTS	Clear to Send	TO
7:SG	Signal Ground	N/A
20:DTR	Data Terminal Ready	FROM

FLOW CONTROL: XON: YES ACK: LEADS THAT MUST BE ON: __ __ __
PRINTER PORT: SERIAL   PARALLEL   FLOW CONTROL: XON/XOFF Hardware
   FLOW CONTROL LEAD(s):   4 11 19 20 __ __   CONNECTOR: DB25 Centronics
SPEEDS: 110 300 600 1200 1800 2400 4800 9600 19.2 56k _____
PARITY: even odd space mark none   CHARACTER LENGTH: 7 8 __
STOP BITS: 1 1.5 2   LINE-ENDING SEQUENCE: cr lf cr/lf
MODE: async sync isoch   EMULATION/COMPATIBLE: ANSI X3.64
   VT100, Televideo 925, ADM-3A, DG100, Hazeltine 1420, HP2621, Regent 25/30
NOTE 1:
NOTE 2:

TERMINAL PORT PROFILE (Underline if supported, circle if selected)
COMPANY: Human Designed Systems, Inc.
PRODUCT: HDS200 terminal

PORT: female(Line 2)   PORT TYPE: serial
CONNECTOR: DB25 9-PIN 8-PIN(modular)   GENDER: male female
PIN CONFIGURATION: C14

PIN	FUNCTION	DIRECTION
1:G	Ground	N/A
2:RD	Receive Data	TO
3:TD	Transmit Data	FROM
4:CTS	Clear to Send	TO
5:RTS	Request to Send	FROM
6:DSR	Data Set Ready	FROM
7:SG	Signal Ground	N/A
8:CD	Carrier Detect	FROM
20:		TO

FLOW CONTROL: 4   XON: YES ACK: LEADS THAT MUST BE ON: __ __ __
PRINTER PORT: SERIAL   PARALLEL   FLOW CONTROL: XON/XOFF Hardware
   FLOW CONTROL LEAD(s):   4 11 19 20 __ __   CONNECTOR: DB25 Centronics
SPEEDS: 110 300 600 1200 1800 2400 4800 9600 19.2 56k _____
PARITY: even odd space mark none   CHARACTER LENGTH: 7 8 __
STOP BITS: 1 1.5 2   LINE-ENDING SEQUENCE: cr lf cr/lf
MODE: async sync isoch   EMULATION/COMPATIBLE: ANSI X3.64
   VT100, Televideo 925, ADM-3A, DG100, Hazeltine 1420, HP2621, Regent 25/30
NOTE 1:
NOTE 2:

TERMINAL PORT PROFILE   (Underline if supported, circle if selected)
COMPANY: Intecolor
PRODUCT: 6000 series terminals

PORT: female(aux)   PORT TYPE: serial
CONNECTOR: DB25 9-PIN 8-PIN(modular)   GENDER: male female
PIN CONFIGURATION: C01

PIN	FUNCTION	DIRECTION	PIN	FUNCTION	DIRECTION
1:PG	Protective Ground	N/A	7:SG	Signal Ground	N/A
2:TD	Transmit Data	FROM	8:DCD	Data Carrier Detect	TO
3:RD	Receive Data	TO	15:TC	Transmit Clock	TO
4:RTS	Request to Send	FROM	17:RC	Rec. Clk/Reverse Chann	TO
5:CTS	Clear to Send	TO	20:DTR	Data Terminal Ready	FROM
6:DSR	Data Set Ready	TO	24:TC	Transmit Clock	FROM

FLOW CONTROL: XON: YES ACK: LEADS THAT MUST BE ON: __ __ __
PRINTER PORT: SERIAL   PARALLEL   FLOW CONTROL: XON/XOFF Hardware
    FLOW CONTROL LEAD(s):   4 11 19 20 __ __ CONNECTOR: DB25 Centronics
SPEEDS: 110 300 600 1200 1800 2400 4800 9600 19.2 56k _____
PARITY: even odd space mark none   CHARACTER LENGTH: 7 8 __
STOP BITS: 1 1.5 2   LINE-ENDING SEQUENCE: cr lf cr/lf
MODE: async sync isoch   EMULATION/COMPATIBLE: ANSI X3.64
    VT100, Televideo 925, ADM-3A, DG100, Hazeltine 1420, HP2621, Regent 25/30
NOTE 1:
NOTE 2:

TERMINAL PORT PROFILE   (Underline if supported, circle if selected)
COMPANY: Intecolor
PRODUCT: 6000 series terminals

PORT: female(host)   PORT TYPE: serial
CONNECTOR: DB25 9-PIN 8-PIN(modular)   GENDER: male female
PIN CONFIGURATION: P10

PIN	FUNCTION	DIRECTION	PIN	FUNCTION	DIRECTION
1:PG	Protective Ground	N/A	7:SG	Signal Ground	N/A
2:TD	Transmit Data	FROM	8:DCD	Data Carrier Detect	TO
3:RD	Receive Data	TO	15:TC	Transmit Clock	TO
4:RTS	Request to Send	FROM	17:RC	Rec. Clk/Reverse Chann	TO
5:CTS	Clear to Send	TO	20:DTR	Data Terminal Ready	FROM
6:DSR	Data Set Ready	TO	24:TC	Transmit Clock	FROM

FLOW CONTROL: XON: YES ACK: LEADS THAT MUST BE ON: __ __ __
PRINTER PORT: SERIAL   PARALLEL   FLOW CONTROL: XON/XOFF Hardware
    FLOW CONTROL LEAD(s):   4 11 19 20 __ __ CONNECTOR: DB25 Centronics
SPEEDS: 110 300 600 1200 1800 2400 4800 9600 19.2 56k _____
PARITY: even odd space mark none   CHARACTER LENGTH: 7 8 __
STOP BITS: 1 1.5 2   LINE-ENDING SEQUENCE: cr lf cr/lf
MODE: async sync isoch   EMULATION/COMPATIBLE: ANSI X3.64
    VT100, Televideo 925, ADM-3A, DG100, Hazeltine 1420, HP2621, Regent 25/30
NOTE 1:
NOTE 2:

TERMINAL PORT PROFILE (Underline if supported, circle if selected)
COMPANY: Intecolor
PRODUCT: 6000 series terminals

PORT: female(printer)   PORT TYPE: serial
CONNECTOR: DB25 9-PIN 8-PIN(modular)   GENDER: male female
PIN CONFIGURATION: C07

PIN	FUNCTION	DIRECTION
1:PG	Protective Ground	N/A
2:TD	Transmit Data	FROM
5:CTS	Clear to Send	TO
7:SG	Signal Ground	N/A
20:DTR	Data Terminal Ready	FROM

FLOW CONTROL: 5   XON: ACK: LEADS THAT MUST BE ON: __ __ __
PRINTER PORT: SERIAL   PARALLEL   FLOW CONTROL: XON/XOFF Hardware
   FLOW CONTROL LEAD(s):   4 11 19 20 __ __ CONNECTOR: DB25 Centronics
SPEEDS: 110 300 600 1200 1800 2400 4800 9600 19.2 56k _____
PARITY: even odd space mark none   CHARACTER LENGTH: 7 8 ___
STOP BITS: 1 1.5 2   LINE-ENDING SEQUENCE: cr lf cr/lf
MODE: async sync isoch   EMULATION/COMPATIBLE: ANSI X3.64
   VT100, Televideo 925, ADM-3A, DG100, Hazeltine 1420, HP2621, Regent 25/30
NOTE 1:
NOTE 2:

TERMINAL PORT PROFILE (Underline if supported, circle if selected)
COMPANY: Intecolor
PRODUCT: 8800/3800 terminals

PORT: female(J2-Host port)   PORT TYPE: serial
CONNECTOR: DB25 9-PIN 8-PIN(modular)   GENDER: male female
PIN CONFIGURATION: P10

PIN	FUNCTION	DIRECTION
1:PG	Protective Ground	N/A
2:TD	Transmit Data	FROM
3:RD	Receive Data	TO
4:RTS	Request to Send	FROM
5:CTS	Clear to Send	TO
7:SG	Signal Ground	N/A
8:DCD	Data Carrier Detect	TO
20:DTR	Data Terminal Ready	FROM

FLOW CONTROL: XON: YES ACK: LEADS THAT MUST BE ON: __ __ __
PRINTER PORT: SERIAL   PARALLEL   FLOW CONTROL: XON/XOFF Hardware
   FLOW CONTROL LEAD(s):   4 11 19 20 __ __ CONNECTOR: DB25 Centronics
SPEEDS: 110 300 600 1200 1800 2400 4800 9600 19.2 56k _____
PARITY: even odd space mark none   CHARACTER LENGTH: 7 8 ___
STOP BITS: 1 1.5 2   LINE-ENDING SEQUENCE: cr lf cr/lf
MODE: async sync isoch   EMULATION/COMPATIBLE: ANSI X3.64
   VT100, Televideo 925, ADM-3A, DG100, Hazeltine 1420, HP2621, Regent 25/30
NOTE 1:
NOTE 2:

TERMINAL PORT PROFILE (Underline if supported, circle if selected)
COMPANY: Intecolor
PRODUCT: Colortrend 210/427 terminals

PORT: female(AUX)   PORT TYPE: serial
CONNECTOR: DB25 9-PIN 8-PIN(modular)   GENDER: male female
PIN CONFIGURATION: C07

PIN	FUNCTION	DIRECTION
1:PG	Protective Ground	N/A
2:TD	Transmit Data	FROM
5:CTS	Clear to Send	TO
7:SG	Signal Ground	N/A
20:DTR	Data Terminal Ready	FROM

FLOW CONTROL: 5   XON: ACK: LEADS THAT MUST BE ON: __ __ __
PRINTER PORT: SERIAL   PARALLEL   FLOW CONTROL: XON/XOFF Hardware
   FLOW CONTROL LEAD(s):   4 11 19 20 __ __ CONNECTOR: DB25 Centronics
SPEEDS: 110 300 600 1200 1800 2400 4800 9600 19.2 56k _____
PARITY: even odd space mark none   CHARACTER LENGTH: 7 8 ___
STOP BITS: 1 1.5 2   LINE-ENDING SEQUENCE: cr lf cr/lf
MODE: async sync isoch   EMULATION/COMPATIBLE: ANSI X3.64
    VT100, Televideo 925, ADM-3A, DG100, Hazeltine 1420, HP2621, Regent 25/30
NOTE 1:
NOTE 2:

TERMINAL PORT PROFILE (Underline if supported, circle if selected)
COMPANY: Intecolor
PRODUCT: Colortrend 210/427 terminals

PORT: female(J1-Host)   PORT TYPE: serial
CONNECTOR: DB25 9-PIN 8-PIN(modular)   GENDER: male female
PIN CONFIGURATION: P10

PIN	FUNCTION	DIRECTION	PIN	FUNCTION	DIRECTION
1:PG	Protective Ground	N/A	7:SG	Signal Ground	N/A
2:TD	Transmit Data	FROM	8:DCD	Data Carrier Detect	TO
3:RD	Receive Data	TO	15:TC	Transmit Clock	TO
4:RTS	Request to Send	FROM	17:RC	Rec. Clk/Reverse Chann	TO
5:CTS	Clear to Send	TO	20:DTR	Data Terminal Ready	FROM
6:DSR	Data Set Ready	TO	24:TC	Transmit Clock	FROM

FLOW CONTROL: XON: YES ACK: LEADS THAT MUST BE ON: __ __ __
PRINTER PORT: SERIAL   PARALLEL   FLOW CONTROL: XON/XOFF Hardware
   FLOW CONTROL LEAD(s):   4 11 19 20 __ __ CONNECTOR: DB25 Centronics
SPEEDS: 110 300 600 1200 1800 2400 4800 9600 19.2 56k _____
PARITY: even odd space mark none   CHARACTER LENGTH: 7 8 ___
STOP BITS: 1 1.5 2   LINE-ENDING SEQUENCE: cr lf cr/lf
MODE: async sync isoch   EMULATION/COMPATIBLE: ANSI X3.64
    VT100, Televideo 925, ADM-3A, DG100, Hazeltine 1420, HP2621, Regent 25/30
NOTE 1:
NOTE 2:

TERMINAL PORT PROFILE (Underline if supported, circle if selected)
COMPANY: Intecolor
PRODUCT: Colortrend 220/920 terminals

PORT: female(serial comm.)   PORT TYPE: serial
CONNECTOR: DB25 9-PIN 8-PIN(modular) GENDER: male female
PIN CONFIGURATION: P10

PIN	FUNCTION	DIRECTION	PIN	FUNCTION	DIRECTION
1:FG	Frame Ground	N/A	7:SG	Signal Ground	N/A
2:TD	Transmit Data	FROM	8:DCD	Data Carrier Detect	TO
3:RD	Receive Data	TO	12:SS	Speed Select	TO
4:RTS	Request to Send	FROM	20:DTR	Data Terminal Ready	FROM
5:CTS	Clear to Send	TO	23:SS	Speed Select	FROM
6:DSR	Data Set Ready	TO			

FLOW CONTROL: XON: YES ACK: LEADS THAT MUST BE ON: __ __ __
PRINTER PORT: SERIAL   PARALLEL   FLOW CONTROL: XON/XOFF Hardware
   FLOW CONTROL LEAD(s):   4 11 19 20 __ __   CONNECTOR: DB25 Centronics
SPEEDS: 110 300 600 1200 1800 2400 4800 9600 19.2 56k _____
PARITY: even odd space mark none   CHARACTER LENGTH: 7 8 ___
STOP BITS: 1 1.5 2   LINE-ENDING SEQUENCE: cr lf cr/lf
MODE: async sync isoch   EMULATION/COMPATIBLE: ANSI X3.64
   VT100, Televideo 925, ADM-3A, DG100, Hazeltine 1420, HP2621, Regent 25/30
NOTE 1:
NOTE 2:

TERMINAL PORT PROFILE (Underline if supported, circle if selected)
COMPANY: Intecolor
PRODUCT: Colortrend 220/920 terminals

PORT: male(9-PIN printer)   PORT TYPE: serial
CONNECTOR: DB25 9-PIN 8-PIN(modular) GENDER: male female
PIN CONFIGURATION: C05

PIN	FUNCTION	DIRECTION
1:FG	Frame Ground	N/A
2:TD	Transmit Data	FROM
3:RD	Receive Data	TO
4:RTS	Request to Send	FROM
5:DTR	Data Terminal Ready	FROM
6:DSR	Data Set Ready	TO
7:SG	Signal Ground	N/A

FLOW CONTROL: 6   XON: YES ACK: LEADS THAT MUST BE ON: __ __ __
PRINTER PORT: SERIAL   PARALLEL   FLOW CONTROL: XON/XOFF Hardware
   FLOW CONTROL LEAD(s):   4 11 19 20 __ __   CONNECTOR: DB25 Centronics
SPEEDS: 110 300 600 1200 1800 2400 4800 9600 19.2 56k _____
PARITY: even odd space mark none   CHARACTER LENGTH: 7 8 ___
STOP BITS: 1 1.5 2   LINE-ENDING SEQUENCE: cr lf cr/lf
MODE: async sync isoch   EMULATION/COMPATIBLE: ANSI X3.64
   VT100, Televideo 925, ADM-3A, DG100, Hazeltine 1420, HP2621, Regent 25/30
NOTE 1: This can be wired as either DTE or DCE
NOTE 2:

TERMINAL PORT PROFILE (Underline if supported, circle if selected)
COMPANY: Intecolor
PRODUCT: CT4100 Model 100 terminal

PORT: male(host)   PORT TYPE: serial
CONNECTOR: DB25 9-PIN 8-PIN(modular)   GENDER: male female
PIN CONFIGURATION: P10

PIN	FUNCTION	DIRECTION	PIN	FUNCTION	DIRECTION
1:CG	Chassis Ground	N/A	7:SG	Signal Ground	N/A
2:TD	Transmit Data	FROM	8:DCD	Data Carrier Detect	TO
3:RD	Receive Data	TO	12:SS	Speed Select	TO
4:RTS	Request to Send	FROM	15:TC	Transmit Clock	TO
5:CTS	Clear to Send	TO	17:RC	Rec. Clk/Reverse Chann	TO
6:DSR	Data Set Ready	TO	20:DTR	Data Terminal Ready	FROM

FLOW CONTROL: XON: YES ACK: LEADS THAT MUST BE ON: __ __ __
PRINTER PORT: SERIAL   PARALLEL   FLOW CONTROL: XON/XOFF Hardware
   FLOW CONTROL LEAD(s):   4 11 19 20 __ __   CONNECTOR: DB25 Centronics
SPEEDS: 110 300 600 1200 1800 2400 4800 9600 19.2 56k _____
PARITY: even odd space mark none   CHARACTER LENGTH: 7 8 ___
STOP BITS: 1 1.5 2   LINE-ENDING SEQUENCE: cr lf cr/lf
MODE: async sync isoch   EMULATION/COMPATIBLE: ANSI X3.64
   VT100, Televideo 925, ADM-3A, DG100, Hazeltine 1420, HP2621, Regent 25/30
NOTE 1:
NOTE 2:

TERMINAL PORT PROFILE (Underline if supported, circle if selected)
COMPANY: Intecolor
PRODUCT: F-8001G terminal

PORT: female   PORT TYPE: serial
CONNECTOR: DB25 9-PIN 8-PIN(modular)   GENDER: male female
PIN CONFIGURATION: P10

PIN	FUNCTION	DIRECTION
1:PG	Protective Ground	N/A
2:TD	Transmit Data	FROM
3:RD	Receive Data	TO
4:RTS	Request to Send	FROM
7:SG	Signal Ground	N/A
20:DTR	Data Terminal Ready	FROM

FLOW CONTROL: XON: YES ACK: LEADS THAT MUST BE ON: __ __ __
PRINTER PORT: SERIAL   PARALLEL   FLOW CONTROL: XON/XOFF Hardware
   FLOW CONTROL LEAD(s):   4 11 19 20 __ __   CONNECTOR: DB25 Centronics
SPEEDS: 110 300 600 1200 1800 2400 4800 9600 19.2 56k _____
PARITY: even odd space mark none   CHARACTER LENGTH: 7 8 ___
STOP BITS: 1 1.5 2   LINE-ENDING SEQUENCE: cr lf cr/lf
MODE: async sync isoch   EMULATION/COMPATIBLE: ANSI X3.64
   VT100, Televideo 925, ADM-3A, DG100, Hazeltine 1420, HP2621, Regent 25/30
NOTE 1:
NOTE 2:

TERMINAL PORT PROFILE (Underline if supported, circle if selected)
COMPANY: Lear Siegler, Inc.
PRODUCT: ADM 11, ADM 11plus terminals

PORT: female (aux)   PORT TYPE: serial
CONNECTOR: DB25 9-PIN 8-PIN(modular)   GENDER: male female
PIN CONFIGURATION: C12

PIN	FUNCTION	DIRECTION
1:FG	Frame Ground	N/A
3:RD	Receive Data	FROM
7:SG	Signal Ground	N/A
20:DTR	Data Terminal Ready	TO

FLOW CONTROL: 20   XON: ACK: LEADS THAT MUST BE ON: __ __ __
PRINTER PORT: SERIAL   PARALLEL   FLOW CONTROL: XON/XOFF Hardware
  FLOW CONTROL LEAD(s):   4 11 19 20 __ __   CONNECTOR: DB25 Centronics
SPEEDS: 110 300 600 1200 1800 2400 4800 9600 19.2 56k _____
PARITY: even odd space mark none   CHARACTER LENGTH: 7 8 ___
STOP BITS: 1 1.5 2   LINE-ENDING SEQUENCE: cr lf cr/lf
MODE: async sync isoch   EMULATION/COMPATIBLE: ANSI X3.64
   VT100, Televideo 925, ADM-3A, DG100, Hazeltine 1420, HP2621, Regent 25/30
NOTE 1:
NOTE 2:

TERMINAL PORT PROFILE (Underline if supported, circle if selected)
COMPANY: Lear Siegler, Inc.
PRODUCT: ADM 11, ADM 11plus terminals

PORT: female (modem)   PORT TYPE: serial
CONNECTOR: DB25 9-PIN 8-PIN(modular)   GENDER: male female
PIN CONFIGURATION: P03

PIN	FUNCTION	DIRECTION
1:FG	Frame Ground	N/A
2:TD	Transmit Data	FROM
3:RD	Receive Data	TO
4:RTS	Request to Send	FROM
5:CTS	Clear to Send	TO
7:SG	Signal Ground	N/A
8:DCD	Data Carrier Detect	TO
20:DTR	Data Terminal Ready	FROM

FLOW CONTROL: 20   XON: YES ACK: LEADS THAT MUST BE ON: __ __ __
PRINTER PORT: SERIAL   PARALLEL   FLOW CONTROL: XON/XOFF Hardware
  FLOW CONTROL LEAD(s):   4 11 19 20 __ __   CONNECTOR: DB25 Centronics
SPEEDS: 110 300 600 1200 1800 2400 4800 9600 19.2 56k _____
PARITY: even odd space mark none   CHARACTER LENGTH: 7 8 ___
STOP BITS: 1 1.5 2   LINE-ENDING SEQUENCE: cr lf cr/lf
MODE: async sync isoch   EMULATION/COMPATIBLE: ANSI X3.64
   VT100, Televideo 925, ADM-3A, DG100, Hazeltine 1420, HP2621, Regent 25/30
NOTE 1: Leads 5 & 8 should be on for data flow.
NOTE 2:

TERMINAL PORT PROFILE (Underline if supported, circle if selected)
COMPANY: Lear Siegler, Inc.
PRODUCT: ADM 12plus terminal

PORT: female (aux)   PORT TYPE: serial
CONNECTOR: DB25 9-PIN 8-PIN(modular)   GENDER: male female
PIN CONFIGURATION: C12

PIN	FUNCTION	DIRECTION
1:FG	Frame Ground	N/A
2:TD	Transmit Data	TO
3:RD	Receive Data	FROM
7:SG	Signal Ground	N/A
20:DTR	Data Terminal Ready	TO

FLOW CONTROL: 20   XON: YES ACK: LEADS THAT MUST BE ON: __ __ __
PRINTER PORT: SERIAL   PARALLEL   FLOW CONTROL: XON/XOFF Hardware
   FLOW CONTROL LEAD(s):   4 11 19 20 __ __   CONNECTOR: DB25 Centronics
SPEEDS: 110 300 600 1200 1800 2400 4800 9600 19.2 56k _____
PARITY: even odd space mark none   CHARACTER LENGTH: 7 8 ___
STOP BITS: 1 1.5 2   LINE-ENDING SEQUENCE: cr lf cr/lf
MODE: async sync isoch   EMULATION/COMPATIBLE: ANSI X3.64
   VT100, Televideo 925, ADM-3A, DG100, Hazeltine 1420, HP2621, Regent 25/30
NOTE 1:
NOTE 2:

TERMINAL PORT PROFILE (Underline if supported, circle if selected)
COMPANY: Lear Siegler, Inc.
PRODUCT: ADM 12plus terminal

PORT: female (modem)   PORT TYPE: serial
CONNECTOR: DB25 9-PIN 8-PIN(modular)   GENDER: male female
PIN CONFIGURATION: P03

PIN	FUNCTION	DIRECTION
1:FG	Frame Ground	N/A
2:TD	Transmit Data	FROM
3:RD	Receive Data	TO
4:RTS	Request to Send	FROM
5:CTS	Clear to Send	TO
7:SG	Signal Ground	N/A
8:DCD	Data Carrier Detect	TO
20:DTR	Data Terminal Ready	FROM

FLOW CONTROL: 20   XON: YES ACK: LEADS THAT MUST BE ON: __ __ __
PRINTER PORT: SERIAL   PARALLEL   FLOW CONTROL: XON/XOFF Hardware
   FLOW CONTROL LEAD(s):   4 11 19 20 __ __   CONNECTOR: DB25 Centronics
SPEEDS: 110 300 600 1200 1800 2400 4800 9600 19.2 56k _____
PARITY: even odd space mark none   CHARACTER LENGTH: 7 8 ___
STOP BITS: 1 1.5 2   LINE-ENDING SEQUENCE: cr lf cr/lf
MODE: async sync isoch   EMULATION/COMPATIBLE: ANSI X3.64
   VT100, Televideo 925, ADM-3A, DG100, Hazeltine 1420, HP2621, Regent 25/30
NOTE 1: Lead 5 & 8 should be on for data flow.
NOTE 2:

TERMINAL PORT PROFILE (Underline if supported, circle if selected)
COMPANY: Lear Siegler, Inc.
PRODUCT: ADM 220 terminal

PORT: female (aux)   PORT TYPE: serial
CONNECTOR: DB25 9-PIN 8-PIN(modular)   GENDER: male female
PIN CONFIGURATION: C12

PIN	FUNCTION	DIRECTION
1:FG	Frame Ground	N/A
2:TD	Transmit Data	TO
3:RD	Receive Data	FROM
7:SG	Signal Ground	N/A
20:DTR	Data Terminal Ready	TO

FLOW CONTROL: 20   XON: YES ACK: LEADS THAT MUST BE ON: __ __ __
PRINTER PORT: SERIAL   PARALLEL   FLOW CONTROL: XON/XOFF Hardware
   FLOW CONTROL LEAD(s):   4 11 19 20 __ __   CONNECTOR: DB25 Centronics
SPEEDS: 110 300 600 1200 1800 2400 4800 9600 19.2 56k _____
PARITY: even odd space mark none   CHARACTER LENGTH: 7 8 ___
STOP BITS: 1 1.5 2   LINE-ENDING SEQUENCE: cr lf cr/lf
MODE: async sync isoch   EMULATION/COMPATIBLE: ANSI X3.64
   VT100, Televideo 925, ADM-3A, DG100, Hazeltine 1420, HP2621, Regent 25/30
NOTE 1:
NOTE 2:

TERMINAL PORT PROFILE (Underline if supported, circle if selected)
COMPANY: Lear Siegler, Inc.
PRODUCT: ADM 220 terminal

PORT: male (modem)   PORT TYPE: serial
CONNECTOR: DB25 9-PIN 8-PIN(modular)   GENDER: male female
PIN CONFIGURATION: P10

PIN	FUNCTION	DIRECTION	PIN	FUNCTION	DIRECTION
1:FG	Frame Ground	N/A	6:DSR	Data Set Ready	TO
2:TD	Transmit Data	FROM	7:SG	Signal Ground	N/A
3:RD	Receive Data	TO	8:DCD	Data Carrier Detect	TO
4:RTS	Request to Send	FROM	12:SS	Speed Select	TO
5:CTS	Clear to Send	TO	20:DTR	Data Terminal Ready	FROM

FLOW CONTROL: XON: YES ACK: LEADS THAT MUST BE ON: __ __ __
PRINTER PORT: SERIAL   PARALLEL   FLOW CONTROL: XON/XOFF Hardware
   FLOW CONTROL LEAD(s):   4 11 19 20 __ __   CONNECTOR: DB25 Centronics
SPEEDS: 110 300 600 1200 1800 2400 4800 9600 19.2 56k _____
PARITY: even odd space mark none   CHARACTER LENGTH: 7 8 ___
STOP BITS: 1 1.5 2   LINE-ENDING SEQUENCE: cr lf cr/lf
MODE: async sync isoch   EMULATION/COMPATIBLE: ANSI X3.64
   VT100, Televideo 925, ADM-3A, DG100, Hazeltine 1420, HP2621, Regent 25/30
NOTE 1:
NOTE 2:

TERMINAL PORT PROFILE   (Underline if supported, circle if selected)
COMPANY: Lee Data Corporation
PRODUCT: 8178/8180 terminal

PORT: COMM   PORT TYPE: serial
CONNECTOR: DB25   9-PIN   8-PIN(modular)   GENDER: male female
PIN CONFIGURATION: P10

PIN	FUNCTION	DIRECTION	PIN	FUNCTION	DIRECTION
1:PG	Protective Ground	N/A	7:SG	Signal Ground	N/A
2:TD	Transmit Data	FROM	8:RLSD	Rec.Line Signal Detect	TO
3:RD	Receive Data	TO	12:SI	Serial In	TO
4:RTS	Request to Send	FROM	20:DTR	Data Terminal Ready	FROM
5:CTS	Clear to Send	TO	23:SS	Speed Select	FROM
6:DSR	Data Set Ready	TO			

FLOW CONTROL: XON: YES   ACK: LEADS THAT MUST BE ON: __ __ __
PRINTER PORT: SERIAL   PARALLEL   FLOW CONTROL: XON/XOFF Hardware
   FLOW CONTROL LEAD(s):   4 11 19 20 __ __   CONNECTOR: DB25 Centronics
SPEEDS: 110 300 600 1200 1800 2400 4800 9600 19.2 56k _____
PARITY: even odd space mark none   CHARACTER LENGTH: 7 8 ___
STOP BITS: 1 1.5 2   LINE-ENDING SEQUENCE: cr lf cr/lf
MODE: async sync isoch   EMULATION/COMPATIBLE: ANSI X3.64
   VT100, Televideo 925, ADM-3A, DG100, Hazeltine 1420, HP2621, Regent 25/30
NOTE 1: This terminal can operate in either VT100
NOTE 2: environments or IBM 3270 synchronous networks

TERMINAL PORT PROFILE   (Underline if supported, circle if selected)
COMPANY: Lee Data Corporation
PRODUCT: 8178/8180 terminals

PORT: 9-PIN printer   PORT TYPE: serial
CONNECTOR: DB25   9-PIN   8-PIN(modular)   GENDER: male female
PIN CONFIGURATION: C05

PIN	FUNCTION	DIRECTION
1:PG	Protective Ground	N/A
2:TD	Transmit Data	FROM
3:RD	Receive Data	TO
4:RTS	Request to Send	FROM
5:DTR	Data Terminal Ready	FROM
6:DSR	Data Set Ready	TO
7:SG	Signal Ground	N/A

FLOW CONTROL: 6   XON: YES   ACK: LEADS THAT MUST BE ON: __ __ __
PRINTER PORT: SERIAL   PARALLEL   FLOW CONTROL: XON/XOFF Hardware
   FLOW CONTROL LEAD(s):   4 11 19 20 __ __   CONNECTOR: DB25 Centronics
SPEEDS: 110 300 600 1200 1800 2400 4800 9600 19.2 56k _____
PARITY: even odd space mark none   CHARACTER LENGTH: 7 8 ___
STOP BITS: 1 1.5 2   LINE-ENDING SEQUENCE: cr lf cr/lf
MODE: async sync isoch   EMULATION/COMPATIBLE: ANSI X3.64
   VT100, Televideo 925, ADM-3A, DG100, Hazeltine 1420, HP2621, Regent 25/30
NOTE 1:
NOTE 2:

TERMINAL PORT PROFILE (Underline if supported, circle if selected)
COMPANY: Liberty Electronics
PRODUCT: Freedom 100/110

PORT: female(printer)   PORT TYPE: serial
CONNECTOR: DB25 9-PIN 8-PIN(modular)   GENDER: male female
PIN CONFIGURATION: C09

PIN	FUNCTION	DIRECTION	PIN	FUNCTION	DIRECTION
1:FG	Frame Ground	N/A	6:DSR	Data Set Ready	FROM
2:RD	Receive Data	TO	7:SG	Signal Ground	N/A
3:TD	Transmit Data	FROM	8:DCD	Data Carrier Detect	FROM
4:RTS	Request to Send	TO	19:PB	Printer Busy	TO
5:CTS	Clear to Send	FROM	20:DTR	Data Terminal Ready	TO

FLOW CONTROL: 19   XON: YES ACK: LEADS THAT MUST BE ON: __ __ __
PRINTER PORT: SERIAL   PARALLEL   FLOW CONTROL: XON/XOFF Hardware
   FLOW CONTROL LEAD(s):   4 11 19 20 __ __   CONNECTOR: DB25 Centronics
SPEEDS: 110 300 600 1200 1800 2400 4800 9600 19.2 56k _____
PARITY: even odd space mark none   CHARACTER LENGTH: 7 8 __
STOP BITS: 1 1.5 2   LINE-ENDING SEQUENCE: cr lf cr/lf
MODE: async sync isoch   EMULATION/COMPATIBLE: ANSI X3.64
   VT100, Televideo 925, ADM-3A, DG100, Hazeltine 1420, HP2621, Regent 25/30
NOTE 1:
NOTE 2:

TERMINAL PORT PROFILE (Underline if supported, circle if selected)
COMPANY: Liberty Electronics
PRODUCT: Freedom 100/110 terminals

PORT: female(Host)   PORT TYPE: serial
CONNECTOR: DB25 9-PIN 8-PIN(modular)   GENDER: male female
PIN CONFIGURATION: P03

PIN	FUNCTION	DIRECTION
1:FG	Frame Ground	N/A
2:TD	Transmit Data	FROM
3:RD	Receive Data	TO
4:RTS	Request to Send	FROM
5:CTS	Clear to Send	TO
6:DSR	Data Set Ready	TO
7:SG	Signal Ground	N/A
8:CD	Carrier Detect	TO
20:DTR	Data Terminal Ready	FROM

FLOW CONTROL: 20   XON: YES ACK: LEADS THAT MUST BE ON: __ __ __
PRINTER PORT: SERIAL   PARALLEL   FLOW CONTROL: XON/XOFF Hardware
   FLOW CONTROL LEAD(s):   4 11 19 20 __ __   CONNECTOR: DB25 Centronics
SPEEDS: 110 300 600 1200 1800 2400 4800 9600 19.2 56k _____
PARITY: even odd space mark none   CHARACTER LENGTH: 7 8 __
STOP BITS: 1 1.5 2   LINE-ENDING SEQUENCE: cr lf cr/lf
MODE: async sync isoch   EMULATION/COMPATIBLE: ANSI X3.64
   VT100, Televideo 925, ADM-3A, DG100, Hazeltine 1420, HP2621, Regent 25/30
NOTE 1:
NOTE 2:

TERMINAL PORT PROFILE (Underline if supported, circle if selected)
COMPANY: Liberty Electronics
PRODUCT: Freedom 200 terminal

PORT: female(AUX)   PORT TYPE: serial
CONNECTOR: DB25 9-PIN 8-PIN(modular)   GENDER: male female
PIN CONFIGURATION: C09

PIN	FUNCTION	DIRECTION	PIN	FUNCTION	DIRECTION
1:CG	Chassis Ground	N/A	6:DSR	Data Set Ready	FROM
2:TD	Transmit Data	TO	7:SG	Signal Ground	N/A
3:RD	Receive Data	FROM	8:DCD	Data Carrier Detect	FROM
4:RTS	Request to Send	TO	19:PB	Printer Busy	TO
5:CTS	Clear to Send	FROM	20:DTR	Data Terminal Ready	TO

FLOW CONTROL: 19   XON: YES ACK: LEADS THAT MUST BE ON: __ __ __
PRINTER PORT: SERIAL   PARALLEL   FLOW CONTROL: XON/XOFF Hardware
   FLOW CONTROL LEAD(s):   4 11 19 20 __ __ CONNECTOR: DB25 Centronics
SPEEDS: 110 300 600 1200 1800 2400 4800 9600 19.2 56k _____
PARITY: even odd space mark none   CHARACTER LENGTH: 7 8 ___
STOP BITS: 1 1.5 2   LINE-ENDING SEQUENCE: cr lf cr/lf
MODE: async sync isoch   EMULATION/COMPATIBLE: ANSI X3.64
   VT100, Televideo 925, ADM-3A, DG100, Hazeltine 1420, HP2621, Regent 25/30
NOTE 1:
NOTE 2:

TERMINAL PORT PROFILE (Underline if supported, circle if selected)
COMPANY: Liberty Electronics
PRODUCT: Freedom 200/220/240 terminals

PORT: female(MAIN)   PORT TYPE: serial
CONNECTOR: DB25 9-PIN 8-PIN(modular)   GENDER: male female
PIN CONFIGURATION: P03

PIN	FUNCTION	DIRECTION		PIN	FUNCTION	DIRECTION
1:CG	Chassis Ground	N/A				
2:TD	Transmit Data			2:TD	Transmit Data	FROM
3:RD	Receive Data	TO				
4:RTS	Request to Send	FROM				
5:CTS	Clear to Send	TO				
6:DSR	Data Set Ready	TO				
7:SG	Signal Ground	N/A				
8:DCD	Data Carrier Detect	TO				
20:DTR	Data Terminal Ready	FROM				

FLOW CONTROL: 20   XON: YES ACK: LEADS THAT MUST BE ON: __ __ __
PRINTER PORT: SERIAL   PARALLEL   FLOW CONTROL: XON/XOFF Hardware
   FLOW CONTROL LEAD(s):   4 11 19 20 __ __ CONNECTOR: DB25 Centronics
SPEEDS: 110 300 600 1200 1800 2400 4800 9600 19.2 56k _____
PARITY: even odd space mark none   CHARACTER LENGTH: 7 8 ___
STOP BITS: 1 1.5 2   LINE-ENDING SEQUENCE: cr lf cr/lf
MODE: async sync isoch   EMULATION/COMPATIBLE: ANSI X3.64
   VT100, Televideo 925, ADM-3A, DG100, Hazeltine 1420, HP2621, Regent 25/30
NOTE 1:
NOTE 2:

TERMINAL PORT PROFILE (Underline if supported, circle if selected)
COMPANY: Liberty Electronics
PRODUCT: Freedom 220/240 terminals

PORT: female(AUX)   PORT TYPE: serial
CONNECTOR: DB25 9-PIN 8-PIN(modular)   GENDER: male female
PIN CONFIGURATION: C14

PIN	FUNCTION	DIRECTION	PIN	FUNCTION	DIRECTION
1:CG	Chassis Ground	N/A	6:DSR	Data Set Ready	FROM
2:TD	Transmit Data	TO	7:SG	Signal Ground	N/A
3:RD	Receive Data	FROM	8:DCD	Data Carrier Detect	FROM
4:RTS	Request to Send	TO	20:DTR	Data Terminal Ready	TO
5:CTS	Clear to Send	FROM			

FLOW CONTROL: 20   XON: YES ACK: LEADS THAT MUST BE ON: __ __ __
PRINTER PORT: SERIAL   PARALLEL   FLOW CONTROL: XON/XOFF Hardware
   FLOW CONTROL LEAD(s):   4 11 19 20 __ __   CONNECTOR: DB25 Centronics
SPEEDS: 110 300 600 1200 1800 2400 4800 9600 19.2 56k _____
PARITY: even odd space mark none   CHARACTER LENGTH: 7 8 ___
STOP BITS: 1 1.5 2   LINE-ENDING SEQUENCE: cr lf cr/lf
MODE: async sync isoch   EMULATION/COMPATIBLE: ANSI X3.64
   VT100, Televideo 925, ADM-3A, DG100, Hazeltine 1420, HP2621, Regent 25/30
NOTE 1:
NOTE 2:

TERMINAL PORT PROFILE (Underline if supported, circle if selected)
COMPANY: Liberty Electronics
PRODUCT: Freedom ONE terminal

PORT: female(main)   PORT TYPE: serial
CONNECTOR: DB25 9-PIN 8-PIN(modular)   GENDER: male female
PIN CONFIGURATION: P03

PIN	FUNCTION	DIRECTION
1:CG	Chassis Ground	N/A
2:TD	Transmit Data	FROM
3:RD	Receive Data	TO
4:RTS	Request to Send	FROM
5:CTS	Clear to Send	TO
6:DSR	Data Set Ready	TO
7:SG	Signal Ground	N/A
8:DCD	Data Carrier Detect	TO
20:DTR	Data Terminal Ready	FROM

FLOW CONTROL: 20   XON: YES ACK: LEADS THAT MUST BE ON: __ __ __
PRINTER PORT: SERIAL   PARALLEL   FLOW CONTROL: XON/XOFF Hardware
   FLOW CONTROL LEAD(s):   4 11 19 20 __ __   CONNECTOR: DB25 Centronics
SPEEDS: 110 300 600 1200 1800 2400 4800 9600 19.2 56k _____
PARITY: even odd space mark none   CHARACTER LENGTH: 7 8 ___
STOP BITS: 1 1.5 2   LINE-ENDING SEQUENCE: cr lf cr/lf
MODE: async sync isoch   EMULATION/COMPATIBLE: ANSI X3.64
   VT100, Televideo 925, ADM-3A, DG100, Hazeltine 1420, HP2621, Regent 25/30
NOTE 1:
NOTE 2:

TERMINAL PORT PROFILE (Underline if supported, circle if selected)
COMPANY: Micro-Term, Inc.
PRODUCT: 400 series terminals

PORT: main(DB-25)   PORT TYPE: serial
CONNECTOR: DB25 9-PIN 8-PIN(modular)   GENDER: male female
PIN CONFIGURATION: P03

PIN	FUNCTION	DIRECTION	PIN	FUNCTION	DIRECTION
1:PG	Protective Ground	N/A	7:SG	Signal Ground	N/A
2:TD	Transmit Data	FROM	8:RLSD	Rec.Line Signal Detect	TO
3:RD	Receive Data	TO	12:SS	Speed Select	TO
4:RTS	Request to Send	FROM	18:+5V		FROM
5:CTS	Clear to Send	TO	20:DTR	Data Terminal Ready	FROM
6:DSR	Data Set Ready	TO	23:SS	Speed Select	FROM

FLOW CONTROL: 20   XON: YES ACK: LEADS THAT MUST BE ON: __ __ __
PRINTER PORT: SERIAL   PARALLEL   FLOW CONTROL: XON/XOFF Hardware
  FLOW CONTROL LEAD(s):   4 11 19 20 __ __   CONNECTOR: DB25 Centronics
SPEEDS: 110 300 600 1200 1800 2400 4800 9600 19.2 56k _____
PARITY: even odd space mark none   CHARACTER LENGTH: 7 8 ___
STOP BITS: 1 1.5 2   LINE-ENDING SEQUENCE: cr lf cr/lf
MODE: async sync isoch   EMULATION/COMPATIBLE: ANSI X3.64
    VT100, Televideo 925, ADM-3A, DG100, Hazeltine 1420, HP2621, Regent 25/30
NOTE 1:
NOTE 2:

TERMINAL PORT PROFILE (Underline if supported, circle if selected)
COMPANY: Micro-Term, Inc.
PRODUCT: 400 series terminals

PORT: PRINTER PORT(DB-9)   PORT TYPE: serial
CONNECTOR: DB25 9-PIN 8-PIN(modular)   GENDER: male female
PIN CONFIGURATION: C05

PIN	FUNCTION	DIRECTION
1:PG	Protective Ground	N/A
2:TD	Transmit Data	FROM
3:RD	Receive Data	TO
4:RTS	Request to Send	FROM
5:CTS	Clear to Send	FROM
6:DSR	Data Set Ready	TO
7:SG	Signal Ground	N/A

FLOW CONTROL: 6   XON: YES ACK: LEADS THAT MUST BE ON: __ __ __
PRINTER PORT: SERIAL   PARALLEL   FLOW CONTROL: XON/XOFF Hardware
  FLOW CONTROL LEAD(s):   4 11 19 20 __ __   CONNECTOR: DB25 Centronics
SPEEDS: 110 300 600 1200 1800 2400 4800 9600 19.2 56k _____
PARITY: even odd space mark none   CHARACTER LENGTH: 7 8 ___
STOP BITS: 1 1.5 2   LINE-ENDING SEQUENCE: cr lf cr/lf
MODE: async sync isoch   EMULATION/COMPATIBLE: ANSI X3.64
    VT100, Televideo 925, ADM-3A, DG100, Hazeltine 1420, HP2621, Regent 25/30
NOTE 1:
NOTE 2:

TERMINAL PORT PROFILE   (Underline if supported, circle if selected)
COMPANY: NemaTron Corporation
PRODUCT: 1000/2000 Industrial Workstations

PORT: female (secondary)   PORT TYPE: serial
CONNECTOR: DB25 9-PIN 8-PIN(modular)   GENDER: male female
PIN CONFIGURATION: C14

PIN	FUNCTION	DIRECTION
1:PG	Protective Ground	N/A
2:DI	Data In	TO
3:DO	Data Out	FROM
4:RTS	Request to Send	TO
5:CTS	Clear to Send	FROM
7:SG	Signal Ground	N/A
8:DCD	Data Carrier Detect	FROM
20:DTR	Data Terminal Ready	TO

FLOW CONTROL: XON: YES ACK: LEADS THAT MUST BE ON: __ __ __
PRINTER PORT: SERIAL   PARALLEL   FLOW CONTROL: XON/XOFF Hardware
  FLOW CONTROL LEAD(s):   4 11 19 20 __ __   CONNECTOR: DB25 Centronics
SPEEDS: 110 300 600 1200 1800 2400 4800 9600 19.2 56k _____
PARITY: even odd space mark none   CHARACTER LENGTH: 7 8 ___
STOP BITS: 1 1.5 2   LINE-ENDING SEQUENCE: cr lf cr/lf
MODE: async sync isoch   EMULATION/COMPATIBLE: ANSI X3.64
   VT100, Televideo 925, ADM-3A, DG100, Hazeltine 1420, HP2621, Regent 25/30
NOTE 1: Lead 4 must be on for IWS to output data.
NOTE 2:

TERMINAL PORT PROFILE   (Underline if supported, circle if selected)
COMPANY: NemaTron Corporation
PRODUCT: 1000/2000/3000 Industrial Workstations

PORT: male (primary port)   PORT TYPE: serial
CONNECTOR: DB25 9-PIN 8-PIN(modular)   GENDER: male female
PIN CONFIGURATION: P09

PIN	FUNCTION	DIRECTION
1:CG	Chassis Ground	N/A
2:DO	Data Out	FROM
3:DI	Data In	TO
4:RTS	Request to Send	FROM
5:CTS	Clear to Send	TO
7:SG	Signal Ground	N/A
20:DTR	Data Terminal Ready	FROM

FLOW CONTROL: 4   XON: YES ACK: LEADS THAT MUST BE ON: __ __ __
PRINTER PORT: SERIAL   PARALLEL   FLOW CONTROL: XON/XOFF Hardware
  FLOW CONTROL LEAD(s):   4 11 19 20 __ __   CONNECTOR: DB25 Centronics
SPEEDS: 110 300 600 1200 1800 2400 4800 9600 19.2 56k _____
PARITY: even odd space mark none   CHARACTER LENGTH: 7 8 ___
STOP BITS: 1 1.5 2   LINE-ENDING SEQUENCE: cr lf cr/lf
MODE: async sync isoch   EMULATION/COMPATIBLE: ANSI X3.64
   VT100, Televideo 925, ADM-3A, DG100, Hazeltine 1420, HP2621, Regent 25/30
NOTE 1: Lead 4 will be on when data may be received. Lead
NOTE 2: 5 should be on for the IWS to output data

TERMINAL PORT PROFILE (Underline if supported, circle if selected)
COMPANY: Perry Data Systems, Inc.
PRODUCT: 9480/9229/9250 terminals

PORT: female(AUX)   PORT TYPE: serial
CONNECTOR: DB25 9-PIN 8-PIN(modular)   GENDER: male female
PIN CONFIGURATION: C14

PIN	FUNCTION	DIRECTION	PIN	FUNCTION	DIRECTION
1:FG	Frame Ground	N/A	5:RTS	Request to Send	FROM
2:RD	Receive Data	TO	6:DTR	Data Terminal Ready	FROM
3:TD	Transmit Data	FROM	7:SG	Signal Ground	N/A
4:CTS	Clear to Send	TO	20:DSR	Data Set Ready	TO

FLOW CONTROL: 4   XON: YES ACK: LEADS THAT MUST BE ON: __ __ __
PRINTER PORT: SERIAL   PARALLEL   FLOW CONTROL: XON/XOFF Hardware
  FLOW CONTROL LEAD(s):   4 11 19 20 __ __   CONNECTOR: DB25 Centronics
SPEEDS: 110 300 600 1200 1800 2400 4800 9600 19.2 56k _____
PARITY: even odd space mark none   CHARACTER LENGTH: 7 8 ___
STOP BITS: 1 1.5 2   LINE-ENDING SEQUENCE: cr lf cr/lf
MODE: async sync isoch   EMULATION/COMPATIBLE: ANSI X3.64
   VT100, Televideo 925, ADM-3A, DG100, Hazeltine 1420, HP2621, Regent 25/30
NOTE 1:
NOTE 2:

TERMINAL PORT PROFILE (Underline if supported, circle if selected)
COMPANY: Perry Data Systems, Inc.
PRODUCT: 9480/9229/9250 terminals

PORT: female(host)   PORT TYPE: serial
CONNECTOR: DB25 9-PIN 8-PIN(modular)   GENDER: male female
PIN CONFIGURATION: P09

PIN	FUNCTION	DIRECTION
1:FG	Frame Ground	N/A
2:TD	Transmit Data	FROM
3:RD	Receive Data	TO
4:RTS	Request to Send	FROM
5:CTS	Clear to Send	TO
6:DSR	Data Set Ready	TO
7:SG	Signal Ground	N/A
8:DCD	Data Carrier Detect	TO
20:DTR	Data Terminal Ready	FROM

FLOW CONTROL: 4   XON: YES ACK: LEADS THAT MUST BE ON: __ __ __
PRINTER PORT: SERIAL   PARALLEL   FLOW CONTROL: XON/XOFF Hardware
  FLOW CONTROL LEAD(s):   4 11 19 20 __ __   CONNECTOR: DB25 Centronics
SPEEDS: 110 300 600 1200 1800 2400 4800 9600 19.2 56k _____
PARITY: even odd space mark none   CHARACTER LENGTH: 7 8 ___
STOP BITS: 1 1.5 2   LINE-ENDING SEQUENCE: cr lf cr/lf
MODE: async sync isoch   EMULATION/COMPATIBLE: ANSI X3.64
   VT100, Televideo 925, ADM-3A, DG100, Hazeltine 1420, HP2621, Regent 25/30
NOTE 1: CTS must be high to transmit
NOTE 2: DCD must be high to receive

TERMINAL PORT PROFILE (Underline if supported, circle if selected)
COMPANY: Prime Computer, Inc.
PRODUCT: PT200 terminal

PORT: female (25-PIN)   PORT TYPE: serial
CONNECTOR: DB25 9-PIN 8-PIN(modular)   GENDER: male female
PIN CONFIGURATION: P10

2:TD	Transmit Data	FROM
3:RD	Receive Data	TO
4:RTS	Request to Send	FROM
5:CTS	Clear to Send	TO
6:DSR	Data Set Ready	TO
7:SG	Signal Ground	N/A
8:DCD	Data Carrier Detect	TO
20:DTR	Data Terminal Ready	FROM

FLOW CONTROL: XON: YES ACK: LEADS THAT MUST BE ON: __ __ __
PRINTER PORT: SERIAL PARALLEL   FLOW CONTROL: XON/XOFF Hardware
   FLOW CONTROL LEAD(s): 4 11 19 20 __ __   CONNECTOR: DB25 Centronics
SPEEDS: 110 300 600 1200 1800 2400 4800 9600 19.2 56k _____
PARITY: even odd space mark none   CHARACTER LENGTH: 7 8 __
STOP BITS: 1 1.5 2   LINE-ENDING SEQUENCE: cr lf cr/lf
MODE: async sync isoch   EMULATION/COMPATIBLE: ANSI X3.64
   VT100, Televideo 925, ADM-3A, DG100, Hazeltine 1420, HP2621, Regent 25/30
NOTE 1:
NOTE 2:

TERMINAL PORT PROFILE (Underline if supported, circle if selected)
COMPANY: Qwint Data, Inc.
PRODUCT: KSR & MSR-743/744/745 terminals

PORT: female   PORT TYPE: serial
CONNECTOR: DB25 9-PIN 8-PIN(modular)   GENDER: male female
PIN CONFIGURATION: P01

PIN	FUNCTION	DIRECTION	PIN	FUNCTION	DIRECTION
1:PG	Protective Ground	N/A	8:RLSD	Rec.Line Signal Detect	TO
2:TD	Transmit Data	FROM	11:SRTS	Secondary Req.to Send	FROM
3:RD	Receive Data	TO	14:STD	Supervisory Trans.Data	FROM
4:RTS	Request to Send	FROM	19:SRTS	Secondary Req.to Send	FROM
5:CTS	Clear to Send	TO	20:DTR	Data Terminal Ready	FROM
6:DSR	Data Set Ready	TO	22:RI	Ring Indicator	TO
7:SG	Signal Ground	N/A			

FLOW CONTROL: 19 11   XON: YES ACK: LEADS THAT MUST BE ON: __ __ __
PRINTER PORT: SERIAL PARALLEL   FLOW CONTROL: XON/XOFF Hardware
   FLOW CONTROL LEAD(s):   4 11 19 20 __ __   CONNECTOR: DB25 Centronics
SPEEDS: 110 300 600 1200 1800 2400 4800 9600 19.2 56k _____
PARITY: even odd space mark none   CHARACTER LENGTH: 7 8 __
STOP BITS: 1 1.5 2   LINE-ENDING SEQUENCE: cr lf cr/lf
MODE: async sync isoch   EMULATION/COMPATIBLE: ANSI X3.64
   VT100, Televideo 925, ADM-3A, DG100, Hazeltine 1420, HP2621, Regent 25/30
NOTE 1:
NOTE 2:

TERMINAL PORT PROFILE (Underline if supported, circle if selected)
COMPANY: Qwint Data, Inc.
PRODUCT: MSR-780 terminal

PORT: female   PORT TYPE: serial
CONNECTOR: DB25 9-PIN 8-PIN(modular)   GENDER: male female
PIN CONFIGURATION: P01

PIN	FUNCTION	DIRECTION	PIN	FUNCTION	DIRECTION
1:PG	Protective Ground	N/A	11:SRTS	Secondary Req.to Send	FROM
2:TD	Transmit Data	FROM	13:SCTS	Secondary Cl'r to Send	TO
3:RD	Receive Data	TO	14:STD	Supervisory Trans.Data	FROM
4:RTS	Request to Send	FROM	16:SRD	Supervisory Rec. Data	TO
5:CTS	Clear to Send	TO	19:SRTS	Secondary Req.to Send	FROM
6:DSR	Data Set Ready	TO	20:DTR	Data Terminal Ready	FROM
7:SG	Signal Ground	N/A	22:RI	Ring Indicator	TO
8:RLSD	Rec.Line Signal Detect	TO			

FLOW CONTROL: 19 11   XON: YES ACK: LEADS THAT MUST BE ON: __ __ __
PRINTER PORT: SERIAL   PARALLEL   FLOW CONTROL: XON/XOFF Hardware
  FLOW CONTROL LEAD(s):   4 11 19 20 __ __   CONNECTOR: DB25 Centronics
SPEEDS: 110 300 600 1200 1800 2400 4800 9600 19.2 56k _____
PARITY: even odd space mark none   CHARACTER LENGTH: 7 8 ___
STOP BITS: 1 1.5 2   LINE-ENDING SEQUENCE: cr lf cr/lf
MODE: async sync isoch   EMULATION/COMPATIBLE: ANSI X3.64
   VT100, Televideo 925, ADM-3A, DG100, Hazeltine 1420, HP2621, Regent 25/30
NOTE 1:
NOTE 2:

TERMINAL PORT PROFILE (Underline if supported, circle if selected)
COMPANY: RCA Data Communications Prod.
PRODUCT: APT (VP4801/3801) terminals

PORT: female   PORT TYPE: serial
CONNECTOR: DB25 9-PIN 8-PIN(modular)   GENDER: male female
PIN CONFIGURATION: P10

PIN	FUNCTION	DIRECTION
1:G	Ground	N/A
2:SO	Serial Out	FROM
3:SI	Serial In	TO
4:RTS	Request to Send	FROM
5:CTS	Clear to Send	TO
7:SG	Signal Ground	N/A
19:F	Fault	FROM
20:DTR	Data Terminal Ready	FROM

FLOW CONTROL: XON: ACK: LEADS THAT MUST BE ON: __ __ __
PRINTER PORT: SERIAL   PARALLEL   FLOW CONTROL: XON/XOFF Hardware
  FLOW CONTROL LEAD(s):   4 11 19 20 __ __   CONNECTOR: DB25 Centronics
SPEEDS: 110 300 600 1200 1800 2400 4800 9600 19.2 56k _____
PARITY: even odd space mark none   CHARACTER LENGTH: 7 8 ___
STOP BITS: 1 1.5 2   LINE-ENDING SEQUENCE: cr lf cr/lf
MODE: async sync isoch   EMULATION/COMPATIBLE: ANSI X3.64
   VT100, Televideo 925, ADM-3A, DG100, Hazeltine 1420, HP2621, Regent 25/30
NOTE 1: Set the terminal to "direct" mode
NOTE 2:

TERMINAL PORT PROFILE   (Underline if supported, circle if selected)
COMPANY: TAB Products Co
PRODUCT: E-22 terminal

PORT: male(9-PIN aux)   PORT TYPE: serial
CONNECTOR: DB25 9-PIN 8-PIN(modular)   GENDER: male female
PIN CONFIGURATION: C05

PIN	FUNCTION	DIRECTION
1:PG	Protective Ground	N/A
2:TD	Transmit Data	FROM
3:RD	Receive Data	TO
4:RTS	Request to Send	FROM
5:DTR	Data Terminal Ready	FROM
6:DSR	Data Set Ready	TO
7:SG	Signal Ground	N/A

FLOW CONTROL: 6   XON: YES ACK: LEADS THAT MUST BE ON: __ __ __
PRINTER PORT: SERIAL   PARALLEL   FLOW CONTROL: XON/XOFF Hardware
  FLOW CONTROL LEAD(s):   4 11 19 20 __ __   CONNECTOR: DB25 Centronics
SPEEDS: 110 300 600 1200 1800 2400 4800 9600 19.2 56k _____
PARITY: even odd space mark none   CHARACTER LENGTH: 7 8 ___
STOP BITS: 1 1.5 2   LINE-ENDING SEQUENCE: cr lf cr/lf
MODE: async sync isoch   EMULATION/COMPATIBLE: ANSI X3.64
    VT100, Televideo 925, ADM-3A, DG100, Hazeltine 1420, HP2621, Regent 25/30
NOTE 1:
NOTE 2:

TERMINAL PORT PROFILE   (Underline if supported, circle if selected)
COMPANY: TAB Products Co.
PRODUCT: E-32/E-22 terminals

PORT: male(host)   PORT TYPE: serial
CONNECTOR: DB25 9-PIN 8-PIN(modular)   GENDER: male female
PIN CONFIGURATION: P09

PIN	FUNCTION	DIRECTION
1:PG	Protective Ground	N/A
2:TD	Transmit Data	FROM
3:RD	Receive Data	TO
4:RTS	Request to Send	FROM
5:CTS	Clear to Send	TO
6:DSR	Data Set Ready	TO
7:SG	Signal Ground	N/A
8:CD	Carrier Detect	TO
20:DTR	Data Terminal Ready	FROM

FLOW CONTROL: 4   XON: YES ACK: LEADS THAT MUST BE ON: __ __ __
PRINTER PORT: SERIAL   PARALLEL   FLOW CONTROL: XON/XOFF Hardware
  FLOW CONTROL LEAD(s):   4 11 19 20 __ __   CONNECTOR: DB25 Centronics
SPEEDS: 110 300 600 1200 1800 2400 4800 9600 19.2 56k _____
PARITY: even odd space mark none   CHARACTER LENGTH: 7 8 ___
STOP BITS: 1 1.5 2   LINE-ENDING SEQUENCE: cr lf cr/lf
MODE: async sync isoch   EMULATION/COMPATIBLE: ANSI X3.64
    VT100, Televideo 925, ADM-3A, DG100, Hazeltine 1420, HP2621, Regent 25/30
NOTE 1:
NOTE 2:

TERMINAL PORT PROFILE (Underline if supported, circle if selected)
COMPANY: Talaris Systems, Inc.
PRODUCT: 7800 terminal

PORT: male(Port A)   PORT TYPE: serial
CONNECTOR: DB25 9-PIN 8-PIN(modular)   GENDER: male female
PIN CONFIGURATION: P03

PIN	FUNCTION	DIRECTION	PIN	FUNCTION	DIRECTION
1:PG	Protective Ground	N/A	11:SS	Speed Select	FROM
2:TD	Transmit Data	FROM	15:TC	Transmit Clock	TO
3:RD	Receive Data	TO	17:RC	Rec. Clk/Reverse Chann	TO
4:RTS	Request to Send	FROM	19:SS	Speed Select	FROM
5:CTS	Clear to Send	TO	20:DTR	Data Terminal Ready	FROM
6:DSR	Data Set Ready	TO	23:SS	Speed Select	FROM
7:SG	Signal Ground	N/A			

FLOW CONTROL: 20   XON: YES ACK: LEADS THAT MUST BE ON: __ __ __
PRINTER PORT: SERIAL   PARALLEL   FLOW CONTROL: XON/XOFF Hardware
  FLOW CONTROL LEAD(s):   4 11 19 20 __ __   CONNECTOR: DB25 Centronics
SPEEDS: 110 300 600 1200 1800 2400 4800 9600 19.2 56k _____
PARITY: even odd space mark none   CHARACTER LENGTH: 7 8 ___
STOP BITS: 1 1.5 2   LINE-ENDING SEQUENCE: cr lf cr/lf
MODE: async sync isoch   EMULATION/COMPATIBLE: ANSI X3.64
     VT100, Televideo 925, ADM-3A, DG100, Hazeltine 1420, HP2621, Regent 25/30
NOTE 1: leads 11/19/23 are on at all times as speed select
NOTE 2:

TERMINAL PORT PROFILE (Underline if supported, circle if selected)
COMPANY: Wang Laboratories, Inc.
PRODUCT: 2110A workstation

PORT: male(aux)   PORT TYPE: serial
CONNECTOR: DB25 9-PIN 8-PIN(modular)   GENDER: male female
PIN CONFIGURATION: C01

PIN	FUNCTION	DIRECTION
1:PG	Protective Ground	N/A
2:TD	Transmit Data	FROM
3:RD	Receive Data	TO
4:RTS	Request to Send	FROM
5:CTS	Clear to Send	TO
6:DSR	Data Set Ready	TO
7:SG	Signal Ground	N/A
8:DCD	Data Carrier Detect	TO
20:DTR	Data Terminal Ready	FROM

FLOW CONTROL: XON: YES ACK: LEADS THAT MUST BE ON: __ __ __
PRINTER PORT: SERIAL   PARALLEL   FLOW CONTROL: XON/XOFF Hardware
  FLOW CONTROL LEAD(s):   4 11 19 20 __ __   CONNECTOR: DB25 Centronics
SPEEDS: 110 300 600 1200 1800 2400 4800 9600 19.2 56k _____
PARITY: even odd space mark none   CHARACTER LENGTH: 7 8 ___
STOP BITS: 1 1.5 2   LINE-ENDING SEQUENCE: cr lf cr/lf
MODE: async sync isoch   EMULATION/COMPATIBLE: ANSI X3.64
     VT100, Televideo 925, ADM-3A, DG100, Hazeltine 1420, HP2621, Regent 25/30
NOTE 1:
NOTE 2:

TERMINAL PORT PROFILE (Underline if supported, circle if selected)
COMPANY: Wang Laboratories, Inc.
PRODUCT: 2110A workstation

PORT: male(main)   PORT TYPE: serial
CONNECTOR: DB25 9-PIN 8-PIN(modular)   GENDER: male female
PIN CONFIGURATION: P10

PIN	FUNCTION	DIRECTION		PIN	FUNCTION	DIRECTION
1:PG	Protective Ground	N/A		7:SG	Signal Ground	N/A
2:TD	Transmit Data	FROM		8:DCD	Data Carrier Detect	TO
3:RD	Receive Data	TO		12:SDCD	Secondary DCD	TO
4:RTS	Request to Send	FROM		20:DTR	Data Terminal Ready	FROM
5:CTS	Clear to Send	TO		23:DRS	Data Rate Select	TO
6:DSR	Data Set Ready	TO				

FLOW CONTROL: XON: YES ACK: LEADS THAT MUST BE ON: __ __ __
PRINTER PORT: SERIAL   PARALLEL   FLOW CONTROL: XON/XOFF Hardware
   FLOW CONTROL LEAD(s): 4 11 19 20 __ __ CONNECTOR: DB25 Centronics
SPEEDS: 110 300 600 1200 1800 2400 4800 9600 19.2 56k _____
PARITY: even odd space mark none   CHARACTER LENGTH: 7 8 __
STOP BITS: 1 1.5 2   LINE-ENDING SEQUENCE: cr lf cr/lf
MODE: async sync isoch   EMULATION/COMPATIBLE: ANSI X3.64
   VT100, Televideo 925, ADM-3A, DG100, Hazeltine 1420, HP2621, Regent 25/30
NOTE 1:
NOTE 2:

TERMINAL PORT PROFILE (Underline if supported, circle if selected)
COMPANY: Wyse Technology
PRODUCT: WY-30 terminal

PORT: female(AUX port)   PORT TYPE: serial
CONNECTOR: DB25 9-PIN 8-PIN(modular)   GENDER: male female
PIN CONFIGURATION: C02

PIN	FUNCTION	DIRECTION
1:FG	Frame Ground	N/A
3:RD	Receive Data	FROM
5:CTS	Clear to Send	FROM
6:DSR	Data Set Ready	FROM
7:SG	Signal Ground	N/A
8:DCD	Data Carrier Detect	FROM
11:DTR	Data Terminal Ready	TO
20:DTR	Data Terminal Ready	TO

FLOW CONTROL: 20 11   XON: ACK: LEADS THAT MUST BE ON: __ __ __
PRINTER PORT: SERIAL   PARALLEL   FLOW CONTROL: XON/XOFF Hardware
   FLOW CONTROL LEAD(s):   4 11 19 20 __ __ CONNECTOR: DB25 Centronics
SPEEDS: 110 300 600 1200 2400 4800 9600 19.2 56k _____
PARITY: even odd space mark none   CHARACTER LENGTH: 7 8 __
STOP BITS: 1 1.5 2   LINE-ENDING SEQUENCE: cr lf cr/lf
MODE: async sync isoch   EMULATION/COMPATIBLE: ANSI X3.64
   VT100, Televideo 925, ADM-3A, DG100, Hazeltine 1420, HP2621, Regent 25/30
NOTE 1: Only connect 11 or 20 for hardware flow control,
NOTE 2: not both.

TERMINAL PORT PROFILE (Underline if supported, circle if selected)
COMPANY: Wyse Technology
PRODUCT: WY-30 terminal

PORT: female(MODEM port)   PORT TYPE: serial
CONNECTOR: DB25 9-PIN 8-PIN(modular)   GENDER: male female
PIN CONFIGURATION: P08

PIN	FUNCTION	DIRECTION
1:FG	Frame Ground	N/A
2:TD	Transmit Data	FROM
3:RD	Receive Data	TO
4:RTS	Request to Send	FROM
7:SG	Signal Ground	N/A
20:DTR	Data Terminal Ready	FROM

FLOW CONTROL: 20   XON: YES ACK: LEADS THAT MUST BE ON: __ __ __
PRINTER PORT: SERIAL PARALLEL   FLOW CONTROL: XON/XOFF Hardware
  FLOW CONTROL LEAD(s):   4 11 19 20 __ __   CONNECTOR: DB25 Centronics
SPEEDS: 110 300 600 1200 1800 2400 4800 9600 19.2 56k _____
PARITY: even odd space mark none   CHARACTER LENGTH: 7 8 __
STOP BITS: 1 1.5 2   LINE-ENDING SEQUENCE: cr lf cr/lf
MODE: async sync isoch   EMULATION/COMPATIBLE: ANSI X3.64
    VT100, Televideo 925, ADM-3A, DG100, Hazeltine 1420, HP2621, Regent 25/30
NOTE 1:
NOTE 2:

TERMINAL PORT PROFILE (Underline if supported, circle if selected)
COMPANY: Wyse Technology
PRODUCT: WY-350 terminal

PORT: female(AUX port)   PORT TYPE: serial
CONNECTOR: DB25 9-PIN 8-PIN(modular)   GENDER: male female
PIN CONFIGURATION: C14

PIN	FUNCTION	DIRECTION
1:FG	Frame Ground	N/A
3:RD	Receive Data	FROM
6:DSR	Data Set Ready	FROM
7:SG	Signal Ground	N/A
20:DTR	Data Terminal Ready	TO

FLOW CONTROL: 20   XON: ACK: LEADS THAT MUST BE ON: __ __ __
PRINTER PORT: SERIAL PARALLEL   FLOW CONTROL: XON/XOFF Hardware
  FLOW CONTROL LEAD(s):   4 11 19 20 __ __   CONNECTOR: DB25 Centronics
SPEEDS: 110 300 600 1200 1800 2400 4800 9600 19.2 56k _____
PARITY: even odd space mark none   CHARACTER LENGTH: 7 8 __
STOP BITS: 1 1.5 2   LINE-ENDING SEQUENCE: cr lf cr/lf
MODE: async sync isoch   EMULATION/COMPATIBLE: ANSI X3.64
    VT100, Televideo 925, ADM-3A, DG100, Hazeltine 1420, HP2621, Regent 25/30
NOTE 1:
NOTE 2:

TERMINAL PORT PROFILE (Underline if supported, circle if selected)
COMPANY: Wyse Technology
PRODUCT: WY-350 terminal

PORT: female(MODEM)   PORT TYPE: serial
CONNECTOR: DB25 9-PIN 8-PIN(modular)   GENDER: male female
PIN CONFIGURATION: P03

PIN	FUNCTION	DIRECTION	PIN	FUNCTION	DIRECTION
1:FG	Frame Ground	N/A	6:DSR	Data Set Ready	TO
2:TD	Transmit Data	FROM	7:SG	Signal Ground	N/A
3:RD	Receive Data	TO	8:DCD	Data Carrier Detect	TO
4:RTS	Request to Send	FROM	20:DTR	Data Terminal Ready	FROM
5:CTS	Clear to Send	TO			

FLOW CONTROL: 20   XON: YES ACK: LEADS THAT MUST BE ON: __ __ __
PRINTER PORT: SERIAL   PARALLEL   FLOW CONTROL: XON/XOFF Hardware
   FLOW CONTROL LEAD(s): 4 11 19 20 __ __   CONNECTOR: DB25 Centronics
SPEEDS: 110 300 600 1200 1800 2400 4800 9600 19.2 56k _____
PARITY: even odd space mark none   CHARACTER LENGTH: 7 8 __
STOP BITS: 1 1.5 2   LINE-ENDING SEQUENCE: cr lf cr/lf
MODE: async sync isoch   EMULATION/COMPATIBLE: ANSI X3.64
   VT100, Televideo 925, ADM-3A, DG100, Hazeltine 1420, HP2621, Regent 25/30
NOTE 1:
NOTE 2:

TERMINAL PORT PROFILE (Underline if supported, circle if selected)
COMPANY: Wyse Technology
PRODUCT: WY-50 terminal

PORT: AUX port   PORT TYPE: serial
CONNECTOR: DB25 9-PIN 8-PIN(modular)   GENDER: male female
PIN CONFIGURATION: C14

PIN	FUNCTION	DIRECTION
1:FG	Frame Ground	N/A
2:TD	Transmit Data	TO
3:RD	Receive Data	FROM
4:RTS	Request to Send	TO
6:DSR	Data Set Ready	FROM
7:SG	Signal Ground	N/A
8:DCD	Data Carrier Detect	FROM
20:DTR	Data Terminal Ready	TO

FLOW CONTROL: XON: YES ACK: LEADS THAT MUST BE ON: __ __ __
PRINTER PORT: SERIAL   PARALLEL   FLOW CONTROL: XON/XOFF Hardware
   FLOW CONTROL LEAD(s): 4 11 19 20 __ __   CONNECTOR: DB25 Centronics
SPEEDS: 110 300 600 1200 1800 2400 4800 9600 19.2 56k _____
PARITY: even odd space mark none   CHARACTER LENGTH: 7 8 __
STOP BITS: 1 1.5 2   LINE-ENDING SEQUENCE: cr lf cr/lf
MODE: async sync isoch   EMULATION/COMPATIBLE: ANSI X3.64
   VT100, Televideo 925, ADM-3A, DG100, Hazeltine 1420, HP2621, Regent 25/30
NOTE 1: Lead 20 is monitored for printer ready condition
NOTE 2:

TERMINAL PORT PROFILE (Underline if supported, circle if selected)
COMPANY: Wyse Technology
PRODUCT: WY-50, WY-75 terminals

PORT: MODEM   PORT TYPE: serial
CONNECTOR: DB25 9-PIN 8-PIN(modular)   GENDER: male female
PIN CONFIGURATION: P03

PIN	FUNCTION	DIRECTION
1:FG	Frame Ground	N/A
2:TD	Transmit Data	FROM
3:RD	Receive Data	TO
4:RTS	Request to Send	FROM
5:CTS	Clear to Send	TO
7:SG	Signal Ground	N/A
8:DCD	Data Carrier Detect	TO
20:DTR	Data Terminal Ready	FROM

FLOW CONTROL: 20   XON: YES ACK: LEADS THAT MUST BE ON: __ __ __
PRINTER PORT: SERIAL   PARALLEL   FLOW CONTROL: XON/XOFF Hardware
    FLOW CONTROL LEAD(s):   4 11 19 20 __ __   CONNECTOR: DB25 Centronics
SPEEDS: 110 300 600 1200 1800 2400 4800 9600 19.2 56k _____
PARITY: even odd space mark none   CHARACTER LENGTH: 7 8 ___
STOP BITS: 1 1.5 2   LINE-ENDING SEQUENCE: cr lf cr/lf
MODE: async sync isoch   EMULATION/COMPATIBLE: ANSI X3.64
    VT100, Televideo 925, ADM-3A, DG100, Hazeltine 1420, HP2621, Regent 25/30
NOTE 1:
NOTE 2:

TERMINAL PORT PROFILE (Underline if supported, circle if selected)
COMPANY: Wyse Technology
PRODUCT: WY-60 terminal

PORT: female(AUX)   PORT TYPE: serial
CONNECTOR: DB25 9-PIN 8-PIN(modular)   GENDER: male female
PIN CONFIGURATION: C14

PIN	FUNCTION	DIRECTION
1:PG	Protective Ground	N/A
2:TD	Transmit Data	TO
3:RD	Receive Data	FROM
6:DSR	Data Set Ready	FROM
7:SG	Signal Ground	N/A
20:DTR	Data Terminal Ready	TO

FLOW CONTROL: 20   XON: YES ACK: LEADS THAT MUST BE ON: __ __ __
PRINTER PORT: SERIAL   PARALLEL   FLOW CONTROL: XON/XOFF Hardware
    FLOW CONTROL LEAD(s):   4 11 19 20 __ __   CONNECTOR: DB25 Centronics
SPEEDS: 110 300 600 1200 1800 2400 4800 9600 19.2 56k _____
PARITY: even odd space mark none   CHARACTER LENGTH: 7 8 ___
STOP BITS: 1 1.5 2   LINE-ENDING SEQUENCE: cr lf cr/lf
MODE: async sync isoch   EMULATION/COMPATIBLE: ANSI X3.64
    VT100, Televideo 925, ADM-3A, DG100, Hazeltine 1420, HP2621, Regent 25/30
NOTE 1: Hardware or software flow control, or both may be
NOTE 2: used

TERMINAL PORT PROFILE (Underline if supported, circle if selected)
COMPANY: Wyse Technology
PRODUCT: WY-60 terminal

PORT: female(MODEM)   PORT TYPE: serial
CONNECTOR: DB25 9-PIN 8-PIN(modular)   GENDER: male female
PIN CONFIGURATION: P10

PIN	FUNCTION	DIRECTION
1:G	Ground	N/A
2:TD	Transmit Data	FROM
3:RD	Receive Data	TO
4:RTS	Request to Send	FROM
5:CTS	Clear to Send	TO
6:DSR	Data Set Ready	TO
7:SG	Signal Ground	N/A
8:DCD	Data Carrier Detect	TO
20:DTR	Data Terminal Ready	FROM

FLOW CONTROL: XON: YES ACK: LEADS THAT MUST BE ON: __ __ __
PRINTER PORT: SERIAL   PARALLEL   FLOW CONTROL: XON/XOFF Hardware
   FLOW CONTROL LEAD(s): 4 11 19 20 __ __   CONNECTOR: DB25 Centronics
SPEEDS: 110 300 600 1200 1800 2400 4800 9600 19.2 56k _____
PARITY: even odd space mark none   CHARACTER LENGTH: 7 8 __
STOP BITS: 1 1.5 2   LINE-ENDING SEQUENCE: cr lf cr/lf
MODE: async sync isoch   EMULATION/COMPATIBLE: ANSI X3.64
     VT100, Televideo 925, ADM-3A, DG100, Hazeltine 1420, HP2621, Regent 25/30
NOTE 1: leads 5/6/8 should be on for the modem protocol
NOTE 2:

TERMINAL PORT PROFILE (Underline if supported, circle if selected)
COMPANY: Wyse Technology
PRODUCT: WY-75 terminal

PORT: AUX port   PORT TYPE: serial
CONNECTOR: DB25 9-PIN 8-PIN(modular)   GENDER: male female
PIN CONFIGURATION: C14

PIN	FUNCTION	DIRECTION
1:FG	Frame Ground	N/A
3:RD	Receive Data	FROM
6:DSR	Data Set Ready	FROM
7:SG	Signal Ground	N/A
20:DTR	Data Terminal Ready	TO

FLOW CONTROL: XON: ACK: LEADS THAT MUST BE ON: __ __ __
PRINTER PORT: SERIAL   PARALLEL   FLOW CONTROL: XON/XOFF Hardware
   FLOW CONTROL LEAD(s): 4 11 19 20 __ __   CONNECTOR: DB25 Centronics
SPEEDS: 110 300 600 1200 1800 2400 4800 9600 19.2 56k _____
PARITY: even odd space mark none   CHARACTER LENGTH: 7 8 __
STOP BITS: 1 1.5 2   LINE-ENDING SEQUENCE: cr lf cr/lf
MODE: async sync isoch   EMULATION/COMPATIBLE: ANSI X3.64
     VT100, Televideo 925, ADM-3A, DG100, Hazeltine 1420, HP2621, Regent 25/30
NOTE 1: PIN 20 is monitored for printer ready condition
NOTE 2:

TERMINAL PORT PROFILE (Underline if supported, circle if selected)
COMPANY: Wyse Technology
PRODUCT: WY-85

PORT: male(COMM port)   PORT TYPE: serial
CONNECTOR: DB25 9-PIN 8-PIN(modular)   GENDER: male female
PIN CONFIGURATION: P03

PIN	FUNCTION	DIRECTION	PIN	FUNCTION	DIRECTION
1:PG	Protective Ground	N/A	7:SG	Signal Ground	N/A
2:TD	Transmit Data	FROM	8:DCD	Data Carrier Detect	TO
3:RD	Receive Data	TO	12:SI	Serial In	TO
4:RTS	Request to Send	FROM	20:DTR	Data Terminal Ready	FROM
5:CTS	Clear to Send	TO	23:SS	Speed Select	FROM
6:DSR	Data Set Ready	TO			

FLOW CONTROL: 20   XON: YES ACK: LEADS THAT MUST BE ON: __ __ __
PRINTER PORT: SERIAL   PARALLEL   FLOW CONTROL: XON/XOFF Hardware
   FLOW CONTROL LEAD(s):   4 11 19 20 __ __ CONNECTOR: DB25 Centronics
SPEEDS: 110 300 600 1200 1800 2400 4800 9600 19.2 56k _____
PARITY: even odd space mark none   CHARACTER LENGTH: 7 8 __
STOP BITS: 1 1.5 2   LINE-ENDING SEQUENCE: cr lf cr/lf
MODE: async sync isoch   EMULATION/COMPATIBLE: ANSI X3.64
   VT100, Televideo 925, ADM-3A, DG100, Hazeltine 1420, HP2621, Regent 25/30
NOTE 1: Modem control mode should be enabled for 5/6/8 to
NOTE 2: be monitored by the terminal--otherwise exclude

TERMINAL PORT PROFILE (Underline if supported, circle if selected)
COMPANY: xycom
PRODUCT: RacPac 4810 terminal

PORT: female   PORT TYPE: serial
CONNECTOR: DB25 9-PIN 8-PIN(modular)   GENDER: male female
PIN CONFIGURATION: P10

PIN	FUNCTION	DIRECTION
1:FG	Frame Ground	N/A
2:TD	Transmit Data	FROM
3:RD	Receive Data	TO
4:RTS	Request to Send	FROM
5:CTS	Clear to Send	TO
6:DSR	Data Set Ready	TO
7:SG	Signal Ground	N/A
20:DTR	Data Terminal Ready	FROM

FLOW CONTROL: XON: YES ACK: LEADS THAT MUST BE ON: __ __ __
PRINTER PORT: SERIAL   PARALLEL   FLOW CONTROL: XON/XOFF Hardware
   FLOW CONTROL LEAD(s):   4 11 19 20 __ __ CONNECTOR: DB25 Centronics
SPEEDS: 110 300 600 1200 1800 2400 4800 9600 19.2 56k _____
PARITY: even odd space mark none   CHARACTER LENGTH: 7 8 __
STOP BITS: 1 1.5 2   LINE-ENDING SEQUENCE: cr lf cr/lf
MODE: async sync isoch   EMULATION/COMPATIBLE: ANSI X3.64
   VT100, Televideo 925, ADM-3A, DG100, Hazeltine 1420, HP2621, Regent 25/30
NOTE 1:
NOTE 2:

TERMINAL PORT PROFILE (Underline if supported, circle if selected)
COMPANY: _____
PRODUCT: _____

PORT: _____   Port Type: serial parallel ___
CONNECTOR: DB25 9-pin 5-pin 8-pin Centronics Gender: male female
Pin Configuration: ___

Pin #	Function	Direction	Pin #	Function	Direction
1	_____	to from n/a	14	_____	to from n/a
2	_____	to from n/a	15	_____	to from n/a
3	_____	to from n/a	16	_____	to from n/a
4	_____	to from n/a	17	_____	to from n/a
5	_____	to from n/a	18	_____	to from n/a
6	_____	to from n/a	19	_____	to from n/a
7	_____	to from n/a	20	_____	to from n/a
8	_____	to from n/a	21	_____	to from n/a
9	_____	to from n/a	22	_____	to from n/a
10	_____	to from n/a	23	_____	to from n/a
11	_____	to from n/a	24	_____	to from n/a
12	_____	to from n/a	25	_____	to from n/a
13	_____	to from n/a			

(complete the next section only with 36-pin cinch connectors)

26	_____	to from n/a	27	_____	to from n/a
28	_____	to from n/a	29	_____	to from n/a
30	_____	to from n/a	31	_____	to from n/a
32	_____	to from n/a	33	_____	to from n/a
34	_____	to from n/a	35	_____	to from n/a
36	_____	to from n/a			

Flow Control Technique: XON/XOFF ENQ/ACK STX/ETX Hardware
Flow Control lead(s):   4 11 19 20 ___ ___ ___
Leads that must be on: 5 6 8 ___ ___ ___
PRINTER PORT: SERIAL PARALLEL   FLOW CONTROL: XON/XOFF Hardware
  FLOW CONTROL LEAD(s):   4 11 19 20 ___ ___   CONNECTOR: DB25 Centronics
Speeds: 110 300 600 1200 1800 2400 4800 9600 19.2 56k _____
Parity: even odd space mark none   CHARACTER LENGTH: 7 8 ___
Stop Bits: 1 1.5 2   Line Ending Sequence: cr lf cr/lf
Mode: async sync isoch   EMULATION/COMPATIBLE: ANSI X3.64
   VT100, Televideo 925, ADM-3A, DG100, Hazeltine 1420, HP2621, Regent 25/30___

NOTE 1:_____
NOTE 2:_____

TERMINAL PORT PROFILE (Underline if supported, circle if selected)
COMPANY: _____
PRODUCT: _____

PORT: _____   Port Type: serial parallel __
CONNECTOR: DB25 9-pin 5-pin 8-pin Centronics Gender: male female
Pin Configuration: ___

Pin #	Function	Direction	Pin #	Function	Direction
1	_____	to from n/a	14	_____	to from n/a
2	_____	to from n/a	15	_____	to from n/a
3	_____	to from n/a	16	_____	to from n/a
4	_____	to from n/a	17	_____	to from n/a
5	_____	to from n/a	18	_____	to from n/a
6	_____	to from n/a	19	_____	to from n/a
7	_____	to from n/a	20	_____	to from n/a
8	_____	to from n/a	21	_____	to from n/a
9	_____	to from n/a	22	_____	to from n/a
10	_____	to from n/a	23	_____	to from n/a
11	_____	to from n/a	24	_____	to from n/a
12	_____	to from n/a	25	_____	to from n/a
13	_____	to from n/a			

(complete the next section only with 36-pin cinch connectors)

26	_____	to from n/a	27	_____	to from n/a
28	_____	to from n/a	29	_____	to from n/a
30	_____	to from n/a	31	_____	to from n/a
32	_____	to from n/a	33	_____	to from n/a
34	_____	to from n/a	35	_____	to from n/a
36	_____	to from n/a			

Flow Control Technique: XON/XOFF ENQ/ACK STX/ETX Hardware
Flow Control lead(s):   4 11 19 20 __ __ __
Leads that must be on: 5 6 8 __ __ __ __
PRINTER PORT: SERIAL PARALLEL   FLOW CONTROL: XON/XOFF Hardware
   FLOW CONTROL LEAD(s):   4 11 19 20 __ __ CONNECTOR: DB25 Centronics
Speeds: 110 300 600 1200 1800 2400 4800 9600 19.2 56k _____
Parity: even odd space mark none   CHARACTER LENGTH: 7 8 ___
Stop Bits: 1 1.5 2   Line Ending Sequence: cr lf cr/lf
Mode: async sync isoch   EMULATION/COMPATIBLE: ANSI X3.64
   VT100, Televideo 925, ADM-3A, DG100, Hazeltine 1420, HP2621, Regent 25/30__

NOTE 1:_____
NOTE 2:_____

TERMINAL PORT PROFILE (Underline if supported, circle if selected)
COMPANY: _____
PRODUCT: _____

PORT: _____   Port Type: serial parallel __
CONNECTOR: DB25 9-pin 5-pin 8-pin Centronics Gender: male female
Pin Configuration: ___

Pin #	Function	Direction	Pin #	Function	Direction
1	_____	to from n/a	14	_____	to from n/a
2	_____	to from n/a	15	_____	to from n/a
3	_____	to from n/a	16	_____	to from n/a
4	_____	to from n/a	17	_____	to from n/a
5	_____	to from n/a	18	_____	to from n/a
6	_____	to from n/a	19	_____	to from n/a
7	_____	to from n/a	20	_____	to from n/a
8	_____	to from n/a	21	_____	to from n/a
9	_____	to from n/a	22	_____	to from n/a
10	_____	to from n/a	23	_____	to from n/a
11	_____	to from n/a	24	_____	to from n/a
12	_____	to from n/a	25	_____	to from n/a
13	_____	to from n/a			

(complete the next section only with 36-pin cinch connectors)

26	_____	to from n/a	27	_____	to from n/a
28	_____	to from n/a	29	_____	to from n/a
30	_____	to from n/a	31	_____	to from n/a
32	_____	to from n/a	33	_____	to from n/a
34	_____	to from n/a	35	_____	to from n/a
36	_____	to from n/a			

Flow Control Technique: XON/XOFF ENQ/ACK STX/ETX Hardware
Flow Control lead(s):   4 11 19 20 __ __ __
Leads that must be on: 5   6   8 __ __ __ __
PRINTER PORT: SERIAL PARALLEL   FLOW CONTROL: XON/XOFF Hardware
  FLOW CONTROL LEAD(s):   4 11 19 20 __ __   CONNECTOR: DB25 Centronics
Speeds: 110 300 600 1200 1800 2400 4800 9600 19.2 56k _____
Parity: even odd space mark none   CHARACTER LENGTH: 7 8 ___
Stop Bits: 1 1.5 2   Line Ending Sequence: cr lf cr/lf
Mode: async sync isoch   EMULATION/COMPATIBLE: ANSI X3.64
   VT100, Televideo 925, ADM-3A, DG100, Hazeltine 1420, HP2621, Regent 25/30__

NOTE 1:_____
NOTE 2:_____

TERMINAL PORT PROFILE (Underline if supported, circle if selected)
COMPANY: _____
PRODUCT: _____

PORT: _____   Port Type: serial parallel __
CONNECTOR: DB25 9-pin 5-pin 8-pin Centronics Gender: male female
Pin Configuration: ___

Pin #	Function	Direction	Pin #	Function	Direction
1	_____	to from n/a	14	_____	to from n/a
2	_____	to from n/a	15	_____	to from n/a
3	_____	to from n/a	16	_____	to from n/a
4	_____	to from n/a	17	_____	to from n/a
5	_____	to from n/a	18	_____	to from n/a
6	_____	to from n/a	19	_____	to from n/a
7	_____	to from n/a	20	_____	to from n/a
8	_____	to from n/a	21	_____	to from n/a
9	_____	to from n/a	22	_____	to from n/a
10	_____	to from n/a	23	_____	to from n/a
11	_____	to from n/a	24	_____	to from n/a
12	_____	to from n/a	25	_____	to from n/a
13	_____	to from n/a			

(complete the next section only with 36-pin cinch connectors)

26	_____	to from n/a	27	_____	to from n/a
28	_____	to from n/a	29	_____	to from n/a
30	_____	to from n/a	31	_____	to from n/a
32	_____	to from n/a	33	_____	to from n/a
34	_____	to from n/a	35	_____	to from n/a
36	_____	to from n/a			

Flow Control Technique: XON/XOFF ENQ/ACK STX/ETX Hardware
Flow Control lead(s):   4 11 19 20 __ __ __
Leads that must be on: 5 6 8 __ __ __ __
PRINTER PORT: SERIAL PARALLEL   FLOW CONTROL: XON/XOFF Hardware
   FLOW CONTROL LEAD(S):   4 11 19 20 __ __   CONNECTOR: DB25 Centronics
Speeds: 110 300 600 1200 1800 2400 4800 9600 19.2 56k _____
Parity: even odd space mark none   CHARACTER LENGTH: 7 8 ___
Stop Bits: 1 1.5 2   Line Ending Sequence: cr lf cr/lf
Mode: async sync isoch   EMULATION/COMPATIBLE: ANSI X3.64
   VT100, Televideo 925, ADM-3A, DG100, Hazeltine 1420, HP2621, Regent 25/30__

NOTE 1:_____
NOTE 2:_____

APPENDIX D. CABLE DIAGRAMS FOR SERIAL CONNECTIONS

Appendix D outlines the connections of computers, terminals, and printers through an RS232 port. When used in conjunction with Appendix C, the proper cables may be constructed to allow data exchange between devices. The following displays the step-by-step procedure for determining how the pins of RS232 cables should be connected:

1. In Appendix C, locate the appropriate devices to be connected, noting their pin configuration. (If your device is not listed, compare its RS232 pinouts with devices in Appendix C until a match is found. Then, use that pin configuration as a surrogate.)
2. Proceed to the appropriate table. Figure D-1 is for connecting computers and terminals to printers. Figure D-2 is for connecting computers to other computers or modems.
3. Find the pin configuration of the computer in the column labeled ''Computer'' at the left of the table.
4. Find the pin configuration of the other computer, modem, printer, or terminal across the top of the table.
5. Note the diagram number at the intersection of the row and column.
6. Find the appropriately labeled graph(Gxx) in this appendix for a display of the cross-connections necessary in the RS232 cable. Construct the cable accordingly.

For example, to connect an IBM PIC(**C01**) to an Okidata Pacemaker 2410 Printer(**P05**), use graph **G04.** It is important to note that when building RS232 cables, many different combinations of pin configurations exist for a connection. The diagrams point out only one of many ways in which RS232 leads may be connected. Neither the author nor the publisher claims responsibility for the accuracy of the diagrams of charts, since they were constructed from information supplied by the vendors. The vendors of these products often provide similar information for device connections. Use their recommendations when possible, as they have been thoroughly tested. This should be done also because, in some cases, more leads are present in these graphs than are actually needed. They are provided for completeness.

For example, often pin 19, 20, or 4 may be used to hold a given lead, such as data set ready, on, or off. The choice may be dictated by a factor such as flow control. If hardware flow control will not be used, pin 4 or 20 would be selected, in which case pin 19 would not even be used. The selection should be based on the options for the particular installation.

Furthermore, different configurations may be possible for ports. The way a port is configured affects the cable to be used. If a port may be set up to emulate either data communications equipment or data terminal equipment, choose the configuration that allows for the most flexibility in your configuration.

Once the cable has been built, the options should be reviewed as outlined in the text and port profiles of Appendix C. Doublecheck to ensure that the options are properly set. Once set, attach the cable between the devices, power up the devices, enable the ports, and test your systems for proper operation, following the ''Steps for Connection'' summarized in Appendix K.

Computer or Modem	Printer or Terminal														
	P01	P02	P03	P04	P05	P06	P07	P08	P09	P10	P11	P12	P13	P14	P15
C01	G01	G02	G03	G04	G04	G05	G06	G05	G07	G08	G05	G07	G01	G09	G10
C02	G11	G12	G12	G13	G13	G12	G13	G12	G14	G12	G12	G14	G11	G15	G16
C03	G13	G12	G17	G13	G13	G17	G13	G17	G12	G12	G17	G12	G13	G15	G16
C04	G19	G18	G20	G21	G21	G20	G21	G20	G18	G18	G22	G18	G19	G09	G10
C05	G19	G18	G20	G21	G21	G20	G21	G20	G18	G18	G22	G18	G19	G09	G10
C06	G23	G12	G23	G23	G23	G12	G23	G12	G23	G23	G23	G24	G23	G38	G23
C07	G26	G18	G27	G21	G21	G22	G21	G22	G07	G25	G08	G18	G01	G09	G10
C08	G01	G07	G08	G04	G04	G03	G06	G22	G07	G22	G08	G18	G19	G09	G10
C09	G12	G28	G29	G12	G12	G29	G12	G29	G28	G12	G29	G28	G12	G15	G29
C10	G30	G30	G30	G30	G30	G12	G12	G12	G30	G30	G12	G30	G30	G15	G30
C11	G01	G18	G03	G04	G04	G05	G06	G05	G07	G08	G05	G07	G01	G09	G10
C12	G24	G24	G31	G32	G32	G12	G32	G12	G33	G31	G12	G33	G24	G09	G34
C13	G24	G24	G31	G32	G32	G31	G35	G31	G33	G34	G31	G33	G24	G15	G36
C14	G24	G34	G12	G37	G37	G73	G37	G73	G14	G30	G12	G14	G11	G38	G34
C15	G24	G24	G31	G32	G32	G31	G35	G31	G33	G31	G39	G33	G24	G40	G41
C16	G50	G51	G52	G53	G53	G52	G53	G52	G51	G52	G52	G51	G50	G54	G55

Figure D-1.   Computer/Modem to Printer/Terminal Hookup logic

Computer or Modem	Computer or Modem															
	C01	C02	C03	C04	C05	C06	C07	C08	C09	C10	C11	C12	C13	C14	C15	C16
C01	G08	G12	G09	G07	G07	G23	G05	G05	G12	G09	G08	G47	G45	G12	G48	G65
C02	G12	G08	G43	G31	G14	G15	G17	G12	G03	G15	G12	G43	G43	G43	G15	G66
C03	G31	G05	G02	G12	G12	G44	G17	G17	G20	G43	G12	G05	G43	G46	G45	G67
C04	G18	G31	G12	G18	G18	G31	G22	G20	G17	G09	G18	G31	G31	G17	G30	G68
C05	G18	G17	G12	G18	G18	G31	G22	G20	G17	G09	G18	G31	G48	G17	G48	G68
C06	G23	G43	G44	G24	G24	G45	G23	G12	G40	G38	G23	G00	G00	G40	G43	G69
C07	G25	G30	G24	G18	G18	G12	G08	G22	G17	G12	G25	G12	G33	G17	G23	G65
C08	G22	G12	G24	G18	G18	G12	G08	G22	G12	G12	G22	G12	G33	G12	G23	G65
C09	G12	G03	G46	G28	G28	G15	G29	G29	G42	G15	G12	G43	G43	G03	G44	G66
C10	G30	G43	G43	G30	G30	G45	G12	G12	G03	G15	G30	G45	G45	G03	G49	G70
C11	G08	G12	G17	G07	G07	G09	G05	G05	G12	G12	G08	G31	G48	G12	G48	G65
C12	G31	G43	G27	G33	G33	G00	G12	G12	G43	G09	G31	G47	G00	G43	G43	G69
C13	G34	G40	G43	G33	G33	G00	G31	G31	G43	G15	G34	G00	G00	G43	G43	G69
C14	G12	G43	G46	G14	G14	G15	G12	G12	G12	G38	G30	G43	G43	G49	G49	G71
C15	G31	G25	G45	G33	G33	G43	G39	G31	G40	G40	G31	G43	G43	G49	G49	G72
C16	G56	G57	G58	G59	G59	G60	G56	G56	G57	G61	G56	G60	G60	G62	G63	G64

Figure D-2.   Computer/Modem to Computer/Modem hookup logic

```
            G01                                  G02                                  G03
Computer        Peripheral           Computer        Peripheral           Computer        Peripheral
(Device-1)      (Device-2)           (Device-1)      (Device-2)           (Device-1)      (Device-2)
   pin             pin                  pin             pin                  pin             pin

   1 ----------- 1                     1 ----------- 1                     1 ----------- 1
   2 ----------> 3                     2 ----------> 3                     2 ----------> 3
   3 <---------- 2                     3 <--------- 2                      3 <---------- 2
   4 ----------> 8                                                        4 ----------> 8

                                       4 --:-------> 8
   5 <-:-------- 19                    5 <-:                              5 <-:-------- 20
   6 <-:                                                                  6 <-:

                                       6 <-:-----:-- 4
   8 <-------:-- 4                     8 <-:       :-> 5                   7 ----------- 7
        :-> 5                                                             8 ----------- 4

                                       7 ----------- 7
   7 ----------- 7                     20 ---------> 6                    20 -------:-> 5
   20 ---------> 6                                                              :-> 6


            G04                                  G05                                  G06
Computer        Peripheral           Computer        Peripheral           Computer        Peripheral
(Device-1)      (Device-2)           (Device-1)      (Device-2)           (Device-1)      (Device-2)
   pin             pin                  pin             pin                  pin             pin

   1 ----------- 1                     1 ----------- 1                     1 ----------- 1
   2 ----------> 3                     2 ----------> 3                     2 ----------> 3
   3 <---------- 2                     3 <---------- 2                     3 <---------- 2
   4 ----------> 8                     4 ----------> 8                     4 ----------> 8

   6 <-:-------- 11                    5 <-:-------- 20                    5 <-:-------- 11
   5 <-:                               6 <-:                               6 <-:
                                       8 <-:                               8 <-:
   8 <-------:-- 4
        :-> 5                          20 -------:-> 5                     20 -------:-> 5
                                             :-> 6                               :-> 6
   7 ----------- 7
   20 ---------> 6                     7 ----------- 7                     7 ----------- 7


            G07                                  G08                                  G09
Computer        Peripheral           Computer        Peripheral           Computer        Peripheral
(Device-1)      (Device-2)           (Device-1)      (Device-2)           (Device-1)      (Device-2)
   pin             pin                  pin             pin                  pin             pin

   1 ----------- 1                     1 ----------- 1                     1 ----------- 1
   2 ----------> 3                     2 ----------> 3                     2 ----------- 2
   3 <---------- 2                     3 <---------- 2                     3 ----------- 3
   4 ----------> 8                     4 ----------> 8                     4 ----------- 4

   5 <-:-----:-- 4                     5 <-:-------- 20                    5 <-:-------- 8
   6 <-:     :-> 5                     6 <-:                               6 <-:
   8 <-:                                                                  8 <-:
                                       7 ----------- 7                    20 <-:
   7 ----------- 7                     8 <---------- 4
   20 ---------> 6                                                        7 ----------- 7
                                       20 -------:-> 5
                                             :-> 6
```

G10	
Computer (Device-1) pin	Peripheral (Device-2) pin

```
1 ----------- 1
2 ----------> 3
3 <---------- 2
4 ----------> 8

5 <-:-------- 25
6 <-:

7 ----------- 7

8 <------:-- 4
         :-> 5
         :-> 6
```

G11	
Computer (Device-1) pin	Peripheral (Device-2) pin

```
1 ----------- 1
2 ----------- 2
3 ----------- 3
4 ----------- 4
5 ----------- 5
6 ----------- 6
7 ----------- 7
8 ----------- 8

              :- 11
20 <--------:- 19

12 ----------- 12
```

G12	
Computer (Device-1) pin	Peripheral (Device-2) pin

```
1 ----------- 1
2 ----------- 2
3 ----------- 3
4 ----------- 4
5 ----------- 5
6 ----------- 6
7 ----------- 7
8 ----------- 8
11 ----------- 11
12 ----------- 12
15 ----------- 15
17 ----------- 17
19 ----------- 19
20 ----------- 20
22 ----------- 22
24 ----------- 24
```

G13	
Computer (Device-1) pin	Peripheral (Device-2) pin

```
1 ----------- 1
2 ----------- 2
3 ----------- 3

4 <-:-----:-- 11
20 <-:    :-- 19

5 ----------- 5
6 ----------- 6
7 ----------- 7
8 ----------- 8
```

G14	
Computer (Device-1) pin	Peripheral (Device-2) pin

```
1 ----------- 1
2 ----------- 2
3 ----------- 3

4 <-:-------- 4
20 <-:

5 --------:-> 5
          :-> 6

7 ----------- 7
8 ----------- 8
```

G15	
Computer (Device-1) pin	Peripheral (Device-2) pin

```
1 ----------- 1
3 <---------- 2
2 ----------> 3

4 --:-------- 8
5 <-:
19 <-:
20 <-:

7 ----------- 7
```

G16	
Computer (Device-1) pin	Peripheral (Device-2) pin

```
1 ----------- 1
2 ----------- 2
3 ----------- 3

4 <-:-------- 25
20 <-:

5 ----------- 5
6 ----------- 6
7 ----------- 7
8 ----------- 8
```

G17	
Computer (Device-1) pin	Peripheral (Device-2) pin

```
1 ----------- 1
2 ----------- 2
3 ----------- 3

4 --:-------- 20
20 <-:

5 ----------- 5
6 ----------- 6
7 ----------- 7

8 --------:-> 4
          :-> 8
```

G18	
Computer (Device-1) pin	Peripheral (Device-2) pin

```
1 ----------- 1
2 ----------> 3
3 <---------- 2

4 --------:-> 5
          :-> 6
          :-> 8

5 <-:-------- 4
6 <-:
8 <-:

7 ----------- 7
```

```
                G19                              G20                              G21
 Computer      Peripheral       Computer      Peripheral       Computer      Peripheral
(Device-1)    (Device-2)       (Device-1)    (Device-2)       (Device-1)    (Device-2)
   pin           pin              pin           pin              pin           pin

   1 ----------- 1               1 ----------- 1                1 ----------- 1
   2 ----------> 3               2 ----------> 3                2 ----------> 3
   3 <---------- 2               3 <---------- 2                3 <---------- 2
                                 4 ----------> 8                7 ----------- 7
   4 -------:-> 5
          :-> 6                  5 <-:-------- 20               5 <-:-------- 11
          :-> 8                  6 <-:                          6 <-:
                                                                8 <-:
                                 7 ----------- 7
   5 <-:-------- 19                                                       :-> 5
   6 <-:                         8 <-------:-- 4                          :-> 6
   8 <-:                                :-> 5                             :-> 8
                                        :-> 6                             :-- 20
   7 ----------- 7
  20 ----------- 20


                G22                              G23                              G24
 Computer      Peripheral       Computer      Peripheral       Computer      Peripheral
(Device-1)    (Device-2)       (Device-1)    (Device-2)       (Device-1)    (Device-2)
   pin           pin              pin           pin              pin           pin

   1 ----------- 1               1 ----------- 1                1 ----------- 1
   2 ----------> 3               2 ----------- 3                2 ----------- 2
   3 <---------- 2               3 ----------- 2                3 ----------- 3
   7 ----------- 7               7 ----------- 7                7 ----------- 7

   4 -------:-> 5                5 <-:                          5 <-:-------- 19
          :-> 6                  6 <-:                         20 <-:
          :-> 8                  8 <-:
                                20 --:                                   :-> 4
   5 <-:-------- 20                                                      :-> 5
   6 <-:                                                                 :-> 6
   8 <-:                                   :-> 5                         :-> 8
                                           :-> 6
                                           :-> 8
                                           :-- 20


                G25                              G26                              G27
 Computer      Peripheral       Computer      Peripheral       Computer      Peripheral
(Device-1)    (Device-2)       (Device-1)    (Device-2)       (Device-1)    (Device-2)
   pin           pin              pin           pin              pin           pin

   1 ----------- 1               1 ----------- 1                1 ----------- 1
   2 ----------> 3               2 ----------- 3                2 ----------> 3
   3 <---------- 2               3 ----------- 2                3 <---------- 2
   4 ----------- 4               7 ----------- 7                7 ----------- 7
   7 ----------- 7
                                 5 <-:-------- 19               5 <-:-------- 20
   5 <-:                         6 <-:                          6 <-:
   6 <-:                         8 <-:                          8 <-:
   8 <-:
  20 --:                        20 -------:-> 5               20 -------:-> 5
                                        :-> 6                         :-> 6
           :-> 5                        :-> 8                         :-> 8
           :-> 6
           :-> 8
           :-- 20
```

```
           G28                              G29                              G30
 Computer      Peripheral        Computer      Peripheral        Computer      Peripheral
(Device-1)     (Device-2)       (Device-1)     (Device-2)       (Device-1)     (Device-2)
   pin            pin              pin            pin              pin            pin

    1 ----------- 1                1 ----------- 1                1 ----------- 1
    2 ----------- 2                2 ----------- 2                2 ----------- 2
    3 ----------- 3                3 ----------- 3                3 ----------- 3
                                   4 ----------- 4
    4 --:-------- 4                5 ----------- 5                  :-- 4
   11 <-:                          6 ----------- 6                  :-> 5
   19 <-:                          7 ----------- 7                  :-> 6
   20 <-:                          8 ----------- 8

    5 ----------- 5               19 <-:-------- 20                7 ----------- 7
    6 ----------- 6               20 <-:                           8 ----------- 8
    7 ----------- 7
    8 ----------- 8                                               20 --:-------- 20
                                                                   4 <-:


           G31                              G32                              G33
 Computer      Peripheral        Computer      Peripheral        Computer      Peripheral
(Device-1)     (Device-2)       (Device-1)     (Device-2)       (Device-1)     (Device-2)
   pin            pin              pin            pin              pin            pin

    1 ----------- 1                1 ----------- 1                1 ----------- 1
    2 ----------- 2                2 ----------- 2                2 ----------- 2
    3 ----------- 3                3 ----------- 3                3 ----------- 3
    7 ----------- 7                7 ----------- 7                7 ----------- 7

      :-- 4                          :-- 4                          :---:-- 4
      :-> 5                          :-> 5              5 <-:        :-> 5
      :-> 6                          :-> 6             20 <-:        :-> 6
      :-> 8                          :-> 8

    4 <-:-------- 20                5 <-:-------- 11
    5 <-:                          20 <-:
    6 <-:
   20 <-:


           G34                              G35                              G36
 Computer      Peripheral        Computer      Peripheral        Computer      Peripheral
(Device-1)     (Device-2)       (Device-1)     (Device-2)       (Device-1)     (Device-2)
   pin            pin              pin            pin              pin            pin

    1 ----------- 1                1 ----------- 1                1 ----------- 1
    2 ----------- 2                2 ----------- 2                2 ----------- 2
    3 ----------- 3                3 ----------- 3                3 ----------- 3
                                   7 ----------- 7                5 <---------- 25
      :-- 4                                                       7 ----------- 7
      :-> 5                        5 <-:-------- 11
      :-> 6                        6 <-:                            :-- 4
      :-> 8                                                         :-> 5

    7 ----------- 7                  :-> 6                          :-> 6
   20 <---------- 25                :-> 8                          :-> 8
                                    :-- 20                          :-- 20
```

```
             G37                            G38                            G39
  Computer      Peripheral      Computer      Peripheral      Computer      Peripheral
 (Device-1)    (Device-2)      (Device-1)    (Device-2)      (Device-1)    (Device-2)
    pin           pin             pin           pin             pin           pin

  1 ----------- 1               1 ----------- 1               1 ----------- 1
  2 ----------- 2               2 ----------> 3               2 ----------- 2
  3 ----------- 3               3 <---------- 2               3 ----------- 3
  4 ----------- 4               4 ----------- 4               7 ----------- 7
  5 ----------- 5               5 ----------- 5
                                7 ----------- 7               5 <-:      :-> 5
             :-> 6             20 <---------- 8               6 <-:---:-- 20
  8 -------:-> 8

  7 ----------- 7
 20 <---------- 11


             G40                            G41                            G42
  Computer      Peripheral      Computer      Peripheral      Computer      Peripheral
 (Device-1)    (Device-2)      (Device-1)    (Device-2)      (Device-1)    (Device-2)
    pin           pin             pin           pin             pin           pin

  1 ----------- 1               1 ----------- 1               1 ----------- 1
  2 ----------> 3               2 ----------> 3               2 ----------- 3
  3 <---------- 2               3 <---------- 2               3 ----------- 2
                                5 <---------- 25              4 ----------> 8
  5 <------:-- 8                7 ----------- 7               8 <---------- 4
         :-> 4                                                6 <---------- 20
         :-> 20                            :-- 4             20 ----------> 6
                                          :-> 5               7 ----------- 7
  7 ----------- 7                         :-> 6

                                          :-> 8
                                          :-> 20


             G43                            G44                            G45
  Computer      Peripheral      Computer      Peripheral      Computer      Peripheral
 (Device-1)    (Device-2)      (Device-1)    (Device-2)      (Device-1)    (Device-2)
    pin           pin             pin           pin             pin           pin

  1 ----------- 1               1 ----------- 1               1 ----------- 1
  2 ----------- 3               7 ----------- 7               7 ----------- 7
  3 ----------- 2               2 ----------- 3               2 ----------- 3
                                3 ----------- 2               3 ----------- 2
  4 <-:      :-> 4             20 ----------- 20
  5 --:---   :-- 5                                            4 --:------> 8
                                4 <-:      :-> 4              5 <-:
  8 --:---   :-- 8              5 <-:      :-> 5
 20 <-:      :-> 20             6 <-:      :-> 8              8 <------:-- 4
                                                                     :-> 5
  7 ----------- 7
                                                            20 ----------> 6
                                                             6 <---------- 20
```

```
              G46                              G47                              G48
Computer      Peripheral         Computer      Peripheral         Computer      Peripheral
(Device-1)    (Device-2)         (Device-1)    (Device-2)         (Device-1)    (Device-2)
   pin           pin                pin           pin                pin           pin

    1 ----------- 1                 1 ----------- 1                 1 ----------- 1
    7 ----------- 7                 7 ----------- 7                 7 ----------- 7
    2 ----------- 3                 2 ----------- 2                 2 ----------- 2
    3 ----------- 2                 3 ---------- 3                  3 ---------- 3
    8 ----------- 8
                                    5 --:-------- 20                4 --:------> 5
    4 --:-------- 5                 6 <-:                           5 <-:
   20 <-:                           8 <-:
                                   20 <-:                           6 <-:        :-> 6
    5 --------:-- 4                                                 8 <-:        :-> 8
              :-- 20                                               20 --:        :-- 20


              G49                              G50                              G51
Computer      Peripheral         Computer      Peripheral         Computer      Peripheral
(Device-1)    (Device-2)         (Device-1)    (Device-2)         (Device-1)    (Device-2)
   pin           pin                pin           pin                pin           pin

    1 ----------- 1                 2 <---------- 2                 2 <---------- 2
    7 ----------- 7                 3 ----------> 3                 3 ----------> 3
    2 ----------- 3                 1 <---------- 19
    3 ----------- 2                                                 1 <-:-------- 4
                                    6 <-:                           6 <-:
    4 --:         :-- 4             8 <-:                           8 <-:
    5 <-:         :-> 5
                                    7 --------:-> 5                 7 --------:-> 5
    8 <-:         :-> 8                       :-> 6                           :-> 6
   20 --:         :-- 20
                                    4 ----------> 8                 4 ----------> 8
                                    5 ----------- 7                 5 ----------- 7


              G52                              G53                              G54
Computer      Peripheral         Computer      Peripheral         Computer      Peripheral
(Device-1)    (Device-2)         (Device-1)    (Device-2)         (Device-1)    (Device-2)
   pin           pin                pin           pin                pin           pin

    2 <---------- 2                 2 <---------- 2                 2 <---------- 3
    3 ----------> 3                 3 ----------> 3                 3 ----------> 2

    1 <-:------- 20                 1 <-:------- 11                 1 <-:-------- 8
    6 <-:                           6 <-:                           6 <-:
    8 <-:                           8 <-:                           8 <-:

    7 --------:-> 5                 7 --------:-> 5                 5 ----------- 7
              :-> 6                           :-> 6

    4 ----------> 8                 4 ----------> 8
    5 ----------- 7                 5 ----------- 7
```

```
            G55                              G56                              G57
Computer      Peripheral       Computer      Peripheral       Computer      Peripheral
(Device-1)    (Device-2)       (Device-1)    (Device-2)       (Device-1)    (Device-2)
   pin           pin              pin           pin              pin           pin

   2 <---------- 2                2 <---------- 2                2 <---------- 3
   3 ----------> 3                3 ----------> 3                3 ----------> 2
   4 ----------> 8                5 ---------- 7                 7 ----------> 4
   5 ---------- 7                                                5 ---------- 7

   1 <-:-------- 25               4 --------:-> 5                4 --------:-> 11
   6 <-:                                   :-> 6                          :-> 19
   8 <-:                                   :-> 8                          :-> 20

   7 --------:-> 5               1 <-:-------- 20                1 <-:-------- 6
            :-> 6                6 <-:                           6 <-:
                                 8 <-:                           8 <-:


            G58                              G59                              G60
Computer      Peripheral       Computer      Peripheral       Computer      Peripheral
(Device-1)    (Device-2)       (Device-1)    (Device-2)       (Device-1)    (Device-2)
   pin           pin              pin           pin              pin           pin

   2 <---------- 3                2 <---------- 2                2 <---------- 3
   3 ----------> 2                3 ----------> 3                3 ----------> 2
   5 ---------- 7
   4 ----------> 8                1 <-:-------- 4                4 --:
   7 ----------> 4                6 <-:                          1 <-:
                                 8 <-:                           6 <-:
   1 <-:-------- 5                                               8 <-|
   6 <-:                          4 --------:-> 5
   8 <-:                                   :-> 6                 7 --------:-> 5
                                           :-> 20                        :-> 20

                                 5 ---------- 7                 5 ---------- 7


            G61                              G62                              G63
Computer      Peripheral       Computer      Peripheral       Computer      Peripheral
(Device-1)    (Device-2)       (Device-1)    (Device-2)       (Device-1)    (Device-2)
   pin           pin              pin           pin              pin           pin

   2 <---------- 3                2 <---------- 3                2 <---------- 3
   3 ----------> 2                3 ----------> 2                3 ----------> 2

   1 <-:-------- 6                1 <-:-------- 8                1 <-:-------- 20
   6 <-:                          6 <-:                          6 <-:
   8 <-:                          8 <-:                          8 <-:

   5 ---------- 7                 4 ----------> 20               4 --------:-> 5
                                  7 ----------> 4                         :-> 8
                                  5 ---------- 7
                                                                5 ---------- 7
```

```
            G64                            G65                            G66
Computer      Peripheral      Computer      Peripheral      Computer      Peripheral
(Device-1)    (Device-2)      (Device-1)    (Device-2)      (Device-1)    (Device-2)
   pin           pin             pin           pin             pin           pin

   2 <---------- 3              2 ----------> 2              2 <---------- 3
   3 ----------> 2              3 <---------- 3              3 ----------> 2

   1 <-:-------- 4             20 --------:-> 1             11 <-:-------- 4
   6 <-:                                 :-> 6             20 <-:
   8 <-:                                 :-> 8             19 <-:

   4 --------:-> 1              5 <-:-------- 4              6 --------:-> 1
            :-> 6              6 <-:                                 :-> 6
            :-> 8              8 <-:                                 :-> 8

   5 ---------- 5              7 ---------- 5              7 ---------- 5
                                                           4 <---------- 7


            G67                            G68                            G69
Computer      Peripheral      Computer      Peripheral      Computer      Peripheral
(Device-1)    (Device-2)      (Device-1)    (Device-2)      (Device-1)    (Device-2)
   pin           pin             pin           pin             pin           pin

   3 ----------> 2              2 ----------> 2              3 ----------> 2
   2 <---------- 3              3 <---------- 3              2 <---------- 3

   8 <---------- 4              4 --------:-> 1                        :-- 4
   4 <---------- 7                       :-> 6                        :-> 1
                                         :-> 8                        :-> 6
   5 --------:-> 1                                                    :-> 8
            :-> 6              5 <-:-------- 4
            :-> 8              6 <-:                         5 <-:-------- 7
                             20 <-:                         20 <-:
   7 ---------- 5
                              7 ---------- 5                7 ---------- 5


            G70                            G71                            G72
Computer      Peripheral      Computer      Peripheral      Computer      Peripheral
(Device-1)    (Device-2)      (Device-1)    (Device-2)      (Device-1)    (Device-2)
   pin           pin             pin           pin             pin           pin

   3 ----------> 2              3 ----------> 2              3 ----------> 2
   2 <---------- 3              2 <---------- 3              2 <---------- 3

   6 --------:-> 1              8 --------:-> 1             20 --------:-> 1
            :-> 6                       :-> 6                        :-> 6
            :-> 8                       :-> 8                        :-> 8

   7 ---------- 5             20 <---------- 4              5 <-:-------- 4
                              4 <---------- 7              8 <-:

                              7 ---------- 5              7 ---------- 5
```

```
            G73                          G74                          G75
Computer    Peripheral       Computer    Peripheral       Computer    Peripheral
(Device-1)  (Device-2)       (Device-1)  (Device-2)       (Device-1)  (Device-2)
   pin         pin              pin         pin              pin         pin

 1 ----------- 1              1 ----------- 1              1 ----------- 1
 2 <---------- 2              2 ----------- 2              2 ----------- 2
 3 ---------->  3             3 ----------- 3              3 ----------- 3
 7 ----------- 7              4 ----------- 4              4 ----------- 4
                             7 ----------- 7              7 ----------- 7
 4 <-:-------- 20           20 ----------- 20            20 ----------- 20
20 <-:
                             8 --------:-> 5              5 --------:-> 5
                                      :-> 6                       :-> 6
                                      :-> 8                       :-> 8


            G76                          G77                          G78
Computer    Peripheral       Computer    Peripheral       Computer    Peripheral
(Device-1)  (Device-2)       (Device-1)  (Device-2)       (Device-1)  (Device-2)
   pin         pin              pin         pin              pin         pin

 1 ----------- 1              1 ----------- 1              1 ----------- 1
 2 ----------- 3              2 ----------- 3              2 ----------- 2
                             3 ----------- 2              3 ----------- 3
 3 ----------- 2              7 ----------- 7              4 ----------- 4
 7 ----------- 7                                          7 ----------- 7
                             8 --------:-> 4             20 ----------- 20
 5 --------:-> 4                      :-> 20
          :-> 20                      :-> 11              5 <-:-------- 8
          :-> 11                                          6 <-:
                             4 <-:-------- 8              8 <-:
 4 <-:-------- 5            20 <-:
20 <-:                      11 <-:
11 <-:


            G79                          G80                          G81
Computer    Peripheral       Computer    Peripheral       Computer    Peripheral
(Device-1)  (Device-2)       (Device-1)  (Device-2)       (Device-1)  (Device-2)
   pin         pin              pin         pin              pin         pin

 1 ----------- 1              1 ----------- 1              1 ----------- 1
 2 ----------- 2              2 ----------- 3              2 ----------- 3
 3 ----------- 3              3 ----------- 2              3 ----------- 2
 7 ----------- 7              7 ----------- 7              7 ----------- 7

 8 --------:-> 5              8 --:                        8 --:-------- 20
          :-> 6              4 <-:                        4 <-:
          :-> 20            20 <-:                       20 <-:

 4 <-:-------- 4                          :-- 8
20 <-:                                    :-> 4
                                          :-> 20
```

```
          G82                          G83                          G84
Computer       Peripheral     Computer       Peripheral     Computer       Peripheral
(Device-1)     (Device-2)     (Device-1)     (Device-2)     (Device-1)     (Device-2)
   pin            pin            pin            pin            pin            pin

   1 ----------- 1              1 ----------- 1              1 ----------- 1
   2 ----------- 3              2 ----------- 3              2 ----------- 3
   3 ----------- 2              3 ----------- 2              3 ----------- 2
   7 ----------- 7              7 ----------- 7              7 ----------- 7

   8 --:------> 5              20 <-------:-- 8              5 <-------:-- 8
   4 <-:                           :-> 4                        :-> 4
  20 <-:                           :-> 20                       :-> 20


          G85                          G86                          G87
Computer       Peripheral     Computer       Peripheral     Computer       Peripheral
(Device-1)     (Device-2)     (Device-1)     (Device-2)     (Device-1)     (Device-2)
   pin            pin            pin            pin            pin            pin

   1 ----------- 1              1 ----------- 1              1 ----------- 1
   2 ----------- 2              2 ----------- 2              2 ----------- 2
   3 ----------- 3              3 ----------- 3              3 ----------- 3
   4 ----------- 4              7 ----------- 7              7 ----------- 7
   7 ----------- 7
                                8 -------:-> 5              8 -------:-> 5
   8 -------:-> 5                   :-> 6                        :-> 6
       :-> 6                        :-> 8                        :-> 8
       :-> 8
                               20 <-:-------- 11            20 <-:-------- 4
  20 <---------- 19              4 <-:                       4 <-:


          G88
Computer       Peripheral
(Device-1)     (Device-2)
   pin            pin

   1 ----------- 1
   2 ----------- 2
   3 ----------- 3
   7 ----------- 7

   8 -------:-> 5
       :-> 6
       :-> 8

  20 <-:-------- 20
   4 <-:
```

APPENDIX E. ASCII CHARACTER SET

BITS B4 B3 B2 B1	ROW \ COLUMN	0 (000)	1 (001)	2 (010)	3 (011)	4 (100)	5 (101)	6 (110)	7 (111)
0 0 0 0	0	NUL CTRL @ — 0 0 0	DLE CTRL p — 20 16 10	SP CTRL (sp) — 40 32 20	0 — 60 48 30	@ — 100 64 40	P — 120 80 50	` — 140 96 60	p — 160 112 70
0 0 0 1	1	SOH CTRL a — 1 1 1	DC1 (XON) CTRL q — 21 17 11	! — 41 33 21	1 — 61 49 31	A — 101 65 41	Q — 121 81 51	a — 141 97 61	q — 161 113 71
0 0 1 0	2	STX CTRL b — 2 2 2	DC2 CTRL r — 22 18 12	" — 42 34 22	2 — 62 50 32	B — 102 66 42	R — 122 82 52	b — 142 98 62	r — 162 114 72
0 0 1 1	3	EXT CTRL c — 3 3 3	DC3 (XOFF) CTRL s — 23 19 13	# — 43 35 23	3 — 63 51 33	C — 103 67 43	S — 123 83 53	c — 143 99 63	s — 163 115 73
0 1 0 0	4	EOT CTRL d — 4 4 4	DC4 CTRL t — 24 20 14	$ — 44 36 24	4 — 64 52 34	D — 104 68 44	T — 124 84 54	d — 144 100 64	t — 164 116 74
0 1 0 1	5	ENQ CTRL e — 5 5 5	NAK CTRL u — 25 21 15	% — 45 37 25	5 — 65 53 35	E — 105 69 45	U — 125 85 55	e — 145 101 65	u — 165 117 75
0 1 1 0	6	ACK CTRL f — 6 6 6	SYN CTRL v — 26 22 16	& — 46 38 26	6 — 66 54 36	F — 106 70 46	V — 126 86 56	f — 146 102 66	v — 166 118 76
0 1 1 1	7	BEL CTRL g — 7 7 7	ETB CTRL w — 27 23 17	' — 47 39 27	7 — 67 55 37	G — 107 71 47	W — 127 87 57	g — 147 103 67	w — 167 119 77

B7 B6 B5 →		0 0 0	0 0 1	0 1 0	0 1 1	1 0 0	1 0 1	1 1 0	1 1 1
BITS B4 B3 B2 B1	ROW \ COLUMN	0	1	2	3	4	5	6	7
1 0 0 0	8	BS CTRL h 10 8 8	CAN CTRL x 30 24 18	(50 40 28	8 70 56 38	H 110 72 48	X 130 88 58	h 150 104 68	x 170 120 78
1 0 0 1	9	HT CTRL i 11 9 9	EM CTRL y 31 25 19	) 51 41 29	9 71 57 39	I 111 73 49	Y 131 89 59	i 151 105 69	y 171 121 79
1 0 1 0	10	LF CTRL j 12 10 A	SUB CTRL z 32 26 1A	* 52 42 2A	: 72 58 3A	J 112 74 4A	Z 132 90 5A	j 152 106 6A	z 172 122 7A
1 0 1 1	11	VT CTRL k 13 11 B	ESC CTRL [33 27 1B	+ 53 43 2B	; 73 59 3B	K 113 75 4B	[133 91 5B	k 153 107 6B	{ 173 123 7B
1 1 0 0	12	FF CTRL l 14 12 C	FS CTRL \ 34 28 1C	, 54 44 2C	< 74 60 3C	L 114 76 4C	\ 134 92 5C	l 154 108 6C	| 174 124 7C
1 1 0 1	13	CR CTRL m 15 13 D	GS CTRL] 35 29 1D	= 55 45 2D	= 75 61 3D	M 115 77 4D	] 135 93 5D	m 155 109 6D	} 175 125 7D
1 1 1 0	14	SO CTRL n 16 14 E	RS CTRL ^ 36 30 1E	. 56 46 2E	> 76 62 3E	N 116 78 4E	^ 136 94 5E	n 156 110 6E	~ 176 126 7E
1 1 1 1	15	SI CTRL o 17 15 F	US CTRL - 37 31 1F	/ 57 47 2F	? 77 63 3F	O 117 79 4F	_ 137 95 5F	o 157 111 6F	DEL CTRL (bs) 177 127 7F

* Keyboard-generated characters.

Legend:

Character	
Octal	
Decimal	
Hex	

Appendix E

APPENDIX F. TRW MODULAR TO DB25 ADAPTERS

The following chart contains several modular to DB25 adapters available from TRW. These provide eight-wire modular access to RS232 input/output connectors. They are available with or without spring latches and come in four types.

Type 1—one-piece hood with two mounting screws
Type 2—one-piece hood with latching blocks and mounting screws
Type 3—two-piece hood with spring latches
Type 4—two-piece hood with filler ends and two mounting screws

PLUG STYLE ADAPTER (MALE)

Part No.	Reference	Modular Jack Position								Jumpers	Type
		D-Subminiature Contact									
		1	2	3	4	5	6	7	8		
002–00035–6	FM-001	7(AB)	4(CA)	2(BA)	20(CD)	3(BB)	8(CF)	7(AB)	5(CB)	—	Type 1
002–00036–9	FM-002	—	8(CF)	1(AA)	2(BA)	7(AB)	3(BB)	20(CD) & 6(CC)	—	4 to 5†	Type 1
002–00037–1	FM-003	—	20(CD) & 6(CC)	1(AA)	3(BB)	7(AB)	2(BA)	8(CF)	—	4 to 5†	Type 1
002–00038–4	FM-004	7(AB)	4(CA)	3(BB)	8(CF)	2(BA)	20(CD)	7(AB)	5(CB)	—	Type 4
002–00039–7	FM-005	1(AA)	5(CB)	2(BA)	20(CD)	3(BB)	8(CF)	7(AB)	4(CA)	—	Type 1
002–00022–6	FM-006	Unassembled Kit (requires plier type termination tool. See page 188.)									Type 4
002–00040–4	FM-007	1(AA)	4(CA)	3(BB)	8(CF)	2(BA)	20(CD)	7(AB)	5(CB)	—	Type 4
002–00041–7	FM-009	1(AA)	5(CB)	2(BA)	20(CD)	3(BB)	8(CF)	7(AB)	4(CA)	—	Type 4
002–00043–2	FM-010	1(AA)	4(CA)	3(BB)	8(CF)	2(BA)	20(CD) & 6(CC)	7(AB)	5(CB)	—	Type 1
002–00044–5	FM-011	1(AA)	4(CA)	3(BB)	8(CF)	2(BA)	20(CD)	7(AB)	5(CB)	—	Type 4
002–00028–9	FM-012	1(AA)	5(CB)	2(BA)	20(CD)*	3(BB)	8(CF)**	7(AB)	4(CA)	—	Type 6
002–00045–8	FM-013	Unassembled Kit (requires plier type termination tool. See page 188. Supplied with 6-position modular jack)									Type 1
002–00047–3	FM-014	—	—	19(SCA)	14(SBA)	7(AB)	16(SBB)	—	—	—	Type 1
002–00048–6	FM-015	—	—	8(CF)	3(BB)	7(AB)	2(BA)	—	—	4 to 5†	Type 1
002–00048–9	FM-016	Unassembled Kit (requires plier type termination tool. See page 188.)									Type 1
002–00060–6	FM-017	7(AB)	5(CB)	3(BB)	8(CF)	2(BA)	20(CD)	7(AB)	4(CA)	—	Type 1
002–00051–9	FM-018	7(AB)	3(BB)	7(AB)	21(CG)	21(CG)	9	2(BA)	7(AB)	4 to 5†	Type 1
002–00024–1	FM-020	7(AB)	5(CB)	3(BB)	6(CC) & 8(CF)	2(BA)	20(CD)	7(AB)	4(CA)	6 to 20†	Type 1
002–00025–4	FM-021	7(AB)	4(CA)	2(BA)	20(CD)	3(BB)	6(CC) & 8(CF)	7(AB)	5(CB)	—	Type 1
002–00026–7	FM-023	6(CC)	20(CD)	7(AB)	2(BA)	4(CA)	3(BB)	8(CF)	5(CB)	—	Type 1
002–00028–2	FM-025	15(DB)	14(SBA)	11	3(BB)	13(SCB)	4(CA)	12(SCF)	2(BA)	—	Type 1
002–00028–5	FM-028	1(AA)	—	2(BA)	4(CA)	3(BB)	5(CB)	7(AB)	—	—	Type 1
002–00030–2	FM-029	1(AA)	5(CB)	2(BA)	20(CD)	3(BB)	8(CF)	7(AB)	4(CA)	9 to 20†	Type 1
002–00031–5	FM-030	5(CB)	6(CC)	3(BB)	20(CD)	2(BA)	7(AB)	22(CE)	4(CA)	—	Type 1
002–00032–8	FM-031	4(CA)	20(CD)	2(BA)	6(CC)	3(BB)	7(AB)	22(CE)	5(CB)	—	Type 1
002–00034–3	FM-032	1(AA)	4(CA)	2(BA)	20(CD)	3(BB)	8(CF)	7(AB)	5(CB)	—	Type 1

* Diode assembled between modular jack position #4 and D-Subminiature position #20.

** Diode assembled between D-Subminiature positions #8 and #20.

† SUPER D positions and jumpered together.

SOCKET STYLE ADAPTER (FEMALE)

Part No.	Reference	Modular Jack Position								Jumpers	Type
		1	2	3	4	5	6	7	8		
		D-Subminiature Contact									
002–00010–9	FF-001	7(AB)	4(CA)	2(BA)	20(CD)	3(BB)	8(CF)	7(AB)	5(CB)	—	Type 1
002–00011–1	FF-002	7(AB)	4(CA)	2(BA)	20(CD)	3(BB)	8(CF)	7(AB)	5(CB)	—	Type 3
002–000012–4	FF-003	Unassembled Kit (requires plier type termination tool. See page 188.)									Type 5
002–00052–1	FF-004	—	8(CF)	1(AA)	2(BA)	7(AB)	3(BB)	20(CD) & 6(CC)	—	4 to 5†	Type 1
002–00120–7	FF-005	—	20(CD) & 6(CC)	1(AA)	3(BB)	7(AB)	2(BA)	8(CF)	—	4 to 5†	Type 1
002–00013–7	FF-006	1(AA)	4(CA)	3(BB)	8(CF)	2(BA)	20(CD)	7(AB)	5(CB)	—	Type 1
002–00016–2	FF-007	1(AA)	4(CA)	3(BB)	8(CF)	2(BA)	20(CD)	7(AB)	5(CB)	—	Type 1
002–00002–2	FF-008	1(AA)	5(CB)	2(BA)	20(CD)	3(BB)	8(CF)	7(AB)	4(CA)	—	Type 4
002–00016–5	FF-009	7(AB)	3(BB)	8(CF)	4(CA)	20(CD)	5(CB)	6(CC)	2(BA)	—	Type 1
002–00017–8	FF-010	1(AA)	4(CA)	3(BB)	8(CF)	2(BA)	20(CD) & 6(CC)	7(AB)	5(CB)	—	Type 1
002–00018–3	FF-011	Unassembled Kit (requires plier type termination tool. See page 188.)									Type 1
002–00021–3	FF-012	7(AB)	4(CA)	2(BA)	20(CD)	3(BB)	6(CC) & 8(CF)	7(AB)	5(CB)	—	Type 1
002–00003–5	FF-013	6(CC)	20(CD)	7(AB)	2(BA)	4(CA)	3(BB)	8(CF)	5(CB)	—	Type 1
002–00004–8	FF-015	2(BA)	3(BB)	4(CA)	6(CC)	8(CF)	7(AB)	9	20(CD)	—	Type 1
002–00006–3	FF-016	7(AB)	5(CB)	3(BB)	8(CF)	2(BA)	20(CD)	7(AB)	4(CA)	—	Type 1
002–00007–8	FF-018	20(CD)	7(AB)	5(CB)	3(BB)	4(CA)	2(BA)	8(CF)	1(AA)	—	Type 1
002–00008–9	FF-030	5(CB)	6(CC)	3(BB)	20(CD)	2(BA)	7(AB)	22(CE)	4(CA)	—	Type 1
002–00009–1	FF-031	4(CA)	20(CD)	2(BA)	6(CC)	3(BB)	7(AB)	22(CE)	5(CB)	—	Type 1

† D-Subminiature positions are jumpered together.

APPENDIX G. PRINTER ESCAPE SEQUENCES

Often, the user or programmer of a system with a printer must set up the hard-copy device to meet certain requirements. For example, when using a spreadsheet or word processor, a control sequence might be required to compress the print to 17 characters per inch. The printer's User Manual should be consulted for the sequence necessary to accomplish this, but it is not always available. The following charts serve as a quick reference for such printer control sequences, recognizing that most printers offer more capabilities than listed.

Normally the escape and control sequences are sent to the device using the CHR$(xx) format if output from a BASIC program. When this is the case, a decimal representation of the ASCII character is required. For example, the sequence for sending a "SO", or Shift-Out, would be of the format, "CHR$(14)". Other sequences may require multiple characters to be sent. The charts that follow include spaces for clarity. However, the actual sequence should not contain them, unless specifically noted with the "sp" notation. It is a common practice to separate the sequences with the ";" character.

Other applications, such as Microsoft Word, allow the user to put control characters in the text. This is done by pressing the "Alt" key while entering the decimal equivalent. For example, to enter the "Escape" character, hold the "Alt" down while entering "27". An arrow will be displayed on the screen to represent the escape sentence.

Lotus 1–2–3 allows the user to provide a setup string when a spreadsheet or other output is destined for a printer. The setup string is entered under the 'print' menu. The string is made up of backslashes (\) followed by the three-digit decimal equivalent of special characters in ASCII code. For example, to set up an Epson dot-matrix printer for compressed print, you would use the string "\015".

Refer to the charts in this appendix to determine the appropriate sequences necessary to cause a printer to compress, underline, superscript, emphasize, or italicize printer output. Consult Appendix E, which provides an ASCII chart, to locate the decimal equivalent of these characters. Use these setup strings for proper control of the printing. Although the vendor's manual is the best source for this type of information, the following charts serve as a summary of this information. Several blank forms are provided for the user to add their own sequences for devices not included.

```
=======================================================================================
PRINTER              | Anadex   Anadex    Anadex    Anadex    Apple    AT&T      AT&T
Model#               | DP-6500  DP-9000   DP-9625B  WP-6000   Dot      455       473
                     |          DP-9500B                      Matrix
=======================|===============================================================
NOTES:               |
                     |
                     |
                     |
PRINT WIDTH COMMANDS  |
---------------------|-----------------------------------------------------------------
10 char/in           | ESC Q    ESC Q     ESC Q     ESC J0    ESC N              DC2
12 char/in           | ESC T    ESC R     ESC T     ESC J2    ESC E
17 char/in           | ESC R              ESC R     ESC J7    ESC Q              SI
Expanded print(1 line)|                                                         SO
Expanded print on    | ESC 5    SO        ESC 5     ESC N     SO                 ESC W 0
Expanded print off   | ESC 6    SI        ESC 6     ESC O     SI                 ESC W 1
                     |
PRINT QUALITY COMMANDS|
---------------------|-----------------------------------------------------------------
Letter quality mode  | ESC r              ESC r     ESC I 5
Near letter quality mode|                 ESC x
DP quality mode      |                              ESC I 6
Draft quality mode   |
Subscript on         | ESC <              ESC <     ESC I 4                      ESC S 1
Subscript off        | ESC :              ESC :     ESC ?                        ESC T
Superscript on       | ESC >              ESC >     ESC I 3                      ESC S 0
Superscript off      | ESC :              ESC :     ESC ?                        ESC T
Underline on         | ESC 8    RS        ESC 8     ESC :     ESC X    ESC I     ESC _ 0
Underline off        | ESC 9    US        ESC 9     ESC ;     ESC Y    ESC J     ESC _ 1
Emphasized on        | ESC p              ESC p               ESC !    ESC Q     ESC E
Emphasized off       | ESC q              ESC q               ESC "    ESC R     ESC F
Doublestrike on      | ESC x              ESC x                        ESC K 1   ESC G
Doublestrike off     | ESC Q              ESC Q                        ESC M     ESC H
Proportional mode on | ESC v              ESC v     ESC P     ESC P    ESC $
Proportional mode off| ESC Q              ESC Q     ESC Q     ESC N    ESC %
Italics on           | ESC t                        ESC X
Italics off          | ESC u                        ESX Y
                     |
PAPER FEED COMMANDS   |
---------------------|-----------------------------------------------------------------
6 lines/in           | ESC H    ESC H     ESC H     ESC E     ESC A    ESC L 0 8 ESC 2
8 lines/in           | ESC I    ESC I     ESC I     ESC F     ESC B    ESC L 0 6 ESC 0
10 lines/in          |                                                 ESC L 0 5 ESC 1
12 lines/in          |                              ESC !     ESC T 12 ESC L 0 4 ESC 3 11
                     |
---------------------|-----------------------------------------------------------------
RESET                |                                                 ESC CR P
=======================================================================================
```

PRINTER Model#	AT&T 470/475	AT&T 477 color	AT&T 5310 5320	Axiom IMP	brother 2024L	brother 2024L	brother HR-15XL
NOTES:		477 mode			DP Mode	WP Mode	
PRINT WIDTH COMMANDS							
10 char/in	ESC N	DC2	ESC [w	ESC 6	ESC P	ESC US 13	ESC US 13
12 char/in	ESC E		ESC [2w	ESC <	ESC M	ESC US 11	ESC US 11
17 char/in	ESC Q	SI	ESC [4w	ESC 7	SI	ESC US 8	ESC US 8
Expanded print(1 line)		SO			SO		
Expanded print on	SO	ESC W 1		ESC SO	ESC W 1		
Expanded print off	SI	ESC W 0		ESC SI	ESC W 0		
PRINT QUALITY COMMANDS							
Letter quality mode	ESC [				ESC x 1	ESC x 1	
Near letter quality mode							
DP quality mode						ESC @	
Draft quality mode	ESC]				ESC x 0	ESC x 0	
Subscript on		ESC S 1			ESC S1	ESC U	
Subscript off		ESC T			ESC T	ESC D	
Superscript on		ESC S 0			ESC SO	ESC D	
Superscript off		ESC T			ESC T	ESC U	
Underline on	ESC X	ESC 1			ESC -1	ESC E	ESC E
Underline off	ESC Y	ESC 0			ESC -0	ESC R	
Emphasized on		ESC E	ESC [5m		ESC E	ESC F	ESC O
Emphasized off		ESC F	ESC [m		ESC F	ESC &	ESC &
Doublestrike on	ESC !	ESC G			ESC G		ESC F
Doublestrike off	ESC "	ESC H			ESC H		ESC &
Proportional mode on	ESC P	ESC p 1			ESC p 1	ESC P	ESC P
Proportional mode off	ESC Q	ESC p 0			ESC p 0	ESC Q	ESC Q
Italics on		ESC 4					
Italics off		ESC 5					
PAPER FEED COMMANDS							
6 lines/in	ESC A	ESC A 10	ESC [z	ESC 4	ESC 2	ESC RS 9	ESC RS 9
8 lines/in	ESC B	ESC 0	ESC [2z		ESC 0	ESC RS 7	ESC RS 7
10 lines/in	ESC T 1 4	ESC A 6			ESC 3 18	ESC RS 6	ESC RS 6
12 lines/in	ESC T 1 2	ESC A 5	ESC [3z	ESC 5	ESC 3 10	ESC RS 5	ESC RS 5
RESET		ESC SUB I			ESC @	ESC CR P	ESC CR P

```
==============================================================================================
PRINTER            | brother    brother      brother    brother      brother    brother
Model#             | HR-25      M-1009       M-1109     M-1109       M-1509     M-1509
                   | HR-35
==============================================================================================
NOTES:             |                         Mode I     Mode II      Mode I     Mode II
                   |
                   |
                   |
PRINT WIDTH COMMANDS |
-------------------|--------------------------------------------------------------------------
10 char/in         | ESC US 13  DC2          DC2        DC2          DC2        DC2
12 char/in         | ESC US 11               ESC M      ESC M        ESC M      ESC M
17 char/in         | ESC US 8   SI           SI         SI           SI         SI
Expanded print(1 line) |
Expanded print on  |           SO           SO         SO           SO         SO
Expanded print off |           DC4          DC4        DC4          DC4        DC4
                   |
PRINT QUALITY COMMANDS |
-------------------|--------------------------------------------------------------------------
Letter quality mode |
Near letter quality mode |                   ESC X 1    ESC X 1      ESC X 1    ESC X 1
DP quality mode    |
Draft quality mode |                         ESC X 0    ESC X 0      ESC X 0    ESC X 0
Subscript on       |           ESC S1        ESC S 1    ESC S 1      ESC S 1    ESC S 1
Subscript off      |           ESC T         ESC T      ESC T        ESC T      ESC T
Superscript on     |           ESC S0        ESC S 0    ESC S 0      ESC S 0    ESC S 0
Superscript off    |           ESC T         ESC T      ESC T        ESC T      ESC T
Underline on       | ESC E     ESC - 1       ESC - 1    ESC - 1      ESC - 1    ESC - 1
Underline off      |           ESC - 0       ESC - 0    ESC - 0      ESC - 0    ESC - 0
Emphasized on      | ESC O     ESC E         ESC E      ESC E        ESC E      ESC E
Emphasized off     | ESC &     ESC F         ESC F      ESC F        ESC F      ESC F
Doublestrike on    | ESC F     ESC G         ESC G      ESC G        ESC G      ESC G
Doublestrike off   | ESC &     ESC H         ESC H      ESC H        ESC H      ESC H
Proportional mode on | ESC P                 ESC P 1                 ESC P 1
Proportional mode off | ESC Q                ESC P 0                 ESC P 0
Italics on         |                         ESC 4                   ESC 4
Italics off        |                         ESC 5                   ESC 5
                   |
PAPER FEED COMMANDS |
-------------------|--------------------------------------------------------------------------
6 lines/in         | ESC RS 9   ESC A 12 ESC 2 ESC 2   ESC A 12 ESC 2 ESC 2    ESC A 12 ESC 2
8 lines/in         | ESC RS 7   ESC 0        ESC 0      ESC 0        ESC 0      ESC 0
10 lines/in        | ESC RS 6   ESC 1        ESC 1      ESC 1        ESC 1      ESC 1
12 lines/in        | ESC RS 5                ESC 3 18   ESC A 6 ESC 2 ESC 3 18  ESC A 6 ESC 2
                   |
-------------------|--------------------------------------------------------------------------
RESET              | ESC CR P
==============================================================================================
```

```
===============================================================================
PRINTER          | brother    brother    Canon       Canon       Centronics  Citizen
Model#           | Twinriter  Twinriter  BJ-80AP/S   LBP-8       351         120-D
                 | 5          5                      A1/A2
===============================================================================
NOTES:           | DP         WP                     Diablo                  Epson
                 | Mode       Mode                   mode                    mode
                 |                                   (ESC :)
                 |
PRINT WIDTH COMMANDS |
------------------------|----------------------------------------------------------
10 char/in       | ESC P      ESC US 13  DC2         ESC US 12   ESC [ 1 w   ESC P
12 char/in       | ESC M      ESC US 11              ESC US 10   ESC [ 2 w   ESC M
17 char/in       | ESC SI     ESC US 8   SI          ESC US 7    ESC [ 4 w   CTRL O
Expanded print(1 line) | SO                                                  CTRL R
Expanded print on | ESC W 1              SO                      ESC [ 5 w   ESC W1
Expanded print off | ESC W 0             DC4                     ESC [ 1 w   ESC WO
                 |
PRINT QUALITY COMMANDS |
------------------------|----------------------------------------------------------
Letter quality mode | ESC x 1   ESC x 1                                      ESC x1
Near letter quality mode |                 ESC I0
DP quality mode  |            ESC a
Draft quality mode | ESC x 0   ESC x 0    ESC I1                             ESC X0
Subscript on     | ESC S1     ESC U      ESC S1      ESC U       ESC K       ESC S1
Subscript off    | ESC T      ESC D      ESC T       ESC D       ESC L       ESC T
Superscript on   | ESC S0     ESC D      ESC S0      ESC D       ESC L       ESC S0
Superscript off  | ESC T      ESC U      ESC T       ESC U       ESC K       ESC T
Underline on     | ESC -1     ESC E      ESC -1      ESC E       ESC [ 4 m   ESC -1
Underline off    | ESC -0     ESC R      ESC -0      ESC R       ESC [ 0 m   ESC -0
Emphasized on    | ESC E      ESC O      ESC E       ESC O                   ESC E
Emphasized off   | ESC F      ESC &      ESC F       ESC &                   ESC F
Doublestrike on  | ESC G      ESC F      ESC G                               ESC G
Doublestrike off | ESC H      ESC X      ESC H                               ESC H
Proportional mode on | ESC p 1   ESC P                ESC P       ESC ) 3     ESC p1
Proportional mode off | ESC p 0  ESC Q                ESC Q       ESC [ 1 w   ESC p0
Italics on       |                                                           ESC 4
Italics off      |                                                           ESC 5
                 |
PAPER FEED COMMANDS |
------------------------|----------------------------------------------------------
6 lines/in       | ESC 2      ESC RS 9   ESC A 12 ESC 2   ESC RS 8   ESC [ 1 z   ESC 2
8 lines/in       | ESC 0      ESC RS 7   ESC 0       ESC RS 6    ESC [ 2 z   ESC 0
10 lines/in      | ESC 3 18   ESC RS 6   ESC 1       ESC RS 5                ESC 1
12 lines/in      | ESC 3 10   ESC RS 5   ESC A 6 ESC 2   ESC RS 4           ESC ~0 CHR$(12)
                 |
------------------------|----------------------------------------------------------
RESET            | ESC a      ESC CR P   ESC a       ESC CR P                ESC a
===============================================================================
```

```
===============================================================================================
PRINTER                 | Citizen      Citizen       Citizen       Citizen      Citizen     Citizen
Model#                  | 120-D        MSP-10/15     MSP-20/25     Premiere     Premiere    Premiere
                        |                                          35           35          35
===============================================================================================
NOTES:                  | IBM          Standard      Standard      Qume         Diablo      NEC
                        | mode         mode          mode          Sprint 11    630         3550
                        |                                          mode         mode        mode
                        |
PRINT WIDTH COMMANDS    |
------------------------|----------------------------------------------------------------------
10 char/in              | CTRL R or ESC P  DC2 or ESC P   DC2 or ESC P                      ESC S
12 char/in              | ESC : or ESCM  ESC M         ESC M                                ESC I
17 char/in              | CTRL O       SI            SI                                     SI
Expanded print(1 line)  | CTRL R
Expanded print on       | ESC W1       SO            SO
Expanded print off      | ESC W0       DC4           DC4
                        |
PRINT QUALITY COMMANDS  |
------------------------|----------------------------------------------------------------------
Letter quality mode     | ESC x1
Near letter quality mode|
DP quality mode         |
Draft quality mode      | ESC X0
Subscript on            | ESC S1       ESC S1        ESC S1
Subscript off           | ESC T        ESC T         ESC T
Superscript on          | ESC S0       ESC S0        ESC S0
Superscript off         | ESC T        ESC T         ESC T
Underline on            | ESC -1                                   ESC I        ESC E       ESC -
Underline off           | ESC -0                                   ESC J, FF    ESC R       ESC '
Emphasized on           | ESC E        ESC E         ESC E         ESC Kd       ESC 0       ESC E
Emphasized off          | ESC F        ESC F         ESC F         ESC M        ___(cr)     ESC F (cr)
Doublestrike on         |              ESC G         ESC G
Doublestrike off        |              ESC H         ESC H
Proportional mode on    | ESC p1                                   ESC $        ESC P       ESC R
Proportional mode off   | ESC p0                                   ESC %        ESC Q       ESC T
Italics on              |              ESC 4         ESC 4
Italics off             |              ESC 5         ESC 5
                        |
PAPER FEED COMMANDS     |
------------------------|----------------------------------------------------------------------
6 lines/in              | ESC 2        ESC 2         ESC 2         ESC L d1,d2  ESC RS 9    ESC 2
8 lines/in              | ESC 0        ESC 0         ESC 0                      ESC RS 7    ESC 0
10 lines/in             | ESC 1        ESC 1         ESC 1                      ESC RS 6    ESC 1
12 lines/in             | ESC ~0 CHR$(12) ESC 3 18   ESC 3 18                  ESC RS 5
                        |
------------------------|----------------------------------------------------------------------
RESET                   | ESC @        ESC @         ESC @         ESC SUB I    ESC CR P    ESC =
===============================================================================================
```

```
===============================================================================================
PRINTER              | C.Itoh      C.Itoh      C.Itoh      DataSouth   DataSouth   DEC
Model#               | 8510/1550   C-310/15    Pro-        180         220         LA 100
                     | S/SC+NLQ                writer
=====================|=========================================================================
NOTES:               |
                     |
                     |
                     |
PRINT WIDTH COMMANDS |
---------------------|-------------------------------------------------------------------------
10 char/in           | ESC N       ESC N       ESC N       ESC [ 1 w   ESC $ 10 M  ESC [ 0 w
12 char/in           | ESC E       ESC E       ESC E       ESC [ 2 w   ESC $ 12 M  ESC [ 2 w
17 char/in           | ESC Q       ESC Q       ESC Q       ESC [ 4 w   ESC $ 16 M  ESC [ 4 w
Expanded print(1 line) |                                               ESC $ 5
Expanded print on    |             SO          SO          ESC $ 5     ESC $ 5     ESC [ 5 w
Expanded print off   |             SI          SI          ESC $ 6     ESC $ 6     ESC [ 0 w
                     |
PRINT QUALITY COMMANDS |
---------------------|-------------------------------------------------------------------------
Letter quality mode  |             ESC m2                              ESC $1 M    ESC [ 3 z
Near letter quality mode | ESC m2   ESC m1
DP quality mode      | ESC m0      ESC m0                              ESC $ 10 M  ESC [ 3 " z
Draft quality mode   | ESC m1                                         ESC $ 13 M  ESC [ 2 " z
Subscript on         | ESC s2      ESC s 2
Subscript off        | ESC s0      ESC s 0
Superscript on       | ESC s1      ESC s 1
Superscript off      | ESC s0      ESC s 0
Underline on         | ESC X       ESC X       ESC X                               ESC [ 4 m
Underline off        | ESC Y       ESC Y       ESC Y                               ESC [ 0 m
Emphasized on        | ESC !       ESC !       ESC !
Emphasized off       | ESC "       ESC "       ESC "
Doublestrike on      |
Doublestrike off     |
Proportional mode on | ESC P       ESC P       ESC P
Proportional mode off |                        ESC N
Italics on           | ESC i1      ESC i 1
Italics off          | ESC i0      ESC i 0
                     |
PAPER FEED COMMANDS  |
---------------------|-------------------------------------------------------------------------
6 lines/in           | ESC A       ESC A       ESC A       ESC [ 1 z   ESC [ 1 z   ESC [ 0 z
8 lines/in           | ESC B       ESC B       ESC B       ESC [ 2 z   ESC [ 2 z   ESC [ 2 z
10 lines/in          | ESC T 1 4   ESC T 1 4   ESC T nn
12 lines/in          | ESC T 1 2   ESC T 1 2   ESC T nn                            ESC [ 3 z
                     |
---------------------|-------------------------------------------------------------------------
RESET                | ESC c1      ESC c
===============================================================================================
```

```
==============================================================================================
PRINTER            | Diablo   Digital Matrix  Epson     Epson      Epson    Ergo Systems
Model#             | 630      9/80 & 9/132    FX-80     Graphtrax  MX-80    HUSH 80
                   |                                    80
==============================================================================================
```

	Diablo 630	Digital Matrix 9/80 & 9/132	Epson FX-80	Epson Graphtrax 80	Epson MX-80	Ergo Systems HUSH 80
NOTES:						
PRINT WIDTH COMMANDS						
10 char/in		ESC 6	DC2	ESC Q	DC2	
12 char/in		ESC 8	ESC M			
17 char/in		ESC 7	SI	ESC P	SI	CTRL O
Expanded print(1 line)			SO	CHR$(14)	SO	CTRL R
Expanded print on		SO	ESC W	ESC S	SO	CTRL N
Expanded print off		SI	DC4	ESC T	DC4	CTRL T
PRINT QUALITY COMMANDS						
Letter quality mode						
Near letter quality mode						
DP quality mode						
Draft quality mode						
Subscript on			ESC S 1			
Subscript off			ESC T			
Superscript on		ESC B	ESC S 0			
Superscript off		ESC C	ESC T			
Underline on	ESC E		ESC - 1			
Underline off	ESC R		ESC - 0			
Emphasized on	ESC O		ESC E	ESC E	ESC E	
Emphasized off	__(cr)		ESC F	ESC F	ESC F	
Doublestrike on		ESC9	ESC G	ESC G	ESC G	
Doublestrike off			ESC H	ESC H	ESC H	
Proportional mode on	ESC P		ESC p 1			
Proportional mode off	ESC Q		ESC p 0			
Italics on			ESC 4	ESC 4		
Italics off			ESC 5	ESC 5		
PAPER FEED COMMANDS						
6 lines/in	ESC RS 9	ESC 4	ESC 2	ESC 2	ESC 2	ESC 2
8 lines/in	ESC RS 7	ESC 5	ESC 0	ESC 0	ESC 0	ESC 0
10 lines/in	ESC RS 6		ESC 1	ESC 1	ESC 1	
12 lines/in	ESC RS 5					ESC A 6
RESET	ESC CR P	ESC R	ESC @	ESC @		

```
==============================================================================================
```

PRINTER Model#	Facit 4565	Facit 4565	Facit C7500	Florida Data OSP-130	Fujitsu DPL24	Fujitsu DPL24
NOTES:	4565 Mode	Diablo 630 mode			TYPE D	TYPE I mode
PRINT WIDTH COMMANDS						
10 char/in			ESC P	ESC US 13	ESC US 13	ESC P
12 char/in			ESC M	ESC US 11	ESC US 11	ESC M
17 char/in			ESC SI	ESC US 8	ESC US 8	SI
Expanded print(1 line)				SO		SO
Expanded print on			ESC SO	SO	ESC w 1	ESC W 1
Expanded print off			DC4	SI	ESC w 0	ESC W 0
PRINT QUALITY COMMANDS						
Letter quality mode			ESC q1	ESC W	ESC # 10	ESC % 30 30
Near letter quality mode			ESC G		ESC # 23	
DP quality mode						
Draft quality mode			ESC H	ESC &	ESC # 34	ESC % 30 32
Subscript on			ESC S0	ESC D		ESC S 1
Subscript off			ESC T	ESC U		ESC T
Superscript on			ESC S1	ESC U		ESC S 0
Superscript off			ESC T	ESC D		ESC T
Underline on	ESC _	ESC E	ESC - 1	ESC E	ESC E	ESC - 1
Underline off	ESC R	ESC R	ESC - 0	ESC R	ESC R	ESC - 0
Emphasized on	ESC O	ESC O	ESC E	ESC O	ESC O	ESC E
Emphasized off	ESC &	ESC &	ESC F	ESC &	ESC &	ESC F
Doublestrike on				ESC # 2		ESC G
Doublestrike off				ESC # 1		ESC H
Proportional mode on	ESC I	ESC P	ESC p1	ESC P	ESC P	ESC p 1
Proportional mode off	ESC J	ESC Q	ESC p0	ESC Q	ESC Q	ESC p 0
Italics on						ESC 4
Italics off						ESC 5
PAPER FEED COMMANDS						
6 lines/in	ESC L 08		ESC 3	ESC RS 9	ESC RS 9	ESC A 10 ESC 2
8 lines/in	ESC L 06		ESC 0	ESC RS 7	ESC RS 7	ESC 0
10 lines/in	ESC L		ESC 1	ESC RS 6	ESC RS 6	ESC A 6 ESC 2
12 lines/in			ESC A 06	ESC RS 5	ESC RS 5	ESC A 5 ESC 2
RESET	ESC SUB I	ESC SUB I		ESC cr P	ESC CR P	ESC @

```
================================================================================
PRINTER          | Fujitsu    Fujitsu     GE      Hewlett      IBM      IBM
Model#           | DX2000     SP320Q      2030    Packard      Color    Graphic
                 |                        2120    LaserJet
================================================================================
NOTES:           |
                 |
                 |
                 |
PRINT WIDTH COMMANDS |
-----------------|--------------------------------------------------------------
10 char/in       | ESC P      ESC US 13   ESC N   ESC (s10H    DC2      DC2
12 char/in       | ESC M      ESC US 11   ESC M   ESC (s12H
17 char/in       | SI         ESC US 8    ESC C   ESC (s16.6H  SI       SI
Expanded print(1 line) | SO                                    SO       SO
Expanded print on  | ESC W SOH                                 ESC W 1  ESC W 1
Expanded print off | ESC W NUL                                 ESC W 0  ESC W 0
                 |
PRINT QUALITY COMMANDS |
-----------------|--------------------------------------------------------------
Letter quality mode |
Near letter quality mode |
DP quality mode  |
Draft quality mode |
Subscript on     | ESC S SOH  ESC U               ESC =        ESC S 1  ESC S 1
Subscript off    | ESC T      ESC D               ESC &a-.5r   ESC T    ESC T
Superscript on   | ESC S NUL  ESC D               ESC &a-.5r   ESC S 0  ESC S 0
Superscript off  | ESC T      ESC U               ESC =        ESC T    ESC T
Underline on     | ESC - SOH  ESC E               ESC &dD      ESC 1    ESC 1
Underline off    | ESC - NUL                      ESC &d@      ESC 0    ESC 0
Emphasized on    | ESC E      ESC O               ESC (s3B     ESC E    ESC E
Emphasized off   | ESC F                          ESC (s0B     ESC F    ESC F
Doublestrike on  | ESC G                                       ESC G    ESC G
Doublestrike off | ESC H                                       ESC H    ESC H
Proportional mode on | ESC p SOH  ESC P           ESC (s1P     ESC P 1  ESC p 1
Proportional mode off | ESC p NUL                 ESC (s0P     ESC P 0  ESC p 0
Italics on       | ESC 4                          ESC (s1S              ESC 4
Italics off      | ESC 5                          ESC (s0S              ESC 5
                 |
PAPER FEED COMMANDS |
-----------------|--------------------------------------------------------------
6 lines/in       | ESC 2      ESC RS 9    ESC 6   ESC &l6D     ESC 2    ESC A 10 ESC 2
8 lines/in       | ESC 0      ESC RS 7    ESC 8   ESC &l8D     ESC 0    ESC 0
10 lines/in      | ESC 1      ESC RS 6                         ESC 3 18 ESC A 6 ESC 2
12 lines/in      | ESC A 6    ESC RS 5    ESC G   ESC &l12D    ESC 3 10 ESC A 5 ESC 2
                 |
-----------------|--------------------------------------------------------------
RESET            | ESC @      ESC CR P            ESC E                 ESC SUB I
================================================================================
```

```
===============================================================================================================
PRINTER                | IDS        Infoscribe  Malibu     Mannesmann  Mannesmann  Mannesmann
Model#                 | P80/P132   1100        200        MT-160      Tally       Spirit
                       |                                               MT600       80
===============================================================================================================
NOTES:                 |
                       |
                       |
                       |
                       |
PRINT WIDTH COMMANDS   |
-----------------------|---------------------------------------------------------------------------------------
10 char/in             | CTRL ]     ESC 6       ESC E 12   ESC [ 4 w   ESC [4w     DC2
12 char/in             | CTRL       ESC 8       ESC E 10   ESC [ 5 w   ESC [5w
17 char/in             | CTRL _     ESC 7       ESC E 07   ESC [ 6 w   ESC 6w      SI
Expanded print(1 line) |                                   SO                      SO
Expanded print on      | CTRL A     CTRL N      ESC @ W 1  ESC W 1     ESC [200;200 B  ESC W 1
Expanded print off     | CTRL B     CTRL O      ESC @ W 0  ESC W 0     ESC [100;100 B  ESC W 0
                       |
PRINT QUALITY COMMANDS |
-----------------------|---------------------------------------------------------------------------------------
Letter quality mode    | ESC R,1,$  ESC 9       ESC @ S L  ESC [ 1 y   ESC [41;71!s SI
Near letter quality mode|                                              ESC [11;1!s SI
DP quality mode        |            ESC 6                              ESC [11;1!s SO
Draft quality mode     | ESC R,2,$  ESC :       ESC @ S D  ESC [  y    ESC [11;1!s SO
Subscript on           | CTRL T     ESC C       ESC U      ESC [ 1 z               ESC S 1
Subscript off          | CTRL Y     cr          ESC D      ESC [ 2 z               ESC T
Superscript on         | CTRL Y     ESC B       ESC D      ESC [ 0 z               ESC S 0
Superscript off        | CTRL T     cr          ESC U      ESC [ 2 z               ESC T
Underline on           |                                   ESC [ 4 m   ESC [4m     ESC - 1
Underline off          |                                   ESC [ 0 m   ESC [0m     ESC - 0
Emphasized on          |                                   ESC [ = z   ESC [200;200!q  ESC E
Emphasized off         |                                   ESC [ > z   ESC [100;100!q  ESC F
Doublestrike on        |            ESC 9                                           ESC G
Doublestrike off       |            ESC 6                                           ESC H
Proportional mode on   |                                   ESC P
Proportional mode off  |                                   ESC Q
Italics on             |            ESC A                                          ESC 4
Italics off            |            ESC @                                          ESC 5
                       |
PAPER FEED COMMANDS    |
-----------------------|---------------------------------------------------------------------------------------
6 lines/in             | ESC B,8,$  ESC 4       ESC L O 8  ESC [ 3 z   ESC [3z     ESC 2
8 lines/in             | ESC B,6,$  ESC 5       ESC L O 6  ESC [ 4 z   ESC [4z     ESC 0
10 lines/in            |                                               ESC [6z     ESC 1
12 lines/in            | ESC B,4,$              ESC L O 4                          ESC 3 18
                       |
-----------------------|---------------------------------------------------------------------------------------
RESET                  |            ESC R       ESC SUB |  ESC [ 6 ~   ESC [ 6 ~   ESC @
===============================================================================================================
```

```
=================================================================================
PRINTER            | NEC      NEC       NEC       NEC          Norcom    Okidata
Model#             | 3550     P560      P660      PC-8023A     DP-80     2410
                   |          P565      P760
=================================================================================
NOTES:             |
                   |
                   |
                   |
                   |
PRINT WIDTH COMMANDS|
-------------------|-------------------------------------------------------------
10 char/in         | ESC S    ESC P     ESC P     ESC N        ESC A0    ESC 6
12 char/in         | ESC I    ESC M     ESC M     ESC E        ESC A1    ESC A
17 char/in         | SI       SI        SI        ESC Q        ESC A2    ESC B
Expanded print(1 line)|       SO        SO
Expanded print on  |          ESC W 1   ESC W 1   DC2          SO        ESC C
Expanded print off |          ESC W 0   ESC W 0   DC4          SI        ESC Z
                   |
PRINT QUALITY COMMANDS|
-------------------|-------------------------------------------------------------
Letter quality mode|          ESC x 1   ESC x 1                          ESC 7
Near letter quality mode|
DP quality mode    |                                                     ESC 8
Draft quality mode |          ESC x 0   ESC x 0                          ESC 9
Subscript on       |          ESC S 1   ESC S 1                          ESC D
Subscript off      |          ESC T     ESC T                            ESC E
Superscript on     |          ESC S 0   ESC S 0                          ESC F
Superscript off    |          ESC T     ESC T                            ESC E
Underline on       | ESC -    ESC -1    ESC -1    ESC X        ESC J1    ESC U
Underline off      | ESC '    ESC - 0   ESC - 0   ESC Y        ESC J0    ESC V
Emphasized on      | ESC E    ESC E     ESC E     ESC !
Emphasized off     | ESC F(cr) ESC F    ESC F     ESC "
Doublestrike on    |          ESC G     ESC G
Doublestrike off   |          ESC H     ESC H
Proportional mode on| ESC R   ESC p 1   ESC p 1   ESC P
Proportional mode off| ESC T  ESC p 0   ESC p 0   ESC N
Italics on         |          ESC 4     ESC 4
Italics off        |          ESC 5     ESC 5
                   |
PAPER FEED COMMANDS|
-------------------|-------------------------------------------------------------
6 lines/in         | ESC 2    ESC 2     ESC 2     ESC A        ESC B6    ESC 4
8 lines/in         | ESC 0    ESC 0     ESC 0     ESC B        ESC B8    ESC 5
10 lines/in        | ESC 1    ESC 3 18  ESC 3 18  ESC T (1)(5)
12 lines/in        |          ESC 3 15  ESC 3 15  ESC T (1)(2)
                   |
-------------------|-------------------------------------------------------------
RESET              | ESC =    ESC @     ESC @                  ESC @0    SI
=================================================================================
```

PRINTER Model#	Okidata 83A	OTC TriMatrix	Panasonic KX-P1090	Primages 90 & 100	Printek 920	Printronix MVP 150B
NOTES:						
PRINT WIDTH COMMANDS						
10 char/in	RS	DC2	ESC + P + (01)	ESC US 13	ESC [1 w	DC2
12 char/in			ESC + P + (00)	ESC US 11	ESC [2 w	ESC V
17 char/in	GS	SI		ESC US 8	ESC [4 w	SI
Expanded print(1 line)		SO				
Expanded print on	US	SO	ESC + W + (01)		SO	SO
Expanded print off	RS	DC4	ESC + W + (00)		SI	DC4
PRINT QUALITY COMMANDS						
Letter quality mode						ESC P
Near letter quality mode						
DP quality mode						ESC R
Draft quality mode		ESC !0				
Subscript on		ESC S1	ESC + S + (00)		ESC [3 x	
Subscript off		ESC T	ESC + T		ESC [1 x	
Superscript on		ESC S0	ESC + S + (00)		ESC [1 x	
Superscript off		ESC T	ESC + T		ESC [3 x	
Underline on		ESC -1	ESC + - + (01)	ESC E	ESC [4 m	ESC - 1
Underline off		ESC -0	ESC + - + (00)	ESC R	ESC [m	ESC - 0
Emphasized on		ESC E	ESC + E	ESC O		ESC E
Emphasized off		ESC F	ESC + F	ESC &		ESC F
Doublestrike on		ESC G	ESC + G			ESC G
Doublestrike off		ESC H	ESC + H			ESC H
Proportional mode on				ESC P		
Proportional mode off				ESC Q		
Italics on			ESC + 4			
Italics off			ESC + 5			
PAPER FEED COMMANDS						
6 lines/in	ESC 6	ESC 2	ESC + 2	ESC RS 9	ESC [1 x	ESC 2
8 lines/in	ESC 8	ESC 0	ESC + 0	ESC RS 7	ESC [2 x	ESC 0
10 lines/in		ESC 1	ESC + 1	ESC RS 6		ESC 1
12 lines/in		ESC 3 18	ESC + A + 6	ESC RS 5	ESC [4 x	
RESET		ESC @	ESC +	ESC SUB I	ESC c	ESC @

```
===============================================================================================
PRINTER            | Qume    Qwint      Qwint      RCA       RCA        Ricoh
Model#             | S/11    KSR/MSR    MSR-780    VP2100    VP2100     RP3400Q
                   |         740 series
===============================================================================================
NOTES:             |                               Mode I    Mode II
                   |
                   |
                   |
PRINT WIDTH COMMANDS|
-------------------|---------------------------------------------------------------------------
10 char/in         |         ESC sp B    ESC [ 10 w   DC2       DC2        ESC US 13
12 char/in         |         ESC " B     ESC [ 12 w   ESC M     ESC M      ESC US 11
17 char/in         |         ESC ' B     ESC [ 15 w   SI        SI         ESC US 8
Expanded print(1 line)|
Expanded print on  |         ESC sp / B  ESC [ 17 w   SO        SO
Expanded print off |         ESC sp B    ESC [ 10 w   DC4       DC4
                   |
PRINT QUALITY COMMANDS|
-------------------|---------------------------------------------------------------------------
Letter quality mode|
Near letter quality mode|                             ESC X 1   ESC X 1
DP quality mode    |
Draft quality mode |                                  ESC X 0   ESC X 0
Subscript on       | ESC U   ESC 9      ESC K        ESC S 1   ESC S 1    ESC U
Subscript off      | ESC D   ESC 8      ESC L        ESC T     ESC T      ESC D
Superscript on     | ESC D   ESC 8      ESC L        ESC S 0   ESC S 0    ESC D
Superscript off    | ESC U   ESC 9      ESC K        ESC T     ESC T      ESC U
Underline on       | ESC I                           ESC - 1   ESC - 1    ESC E
Underline off      | ESC J                           ESC - 0   ESC - 0    ESC R
Emphasized on      | ESC Q                           ESC E     ESC E      ESC O
Emphasized off     | ESC R                           ESC F     ESC F      ESC &
Doublestrike on    | ESC K 1                         ESC G     ESC G
Doublestrike off   | ESC M                           ESC H     ESC H
Proportional mode on| ESC $                          ESC P 1              ESC P
Proportional mode off| ESC %                         ESC P 0              ESC Q
Italics on         |                                 ESC 4
Italics off        |                                 ESC 5
                   |
PAPER FEED COMMANDS|
-------------------|---------------------------------------------------------------------------
6 lines/in         | ESC L 0 8  ESC :    ESC [ 1 z    ESC 2     ESC A 12 ESC 2  ESC RS 9
8 lines/in         | ESC L 0 6  ESC ;    ESC [ 2 z    ESC 0     ESC 0     ESC RS 7
10 lines/in        | ESC L 0 5                        ESC 1     ESC 1     ESC RS 6
12 lines/in        | ESC L 0 4           ESC [ 3 z    ESC 3 18  ESC A 6 ESC 2  ESC RS 5
                   |
-------------------|---------------------------------------------------------------------------
RESET              | ESC CR P                                             ESC SUB I
===============================================================================================
```

```
================================================================================
PRINTER                 | Siemens    Singer    Star       Star        Swintec    Toshiba
Model#                  | PT 88/89   Data      Gemini     Micronics   2100       1350
                        |            HR12E     10         NB-15
========================|=======================================================
NOTES:                  |
                        |
                        |
                        |
PRINT WIDTH COMMANDS    |
------------------------|----------------------------------------------------------
10 char/in              | ESC [ 1 w              DC2        ESC P       ESC US 13  ESC E 12
12 char/in              | ESC [ 2 w              ESC B 2    ESC M       ESC US 11  ESC E 10
17 char/in              | ESC [ 4 w    SI        SI         SI          ESC US 8   ESC E 07
Expanded print(1 line)  |              DC2       SO         SO
Expanded print on       | ESC 8        SO        ESC W 1    ESC W1                 ESC !
Expanded print off      | ESC <        DC4       ESC W 0    ESC W0                 ESC "
                        |
PRINT QUALITY COMMANDS  |
------------------------|----------------------------------------------------------
Letter quality mode     |                                   ESC x1                 ESC * 2
Near letter quality mode|
DP quality mode         |                                                          ESC * 0
Draft quality mode      |                                   ESC x0                 ESC * 1
Subscript on            | ESC K        ESC FS    ESC S 1    ESC S1      ESC U      ESC U
Subscript off           | ESC L        ESC RS    ESC T      ESC T       ESC D      ESC D
Superscript on          | ESC L        ESC RS    ESC S 0    ESC S0      ESC D      ESC D
Superscript off         | ESC K        ESC FS    ESC T      ESC T       ESC U      ESC U
Underline on            | ESC 0        ESC U     ESC - 1    ESC -1      ESC E      ESC I
Underline off           | ESC 9        ESC V     ESC - 0    ESC -0      ESC R      ESC J
Emphasized on           |              ESC E     ESC E      ESC E       ESC O
Emphasized off          |              ESC F     ESC F      ESC F       ESC &
Doublestrike on         |                        ESC G
Doublestrike off        |                        ESC H
Proportional mode on    | ESC [ 2 SP E                      ESC p1
Proportional mode off   | ESC [ SP E                        ESC p0
Italics on              |                        ESC 4
Italics off             |                        ESC 5
                        |
PAPER FEED COMMANDS     |
------------------------|----------------------------------------------------------
6 lines/in              | ESC [ 12 x  ESC 2      ESC 2      ESC 2       ESC RS 9   ESC L 08
8 lines/in              | ESC [ 9 x   ESC 0      ESC 0      ESC 0       ESC RS 7   ESC L 06
10 lines/in             | ESC [ 7 x   ESC 1      ESC 1      ESC 3 18    ESC RS 6
12 lines/in             | ESC [ 6 x   ESC A 06                          ESC RS 5   ESC L 04
                        |
------------------------|----------------------------------------------------------
RESET                   | ESC c                  ESC @      ESC @       ESC cr P   ESC SUB I
================================================================================
```

```
=============================================================================================
PRINTER              |
Model#               |
                     |
=====================|=======================================================================
NOTES:               |
                     |
                     |
                     |
PRINT WIDTH COMMANDS |
---------------------|-----------------------------------------------------------------------
10 char/in           |
12 char/in           |
17 char/in           |
Expanded print(1 line) |
Expanded print on    |
Expanded print off   |
                     |
PRINT QUALITY COMMANDS |
---------------------|-----------------------------------------------------------------------
Letter quality mode  |
Near letter quality mode |
DP quality mode      |
Draft quality mode   |
Subscript on         |
Subscript off        |
Superscript on       |
Superscript off      |
Underline on         |
Underline off        |
Emphasized on        |
Emphasized off       |
Doublestrike on      |
Doublestrike off     |
Proportional mode on |
Proportional mode off |
Italics on           |
Italics off          |
                     |
PAPER FEED COMMANDS  |
---------------------|-----------------------------------------------------------------------
6 lines/in           |
8 lines/in           |
10 lines/in          |
12 lines/in          |
                     |
---------------------|-----------------------------------------------------------------------
RESET                |
=============================================================================================
```

```
==============================================================================================
PRINTER             |
Model#              |
                    |
==============================|===============================================================
NOTES:              |
                    |
                    |
                    |
PRINT WIDTH COMMANDS|
----------------------------|------------------------------------------------------------------
10 char/in          |
12 char/in          |
17 char/in          |
Expanded print(1 line) |
Expanded print on   |
Expanded print off  |
                    |
PRINT QUALITY COMMANDS|
----------------------------|------------------------------------------------------------------
Letter quality mode |
Near letter quality mode |
DP quality mode     |
Draft quality mode  |
Subscript on        |
Subscript off       |
Superscript on      |
Superscript off     |
Underline on        |
Underline off       |
Emphasized on       |
Emphasized off      |
Doublestrike on     |
Doublestrike off    |
Proportional mode on|
Proportional mode off|
Italics on          |
Italics off         |
                    |
PAPER FEED COMMANDS |
----------------------------|------------------------------------------------------------------
6 lines/in          |
8 lines/in          |
10 lines/in         |
12 lines/in         |
                    |
----------------------------|------------------------------------------------------------------
RESET               |
==============================================================================================
```

```
===============================================================================================
PRINTER                   |
Model#                    |
                          |
==========================|====================================================================
NOTES:                    |
                          |
                          |
                          |
PRINT WIDTH COMMANDS      |
--------------------------|--------------------------------------------------------------------
10 char/in                |
12 char/in                |
17 char/in                |
Expanded print(1 line)    |
Expanded print on         |
Expanded print off        |
                          |
PRINT QUALITY COMMANDS     |
--------------------------|--------------------------------------------------------------------
Letter quality mode       |
Near letter quality mode  |
DP quality mode           |
Draft quality mode        |
Subscript on              |
Subscript off             |
Superscript on            |
Superscript off           |
Underline on              |
Underline off             |
Emphasized on             |
Emphasized off            |
Doublestrike on           |
Doublestrike off          |
Proportional mode on      |
Proportional mode off     |
Italics on                |
Italics off               |
                          |
PAPER FEED COMMANDS       |
--------------------------|--------------------------------------------------------------------
6 lines/in                |
8 lines/in                |
10 lines/in               |
12 lines/in               |
                          |
--------------------------|--------------------------------------------------------------------
RESET                     |
===============================================================================================
```

```
================================================================================
PRINTER            |
Model#             |
                   |
================================|================================================
NOTES:             |
                   |
                   |
                   |
PRINT WIDTH COMMANDS |
--------------------|-----------------------------------------------------------
10 char/in         |
12 char/in         |
17 char/in         |
Expanded print(1 line) |
Expanded print on  |
Expanded print off |
                   |
PRINT QUALITY COMMANDS |
--------------------|-----------------------------------------------------------
Letter quality mode |
Near letter quality mode |
DP quality mode    |
Draft quality mode |
Subscript on       |
Subscript off      |
Superscript on     |
Superscript off    |
Underline on       |
Underline off      |
Emphasized on      |
Emphasized off     |
Doublestrike on    |
Doublestrike off   |
Proportional mode on |
Proportional mode off |
Italics on         |
Italics off        |
                   |
PAPER FEED COMMANDS |
--------------------|-----------------------------------------------------------
6 lines/in         |
8 lines/in         |
10 lines/in        |
12 lines/in        |
                   |
--------------------|-----------------------------------------------------------
RESET              |
================================================================================
```

APPENDIX H. TERMINAL ESCAPE SEQUENCES

When writing application programs for various terminals, the programmer must often know the specific terminal escape sequences for items such as homing the cursor, erasing the screen, cursor positioning, etc. The specific terminal user's manuals should be consulted for such sequences but are not always available. The following charts have been compiled to fulfill this need.

Furthermore, as multi-user systems using the UNIX operating system proliferate, there is a need to have the type of information in this appendix available. Files within the operating system must contain terminal definitions. In particular, TERMCAP and CURSES/TERMINFO entries allow users to capitalize on the terminals' capabilities. The control sequences that allow these capabilities consist of escape sequences as outlined in this appendix. Should the system files lack these sequences, extract the information from these charts and update the operating system files.

The reader is advised that most terminals offer more capabilities than listed in these charts. Every attempt was made to provide accurate and complete information on the more prevalent features. As new terminals become available, the user is encouraged to use the blank forms at the end of this appendix to summarize the capabilities.

```
=================================================================================================
VENDOR              | ADDS        ADDS          ADDS         ADDS         AT&T         AT&T
MODEL               | 1010        Regent 25     Regent 30    Viewpoint    5420 &       610
                    |                                        60           4425
=================================================================================================
NOTES:              | Viewpoint                                          pn=#
                    | A1 mode                                            r=row
                    |                                                    c=column
                    |
GENERAL COMMANDS    |
--------------------|----------------------------------------------------------------------------
Reset device        |                                                    ESC c        ESC c
Horizontal tab set  |             ESC 1                                  ESC H        ESC H
Horizontal tab clear|             ESC 2                                  ESC [ 0 g    ESC [ g
Clear all tabs      |             ESC -                                  ESC [ 3 g    ESC [ 3 g
Lock keyboard       | ESC 5       ESC 5         ESC 5        ESC 5       ESC `
Unlock keyboard     | ESC 6       ESC 6         ESC 6        ESC 6       ESC b
                    |
CURSOR CONTROL COMMANDS |
--------------------|----------------------------------------------------------------------------
Read cursor position|             ESC ?         ESC ENQ      ESC ENQ     ESC [ 6 n    ESC [ 6 n
Cursor up           | SUB         CTRL Z        CTRL Z       CTRL Z      ESC [ pn A   ESC [ pn A
Cursor down         | LF          CTRL J        CTRL J       CTRL J      ESC [ pn B   ESC [ pn B
Cursor right        | ACK         CTRL F        CTRL F       CTRL F      ESC [ pn C   ESC [ pn C
Cursor left         | NAK         CTRL U        CTRL U       CTRL U      ESC [ pn D   ESC [ pn D
Home cursor         | SOH         CTRL A        CTRL A       CTRL A      ESC [ H      ESC [ H
Position cursor     | ESC Y r c   ESC Y r c     ESC Y r c    ESC Y r c   ESC [ r;c f  ESC [ r;c h
                    |
DISPLAY CONTROL COMMANDS |
--------------------|----------------------------------------------------------------------------
Clear to end of page| ESC k       ESC y         ESC k        ESC k       ESC [ 0 J    ESC [ 0 J
Clear to end of line| ESC K       ESC t         ESC K        ESC K       ESC [ 0K     ESC [ 0 K
Clear screen(to nulls)| FF        ESC *         CTRL L       CTRL F      ESC [ 2J     ESC [ 2 J
Underscore          | ESC 0 \                   ESC n '      ESC 0 '     ESC [ 4 m    ESC [ 4 m
Blink               | ESC 0 B                   ESC n B      ESC 0 b     ESC [ 5 m    ESC [ 5 m
Reverse video       | ESC 0 P                   ESC n P      ESC 0 P     ESC [ 7 m    ESC [ 7 m
Blank video(invisible)| ESC 0 D                              ESC 0 D     ESC [ 8 m    ESC [ 8 m
132 Column mode     |                                                    ESC [ ? 3h   ESC [ ? 3h
80 Column mode      |                                                    ESC [ ? 3 l  ESC [ ? 3 l
Next page           |                           DC1                      ESC [ U
Previous page       |                           SOH                      ESC [ V
Protect mode on     |             ESC )         ESC P        ESC 0 H     ESC V
Protect mode off    |             ESC (         ESC p        ESC 0 @     ESC W
                    |
EDITING COMMANDS    |
--------------------|----------------------------------------------------------------------------
Line insert         |             ESC M         ESC M        ESC M       ESC [ pn L   ESC [ pn L
Line delete         |             ESC 1         ESC 1        ESC 1       ESC [ pn M   ESC [ pn M
Character insert    |             ESC F         ESC F        ESC F       ESC [ pn @   ESC [ pn @
Character delete    |             ESC E         ESC E        ESC E       ESC [ pn P   ESC [ pn P
                    |
ATTACHED PRINTER COMMANDS |
--------------------|----------------------------------------------------------------------------
Print screen        |             ESC x         ESC x        ESC [ 0 i
Print on line(POL) on| DC2        CTRL R        DC2          CTRL R      ESC [ ? 5 i  ESC [ ? 5 i
Print on line(POL) off| DC4       CTRL T        DC4          CTRL T      ESC [ ? 4 i  ESC [ ? 4 i
Transparent print mode on | ESC 3 ESC a        ESC 3        ESC 3       ESC [ 5 i    ESC [ 5 i
Transparent print mode off| ESC 4 ESC A        ESC 4        ESC 4       ESC [ 4 i    ESC [ 4 i
=================================================================================================
```

```
===============================================================================
VENDOR            | Beehive    Data General  DEC          DEC          DEC
MODEL             | ATL-008    D100/D200     VT52         VT100        VT220
                  |
===============================================================================
NOTES:            |            Codes                      ANSI mode    VT200 mode
                  |            below are                                pn=#
                  |            in octal                                 pl=line
                  |                                                     pc=column
GENERAL COMMANDS  |
------------------|------------------------------------------------------------
Reset device      | ESC c                                 ESC c        ESC c
Horizontal tab set| ESC H                                 ESC H        ESC H
Horizontal tab clear| ESC [ g                             ESC [ g      ESC [ g
Clear all tabs    | ESC [ 3 g                             ESC [ 3 g    ESC [ 3 g
Lock keyboard     |                                                    ESC [ 2 h
Unlock keyboard   |                                                    ESC [ 2 l

CURSOR CONTROL COMMANDS |
------------------|------------------------------------------------------------
Read cursor position | ESC [ 6 n  005                     ESC [ 6 n    ESC [ 6 n
Cursor up         | ESC [ pn A  027        ESC A          ESC [ pn A   ESC [ pn A
Cursor down       | ESC [ pn B  032        ESC B          ESC [ pn B   ESC [ pn B
Cursor right      | ESC [ pn C  030        ESC C          ESC [ pn C   ESC [ pn C
Cursor left       | ESC [ pn D  031        ESC D          ESC [ pn D   ESC [ pn D
Home cursor       | ESC [ H     010        ESC H          ESC [ H      ESC [ H
Position cursor   | ESC [ r;c h 020 xxx yyy ESC Y r+31 c+31 ESC [ r;c h ESC [ pl ; pc H

DISPLAY CONTROL COMMANDS |
------------------|------------------------------------------------------------
Clear to end of page | ESC [ J  014          ESC J         ESC [ J      ESC [ J
Clear to end of line | ESC [ K  013          ESC K         ESC [ K      ESC [ K
Clear screen(to nulls) | ESC [ 2 J                         ESC [ 2 J    ESC [ 2 J
Underscore        | ESC [ 4 m  024                         ESC [ 4 m    ESC [ 4 m
Blink             | ESC [ 5 m  016                         ESC [ 5 m    ESC [ 5 m
Reverse video     | ESC [ 7 m  036                         ESC [ 7 m    ESC [ 7 m
Blank video(invisible) | ESC [ 8 m                         ESC [ 8 m    ESC [ 8 m
132 Column mode   | ESC [ ? 3h                             ESC [ ? 3h   ESC [ ? 3 h
80 Column mode    | ESC [ ? 3 l                            ESC [ ? 3 l  ESC [ ? 3 l
Next page         |
Previous page     |
Protect mode on   |
Protect mode off  |

EDITING COMMANDS  |
------------------|------------------------------------------------------------
Line insert       |                                                    ESC [ pn L
Line delete       |                                                    ESC [ pn M
Character insert  |                                                    ESC [ pn @
Character delete  |                                                    ESC [ pn P

ATTACHED PRINTER COMMANDS |
------------------|------------------------------------------------------------
Print screen      |            021          ESC ]                      ESC [ i
Print on line(POL) on |                     ESC ^                      ESC [ ? 5 i
Print on line(POL) off |                    ESC _                      ESC [ ? 4 i
Transparent print mode on |                 ESC W                      ESC [ 5 i
Transparent print mode off|                 ESC X                      ESC [ 4 i
===============================================================================
```

```
===============================================================================
VENDOR          | Esprit     Esprit     Hazeltine   Hewlett     Hewlett
MODEL           | 6310       III        1420        Packard     Packard
                |                                    2624        2648
===============================================================================
NOTES:          | Hazeltine   n=#
                | 1500 mode
                | ESC or ~
                | prefix

GENERAL COMMANDS
----------------|--------------------------------------------------------------
Reset device    |                                   ESC E       ESC E
Horizontal tab set  | ESC 1   ESC 1      ESC 1
Horizontal tab clear| ESC 2   ESC 2      ESC 3
Clear all tabs      | ESC 3   ESC 3      ESC 2
Lock keyboard       | ESC NAK ESC #      ESC CTRL U
Unlock keyboard     | ESC ACK ESC "      ESC CTRL F
                |
CURSOR CONTROL COMMANDS |
----------------|--------------------------------------------------------------
Read cursor position | ESC ENQ  ESC ?    ESC CTRL E  ESC ` DC1   ESC ` DC1
Cursor up       | ESC FF   VT(CTRL K)    ESC CTRL L  ESC A       ESC A
Cursor down     | ESC VT   SYN(CTRL V)   ESC CTRL K  ESC B       ESC B
Cursor right    | DLE      FF(CTRL L)    CTRL P      ESC C       ESC C
Cursor left     | BS       BS            CTRL H      ESC D       ESC D
Home cursor     | ESC DC2  RS(CTRL ^)    ESC CTRL R  ESC H       ESC H
Position cursor | ESC DC1 c r  ESC = n n             ESC & a r c ESC & a r c
                |
DISPLAY CONTROL COMMANDS |
----------------|--------------------------------------------------------------
Clear to end of page | ESC SI   ESC y     ESC y       ESC J       ESC J
Clear to end of line | ESC CAN  ESC t     ESC t       ESC K       ESC K
Clear screen(to nulls)| ESC FS  ESC *     ESC CTRL L  ESC g       ESC g
Underscore      |                                    ESC & d D   ESC & d D
Blink           |                                    ESC & d A   ESC & d A
Reverse video   |          ESC b                     ESC & d B   ESC & d B
Blank video(invisible) |  ESC o                      ESC & d S   ESC & d S
132 Column mode |
80 Column mode  |
Next page       | ESC K    ESC K                     ESC V       ESC V
Previous page   | ESC J    ESC J                     ESC U       ESC U
Protect mode on |                        ESC CTRL Y  ESC ]       ESC & d J
Protect mode off|                        ESC CTRL _  ESC [       ESC & d @
                |
EDITING COMMANDS |
----------------|--------------------------------------------------------------
Line insert     | ESC SUB  ESC E         ESC CTRL Z  ESC L       ESC L
Line delete     | ESC DC3  ESC R         ESC CTRL S  ESC M       ESC M
Character insert| ESC P    ESC Q         ESC Q       ESC Q       ESC Q
Character delete| ESC T    ESC W         ESC W       ESC P       ESC P
                |
ATTACHED PRINTER COMMANDS |
----------------|--------------------------------------------------------------
Print screen    | ESC RS   ESC L
Print on line(POL) on  | ESC /   ESC @    ESC /
Print on line(POL) off | ESC ?   ESC A    ESC ?
Transparent print mode on  | ESC *  ESC `  ESC *
Transparent print mode off | ESC ?  ESC a  ESC ?
===============================================================================
```

```
========================================================================
VENDOR          | IBM    Lear        Lee Data     Liberty      Micro-Term
MODEL           | 3101   Siegler     8178/8180    Electronics  Ergo 320
                |        ADM3A                     Freedom 100
========================|===============================================
NOTES:          |                    VT100        Native       VDT200
                |                    mode         mode         mode
                |                                 n=#
                |
GENERAL COMMANDS|
----------------|-------------------------------------------------------
Reset device    |                    ESC c                     ESC c
Horizontal tab set   | ESC 0   ESC 1        ESC H        ESC 1        ESC H
Horizontal tab clear |         ESC 2        ESC [ g      ESC 2        ESC [ 0 g
Clear all tabs       |         ESC 3        ESC [ 3 g    ESC 3        ESC [ 3 g
Lock keyboard   | ESC :   SI                        ESC #        ESC [ 2 h
Unlock keyboard | ESC ;   SO                        ESC "        ESC [ 2 l
                |
CURSOR CONTROL COMMANDS |
----------------|-------------------------------------------------------
Read cursor position | ESC 5   ESC ?       ESC [ 6 n    ESC ?        ESC [ 6 n
Cursor up       | ESC A   VT(CTRL K)   ESC [ pn A   CTRL K       ESC [ pn A
Cursor down     | ESC B   SYN(CTRL V)  ESC [ pn B   CTRL J       ESC [ pn B
Cursor right    | ESC C   FF(CTRL L)   ESC [ pn C   CTRL L       ESC [ pn C
Cursor left     | ESC D   BS           ESC [ pn D   CTRL H       ESC [ pn D
Home cursor     | ESC H   RS(CTRL ^)   ESC [ H      CTRL ^       ESC [ H
Position cursor | ESC Y x y  ESC = r c  ESC [ r;c h  ESC = n n    ESC [ pr ; pc H
                |
DISPLAY CONTROL COMMANDS |
----------------|-------------------------------------------------------
Clear to end of page | ESC J   ESC y        ESC [ J      ESC y        ESC [ ? 0 J
Clear to end of line | ESC I   ESC t        ESC [ K      ESC t        ESC [ ? 0 K
Clear screen(to nulls) | ESC L   ESC *      ESC [ 2 J    ESC *        ESC [ ? 2 J
Underscore      |         ESC G 8      ESC [ 4 m    ESC G 8      ESC [ 4 m
Blink           | ESC 3 I   ESC G 2      ESC [ 5 m    ESC G 2      ESC [ 5 m
Reverse video   | ESC 3 E   ESC G 4      ESC [ 7 m    ESC G 4      ESC [ 7 m
Blank video(invisible) | ESC 3 M  ESC G 18  ESC [ 8 m   ESC G 18
132 Column mode |                    ESC [ ? 3h                ESC [ ? 3 h
80 Column mode  |                    ESC [ ? 3 l               ESC [ ? 3 l
Next page       |         ESC K
Previous page   |         ESC J
Protect mode on | ESC 3 C   ESC &                     ESC )
Protect mode off| ESC 3 B   ESC '                     ESC (
                |
EDITING COMMANDS|
----------------|-------------------------------------------------------
Line insert     | ESC N   ESC E                     ESC E        ESC [ pn L
Line delete     | ESC O   ESC R                     ESC R        ESC [ pn M
Character insert| ESC P   ESC Q                     ESC Q        ESC [ pn @
Character delete| ESC Q   ESC W                     ESC W        ESC [ pn P
                |
ATTACHED PRINTER COMMANDS |
----------------|-------------------------------------------------------
Print screen    | ESC W   ESC P                     ESC P        ESC [ i
Print on line(POL) on  |  ESC @                      ESC @        ESC [ ? 5 i
Print on line(POL) off |  ESC A                      ESC A        ESC [ ? 4 i
Transparent print mode on |  ESC \                   ESC `        ESC [ 5 i
Transparent print mode off|  ESC a                   ESC a        ESC [ 4 i
========================================================================
```

```
=====================================================================================
VENDOR                 | RCA      Televideo  Televideo  Televideo  Wyse        Wyse
MODEL                  | APT      910        920        925        Technology  Technology
                       |                                           WY-30       WY-50
                       |
=====================================================================================
NOTES:                 |          Native     Native     Native     WY-30       WY-50
                       |          mode       mode       mode       mode        mode
                       |          l=line     l=line     l=line     r=row       r=row
                       |          c=column   c=column   c=column   c=column    c=column
GENERAL COMMANDS       |
-----------------------|-----------------------------------------------------------------
Reset device          |
Horizontal tab set    |          ESC 1      ESC 1      ESC 1      ESC 1       ESC 1
Horizontal tab clear  |          ESC 2      ESC 2      ESC 2      ESC 2       ESC 2
Clear all tabs        |          ESC 3      ESC 3      ESC 3      ESC 0       ESC 0
Lock keyboard         | ESC b    ESC #                 ESC #      ESC #       ESC #
Unlock keyboard       | ESC c    ESC "                 ESC "      ESC "       ESC "
                      |
CURSOR CONTROL COMMANDS|
-----------------------|-----------------------------------------------------------------
Read cursor position  | ESC a    ESC ?      ESC ?      ESC ?      ESC ?       ESC ?
Cursor up             | ESC A    CTRL K     CTRL K     CTRL K     CTRL K      CTRL K
Cursor down           | ESC B    CTRL J     CTRL J     CTRL V     CTRL J      CTRL J
Cursor right          | ESC C    CTRL L     CTRL L     CTRL L     CTRL L      CTRL L
Cursor left           | ESC D    CTRL H     CTRL H     CTRL H     CTRL H      CTRL H
Home cursor           | ESC H    ESC {      CTRL ^     CTRL ^     ESC {       ESC {
Position cursor       | ESC Y r c  ESC = l c  ESC = l c  ESC = l c  ESC = rc    ESC = rc
                      |
DISPLAY CONTROL COMMANDS|
-----------------------|-----------------------------------------------------------------
Clear to end of page  | ESC J    ESC y      ESC y      ESC y      ESC Y       ESC y
Clear to end of line  | ESC K    ESC t      ESC t      ESC t      ESC t       ESC t
Clear screen(to nulls)| ESC j    ESC *      ESC *      ESC *      ESC y       ESC *
Underscore            |          ESC G 8    ESC G 8    ESC G 8    ESC A 0 8   ESC A 0 8
Blink                 | ESC ESC S 4  ESC G 2  ESC G 2  ESC G 2    ESC A 0 2   ESC A 0 2
Reverse video         | ESC ESC S 3  ESC G 4  ESC G 4  ESC G 4    ESC A 0 4   ESC A 0 4
Blank video(invisible)|          ESC G 3    ESC G 3    ESC G 3    ESC A 0 3   ESC A 0 3
132 Column mode       |                                                       ESC ;
80 Column mode        | ESC ESC D 3                                           ESC :
Next page             |          ESC J      ESC J      ESC J      ESC }       ESC }
Previous page         |          ESC K      ESC K      ESC K      ESC ]       ESC ]
Protect mode on       |          ESC (      ESC (      ESC (      ESC &       ESC &
Protect mode off      |          ESC )      ESC )      ESC )      ESC '       ESC '
                      |
EDITING COMMANDS      |
-----------------------|-----------------------------------------------------------------
Line insert           | ESC L    ESC E      ESC E      ESC E      ESC E       ESC E
Line delete           | ESC M    ESC R      ESC R      ESC R      ESC R       ESC R
Character insert      | ESC P    ESC Q      ESC Q      ESC Q      ESC Q       ESC Q
Character delete      | ESC Q    ESC W      ESC W      ESC W      ESC W       ESC W
ATTACHED PRINTER COMMANDS|
-----------------------|-----------------------------------------------------------------
Print screen          | ESC O    ESC P      ESC P      ESC P      ESC P       ESC P
Print on line(POL) on | DC2(CRTL T) ESC @   DC2        DC2        CTRL R      DC2
Print on line(POL) off| DC4(CTRL T) ESC a   DC4        DC4        CTRL T      DC4
Transparent print mode on |       ESC `     ESC ` n    ESC ` n    CTRL X      CAN
Transparent print mode off|       ESC a     ESC a      ESC a      CTRL T      DC4
=====================================================================================
```

VENDOR MODEL	Wyse Technology WY-60	Wyse Technology WY-75	Wyse Technology WY-85	Wyse Technology WY-350	xycom RacPac 4810
NOTES:	Native mode l=line c=column	Native mode n1=line# n2=column#	Native mode n1=line# n2=column#	Native mode l=line c=column	
GENERAL COMMANDS					
Reset device		ESC c	ESC c		
Horizontal tab set	ESC 1	ESC [0 w	ESC [0 w	ESC 1	
Horizontal tab clear	ESC 2	ESC [0 g	ESC [0 g	ESC 2	
Clear all tabs	ESC 0	ESC [3 g	ESC [3 g	ESC 0	
Lock keyboard	SI or ESC #	ESC [2 h	ESC [2 h	SI or ESC #	ESC '
Unlock keyboard	SO or ESC "	ESC [2 l	ESC [2 l	SO or ESC "	ESC b
CURSOR CONTROL COMMANDS					
Read cursor position	ESC ?	ESC [6 n	ESC [6 n	ESC ?	
Cursor up	CTRL K	ESC [1 A	ESC [1 A	CTRL K	ESC [A
Cursor down	CTRL J	ESC [1 B	ESC [1 B	CTRL J	ESC [B
Cursor right	CTRL L	ESC [1 C	ESC [1 C	CTRL L	ESC [C
Cursor left	CTRL H	ESC [1 D	ESC [1 D	CTRL H	BS
Home cursor	ESC (	ESC [H	ESC [H	ESC (	ESC [H
Position cursor	ESC = l c	ESC [n1;n2 H	ESC [n1;n2 H	ESC = l c	ESC [l ; c H
DISPLAY CONTROL COMMANDS					
Clear to end of page	ESC y	ESC [0 J	ESC [0 J	ESC y	ESC [0 J
Clear to end of line	ESC t	ESC [0 K	ESC [0 K	ESC t	ESC [K
Clear screen(to nulls)	ESC *	ESC [2 J	ESC [2 J	ESC *	ESC [2 J
Underscore	ESC ' E	ESC [8 p	ESC [4 m	ESC G 8	ESC [1;4;0p
Blink	ESC ' B	ESC [2 p	ESC [5 m	ESC G 2	ESC [1;8;0p
Reverse video	ESC ' F	ESC [16 p	ESC [7 m	ESC G 4	ESC [1;1;0p
Blank video(invisible)	ESC ' C	ESC [6 p	ESC [8 m	ESC G 3	
132 Column mode	ESC ' ;	ESC [? 3 h	ESC [? 3 h	ESC ' ;	
80 Column mode	ESC ' :	ESC [? 3 l	ESC [? 3 l	ESC ' :	
Next page	ESC w C			ESC)	
Previous page	ESC w B			ESC]	
Protect mode on	ESC (			ESC (	
Protect mode off	ESC)			ESC)	
EDITING COMMANDS					
Line insert	ESC E	ESC [1 L	ESC [1 L	ESC E	ESC L
Line delete	ESC R	ESC [1 M	ESC [1 M	ESC R	ESC M
Character insert	ESC Q	ESC [1 @	ESC [1 @	ESC Q	
Character delete	ESC W	ESC [1 P	ESC [1 P	ESC W	
ATTACHED PRINTER COMMANDS					
Print screen	ESC @ or L o	ESC [? 19 h	ESC [? 19 h	ESC @ or L or P	
Print on line(POL) on	DC2	ESC [? 5 i	ESC [? 5 i	DC2	
Print on line(POL) off	DC4	ESC [? 4 i	ESC [? 4 i	DC4	
Transparent print mode on	ESC d #	ESC [5 i	ESC [5 i	CAN	
Transparent print mode off	DC4	ESC [4 i	ESC [4 i	DC4	

```
===============================================================================
VENDOR             |
MODEL              |
                   |
                   |
===============================|===============================================
NOTES:             |
                   |
                   |
                   |
GENERAL COMMANDS   |
-------------------|-----------------------------------------------------------
Reset device       |
Horizontal tab set |
Horizontal tab clear |
Clear all tabs     |
Lock keyboard      |
Unlock keyboard    |
                   |
CURSOR CONTROL COMMANDS |
-----------------------|-------------------------------------------------------
Read cursor position |
Cursor up          |
Cursor down        |
Cursor right       |
Cursor left        |
Home cursor        |
Position cursor    |
                   |
DISPLAY CONTROL COMMANDS |
------------------------|-------------------------------------------------------
Clear to end of page |
Clear to end of line |
Clear screen(to nulls) |
Underscore         |
Blink              |
Reverse video      |
Blank video(invisible) |
132 Column mode    |
80 Column mode     |
Next page          |
Previous page      |
Protect mode on    |
Protect mode off   |
                   |
EDITING COMMANDS   |
-------------------|-----------------------------------------------------------
Line insert        |
Line delete        |
Character insert   |
Character delete   |
                   |
ATTACHED PRINTER COMMANDS |
-------------------------|------------------------------------------------------
Print screen       |
Print on line(POL) on |
Print on line(POL) off |
Transparent print mode on |
Transparent print mode off|
===============================================================================
```

```
=================================================================================
VENDOR                       |
MODEL                        |
                             |
=============================|===================================================
NOTES:                       |
                             |
                             |
                             |
GENERAL COMMANDS             |
-----------------------------|--------------------------------------------------
Reset device                 |
Horizontal tab set           |
Horizontal tab clear         |
Clear all tabs               |
Lock keyboard                |
Unlock keyboard              |
                             |
CURSOR CONTROL COMMANDS       |
-----------------------------|--------------------------------------------------
Read cursor position         |
Cursor up                    |
Cursor down                  |
Cursor right                 |
Cursor left                  |
Home cursor                  |
Position cursor              |
                             |
DISPLAY CONTROL COMMANDS      |
-----------------------------|--------------------------------------------------
Clear to end of page         |
Clear to end of line         |
Clear screen(to nulls)       |
Underscore                   |
Blink                        |
Reverse video                |
Blank video(invisible)       |
132 Column mode              |
80 Column mode               |
Next page                    |
Previous page                |
Protect mode on              |
Protect mode off             |
                             |
EDITING COMMANDS             |
-----------------------------|--------------------------------------------------
Line insert                  |
Line delete                  |
Character insert             |
Character delete             |
                             |
ATTACHED PRINTER COMMANDS    |
-----------------------------|--------------------------------------------------
Print screen                 |
Print on line(POL) on        |
Print on line(POL) off       |
Transparent print mode on    |
Transparent print mode off   |
=================================================================================
```

```
===================================================================================
VENDOR                 |
MODEL                  |
                       |
===================================================================================
NOTES:                 |
                       |
                       |
                       |
                       |
GENERAL COMMANDS       |
-----------------------|-----------------------------------------------------------
Reset device           |
Horizontal tab set     |
Horizontal tab clear   |
Clear all tabs         |
Lock keyboard          |
Unlock keyboard        |
                       |
CURSOR CONTROL COMMANDS |
-----------------------|-----------------------------------------------------------
Read cursor position   |
Cursor up              |
Cursor down            |
Cursor right           |
Cursor left            |
Home cursor            |
Position cursor        |
                       |
DISPLAY CONTROL COMMANDS|
-----------------------|-----------------------------------------------------------
Clear to end of page   |
Clear to end of line   |
Clear screen(to nulls) |
Underscore             |
Blink                  |
Reverse video          |
Blank video(invisible) |
132 Column mode        |
80 Column mode         |
Next page              |
Previous page          |
Protect mode on        |
Protect mode off       |
                       |
EDITING COMMANDS       |
-----------------------|-----------------------------------------------------------
Line insert            |
Line delete            |
Character insert       |
Character delete       |
                       |
ATTACHED PRINTER COMMANDS|
-----------------------|-----------------------------------------------------------
Print screen           |
Print on line(POL) on  |
Print on line(POL) off |
Transparent print mode on |
Transparent print mode off|
===================================================================================
```

```
=====================================================================================
VENDOR                  |
MODEL                   |
                        |
                        |
========================|=============================================================
NOTES:                  |
                        |
                        |
                        |
GENERAL COMMANDS        |
------------------------|-------------------------------------------------------------
Reset device           |
Horizontal tab set     |
Horizontal tab clear   |
Clear all tabs         |
Lock keyboard          |
Unlock keyboard        |
                        |
CURSOR CONTROL COMMANDS |
------------------------|-------------------------------------------------------------
Read cursor position   |
Cursor up              |
Cursor down            |
Cursor right           |
Cursor left            |
Home cursor            |
Position cursor        |
                        |
DISPLAY CONTROL COMMANDS|
------------------------|-------------------------------------------------------------
Clear to end of page   |
Clear to end of line   |
Clear screen(to nulls) |
Underscore             |
Blink                  |
Reverse video          |
Blank video(invisible) |
132 Column mode        |
80 Column mode         |
Next page              |
Previous page          |
Protect mode on        |
Protect mode off       |
                        |
EDITING COMMANDS        |
------------------------|-------------------------------------------------------------
Line insert            |
Line delete            |
Character insert       |
Character delete       |
                        |
ATTACHED PRINTER COMMANDS|
------------------------|-------------------------------------------------------------
Print screen           |
Print on line(POL) on  |
Print on line(POL) off |
Transparent print mode on |
Transparent print mode off|
=====================================================================================
```

APPENDIX I. INTELLIGENT MODEM COMMANDS

With the advent of the intelligent modem, a set of modem commands has emerged. These commands are to provide the user, either directly or through communication software, with an ability to control communications with a remote system.

The Hayes Smartmodem series has established a "standard" command set for the industry. Other vendors offer their own commands, a duplication of the Hayes command set, or a superset/subset of the Hayes command set. Even as Hayes has announced new and faster modems, they have provided a superset of commands to the original "AT" command set. Vendors claim compatibility with this "AT" command set. This appendix summarizes the different commands sets offered for a variety of modems. Although many different commands are offered, the list provides the user with the more common modem capabilities.

The commands are summarized by arbitrarily set categories: answer, dialing, general, port, registers and options, tests, and user interface commands. If certain features were neglected, it was not intentional. The user should merely update this appendix with the new information. Blank command forms are provided at the end of the appendix, allowing the reader to keep an up-to-date list of commands necessary to operate intelligent modems.

MODEM VENDOR / Model	Anchor Automation Volksmodem 12	AT&T 2212C string mode	AT&T 2212C friendly mode	AT&T 4000 modem
NOTES:		string mode	string mode	
ANSWER COMMANDS				
Answer call w/o ring	ATA			
Auto answer	ATS0=1	ato7=y/n	o7=y/n	ATS0=X X=(0)-255
DIALING COMMANDS				
Blind dial/ext. result codes/busy detection				
Blind dial/ext. result codes/no busy det.				
Dial a number	ATDs (S=0..9)	atd(1-19)	d(1-19)	ATD #
Dial stored number				
List dial(multiple # dialing)				
List directories			l or l(1-19)	
No Blind dial/ext. result codes/no busy det.				
No Blind dial/ext.codes/busy detection				
Pause	,	,	,	,
Pulse dial	P	p	p	P
QUIT (exit dialer mode)	any key			
Redial last #		atr	r	
Redial(continuously)		atm	m	
Return to command state after dialing	;			;
Reverse mode(call "originate-only" modem)				R
Store directory entry			u(1-19)	
Touch-Tone dial	T	t	t	T
Wait for second dial tone				T
GENERAL COMMANDS				
Enter answer mode		atans	ans	ATA
Enter originate mode		atorig	orig	ATO
Enter talk mode		attalk	talk	
Exit Data mode		$:	$:	
Help command		n/a	h	AT$
Inactivity timer(hang-up)				
Long space disconnect disabled				
Long space disconnect enabled				
Off-hook				ATH1
Off-hook(special)	ATH1			
On-hook (Hang-up)	ATH0			ATH0
Prefix to commands	AT	at	(carriage return)	
Repeat last command	A/			A/
Reset modem(sets to default values)	ATZ	atod	od	ATZ
Resume Data mode		atdata	data	
Return to command mode(from online)	ATO0			+++
Return to on-line state				ATO
Return to on-line state & begin eq-retrain				
Transmitter off	ATC0			
Transmitter on	ATC1			

MODEM VENDOR Model	Anchor Automation Volksmodem 12	AT&T 2212C string mode	AT&T 2212C friendly mode	AT&T 4000 modem
PORT COMMANDS				
212A operation at 1200 bps(Bell mode)				
Asynchronous mode				
CCITT V.22 operation at 1200 bps				
Clear to send always on				
Clear to send(lead 5) tracks RTS(lead 4)				
DSR on according to EIA standard				
DSR on while onhook				
DSR(lead 6) always on				
DTR ON/OFF transition causes modem reset				
DTR delay				
DTR transition ON/OFF causes modem cmd state				
DTR(lead 20) signal ignored by modem				
DTR ON/OFF transition causes on-hook, modem to enter command state, and no auto- answer until DTR turned back on.				
Data carrier detect on while on-hook				
Data carrier detect tracks actual carrier				
Data carrier detect(lead 8) always on				
External timing enabled				
Flow control off	ATF1		f0	
Flow control on	ATF0		f1	
Full-duplex				
Half duplex				
Internal timing enabled				
RJ-11/RJ-41S/RJ-45S Telephone jack				
RJ-12/RJ-13 Telephone jack				
RTS/CTS delay				
Slave timing enabled				
Sync Mode 1(sync/async)				
Sync Mode 2 (stored number dial)				
Sync Mode 3 (manual dial)				
REGISTERS & OPTIONS				
Register set	ATSr=n (r=0..16) (n=0..255)	ato(1-26)=	o(1-26)=	
Register read	ATSr? r=REGISTER (r=0..16)		o,o(1-26)	ATSr? r=REGISTER
10 bit character		ato17=y	o17=y	
1800-Hz preamble		ato10=n/y	o10=n/y	
2100-Hz preamble		ato9=n/y	o9=n/y	
9 bit character		ato17=n	o17=n	
Answer on ring #	ATS0=0 (0-255 rings)	ato20=N (N= 1-99)	o20=N (N=1-99)	ATS1=X X=(0)-255
Answertone = 2225-Hz		ato14=n	o14=n	
Backspace character	ATS5=08 (0-32, 127 ASCII)			ATS5=8 (0-32 ASCII)
Cancel character		ato24=0 (any)	o24=0 (any)	ATS2=43 (0-95 ASCII)
Carriage Return	ATS3=13 (0-127 ASCII)			ATS3=13 (0-95 ASCII)

MODEM VENDOR / Model	Anchor Automation Volksmodem 12	AT&T 2212C string mode	AT&T 2212C friendly mode	AT&T 4000 modem
Carrier detect response time				
Character delete	ATS2=43 (0-127 ASCII)	ato23=^H (any)	o23=^H (any)	
Comma (pause)		ato6=y/n	o6=y/n	ATS8=2 (0-255 sec's)
Common CTS-RLSD				
DTMF dialing speed				
Dialing delay				ATS6=2 (2-255 sec's)
Display active profile				
Drop call on timeout		ato18=n/y	o18=n/y	
Enable speed conversion(match DTE)				
Escape character		ato26=$:(any pair)	o26=$:(any pair)	
Escape code guard time				ATS12=50 (0-255 1/50sec)
Exit DATA mode		ato1=y/n	o1=y/n	
Far end sends first		ato16=n/y	o16=n/y	
Flow control		ato8=y/n	o8=n/y	
High speed only				
Immediate dial from dir X		ato21=X (X=0,0-19)	o21=X (X=0,0-19)	
Line feed character	ATS4=10 (0-127 ASCII)			ATS4=10 (0-95 ASCII)
Local echo		ato15=y/n	o15=y/n	
Loss of carrier disconnect		ato3=y/n	o3=y/n	
Lost carrier to hang-up delay				ATS10=7 (1-255)
Prompt character		ato22=: (any)	o22=: (any)	
Received space disconnect		ato4=y/n	o4=y/n	
Responds to Remote Loop		ato2=y/n	o2=y/n	
Ring Indicator on until disconnect		ato11=n/y	o11=n/y	
Ring count	ATS1=00 (0-255 rings)			
Select factory profile		ato25=$B(any pair)	o25=$B(any pair)	
Send break		ato13=n/y	o13=n/y	
Send break enable		ato5=y/n	o5=y/n	
Send space disconnect				
Set default profile				
Set disconnect character				
Set halt character(for operator intervention)				
Set terminator(marks end of number/login)				
Set password				
Set sequence of multiple # dialing				
Set wait char(delay prior to login after DCD)				
Skip header message		ato19=n/y	o19=n/y	
Transparent data mode		ato12=n/y	o12=n/y	
UM answertone		ato14=y	o14=y	
Wait for carrier				ATS7=30 (1-255 sec's)
Write configurations to memory				

MODEM VENDOR Model	Anchor Automation Volksmodem 12	AT&T 2212C string mode	AT&T 2212C friendly mode	AT&T 4000 modem
TESTS				
Analog loopback test		atll	ll	AT&T1
Cancel all tests		atct	ct	AT&T0
Denies remote digital loopback request				AT&T5
Digital loop test		atdl	dl	AT&T4
Grants remote digital loopback request				AT&T6
Initiate RDL test		atrl	rl	
Perform checksum & return status message	ATI1			ATI1
Perform checksum 7 return checksum				
Remote loop test				
Request firmware revision #	ATI0			ATI0
Request product code				
Self-test		atst	st	
Test timer				ATS18=0 (0-255 sec)
Touchtone frequency test				
USER INTERFACE				
Cancel character		@	@	
Change cancel character		atcx x=new	cx x=new	
Delete character(backspace)		backspace	backspace	backspace
Echo characters in command modem(on)	ATE1	ate1	e1	ATE1
Echo characters(off)	ATE0	ate0	e0	ATE0
Escape code	+++			
Flash				
High speaker volume				
Low speaker volume				
Medium speaker volume				
Result code set(basic)	ATX0			ATX0
Result code set(extended)	ATX1			ATX1
Result code set(full)				
Result codes not sent	ATQ1			ATQ1
Result codes sent	ATQ0			ATQ0
Result codes transmitted as digits	ATV0			ATV0
Result codes transmitted as words	ATV1			ATV1
Send break		$B		$B
Speaker off always	ATM0			ATM0
Speaker on always	ATM2			ATM2
Speaker on until carrier detected	ATM1			ATM1
Spkr on until carr-det except during dialing				
Wait for silence(quiet answer)				

	FastComm 9600/2496/2400 modems	Hayes Smartmodem 300	Hayes Smartmodem 1200	Hayes Smartmodem 2400
NOTES:				
ANSWER COMMANDS				
Answer call w/o ring	ATA	ATA	ATA	ATA
Auto answer	ATS0=1	ATS0=1	ATS0=1	ATS0=1
DIALING COMMANDS				
Blind dial/ext. result codes/busy detection				ATX3
Blind dial/ext. result codes/no busy det.				ATX1
Dial a number	ATDs (S=0..9)	ATDs (S=0..9)	ATDs (S=0..9)	ATDs (S=0..9)
List dial(multiple # dialing)				ATDS=n (n=0-3)
List directories				
No Blind dial/ext. result codes/no busy det.				ATX2
No Blind dial/ext.codes/busy detection				ATX4
Pause		,	,	,
Pulse dial	P	P	P	P
QUIT (exit dialer mode)				any key
Redial last #				
Redial(continuously)				
Return to command state after dialing		;	;	;
Reverse mode(call "originate-only" modem)		R	R	R
Store directory entry				AT&Zn=# (n=0-3, #=PHONE#)
Touch-Tone dial	T	T	T	T
Wait for second dial tone		,	,	,
GENERAL COMMANDS				
Enter answer mode				
Enter originate mode				
Enter talk mode				
Exit Data mode				
Help command				
Inactivity timer(hang-up)				
Long space disconnect disabled				ATY0
Long space disconnect enabled				ATY1
Off-hook	ATH1	ATH1	ATH1	ATH1
Off-hook(special)		ATH2	ATH2	
On-hook (Hang-up)	ATH0	ATH0	ATH0	ATH0
Prefix to commands	AT	AT	AT	AT
Repeat last command	A/	A/	A/	A/
Reset modem(sets to default values)	ATZ	ATZ	ATZ	ATZ
Resume Data mode				
Return to command mode(from online)				
Return to on-line state	ATO0	ATO	ATO0	ATO0
Return to on-line state & begin eq-retrain				ATO1
Transmitter off	ATC0	ATC0	ATC0	ATC0
Transmitter on	ATC1	ATC1	ATC1	ATC1

MODEM VENDOR / Model

Model	FastComm 9600/2496/2400 modems	Hayes Smartmodem 300	Hayes Smartmodem 1200	Hayes Smartmodem 2400
PORT COMMANDS				
212A operation at 1200 bps(Bell mode)				ATB1
Asynchronous mode				AT&M0
CCITT V.22 operation at 1200 bps				ATB
Clear to send always on				AT&R1
Clear to send(lead 5) tracks RTS(lead 4)				AT&R0
DSR on according to EIA standard	AT#LMN			AT&S1
DSR on while onhook				
DSR(lead 6) always on	AT#LMO			AT&S0
DTR ON/OFF transition causes modem reset				AT&D3
DTR delay				ATS25=05 (0-255 1/100sec)
DTR transition ON/OFF causes modem cmd state				AT&D1
DTR(lead 20) signal ignored by modem	AT#LDI			AT&D0
DTR ON/OFF transition causes on-hook, modem to enter command state, and no auto-answer until DTR turned back on.				AT&D2
Data carrier detect on while on-hook				
Data carrier detect tracks actual carrier	AT#LCN			AT&C1
Data carrier detect(lead 8) always on	AT#LCO			AT&C0
External timing enabled				AT&X1
Flow control off				
Flow control on				
Full-duplex	ATF1	ATF1	ATF1	ATF1
Half duplex	ATF0	ATF0	ATF0	ATF0
Internal timing enabled				AT&X0
RJ-11/RJ-41S/RJ-45S Telephone jack				AT&J0
RJ-12/RJ-13 Telephone jack				AT&J1
RTS/CTS delay				ATS26=01 (0-255 1/100sec)
Slave timing enabled				AT&X2
Sync Mode 1(sync/async)				AT&M1
Sync Mode 2 (stored number dial)				AT&M2
Sync Mode 3 (manual dial)				AT&M3
REGISTERS & OPTIONS				
Register set	ATSr=n (r=0..16) (n=0..255)	ATSr=n (r=0..16) (n=0..255)	ATSr=n (r=0..16) (n=0..255)	ATSr=n (r=0..16) (n=0..255)
Register read	ATSr? r=REGISTER (r=0..16)	ATSr? r=REGISTER (r=0..16)	ATSr? r=REGISTER (r=0..16)	ATSr? r=REGISTER (r=0..16)
10 bit character				
1800-Hz preamble				
2100-Hz preamble				
9 bit character				
Answer on ring #	ATS0=0 (0-255 rings)	ATS0=0 (0-255 rings)	ATS0=0 (0-255 rings)	ATS0=0 (0-255 rings)
Answertone = 2225-Hz				
Backspace character	ATS5=08 (0-32, 127 ASCII)	ATS5=08 (0-32, 127 ASCII)	ATS5=08 (0-32, 127 ASCII)	ATS5=08 (0-32, 127 ASCII)
Cancel character				
Carriage Return	ATS3=13 (0-127 ASCII)	ATS3=13 (0-127 ASCII)	ATS3=13 (0-127 ASCII)	ATS3=13 (0-127 ASCII)

REGISTERS & OPTIONS continued

MODEM VENDOR Model	FastComm 9600/2496/2400 modems	Hayes Smartmodem 300	Hayes Smartmodem 1200	Hayes Smartmodem 2400
Carrier detect response time	ATS9=06 (1-255 1/10secs)	ATS9=06 (1-255 1/10secs)	ATS9=06 (1-255 1/10secs)	ATS9=06 (1-255 1/10secs)
Character delete				
Comma (pause)	ATS8=2 (0-255secs)	ATS8=2 (0-255secs)	ATS8=2 (0-255secs)	ATS8=2 (0-255secs)
Common CTS-RLSD				
DTMF dialing speed	ATS11=95 (50-255 msec)	ATS11=95 (50-255 msec)	ATS11=95 (50-255 msec)	ATS11=95 (50-255 msec)
Dialing delay	ATS6=02 (0-255sec)	ATS6=02 (0-255sec)	ATS6=02 (0-255sec)	ATS6=02 (0-255sec)
Display active profile	AT?			AT&V
Drop call on timeout				
Enable speed conversion(match DTE)				
Escape character	ATS2=43 (0-127 ASCII)	ATS2=43 (0-127 ASCII)	ATS2=43 (0-127 ASCII)	ATS2=43 (0-127 ASCII)
Escape code guard time	ATS12=50 (0-255 1/50sec)	ATS12=50 (0-255 1/50sec)	ATS12=50 (0-255 1/50sec)	ATS12=50 (0-255 1/50sec)
Exit DATA mode				
Far end sends first				
Flow control	AT#L?			
High speed only				
Immediate dial from dir X				
Line feed character	ATS4=10 (0-127 ASCII)	ATS4=10 (0-127 ASCII)	ATS4=10 (0-127 ASCII)	ATS4=10 (0-127 ASCII)
Local echo				
Loss of carrier disconnect				
Lost carrier to hang-up delay	ATS10=14 (1-255 1/10secs)	ATS10=14 (1-255 1/10secs)	ATS10=14 (1-255 1/10secs)	ATS10=14 (1-255 1/10secs)
Prompt character				
Received space disconnect				
Responds to Remote Loop				
Ring Indicator on until disconnect				
Ring count	ATS1=00 (0-255 rings)	ATS1=00 (0-255 rings)	ATS1=00 (0-255 rings)	ATS1=00 (0-255 rings)
Select factory profile	AT#F			AT&F
Send break				
Send break enable				
Send space disconnect				
Set default profile		ATZ	ATZ	AT&Yn (n=0-1)
Set disconnect character				
Set halt character(for operator intervention)				
Set terminator(marks end of number/login)				
Set password				
Set sequence of multiple # dialing				
Set wait char(delay prior to login after DCD)				
Skip header message				
Transparent data mode				
UM answertone				
Wait for carrier	ATS7=30 (1-30 secs)	ATS7=30 (1-30 secs)	ATS7=30 (1-30 secs)	ATS7=30 (1-30 secs)
Write configurations to memory	AT#W			AT&Wn (n=0-1)

MODEM VENDOR / Model	FastComm 9600/2496/2400 modems	Hayes Smartmodem 300	Hayes Smartmodem 1200	Hayes Smartmodem 2400
TESTS				
Analog loopback test		ATS16=1	ATS16=1	AT&T1
Cancel all tests		ATS16=0	ATS16=0	AT&T0
Denies remote digital loopback request				AT&T5
Digital loop test				AT&T3
Grants remote digital loopback request				AT&T4
Initiate RDL test				AT&T6
Perform checksum & return status message	ATI2			ATI2
Perform checksum 7 return checksum	ATI1			ATI1
Remote loop test				
Request firmware revision #			ATI1	
Request product code	ATI0		ATI0	ATI0
Self-test				AT&T8
Test timer				ATS18=00 (0-255)
Touchtone frequency test				
USER INTERFACE				
Cancel character				
Change cancel character				
Delete character(backspace)				
Echo characters in command modem(on)	ATE1	ATE1	ATE1	ATE1
Echo characters(off)	ATE0	ATE0	ATE0	ATE0
Escape code		+++	+++	+++
Flash				!
High speaker volume				ATL3
Low speaker volume				ATL1
Medium speaker volume				ATL2
Result code set(basic)	ATX0		ATX0	ATX0
Result code set(extended)	ATX1		ATX1	ATX1
Result code set(full)	ATX2			
Result codes not sent	ATQ1	ATQ1	ATQ1	ATQ1
Result codes sent	ATQ0	ATQ0	ATQ0	ATQ0
Result codes transmitted as digits	ATV0	ATV0	ATV0	ATV0
Result codes transmitted as words	ATV1	ATV1	ATV1	ATV1
Send break				
Speaker off always	ATM0	ATM0	ATM0	ATM0
Speaker on always	ATM2	ATM2	ATM2	ATM2
Speaker on until carrier detected	ATM1	ATM1	ATM1	ATM1
Spkr on until carr-det except during dialing	ATM3			ATM3
Wait for silence(quiet answer)				@

MODEM VENDOR / Model	Microcom AX/1200 & AX/2400 modems	Microcom AX/1200 & AX/2400 modems	MultiTech Multimodem 224/224E	MultiTech Multimodem 300/1200
NOTES:	SX Mode-Type several 4's to get in command mode	AT mode		RETURN key executes most commands
ANSWER COMMANDS				
Answer call w/o ring	A	ATA	ATA	ATA
Auto answer	AAON		ATS0=1	
DIALING COMMANDS				
Blind dial/ext. result codes/busy detection		ATX3	ATB0	ATB0
Blind dial/ext. result codes/no busy det.		ATX1		
Dial a number	D# (#=phone no.)	ATD #	ATDs (S=0..9)	ATDs (S=0..9)
Dial stored number	S or D/n (n=1-9)	ATD/n (n=1-9)	ATNn (n=1-9)	ATNd (d=0-9)
List dial(multiple # dialing)	Nn (n=1-9)	Nn (n=1-9)	ATNnNn (n=1-9)	ATNdNe (d/e = 1-9)
List directories	RP	AT\F	ATL	ATL
No Blind dial/ext. result codes/no busy det.		ATX2	ATB1	ATB1
No Blind dial/ext.codes/busy detection		ATX4		
Pause	,	,	,	
Pulse dial	P	P	P	P
QUIT (exit dialer mode)	DL	ATDL		
Redial last #	RDL or RD# or RD/n (n=1-9)		ATA: or :	A:
Redial(continuously)	;	;	;	; (at end of dial command)
Return to command state after dialing	R	R	R	R
Reverse mode(call "originate-only" modem)		AT\Pn # (n=1-9)	AT#Nn (n=1-9)	ATD#Nd (#=phone,d=0-9)
Store directory entry	WPn # (n=1-36)			
Touch-Tone dial	T	T	T	T
Wait for second dial tone	W	W	W	,
GENERAL COMMANDS				
Enter answer mode				
Enter originate mode				
Enter talk mode				
Exit Data mode		AT\T		
Help command	HELP or RS3		$H	AT$HN (n=1-4)
Inactivity timer(hang-up)	SITn (0-90min)			
Long space disconnect disabled				
Long space disconnect enabled				
Off-hook	H	ATH	ATH1	ATH1
Off-hook(special)				
On-hook (Hang-up)			ATH0	ATH0
Prefix to commands		AT	AT	AT
Repeat last command		A/	A/	A/
Reset modem(sets to default values)	INIT	AT\M or ATZ	ATZ	ATZ
Resume Data mode				
Return to command mode(from online)				
Return to on-line state	E	ATO0	ATO0	ATO
Return to on-line state & begin eq-retrain	ER	ATO1		
Transmitter off				ATC0
Transmitter on				ATC1

MODEM VENDOR / Model	Microcom AX/1200 & AX/2400 modems	Microcom AX/1200 & AX/2400 modems	MultiTech Multimodem 224/224E	MultiTech Multimodem 300/1200
PORT COMMANDS				
212A operation at 1200 bps(Bell mode)	BELLON	ATB1		
Asynchronous mode	SNC0	AT&M0	AT&M0	AT&V0
CCITT V.22 operation at 1200 bps	BELLOFF	ATB		AT&V1
Clear to send always on	S1D0	AT/D0	AT&R1	AT&R1
Clear to send(lead 5) tracks RTS(lead 4)	CRTS0	AT&R0	AT&R0	AT&R0
DSR on according to EIA standard	S1D1	AT/D1		
DSR on while onhook	S1D1	AT/D1		
DSR(lead 6) always on	S1D0	AT/D0		
DTR ON/OFF transition causes modem reset	SD3	AT&D3		
DTR delay	ATS25=05 (0-255 1/100sec)	ATS25=05 (0-255 1/100sec)	ATS25=0 (0-255 100msec)	
DTR transition ON/OFF causes modem cmd state	SD1	AT&D1		
DTR(lead 20) signal ignored by modem	SD0	AT&D0	ATS18=1	
DTR ON/OFF transition causes on-hook, modem		AT&D2	ATS18=0	
to enter command state, and no auto-answer until DTR turned back on.				
Data carrier detect on while on-hook	S1C2	AT&C2		
Data carrier detect tracks actual carrier	S1C1	AT&C1	AT&C1	
Data carrier detect(lead 8) always on	S1C0	AT&C0	AT&C0	
External timing enabled				
Flow control off		AT\G0		
Flow control on		AT\G1		
Full-duplex		AT\E1	ATF1	ATF1
Half duplex		AT\E0	ATF0	ATF0
Internal timing enabled				
RJ-11/RJ-41S/RJ-45S Telephone jack				
RJ-12/RJ-13 Telephone jack				
RTS/CTS delay	ATS26=01 (0-255 1/100sec)	ATS26=01 (0-255 1/100sec)		
Slave timing enabled				
Sync Mode 1(sync/async)	SNC1	AT&M1	AT&M1	
Sync Mode 2 (stored number dial)	SNC2	AT&M2		
Sync Mode 3 (manual dial)	SNC3	AT&M3		
REGISTERS & OPTIONS				
Register set	Sn=x (n=register#) (x=value)		ATSr=n (r=0..16) (n=0..255)	ATSr=n (r=0..16) (n=0..255)
Register read	Sn? n=REGISTER (n=0..27)	ATSr? r=REGISTER (r=0..16)	ATSr? r=REGISTER (r=0..16)	ATSr? r=REGISTER (r=0..16)
10 bit character				
1800-Hz preamble				
2100-Hz preamble				
9 bit character				
Answer on ring #	ATS0=0 (0-255 rings)	ATS0=0 (0-255 rings)	ATS0=0 (0-255 rings)	
Answertone = 2225-Hz				
Backspace character	ATS5=08 (0-32, 127 ASCII)	ATS5=08 (0-32, 127 ASCII)	ATS5=08 (0-32, 127 ASCII)	
Cancel character				
Carriage Return	ATS3=13 (0-127 ASCII)	ATS3=13 (0-127 ASCII)	ATS3=13 (0-127 ASCII)	

REGISTERS & OPTIONS continued

MODEM VENDOR / Model	Microcom AX/1200 & AX/2400 modems	Microcom AX/1200 & AX/2400 modems	MultiTech Multimodem 224/224E	MultiTech Multimodem 300/1200
Carrier detect response time	ATS9=06 (1-255 1/10secs)	ATS9=06 (1-255 1/10secs)	ATS9=06 (1-255 1/10secs)	
Character delete				
Comma (pause)	ATS8=2 (0-255secs)	ATS8=2 (0-255secs)	ATS8=2 (0-255secs)	
Common CTS-RLSD	S1D2			
DTMF dialing speed			ATS11=95 (50-255 msec)	
Dialing delay	SPTn (n=0-255sec)	ATS6=02 (0-255sec)	ATS6=02 (0-255sec)	
Display active profile	REGS	AT\S or AT%R	ATL5	ATL5
Drop call on timeout				
Enable speed conversion(match DTE)				
Escape character	ATS2=43 (0-127 ASCII)	ATS2=43 (0-127 ASCII)	ATS2=43 (0-127 ASCII)	
Escape code guard time	ATS12=50 (0-255 1/50sec)	ATS12=50 (0-255 1/50sec)	ATS12=50 (0-255 1/50sec)	
Exit DATA mode				
Far end sends first				
Flow control	SF11			
High speed only				
Immediate dial from dir X				
Line feed character	ATS4=10 (0-127 ASCII)	ATS4=10 (0-127 ASCII)	ATS4=10 (0-127 ASCII)	
Local echo				
Loss of carrier disconnect				
Lost carrier to hang-up delay	ATS10=14 (1-255 1/10secs)	ATS10=14 (1-255 1/10secs)	ATS10=14 (1-255 1/10secs)	
Prompt character				
Received space disconnect				
Responds to Remote Loop				
Ring Indicator on until disconnect	S1R0	AT\R0		
Ring count	ATS1=00 (0-255 rings)	ATS1=00 (0-255 rings)	ATS1=00 (0-255 rings)	
Select factory profile		AT&F	AT&F	AT&F
Send break				
Send break enable				
Send space disconnect				
Set default profile				
Set disconnect character	SE/c (c=character)			
Set halt character(for operator intervention)				
Set terminator(marks end of number/login)				
Set password				
Set sequence of multiple # dialing				
Set wait char(delay prior to login after DCD)				
Skip header message				
Transparent data mode				
UM answertone				
Wait for carrier	ATS7=30 (1-30 secs)	ATS7=30 (1-30 secs)	ATS7=30 (1-30 secs)	
Write configurations to memory		AT&W	AT&W	AT&W0

MODEM VENDOR Model	Microcom AX/1200 & AX/2400 modems	Microcom AX/1200 & AX/2400 modems	Multitech Multimodem 224/224E	Multitech Multimodem 300/1200
TESTS				
Analog loopback test	^A or XA	AT&T1	ATU0	ATU0
Cancel all tests	ET	AT&T0	ATS16=0	
Denies remote digital loopback request	RLBOFF	AT&T5	AT&T5	AT&T5
Digital loop test	^D OR XL	AT&T3	ATU3	ATU3
Grants remote digital loopback request	RLBON	AT&T4	AT&T4	AT&T4
Initiate RDL test	RLT or XD# or XD/n (n=1-9)	AT&T6	ATU2	ATU2
Perform checksum & return status message		ATI2		
Perform checksum 7 return checksum		ATI1		
Remote loop test				
Request firmware revision #	ID	ATI0	ATI1	ATI2
Request product code	YA OR YD (A=AL, D=RDL)	AT&T8	ATI0	ATI1
Self-test	ATS18=00 (0-255)	ATS18=00 (0-255)		ATI0
Test timer				
Touchtone frequency test				
USER INTERFACE				
Cancel character				
Change cancel character				
Delete character(backspace)				
Echo characters in command modem(on)	SDEON	ATE1	ATE1	ATE1
Echo characters(off)	SDEOFF	ATE0	ATE0	ATE0
Escape code	!	!	+++	+++
Flash				
High speaker volume				
Low speaker volume				
Medium speaker volume				
Result code set(basic)			ATX0	ATX0
Result code set(extended)			ATX1	ATX1
Result code set(full)				
Result codes not sent	SCENO	ATQ1	ATQ1	ATQ1
Result codes sent	SCEOFF	ATQ0	ATQ0	ATQ0
Result codes transmitted as digits		ATV0	ATV0	ATV0
Result codes transmitted as words		ATV1	ATV1	ATV1
Send break	Bn (n=1-9, 100 msec)	AT/Bn (n=1-9 100msec)		
Speaker off always	SA2	ATM0	ATM0	ATM0
Speaker on always	SA1	ATM2	ATM2	ATM2
Speaker on until carrier detected	SA0	ATM1	ATM1	ATM1
Spkr on until carr-det except during dialing	SA3	ATM3		
Wait for silence(quiet answer)	@	@		

MODEM VENDOR / Model	NEC AUTO-DIAL/LOGIN N1220/30HN	NEC AUTO-DIAL/LOGIN N1220/30HN	NEC N2420/30 modem	NEC N2420/30 modem
NOTES:	NEC commands	AT Mode Enter "G" from main menu	NEC commands	"AT" Mode Enter "G"

ANSWER COMMANDS

	N1220/30HN (NEC commands)	N1220/30HN (AT Mode)	N2420/30 (NEC commands)	N2420/30 (AT Mode)
Answer call w/o ring				
Auto answer		ATA		ATA

DIALING COMMANDS

	N1220/30HN (NEC commands)	N1220/30HN (AT Mode)	N2420/30 (NEC commands)	N2420/30 (AT Mode)
Blind dial/ext. result codes/busy detection				
Blind dial/ext. result codes/no busy det.				
Dial a number	K# (# is number)	ATDs (S=0..9)	K# (# is number)	ATDs (S=0..9)
Dial stored number	M# (#=1-12)		M# (#=1-12)	
List dial(multiple # dialing)	L		L	
List directories	D		D	
No Blind dial/ext. result codes/no busy det.				
No Blind dial/ext.codes/busy detection				
Pause		´		´
Pulse dial	S (P)	P	S (P)	P
QUIT (exit dialer mode)	Q (Y)		Q (Y)	
Redial last #	A		A	
Redial(continuously)				
Return to command state after dialing		;		;
Reverse mode(call "originate-only" modem)	I # (# is entry to store)		I # (# is number)	I # (# is the entry to store)
Store directory entry	S (T)		S (T)	S (T)
Touch-Tone dial	T	T		T
Wait for second dial tone	,	,		,

GENERAL COMMANDS

	N1220/30HN (NEC commands)	N1220/30HN (AT Mode)	N2420/30 (NEC commands)	N2420/30 (AT Mode)
Enter answer mode				
Enter originate mode				
Enter talk mode				
Exit Data mode				
Help command	H		H	
Inactivity timer(hang-up)				
Long space disconnect disabled				
Long space disconnect enabled				
Off-hook		´		´
Off-hook(special)		ATH1		ATH1
On-hook (Hang-up)		ATH0		ATH0
Prefix to commands		AT		AT
Repeat last command		A/		A/
Reset modem(sets to default values)		ATZ		ATZ
Resume Data mode				
Return to command mode(from online)				
Return to on-line state				
Return to on-line state & begin eq-retrain				
Transmitter off		ATO0		ATO0
Transmitter on				

MODEM VENDOR Model	NEC AUTO-DIAL/LOGIN N1220/30HN	NEC AUTO-DIAL/LOGIN N1220/30HN	NEC N2420/30 modem	NEC N2420/30 modem
PORT COMMANDS				
212A operation at 1200 bps(Bell mode)				
Asynchronous mode		+++		+++
CCITT V.22 operation at 1200 bps				
Clear to send always on		;		;
Clear to send(lead 5) tracks RTS(lead 4)				
DSR on according to EIA standard				
DSR on while onhook				
DSR(lead 6) always on				
DTR delay				
DTR ON/OFF transition causes modem reset				
DTR transition ON/OFF causes modem cmd state				
DTR(lead 20) signal ignored by modem				
DTR ON/OFF transition causes on-hook, modem to enter command state, and no auto-answer until DTR turned back on.				
Data carrier detect on while on-hook				
Data carrier detect tracks actual carrier				
Data carrier detect(lead 8) always on				
External timing enabled				
Flow control off				
Flow control on				
Full-duplex	F (Y)	ATF1	F (Y)	ATF1
Half-duplex	F (N)	ATF0	F (N)	ATF0
Internal timing enabled				
RJ-11/RJ-41S/RJ-45S Telephone jack				
RJ-12/RJ-13 Telephone jack				
RTS/CTS delay				
Slave timing enabled				
Sync Mode 1(sync/async)				
Sync Mode 2 (stored number dial)				
Sync Mode 3 (manual dial)				
REGISTERS & OPTIONS				
Register set		ATSr=n (r=0..16) (n=0..255)		ATSr=n (r=0..16) (n=0..255)
Register read		ATSr? r=REGISTER (r=0..16)		ATSr? r=REGISTER (r=0..16)
10 bit character				
1800-Hz preamble				
2100-Hz preamble				
9 bit character				
Answer on ring #		ATS0=0 (0-255 rings)		ATS0=0 (0-255 rings)
Answertone = 2225-Hz				
Backspace character		ATS5=08 (0-32, 127 ASCII)		ATS5=08 (0-32, 127 ASCII)
Cancel character				
Carriage Return		ATS3=13 (0-127 ASCII)		ATS3=13 (0-127 ASCII)

REGISTERS & OPTIONS continued

MODEM VENDOR / Model	NEC AUTO-DIAL/LOGIN N1220/30HN	NEC N2420/30 modem
Carrier detect response time	ATS9=06 (1-255 1/10secs)	ATS9=06 (1-255 1/10secs)
Character delete		
Comma (pause)	ATS8=2 (0-255secs)	ATS8=2 (0-255secs)
Common CTS-RLSD		
DTMF dialing speed	ATS11=95 (50-255 msec)	ATS11=95 (50-255 msec)
Dialing delay	ATS6=02 (0-255sec)	ATS6=02 (0-255sec)
Display active profile		
Drop call on timeout		
Enable speed conversion(match DTE)		
Escape character	ATS2=43 (0-127 ASCII)	ATS2=43 (0-127 ASCII)
Escape code guard time	ATS12=50 (0-255 1/50sec)	ATS12=50 (0-255 1/50sec)
Exit DATA mode		
Far end sends first		
Flow control		
High speed only		
Immediate dial from dir X		
Line feed character	ATS4=10 (0-127 ASCII)	ATS4=10 (0-127 ASCII)
Local echo		
Loss of carrier disconnect		
Lost carrier to hang-up delay	ATS10=14 (1-255 1/10secs)	ATS10=14 (1-255 1/10secs)
Prompt character		
Received space disconnect		
Responds to Remote Loop		
Ring Indicator on until disconnect		
Ring count	ATS1=00 (0-255 rings)	ATS1=00 (0-255 rings)
Select factory profile		
Send break		
Send break enable		
Send space disconnect		
Set default profile		
Set disconnect character	I D (& up to 7 chars)	I D (& up to 7 chars)
Set halt character(for operator intervention)	I H (& any char)	I H (& any char)
Set terminator(marks end of number/login)	I T (& any char)	I T (& any char)
Set password	I P (& up to 7 char)	I P (& up to 7 char)
Set sequence of multiple # dialing	I L (& #, #, #)	I L (& #, #, #)
Set wait char(delay prior to login after DCD)	I W (& any char)	I W (& any char)
Skip header message		
Transparent data mode		
UM answertone		
Wait for carrier	ATS7=30 (1-30 secs)	ATS7=30 (1-30 secs)
Write configurations to memory		

MODEM VENDOR Model	NEC AUTO-DIAL/LOGIN N1220/30HN	NEC AUTO-DIAL/LOGIN N1220/30HN	NEC N2420/30 modem	NEC N2420/30 modem
TESTS				
Analog loopback test		ATS16=1		ATS16=1
Cancel all tests		ATS16=0		ATS16=0
Denies remote digital loopback request				
Digital loop test				
Grants remote digital loopback request				
Initiate RDL test				
Perform checksum & return status message				
Perform checksum 7 return checksum				
Remote loop test				
Request firmware revision #				
Request product code		ATIO		ATIO
Self-test				
Test timer				
Touchtone frequency test		ATS16=2		ATS16=2
USER INTERFACE				
Cancel character				
Change cancel character				
Delete character(backspace)				
Echo characters in command modem(on)	E (Y)	ATE1	E (Y)	ATE1
Echo characters(off)	E (N)	ATE0	E (N)	ATE0
Escape code		+++		+++
Flash				
High speaker volume				
Low speaker volume				
Medium speaker volume				
Result code set(basic)		ATX0		ATX0
Result code set(extended)		ATX1		ATX1
Result code set(full)				
Result codes not sent		ATQ1		ATQ1
Result codes sent		ATQ0		ATQ0
Result codes transmitted as digits		ATV0		ATV0
Result codes transmitted as words		ATV1		ATV1
Send break				
Speaker off always		ATM0		ATM0
Speaker on always		ATM2		ATM2
Speaker on until carrier detected		ATM1		ATM1
Spkr on until carr-det except during dialing				
Wait for silence(quiet answer)				

MODEM VENDOR Model	Penril CADET 1200	Penril DataComm CADET 2400 modem	Penril DataComm PACER 2400 modem	Prentice P-2122X modem
NOTES:				Commands are preceded with AT and trailed by RETURN
ANSWER COMMANDS				
Answer call w/o ring	ATA	ATA	ATA	ATA
Auto answer	ATS0=1			
DIALING COMMANDS				
Blind dial/ext. result codes/busy detection				
Blind dial/ext. result codes/no busy det.				
Dial a number	ATDs (S=0..9)	ATDs (S=0..9)	ATDs (S=0..9)	ATDs (S=0..9)
Dial stored number				
List dial(multiple # dialing)				
List directories				
No Blind dial/ext. result codes/no busy det.				
No Blind dial/ext.codes/busy detection				
Pause	,	,	,	,
Pulse dial	P	P	P	P
QUIT (exit dialer mode)				
Redial last #				
Redial(continuously)				
Return to command state after dialing	;	;	;	;
Reverse mode(call "originate-only" modem)	R	R	R	R
Store directory entry				
Touch-Tone dial	T	T	T	T
Wait for second dial tone	W			
GENERAL COMMANDS				
Enter answer mode				
Enter originate mode				
Enter talk mode				
Exit Data mode				
Help command				
Inactivity timer(hang-up)				
Long space disconnect disabled				
Long space disconnect enabled				
Off-hook	ATH1	ATH1	ATH1	ATH1
Off-hook(special)	ATH2			
On-hook (Hang-up)	ATH0	ATH0	ATH0	ATH0
Prefix to commands	AT	AT	AT	AT
Repeat last command	ATA/	A/	A/	
Reset modem(sets to default values)	ATZ			ATZ
Resume Data mode				ATO
Return to command mode(from online)				
Return to on-line state	ATO	ATO	ATO	ATO0
Return to on-line state & begin eq-retrain				
Transmitter off	ATC0			
Transmitter on	ATC1			

MODEM VENDOR Model	Penril CADET 1200	Penril DataComm CADET 2400 modem	Penril DataComm PACER 2400 modem	Prentice P-2122X modem
PORT COMMANDS				
212A operation at 1200 bps(Bell mode)				ATS18=1
Asynchronous mode				
CCITT V.22 operation at 1200 bps				ATS18=2
Clear to send always on				
Clear to send(lead 5) tracks RTS(lead 4)				
DSR on according to EIA standard				ATS18=0
DSR on while onhook				
DSR(lead 6) always on				ATS18=2
DTR ON/OFF transition causes modem reset				
DTR delay				
DTR transition ON/OFF causes modem cmd state				
DTR(lead 20) signal ignored by modem				
DTR ON/OFF transition causes on-hook, modem to enter command state, and no auto-answer until DTR turned back on.				
Data carrier detect on while on-hook				
Data carrier detect tracks actual carrier				ATS18=0
Data carrier detect(lead 8) always on				ATS18=2
External timing enabled				
Flow control off				
Flow control on				
Full-duplex	ATF1	ATF1	ATF1	
Half duplex	ATF0	ATF0	ATF0	
Internal timing enabled				
RJ-11/RJ-41S/RJ-45S Telephone jack				
RJ-12/RJ-13 Telephone jack				
RTS/CTS delay				
Slave timing enabled				
Sync Mode 1(sync/async)				
Sync Mode 2 (stored number dial)				
Sync Mode 3 (manual dial)				
REGISTERS & OPTIONS				
Register set	ATSr=n (r=0..16) (n=0..255)	ATSr=n (r=0..16) (n=0..255)	ATSr=n (r=0..16) (n=0..255)	ATSr=n (r=0..16) (n=0..255)
Register read	ATSr? (r=0..16)	ATSr? r=REGISTER (r=0..16)	ATSr? r=REGISTER (r=0..16)	ATSr? r=REGISTER (r=0..16)
10 bit character				
1800-Hz preamble				
2100-Hz preamble				
9 bit character				
Answer on ring #	ATS0=0 (0-255 rings)	ATS0=0 (0-255 rings)	ATS0=0 (0-255 rings)	ATS0=2 (0-255 rings)
Answertone = 2225-Hz				
Backspace character	ATS5=08 (0-32, 127 ASCII)	ATS5=08 (0-32, 127 ASCII)	ATS5=08 (0-32, 127 ASCII)	ATS5=08 (0-32, 127 ASCII)
Cancel character				
Carriage Return	ATS3=13 (0-127 ASCII)	ATS3=13 (0-127 ASCII)	ATS3=13 (0-127 ASCII)	ATS3=13 (0-127 ASCII)

MODEM VENDOR / Model

REGISTERS & OPTIONS continued

	Penril CADET 1200	Penril DataComm CADET 2400 modem	Penril DataComm PACER 2400 modem	Prentice P-212ZX modem
Carrier detect response time	ATS9=06 (1-255 1/10secs)	ATS9=06 (1-255 1/10secs)	ATS9=06 (1-255 1/10secs)	
Character delete				
Comma (pause)	ATS8=2 (0-255secs)	ATS8=2 (0-255secs)	ATS8=2 (0-255secs)	ATS8=2 (0-255secs)
Common CTS-RLSD				
DTMF dialing speed	ATS11=95 (50-255 msec)	ATS11=95 (50-255 msec)	ATS11=95 (50-255 msec)	
Dialing delay	ATS6=02 (0-255sec)	ATS6=02 (0-255sec)	ATS6=02 (0-255sec)	ATS6=02 (0-255sec)
Display active profile				ATI1
Drop call on timeout				
Enable speed conversion(match DTE)				
Escape character	ATS2=43 (0-127 ASCII)	ATS2=43 (0-127 ASCII)	ATS2=43 (0-127 ASCII)	ATS2=43 (0-127 ASCII)
Escape code guard time	ATS12=50 (0-255 1/50sec)	ATS12=50 (0-255 1/50sec)	ATS12=50 (0-255 1/50sec)	ATS12=50 (0-255 1/50sec)
Exit DATA mode				
Far end sends first				
Flow control				
High speed only				
Immediate dial from dir X				
Line feed character	ATS4=10 (0-127 ASCII)	ATS4=10 (0-127 ASCII)	ATS4=10 (0-127 ASCII)	ATS4=10 (0-127 ASCII)
Local echo				
Loss of carrier disconnect				
Lost carrier to hang-up delay	ATS10=14 (1-255 1/10secs)	ATS10=14 (1-255 1/10secs)	ATS10=14 (1-255 1/10secs)	ATS10=70 (1/10th sec)
Prompt character				
Received space disconnect				
Responds to Remote Loop				
Ring Indicator on until disconnect				
Ring count	ATS1=00 (0-255 rings)	ATS1=00 (0-255 rings)	ATS1=00 (0-255 rings)	ATS1=00 (0-255 rings)
Select factory profile				
Send break				
Send break enable				
Send space disconnect				
Set default profile				
Set disconnect character				
Set halt character(for operator intervention)				
Set terminator(marks end of number/login)				
Set password				
Set sequence of multiple # dialing				
Set wait char(delay prior to login after DCD)				
Skip header message				
Transparent data mode				
UM answertone				
Wait for carrier	ATS7=30 (1-30 secs)	ATS7=30 (1-30 secs)	ATS7=30 (1-30 secs)	ATS7=30 (1-30 secs)
Write configurations to memory				

MODEM VENDOR Model	Penril CADET 1200	Penril DataComm CADET 2400 modem	Penril DataComm PACER 2400 modem	Prentice P-212ZX modem
TESTS				
Analog loopback test	ATS16=1	ATS16=1	ATS16=1	ATS16=1
Cancel all tests	ATS16=0	ATS16=0	ATS16=0	ATS16=0
Denies remote digital loopback request				
Digital loop test	ATS16=4	ATS16=4	ATS16=4	
Grants remote digital loopback request		ATS16=6	ATS16=6	
Initiate RDL test				
Perform checksum & return status message	ATI1	ATI1	ATI1	
Perform checksum 7 return checksum				
Remote loop test				
Request firmware revision #				
Request product code	ATI0	ATI0	ATI0	ATI0
Self-test		ATS16=3	ATS16=3	
Test timer		ATS18=00 (0-255)	ATS18=00 (0-255)	
Touchtone frequency test				
USER INTERFACE				
Cancel character				+++
Change cancel character				
Delete character(backspace)				^H
Echo characters in command modem(on)	ATE1	ATE1	ATE1	ATE1
Echo characters(off)	ATE0	ATE0	ATE0	ATE0
Escape code	+++			+++
Flash				
High speaker volume		ATL3	ATL3	
Low speaker volume		ATL1	ATL1	
Medium speaker volume		ATL2	ATL2	
Result code set(basic)	ATX0	ATX0	ATX0	ATX0
Result code set(extended)	ATX1	ATX1	ATX1	ATX1
Result code set(full)				ATX2
Result codes not sent	ATQ1	ATQ1	ATQ1	ATQ1
Result codes sent	ATQ0	ATQ0	ATQ0	ATQ0
Result codes transmitted as digits	ATV0	ATV0	ATV0	ATV0
Result codes transmitted as words	ATV1	ATV1	ATV1	ATV1
Send break				
Speaker off always	M0	ATM0	ATM0	ATM0
Speaker on always	M2	ATM2	ATM2	ATM2
Speaker on until carrier detected	M1	ATM1	ATM1	ATM1
Spkr on until carr-det except during dialing				
Wait for silence(quiet answer)				

MODEM VENDOR Model	Prentice P224 modem	Prentice POPCOM X100 modem	Prentice POPCOM C200 modem	QUBIE' 1200 & 1200E modem
NOTES:	Commands are preceded with AT and trailed by RETURN	Commands are preceded with AT and trailed by RETURN	Commands are preceded with AT and trailed by RETURN	Commands are preceded with AT and trailed by RETURN
ANSWER COMMANDS				
Answer call w/o ring	ATA	ATA	ATA	ATA
Auto answer				ATS0=1
DIALING COMMANDS				
Blind dial/ext. result codes/busy detection				
Blind dial/ext. result codes/no busy det.				
Dial a number	ATDs (S=0..9)	ATDs (S=0..9)	ATDs (S=0..9)	ATDs (S=0..9)
Dial stored number				
List dial(multiple # dialing)				
List directories				
No Blind dial/ext. result codes/no busy det.				
No Blind dial/ext.codes/busy detection				
Pause	P	P	P	P
Pulse dial				
QUIT (exit dialer mode)				
Redial last #				
Redial(continuously)				
Return to command state after dialing	;	;	;	;
Reverse mode(call "originate-only" modem)	R	R		R
Store directory entry				
Touch-Tone dial	T	T	T	T
Wait for second dial tone				
GENERAL COMMANDS				
Enter answer mode				
Enter originate mode				
Enter talk mode				
Exit Data mode				
Help command				$
Inactivity timer(hang-up)				
Long space disconnect disabled				
Long space disconnect enabled				
Off-hook	ATH1	ATH1	ATH1	ATH1
Off-hook(special)				
On-hook (Hang-up)	ATH0	ATH0	ATH0	ATH0
Prefix to commands	AT	AT	AT	AT
Repeat last command				A/
Reset modem(sets to default values)	ATZ	ATZ	ATZ	ATZ
Resume Data mode	ATO	ATO	ATO	
Return to command mode(from online)				
Return to on-line state	ATO0	ATO0	ATO0	ATO0
Return to on-line state & begin eq-retrain				
Transmitter off				ATC0
Transmitter on				ATC1

Appendix I

MODEM VENDOR Model	Prentice P224 modem	Prentice POPCOM X100 modem	Prentice POPCOM C200 modem	QUBIE' 1200 & 1200E modem
PORT COMMANDS				
212A operation at 1200 bps(Bell mode)	ATS18=1	ATS18=1	ATS18=1	
Asynchronous mode				
CCITT V.22 operation at 1200 bps				
Clear to send always on	ATS18=2	ATS18=2	ATS18=2	
Clear to send(lead 5) tracks RTS(lead 4)				
DSR on according to EIA standard	ATS18=0	ATS18=0	ATS18=0	
DSR on while onhook				
DSR(lead 6) always on				
DTR ON/OFF transition causes modem reset	ATS18=2	ATS18=2	ATS18=2	
DTR delay				
DTR transition ON/OFF causes modem cmd state				
DTR(lead 20) signal ignored by modem				
DTR ON/OFF transition causes on-hook, modem to enter command state, and no auto-answer until DTR turned back on.				
Data carrier detect on while on-hook		ATS18=0		
Data carrier detect tracks actual carrier		ATS18=2		
Data carrier detect(lead 8) always on				
External timing enabled				
Flow control off				
Flow control on				
Full-duplex	ATF1			ATF1
Half duplex	ATF0			ATF0
Internal timing enabled				
RJ-11/RJ-41S/RJ-45S Telephone jack				
RJ-12/RJ-13 Telephone jack				
RTS/CTS delay				
Slave timing enabled				
Sync Mode 1(sync/async)				
Sync Mode 2 (stored number dial)				
Sync Mode 3 (manual dial)				
REGISTERS & OPTIONS				
Register set	ATSr=n (r=0..16) (n=0..255)	ATSr=n (r=0..16) (n=0..255)	ATSr=n (r=0..16) (n=0..255)	ATSr=n (r=0..16) (n=0..255)
Register read	ATSr? r=REGISTER (r=0..16)	ATSr? r=REGISTER (r=0..16)	ATSr? r=REGISTER (r=0..16)	ATSr? r=REGISTER (r=0..16)
10 bit character				
1800-Hz preamble				
2100-Hz preamble				
9 bit character				
Answer on ring #	ATS0=2 (0-255 rings)	ATS0=2 (0-255 rings)	ATS0=2 (0-255 rings)	ATS0=0 (0-255 rings)
Answertone = 2225-Hz				
Backspace character	ATS5=08 (0-32, 127 ASCII)	ATS5=08 (0-32, 127 ASCII)	ATS5=08 (0-32, 127 ASCII)	ATS5=08 (0-32, 127 ASCII)
Cancel character				
Carriage Return	ATS3=13 (0-127 ASCII)	ATS3=13 (0-127 ASCII)	ATS3=13 (0-127 ASCII)	ATS3=13 (0-127 ASCII)

MODEM VENDOR Model	Prentice P224 modem	Prentice POPCOM X100 modem	Prentice POPCOM C200 modem	QUBIE' 1200 & 1200E modem
Carrier detect response time	ATS9=7 (1/10sec.)		ATS9=7 (1/10sec.)	ATS9=06 (1-255 1/10secs)
Character delete				
Comma (pause)	ATS8=2 (0-255secs)	ATS8=2 (0-255secs)	ATS8=2 (0-255secs)	ATS8=2 (0-255secs)
Common CTS-RLSD				
DTMF dialing speed	ATS11=70 (msec.)		ATS11=70 (msec.)	ATS11=95 (50-255 msec)
Dialing delay	ATS6=02 (0-255sec)	ATS6=02 (0-255sec)	ATS6=02 (0-255sec)	ATS6=02 (0-255sec)
Display active profile	ATI1	ATI1	ATI1	
Drop call on timeout				
Enable speed conversion(match DTE)				
Escape character	ATS2=43 (0-127 ASCII)	ATS2=43 (0-127 ASCII)	ATS2=43 (0-127 ASCII)	ATS2=43 (0-127 ASCII)
Escape code guard time	ATS12=50 (0-255 1/50sec)	ATS12=50 (0-255 1/50sec)	ATS12=50 (0-255 1/50sec)	ATS12=50 (0-255 1/50sec)
Exit DATA mode	ATS18=47 (>127 disables)		ATS18=47 (>127 disables)	
Far end sends first				
Flow control				
High speed only				
Immediate dial from dir X				
Line feed character	ATS4=10 (0-127 ASCII)	ATS4=10 (0-127 ASCII)	ATS4=10 (0-127 ASCII)	ATS4=10 (0-127 ASCII)
Local echo				
Loss of carrier disconnect				
Lost carrier to hang-up delay	ATS10=70 (1/10th sec)	ATS10=70 (1/10th sec)	ATS10=70 (1/10th sec)	ATS10=14 (1-255 1/10secs)
Prompt character				
Received space disconnect				
Responds to Remote Loop				
Ring Indicator on until disconnect				
Ring count	ATS1=00 (0-255 rings)	ATS1=00 (0-255 rings)	ATS1=00 (0-255 rings)	ATS1=00 (0-255 rings)
Select factory profile				
Send break				
Send break enable				
Send space disconnect				
Set default profile				
Set disconnect character				
Set halt character(for operator intervention)				
Set terminator(marks end of number/login)				
Set password				
Set sequence of multiple # dialing				
Set wait char(delay prior to login after DCD)				
Skip header message				
Transparent data mode				
UM answertone				
Wait for carrier	ATS7=30 (1-30 secs)	ATS7=30 (1-30 secs)	ATS7=30 (1-30 secs)	ATS7=30 (1-30 secs)
Write configurations to memory				

Appendix I

MODEM VENDOR Model	Prentice P224 modem	Prentice POPCOM X100 modem	Prentice POPCOM C200 modem	QUBIE' 1200 & 1200E modem
TESTS				
Analog loopback test	ATS16=1	ATS16=1	ATS16=1	ATS16=1 or 5 (5=ALST)
Cancel all tests	ATS16=0	ATS16=0	ATS16=0	ATS16=0
Denies remote digital loopback request				
Digital loop test				
Grants remote digital loopback request				
Initiate RDL test				
Perform checksum & return status message				
Perform checksum 7 return checksum				
Remote loop test				
Request firmware revision #				ATI1
Request product code	ATI	ATI0	ATI	ATI0
Self-test				ATS16=4
Test timer				
Touchtone frequency test				ATS16=2
USER INTERFACE				
Cancel character	+++	+++	+++	+++
Change cancel character				
Delete character(backspace)	^H	^H	^H	
Echo characters in command modem(on)	ATE1	ATE1	ATE1	ATE1
Echo characters(off)	ATE0	ATE0	ATE0	ATE0
Escape code	+++	+++	+++	+++
Flash				!
High speaker volume				
Low speaker volume				
Medium speaker volume				
Result code set(basic)	ATX0	ATX0	ATX0	ATX0
Result code set(extended)	ATX1	ATX1	ATX1	ATX1
Result code set(full)	ATX2	ATX2	ATX2	
Result codes not sent	ATQ1	ATQ1	ATQ1	ATQ1
Result codes sent	ATQ0	ATQ0	ATQ0	ATQ0
Result codes transmitted as digits	ATV0	ATV0	ATV0	ATV0
Result codes transmitted as words	ATV1	ATV1	ATV1	ATV1
Send break				
Speaker off always	ATM0	ATM0	ATM0	ATM0
Speaker on always	ATM2	ATM2	ATM2	ATM2
Spkr on until carrier detected	ATM1	ATM1	ATM1	ATM1
Spkr on until carr-det except during dialing				
Wait for silence(quiet answer)				@

MODEM VENDOR / Model	Racal-Vadic 2400PA modem	Racal-Vadic 2400PA modem	Racal-Vadic 2400VP modem	Racal-Vadic 2400VP modem
NOTES:	Interactive mode Wake up modem by	AT mode entered anytime	Interactive mode Wake up modem by	ATplus mode entered anytime
ANSWER COMMANDS				
Answer call w/o ring		ATA		ATA
Auto answer	O(cr) 4(cr) 1(cr)	O(cr) 4(cr) 1(cr)	O(cr) 4(cr) 1(cr)	O(cr) 4(cr) 1(cr)
DIALING COMMANDS				
Blind dial/ext. result codes/busy detection	O(cr) 7(cr) 2(cr)	O(cr) 7(cr) 2(cr)	O(cr) 7(cr) 2(cr)	ATX3
Blind dial/ext. result codes/no busy det.				ATX1
Dial a number	D(cr) #(cr) (#=phone no.)	D(cr) #(cr) (#=phone no.)	D(cr) #(cr) (#=phone no.)	ATDs (S=0..9)
Dial stored number	# (#=1-15)	# (#=1-15)	# (#=1-15)	ATDS=n (n=0-3)
List dial(multiple # dialing)	L(cr) 1-15/1-15(cr)	L(cr) 1-15/1-15(cr)	L(cr) 1-15/1-15(cr)	L(cr) 1-15/1-15(cr)
List directories	M	M	M	M
No Blind dial/ext. result codes/no busy det.				ATX2
No Blind dial/ext.codes/busy detection	O(cr) 7(cr) 1(cr)	O(cr) 7(cr) 1(cr)	O(cr) 7(cr) 1(cr)	ATX4
Pause	O(cr) 6(cr) 3(cr)	,	O(cr) 6(cr) 3(cr)	,
Pulse dial	,		,	
QUIT (exit dialer mode)		ATZ		ATZ
Redial last #	R(cr) #(cr) (#=retries)	AT*R0	R(cr) #(cr) (#=retries)	R(cr) #(cr) (#=retries)
Redial(continuously)		AT*Rn (n times)		
Return to command state after dialing		;		;
Reverse mode(call "originate-only" modem)	R	R	R	R
Store directory entry	C (cr) 1-15(cr) # (cr)	AT&Zn=# (n=0-3, #=PHONE#)	C (cr) 1-15(cr) # (cr)	AT&ZT# (#=phone no.)
Touch-Tone dial	O(cr) 6(cr) 2(cr)	O(cr) 6(cr) 2(cr)	O(cr) 6(cr) 2(cr)	O(cr) 6(cr) 2(cr)
Wait for second dial tone	K	W	K	W
GENERAL COMMANDS				
Enter answer mode				
Enter originate mode				
Enter talk mode				
Exit Data mode				
Help command	P or ?		P or ?	
Inactivity timer(hang-up)		AT*T1		AT*T1
Long space disconnect disabled				
Long space disconnect enabled				
Off-hook		ATH1		ATH1
Off-hook(special)	^C D		^CD	
On-hook (Hang-up)		ATH0		ATH0
Prefix to commands		AT		AT
Repeat last command		A/		A/
Reset modem(sets to default values)		ATZ		ATZ
Resume Data mode				
Return to command mode(from online)				
Return to on-line state		ATO0		ATO0
Return to on-line state & begin eq-retrain		ATO1		ATO1
Transmitter off				
Transmitter on				

MODEM VENDOR Model	Racal-Vadic 2400PA modem	Racal-Vadic 2400PA modem	Racal-Vadic 2400VP modem	Racal-Vadic 2400VP modem
PORT COMMANDS				
212A operation at 1200 bps(Bell mode)	0(cr) 14(cr) 1(cr)	AT&M0	0(cr) 14(cr) 1(cr)	AT&M0
Asynchronous mode				
CCITT V.22 operation at 1200 bps				
Clear to send always on	0(cr) 21(cr) 3(cr)	AT&R1	0(cr) 21(cr) 3(cr)	AT&R1
Clear to send(lead 5) tracks RTS(lead 4)	0(cr) 21(cr) 1(cr)	AT&R0	0(cr) 21(cr) 1(cr)	AT&R0
DSR on according to EIA standard	0(cr) 2(cr) 3(cr)	0(cr) 2(cr) 3(cr)	0(cr) 2(cr) 3(cr)	AT&S1
DSR on while onhook		0(cr) 02(cr) 1(cr)	0(cr) 02(cr) 1(cr)	AT&S0
DSR(lead 6) always on	0(cr) 2(cr) 2(cr)	0(cr) 2(cr) 2(cr)	0(cr) 2(cr) 2(cr)	
DTR ON/OFF transition causes modem reset		AT&D3		AT&D3
DTR delay				
DTR transition ON/OFF causes modem cmd state		AT&D1	0(cr) 22(cr) 2(cr)	AT&D1
DTR(lead 20) signal ignored by modem		AT&D0		AT&D0
DTR ON/OFF transition causes on-hook, modem to enter command state, and no auto-answer until DTR turned back on.		AT&D2		AT&D2
Data carrier detect on while on-hook	0(cr) 3(cr) 2(cr)	AT&C1	0(cr) 3(cr) 2(cr)	AT&C1
Data carrier detect tracks actual carrier	0(cr) 3(cr) 1(cr)	AT&C0	0(cr) 3(cr) 1(cr)	AT&C0
Data carrier detect(lead 8) always on	0(cr) 3(cr) 3(cr)	AT&X1	0(cr) 3(cr) 3(cr)	AT&X1
External timing enabled				
Flow control off				
Flow control on				
Full-duplex				
Half duplex				
Internal timing enabled	0(cr) 13(cr) 1(cr)	AT&X0	0(cr) 13(cr) 1(cr)	AT&X0
RJ-11/RJ-41S/RJ-45S Telephone jack				
RJ-12/RJ-13 Telephone jack				
RTS/CTS delay				ATS26=01 (0-255 1/100sec)
Slave timing enabled	0(cr) 13(cr) 2(cr)	AT&X2	0(cr) 13(cr) 2(cr)	AT&X2
Sync Mode 1(sync/async)	0(cr) 14(cr) 2(cr)	AT&M1	0(cr) 14(cr) 2(cr)	AT&M1
Sync Mode 2 (stored number dial)		AT&M2		AT&M2
Sync Mode 3 (manual dial)		AT&M3		AT&M3
REGISTERS & OPTIONS				
Register set		ATSr=n (r=0..16) (n=0..255)		ATSr=n (r=0..16) (n=0..255)
Register read		ATSr? r=REGISTER (r=0..16)		ATSr? r=REGISTER (r=0..16)
10 bit character	0(cr) 10(cr) 1(cr)	0(cr) 10(cr) 1(cr)	0(cr) 10(cr) 1(cr)	0(cr) 10(cr) 1(cr)
1800-Hz preamble				
2100-Hz preamble				
9 bit character	0(cr) 10(cr) 3(cr)	0(cr) 10(cr) 3(cr)	0(cr) 10(cr) 3(cr)	0(cr) 10(cr) 3(cr)
Answertone = 2225-Hz				
Answer on ring #	0(cr) 4(cr) 3(cr)	ATS0=0 (0-255 rings)	0(cr) 4(cr) 3(cr)	ATS0=0 (0-255 rings)
Backspace character		ATS5=08 (0-32, 127 ASCII)		ATS5=08 (0-32, 127 ASCII)
Cancel character				
Carriage Return		ATS3=13 (0-127 ASCII)		ATS3=13 (0-127 ASCII)

REGISTERS & OPTIONS continued

MODEM VENDOR Model	Racal-Vadic 2400PA modem	Racal-Vadic 2400PA modem	Racal-Vadic 2400VP modem	Racal-Vadic 2400PA modem	Racal-Vadic 2400VP modem	Racal-Vadic 2400VP modem
Carrier detect response time						ATS9=06 (1-255 1/10secs)
Character delete						
Comma (pause)		ATS8=2 (0-255secs)				ATS8=2 (0-255secs)
Common CTS-RLSD	O(cr) 21(cr) 2(cr)	O(cr) 21(cr) 2(cr)	O(cr) 21(cr) 2(cr)	O(cr) 21(cr) 2(cr)	O(cr) 21(cr) 2(cr)	O(cr) 21(cr) 2(cr)
DTMF dialing speed						ATS11=95 (50-255 msec)
Dialing delay		ATS6=02 (0-255sec)				ATS6=02 (0-255sec)
Display active profile	T	AT*T	T	T	T	AT*T
Drop call on timeout						
Enable speed conversion(match DTE)		AT*C1				AT*C1
Escape character	O(cr) 18(cr) 2(cr)	ATS2=43 (0-127 ASCII)	O(cr) 18(cr) 2(cr)	O(cr) 18(cr) 2(cr)	O(cr) 18(cr) 2(cr)	ATS2=43 (0-127 ASCII)
Escape code guard time		ATS12=50 (0-255 1/50sec)				ATS12=50 (0-255 1/50sec)
Exit DATA mode						
Far end sends first						
Flow control	O(cr)17(cr)x(cr) (x,2=XON) AT*F1 OR AT*F4 (1=local)	O(cr)17(cr)x(cr) (x,2=XON) AT*F1 OR AT*F4 (1=local)	O(cr)17(cr)x(cr) (x,2=XON) AT*F1 OR AT*F4 (1=local)	O(cr)17(cr)x(cr) (x,2=XON) AT*F1 OR AT*F4 (1=local)	O(cr)17(cr)x(cr) (x,2=XON) AT*F1 OR AT*F4 (1=local)	O(cr)17(cr)x(cr) (x,2=XON) AT*F1 OR AT*F4 (1=local)
High speed only						
Immediate dial from dir X						
Line feed character		ATS4=10 (0-127 ASCII)				ATS4=10 (0-127 ASCII)
Local echo	O(cr)16(cr)x(cr) (x,1=on)	O(cr)16(cr)x(cr) (x,1=on)	O(cr)16(cr)x(cr) (x,1=on)	O(cr)16(cr)x(cr) (x,1=on)	O(cr)16(cr)x(cr) (x,1=on)	O(cr)16(cr)x(cr) (x,1=on)
Loss of carrier disconnect						
Lost carrier to hang-up delay						ATS10=14 (1-255 1/10secs)
Prompt character						
Received space disconnect						
Responds to Remote Loop						
Ring Indicator on until disconnect						
Ring count		ATS1=00 (0-255 rings)				ATS1=00 (0-255 rings)
Select factory profile		AT&F				AT&F
Send break						
Send break enable						
Send space disconnect						
Set default profile	O(cr) 1(cr) 1(cr)	O(cr) 1(cr) 1(cr)	O(cr) 1(cr) 1(cr)	O(cr) 1(cr) 1(cr)	O(cr) 1(cr) 1(cr)	O(cr) 1(cr) 1(cr)
Set disconnect character	^C D		^C D	^C D	^C D	
Set halt character(for operator intervention)						
Set terminator(marks end of number/login)						
Set password						
Set sequence of multiple # dialing						
Set wait char(delay prior to login after DCD)						
Skip header message						
Transparent data mode						
UM answertone						
Wait for carrier		ATS7=30 (1-30 secs)				ATS7=30 (1-30 secs)
Write configurations to memory		AT&W				AT&W

MODEM VENDOR / Model	Racal-Vadic 2400PA modem	Racal-Vadic 2400PA modem	Racal-Vadic 2400VP modem	Racal-Vadic 2400VP modem
TESTS				
Analog loopback test		ATS16=1		AT&T1
Cancel all tests	ATS16=0	ATS16=0		AT&T0
Denies remote digital loopback request	O(cr) 20(cr) 2(cr)	O(cr) 20(cr) 2(cr)		AT&T5
Digital loop test		ATS16=2		AT&T3
Grants remote digital loopback request	O(cr) 20(cr) 1(cr)	O(cr) 20(cr) 1(cr)		AT&T4
Initiate RDL test	^R I	^R I	^R I	AT&T6 AT&T7 (7 initiates)
Perform checksum & return status message		ATI2	ATI2	ATI2
Perform checksum 7 return checksum		ATI1	ATI1	ATI1
Remote loop test				
Request firmware revision #				
Request product code		ATI0	ATI0	ATI0
Self-test	ATS16=6	ATS16=6		AT&T8
Test timer				ATS18=00 (0-255)
Touchtone frequency test				
USER INTERFACE				
Cancel character	^D or ^H	^D or ^H	^D or ^H	^D or ^H
Change cancel character	O(cr) 5(cr) 1(cr)		O(cr) 5(cr) 1(cr)	
Delete character(backspace)	O(cr) 5(cr) 2(cr)		O(cr) 5(cr) 2(cr)	
Echo characters in command modem(on)		ATE1		ATE1
Echo characters(off)		ATE0		ATE0
Escape code	(Esc) key	+++	(Esc) key	+++
Flash		!		!
High speaker volume				
Low speaker volume				
Medium speaker volume				
Result code set(basic)		ATX0		ATX0
Result code set(extended)		ATX1		ATX1
Result code set(full)		ATX9		ATX9
Result codes not sent	O(cr) 9(cr) 3(cr)	ATQ1	O(cr) 9(cr) 3(cr)	ATQ1
Result codes sent	O(cr) 9(cr) 1(cr)	ATQ0	O(cr) 9(cr) 1(cr)	ATQ0
Result codes transmitted as digits				
Result codes transmitted as words	O(cr) 9(cr) 1(cr)	O(cr) 9(cr) 1(cr)	O(cr) 9(cr) 1(cr)	O(cr) 9(cr) 1(cr)
Send break				
Speaker off always				ATM0
Speaker on always				ATM2
Speaker on until carrier detected				ATM1
Spkr on until carr-det except during dialing				ATM3
Wait for silence(quiet answer)		@		@

MODEM VENDOR	Racal-Vadic	Racal-Vadic	USRobotics	USRobotics
Model	MAXWELL modem 2400V/2400PC	MAXWELL modem 2400V/2400PC	Auto Dial 212A	Courier modem 1200 & 2400
NOTES:	Interactive mode / Wake up modem by	AT mode		
ANSWER COMMANDS				
Answer call w/o ring	0(cr) 4(cr)	ATA	ATA	ATA
Auto answer	1(cr)	ATS0=1	ATS0=1	ATS0=1
DIALING COMMANDS				
Blind dial/ext. result codes/busy detection	0(cr) 7(cr) 2(cr)	0(cr) 7(cr) 2(cr)		
Blind dial/ext. result codes/no busy det.				
Dial a number	D(cr) #(cr) (#=phone no.)	ATDs (S=0..9)	ATDs (S=0..9)	ATDs (S=0..9)
Dial stored number		# (#=1-15)		
List dial(multiple # dialing)		L(cr) 1-15/1-15(cr)		
List directories		M		
No Blind dial/ext. result codes/no busy det.	0(cr) 7(cr) 1(cr)	0(cr) 7(cr) 1(cr)		
No Blind dial/ext.codes/busy detection				
Pause	,	,	,	,
Pulse dial	P	P	P	P
QUIT (exit dialer mode)	0(cr) 6(cr) 3(cr)	I(cr)		
Redial last #	R(cr) #(cr) (#=retries)	R(cr) #(cr) (#=retries)		
Redial(continuously)				>
Return to command state after dialing		;		;
Reverse mode(call "originate-only" modem)			R	R
Store directory entry	0(cr) 6(cr) 2(cr)	C (cr) 1-15(cr) # (cr)		
Touch-Tone dial		T	T	T
Wait for second dial tone	K	K		W
GENERAL COMMANDS				
Enter answer mode				
Enter originate mode				
Enter talk mode				
Exit Data mode				
Help command	P or ?	P or ?		$
Inactivity timer(hang-up)				
Long space disconnect disabled				
Long space disconnect enabled				ATH1
Off-hook		ATH1		
Off-hook(special)	^CD			
On-hook (Hang-up)		ATH0		ATH0
Prefix to commands		AT	AT	AT
Repeat last command		A/	A/	A/
Reset modem(sets to default values)		ATZ	ATZ	ATZ
Resume Data mode				
Return to command mode(from online)				
Return to on-line state		ATO0		ATO0
Return to on-line state & begin eq-retrain		ATO1		
Transmitter off				ATC0
Transmitter on				ATC1

MODEM VENDOR / Model	Racal-Vadic MAXWELL modem 2400V/2400PC	Racal-Vadic MAXWELL modem 2400V/2400PC	USRobotics Auto Dial 212A	USRobotics Courier modem 1200 & 2400
PORT COMMANDS				
212A operation at 1200 bps(Bell mode)		O(cr) 14(cr) 1(cr)		
Asynchronous mode				
CCITT V.22 operation at 1200 bps		O(cr) 21(cr) 3(cr)		
Clear to send always on		O(cr) 21(cr) 1(cr)		
Clear to send(lead 5) tracks RTS(lead 4)		O(cr) 2(cr) 3(cr)		
DSR on according to EIA standard	O(cr) 2(cr) 3(cr)	O(cr) 02(cr) 1(cr)		
DSR on while onhook	O(cr) 02(cr) 1(cr)	O(cr) 2(cr) 2(cr)		
DSR(lead 6) always on	O(cr) 02(cr) 2(cr)			
DTR ON/OFF transition causes modem reset				
DTR delay				
DTR transition ON/OFF causes modem cmd state				
DTR(lead 20) signal ignored by modem		O(cr) 22(cr) 2(cr)		
DTR ON/OFF transition causes on-hook, modem to enter command state, and no auto-answer until DTR turned back on.				
Data carrier detect on while on-hook	O(cr) 3(cr) 2(cr)	O(cr) 3(cr) 2(cr)		
Data carrier detect tracks actual carrier	O(cr) 3(cr) 1(cr)	O(cr) 3(cr) 1(cr)		
Data carrier detect(lead 8) always on	O(cr) 3(cr) 3(cr)	O(cr) 3(cr) 3(cr)		
External timing enabled				
Flow control off				
Flow control on				
Full-duplex		ATF1	ATF1	ATF1
Half duplex		ATF0	ATF0	ATF0
Internal timing enabled		O(cr) 13(cr) 1(cr)		
RJ-11/RJ-41S/RJ-45S Telephone jack				
RJ-12/RJ-13 Telephone jack				
RTS/CTS delay				
Slave timing enabled				
Sync Mode 1(sync/async)		O(cr) 13(cr) 2(cr)		
Sync Mode 2 (stored number dial)		O(cr) 14(cr) 2(cr)		
Sync Mode 3 (manual dial)				
REGISTERS & OPTIONS				
Register set		ATSr=n (r=0..16) (n=0..255)	ATSr=n (r=0..16) (n=0..255)	ATSr=n (r=0..16) (n=0..255)
Register read	O(cr)17(cr)x(cr) (x,2=XON)	ATSr? r=REGISTER (r=0..16)	ATSr? r=REGISTER (r=0..16)	ATSr? r=REGISTER (r=0..16)
10 bit character	O(cr) 10(cr) 1(cr)	O(cr) 10(cr) 1(cr)		
1800-Hz preamble				
2100-Hz preamble				
9 bit character		O(cr) 10(cr) 3(cr)		
Answer on ring #		ATS0=0 (0-255 rings)		ATS0=0 (0-255 rings)
Answertone = 2225-Hz				
Backspace character		ATS5=08 (0-32, 127 ASCII)		ATS5=08 (0-32, 127 ASCII)
Cancel character				
Carriage Return		ATS3=13 (0-127 ASCII)		ATS3=13 (0-127 ASCII)

REGISTERS & OPTIONS continued

MODEM VENDOR Model	Racal-Vadic MAXWELL modem 2400V/2400PC	Racal-Vadic MAXWELL modem 2400V/2400PC	USRobotics Auto Dial 212A	USRobotics Courier modem 1200 & 2400
Carrier detect response time		ATS9=06 (1-255 1/10secs)		ATS9=06 (1-255 1/10secs)
Character delete				
Comma (pause)		ATS8=2 (0-255secs)		ATS8=2 (0-255secs)
Common CTS-RLSD		0(cr) 21(cr) 2(cr)		
DTMF dialing speed		ATS11=95 (50-255 msec)		ATS11=95 (50-255 msec)
Dialing delay		ATS6=02 (0-255sec)		ATS6=02 (0-255sec)
Display active profile	T	T		
Drop call on timeout				
Enable speed conversion(match DTE)		0(cr) 18(cr) 2(cr)		
Escape character		ATS2=43 (0-127 ASCII)	ATS2=43 (0-127 ASCII)	ATS2=43 (0-127 ASCII)
Escape code guard time		ATS12=50 (0-255 1/50sec)		ATS12=50 (0-255 1/50sec)
Exit DATA mode				
Far end sends first				
Flow control		0(cr)17(cr)x(cr) (x,2=XON)		
High speed only				
Immediate dial from dir X				
Line feed character		ATS4=10 (0-127 ASCII)		ATS4=10 (0-127 ASCII)
Local echo				
Loss of carrier disconnect		0(cr)16(cr)x(cr) (x,1=on)		
Lost carrier to hang-up delay		ATS10=14 (1-255 1/10secs)		ATS10=14 (1-255 1/10secs)
Prompt character				
Received space disconnect				
Responds to Remote Loop				
Ring Indicator on until disconnect				
Ring count		ATS1=00 (0-255 rings)		ATS1=00 (0-255 rings)
Select factory profile		0(cr) 1(cr) 1(cr)		
Send break				
Send break enable				
Send space disconnect				
Set default profile		0(cr) 1(cr) 1(cr)		
Set disconnect character				
Set halt character(for operator intervention)				
Set terminator(marks end of number/login)				
Set password				
Set sequence of multiple # dialing				
Set wait char(delay prior to login after DCD)				
Skip header message				
Transparent data mode				
UM answertone				
Wait for carrier		ATS7=30 (1-30 secs)	ATS7=30 (1-30 secs)	ATS7=30 (1-30 secs)
Write configurations to memory				

Appendix I

MODEM VENDOR / Model	Racal-Vadic MAXWELL modem 2400V/2400PC	Racal-Vadic MAXWELL modem 2400V/2400PC	USRobotics Auto Dial 212A	USRobotics Courier modem 1200 & 2400
TESTS				
Analog loopback test		^A		ATS16=1 or 5 (5=ALST)
Cancel all tests				ATS16=0
Denies remote digital loopback request				
Digital loop test		^D		
Grants remote digital loopback request				
Initiate RDL test		^R		
Perform checksum & return status message				ATI1
Perform checksum 7 return checksum				
Remote loop test				
Request firmware revision #		^V		ATI0
Request product code		ATI0		ATS16=4
Self-test				
Test timer		ATS18=00 (0-255)		
Touchtone frequency test				ATS16=2
USER INTERFACE				
Cancel character				
Change cancel character				
Delete character(backspace)	^H	^D or ^H		
Echo characters in command modem(on)	O(cr) 5(cr) 1(cr)	ATE1	ATE1	ATE1
Echo characters(off)	O(cr) 5(cr) 2(cr)	ATE0	ATE0	ATE0
Escape code		+++	+++	+++
Flash				!
High speaker volume				
Low speaker volume				
Medium speaker volume				
Result code set(basic)		ATX0	ATX0	ATX0
Result code set(extended)		ATX1	ATX1	ATX1
Result code set(full)				
Result codes not sent		ATQ1	ATQ1	ATQ1
Result codes sent		ATQ0	ATQ0	ATQ0
Result codes transmitted as digits	O(cr) 9(cr) 3(cr)	ATV0	ATV0	ATV0
Result codes transmitted as words	O(cr) 9(cr) 1(cr)	ATV1	ATV1	ATV1
Send break				
Speaker off always		ATM0	ATM0	ATM0
Speaker on always		ATM2	ATM2	ATM2
Speaker on until carrier detected		ATM1	ATM1	ATM1
Spkr on until carr-det except during dialing		ATM3	ATM3	ATM3
Wait for silence(quiet answer)				@

MODEM VENDOR Model	USRobotics Microlink 1200 modem	USRobotics Microlink 2400 modem	USRobotics Password modem
NOTES:			
ANSWER COMMANDS			
Answer call w/o ring	ATA	ATA	ATA
Auto answer	ATS0=1	ATS0=1	ATS0=1
DIALING COMMANDS			
Blind dial/ext. result codes/busy detection			
Blind dial/ext. result codes/no busy det.			
Dial a number	ATDs (S=0..9)	ATDs (S=0..9)	ATDs (S=0..9)
Dial stored number			
List dial(multiple # dialing)			
List directories			
No Blind dial/ext. result codes/no busy det.			
No Blind dial/ext.codes/busy detection			
Pause	,	,	,
Pulse dial	P	P	P
QUIT (exit dialer mode)			
Redial last #		>	
Redial(continuously)		:	
Return to command state after dialing	R	R	R
Reverse mode(call "originate-only" modem)			
Store directory entry			
Touch-Tone dial	T	T	T
Wait for second dial tone		W	
GENERAL COMMANDS			
Enter answer mode			
Enter originate mode			
Enter talk mode			
Exit Data mode			
Help command		$	
Inactivity timer(hang-up)			
Long space disconnect disabled			
Long space disconnect enabled			
Off-hook		ATH1	
Off-hook(special)			
On-hook (Hang-up)		ATH0	
Prefix to commands	AT	AT	AT
Repeat last command	A/	A/	A/
Reset modem(sets to default values)	ATZ	ATZ	ATZ
Resume Data mode			
Return to command mode(from online)			
Return to on-line state		ATO0	
Return to on-line state & begin eq-retrain			
Transmitter off		ATC0	
Transmitter on		ATC1	

MODEM VENDOR Model	USRobotics Microlink 1200 modem	USRobotics Microlink 2400 modem	USRobotics Password modem
PORT COMMANDS			
212A operation at 1200 bps(Bell mode)			
Asynchronous mode			
CCITT V.22 operation at 1200 bps			
Clear to send always on			
Clear to send(lead 5) tracks RTS(lead 4)			
DSR on according to EIA standard			
DSR on while onhook			
DSR(lead 6) always on			
DTR ON/OFF transition causes modem reset			
DTR delay			
DTR transition ON/OFF causes modem cmd state			
DTR(lead 20) signal ignored by modem			
DTR ON/OFF transition causes on-hook, modem			
to enter command state, and no auto-			
answer until DTR turned back on.			
Data carrier detect on while on-hook			
Data carrier detect tracks actual carrier			
Data carrier detect(lead 8) always on			
External timing enabled			
Flow control off			
Flow control on			
Full-duplex	ATF1	ATF1	ATF1
Half duplex	ATF0	ATF0	ATF0
Internal timing enabled			
RJ-11/RJ-41S/RJ-45S Telephone jack			
RJ-12/RJ-13 Telephone jack			
RTS/CTS delay			
Slave timing enabled			
Sync Mode 1(sync/async)			
Sync Mode 2 (stored number dial)			
Sync Mode 3 (manual dial)			
REGISTERS & OPTIONS			
Register set	ATSr=n (r=0..16) (n=0..255)	ATSr=n (r=0..16) (n=0..255)	ATSr=n (r=0..16) (n=0..255)
Register read	ATSr? r=REGISTER (r=0..16)	ATSr? r=REGISTER (r=0..16)	ATSr? r=REGISTER (r=0..16)
10 bit character			
1800-Hz preamble			
2100-Hz preamble			
9 bit character			
Answer on ring #		ATS0=0 (0-255 rings)	
Answertone = 2225-Hz			
Backspace character		ATS5=08 (0-32, 127 ASCII)	
Cancel character			
Carriage Return		ATS3=13 (0-127 ASCII)	

MODEM VENDOR Model	USRobotics Microlink 1200 modem	USRobotics Microlink 2400 modem	USRobotics Password modem
REGISTERS & OPTIONS continued			
Carrier detect response time		ATS9=06 (1-255 1/10secs)	
Character delete			
Comma (pause)		ATS8=2 (0-255secs)	
Common CTS-RLSD			
DTMF dialing speed		ATS11=95 (50-255 msec)	
Dialing delay		ATS6=02 (0-255sec)	
Display active profile			
Drop call on timeout			
Enable speed conversion(match DTE)			
Escape character	ATS2=43 (0-127 ASCII)	ATS2=43 (0-127 ASCII)	ATS2=43 (0-127 ASCII)
Escape code guard time		ATS12=50 (0-255 1/50sec)	
Exit DATA mode			
Far end sends first			
Flow control			
High speed only			
Immediate dial from dir X			
Line feed character		ATS4=10 (0-127 ASCII)	
Local echo			
Loss of carrier disconnect			
Lost carrier to hang-up delay		ATS10=14 (1-255 1/10secs)	
Prompt character			
Received space disconnect			
Responds to Remote Loop			
Ring Indicator on until disconnect			
Ring count		ATS1=00 (0-255 rings)	
Select factory profile			
Send break			
Send break enable			
Send space disconnect			
Set default profile			
Set disconnect character			
Set halt character(for operator intervention)			
Set terminator(marks end of number/login)			
Set password			
Set sequence of multiple # dialing			
Set wait char(delay prior to login after DCD)			
Skip header message			
Transparent data mode			
UM answertone			
Wait for carrier	ATS7=30 (1-30 secs)	ATS7=30 (1-30 secs)	ATS7=30 (1-30 secs)
Write configurations to memory			

MODEM VENDOR Model	USRobotics Microlink 1200 modem	USRobotics Microlink 2400 modem	USRobotics Password modem
TESTS			
Analog loopback test		ATS16=1 or 5 (5=ALST)	
Cancel all tests		ATS16=0	
Denies remote digital loopback request			
Digital loop test			
Grants remote digital loopback request			
Initiate RDL test			
Perform checksum & return status message		ATI1	
Perform checksum 7 return checksum			
Remote loop test		ATI0	
Request firmware revision #		ATS16=4	
Request product code			
Self-test			
Test timer		ATS16=2	
Touchtone frequency test			
USER INTERFACE			
Cancel character			
Change cancel character			
Delete character(backspace)			
Echo characters in command modem(on)	ATE1	ATE1	ATE1
Echo characters(off)	ATE0	ATE0	ATE0
Escape code	+++	+++	+++
Flash		!	
High speaker volume			
Low speaker volume			
Medium speaker volume			
Result code set(basic)	ATX0	ATX0	ATX0
Result code set(extended)	ATX1	ATX1	ATX1
Result code set(full)			
Result codes not sent	ATQ1	ATQ1	ATQ1
Result codes sent	ATQ0	ATQ0	ATQ0
Result codes transmitted as digits	ATV0	ATV0	ATV0
Result codes transmitted as words	ATV1	ATV1	ATV1
Send break			
Speaker off always	ATM0	ATM0	ATM0
Speaker on always	ATM2	ATM2	ATM2
Speaker on until carrier detected	ATM1	ATM1	ATM1
Spkr on until carr-det except during dialing	ATM3	ATM3	ATM3
Wait for silence(quiet answer)		@	

===
MODEM VENDOR
Model

===
NOTES:

ANSWER COMMANDS

Answer call w/o ring
Auto answer

DIALING COMMANDS

Blind dial/ext. result codes/busy detection
Blind dial/ext. result codes/no busy det.
Dial a number
Dial stored number
List dial(multiple # dialing)
List directories
No Blind dial/ext. result codes/no busy det.
No Blind dial/ext.codes/busy detection
Pause
Pulse dial
QUIT (exit dialer mode)
Redial last #
Redial(continuously)
Return to command state after dialing
Reverse mode(call "originate-only" modem)
Store directory entry
Touch-Tone dial
Wait for second dial tone

GENERAL COMMANDS

Enter answer mode
Enter originate mode
Enter talk mode
Exit Data mode
Help command
Inactivity timer(hang-up)
Long space disconnect disabled
Long space disconnect enabled
Off-hook
Off-hook(special)
On-hook (Hang-up)
Prefix to commands
Repeat last command
Reset modem(sets to default values)
Resume Data mode
Return to command mode(from online)
Return to on-line state
Return to on-line state & begin eq-retrain
Transmitter off
Transmitter on

PORT COMMANDS

212A operation at 1200 bps(Bell mode)
Asynchronous mode
CCITT V.22 operation at 1200 bps
Clear to send always on
Clear to send(lead 5) tracks RTS(lead 4)
DSR on according to EIA standard
DSR on while onhook
DSR(lead 6) always on
DTR ON/OFF transition causes modem reset
DTR delay
DTR transition ON/OFF causes modem cmd state
DTR(lead 20) signal ignored by modem
DTR ON/OFF transition causes on-hook, modem
  to enter command state, and no auto-
  answer until DTR turned back on.
Data carrier detect on while on-hook
Data carrier detect tracks actual carrier
Data carrier detect(lead 8) always on
External timing enabled
Flow control off
Flow control on
Full-duplex
Half duplex
Internal timing enabled
RJ-11/RJ-41S/RJ-45S Telephone jack
RJ-12/RJ-13 Telephone jack
RTS/CTS delay
Slave timing enabled
Sync Mode 1(sync/async)
Sync Mode 2 (stored number dial)
Sync Mode 3 (manual dial)

REGISTERS & OPTIONS

Register set

Register read

10 bit character
1800-Hz preamble
2100-Hz preamble
9 bit character
Answer on ring #
Answertone = 2225-Hz
Backspace character
Cancel character
Carriage Return

MODEM VENDOR
Model

REGISTERS & OPTIONS continued

Carrier detect response time
Character delete
Comma (pause)
Common CTS-RLSD
DTMF dialing speed
Dialing delay
Display active profile
Drop call on timeout
Enable speed conversion(match DTE)
Escape character
Escape code guard time
Exit DATA mode
Far end sends first
Flow control
High speed only
Immediate dial from dir X
Line feed character
Local echo
Loss of carrier disconnect
Lost carrier to hang-up delay
Prompt character
Received space disconnect
Responds to Remote Loop
Ring Indicator on until disconnect
Ring count
Select factory profile
Send break
Send break enable
Send space disconnect
Set default profile
Set disconnect character
Set halt character(for operator intervention)
Set terminator(marks end of number/login)
Set password
Set sequence of multiple # dialing
Set wait char(delay prior to login after DCD)
Skip header message
Transparent data mode
UM answertone
Wait for carrier
Write configurations to memory

Appendix I

601

MODEM VENDOR
Model

TESTS

Analog loopback test
Cancel all tests
Denies remote digital loopback request
Digital loop test
Grants remote digital loopback request
Initiate RDL test
Perform checksum & return status message
Perform checksum 7 return checksum
Remote loop test
Request firmware revision #
Request product code
Self-test
Test timer
Touchtone frequency test

USER INTERFACE

Cancel character
Change cancel character
Delete character(backspace)
Echo characters in command modem(on)
Echo characters(off)
Escape code
Flash
High speaker volume
Low speaker volume
Medium speaker volume
Result code set(basic)
Result code set(extended)
Result code set(full)
Result codes not sent
Result codes sent
Result codes transmitted as digits
Result codes transmitted as words
Send break
Speaker off always
Speaker on always
Speaker on until carrier detected
Spkr on until carr-det except during dialing
Wait for silence(quiet answer)

APPENDIX J. CONNECTION SYMPTOMS AND SOLUTIONS

Often the user faces problems getting two devices to work together. The case studies presented step-by-step approaches to device connections. Once two devices are connected, they still may not function together properly. The next few sections summarize some of the symptoms that may be noticed when connecting devices. Furthermore, possible cures to clear the problem are proposed. This list is far from complete yet gives the user a place to begin in isolating the problems. These cures, separated by the categories, computers, modems, printers, and terminals, are covered in greater detail in the tutorial modules. First the symptoms and data-appearance problems will be covered, followed by some device-specific problems.

Common Connection Symptoms and Causes

Symptom	Causes
1. Garbled characters	Parity, speed, character length, stop bits, bad phone line
2. Lost data	Flow control
3. Double spacing	Translation of received carriage returns or line feeds
4. Overwriting	Translation of received carriage returns or line feeds
5. No display of typed characters	Far end is not echoplexing, duplex option
6. Double characters	Duplex option

Common Data Appearance Problems

If the data you receive look like . . .	Problem	Resolution
1. line1 . . . . . . (your output will vary) line2 . . . . . . (your output will vary) line3	Too many line feeds	Insure that both CR & LF are not being performed with receipt of line ending sequence. Or disable one at the sending end of the connection.
2. line1 . . . . . 　　　　line2 . . . . 　　　　　　　line3	No carriage Return is being performed	Enable receiving device to perform CR/LF upon receipt of line ending sequence.
3. Lines 1 & 2 & 3 overwriting each other causing illegible lines	No Line Feed is being performed	Change option so that receipt of line ending sequence is interpreted as CR/LF, instead of just a CR.
4. The qpoic ýrÜwn fox xwpeorlk fs	Mismatched options	Compare options of both ports to insure that the parity, speed char-length, # of stop bits match.
5. The qpoic broke fox xwpeorlk fslk	Bad phone line	Hang-up & redial
6. Lost data or only partially received	Improper or no flow control	Insure that both ports are set up for the same flow control
7. No data being displayed while you type	Duplex problem	Insure that both ports gee-haw. If the attached device is not echoplexing, then your port should be set up for half-duplex.
8. DDoouubbllee CChhaarraacctteerrss	Duplex problem	The other device is set up to echoplex. Change your device to full-duplex, or no local display.

Computers: Failure to Get the "Login:" Prompt

1. The cable is not securely connected, is connected to the wrong port, or has the wrong ends connected to the wrong port. Check all cabling and connections.
2. The far-end computer is not on. Insure that the attached computer is up and running.
3. Your port is not enabled. Have the Systems Administrator enable the port.
4. Options are set incorrectly at one or both of the computers. Make sure that the options match at both ports, specifically the speed, character length, parity, and duplex. Compare the Port Profiles for the common options.
5. Reload the communication software on your device, as appropriate.

Modems—Failure to Complete Dialing

1. Check to insure that the phone line works. Usually you can connect any telephone to the phone plug outlet and check to see if you can call a local number
2. Check to see that a modular cord is connecting the modem to the outlet
3. Check to see that your cable is securely connected
4. Check to see that the modem is optioned to match the attached device. Compare the two Port Profiles for common settings.
5. Check to insure that your communication software, is set to the proper speed, parity, character length, port.
6. Insure that the power cable is plugged into the modem, and the modem is turned on. Light indicators on the front should be present.
7. Check that you are dialing the correct number.
8. If you are calling from behind a PBX, you may need to include a dial access code. This is usually a "9" or an "8," but check to make sure.
9. Check that the remote computer is up and running, with this port enabled
10. Check with the remote computer systems analyst or systems administrator to insure that the modem you are calling, is set up to receive calls and automatically answer.

Printers—Lack of Printing

1. The cable is not securely connected, is connected to the wrong port, or has the wrong ends connected to the wrong port. Check the cabling.
2. The computer or printer is not on. Insure that both devices are up and running.
3. Your port is not setup as the default printer port. Check with the administrator, or issue the commands, to insure that the desired printer is the default output device for you.
4. Options are set incorrectly. Compare Port Profiles for common optioning. Make sure that the options match at both ports, specifically the speed, character length, parity, and duplex.
5. Check to see that there are no printer error conditions. Reset the printer to clear any of these conditions.

Terminals—Failure to Get a "login:" Prompt

1. Check the terminal options. Compare the Port Profiles and set both devices to common options of speed, character length, parity, and duplex.
2. Insure that the terminal is connected to the correct port with the right cable and that the terminal has power.
3. The attached computer is not on—double check.

APPENDIX K. STEPS FOR CONNECTION

This appendix contains the recommended steps that the reader should follow when connecting any two devices together. Adherence to these steps should reduce the confusion that can arise when attempting to connect computers, modems, printers, and terminals together. The case studies in the text follow these steps.

Steps for Connection

1. Determine compatibility. (Should it work?)
2. Determine signs of success.
3. Determine the type of connector used.
4. Determine gender of the ports.
5. Determine which leads (pins) are provided by each device.
6. Determine which leads are required to be on by each device.
7. Design the cable.
8. Build the cable.
9. Test the cable for continuity.
10. Cable the two systems together with the cable.
11. From step two, measure success.

APPENDIX L. RULES FOR CABLE DESIGN

The following rules should be applied when a serial or parallel cable is being designed to connect computers, modems, printers, and terminals. The connector size or number of pins is irrelevant to these rules. The case studies applied these in every case. These are general rules that should be applied by the reader.

1. **CONNECT LIKE-CATEGORIES OF LEADS TOGETHER.** Connect ground leads to ground leads, data to data, control to control, and timing to timing leads. Do not connect a control lead to a data lead. Separate the leads into the different categories as an aid to avoid misconnections.

2. **ALWAYS CONNECT AN "OUT" TO AN "IN", AND AN "IN" TO AN "OUT".** Simply put, this means that a lead that is provided by a device should be connected to one of the leads required by the device. Leads provided by a device should not be connected to another lead that is provided by a device. The direction of the leads is very important for proper cable design.

3. **A LEAD THAT IS INPUT SHOULD ONLY BE CONNECTED TO ANOTHER LEAD THAT IS AN INPUT IF BOTH OF THESE ARE CONNECTED TO AN OUTPUT LEAD.** The goal is to keep input leads on (high), using the leads that are output from a port. We may have to use one output lead to keep more than one input lead on. This is why you may need to connect multiple input leads together. This is the "jumpering" concept.

4. **IN SYNCHRONOUS CONNECTIONS, ONLY USE ONE SOURCE OF TIMING.** If multiple timing leads are available with a timing signal on them, use only one of them. The others should be driven off this single lead to get their timing. The goal is to minimize the number of timing sources to avoid clocks that are out of phase. In asynchronous connections this rule is not applicable.

APPENDIX M. RS449, RS232-C, AND CCITT-V.24 CROSS-REFERENCE CHART

RS-449A FUNCTION	PIN	ABBR	PIN	ABBR	CODE	V.24 #	DIR.	RS-232C/V.24 FUNCTION
Shield	1	—	1	RG	AA	Shd.	—	Protective Ground
Signalling Rate Indicator	2	SI	12	—	CI	112	To DTE	Data Signal Rate Selector (CH or CI)
—	3	Spare	—	—	—	—	—	
Send Data	4	SD	2	TD	BA	103	To DCE	Transmitted Data
Send Timing	5	ST	15	TC	DB	114	To DTE	Transmit Clock (DCE source)
Receive Data	6	RD	3	RD	BB	104	To DTE	Received Data
Request to Send	7	RS	4	RTS	CA	105	To DCE	Request to Send
Receive Timing	8	RT	17	RC	DD	115	To DTE	Receive Clock
Clear to Send	9	CS	5	CTS	CB	106	To DTE	Clear to Send
Local Loopback	10	LL	—	—	—	141	To DCE	
Data Mode	11	DM	6	DSR	CC	107	To DTE	Data Set Ready
Terminal Ready	12	TR	20	DTR	CD	108	To DCE	Data Terminal Ready
Receiver Ready	13	RR	8	DCD	CF	109	To DTE	Carrier Detect
Remote Loopback	14	RL	—	—	—	140	To DCE	
Incoming Call	15	IC	22	RI	CE	125	To DTE	Ring Indicator
Select Frequency/	16	SF/	23	—	CH/	111/	To DCE/	Data Signal Rate Selector/
Signalling Rate Selector		SR			CI	112	To DTE	Data Signal Rate Selector
Terminal Timing	17	TT	24	TC	DA	113	To DCE	Transmit Clock (DTE Source)
Test Mode	18	TM	—	—	—	142	To DTE	
Signal Ground	19	SG	7	SG	AB	102	—	Signal Ground
Receive Common	20	RC	7	SG	AB	102	To DTE	
—	21	Spare	—	—	—	—	—	
RS-422 Return Lead	22	SD	—	—	—	—	To DCE	
RS-422 Return Lead	23	ST	—	—	—	—	To DTE	
RS-422 Return Lead	24	RD	—	—	—	—	To DTE	
RS-422 Return Lead	25	RS	—	—	—	—	To DCE	
RS-422 Return Lead	26	RT	—	—	—	—	To DTE	
RS-422 Return Lead	27	CS	—	—	—	—	To DTE	
Terminal in Service	28	IS	25	—	CN	135	To DCE	Busy out
RS-422 Return	29	DM	—	—	—	—	To DTE	
RS-422 Return	30	TR	—	—	—	—	To DCE	
RS-422 Return	31	RR	—	—	—	—	To DTE	
Select Standby	32	SS	—	—	—	116	To DCE	
Signal Quality	33	SQ	21	SQ	CG	110	To DTE	Signal Quality Detector
New Signal	34	NS	18	NS	—	136	To DCE	New Sync

RS-449A FUNCTION	PIN	ABBR	PIN	ABBR	CODE	V.24 #	DIR.	RS-232C/V.24 FUNCTION
RS-422 Return	35	TT	—	—	—	—	To DCE	
Standby Indicator	36	SB	—	—	—	117	To DTE	
Send Common	37	SC	7	SG	AB	102	To DCE	Signal Ground
9 PIN COMMON								
Shield	1	Shd.	1	FG	AA	Shd.	—	Frame Ground
Secondary Receiver Ready	2	SRR	12	—	SCF	122	To DTE	Secondary Carrier Detect
Secondary Send Data	3	SSD	14	—	SBA	118	To DCE	Secondary Transmitted Data
Secondary Receive Data	4	SRD	16	—	SBB	119	To DTE	Secondary Received Data
Signal Ground	5	SG	7	SG	AB	102	To DCE	Signal Ground
Receive Common	6	RC	7	SG	AB	102B	To DTE	
Secondary Request to Send	7	SRS	19	SRS	SCA	120	To DCE	Secondary Request to Send
Secondary Clear to Send	8	SCS	13	SCS	SCB	121	To DTE	Secondary Clear to Send
Send Common	9	SC	7	SG	AB	102A	To DCE	

INDEX

D